# THE JURISTS

# The Jurists

*A Critical History*

JAMES GORDLEY

Great Clarendon Street, Oxford, OX2 6DP,
United Kingdom

Oxford University Press is a department of the University of Oxford.
It furthers the University's objective of excellence in research, scholarship,
and education by publishing worldwide. Oxford is a registered trade mark of
Oxford University Press in the UK and in certain other countries

© J. Gordley 2013

The moral rights of the authors have been asserted

First Edition published in 2013

All rights reserved. No part of this publication may be reproduced, stored in
a retrieval system, or transmitted, in any form or by any means, without the
prior permission in writing of Oxford University Press, or as expressly permitted
by law, by licence or under terms agreed with the appropriate reprographics
rights organization. Enquiries concerning reproduction outside the scope of the
above should be sent to the Rights Department, Oxford University Press, at the
address above

You must not circulate this work in any other form
and you must impose this same condition on any acquirer

Crown copyright material is reproduced under Class Licence
Number C01P0000148 with the permission of OPSI
and the Queen's Printer for Scotland

Published in the United States of America by Oxford University Press
198 Madison Avenue, New York, NY 10016, United States of America

British Library Cataloguing in Publication Data
Data available

Library of Congress Control Number: 2013940019

ISBN 978–0–19–968939–2

Links to third party websites are provided by Oxford in good faith and
for information only. Oxford disclaims any responsibility for the materials
contained in any third party website referenced in this work.

*Magistris antiquis discipulus pius*

# Contents

Prologue ... ix

## I *Ius Civile*: The Roman Jurists — 1
Origins ... 1
Method ... 7
Roman law and Greek philosophy ... 12
Roman law and later civil law ... 18
Roman law and common law ... 21

## II *Ius Commune*: The Medieval Jurists — 28
i The civilians ... 28
  Origins ... 28
  Method ... 32
ii The canonists ... 51
  Origins ... 51
  A similar method, different authorities ... 53
  The interaction of civil and canon law ... 55
  The external and the internal forum ... 66

## III *Ius et Iustitia*: The Late Scholastics — 82
Origins ... 82
Commutative justice and private law ... 84
The late scholastics and Roman law ... 99
The development of international public law ... 101
The late scholastics and canon law ... 105
The late scholastics and metaphysics ... 107

## IV *De Iure Civile in Artem Redigendo*: The Humanist Ideal — 111
i *Studia humanitatis*: the Renaissance humanists ... 111
ii *Mos gallicus*: the French humanists ... 118

## V *Ius Naturae et Gentium*: The Iusnaturalists — 128

## VI *Droit Civil Français*: The French Alternative — 141
i *Droit civil selon l'ordre naturel* ... 141
ii *Code civil* ... 147

## VII *Usus Modernus Pandectarum*: The German-Dutch Alternative — 156

## VIII  *Mos Geometricus*: The Coming of Rationalism — 165
    An innovation in metaphysics — 166
    An innovation in method — 177
    An innovation in principle — 181
    Conclusion — 193

## IX  *Novus Ordo*: Positivism and Conceptualism — 195
    Positivism — 196
        *L'école de l'exégèse* in France — 196
        *Pandektenrecht* in Germany — 199
        Anglo-American common law — 204
    Conceptualism — 212
        International law — 215
        Private law — 222

## X  *Ubinam Gentium Sumus?* After Positivism and Conceptualism — 275
    The revolt — 275
    The appeal to intuition — 281
    The evaluation of interests — 287
    The appeal to social purpose: *abus de droit* — 292
    The appeal to the social sciences — 297
    Whither? — 309

*Index* — 313

# *Prologue*

A modern insight that has transformed the writing of history is that people now are not as they once were. Some trace this insight to the Renaissance. Humanists such as Petrarch thought that classical Rome was much different than his own time. Nevertheless, he thought that the difference was the result of barbarism and degeneracy. His contemporaries were not nearly as virtuous as the ancient Romans, but, to the extent that they were virtuous, they were virtuous in the same way. His educational program was to revive the study of ancient authors so that people would become more virtuous.

The modern insight goes back only to the nineteenth century. As a result, important as it is, it has a dubious pedigree. In the nineteenth century, scholars became skeptical of universals such as "virtue." Under the influence of romanticism and philosophical idealism, many believed that the ideas have meaning only within the historical or cultural context in which they were expressed. The context was said to be the *Zeitgeist* of an era, the *Volksgeist* of a people, a "world view," a "culture," the "consciousness" of a social class, and more recently a "mindset," a "value-system," or an "intellectual horizon."

According to this view, taken to its extreme, each idea had meaning only in relation to other ideas within the same cultural or historical context, and no meaning outside this context. Gothic man understood the world one way; Renaissance man, in another way; Baroque man, in yet another. By this approach, it was difficult to explain elements of continuity between the Middle Ages, the Renaissance, and the Baroque. It was difficult to explain transitions between one period and the next, since they were not marked by radical changes in the understanding of everything. It was difficult to explain what sort of unity the elements of a culture or an historical period could have for it to be possible to understand each element only in terms of the others. What could Renaissance philology have to do with Renaissance styles of dress?

Proponents of a more moderate approach, which is still with us, without insisting that ideas have meaning only within an historical or cultural context, nevertheless think that one idea or event is well explained when it can be linked to another idea or event that happened to occur at the same time, even without evidence that the two were linked in the minds of people then alive. Metaphysical theories have been explained by class structures that have no apparent relation to the metaphysical problems that interested the theorists. The form of Gothic cathedrals has been explained by the form of scholastic arguments.

The parallels are not only fanciful and forced. They also undercut the truth that underlies the modern insight as to how history should be written. To write history is to write about what occurred in the past. When we write about how people once thought, we must write about what they actually were thinking. The best evidence is what they said and what they themselves were trying to do.

This book is concerned with what jurists said and what they were trying to do. Rarely have jurists worked alone. Rather, they have worked in schools of similarly minded jurists. Each school can be described by the project that it was pursuing. The project can be described by the goal that the jurists sought and the methods that they used to achieve it. The goal and methods can be seen from what they wrote, and can explain why they wrote what they did. The goals and methods may or may not have had anything to do with whatever else was going on at the same time. The only solid proof that they did would be an acknowledgment by the jurists themselves.

This approach supports the modern insight that people at different times thought differently. The jurists thought differently because they were engaged in different projects: they pursued different goals by different methods. To describe their work in terms of the projects that they undertook is faithful to the truth behind the modern insight that history must be understood in terms of what people in the past were trying to do. But that does not mean that their goals and methods were meaningful only to themselves or only within their historical or cultural context. Later jurists found the work of earlier jurists meaningful even though their own projects were different. They tried to learn from the successes and to avoid the failures of earlier projects.

Consequently, this approach permits critical history—history that is critical in the sense that it considers the extent to which, given its methods, a school of jurists achieved or failed to achieve its goals. One can see how its goals and methods set limits to what it could achieve. When it failed, one can identify the source of its difficulties.

The work of the jurists will be described as a series of such projects. Not all history can be written in this way. This approach works only when, like the jurists, one is writing about people who were team players in the sense that they worked on the same projects. I doubt if one could write a similar history of artists or philosophers.

For that matter, not all legal history should be written in this way. The projects of the jurists had one element in common: they were attempts to understand and explain the law. Commitment to that project is the defining characteristic of a jurist. But legal history is not only about the work of jurists. Those who administered the law resolved practical problems, sometimes drawing on the writings of the jurists and sometimes not. Their work, despite its importance, figures here only to the extent that the jurists faced these problems themselves or drew on the solutions of those who did.

Again, to write about schools of jurists is to neglect occasional brilliant mavericks whose work may have been influential, but who were not committed to the project of any school. Examples are sixteenth-century jurist Charles du Moulin, who developed the doctrine that damages for breach of contract should be limited to those foreseeable when the contract was made, or eighteenth-century jurist Christian Thomasius, who criticized negligence law and defended strict liability.

Moreover, for this book to be readable—and indeed writable—it had to be confined to a limited number of related projects, and only a limited amount can be said about each of these. Each of the projects dealt with here will be treated by describing, although in some detail, the work of a few key figures, or, when we reach the nineteenth century, a few jurisdictions. The projects chosen are related because they concern similar legal problems, mostly problems of private law, although it will be noted from time to time how other problems branched off from these. One could write about the project of explaining American constitutional law or French administrative law, but they would be distinct stories.

A final limitation concerns what this history can account for and what it cannot. It describes the work of jurists as a series of projects, each distinguished by its goal and methods. It explains, in terms of these goals and methods, the achievements of the jurists committed to each project, the limits to what they could achieve, and their failures. It explains why jurists committed to different projects wrote differently. What it does not explain is why any of these projects ever got started. We will describe the origin of each and come away puzzled. Not one of them had to have happened. Indeed, one can say the same of the entire tradition. Had it not been for an intellectual innovation in the late Roman Republic, there might have been no jurists.

James Gordley

*New Orleans, LA*
*June 2013*

# I

## *Ius Civile*

### The Roman Jurists

### Origins

Intellectual traditions have beginnings in time. Western philosophy began with the Greeks, modern physics with Galileo and Newton, and modern economics with Adam Smith. The intellectual tradition that shaped Western law began in the late Roman Republic in the second century BC when the Romans began to produce jurists.

Most of the jurists whose writings survived wrote later, during the classical period of Roman law, usually dated from the beginning of the Empire in 27 BC. They wrote more than two thousand books in which, as Fritz Schulz noted, "the picture sketched in bare outline by the Republican jurists was filled in down to the last detail."[1]

The end of the classical period has been dated from the death of the jurist Modestinus in 235 AD. Jurists stopped writing commentaries on law. The work of the great jurists such as Pomponius, Ulpian, and Paul became "classicized," and was taught in law schools by teachers who themselves never attempted to develop it further. In part, the reason may have been the bureaucratization of the state after the accession of the Emperor Diocletian forty years later. In part, it may have been a conviction that the works of the classical jurists could not be surpassed. In any event, if one looks to what was written and taught, according to Shultz, "one is baffled by the sudden and unexpected collapse of classical jurisprudence in the second half of the third century...," although, as he notes, the graduates of law schools assumed important positions in the state as judges, advisers, and drafters of imperial decrees.[2]

In the sixth century, the Emperor Justinian ordered a compilation of legal texts to be made that later became known as the *Corpus iuris civilis*. These texts were the only ones that were to have the force of law. The largest part, the *Digest*, was made up of short excerpts mostly from the works of the classical jurists, amounting, in all, to about 5 percent of what they had written. Two further sections, the *Codex* and the *Novellae*, consisted of imperial decrees. Another, the *Institutes*, was a short

---

[1] Fritz Schulz, *History of Roman Legal Science* (Oxford, 1946), 126.
[2] Schulz (n. 1), 263.

revision of an introduction to law written by the classical jurist Gaius. The *Corpus iuris* fell out of use in the eastern Roman Empire. Classical Roman law was forgotten, not to be revived until the Middle Ages, and then on the basis of a single manuscript copy, known as the *Pisana* or *Fiorentina*. The *Corpus iuris*, as transmitted through this single document, contains all that has survived of Roman law except for a copy of the original version of the *Institutes* of Gaius that was rediscovered in the nineteenth century.

Although Roman law was perfected during the classical period, as Schulz observed, "[t]he heroic age of creative genius and daring pioneers" was not the Empire, but the late Republic.[3] It was then that jurists first appeared and assumed a unique position in Roman society that they kept throughout the classical period. We know little about the first jurists. The only surviving description of them is in a few lines written by the classical jurist Pomponius about 130–140 AD. He said that the civil law was "founded" by M. Manilus, M. Junius Brutus, and P. Mucius Scaevola, all of whom lived in the late second century BC. In the following generation, the first commentary on civil law was written by Q. Mucius Scaevola.[4] Only fragments of their writings survive. Yet, by the end of the Republic, the jurists had identified the concepts that became the foundations of Western private law. They had developed a unique method for analyzing and refining these concepts that the classical jurists perfected.

At the time that the civil law was founded according to Pomponius, the late second century, a new procedure—the so-called "formulary procedure"—became increasingly common. Its use was extended by the *lex Aebutia* in 143 BC, although it is hard to tell in what way. The part that the jurists played in this procedure defined their role throughout classical times. They held no official position. Upon request, they advised those who conducted the formulary procedure: the praetor, the iudex, and the advocates or oratores.

In this procedure, a lawsuit was conducted in two phases. In the first, a litigant appeared before a magistrate—a praetor or aedile—and asked that a iudex be appointed to hear his case, and that the iudex be given certain instructions—the *formula*. The iudex was a private person with no specialized legal training appointed ad hoc for a single lawsuit. The *formula* told the iudex what he was to do. For example:

If it appears that C. Marcius Saturninus ought to give 18,000 sesterces to C. Sulpicius Cinnamus, which is the matter in dispute, C. Blossius Celadus, the iudex, shall condemn C. Marcius Saturninus for 18,000 sesterces in favor of C. Blossius Celadus; otherwise he shall absolve.[5]

In the second phase of the lawsuit, the parties appeared before the iudex, represented, if at all, by advocates—oratores—who also lacked specialized legal training,

---

[3] Schulz (n. 1), 99. *See* Aldo Schiavone, *The Invention of Law in the West*, trans. Jeremy Carden and Anthony Shugaar (Cambridge, MA, 2012), 158.
[4] D. 1.2.2.39, 41.
[5] A formula from the first century AD, translated in Ernest Metzger, "Actions," in *A Companion to Justinian's Institutes*, ed. Ernest Metzger (Ithaca, NY, 1998), 208 at 213.

although they might be trained in rhetoric. Cicero was an "orator." The judge heard whatever evidence he saw fit and then decided the case in accordance with the *formula*. There was no appeal. Nor was there state machinery to enforce the iudex's decision. The effect of the decision was to legalize self-help.

To get before a iudex, a litigant had to bring his claim within the words of the *formula* that the praetor would accept and send to the iudex. The praetor would issue an "edict" at the beginning of his term describing the *formulae* that he would recognize. He might recognize new *formulae* when he thought there was a gap in the existing law. The praetor served for only a year, however, and usually had no specialized legal training. The jurists would advise him as to what *formulae* he ought to accept. They would also help litigants to propose a suitable *formula* and advise iudices on how to apply a formula submitted to them. Much of the jurists' work from late Republican through classical times concerned the perfection and interpretation of the praetor's edict. Even after the edict was put in final form under Hadrian around 130 AD, jurists continued to write commentaries on it. Many passages in Justinian's *Digest* were taken from the commentary on the edict of the late classical jurist Ulpian.

The formulary procedure replaced an earlier one, the so-called *legis actio*, in which a litigant had to state his claim before the praetor by reciting a set form of words. The smallest mistake in the form could be fatal. According to Gaius, a plaintiff would lose if he were to claim that the defendant had cut down his "vines" (*vites*), since the set form that he needed to recite spoke of "trees" (*arbores*) rather than vines.[6] If the plaintiff stated his claim correctly, then, as in the formulary procedure, the praetor would appoint a iudex to decide the case.

The *legis actio* has one feature that was common in early law, at least in Europe: the plaintiff could prevail only if he flawlessly performed certain prescribed actions such as the recitation of a set form of words. If he did so, then, typically, the dispute was resolved in some mechanical way, for example by the taking of oaths, or by ordeal, or by combat, or by referring the case to a panel chosen by a specified procedure, which would decide it without hearing evidence or legal argument. The unusual feature of the *legis actio* is not that a litigant must flawlessly recite certain words, but rather that the case is referred to a iudex, who seems to have had power to decide it informally according to his own judgment. Scholars have suggested that, initially, instead of being resolved by a iudex, cases were decided in some mechanical way such as by oaths or ordeals or combat.[7] Nevertheless, the sources contain almost no evidence as to what the Romans might have done in the beginning.

Scholars have said that the *legis actio* procedure originally had a religious or "sacral" character. There is evidence that originally each party initiated the procedure by swearing an oath as to the rightness of his claim, thereby appealing to the gods. Some scholars imply that the procedure had to be performed flawlessly for

---

[6] G. 4.11.
[7] Arthur Schiller, *Roman Law Mechanisms of Development* (New York, 1978), 193–96; Peter Stein, *Regulae Iuris: From Juristic Rules to Legal Maxims* (Edinburgh, 1966).

much the same reason as the procedure for taking the auspices had to be performed flawlessly. Otherwise, it would not work. The gods would not intervene unless they were invoked properly. And indeed, in ancient Rome, the persons charged with determining whether the correct form of words for a lawsuit had been followed were the "college of priests," the group also charged with taking the auspices.

Perhaps the *legis actio* originally did have a sacral character and, for that reason, its proper performance was entrusted to priests. Nevertheless, other societies have used formalistic procedures in which the least flaw was fatal even when there was nothing sacral about its performance. In *Nyal's Saga*, the protagonists who brought suit over the burning to death of Nyal nearly lost because they committed technical procedural flaws when they choose jurors.[8] Those who determined whether the correct procedure had been followed were not priests. They were laymen who had gained a reputation for their knowledge of the law. In a medieval manorial court in England, a plaintiff would recite a set formula before the lord or steward, and would lose if he were to make a slip. In one case, the slip was the failure to state, at the end of his claim, that he had brought his "suit," meaning that he had with him a prescribed number of people who would swear to the rightness of his cause. The "court"—meaning the steward, perhaps with the advice of the villagers present—ruled that the plaintiff had lost because he had failed to state his claim properly.[9]

Procedures such as these permit a case to be decided by law without investing anyone with the authority to judge the merits of the case. Either the litigant stated his claim or defense in a form sanctioned by tradition or he did not. Whether he did was a question to be answered not by the judge of the particular case, but by the custodians of the tradition, whether they were priests or well-versed laymen. A litigant may lose, however, simply because the procedure is inflexible. The traditional forms for presenting claims or defenses may not be suited to his case. He may say "vines" instead of "trees," or choose a juror subject to a procedural objection, or fail to mention his "suit." He loses not because anyone believes that the flaw should matter, but because no one has the authority to decide which flaws matter and which do not.

In contrast, under the formulary procedure, jurists and praetors decided whether a claim or defense ought to prevail. It then became possible for the first time to disentangle substantive law from procedure. Alan Watson has claimed that the Romans had understood the difference between substance and procedure long before the time of the formulary procedure.[10] He may be quite right. But, in the late Republic, the difference took on a new significance. In the formulary procedure, the question that arose was whether a certain kind of claim or defense ought to be recognized, not merely whether the right procedures had been followed in raising a claim or defense.

---

[8] *Nyal's Saga*, trans. M. Magusson and H. Palsson (London, 1960), c. 142.
[9] "*De Placitis et Curiis Tenendis*," in *The Court Baron*, eds. F. W. Maitland and W. P. Baildon (London, 1891), 68.
[10] Alan Watson, *The Spirit of Roman Law* (Athens, GA, 1995).

Moreover, it became possible to disentangle questions of law from questions of fact. Under the *legis actio*, if the plaintiff recited a claim for damage to his trees and the defendant denied it, the defendant might be claiming that he did no damage at all, thus raising what we would call a "question of fact." Or he might be claiming that it did not matter whether he had damaged the plaintiff's vines, since the proper form for the *legis actio* spoke only of "trees," and vines are not trees. His defense would then raise what we call a "question of law." Under the *legis actio*, there was no way to disentangle these questions, and hence no way to build up a body of substantive law.

Under the formulary procedure, substantive law was built up by the praetor and the jurists working in a symbiotic relationship. The praetor gave official sanction to a *formula* by including it in his edict and submitting it to a iudex to decide a particular lawsuit. The jurists advised him on what *formulae* to recognize, often proposing new *formulae*, but basing their advice on a consideration of the *formulae* that had been recognized in the past. The work of the praetors was the starting point for the work of the jurists, which in turn shaped the work of the praetors.

The substantive law became ever more detailed until it took a long period of specialized study to master it, which was spent not in a law school, but under the guidance of a recognized jurist. Jurists became a cadre of experts learned in law. In this respect, they differed from everyone else who played a role in Roman government.[11] Rome was governed by nonspecialists who came, typically, from upper-class families, and received an all-round education that was supposed to prepare them to serve as a praetor or a consul, to make speeches, to lead armies, and eventually to take a place in the Senate. The jurists, who typically were from the upper classes, sometimes played these roles as well. As Alan Watson notes, "[u]ntil the first century B.C., the senators dominated the ranks of the jurists; and up to 95 B.C. eighteen jurists had held the consulate."[12] Of the founders of Roman law, M. Manilius was consul in 149 BC, P. Mucius Scaevola in 133 BC, and Q. Mucius Scaevola in 95 BC. Aulus Cascellius was offered the consulship by Augustus, but turned it down in order to devote himself to law. Nevertheless, educated upper-class Romans, although they could hold these offices, could not be jurists without specialized study.

In this respect, the jurists differed from the priests who had traditionally decided whether a certain form of action could be approved by the praetor. The priests were not a class of religious specialists expounding esoteric knowledge. They consulted books to learn how sacrifices were to be made, how auspices were to be taken, and how lawsuits were to be brought. These books were kept secret. The priests, however, were educated upper-class Romans who might serve as priests one year and in some other position the next. They could read the books without specialized training. According to Roman historians, the books were kept secret so that the law could serve as a weapon in the hands of the upper classes. For that reason, supposedly, the plebians demanded that the law be made public and, in 451–50

[11] *See* Schiavone (n. 3), 113.    [12] Watson (n. 10), 39.

BC, the law was finally written down on Twelve Tables erected in the forum. Around 300 BC, supposedly, Gnaeus Flavius, a freedman, stole the books describing the forms for bringing actions from Appius Claudius and made them public.

Since the work of the priests passed seamlessly into the work of the jurists, modern scholars have spoken of a "secularization" of Roman law. The expression is misleading. Perhaps, in the transition, law did become more secular by losing some of its sacral character. But it never could have become religious law like the Talmud or Shari'a—law expounded by religious experts who interweave questions of private law with ceremonial precepts that govern the life of a believer. The Roman gods had far less to say than Jehovah and Allah about how a believer should live his life. In any event, the Roman priests were not religious experts. Secularization meant that the law left the hands of generalists and passed into the custody of jurists, a new order of secular experts that had never existed before.

It need not have happened. There might never have been jurists. In Greece, the law may have originally been as formalistic as the *legis actio*. The procedure became more flexible and yet no class of jurists emerged. Instead, discretion to decide cases was given to laypeople such as the Athenian jurors, who made such decisions without learned advice. The Romans might have done the same. Criminal cases in the late Republic were decided by assemblies of several dozen laymen, and the jurists had little to say about criminal law. There were some courts for civil cases: one type with thirty or forty members; another with five.[13] In other cultures, such as traditional China, lawsuits were decided by judges who had received a generalized education that was thought to fit them for any important role in government. It is almost surprising that, despite their own confidence in a general education, the Romans entrusted their law to the jurists.

Like the Roman jurists, modern jurists are also a cadre with specialized legal training. Like the Romans, they have a symbiotic relationship with state authority. They interpret the law as laid down by state authorities, who themselves then draw upon the jurists' work to modify the law, and thereby lay down new law for the jurists to interpret. But there are differences. Today, the state authorities are legislators, who may have specialized legal training, or judges, who must. The Roman jurists held no official position. The state authorities who laid down the law—the legislative assemblies and praetor—were laymen. So was the iudex, whose decisions were not preserved and who played no part in the development of the law.

Moreover, as David Daube observed, in Rome, the promulgation of law by state authority was a matter of "continuous day-to-day adjustment." Legislation was rare because it was regarded as "cumbrous."[14] A praetor could change his edict as he saw fit. The bulk of it would track the edict of his predecessor and the changes would be made with the advice of the jurists.[15] The jurists could not revise the law except by

---

[13] John P. Dawson, *The Oracles of the Law* (Ann Arbor, MI, 1968), 101.
[14] David Daube, "Texts and Interpretation in Roman and Jewish Law," in vol. 1 of *Collected Works of David Daube*, ed. Calum Carmichael (Berkeley, CA, 1992), 173 at 174.
[15] Watson (n. 10), 74–81.

working though the praetor. The praetor, whatever his prominence and political acumen, was likely to listen. He was not an expert and he knew that any enduring change would need the approval of future praetors, who would receive the advice of jurists. Indeed, enduring change depended on the praetors and the jurists making the sort of changes that would be preserved because they commended themselves to other praetors and jurists. Consequently, while the task of the jurists was to explain the *ius civile* as promulgated by state authority, it was, at the same time, to determine what state authority should say. The task was ongoing. The jurists explained what the law should be, not occasionally, when suggestions were made for law reform, but continually, as part of their normal work.

Also, the law promulgated by state authority was relatively sparse. There was a great gap between anything that the legislative assemblies enacted, or that the praetor said, and the knowledge of law that the iudex needed to decide a case. For example, the praetor had devised an action for protecting possession of land: the interdict *uti possidetis*. The *formula* ran: "I forbid the use of force to prevent whichever of you is presently in possession without force, leave or license from continuing to possess...."[16] But the jurists explained what constituted possession. The *lex Aquilia*, enacted by the plebian assembly in the early third century BC,[17] said that the plaintiff could recover for harm, or *damnum* done to him, *iniuria*, which, according to the jurists, meant harm done in a way that was *non iure* or unlawful. Harm done unlawfully, they said, was harm done by fault, either intentionally or by negligence. They then explained what constituted fault. Similarly, the praetor gave an action on a sale, but the jurists explained when the sale might be invalid, for example for lack of consent.

Thus the elucidation of such concepts as possession, fault, and consent, which became basic in Western private law, was left to the jurists. Their conclusions were not incorporated into the *formulae* that the praetor would grant in future cases. The *formulae* remained general. Nor were they affected by the opinions of a iudex in a particular case. Consequently, there was little in the legislative texts or the *formulae* of the praetors, and almost nothing in the decisions of the iudices, to serve as authority for the jurists. When they cited authority for their conclusions, it was nearly always the opinions of other jurists.

## Method

The Roman jurists, like those engaged in other intellectual disciplines, identified and refined a set of concepts to explain a large and varied realm of experience. Alan Watson has spoken of the "very high degree of conceptualization of

---

[16] D. 43.17.1.pr.
[17] That seems to be the most plausible date: Reinhard Zimmermann, *The Law of Obligations: Roman Foundations of the Civilian Tradition* (Cape Town, 1990), 955–57. Honoré puts the date at the end of that century: A. M. Honoré, "Linguistic and Social Context of the *Lex Aquilia*," *The Irish Jurist* 7 (1972): 145, 149.

Roman law."[18] Nevertheless, although the Romans explored the meaning and implications of concepts, they did so in a different way than, for example, those in fields such as philosophy, physics, and economics. Although the concepts used by a Greek philosopher, a modern physicist, or a modern economist are meant to explain ordinary experience, they are not found in ordinary experience. Only a philosopher, an economist, or a physicist understands concepts such as substance and accident, matter and energy, or supply and demand. By and large, the concepts used by the Romans were familiar from ordinary experience. For example, they explored the meaning of concepts such as sale and lease, which are familiar to everyone who sells or leases, and concepts such as slavery, which were familiar to everyone in Roman society. Moreover, a Greek philosopher, or a modern physicist or economist, defines concepts abstractly and then works out their implications one step after another. The Roman jurists explained their concepts not by defining them, but by testing them against particular cases. The jurist Javolenus said that, "in civil law, all definitions are dangerous for there are few that cannot be upset."[19] He meant, as Peter Stein noted, that "all definitions are dangerous for they give the impression that they have a general application and cover all the cases when in fact they do not."[20] Unlike a philosopher, physicist, or economist, the Roman jurists moved from a concept to its application in a particular case all at once, without explaining how they got from one to the other.

One can see these features of their method in a case put by the Roman jurist Gaius that Alan Watson used to illustrate their work.[21] A contract was made to provide slaves as gladiators to fight in the arena. The contract provided that the slaves' owner would receive twenty denarii for each one who returned and one thousand denarii for each one who was killed. The question was whether the contract was a sale of the slaves or a lease of their services. Either conclusion seems odd. A lessor, unlike a seller, can demand the return of his property. But here the owner of the gladiators could demand the return of only the slaves who survived. The answer according to most jurists, Gaius said, was that the contract was a sale of every slave who was killed and a lease of every slave who returned.

Another illustration used by Watson is a case put by the Tryphonius.[22] A slave woman was to be freed after she had borne three children. The children born before she was free would remain the slaves of her master. She bore one child and, later, she bore triplets. Which of her children, if any, were to be free? It would be odd to

---

[18] Watson (n. 10), 90. That statement might seem squarely to contradict Stein and Behrens. Stein said that the Roman jurists "did not consciously think of law in terms of concepts; indeed the notion of a concept was not found in their mental equipment": Stein (n. 7), 47–48. Behrens made similar statements, pointing to the lack of abstraction in Roman law and the limited use of definitions: Dietrich Behrens, "Begriff und Definition in den Quellen," *Zeitschrift des Savingy-Stiftung für Rechtsgeschichte Rom. Abt.* 74 (1957): 352. The contradiction is only apparent. Stein and Behrens certainly did not wish to deny the importance to the Roman jurists of concepts such as sale, lease, possession, fault, or consent. They seem to mean that, as noted in the text, concepts such as these were familiar from ordinary experience and that the Romans were not concerned with defining them.

[19] D. 50.17.202.   [20] Stein (n. 7), 70.   [21] G. 3.146.   [22] D. 1.5.15.

think that the triplets were slaves and odd to think that they were free. Tryphonius answered that only one child was free: the last of the triplets to be born.

Watson thought that these cases exemplified the method of the Roman jurists, yet for that reason he found their method puzzling. He could not understand why the jurists were concerned about such problems. He thought that, in the case of the gladiators, the reason was procedural. In Roman procedure, there was one action for sale and another action for lease. Therefore "enormous effort [was] expended... to determine what counted as the sale and what as the hire of a thing."[23] Perhaps. But the reason why the jurists were interested in the problem was probably not that they wanted to know what procedure to follow the next time an owner of gladiators brought suit on such a contract. It is more likely that they were interested because the case showed that it might not be possible to tell whether a contract was a sale or a lease at the time that the contract was made, but only thereafter. The contract was like Schroedinger's cat in quantum physics, which, at a certain moment, cannot be said to be either alive or dead, but, at a later moment, turns out to have been alive or dead all along.

Watson found the case of triplets still more puzzling. Why would the jurists worry about it, since the birth of triplets must have been a "rare event"? Why would the master free the slave woman under such a condition even though, "[o]bviously, he wanted a financial benefit from slave breeding"? "Presumably," Watson continues, "[h]e was well disposed toward this slave but the very condition in the will is indicative of the callousness that arises from slave-owning." Nevertheless, there is "no trace of humanitarianism in the argument of the jurist." The jurist, Watson concluded, "is interested only in the legal problem."[24]

That interest in only the legal problem, however, is precisely why the case did matter to Tryphonius and why he stated it as he did, mentioning only those facts that bore upon the legal problem. The legal problem was of interest whether or not a master was likely to impose such a condition, and whether or not, if he did so, the slave was likely to have triplets. Since slavery was recognized by Roman law, it was not necessary for Tryphonius to discuss humanity toward slaves or the legitimacy of slavery to resolve the legal problem, any more than it is necessary for a modern lawyer to discuss the justification for private property or capitalism to resolve a problem in property or corporation law. Watson concluded that the Roman jurists wrote "as if they lived in a vacuum, remote from economic, social, or spiritual considerations."[25] They did indeed, because they had a method in which cases were stated abstractly to include only those features that were relevant to a legal problem.

Watson is not the only one to have thought it odd that the Roman jurists paid attention to cases of such little practical significance. Schulz said:

With untiring patience and unvarying acumen the classical writers subject the institutions of the law ever and again to a searching casuistic examination which, by applying it in concrete cases, real or imaginary, pursues each principle to its most remote and minute

---

[23] Watson (n. 10), 90.   [24] Watson (n. 10), 69.
[25] Watson (n. 10), 66. Similarly, Schiavone (n. 3), 200.

consequences. No problem of private law, however petty or singular, but was welcomed and probed. One is astonished at the number of insignificant and practically useless cases that are discussed.... One wonders whether it was really justifiable to spend so much time and labour on these difficult, tortuous questions, the practical importance of which was so small.[26]

The Roman jurists, however, did not regard the intellectual problems raised by such cases as "useless," "petty," and "insignificant." It was those problems that interested them, not the practical significance of the cases. Nevertheless, the practical significance of their work cannot be understated. They identified and refined concepts that are basic in modern legal systems, in both civil law and common law jurisdictions, for example possession, fault, and consent.

As noted, one feature of the method of the Roman jurists was that they elaborated the meaning of concepts familiar from ordinary experience. Indeed, it is hard to imagine a society in which some of these concepts, such as possession, fault, and consent, would not be familiar. Possession will be a familiar idea in any society in which certain objects belong to certain people. A person will sometimes possess an object that does not belong to him. He may pick up another's spear or blanket. It is hard to imagine a society in which people are unfamiliar with the idea that a person is at fault if he harms someone intentionally (which the Romans called *dolus*) or if he does so negligently (which the Romans called *culpa* in the narrow sense of the term). Children will be taught to be careful not to burn down the house, hut, or tent, and not to wound someone with a kitchen knife, javelin, or rock. Similarly, it is hard to imagine a society in which it never matters whether a person gave his consent. The genius of the Roman jurists lay not in finding new concepts, but in seeing the legal significance of familiar ones.

Another feature of their method was that they refined these concepts by putting particular cases. They did so in three different ways, which are illustrated by their discussion of possession, fault, and consent.

Sometimes, as when they explained the meaning of possession, they put cases that lay at the boundaries of a concept. A person who had been deprived of possession had an action even if he were not the owner. But could a person be in possession of an object of which he no longer had physical control? Certainly. As Ulpian said, "if someone has gone away from his field or house leaving none of his household there, and on his return was... prevented from entering the premises," he has been deprived of possession.[27] But what sort of physical control was necessary to acquire possession? According to Paulus, although possession must be taken physically:

> ...that should not be taken to mean that one seeking to possess an estate must go round every part of it. It is enough that he enters some part of the estate, but with the intent and awareness that he seeks to possess the estate to its furthest boundaries.[28]

---

[26] Schulz (n. 1), 126.   [27] D. 43.16.1.24.   [28] D. 41.2.3.1.

## Ius Civile: *The Roman Jurists*

According to Celsus:

If I instruct the seller to leave what I bought at my house, it is certain that I possess it, even though no one has yet touched it. Again, if my seller points out to me from my turret the neighboring land which I have bought, and declares that he is giving me vacant possession, I begin to possess it no less than if I set foot within its boundary.[29]

A buyer of wine is in possession when he is given the key to the cellar.[30] The buyer of a pile of logs who has been told by the seller to take them away is in possession as soon as he puts a guard on them.[31]

Sometimes, as when they explained the meaning of negligence, the Roman jurists put typical cases in which the concept would apply. A pruner is negligent if he harms someone by cutting off a branch over a public way without calling out.[32] If a farmer burns stubble and the fire gets of control, he is negligent if he did so on a windy day, but not if the day was calm and the fire spread because of a sudden gust of wind.[33] A javelin thrower is negligent if he kills someone by throwing the javelin in an inappropriate place,[34] as is the stoker of a furnace if a fire starts because he fell asleep instead of watching it,[35] and a barber who shaves a customer out of doors near a playing field and cuts him when a ball strikes the hand holding the razor.[36] So too is someone who digs a pit to catch a deer or bear in a public place where someone might fall into the pit rather than in the usual place for such pits.[37] A mule driver is negligent if he is too inexperienced to control his mules,[38] as is a carter if he loaded stones badly so that one fell out of his cart,[39] and a doctor if he lacked the skill to perform an operation properly[40] or to prescribe the right drug.[41]

Sometimes, the jurists put cases that indicated distinct types of situation to which a single concept would apply. An example is the way in which they explained consent in contract formation. Ulpian said:

It is obvious that in contracts of sale there must be consent. The sale is invalid if there is disagreement either as to the fact of sale (*in ipsa emptione*) or the price or any other matter. If, therefore, I thought I was buying the Cornelian estate, and you that you were selling the Sempronian, the sale is void on the ground that we were not at one as to the physical thing sold (*in corpore*).... Of course, if we are merely in disagreement over the name but at one on the actual thing, there is no doubt that the sale is good; for if the thing is identified, a mistake over its name is irrelevant. Next comes the question whether there is a good sale if there is no mistake as to the physical thing (*in corpore*), but there is in regard to its substance (*in substantia*), for example where vinegar is sold for wine, or copper for gold, or lead or something else resembling silver for silver.[42]

Ulpian concluded that consent had not validly been given at least in the case of the copper sold for gold and the lead sold for silver. Curiously, he claimed that, in the

---

[29] D. 41.2.18.2. [30] D. 18.2.1.21. [31] D. 18.2.51. [32] D. 9.2.31.
[33] D. 9.2.30.3. [34] D. 9.2.9.4. [35] D. 9.2.27.9. [36] D. 9.2.11.pr.
[37] D. 9.2.28.pr.; see D. 9.2.29.pr. [38] D. 9.2.8.1. [39] D. 9.2.27.33.
[40] D. 9.2.7.8. [41] D. 9.2.8.pr. [42] D. 18.1.9.

case of the vinegar sold for wine, the parties had consented when the wine happened to sour, but not if it had been deliberately soured to produce vinegar.

Sometimes, the question was not the meaning of a single concept, but which of several concepts would apply to a given factual situation. An example is the case of the gladiators mentioned earlier, in which the question was whether the transaction was a sale or a lease. As that case illustrates, the Roman jurists also answered this question by putting particular cases. Suppose a goldsmith is paid to make a ring of a given weight and design using his own gold. Cassius had said that the transaction was a sale of the material and a lease of the work,[43] but, according to Gaius, most jurists regarded it as a sale unless the smith was given the gold and a charge fixed for his work, in which case it was a lease.[44] But suppose a contractor were to build for the owner of the building site, acquiring all of the materials himself and providing all of the labor. According to Paul, it was a lease of the contractor's services.[45]

The manner in which the jurists stated their cases was in one way concrete and in another abstract.[46] It was concrete in that each case concerned a particular factual situation that might actually occur. It was abstract in that, among all of the facts that might be encountered in real life, the jurists mentioned only those that bore upon the legal problem that they wished to solve.

As we will see, this method was not that of later jurists, although with it the Roman jurists identified and refined the concepts that are basic to modern civil and common law.

## Roman law and Greek philosophy

As it has just been described, the method of the Roman jurists looks nothing like that of Greek philosophers such as Aristotle. As we have seen, unlike the philosophers, the jurists drew their concepts from ordinary experience. Unlike the philosophers, the jurists did not define these concepts and work out the implications of the definitions, but explained them by putting particular cases. They leapt from a concept to a conclusion about how it applied in a particular cases without explaining how they got there—a feature of their method that can be unsettling to those familiar with intellectual traditions such as Greek philosophy, or modern physics or economics, in which one is supposed to describe the path that leads from premise to conclusion.

Perhaps because the method of the Roman jurists was so different, modern scholars have had trouble seeing how it could have taken them so far. Many scholars have thought that the jurists' success must have resulted not from a concern for particular cases, but from an effort to transcend this concern. Many have thought that they did so by borrowing from the Greeks. Thus, according to Paul Jörs, the Roman jurists succeeded because they advanced from an approach based on particular cases (*Cautelarjurisprudenz*) toward one based on rules

[43] D. 19.2.22.  [44] G. 3.147.  [45] D. 19.2.22.
[46] This paragraph owes a great deal to a conversation with Patrick Hanlon.

(*Regularjurisprudenz*).⁴⁷ According to Giorgio La Pira,⁴⁸ Fritz Pringsheim,⁴⁹ Fritz Schulz, and Peter Stein, they did so by borrowing the method of Greek philosophy, and particularly that of Aristotle.⁵⁰ According to Aldo Schiavone, their method came from a "delicate and crucial process of integration" with Greek philosophy, which managed to "project Roman legal knowledge beyond previously attained horizons...."⁵¹

In Stein's account:

> By the end of the [second] century the whole field of private law was covered by juristic opinions given piecemeal, and it became necessary to organise the mass of material in some way. The material remained Roman, but the methods by which it was organised were Greek. It was from Aristotle, in particular, that the Roman jurists learned these methods. In his works they found a statement of the general technique by which any science should be constructed....⁵²

The result, according to Stein, was a "scientific revolution."

According to Schulz, the use of Aristotelian dialectic:

> ... was a matter of extreme significance in the history of Roman jurisprudence and therefore of jurisprudence generally. It introduced Roman jurisprudence into the circle of the Hellenistic professional sciences and turned it into a science in the sense in which that term is used by Plato and Aristotle no less than by Kant.⁵³

These conclusions cannot be correct. They truly obscure the unique contribution that the Roman jurists made, which was not to borrow from Greek philosophy, but rather to found an intellectual tradition of their own that approached problems in a different way.

These modern scholars correctly understood Aristotle's idea of the proper method to be followed in investigating a subject. Stein described it very well:

> We begin by accumulating experience.... From the stage of experience we pass to the stage of science by finding the common element in the particular cases which have been observed.... [D]iscovery of the common element... is the method by which first principles are reached.... The final act of insight, whereby we are led on to recognise the principle which lies behind all the particular instances [is] itself an act of intuition ($νοῦς$)... [W]hen the fundamental principles have been discovered... deduction is possible.... Thus Aristotle conceived the development of a science as an upward movement of thought... [by] which first principles are discovered and stated, followed by a downward deductive process in which the necessary consequences of those principles are worked out... The material organized by these two movements [can then be] organized according to its various parts, *genera* and *species*.⁵⁴

---

⁴⁷ Paul Jörs, *Römische Rechtswissenschaft zur Zeit der Republik, I: Bis auf die Catonen* (Berlin, 1888), 295–313. For criticism of his use of evidence, *see* Stein (n. 7), 32–33.

⁴⁸ Giorgio La Pira, "La genesi del sistema nella giurisprudenza romana," in *Studia et Documenta Historiae et Iuri*, ed. Aemilius Albertario (Rome, 1935), 319.

⁴⁹ Fritz Pringsheim, "Beryt und Bologna," *Festschrift Otto Lenel* (Leipzig, 1921), 246. *See* Stephan Meder, *Rechtsgeschichte Eine Einführung*, 2d ed. (Cologne, 2005), 53–54.

⁵⁰ In contrast, Jörs thought that there was no evidence to support any conclusion about Greek influence on the development of what he called *Regularjurisprudenz*: Jörs (n. 47), 312–13.

⁵¹ Schiavone (n. 3), 186.   ⁵² Stein (n. 7), 33–35.
⁵³ Schulz (n. 1), 67.   ⁵⁴ Stein (n. 7), 34–36.

But the jurists did not use such a method. To show that they did, Schulz and Stein note that Q. Mucius Scaevola used a general term when he might have used one that was more particular. He spoke of the theft of an "object," whereas M. Junius Brutus, forty years earlier, had spoken of the theft of a "horse." That difference hardly supports the conclusion of Schulz and Stein that Scaevola was seizing on the common element in the manner commended by Aristotle.[55]

According to Schiavone, "the achievement of abstractions and concepts developed in Roman legal thought, not before, but in conjunction with the use" of Greek models.[56] But, as we have seen, Roman legal concepts were not abstract in the same way as those of Greek philosophy. For the most part, they were taken from ordinary experience. Nor were they defined abstractly and the implications of the definitions logically explored.

According to Schiavone, "the logical foundation" of the thought of Q. Mucius Scaevola was "an new analytical structure…identified in the articulation of the content into modules by division into genera and species"—an idea that Mucius supposedly took from Plato and Aristotle.[57] In a similar vein, Schulz noted that Mucius distinguished several genera of possession, P. Mucius Scaevola distinguished five kinds of tutorship, and S. Sulpicius Rufus four kinds of theft.[58] But these distinctions were not general in the Aristotelian sense. For Aristotle, science depended on the abstraction of first principles. The principles could be stated in a definition that consisted of a genus containing several different species and a distinction that made one species different from all others. For example, in the statement "Man is a rational animal," the genus is "animal," the distinction is "rational," and taken together they define the species to which man belongs. The Roman jurists' lists of types of possession, tutorship, and theft do not attempt anything of the sort. They are simply lists. The Roman jurists are doing no more than common lawyers do when they say that there are four traditional types of negative easement: light, view, support, and the passage of water; or that there are three types of burden that run with the land: easements, real covenants, and equitable servitudes. As Watson said, "the drawing of these distinctions could easily have occurred without the influence of Greek dialectics; moreover, without the further division of a genus into its species, the essential Greek contribution is lacking."[59]

Schulz and Stein also noted that, sometimes, the Roman jurists phrased their opinions as general rules. Schulz cited two instances in which they did so. Stein cited another seven. Certainly, the Roman jurists sometimes found it useful to formulate general rules. Stein may even be right that "[t]hese propositions show a confident mastery of the relevant material coupled with an ability to pick out the universal element from the mass of opinions and express it in precise terms."[60]

---

[55] Schulz (n. 1), 65–66; Stein (n. 7), 45.   [56] Schiavone (n. 3), 198.
[57] Schiavone (n. 3), 184–85.   [58] Schulz (n. 1), 65.
[59] Watson (n. 10), 163.   [60] Stein (n. 7), 38.

Nevertheless, none of the rules that Schulz[61] and Stein[62] mention look like an Aristotelian first principle. Rather, they were statements about regularities that had been observed in particular cases. As the jurist Paulus explained:

> A rule (*regula*) briefly explains a *res* [a thing, event, or fact]. The law is not taken from rules, but the rule comes from the law. Therefore the rule is a brief statement of the *res* which is handed down (*traditur*). So, as Sabinus says, it is a putting together (*coniectio*) of *causae* [meaning cases, or arguments and reasons[63]] which loses its force as soon as it is defective in any way.[64]

After a detailed analysis of this passage and others, Stein himself concluded that some jurists thought that a rule "was merely a reflection of the actual state of the law and had no independent normative force"[65]: "In the classical period, the term *regula* connoted a juristic rule, which summed up what had been handed down (*tradita*) by juristic practice."[66] Given the examples that Stein mentions, it is hard to think that rules in the late Republic were regarded differently.

In a celebrated study, Theodor Viehweg pointed out that the Roman jurists' method was not based on the kind of reasoning that Aristotle ascribed to science.[67] Critics such as Max Kaser and Franz Horak attacked his conclusion.[68] Arthur Schiller tried to keep the peace by claiming that the Romans used "all the types of reasoning for decision-making which modern legal thinkers are accustomed to employ."[69] Yet the text that Schiller presented as an example of Roman legal reasoning is that quoted earlier in which Paulus explained possession by putting particular cases. Viehweg's critics did not cite texts in which the Romans used a method of reasoning that abstracted first principles and then drew conclusions.

---

[61] The only kind of work one could do on public holidays was work that would prevent damage from occurring: Macrob. Sta. 1.16.10. 2. The widow of C. Gracchus could not obtain the return of her property from his heirs after her husband's murder for his political activities on the ground that a husband is responsible for damage caused by himself intentionally or through negligence: D. 24.3.66. pr.; Schulz (n. 1), 65.

[62] An act is done by force [and therefore a party's possession gained by force is not protected] when the act is prohibited: D. 50.17.73.2. Whatever is not attached to the soil or part of a building does not pass to the buyer of land: D. 50.16.241. Whatever is written in a testament, and cannot be understood, is treated as though it had not been written: D. 50.17.73.3. One cannot provide a benefit for another by making an agreement or stipulation in his favor: D. 50.17.73. No one can appoint a tutor except to one whom he has as his heir: D. 50.17.73.1. Whoever is a tutor for a person has a tutor's power over his estate [when he dies] except when the heirs are female: D. 50.17.73.pr. If C steals goods from B that B had stolen from A, B cannot get them back because the *actio furti* protects only "the person whose interest it was that the thing which was taken should be untouched": D. 47.2.77. *See* Stein (n. 7), 36–38, 46.

[63] In context, *causae* seems to mean cases, but, according to Gaius, the parties would summarize their case before the iudex "and [t]his was called *causae coniectio*....": G. 4.17. The parties were bringing together the arguments or reasons why they should prevail.

[64] D. 50.17.1.   [65] Stein (n. 7), 73.   [66] Stein (n. 7), 110.

[67] Theodor Viehweg, *Topik und Jurisprudenz*, 5th ed. (Munich, 1974).

[68] Max Kaser, *Zur Methodologie der römischen Rechts Quellenforschung* (Vienna, 1972), 53; Franz Horak, *Rationes decidendi: Entscheidungsbegründungen bei den älteren römischen Juristen bis Labeo* (Innsbruck, 1969), 45–64.

[69] Schiller (n. 7), 383–84.

Indeed, Seidl has shown that the Romans did not do so.[70] Rather, Viehweg's critics assumed that, since valid reasoning demonstrates its conclusions, the Roman jurists must have been using it.

Nevertheless, Viehweg himself thought that the Roman jurists took their method from Aristotle. It was not the method of science, which is based on the abstraction of first principles, but the problem-based method that Aristotle described in the *Topics*, which reaches conclusions that are tentative rather than certain. There, Aristotle distinguished demonstration, which reasons from first principles and is characteristic of science, from dialectical argument, which reasons from "reputable opinions." Dialectical argument may proceed by "deduction," which shows that "certain things being laid down, something other than these necessarily comes about through them."[71] It may also proceed by "induction," which "is a passage from particulars to universals, e.g., the argument that supposing the skilled pilot is the most effective, then likewise the skilled charioteer, then in general the skilled man is the best at his particular task."[72] As we have seen, however, the Roman jurists were not reasoning from reputable opinions. They were giving their own opinions as jurists as to how legal concepts applied to particular cases. They were neither deducing the results in the cases from the concepts, nor deriving general conclusions about the concepts from the results in the cases. As Blühdorn has shown,[73] in identifying the method of the *Topics* with that of the Roman jurists, Viehweg misread the *Topics*.

Cicero understood how different the work of the jurists was from the treatises of the Greeks. He lived during the period that Schulz called "[t]he heroic age of creative genius and daring pioneers,"[74] during which the jurists developed the method that classical jurists were to perfect. If Pomponius is correct,[75] the civil law was "founded" in the half-century before Cicero's birth. As a young man, Cicero attended the legal consultations of Q. Mucius Scaevola. Cicero did not like what he saw, especially as compared with Greek learning. The jurists concerned themselves with trifles. According to Atticus, a character in one of his dialogues, "though they have made great claims, they have spent their time on unimportant details...." They write about "the law of eaves and house-walls [*de parietum*]," and about "the *formulae* for making a *stipulatio* or bringing a legal action"—and "all this amounts to little so far as learning is concerned...."[76]

---

[70] Erwin Seidl, "Labeos geistiges Profil," in vol. 1 of *Studi in onore di Edoardo Volterra* (Milan, 1971), 63 at 64–68. Seidl did believe that the Roman jurists used deductive reasoning in two cases: in interpreting the words of a testament and in interpreting those of the edict of the praetor. In both cases, their reasoning began, of course, with the word in question. But that would not show that their reasoning was deductive unless they were treating the word as an abstract concept from which conclusions could be derived by deductive logic. Instead, as his examples indicated, they were trying to determine what the testator or the praetor meant by the word—a question that turned on conventional usage and common sense.

[71] *Topics* I.i 100$^a$ 25–26.   [72] *Topics* I.xii 105$^a$ 10–15.

[73] Jürgen Blühdorn, "Kritische Bermerkungen zu Theodor Viewegs Schrift: Topic und Juriprudenz," *Tijdschrift voor Rechtsgeschiedenis* 38 (1970): 269, 278–307.

[74] Schulz (n. 1), 99.   [75] D. 1.2.2.39, 41.   [76] *De legibus* I.iv.14.

Cicero also thought that the method of the jurists was too unsystematic to be intellectually respectable. In his dialogue *De oratore*, Licinius Crassus explained that the reason why the study of law was "a matter of great difficulty" was that "no one [had been] able to distribute these matters into their kinds and arrange them as an *ars*."[77] By an *ars*, Cicero did not mean a science as Aristotle had conceived it: an exercise of theoretical, as opposed to practical, reason in which first principles are abstracted and conclusions follow deductively. For Cicero, an *ars* was an orderly and systematic presentation of practical knowledge, like a Greek treatise on rhetoric. He said: "*Ars* is the synthesis of disciplined observations for some purpose useful to life."[78] It was a definition taken from the Stoics and has been attributed to Zeno.[79] The word he was translating as *ars* was the Greek word *techne*, which means a useful or applied body of knowledge.[80]

Cicero believed that law should be made into an *ars*, but the jurists had failed to do so. In a dialogue, his character Licinius explains that one should proceed by:

...dividing the entire civil law into its genera, which are very few, and next distributing what I may call the members of those classes, and after that making the proper significance of each plain by definition, [and] then you will have a perfect *ars* of the civil law, magnificent and copious but neither inaccessible nor mysterious.[81]

The disorderly work of the jurists did not rise to the level of an *ars*.

Later, in the same dialogue, Antonius complained:

[T]he jurists embarrass us and frighten us away from learning. For I observe that in the treatises of Cato and Brutus the advice given to clients of either sex is generally set down with the parties named, I suppose, to make us think that some reason for seeking advice or for the discussion originated in the parties and not in the circumstances, to the end that, seeing the parties to be innumerable, we might be discouraged from studying the law, and might cast away our inclination to learn at the same moment as our hope of mastery. But these matters Crassus will one day disentangle for us and set forth arranged under heads.

To judge from the texts that have survived, to reproach the jurists for mentioning the names of the parties seems unfair. Names are rare and the cases are usually stated so abstractly that one cannot tell whether they are real or hypothetical. But Cicero evidently did not see why the jurists should discuss particular cases instead of presenting the law "under heads" as an *ars*. Once that task had been accomplished, Crassus explained, "no *ars* would be easier of attainment."[82] It could be learned by the nonspecialists along with other *artes*, such as rhetoric. It could be learned by the *oratores* who actually argued cases, but had no specialized legal training. Would there then be any need for jurists? Cicero does not say. According

---

[77] *De oratore* I.xli, 185–86.
[78] Volume 1 of *Storicorum Veterum Fragmenta*, ed. Johannnes ab Arnim (Lipsiae, 1905), 21 ll. 19–20.
[79] By Olympiodorus: *Storicorum Veterum Fragmenta* (n. 78), 21 ll. 3–6. On Stoic doctrines of art, see Neal W. Gilbert, *Renaissance Concepts of Method* (New York, 1960), 11–13.
[80] See the definitions of Olympiodorus and Lucianus in *Storicorum Veterum Fragmenta* (n. 78), 21 ll. 3–8.
[81] *De oratore* I.xli, 191.   [82] *De oratore* I.xli, 185.

to Aulius Gellius, Cicero wrote a work, *De iure civile in artem redigendo* [The civil law redacted as (or reduced to) an art],[83] but it disappeared and left no trace on the work of the jurists,[84] who, as Stein observed, "turned their backs on Cicero's idea of converting the law into a science composed of clear cut rules...."[85] There was no doubt in Cicero's mind that jurists had not learned their method from the Greeks. The jurists' innovation was as strikingly original as that of the Greeks themselves, or that of the founders of modern physics and economics.

## Roman law and later civil law

Much of modern civil law is based on concepts that the Roman jurists identified and refined. Nevertheless, today it is commonly said that a distinctive feature of civil law is that it depends on principle and on system. The civil law is organized into fields such as property, tort, contract, and unjust enrichment. Each is explained by a series of rules and principles that are to govern it.

Roman law was not based on a set of rules or principles that the jurists themselves articulated. Neither did Roman law have a systematic doctrinal structure. Because of their method, the Roman jurists did not feel a need for them. Their method required a stock of concepts of legal significance that they could refine by putting particular cases. When they had to decide which of two concepts to apply to a particular situation, such as sale or lease, they resolved that question as well by putting particular cases. Their method did not require a set of general principles or an explanation of the relationship between a concept and some higher-level concept.

In modern civil law, doctrines are organized into categories such as tort, contract, and unjust enrichment, which are explained by general principles. Property is typically explained by the general principle that an owner can deal as he wishes with what he owns. The principle is then qualified by doctrines, such as necessity, which sometimes allows another person to use the owner's property, or nuisance, which limits the owner's use of his property in order to protect others. Both the *Digest* and the *Institutes* of Justinian contain introductory sections on property law modeled on the treatise of Gaius. These introductions do not explain property by means of a general principle or describe the doctrines that qualify it. Rather, they discuss the rights that a person can have in his own things, and also to things that have no owner or are owned by someone else. These rights are discussed by putting particular cases in the way described earlier. The sea and seashore are "common things" that belong to everyone, and so everyone can use them.[86] But an individual

---

[83] *Noctes Atticae* 1.22.7.

[84] In *Brutus* 41.152, Cicero praised his friend, the jurist Servius Sulpicius Rufus, for using dialectic and treating law as an *ars*. Schulz called that statement a "gross exaggeration": Schulz (n. 1), 69. Even if it were true, it did not shape the work of later jurists or even their use of Servius' work. As Stein noted, the surviving references to Servius' writings do not suggest a systematic treatment of law: Stein (n. 7), 42.

[85] Stein (n. 7), 102.    [86] I. 2.1.1; I. 2.1.5; D. 1.8.2.1.

owns gems or pebbles that he takes from the shore.[87] Moreover, an individual can build a hut on the shore[88] and others must keep clear of the hut.[89] But his ownership lasts only as long as the building remains: if it collapses, someone else can build on the site.[90] Wild animals, birds, and fish belong to no one, but become the property of the person who captures them.[91] Rivers and harbors are "public things": they belong to the public, and everyone can fish or boat on them.[92] The banks are owned by those whose lands border them, yet everyone using the river is free to beach boats, dry nets, and haul fish onto the banks, and to tie up to trees there, even though the trees belong to the owner of the land.[93] Theaters and stadiums are "civic things": they belong to the citizen body as a whole, not to the citizens as individuals.[94] An individual citizen, however, has a right of action against anyone who prevents him from using them.[95] Some things cannot become private property: consecrated things (*res sacrae*), such as temples,[96] hallowed things (*res religiosae*), such as tombs, which, unlike temples, can cease to be private property by the act of a private person who buries a corpse on a plot;[97] and city walls and gates (*res sanctae*), which are not only incapable of private ownership,[98] but also of private use by a person who wishes to build against them.[99]

The Roman jurists did not explain tort and contract law by general principles.[100] Theirs was a law of particular torts and contracts. Even the categories of tort and contract arrived late. Gaius was the first to distinguish the general classes of obligations *delictus* and *contractus*.[101] Justinian's compilers supplemented them with two more. One was "quasi-tort" (*quasi ex maleficio*) to cover cases of what we would call strict liability: for example the defendant was liable when harm was done by objects thrown out of windows,[102] or hung over the street,[103] or when harm was done by those he employed to a guest in an inn.[104] He was also liable without fault in an *actio de pauperie* for harm done by animals that he owned.[105] The other was "quasi-contract" (*quasi ex contractu*) to cover certain cases of what we would call unjust enrichment.[106] The defendant was liable when the plaintiff had paid him money by mistake or taken care of his property without being asked to do so. The categories of tort and contract may not have been of Roman origin. They are similar to a distinction that Aristotle drew between involuntary and voluntary commutative justice. Modern scholars believe that Gaius took them from Aristotle.[107] In any event, Gaius did not discuss these categories and their implications. Having introduced them, he immediately turned to the particular torts and contracts of Roman law.

---

[87] D. 1.8.3.  [88] I. 2.1.5; D. 1.8.3.  [89] D. 1.8.4.  [90] D. 1.8.6.pr.
[91] I. 2.1.12.  [92] I. 2.1.2; D. 1.8.5.pr.  [93] I. 2.1.4; D. 1.8.5.pr.
[94] I. 2.1.6; D. 1.8.6.1.  [95] D. 47.10.15.7.  [96] I. 2.1.8; D. 1.8.6.3.
[97] D. 1.8.6.4; I. 2.1.9.  [98] I. 2.1.10; D. 1.8.6.2; D. 1.8.8.2.  [99] D. 1.8.8.2.
[100] *See* Watson (n. 10), 169–70; J. A. C. Thomas, *Textbook of Roman Law* (Oxford, 1976), 226.
[101] G. 3.88.  [102] D. 9.3.1.pr; I. 4.5.1.  [103] I. 4.5.1.2; D. 9.3.5.6–13.
[104] D. 47.5; I. 4.5.3.  [105] D. 9.1; I. 4.9.  [106] I. 3.13.2.
[107] Zimmermann (n. 17), 10–11; Max Kaser, *Römische Privatrecht* (Munich, 1959), 522; A. M. Honoré, *Gaius* (Oxford, 1962), 100; Helmut Coing, "Zum Einfluß der Philosophie des Aristoteles aud die Entwicklung des römischen Rechts," *Zeitschrift der Savigny-Stiftung für Rechtsgeschichte, Rom. Abt.* 69 (1952): 24, 59.

Modern civil lawyers typically explain tort by the general principle that one who intentionally or negligently causes harm must pay compensation, at least for causing certain types of harm. That principle is then qualified to allow for certain cases of strict liability. In his introduction to tort law, Gaius did not state a general principle. He explained that obligations in tort could arise in four ways.[108] Two of them, theft (*furtum*) and robbery (*rapina*), are penal actions. The plaintiff could recover a multiple of the value of the property threatened. These actions had been instituted before the Romans had an effective system of criminal justice. They fell into disuse with the advent of a procedure called *cognitio extraordinaria*, in which cases could be tried and penalties could be imposed by magistrates.[109] A third way in which an obligation in tort could arise was an action under the *lex Aquilia* for physical harm done by fault, either intentionally or negligently. In the texts, the physical harm is nearly always to one's property, although in two texts it is to one's son. The fourth way was an action for *iniuria*, which, in most cases, was an action for harm done to one's dignity or reputation.

Modern civil lawyers typically explain contract in terms of the consent of the parties and then qualify the general principle to limit the agreements that are enforceable. Gaius no sooner mentioned contract as a general category of obligations than he described the particular contracts recognized in Roman law. While the Romans knew that all contracts require consent to be binding, only some—the "consensual" contracts (contracts *consensu*)—are binding by consent alone. Gaius mentioned sale, lease (or hire), partnership, and mandate, which is a kind of gratuitous agency. Others, the "real" contracts (contracts *re*), are binding when an object is actually delivered. Gaius mentions loans for use or for consumption, deposit, and pledge. Other contracts were binding upon the execution of a formality. The all-purpose formality was *stipulatio*, which was originally oral, although eventually writing could be used to prove a *stipulatio* had been made. One party would ask the other "Do you promise such and such?" and the other would answer that he did. For each party to be bound, each party would make a *stipulatio* in which his obligation was conditional on the other party's fulfillment of his own. In contrast to a sale or lease, which were contracts "of good faith" (*bonae fidei*), *stipulatio* was a contract of strict law (*stricti iuris*). That meant that, in a sale or lease, the parties were bound not only to what they said, but also to whatever else good faith required. In contrast, in a *stipulatio*, a party was bound only to what he had said, fairly interpreted, but not supplemented by obligations that he had not expressly undertaken. Eventually, a special formality, *insinuatio*, was required for the promises of gifts. The promise had to be officially registered. Finally, there were "innominate" contracts—contracts "without names"—that were not enforceable before performance. An example was barter.

The Roman jurists had no general explanation why different contracts should be formed in different ways. Rules had grown up around each particular contract and

---

[108] G. 3.182.  [109] Zimmermann (n. 17), 944.

Gaius, in classifying these contracts, was noting resemblances among the rules. As Alan Watson observed, for the Roman jurists:

Each individual type of contract, such as stipulation, loan for use, or loan for consumption, sale, hire, or mandate, remains intact with its own sui generis body of rules.... [F]or a Roman jurist it was unthinkable... to write a commentary on the law of contracts or even on the law of a group of contracts, such as consensual contracts. The same is equally true of other fields, for instance of delicts.[110]

We have seen why the Romans would not have felt the need to write such a commentary. Their method was to identify a concept of legal significance and then refine it by putting particular cases. As we will see in a later chapter,[111] private law acquired a systematic structure based on general principles for the first time in the sixteenth century, when a group centered in Spain and known to historians as the "late scholastics" synthesized Roman law with the moral philosophy of their intellectual heroes, Aristotle and Thomas Aquinas. In the seventeenth century, many of their conclusions were taken over by a school of jurists founded by Hugo Grotius and passed eventually into modern law. Paradoxically, their conclusions were disseminated throughout Europe even though the philosophical ideas on which these conclusions had been founded were falling from favor.

## Roman law and common law

A distinctive feature of common law is that it has been based on decided cases. Peter Stein noted that the work of the Roman jurists and that of the common law judges is similar in that it depends on the use of particular cases.[112] But it would be a mistake to think that the method of the English judges who founded the common law was like that of the Roman jurists. They were using their cases in very different ways.

The Roman jurists used cases to clarify the meaning of general concepts such as ownership, possession, fault, sale, and lease. Traditionally, English judges used cases to determine the boundaries of the writs recognized by the common law courts. To bring a case before the common law courts, the plaintiff had to obtain a "writ" from the royal chancellor. At first, the chancellor created new writs as new cases arose that, in his judgment, the royal courts ought to hear. Eventually, the number of writs became frozen, so that, by the fourteenth century, no new writs were being created. Until the nineteenth century, to obtain relief, the facts of the plaintiff's case had to fit one of the existing writs—often called the "forms of action." Whether or not they did so was decided by reference to the cases that had previously been decided. The judges did not try to determine the scope of writs

---

[110] Watson (n. 10), 170. [111] *See* Chapter III, pp. 84–98.
[112] Peter G. Stein, "Roman Law, Common Law and Civil Law," *Tulane Law Review* 66 (1992): 1591, 1591–92.

by such general concepts as possession, fault, or consent, nor did they regard cases as significant because they clarified such concepts. The cases gave rise to a body of lore that grew up around each writ without reference to any such general concept. Consequently, while the Roman jurists developed a substantive law based on these concepts that was largely independent of procedure, the English judges never developed a substantive law that stood apart from the procedural question of what writ the plaintiff could bring. As Sir Henry Maine said of the writ system, substantive law was secreted in the interstices of procedure.[113]

The great historian Frederic William Maitland once said that, when the history of the common law is finally written, we will understand how the common lawyers arrived at "the great elementary conceptions, ownership, possession, contract, tort and the like."[114] As Charles Donahue has said:

[W]e know a considerable amount more today than we did when Maitland wrote.... What we have learned, however, is puzzling. Relatively little of the history of the forms of action seems to deal with "the great elementary conceptions," like ownership, possession, tort and contract.[115]

As we will see later,[116] these conceptions and a great deal else were borrowed from the civil law in the nineteenth century, and grafted onto the English common law.

It seems surprising that the common lawyers took so long to arrive at the point that the Romans had reached centuries before and that they did so only by borrowing from civil law. It is all the more surprising because, like the Romans, the common law judges and practitioners belonged to a learned tradition concerned with the interpretation of the law in force. They both were cadres of experts who, having spent a long apprenticeship mastering that law, could speak with authority on how the law in force should be understood.

Indeed, both legal traditions emerged in a similar way. In England, as in Rome, an earlier formal procedure was replaced by one in which a judgment had to be made as to whether a claim was good. In Rome, the learned men who made that judgment were the jurists. In England, they were the common law judges and practitioners. In Rome, as we have seen, that change took place when the formulary procedure replaced that of the *legis actio*. In England, it took place soon after the king decided that certain types of claim would be heard by his central courts in Westminster.

Initially, proceedings in the king's courts may have been much like those in the English manorial courts described earlier. In the king's courts, as in the manorial court, a lawsuit comprised two stages. In the first, the plaintiff formally made a claim, which the defendant formally denied. In the second, the case was decided by some mechanical procedure, such as the use of oath helpers—the so-called "wager

---

[113] Henry Maine, *Dissertations on Early Law and Custom* (London, 1883), 389.
[114] Frederic William Maitland, "Why the History of English Law is Not Yet Written," in vol. 1 of *The Collected Papers of Fredric William Maitland* (Cambridge, 1911), 480 at 484.
[115] Charles Donahue, "Why the History of Canon Law is Not Written," Selden Society lecture, Old Hall of Lincoln's Inn, London, July 3, 1984 (London, 1986), 6.
[116] *See* Chapter IX, pp. 204–12.

of law." If the defendant appeared on a set day with a prescribed number of people who would swear that he was in the right, then he prevailed with no further appeal. Later, for some writs, the procedure was trial by jury, but it was not a jury in a modern sense. It heard no evidence and was not instructed on the substantive law. Rather, it was a body of laypeople who were simply to say whether or not they believed an allegation to be true. In the king's courts, the first phase was carried out by pleading before the king's judges in London. The second was carried out in whatever place the dispute had arisen. Initially, then, substantive and procedural law, and questions of law and fact, were entangled, as they were in the Roman *legis actio*. The defendant who denied that he had struck the plaintiff wrongfully might mean that he had never struck him at all or that he had had every right to strike him.

Matters changed when the pleadings were no longer limited to a claim by one party and a denial by the other. Each party could respond in one of three ways to the other party's pleading. He could "traverse," which meant that he could deny the other party's claim. He could "demur," which meant that he could concede the truth of it, but claim that he should prevail anyway. Or he could "plead new matter," which meant that he could plead some additional fact that, if true, might entitle him to prevail. For example, if the plaintiff were to plead that the defendant had struck him, the defendant might concede that he had done so and plead that he had been defending himself after the plaintiff had attacked him with a knife. The parties would plead new matter until one of them traversed or demurred. If a party traversed, the question of whose account of the facts was true would be settled in the second phase of the procedure, by oath helpers or by a jury, in the locality in which the dispute had arisen. If he demurred, then there would be no second phase. The judges would decide then and there which party was entitled to prevail on the facts that had been conceded. If they decided against the party who had demurred, that party had no chance to change his mind and to put into issue the facts that he had conceded. He lost.

It then became possible to build up a body of law governing what should constitute a good claim. The judges had to decide who should prevail on a given state of the facts. One might have expected events to take the same course that they had in Rome. By comparing one case with another, the English might have arrived at "great elementary conceptions" on which the parties' rights would depend. Instead, the English judges did not employ such "great elementary conceptions" to determine whether the plaintiff could bring his case within an existing writ. They merely consulted the lore that had grown up around that writ. That lore was developed to delimit the writs, so as, if possible, to give relief in deserving cases. It was not an attempt to delimit relief by general ideas as to when relief ought to be given.

Indeed, it was not until the nineteenth century that English courts arrived at the "elementary conceptions" that we have used to illustrate Roman law: the protection of possession, as distinct from ownership; liability for fault, as distinct from strict liability; consent in contract formation that could be vitiated by mistake.

The English courts were never clear about whether they were protecting ownership or possession until the Court of Queen's Bench decided *Asher v. Whitlock* in 1865.[117] In that case, the Court allowed a prior possessor to recover land to which it was clear he did not have title. In a series of prior cases, the courts had allowed the possessor to recover, saying that the plaintiff's prior possession was evidence of title. The principle was laid down by Lord Holt at the end of the seventeenth century. He said that twenty years of possession raised a presumption that the plaintiff had title.[118] In 1777, Lord Mansfield repeated Holt's rule, but paradoxically allowed a plaintiff to recover who could not prove possession for that length of time.[119] In 1829, a plaintiff won by proving that, after he had been in possession a year, the "defendant had forcibly taken possession."[120] The Court did not explain whether he won because he had possession or because possession was regarded as evidence of title.[121] In 1841, a jury was instructed that it could find that the plaintiff had title since he had been in possession, although for less than twenty years.[122] In short, as long as the plaintiff had been in possession and it was possible that he had title, the courts would protect him without facing the question of whether what mattered was possession or title. They confronted that question only when they were forced to: when it was clear that the plaintiff once had possession, but never had title. The first such case was *Doe dem. Carter v. Barnard*, decided in 1849.[123] The plaintiff lost because, according to the Court, prior possession was only evidence of title. Then, in 1865, in *Asher v. Whitlock*, in which again it was clear the plaintiff did not have title, the Court finally laid down the rule that is accepted in common law jurisdictions today: the plaintiff who had possession, but not title, can recover.

As late as the eighteenth century it was still impossible to know whether the fault of the defendant mattered in common law when the plaintiff was trying to recover for harm done to him. The reason was not that the common law judges distinguished fault-based and strict liability, and had trouble making up their minds what rule to adopt. As Milsom and Fifoot have pointed out, they failed to draw that distinction.[124] The plaintiff did not need to allege fault when he sued for trespass in assault and battery, trespass to land (*quare clausum fregit*), trespass to chattels (*de bonis asportatis*), and so forth. He might simply allege that the defendant had struck him, or set fire to his house, or killed his horse. The defendant could then traverse—that is, he could deny that he had done so—or he could plead new

---

[117] 1 L.R. 1 Q.B. For a fuller account, *see* James Gordley and Ugo Mattei, "Protecting Possession," *California Law Review* 44 (1996): 293, 319–27.

[118] *Stokes v. Berry*, 2 Salk. 421, 91 E.R. 366 (K.B. 1699).

[119] *Denn ex dem. Tarzwell v. Barnard*, Cowp. 595, 98 E.R. 1259 (K.B. 1777).

[120] *Doe dem Hughes v. Dyeball*, M. & M 345, 173 E.R. 1184 (N.P. 1829).

[121] Chitty, for the defendant, objected that the plaintiff had not proven title. Lord Tenterden, C.J., answered: "That does not signify; there is ample proof; the plaintiff is in possession, and you come and turn him out; you must show your title." Dispossession, then, was proof of title. The headnote summarized: "Prior possession, however short, is sufficient prima facie title in ejectment against a mere wrongdoer."

[122] *Doe dem. Humphrey v. Martin*, Carr & M. 32, 174 E.R. 395 (N.P. 1841).

[123] 13 Q.B. 945, 116 E.R. 1524 (1849).

[124] S. F. C. Milsom, *Historical Foundations of the Common Law* (London, 1981), 392–98; C. H. S. Fifoot, *History and Sources of the Common Law Tort and Contract* (London, 1949), 189, 191.

matter that he hoped would exonerate him. If he traversed, the question of whether the defendant had shot or struck him would go to a jury. It is hard to know whether juries cared whether or not the defendant was at fault.[125] If, for example, the plaintiff had been struck when the defendant's horse had bolted, a jury might hold the defendant liable, or they might conclude that it was not the defendant but the horse that had struck the plaintiff, or, possibly, that he had not committed a trespass or wrong, whatever that might have meant to the jurymen. There is no way to know.

The defendant's other alternative was to plead in justification that he was not at fault. It was not clear what would happen then. Defendants did so in only a few cases, and the remarks of the judges are confusing and seem contradictory. Some judges said that the defendant was not liable if he had done his best;[126] some said that he was;[127] and some said that he could escape liability if his conduct were the product of "unavoidable necessity."[128] It is hard to know what these statements meant to the judges who made them. For example, in *Weaver v. Ward*, a member of a company of part-time soldiers injured another when his musket accidentally fired. He pled that he was not at fault. The Court said that he was liable anyway, but would be excused if he were "utterly without fault," if the accident were "inevitable," and if he "had committed no negligence to give occasion to the hurt."[129] As Fifoot said of this case, "'[f]ault,' 'inevitable accident,' 'negligence' are words used indiscriminately without reflection and almost without meaning."[130] As in the case of possession, rather than looking for a "great elementary conception" that would

---

[125] Milsom (n. 124), 393.

[126] For example, *The Thorns Case*, Y.B. Mich. 6 Ed. 4, f. 7, pl. 18 (1466) (Choke, C.J.: "As to what has been said that they [thorns] fell ipso invito [on another's land], this is not a good plea; but he should have said that he could not do it in any other manner or that he did all that was in his power to keep them out"); *Mitten v. Fandrye*, Popham 161, 79 E.R. 1259 (K.B. 1626) (defendant excused because he has "done his best endeavor"); *Wakeman v. Robinson*, 1 Bing. 213, 130 E.R. 86 (C.P. 1823) (Dallas, C.J.: "If the accident happened entirely without default on the part of the defendant or blame imputable to him, the action does not lie").

[127] *The Thorns Case* (n. 126) (Littleton, J.: "If a man suffers damage, it is right that he be recompensed"); *Lambert v. Bessey*, Sir T. Raym. 421, 467, 83 E.R. 220, 221 (K.B. 1682) (Sir Thomas Raymond: "in all civil acts the law doth not so much regard the intent of the actor as the loss and damage of the party suffering"); *Leame v. Bray*, 3 East. 593, 102 E.R. 724 (K.B. 1803) (Grose, J.: "if the injury be done by the act of the party himself at the time or he be the immediate cause of it, though it happen accidentally or by misfortune, yet he is answerable in trespass").

[128] *Dickenson v. Watson*, Sir T. Jones 205, 84 E.R. 218, 219 (K.B. 1682) (defendant who had shot the plaintiff and pleaded accident not excused, "for in trespass the defendant shall not be excused without unavoidable necessity").

[129] *Weaver v. Ward*, Hobart 134, 80 E.R. 284 (K.B. 1616).

[130] Fifoot (n. 124), 191. On account of these uncertainties, the plaintiff might sue not in a trespass action, but in trespass on the case, and allege that the defendant acted negligently in his statement of the facts that supposedly called for relief. Sometimes, the plaintiff did so: Milsom (n. 124), 394. But even then, it is not clear what the allegation meant: Milsom (n. 124), 399; A. I. Ogus, "Vagaries in Liability for the Escape of Fire," *Cambridge Law Journal* 27 (1969): 104, 105–06. It might or might not mean negligence in the modern (or ancient Roman) sense. Certainly, judges did not instruct the jury to ask themselves whether the defendant had behaved like a reasonable person. In any event, the defendants also brought actions of trespass on the case without alleging negligence: Milsom (n. 124), 394.

make sense of their particular cases, the common law judges almost seem bent on avoiding one.

The principle that mistake could prevent formation of a contract because the parties must consent to the same thing was acknowledged by an English court in 1865, in the now-famous case of *Raffles v. Wichelhaus*.[131] It concluded that there was no valid contract when one party intended to buy the cotton arriving on a ship named *Peerless* and the other party intended to sell the cotton arriving on another ship of the same name. Until then, the courts avoided a discussion of whether mistake destroys consent even in situations that might seem to cry out for it. As A. W. B. Simpson has said, the common law judges said very little about mistake until the nineteenth century.[132] Even then, they avoided saying much about it for a long time. In 1815, in *Cox v. Prentice*, a buyer of a bar of silver was mistaken as to how many ounces it contained.[133] In 1846, in *Smith v. Jeffryes*, a buyer of "ware potatoes" mistakenly thought that he was getting one kind of ware potatoes, "Regent's ware," when the potatoes in question were actually "Kidney wares."[134] In 1858, in *Scott v. Littledale*, a buyer purchased one hundred chests of Conguo tea when the seller had mistakenly shown him a sample of a quite different tea.[135] These are the kind of cases that the Romans might have put to probe the question of when the parties should be deemed to have consented. The common law judges decided them without ever raising that question: there was no warranty covering the ounces of silver in the bar; the parol evidence rule prevented the buyer from proving what kind of potatoes he intended; the buyer needed to compensate the seller only for any difference in the quality of the tea.

The point of these examples is not to disparage the work of the common lawyers. They cannot be criticized for failing to achieve what they never attempted. For the Roman jurists, the question of whether a party could recover turned on the meaning of concepts clarified by putting particular cases. In common law, whether a party could do so depended on the scope of a writ, as determined by a patchwork of unrationalized decisions laid down as the judges dealt with particular cases.

Maine seems to have thought that the writ system marked a mid-point in a natural process that leads all societies from formalistic procedures like those of early Germanic societies to a substantive law like that which the Romans developed and the English eventually adopted. That is not what happened. Although Romans had particular actions, they never had anything like the English writ system, let alone the English method for determining the scope of a writ. Moreover, once the English had established their writ system, there was no natural process that required it to disappear. It may have worked well enough for practical purposes. It was still intact when the English had developed a commercial empire in the seventeenth and eighteenth centuries, and began to industrialize in the early nineteenth century.

---

[131] 2 H. & C. 906, 159 E.R. 304 (1858).
[132] A. W. B. Simpson, "Innovation in 19th Century Contract Law," *Law Quarterly Review* 91 (1975): 247, 265–69.
[133] 3 M. & S. 344, 16. Rev. Rep. 288.
[134] 3 Ad. & El. 355, 11 E.R. 448.   [135] 8 Eliz. & Bl. 815, 120 E.R. 304.

It was displaced in the nineteenth century when common lawyers became concerned not with results that courts were reaching, which they accepted and tried to explain, but with explaining these results. As mentioned, they did so by borrowing much from the civil law. Before the nineteenth century, the English had a learned tradition, but not an intellectual tradition, if by that we mean one that is concerned with explanations. In the nineteenth century, the tradition became intellectual as well as learned. The cases were now significant because they were illustrations of general concepts of substantive law. For that reason, we will leave the common law aside until we come to the changes that took place in the nineteenth century.

# II

## *Ius Commune*
### The Medieval Jurists

### i THE CIVILIANS

#### Origins

In the first half of the twelfth century, the academic study of law began so rapidly that Kenneth Pennington has spoken of the "big bang."[1] One event was the renewed study of the *Corpus iuris civilis*. Another was the study of canon law based on the *Decretum*, a collection of excerpts from Church councils, the writings of the fathers, and other sources regarded as authoritative by Christians, which, according to tradition, was compiled by Gratian in 1140. For the medieval jurists, the civil and canon law constituted the *ius commune*, or "common law," applicable whenever a local ordinance or custom did not contradict it.

Traditionally, the university study of Roman and civil law is said to have begun in Bologna. According to the jurist Odofredus, writing in the thirteenth century, the first great teacher of Roman law was Irnerius, "the lamp of the law among us, that is, the first who taught law in this city ... he was of great fame and the first illuminator of the science, and he was the first who glossed our book."[2] Irnerius, he said, taught the Four Doctors of Bologna—Bulgarus, Martinus, Ugo, and Iacobus—through whom later doctors of law traced their pedigree.

Odofredus was writing well over a century after the events he described, much like Pomponius, who wrote about the founding of Roman civil law after more than a century. Odofredus' account has been questioned by Charles Radding and Antonio Ciaralli,[3] who believe that the study of Roman law was revived before Irnerius in the late eleventh century, and by Anders Winroth[4], who doubts that Irnerius had much to do with reviving it. Winroth believes that Roman law may not have been taught in Bologna before 1140.

---

[1] Kenneth Pennington, "The 'Big Bang': Roman Law in the Early Twelfth Century," *Rivista internazionale di diritto comune* 18 (2007): 43, 70.
[2] *The Origins of Medieval Jurisprudence: Pavia and Bologna 850–1150*, trans. Charles M. Radding (New Haven, CT, 1988), 159.
[3] Charles M. Radding and Antonio Ciaralli, *The* Corpus Iuris Civilis *in the Middle Ages: Manuscripts and Transmission from the Sixth Century to the Juristic Revival* (Leiden, 2007).
[4] Anders Winroth, *The Making of Gratian's* Decretum (Cambridge, 2000), 157–74.

## Ius Commune: *The Medieval Jurists*

However correct their conclusions may be about the revival of Roman law, their research does show the steps by which it was revived. A first step was to produce a version of the *Corpus iuris civilis* as close as possible to the one originally promulgated by Justinian. The result was the "vulgate," the version that was in standard use in the Middle Ages. A second step was to write "glosses," or notes to the text, directing the reader's attention to some important passage or to a related text, or explaining a difficult word or phrase. A final step took the medieval jurists to what became their main enterprise: to apply the texts to new cases and, so far as possible, to explain each of its texts in terms of every other.

Scholars agree that whoever prepared the vulgate worked from the only surviving manuscript of the *Corpus iuris* known to us, written in the sixth century, and now called the *Pisana*, or the *Fiorentina*, because Florentines took it from Pisa as war booty in 1406. That manuscript was not merely transcribed, but sometimes changed. Some changes corrected grammatical or scribal errors. Some may have been made by using other ancient sources that have since disappeared. Others, as Radding and Chiarelli point out, altered the text so that it would make better sense.[5] These changes must have been made by someone with a good knowledge of Roman law.[6] Hermann Kantorowicz imagined him as a genius working alone—quite possibly, the legendary Irnerius.[7] As Kanorowicz recognized, however, and as Radding and Ciarelli pointed out, the vulgate must have been finished by 1085 at the latest.[8] Irnerius appears in documents dating from 1112 to 1125 (with his name spelled "Wernerius" or "Guarnerius").[9] It is hard to believe that the work could have been done by a person so young. Moreover, it is hard to believe that the work would have been done unless there already were jurists with a strong interest in Roman law. Radding and Chiarelli believed that these jurists had previously studied Lombard law and worked in Pavia, before Roman law was studied in Bologna.[10]

In any event, this attempt to bring an ancient text closer to the original version was unique for its time. According to Radding and Chiaralli, one cannot find this sort of textual criticism in fields other than law before the thirteenth century.[11] The production of the vulgate shows how far such efforts could go even before the advent of the philological techniques of the Renaissance humanists. But the humanists proceeded in a different way. As will be seen in a later chapter,[12] they corrected texts by paying close attention to grammar and syntax, and by comparing the use of a word or phrase in the *Corpus iuris* with its use in other ancient texts. The philological method that they developed is still basic to historians' study of ancient documents. In contrast, the vulgate was produced by identifying passages that did not make legal sense and correcting them so that they would. As Radding and Chiaralli explained,

---

[5] Radding and Ciaralli (n. 3), 185–90.  [6] Radding and Ciaralli (n. 3), 185–90.
[7] Hermann Kantorowicz, *Über die Entstehung der Digestenvulgata* (Weimar, 1910).
[8] Radding and Ciaralli (n. 3), 187, n. 44.  [9] Winroth (n. 4), 162–63.
[10] Radding and Ciaralli (n. 3), 212.  [11] Radding and Ciaralli (n. 3), 190.
[12] *See* Chapter IV, pp. 112–15.

"these jurists were prepared to substitute their understanding of what a text should mean for what the text actually said."[13]

While these scholars found evidence of the serious study of Roman law before Irnerius, Winroth found little evidence of the role of Irnerius.[14] Little that he wrote has survived other than some brief observations called the *Materia Codicis*, compiled, perhaps, from his glosses, and a series of glosses to the *Corpus iuris* traditionally ascribed to him. The writing of glosses, which are marginal or interlinear notes to a text, was characteristic of medieval jurists. A gloss is what a computer technician today would call a hypertext. A hypertext "allows a user... to link fields of information... and to retrieve the data non-sequentially."[15] One could read a Roman legal text from beginning to end, as it appeared in the *Corpus iuris*, or one could skip from a word or phrase in that text to a note on the text in a gloss.

Gero Dolazalek, followed by Winroth, questioned whether Irnerius wrote the glosses that have been traditionally ascribed to him.[16] Whoever may have written them, modern scholars have been dissatisfied by their intellectual content and that

---

[13] Radding and Ciaralli (n. 3), 192. For example, the word "without" (*sine*) was inserted to make a text say that an emancipated son could marry without, rather than with, his father's consent: D. 23.2.25. The word "not" (*non*) was inserted to make a text read that a grandfather could not arrange the marriage of two of his grandchildren: D. 23.2.3.

[14] He found no proof that a law school existed in Bologna before 1140, or that Irnerius had much to do with its beginnings: Winroth (n. 4), 162. Pennington, however, has found a good deal of evidence that the law school was in full swing in the early twelfth century and was influencing secular legislation elsewhere in the 1120s and 1130s: Pennington (n. 1); Kenneth Pennington, "The Birth of the *Ius commune*: King Roger II's Legislation," *Revista internazionale del diritto commune* 17 (2006): 1–40; Kenneth Pennington, "*Lex* and *ius* in the twelfth and thirteenth centuries," in Lex *and* Ius: *Essays on the Foundation of Law in Medieval and Early Modern Philosophy*, eds. A. Fidora, M. Lutz-Bachman, and A. Wagner (Stuttgart, 2010), 1–25.

[15] *Random House Webster's Unabridged Dictionary*, 2nd ed. s. v. "hypertext."

[16] Medieval manuscripts often identify the author of a gloss by marking it with letters indicating his name and known as his *siglum*: for example "B." for Bulgarus or "Bar." for Bartolus. Many early glosses are marked "Y," which has been thought to be the *siglum* of "Yrnerius" or "Irnerius." Dolazalek, followed by Winroth, suggested that Irnerius did not write them. To begin with, his name appears as "Wernerius" or "Guarnerius" in the court records that have survived, not as "Irnerius" or "Yrnerius": Winroth (n. 4), 166; *see* Gero Dolazalek, *Repertorium manuscriptorum veterum Codicis Iustiniani* (Frankfurt am Main, 1985), 465, n. 11. The *Materia Codicis* is signed "Guar." Moreover, as Dolazalek noted, sometimes letters next to a gloss merely indicated the owner of the manuscript from which the gloss had been transcribed. He developed what Winroth calls "the very attractive hypothesis" that "Y" was an owner, not an author: Dolazalek, *Repertorium* 49; Winroth (n. 4), 165. Dolazalek also noted that, most often, "Y" appears at the beginning of a gloss, although later in the twelfth century, *sigla* appear at the end of it. The symbol "§" often appeared at the beginning of a gloss to indicate that it was not part of the text. By scribal errors, the symbol could have been falsely transcribed as "Y," because it looks similar: Gero Dolazalek, "Review of Spagnesi, *Wernius Bononiensis iudex*," *Zeitscrift der Savigny-Stiftung für Rechtsgeschichte, Römische Abteilung* 88 (1971): 497; Winroth (n. 4), 166.

Their doubts may not be justified. If "Y" was the owner of a book, that book must have been uniquely rich in glosses and copyists must have had an exceptional desire to preserve the owner's identity. If "Y" was a scribal error for "§," scribes must have been careless in the same way many times. Moreover, as André Gouron observed, sometimes "Y" could not have been meant to show where a gloss began. It sometimes appears at the end of a gloss, or, as Andrea Errera noted, in an interlineal gloss, which is one written between lines of text where there would be no need to indicate that what follows is a gloss: André Gouron, "Le Droit romain a-t-il été la 'servante' du droit canonique?," *Initium Revista Catalana d'Història del Dret* 12 (2007): 231, 235; Andrea Errera, *Arbor Actionum* (Bologna, 1995), 128, n. 15. Dolzalek also noted, and Winroth acknowledged, that sometimes one finds "Y§" or "§Y": Dolzalek, *Repertorium* 472, n. 24; Winroth (n. 4), 166.

of the *Materia Codicis*. As Winroth notes, Kantorwicz said of the *Materia Codicis* "The first impression is very disappointing.... We are faced with a disorderly set of eight observations."[17] Dolazalek observed that the glosses traditionally ascribed to Irnerius would disappoint anyone looking for "long doctrinal expositions" like those of later jurists.

It would be fairer to say that, whoever may have written them, these glosses constituted a further step in the revival of the study of Roman law. Dolazalek divided them into three categories: "notabilia," which simply direct the reader's attention to some important passage in the text; "allegations," which draw attention to related texts elsewhere in the *Corpus iuris*; and "explicatory glosses," which are, for the most part, between one and four words long, and explain a difficult word or phrase, for example *transactum, id est, pactum* ("transaction [in this text] means agreement").[18] These, are, indeed, steps that one would take initially to clarify a text: to draw attention to important passages, to refer to related texts, and to explain difficult terms. These categories are a good description of the notes that a law professor might make on the pages of case books before teaching a class: underlining a passage in a case or statute to which students' attention is to be drawn; adding a reference in the margin to another case or statutory provision that students are to consider; or circling a term that students may find unfamiliar and which should be explained. Like the early glosses, such notes are a checklist of points to be made to clarify a text before going any further.

The teaching of the early twelfth-century jurists did go further. They were engaged in what became the main enterprise of the medieval civilians: the resolution of every case that might arise by reference to a text in the *Corpus iuris* and the explanation of each of its texts in terms of every other. Because they pursued this enterprise in glosses that they wrote in the margins of the *Corpus iuris*, historians have called them the "Glossators." Their work culminated in the *Glossa ordinaria*, or Standard Gloss of Accursius, which contained around a hundred thousand individual glosses, most taken from the work of his predecessors. Later medieval jurists are generally called the "Commentators," because they characteristically wrote commentaries on texts rather than glosses in the margins next to them. Two of the greatest were Bartolus of Saxoferrato and his pupil Baldus degli Ubaldi. The change was not simply one in literary form. The Commentators, as many scholars have noted, interpreted their texts more freely and applied them more often to the problems of their own time. We will see a striking example later. Nevertheless, the Commentators were engaged in the same enterprise as their predecessors: the resolution of every legal problem by a text and the explanation of every text by means of another. As we will see, they pursued this goal by the same methods.

This enterprise presupposed a different idea of what it meant to be a jurist, and of how law was to be interpreted, than that of the Romans. Among the Romans, a

---

[17] Gouron noted that Kantorwicz, "after saying that he had been deceived on first impression by their chaotic order, succeeded in showing that it was a question of glosses written by the master that had been compiled without order by his students": Gouron (n. 16), 234. But evidently the content of the glosses did not impress Kantorowicz either.

[18] Dolezalek, *Repertorium* (n. 16), 471.

jurist was someone who, by virtue of his specialized training, could give an opinion about Roman law that would be respected by other jurists. If a jurist cited an authority for his opinion, it was likely to be the opinion of another jurist. In the Middle Ages, a jurist was one who, by virtue of his specialized training, knew the Roman texts and could cite them to support his opinions. Law was based, as much of it still is, on the exposition of authoritative texts.

This chapter will describe the method by which the medieval jurists engaged in their enterprise. The historical consequences are hard to understate. Yet it is as difficult to say why the medieval jurists developed this method as it is to say why the Roman jurists developed theirs in the late Republic. Those who prepared the vulgate, even if they had been completely successful, would only have recreated the situation in which law had been taught in the late Roman Empire: instructors taught the texts of the classical jurists, but taught them more or less as written, without adding more. The medieval jurists launched the enterprise of understanding and applying law by comparing and reconciling authoritative texts.

## Method

One part of the medieval jurists' enterprise was to apply texts to situations that the texts did not expressly cover. Another part was to make sense of these texts by understanding each in terms of every other.

The first task was like that which modern lawyers face when they have to apply their own authoritative texts, whether judicial decisions or statutes, to new cases. Indeed, we will see that the method of the medieval lawyers was like that which modern lawyers still use. As one can say that the Renaissance humanists developed techniques of philology that are still used by historians, one can also say that the medieval jurists developed techniques of applying authoritative texts to new situations that are still used by lawyers. In this sense, Charles Homer Haskins was correct when he observed in his study of the twelfth century that law (as practiced today) is inherently scholastic.[19]

There were, of course, differences. A major one was that the texts that modern lawyers apply are comparatively recent, or at least not as remote from their own time as the Roman texts were from the time of the medieval civilians. Moreover, when new problems arise, modern jurists can often turn to new judicial decisions and statutes that address them, which have become authoritative texts. Accordingly, medieval jurists were more likely to be confronted with a problem that had no parallel at the time that their authoritative texts were written—a problem that the authors of these texts could not have imagined, let alone addressed. In such cases, the medieval jurists had to make bricks without clay: they had to cite texts that had nothing to do with the problems that they addressed.

---

[19] Charles Homer Haskins, *The Twelfth Century Renaissance* (New York, 1957), 204–05.

Another part of the medieval enterprise was to understand every text in terms of every other. By doing so, the jurists gave law a unity that it had lacked among the Romans. As we have seen, Roman law had little overall structure or organization, and the Roman jurists did not feel the need for one. Their method required a good stock of concepts and adeptness at refining them by putting particular cases. Modern law does have an overall structure. As described in the last chapter, modern law is organized into fields of law such as property, contract, and tort, and these fields are then organized into doctrines. In contrast, medieval jurists did not organize the law systematically and doctrinally. They sought an order among their texts, but, as we will see, by linking their texts together in various ways.

We will consider first how the medieval civilians applied their texts to situations that the texts did not expressly cover; then, we will look at how they linked them to form this larger order.

## The application of texts to new situations

The problem of applying authoritative texts to situations that they do not expressly cover is one that modern lawyers face as well. The medieval jurists found ways of doing so that modern lawyers still use. One is to generalize a text that deals with one situation so that it can be applied to others. Another is to limit a text framed in general terms by distinguishing situations to which it should be applied from those to which it should not. The third way is to move directly and by analogy from the situations dealt with expressly in the texts to a different situation. Modern jurists proceed in these ways when they apply a code, a statute, or a precedent. Since the task is similar, this similarity is not surprising. Beginning with an authoritative text, one can move up, down, or sideways. These are the only directions in which one can move.

The medieval jurists discussed their method in glosses to a text quoted earlier that said:

A rule (*regula*) briefly explains a *res* [a thing, event or fact]. The law is not taken from rules, but the rule comes from the law. Therefore the rule is a brief statement of the *res* [the thing, event or fact] which is handed down (*traditur*).[20]

The text added that a rule "loses its force as soon as it is defective in any way."[21]

Accursius gave an example that had been used by Bulgarus, Placentinus, and Iohnannes Bassianus:[22] the first person to take possession of a fish becomes its owner, and so it is with lions and other wild animals, and with birds; none of these things previously belonged to anyone. And so one can arrive at the rule stated in I. 2.1.12: "That, indeed, which previously belonged to no one by natural reason is yielded to the first possessor." But, thus stated, the rule is too broad. It applies to these situations, but not to others. Free men do not belong to anyone and neither do consecrated things (*res sacrae*), such as temples, or hallowed things (*res religiosae*),

---

[20] D. 50.17.1.   [21] D. 50.17.1.
[22] Peter Stein, Regulae Iuris: *From Juristic Rules to Legal Maxims* (Edinburgh, 1966), 132–42.

such as tombs.²³ Yet they do not belong to the first person to take possession of them.²⁴ They are exceptions to the rule. In Accursius' explanation of rules, one can see the use of texts in the three ways that were just described. The jurist can move sideways by analogy to see that fish, lions, other wild beasts, and birds should be treated alike: they are owned by the first possessor. He moves upward to frame a general rule: whatever belongs to no one belongs to the first possessor. He moves downward to limit the rule by distinguishing those situations to which it should be applied.

Movement in each of these directions can be illustrated by the medieval civilians' discussion of the harm for which the plaintiff could recover under the *lex Aquilia*. In nearly all of the Roman texts, the harm was to property. Two texts, both by Ulpian, implied there could be recovery for the death of a free person. In one, a shoemaker struck a boy who had done his work badly and, in doing so, the shoemaker knocked out the boy's eye. The shoemaker was liable.²⁵ According to another text, a person who kills another in a public boxing or wrestling match is not liable since "the harm appears to have been done in the cause of glory and virtue and not for the sake of injury...."²⁶ Both texts dealt with a son under the authority of his father.

The second of these texts suggested that the defendant would be liable if the boxing or wrestling match were not public. Nevertheless, Bulgarus rejected that conclusion because it seemed to contradict other texts that said that damages could not be awarded when a free person was injured, "because as to the body of a freeman, estimation [of its value] cannot be made."²⁷ Azo avoided this conclusion by claiming that although the plaintiff would not have an *actio directa* under the *lex Aquilia*, he would have an *actio utilis*. He thereby invented the personal injury action. He cited a text that said that if harm was done in a physically indirect manner, the plaintiff could not have an *actio directa*, but he could have an *actio utilis* or an *actio in factum*.²⁸ Azo was reading that text broadly to remove the limits that the Roman jurists had placed on the harm for which one could recover under the *lex Aquilia*. This solution was adopted in the Standard Gloss of his pupil Accursius and was widely accepted thereafter.²⁹

With these limits gone, medieval jurists simply said that the plaintiff could recover if he suffered damage, and that "damage" meant a diminution in his *patrimonium*.³⁰ They did not distinguish between loss of a physical asset and other kinds of loss. Indeed, they sometimes put cases in which, they said, the plaintiff could recover although he suffered what we today would call pure economic loss. The medieval jurist Durandus said that the plaintiff can recover if the defendant put dung in the street in front of his house, and he consequently had

---

²³ *See* Chapter I, p. 000.   ²⁴ *Gl. ord.* to D. 50.17.1 to *Regula est*.
²⁵ D. 9.2.5.3.   ²⁶ D. 9.2.7.4.   ²⁷ D. 9.3.1.5.
²⁸ I. 4.3.16. The text was an attempt by Justinian's compilers to rationalize the distinction among these actions: Reinhard Zimmermann, *The Law of Obligations: Roman Foundations of the Civilian Tradition* (Cape Town, 1990), 996–97.
²⁹ *Gl. ord.* to D. 9.2.7.4 to *in publico* (describing the opinions of Bulgarus and Azo).
³⁰ Azo, *Summa Codicis* (Lyons, 1557), to D. 9.2; Hostiensis, *Summa aurea* (Lyon, 1556), lib. 5, rubr. "de damno dato," no. 1.

to pay a fine imposed by statute.[31] Baldus degli Ubaldi said that the plaintiff could recover against a secretary who revealed his secrets.[32]

As this example shows, although the medieval jurists expected their conclusions to be logically consistent with the texts, nevertheless different conclusions could be logically consistent with the same texts. There was no reason, logically, why one had to reach the same conclusion as Bulgarus or Azo. As a result, the medieval method has the same unsettling feature as that of the Romans. Their starting points are different: the Roman jurist began with a concept and the medieval jurist with a text. But they both moved to their conclusions without pretending that only one conclusion was logically possible and without explaining why one conclusion was more appropriate than another. In this example, one can see that the jurists preferred the solution of Azo to that of Bulgarus. The jurists adopted it without discussion once Azo had shown how to get around some awkward texts. But because they did so without discussion, we cannot know why they preferred it.

Another example is the medieval civilians' discussion of the relief to be given if a price is disproportionately low or high. Again, the jurists generalized some texts, limited others, and worked by analogy. Again, they agreed on a solution. But again, because they did so without discussion, we cannot know why they preferred it.

They generalized a post-classical text that dealt with the sale of land:

If you or your father part with an estate for a lesser price when it is worth a greater, it is equitable that you return the price to the buyer and recover the land by the authority of the court, or, if the buyer chooses, that you recover the amount of the deficiency in the just price. The price is considered to be too low if less than half of the true price was paid.[33]

At an early date, the medieval civilians applied this text to protect sellers of things other than land, and to protect buyers, as well as sellers.[34] The result was the general remedy for a one-sided contract that became known as *laesio enormis*.

In order to generalize this text, the medieval civilians had to limit the scope of another, a classical text that read: "Pomponius says with regard to the price in sale that the contracting parties are naturally permitted to take advantage of each other."[35] Accursius added: "... unless he is deceived beyond half the just price."[36]

The civilians then proceeded by analogy to explain when a price is just. On the basis of texts that described how prices were determined in other situations, they

---

[31] Durandus, *Speculum iuris* (Basil, 1574) lib. iv, par. iv, *De iniuriis et damno dato*, § 2 (*sequitur*), no. 15.
[32] Baldus de Ubaldi, *Commentaria Corpus iuris civilis* (Venice, 1577), to Dig. 9.2.41 [vulg. 42]. pr. in fine.
[33] C. 4.44.2.
[34] The *Brachylogus*, written at the beginning of the twelfth century, does not speak of land, but of objects sold: *Corpus legum: sive Brachylogus iuris civilis*, ed. Eduard Böcking (Berlin, 1829), iii.xiii.8. The *Dissensiones dominorum* of the early thirteenth century reports a dispute in which all participants take it for granted that the buyer has a remedy. The disputed question is whether, for him to have it, the sales price must be twice or one-and-a-half times the just price. The participants are said to be Placentinus and Albericus, who wrote in the twelfth century, and Martinus, a student of Irnerius: Hugolinus de Presbyteris, *Diversitates sive dissensiones dominorum*, ed. G Haenel (1834), § 253. According to Accursius, it was agreed among the jurists that the remedy would be available generally in contracts *bonae fidei*: *Gl. ord.* to C. 4.44.2 to *auctoritate iudicis*.
[35] D. 4.4.16.4; *see also* D. 19.2.22.3.  [36] *Gl. ord.* to D. 44.16.4 to *naturaliter licere*.

concluded that the just price is the price prevailing at the time and place that the contract was made. According to Accursius,[37] that conclusion was supported by two texts that said that the value of a slave is not his value to individuals, but to people in general. One text concerned a slave who was to be redeemed by paying his value.[38] The other dealt with the amount to be paid for a slave who was killed.[39] The value of land, according to Accursius, is to be determined by its quality and rents. He cited two imperial rescripts and a text calling into question the sale by a guardian of land that was "infertile, stony and pestilential."[40] The value of chattels was their price as of the time and place of sale, although, in opposition to his own view, Accursius cited a text that concerned the difficulties of valuing a stolen cow.[41]

It would have been just as logically consistent to have generalized the text that allowed the buyer and seller to take advantage of each other, and to have limited the one that gave the seller a remedy when he had received less than half the just price. The jurists did not explain why one conclusion was more appropriate than another. As a result, it is difficult to tell why they preferred it.

In the view of some modern scholars, they did so because they regarded the text that allowed the parties to take advantage of each other as repugnant to their Christian values.[42] That suggestion may go beyond what we can know. Accursius merely said that "it is permitted for the contracting parties to deceive each other up to half the just price." He did not say anything about whether it was contrary to Christian values for them to do so and, if it were, why they should be allowed to deceive each other at all. His contemporaries did not seem to find this position troubling. A papal decretal provided that, in canon law, as in civil law, relief would not be given unless the contract price deviated by half from the just price.[43] Although France was a Christian country, the French never went as far as the medieval civilians. They maintained into modern times that the remedy should be given only to sellers of land.[44] England was a Christian country and never developed a similar remedy. In the nineteenth century, in Germany, which still considered itself a Christian country, jurists were still arguing about how to read these two texts: to provide a remedy only for sellers of land,[45] or for buyers as well and parties to similar transactions.[46] In considering why the medieval civilians reached their conclusions, we must go by what they tell us. Here, they tell us almost nothing.

---

[37] *Gl. ord.* to C. 4.44.2 to *autoritate iudicis*.    [38] D. 35.2.63.    [39] D. 8.2.33.
[40] D. 27.9.13.pr.    [41] D. 13.1.14.3.
[42] James Q. Whitman, "Long Live the Hatred of Roman Law!" *Rechtsgeschichte* 2 (2003): 40, 48–49.
[43] X 3.17.3.
[44] Volume II of *Dictionnaire de droit et de pratique*, ed. C. de Ferrière, nouv. ed. (Paris, 1769) s. v "lézion d'outre moité de juste prix"; vol. II of *Dictionnaire portatif de jurisprudence et de pratique*, ed. Honoré Lacombe de Prezel (Paris, 1763) s. v. "lesion."
[45] For example, Rudolph von Holzschuher, vol. 3 of *Theorie und Casuistik des gemeinen Civilrechts* (Leipzig, 1864) 729–30; Karl von Vangerow, vol. 3 of *Leitfaden für Pandekten-Vorlesungen* (Marburg, 1847), § 611; Carl von Wächter, vol. 3 of *Pandekten* (Leipzig, 1881) § 207.
[46] For example, Johann Adam Seuffert, vol. 2 of *Praktisches Pandektenrecht* (Warburg, 1852), § 272.

One can get a sense of why the jurists preferred one conclusion to another by looking at instances in which they disagreed or changed their views over time. We will examine their approach to three problems: whether a person is liable if his use of his land bothers a neighbor; whether he is liable if he makes a true statement that injures the reputation of another; and whether he is liable if he builds a watermill that cuts off the flow of current to a nearby mill owner on the same stream. To resolve the first problem, the medieval civilians generalized a text; to resolve the second, they limited one; to resolve the third, they applied their texts by analogy. We have seen that there was nothing distinctively medieval in applying a text to a new situation in these three ways. We will now see that, in each of these instances, there was nothing distinctively medieval about the way in which the jurists looked for the best solution. In each case, there are direct parallels in the work of later jurists.

The problem of the person who bothers his neighbor by making smoke was governed chiefly by two short Roman texts. According to one, the jurist Aristo "does not think that smoke can lawfully be discharged from a cheese shop onto the buildings above it." The text added:

He also holds that it is not permissible to discharge water or any other substance from the upper onto the lower property, as a man is only permitted to carry out operations on his own premises to this extent, that he discharge nothing onto those of another.[47]

The other text suggested that, nevertheless, a person could "create a moderate amount of smoke on his own premises, for example, smoke from a hearth."[48] So the question arose: what general rule could explain why there was an action for the smoke of the cheese shop, but none for that of the hearth?

Accursius distinguished the discharge of smoke from that of water on the basis that "smoke naturally disperses." The owner himself is not putting it on another person's property. Accursius was then unable to distinguish the smoke from a cheese shop from that from a hearth. He concluded that the text about the cheese shop could not mean what it said. Instead, "the person with the upper premises is required to bear the smoke, and on that account not to have windows."[49] His inveterate critic, Iacobus de Ravanis, had little difficulty pointing out why this solution was unsatisfactory: the text "says the complete opposite of what the *Gloss* [of Accursius] says."[50]

According to Odofredus, the owner of the cheese shop was liable because one cannot use one's own property in a way that harms another: *unusquisque debet facere in suo quod non officiat alieno*.[51] That rule appeared to rest on a straightforward principle, and perhaps for that reason it lived on. Rephrased by Blackstone—*sic utere tuo ut neminem laedas*[52]—it passed into the common law. Nevertheless, it did

---

[47] D. 8.5.8.5.   [48] D. 8.5.8.6.   [49] *Gl. ord.* to D. 8.5.8.5 to *ad iure*.

[50] Albericus de Rosate Bergamensis, *In primam Digesti veteris partem commentarii* (Venice, 1585) (photographic reproduction, *Opera iuridica rariora*, vol. 21, 1974), to D. 8.5.8.5, no. 5 (describing the opinion of Iacobus de Ravanis).

[51] Odofredus, *Lectura super digesto veteri* (Lyon, 1550) (photographic reproduction, *Opera iuridica rariora*, vol. 2), to D. 8.5.8.5.

[52] William Blackstone, vol. 2 of *Commentaries on the Laws of England* (London, 1766), *306.

not explain why one person could annoy another with the smoke from his hearth. It has been criticized by modern jurists because it does not explain why one can harm another in cases like that of the hearth, but not like that of the cheese shop.[53]

Iacobus de Ravanis proposed a different distinction: a person cannot discharge anything onto another's property.[54] That solution was suggested by Aristo's remark that one must "discharge nothing onto [the premises] of another." It sounded like a clear rule. Perhaps for that reason it was accepted by Baldus,[55] and became popular among the Dutch and German jurists of the seventeenth and eighteenth centuries.[56] But, again, it does not explain why one is not liable for the hearth, which does discharge smoke onto another's property.

Bartolus found another solution:

> I think the following is to be said: Sometimes the owner of the lower premises makes fire in the usual way for the ordering of his family, and then he may do it lawfully, and he is not liable if the smoke ascends unless he acts with an intention to injure. In the same way, if the owner of the upper premises lets water flow in some way that is normal, for his water clock, he is not liable if some descends unless he acts with an intention to injure. But if the owner of the lower premises wants to make a shop or inn where he is continually making a fire and a great deal of smoke, he is not allowed to do so, as in this text. In the same way, if the owner of the upper premises lets water flow beyond what is normal, he is not allowed to do so, as this text says.[57]

For Bartolus, then, two things mattered: the extent of the interference, and whether the interfering use of the land was usual. This is a solution that has been adopted in many modern legal systems.[58]

Unlike the rule of Odofredus that one landowner cannot harm another, Bartolus' solution does not seem to rest on a straightforward principle. Nor is it as clear as the rule of Iacobus de Ravanis that no one can discharge anything on another person's land. To apply Bartolus' rule, one must decide how much smoke is a "great deal" and what activities are "usual." But his rule did distinguish the hearth from the cheese shop. Presumably, the jurists would have agreed on a single rule if they had found one that did seem to rest on a straightforward principle, which was also clear and which could distinguish the hearth from the cheese shop. Since they could not find a rule that was satisfactory in all of these ways, they disagreed as to what the proper rule should be.

Because they disagreed, we can get a sense of the sort of rule that they would have regarded as satisfactory. We can also see that, in this instance, there was nothing

---

[53] Jesse Dukeminier, James E. Krier, Gregory S. Alexander, and Michael H. Schilll, *Property*, 7th ed. (Austin, TX, 2010), 731.
[54] Albericus de Rosate (n. 50), to D. 8.5.8.5, no. 5 (describing the opinion of Iacobus de Ravanis).
[55] Baldus (n. 32), to D. 8.5.8.5.
[56] For example, Dionysius Gothofredus, *Corpus iuris civilis... cum notis integris Dionysii Gothofredi, Antonii Anselmo, Simonis von Leuwen* (Antwerp, 1726) to D 8.5.8.5, n. 37; Johann Voet, *Commentarius ad Pandectas* (The Hague, 1726), lib. VIII, tit. 5, § 5.
[57] Bartolus de Saxoferrato, *Commentaria Corpus iuris civilis* (Venice, 1615), to D. 8.5.8.5.
[58] James Gordley, *Foundations of Private Law* (Oxford, 2006), 68–69.

distinctively medieval about their ideas of what a satisfactory rule would look like. There is nothing distinctively medieval about wanting a rule that seems to rest on a straightforward principle, a rule that is clear, and a rule that distinguishes cases like the hearth from cases like the cheese shop. Since modern jurists did not find a rule that was satisfactory in all of these ways, they continued to disagree over which of the three rules proposed by the medieval jurists is the best.

In this example, the jurists started with texts that dealt with a specific situation and tried to formulate a general rule. At other times, they tried to limit the scope of a general text. An example is the way in which they dealt with the question of whether a person is liable for making a statement that is truthful, but which detracts from another's honor or reputation. If the statement had been untruthful, the person who made it would be liable in an action for *iniuria*. One text suggested that he would not be liable if the statement were true: "It would not be fair (*bonum aequum*) for one who defames a pernicious person to be condemned, for the wrongs of such a person ought to be observed and made known."[59] The medieval civilians were faced with two alternatives: to conclude that a person who reveals another's wrongs is never liable, or to find some way in which to limit this text.

Accursius mentioned one possible limitation, only to reject it: the text might apply only to statements made in judicial proceedings.[60] But that limitation was too strict if "wrongs... ought to be observed and made known."

Cinus de Pistoia cited another text that said it would be "inhumane" to disclose the extent of another's wealth.[61] He suggested that it would be wrong and inhumane (*iniuriosus et inhumanus*) to disclose another person's defects.[62] But could one disclose another's moral, as well as his physical, defects? Could one never disclose a physical defect?

Iacobus de Ravanis thought that one could disclose conduct for which the plaintiff would be legally answerable. In that event, he said, the defendant should not be liable, since there was a public interest in the revelation.[63] This position was taken by Petrus de Bellapertica in his *Lectura Institutionum*,[64] and later adopted by Dinus de Mugello.[65] But Petrus refined it in a comment on C. 9.35.5. The important question, he said, is whether the disclosure is of aid or interest to the commonwealth. The defendant should be able to reveal matters of public interest even when the plaintiff would not be legally answerable, for example if the plaintiff had leprosy and might infect the city.[66] This solution became standard. It was accepted by Cinus himself[67] and by Bartolus.[68]

Here, although the jurists finally settled on a rule, they did so only after several different rules were tried and found wanting. Cinus' proposal—that one could not

---

[59] D. 47.10.18.pr.    [60] *Gl. ord.* to D. 47.10.18.pr. to *infamavit*.
[61] C. 10.35.2 [vulg. 34.2].
[62] Cinus de Pistoia, *In Codicem commentaria* (Frankfurt-am-Main, 1578), to C. 9.35.5, no. 10.
[63] According to Cinus (n. 62).
[64] Petrus de Bellapertica, *Lectura Institutionum* (Lyon, 1536), to I. 4 *de iniuriis*.
[65] According to Cinus (n. 62), no. 12.
[66] Petrus de Bellapertica, *Super ix libros Codicis* C. 9.35.5, no. 16.
[67] Cinus (n. 62), no. 12.    [68] Bartolus (n. 57), to D. 47.10.18, no. 1.

reveal another's defect—was ambiguous. Cinus himself must have thought that, standing alone, it was inadequate, since he accepted the rule that became standard. Other rules seemed narrow: that one could reveal another's conduct only in legal proceedings or if that person would be legally answerable for it. The jurists finally concluded that there must be a public interest in the disclosure.

Once again, there was nothing distinctively medieval about the way in which the medieval jurists arrived at this solution. Modern jurists have walked the same path. They have faced the same alternatives: to exclude liability for any truthful statement, or to impose liability, but to limit it. The common law, traditionally, excluded liability. Most jurisdictions today impose liability, but limit it in the same way as the medieval jurists: the defendant is not liable for disclosures in the public interest.[69] The defendant is liable in the United States for the new tort of "intentional disclosure of embarrassing private facts" except for information "of legitimate concern to the public."[70] In England, the defendant is now liable for "breach of confidence" even if no information had been confided to that defendant unless "there is a sufficient public interest . . . to justify curtailment of the conflicting right."[71] In France, a defendant will be liable for revealing facts about a celebrity's private life in a tabloid, yet not for revealing the same information in an historical work.[72] In Germany, a defendant is liable for disclosing the crimes that a person committed in the past, but not if they were war crimes, since the press has a "legitimate interest" in "informing, instructing and . . . shaping public opinion."[73] According to the European Court of Human Rights, there is "a fundamental distinction" between merely "reporting details of the private life of an individual" and "impart[ing] information and ideas on matters of public interest."[74]

There have been different views of what information is a matter of public interest. The view in the United States is notoriously broader than that in Continental countries. The view in modern democracies informed by mass media is necessarily broader than that in medieval society. Nevertheless, it is not surprising that jurists, medieval and modern, have limited liability for disclosing truthful information by asking whether there is a public interest in the disclosure. Any narrower limit seems arbitrarily to prohibit some disclosures while allowing others, which is the objection that Accursius made against permitting only disclosures in legal proceedings, and which Iacobus de Ravanis made against permitting disclosures only about conduct for which the plaintiff was legally answerable. There is nothing distinctly medieval about the discomfort that the jurists felt about stopping short of a rule that protected disclosures provided that they were in the public interest.

The third way in which the medieval civilians applied their texts to new situations was by drawing analogies to situations that were dealt with by their

---

[69] Gordley (n. 58), 250–52.   [70] *Restatement (Second) of Torts* § 652(D) (1976).
[71] *Campbell v. MGN Ltd.* [2004] 2 AC 457.
[72] Cass., 2$^e$ ch. civ., November 14, 1975, arrêt no. 729, pourvoi no. 74-11.278 (unpublished).
[73] OLG, Frankfurt, September 6, 1979, NJW 1980, 597.
[74] *Von Hannover v. Germany*, June 24, 2004 (Application no. 59320/00) no. 63.

texts. An example is their discussion of a question put by Bartolus: "[I]f I have a mill below, and others make a mill above so that they impede me, may they do this?"[75] As Alan Watson pointed out, no Roman text dealt expressly with this problem.[76] Bartolus said that it was an old question, which had been argued by "Franciscus Accursius (not the author of the Standard Gloss) and other doctors of Bologna."[77] It had become important in the Middle Ages because of a revolution in mill technology.[78] When mills became more efficient and could be used for a greater variety of tasks, rivers became crowded with them. Accursius, the author of the Standard Gloss, cited one text in favor of the builder of the first mill.[79] It said that usage should be respected.[80] But, he added, the opposite result was supported by three other texts, which allowed a proprietor to divert water that had its source on his own land,[81] and a fourth, which dealt with a more remote problem.[82]

Bartolus concluded that:

[I]f, indeed, the river was public, as is every river that flows perpetually[83] ... [and] the first person had his mill lawfully ... the second person cannot act or take away from him the advantage that he lawfully began [to derive] from what is public.[84]

The result should be the same, he added, if the second person builds below the first mill and backs up the water.[85] In his view, the key to the problem is that the river is "public." He relied on a text that stated that, "whenever anything is done in a public place, it should be permitted on condition that it causes no injury to anyone."[86] He supported his conclusion by citing texts that dealt with things done in public places. The building of the mills was like an encounter between carts on a public road: the first one to enter prevails. It was like two people who want to build on a strip of beach where anyone was entitled to build: the first to begin building prevails.[87] Similarly, the first to draw water from a public river may do so if it is "without injury to those nearby."[88]

Again, there is nothing distinctly medieval about Bartolus' use of analogy to resolve a new problem. Blackstone did so when he discussed the same problem. Like Bartolus, he thought that the first person to build a mill was protected against latecomers. He drew an analogy to a wild animal, which belongs to the first person to capture it.[89] In the early nineteenth century, Justice Shaw defended the same

---

[75] Bartolus (n. 57), to D. 43.12.2 [vulg. 11.2], no. 2.
[76] Alan Watson, "The Transformation of American Property Law: A Comparative Law Approach," *Georgia Law Review* 24 (1990): 163, 175.
[77] Bartolus (n. 57), to D. 43.12.2 [vulg. 11.2], no. 2.
[78] Jean Gimpel, *The Medieval Machine: The Industrial Revolution of the Middle Ages* (New York, 1977), 7–15.
[79] Gl. ord. to C. 3.34.7 to *procurator*. He mentioned the problem without resolving it in his gloss to D. 2.13.6.6 to *rationis*.
[80] C. 3.34.7.    [81] D. 39.3.21; D. 38.2.24.12; D. 38.2.26.
[82] D. 50.17.61 [vulg. 62] (the problem of repairing one's own house).
[83] Citing D. 43.12.1.3.    [84] Bartolus (n. 57), to D. 43.12.2 [vulg 11.2], no. 2.
[85] Bartolus (n. 57), to D. 43.12.2 [vulg. 11.2], no. 8.    [86] D. 43.8.2.10.
[87] Bartolus (n. 57), to D. 43.12.2 [vulg. 11.2], no. 10.
[88] Bartolus (n. 57), to D. 43.12.2 [vulg. 11.2], no. 10.    [89] Blackstone (n. 52), *403.

position by drawing the same analogy as that of Bartolus to an encounter between the first person to occupy a spot on a public road and one who came later.[90] Ultimately, American courts rejected Shaw's position. An important reason, I have argued elsewhere, is that Roman law was a richer source than the common law of analogies that would support it.[91] Bartolus could cite texts about people who build on a public beach and those who draw water from a public river. In contrast, it is hard to think of a common law action to vindicate a right to use a public place.[92] Like Bartolus, Shaw drew an analogy to an encounter on a public road, but the case was hypothetical and, to common lawyers, might have seemed recherché. If a person were pushed out of a spot that he occupied on a road, he would recover at common law for battery simply because he was pushed, and not by asserting a quasi-proprietary right to the spot on which he was standing. When Bartolus drew the analogy, he could cite a text.

In these instances, modern jurists work from their authoritative texts in much the same way as medieval jurists. They are using a method that the medieval jurists first developed. Nevertheless, it would be wrong to overlook the differences. One difference is that modern jurists use other methods as well. Another, mentioned earlier, is that the medieval jurists had to work with a closed corpus of texts written centuries before their own time.

Modern jurists use other methods as well. At various times, one or another of these newer methods has taken the limelight, leaving the older one in the shadows. We think of the nineteenth century as an age of conceptualism, or *Begriffsjurisprudenz*. The conceptualist method was to define legal concepts such as contract or property abstractly and then try to extract conclusions from the definitions. For example, contract was defined in terms of the will of the parties. It was thought to follow that a contract, even at an unfair price, was valid in principle if it was freely entered into.[93] Property was defined in terms of the will of the owner: he could use his property as he chose. The nineteenth-century conceptualists then found it hard to explain why, sometimes, an owner could not use his property as he wished, as in cases like that of the cheese shop.[94] Since the late nineteenth and early twentieth centuries, when jurists became aware of the limits of conceptualism, the favored method has been to reason functionally, in terms of the policies that the law should serve. Although modern jurists often interpret authoritative texts in much the same way as medieval jurists, they use these newer methods as well.

The reason for the difference is not that the medieval jurists were incapable of making what we would call conceptualist or functionalist arguments. Occasionally, they did so. But they did so sporadically, without regarding these arguments as the basis for an alternative method for applying their texts. An example is Bartolus' response to the question of whether the first person to build a mill on river has

---

[90] *Carey v. Daniels*, 49 Mass. (8 Met.) 466, 478 (1839).
[91] Gordley (n. 58), 116–19.
[92] The only one that comes readily to mind is an action for public nuisance, and it can be brought only privately, when the plaintiff has been specially affected.
[93] *See* Chapter IX, pp. 248–54.   [94] *See* Chapter IX, pp. 223–27.

injured those who later want to build a mill near his: "Is it not always an injury to those nearby since then one cannot make his own building?" Bartolus made what we would call a conceptualist response: "I answer that he does not suffer injury or harm but he does not acquire an advantage; and these are not equivalent or the same in meaning (*ratio*)."[95] According to this argument, it is not an injury to prevent another from acquiring an advantage; therefore the latecomer is not injured. In the nineteenth century, Joseph Story made the same argument as Bartolus' hypothetical interrogator: to take possession of a wild animal "presupposes no ownership already existing," but if he who builds the first mill could prevent others from doing likewise, he would deprive them of a right that they previously possessed.[96]

Similarly, the medieval jurists occasionally made what we would call functionalist arguments or arguments of public policy. In discussing what we call the conflict of laws, Bartolus considered whether a city or principality could punish its own citizens for crimes committed elsewhere. He answered that it could, "for it is in the interest of the republic to have good subjects... but men are made good by punishments imposed for wrongs."[97]

Medieval jurists such as Bartolus would not have made such arguments if they had regarded them as improper or antithetical to their usual method. The reason why they made them so rarely seems to be that they thought that their usual method was quite satisfactory and, indeed, that their method epitomized the proper way in which to apply an authoritative text. Ernst Gombrich described a similar phenomenon in the history of art. In ancient Egyptian relief sculpture, one can find, on rare occasions, touches of realism: the bent back and the tension in the muscles of a man pulling on a rope. But these were "isolated instances" that "remained without consequence": "They do not become part of the tradition to be improved and extended...." Gombrich likened them to "random mutations... weeded out by a principle of natural selection."[98] That may be a bad simile. They were not random: the Egyptian sculptor and the medieval jurists must have regarded them as nice touches, although not the basis for a new method. The principle of natural selection did not work against them, but neither did it work for them so that they could be developed and refined.

Another difference between the medieval and modern jurists is that, in modern law, jurists apply texts that are not as remote from their own time as the Roman texts were from the Middle Ages. Moreover, when new problems arise, new cases may be decided and new statutes passed to address them, which then become authoritative texts. In contrast, the medieval jurists worked with a closed body of ancient texts, those of the *Corpus iuris*. Supposedly, the Holy Roman Emperors, as

---

[95] Bartolus (n. 57), to D. 43.12.2 [vulg. 11.2], no. 5.
[96] *Tyler v. Wilkinson*, 24 Fed. Cas. 472, 474 (1827) (Case no. 14312).
[97] Bartolus (n. 57), to C. 1.4, no. 47.
[98] E. M. Gombrich, *Art and Illusion: A Study in the Psychology of Pictorial Representation*, 2nd ed. (New York, 1961), 143.

successors of the Caesars, could alter or add to these texts, but they rarely did so.[99] Much of medieval legislation did deal with new problems, but it was the work of princes or municipal authorities. It did not become part of the *ius commune*, which, in the eyes of the civilians, was common to all principalities and cities. Consequently, the medieval jurists were more likely than moderns to find themselves confronted with a problem that had no parallel at the time that their texts were written. When the medieval jurists tried to resolve such a problem, they became creative in the extreme. Their method required them to cite texts, so they cited texts that had nothing to do with the problem.

This creativity was particularly characteristic of the later medieval jurists, the Commentators. They were more interested than their predecessors, the Glossators, in applying Roman texts to the problems of their own age. To do so, they had to apply the texts more flexibly. A striking illustration is their discussion of what we call conflict of laws. Suppose the statutes or customs of Bologna, Padua, and Modena differ. Which law should apply when suit was brought in one city over an event that had occurred in a different city or between citizens of different cities? The Roman jurists had never addressed the problem. They had distinguished the *ius gentium*, which governed matters such as sales and applied to people regardless of their nationality, from the *ius civile* in the strict sense, which governed matters such as marriage and applied only to Romans. They allowed subject peoples in the Roman Empire to keep much of their own law. But they had never addressed the question of whether a Roman court should apply someone else's law instead of its own. The Commentators believed that the question of which law to apply should be resolved by the *ius commune* rather than by the statute or custom of a particular principality or city. So they tried to answer the question from their Roman texts.

Iacobus de Arena proposed some basic rules that were accepted by Cinus of Pistoia[100] and refined by his pupil Bartolus.[101] They still sound familiar. According to Iacobus, if a question concerns procedure, it is to be resolved by the law of the forum; if contract, by the law of the place of contracting; if delict (meaning tort or crime), by the law of the place where the wrong was done; if property, by the law of the place where the property was located.[102] As a medieval civilian, Iacobus was required by his method to cite a Roman text for each of these propositions. The texts that he cited show the lengths to which a medieval jurist might go when there were no good texts on hand.

For the proposition that, in matters of procedure, the judge should apply the law of his own court, he cited a text that advised a Roman judge that, "although witnesses should not be lightly summoned from long distances," "he should find out what the practice is in the province of which he is the judge" and summon witnesses from another city if that is the practice.[103] To show that a contract should

---

[99] Manilio Bellomo, *The Common Legal Past of Europe 1000–1800* (Washington, D.C., 1995), 67–68.
[100] Cinus de Pistoia, *Super codice cum additionibus* (Frankfort-am-Main, 1493) to C. 8.53.1.
[101] Bartolus (n. 57), to C. 1.1.
[102] Iacobus de Arena Parmensis, *Super iure civile* (Lyon, 1541) to C. 8.53.1.
[103] D. 22.5.3.6.

be governed by the law of the place where the contract was made, he cited two texts: one said that the rate of interest fixed by a judge should be governed by the custom of the region,[104] and the other, that the warranty of eviction in a sale of land should be adapted to that custom.[105] To show that, in delict, one should look to the place where the wrong was committed, he cited a text that discussed what a master must pay when his slave cuts down a neighbor's tree, and a law imposes a "particular fine" on a man who does so.[106] Here, he was helped by a gloss of Accursius, which said that the fine was imposed by the law "of the place where the trees were."[107] Iacobus also cited a text that said that some crimes that occur in one province do not occur in others. For example, in Arabia, the enemies of a person commit a crime called σκοπελίσμον by piling stones on a person's land as a sign that anyone who cultivates it will die horribly. That crime should be punished, according to the text, because it violates the principle that it is wrong to threaten another's life.[108] On the law that applies to suits over property, Iacobus cited one text that concerns what a magistrate should do when a house is in a ruinous state[109] and another that deals with a guardian who paid taxes on a ward's estate that were not legally due, but were paid by the landowner, rather than his tenants, by the custom of the region.[110] These texts merely show that, in Roman times, local practice mattered when it was a question of summoning witnesses, fixing interest in court, construing implied warranties, fining people who cut down trees, keeping buildings in good repair, and paying taxes that are customary, but not legally due. Moreover, vengeance can take odd forms in places like Arabia. None of the texts concerns the conflict of laws.

By the fourteenth century, the creativity of the jurists was drawing criticism. Richardus Malumbra complained that "our older fathers and doctors...argued from the witness of our laws which were close to the matter in question." Now, he said, instead of "sticking to the text and the gloss and the opinions of the most respected doctors," the jurists "turn to fables or make arguments so logistic and sophistic that they have no truth but only its appearance."[111] Perhaps he had in mind imaginative uses of the Roman texts like that which we have just seen. If so, the criticism may have been a bit unfair. There were only so many Roman texts, and no legal problem could be resolved without citing them.

## Seeking order

As mentioned earlier, the concern of the medieval jurists was not solely to apply their texts to situations that the texts did not expressly cover. They also wanted to explain each text of the *Corpus iuris* in terms of every other. That effort led them to impose an order on the texts that the Romans had not contemplated.

Their method of finding order in the law was neither Roman nor modern. The Roman jurists worked by testing their concepts against particular cases. They did

---

[104] D. 22.1.1.pr.   [105] D. 21.2.6.   [106] C. 3.42.2.
[107] *Gl. ord.* to 3.42.2 to *saltum.*   [108] D. 47.11.9.   [109] C. 8.10.3.
[110] D. 26.7.37.6.   [111] Quoted in Albericus de Rosate (n. 50), *Proemium.*

not need much structure. Since early modern times, jurists have sought order by trying to explain rules by higher-level principles or concepts. Medieval jurists sought order, but not in this way.[112] They sought order by linking related texts. Sometimes, they juxtaposed Roman texts that used the same word or expression: the meaning of a word in one text was identified or distinguished from the meaning of the same word in another. Sometimes, they ascribed explanatory power to a term found in one text: they treated it as the key to understanding other texts that may not have used the same term. Sometimes, they created a schema: differences or similarities in results were explained by identifying an element that the texts had in common, although they might not mention it expressly, and then a circumstance that supposedly accounted for the difference or the similarity between the texts.

Linking texts might illuminate an area of law. In these instances, a modern reader is apt to imagine that the medieval jurists were groping towards a principled explanation of that area. It is the sort of explanation to which the modern reader is accustomed. Yet it would be a mistake to regard the medieval jurists' work as a primitive attempt in that direction. At other times, by linking texts, the medieval jurists did little more than cross-reference them and classify the ones that bore upon the same legal problems, but were dispersed in the *Corpus iuris*. The modern reader is apt to think that the medieval jurists were attempting to make something like an index or a card file. It is true that the order that the medieval jurists found in their texts served for them the purposes that would be served, for a modern jurist, either by a principled explanation or by an indexing system: in the one case, illuminating an area of law; in the other, labeling and cross-referencing. Nevertheless, the medieval jurists themselves were neither searching for principled explanations nor merely trying to label and cross-reference. Rather, their goal was to assign to each text a place in the scheme of things by relating it so far as possible to every other text.

## Order through the juxtaposition of texts

One way in which the medieval jurists found order was by explaining one text by juxtaposing others that used the same word or expression. One of the other texts might use a different word or expression that appeared in still a further text, which could then be linked to the second text and through it back to the first. The end result was a chain of interconnections among texts in which each text was supposed to shed light on the meaning of every other.

Sometimes, the juxtaposition of texts led to a deeper insight than one might obtain by reading the texts in isolation. An example is the jurists' discussion of the role of consent in contract formation. In Roman law, as we have seen, only certain contracts such as sale and lease were legally binding upon consent. Others, such as gratuitous loans for use and consumption, were binding when a certain object was handed over. Still others were binding upon completion of a formality that involved the use of certain words. All of these contracts required consent. As Ulpian said,

---

[112] Franz Wieacker, *Privatrechtsgeschicte der Neuzeit under besonderer Berücktsichtigung der deutschen Entwicklung*, 2nd ed. (Göttingen, 1967), 66–67.

quoting Pedius, "there is no contract, no obligation that does not consist of consent, whether it is formed by the handing over of something or by the use of certain words...."[113] But each contract had its own rules as to when it became binding.

By juxtaposing Roman texts, the medieval civilians arrived at or sharpened the insight that, in principle or by nature, all contracts are binding by consent, although not all are legally enforceable. That insight may have been glimpsed by the Roman jurists. When the texts were linked, it appeared more clearly.

Accursius explained:

There are two roots of an effective obligation. One is natural. The natural root arises out of consent which can be given by all men, even slaves. D. 2.14.1.3 ... Nevertheless this natural root does not have the force to compel performance of the obligation. It does prevent a person who has performed from taking back his performance. D. 46.1.16.3. To this natural root a civil root is sometimes joined which gives efficacy or form or clothing to the natural root so that it can produce an obligation.[114]

In this passage, Accursius pulled together two lines of Roman authority. The first text he cited, D. 2.14.1.3., is that just mentioned in which Ulpian said that all contracts require consent. The second text concerns the Roman distinction between natural and civil obligations. Natural obligations were created by certain contracts that were not directly enforceable, such as a contract made by a slave or by a father with his son. These contracts nevertheless had certain legal consequences, two of which are mentioned in D. 46.1.17, the text that Accursius cited: a natural obligation could be the subject of a guarantee, and it could be raised as a defense if a party performed and later sued to recover his performance. In Accursius's view, then, consent to real and formal contracts produces a natural obligation that must then be "clothed" by the delivery of the object or the formality to produce a civil obligation.

Another Roman text said that "an obligation is a legal bond which ties us to the necessity of delivering some thing in accordance with the laws of our state."[115] Accursius thought that the text applied to both natural and civil obligations. Since the civil law did not compel performance of a natural obligation, Accursius concluded that, "whenever a person is said to be bound by a natural obligation, the statement should be understood of the *ius gentium*."[116]

According to other texts, the *ius gentium* was a law governing matters such as sales that applied to people regardless of their nationality. It was distinguished from the *ius civile*, which governed such matters as marriage and applied only to Romans. In several texts, the distinction is dressed up with some philosophical speculation. The *ius gentium* is the law "established among all men by natural reason."[117] The *ius gentium* emerged in response to human necessities; such things as war, captivity, and slavery pertain to it, since by the law of nature all were born free. "And by the *ius gentium*, nearly all contracts were introduced such as sale and purchase, lease and

---

[113] D. 2.14.1.3.   [114] *Gl. ord.* to I. 3.14 pr. to *necessitate.*
[115] I. 3.13 [vulg. 14].pr.   [116] *Gl. ord.* to I. 3.13.pr [vulg. 14].pr. to *Obligatio.*
[117] I. 1.2.1. The same phrase appears in D. 1.1.9.

hire, partnership, loan for consumption and others without number."[118] Thus, by pulling all of these texts together, Accursius concluded that, according to the law established by natural reason, all contracts give rise to an obligation upon consent, although the obligation was natural and not civil. One cannot say whether, by linking these texts, he derived a new insight or merely clarified the insights of the Roman jurists. Be that as it may, he had reached a conclusion that, at the most, was only implicit in the texts.

At other times, by juxtaposing their texts, the medieval jurists classified them without coming closer to an insight that would explain them. An example is a distinction that they drew between "natural" and "civil" possession. In one text,[119] Ulpian had said that "if someone has gone away from his field or house leaving none of his household there, and on his return was... prevented from entering the premises," he had not lost possession by going away.[120] In another text, Paul said that a person "naturally" possesses what he stands upon, and that "the ownership of things originated in natural possession... a relic of which survives in those things that are captured on land, sea and in the air, for they become the property of those who first take possession of them."[121] Ulpian had said that both "natural" and "civil" possession are protected, although in the context of a different problem: protecting a possessor who does not have legal title.[122] Putting their statements together, the twelfth-century jurist Hugo concluded that there were two kinds of possession: natural, when one was in physical control, and civil, as in the case Ulpian put in which "someone has gone away from his field or house"[123]—a conclusion that was adopted by Accursius.[124]

The distinction between natural and civil possession appeared in leading treatises into the eighteenth century such as that of Johannes Voet.[125] It was useful as a label for the obvious point made by Ulpian: that one does not lose possession merely by leaving one's house. But it is merely a label. It does not shed light on why possession ought to be protected.

### Order by ascribing explanatory power to terms in certain texts

Another way in which the medieval civilians found order in their texts was to ascribe explanatory power to a term found in one text, treating it as the key to understanding other texts. Again, some of the conclusions that they reached were more illuminating than others.

A success, to judge by its later history, was the formulation by Bartolus and his pupil Baldus of what came to be called the doctrine of *causa*. According to this doctrine, for the parties to enter into a contract that the law will respect, they must have done so for one of two *causae*, or reasons: either to receive something in return,

---

[118] I. 1.2.1. [119] D. 43.16.1.24; *see* Chapter I, p. 10. [120] D. 43.16.1.24.
[121] D. 41.2.1.pr.; D. 41.2.1.1. [122] D. 43.16.1.9.
[123] *Gl. ord.* to D. 43.16 [vulg. 15].1.9 to *civiliter*.
[124] *Gl. ord.* to D. 43.16 [vulg. 15].1.9 to *civiliter*.
[125] For example, Johannes Voet, *Compendium iuris iuxta seriem Pandectarum adjectis differentiis iuris civilis et canonici* (1688), lib. 41, tit. 2, § 3.

or out of liberality. As I have described elsewhere, Bartolus and Baldus were probably drawing on the distinction that Aristotle and Thomas Aquinas had drawn between acts of commutative justice and acts of liberality,[126] although they do not refer to it expressly. They read this distinction into three key Roman texts. One explained that, in Roman law, not all contracts were actionable: "When there is no *causa*, it is accepted that no obligation can be constituted by an agreement; therefore a naked agreement does not give rise to an action although it does give rise to a defense (*exceptio*)."[127] Accursius and Iacobus de Ravanis had described the *causa* referred to by this text as simply "something given or done."[128] The other two texts said that the formal contract of *stipulatio* had to have a *causa*.[129] The *causa* in those texts, according to Accursius, was *re* or *spe*, a thing or the hope of a thing.[130] According to Iacobus de Ravanis and Petrus de Bellapertica, the texts meant that a *stipulatio* is not valid if a party mistakenly believes there to be a *causa* or reason for obligating himself.[131] These texts might seem an unpromising source for a general ordering principle of contract law. Yet Bartolus found one. When the first text spoke of an agreement without a *causa*, he said, it meant "no *causa* fulfilled (*impleta*), but the agreement was certainly made for a *causa*."[132] Consequently, one sort of *causa* was the receipt of something in return. The receipt of something in return might also be the *causa* of a *stipulatio*, but a *stipulatio* was also binding if a promise was gratuitous. If so, Bartolus explained, the *causa* was "liberality." There were, then, two kinds of *causa*.[133] This doctrine was accepted by his pupil Baldus, who read it into the canon law.[134]

Less successful in retrospect was the jurist's attempt to find a basis in the *ius gentium* for the Roman distinction between contracts that were and were not binding upon consent. Bartolus did not reject Accursius' view that consent gives rise to a natural obligation by the *ius gentium*. Nevertheless, he tried to find a basis in the *ius gentium* for the distinction between consensual and real contracts. He claimed that the *ius gentium* gave these contracts their "name." The "name" made these contracts actionable, for "nominate contracts give rise to an action by this alone: that they exist and have a name."[135] Consensual contracts were binding on consent and real contracts only on delivery of an object because of a difference in their names. Consensual contracts such as sale took their names from an act that a party performs by agreeing: I can sell you my house today by so agreeing even if I do not deliver it to you until next month. Real contracts such as deposit took their

---

[126] James Gordley, *The Philosophical Origins of Modern Contract Doctrine* (Oxford, 1991), 49–57.
[127] D. 2.14.7.1.
[128] *Gl. ord.* to D. 2.14.7.1 to *causa*; Iacobus de Ravanis, *Lectura super Codicis* (published under the name of Petrus de Bellapertica, Paris, 1519), to C. 2.3.10 (on the authorship, see E. H. Meiers, *Etudes d'histoire du droit III Le Droit romain au moyen âge* (Leiden, 1959), 70–77).
[129] D. 12.7.1; D. 44.4.2.3.   [130] *Gl. ord.* to 44.4.2.3 to *idoneum*.
[131] Iacobus de Ravanis (n. 128), to C. 2.3.5; Petrus de Bellapertica, *Commentaria in Digestum Novum* to D. 44.4.2.
[132] Bartolus (n. 57), to D. 12.4.7.2.   [133] Bartolus (n. 57), to D. 12.4.7.2.
[134] Baldus (n. 32), to C. 3.36.15, no. 3; *see* Baldus, *In Decretalium volumen commentaria* (Venice, 1595), to X 1.35.1.
[135] Bartolus (n. 57), to D. 12.4.7.2, nos. 14–16; to D. 2.14.7, no. 2.

names from an act that a party performs by delivering: I cannot say that I am depositing an object with you unless I am actually depositing it right now.[136] Baldus not only accepted this explanation, but also concluded that innominate contracts were unenforceable in canon law.[137]

Later jurists accepted the doctrine of *causa*, but thought that the distinction between nominate and innominate contracts made no sense at all. In both cases, however, Bartolus and Baldus arrived at their explanations in the same way: by taking a term that appeared in their texts—in the one case, *causa*; in the other, "name"—and treating it as the key to understanding other texts.

### *Order through a schema*

Another way in which the medieval civilians ordered their texts was by making a schema. Differences or similarities in results were explained by identifying an element that they had in common and then a circumstance that supposedly accounted for the difference or the similarity.

Sometimes, the result was a mere list. An example is Accursius' account of the mistakes that vitiate consent to a sale. He merely listed the types of mistake described by Ulpian in a passage quoted earlier. Consent was lacking if the parties were in error about (1) whether there was a sale, (2) the price, (3) the particular object (*in corpore*), (4) the substance (*substantia*), and (5) the *materia*.[138] The schema does not tell us much more than we could see from Ulpian's examples.

Sometimes, the schema explained nothing. For example, Accursius proposed a threefold classification of fault (*culpa*): "[T]he fault is sometimes within the act; sometimes it precedes the act; sometimes it follows the act."[139] He found instances of each in his texts. Fault is within the act when a man throws another off a bridge,[140] or a doctor operates negligently on a slave.[141] It precedes the act when someone digs a pit to catch bears or deer in a public place and someone falls in,[142] or when a person who has borrowed silver for a dinner party takes it aboard a ship, where it is lost to shipwreck or pirates.[143] It follows the act when a doctor operates correctly, but neglects to care for his patient thereafter.[144] His texts fit into these three categories, but the classification does not tell us much about fault.

Nevertheless, sometimes the schema suggests a reason why results should be similar or different. An example is a series of distinctions concerning fraud that seem to have first appeared in a gloss to the *Liber pauperum* of the eleventh-century jurist Vacarius,[145] and which were subsequently picked up by Azo and

---

[136] Bartolus (n. 57), to D. 2.14.7, no. 2.
[137] Baldus (n. 134), to X 1.4.11, no. 30; Baldus (n. 32), to C. 3.36.15, no. 3.
[138] *Gl. ord.* to D. 18.1.9 to *aliquo alio*. He had a sixth category as well: error in "sex." That category was based on D. 18.1.11.1, which said that the buyer of a slave could void the sale if he mistakenly thought that the slave was male, but not if he knew that she was female, but mistakenly thought she was a virgin.
[139] *Gl. ord.* to D. 9.2.8.pr. to *sed culpa reus*.   [140] D. 9.2.7.7.   [141] D. 9.2.7.8.
[142] D. 9.2.28.pr.   [143] D. 44.7.1.4.   [144] D. 9.2.8.pr.
[145] Vacarius, *Liber pauperum*, ed. F. Zulueta (London, 1927), 51, to D. 19.2.23.3.

Accursius.[146] One sort of fraud is fraud in the *causa* or motive that led a person to contract who otherwise would not have contracted. Another sort is incidental fraud that led a person to contract on worse terms than he otherwise would have accepted. Incidental fraud was distinguished into fraud *ex proposito* if it was practiced intentionally, and fraud *ex re ipsa* if a party paid too much or too little, even though the other party had done nothing intentionally to defraud him. In the first case, the victim had an action for the difference between the amount that he paid and the amount that he should have paid, however small that difference might be. In the case of fraud *ex re ipsa*, he had an action for *laesio enormis*, but only if the difference exceeded half the just price. Azo and Accursius cited a text for each branch of these distinctions. Here, the schema was not merely a list. It identified an evil to be remedied—an unfair price—which was the same in the case of intentional incidental fraud and *laesio enormis*. The difference was that, in the one case, the unfairness was brought about intentionally and would be remedied however small it was, while in the other, it was not, and would be remedied only if it was greater than half the just price.

In these ways, the medieval jurists sought order by linking one Roman text to another. Modern jurists seek order in a quite different way. They explain rules by means of higher-level rules and concepts. As we will see in a later chapter,[147] this approach began in the sixteenth century with the work of the late scholastics, who, for the first time, organized Roman law into doctrines that they tried to explain by higher principles. Their approach was taken up in the seventeenth and eighteenth centuries by the founders of the northern natural law school, Hugo Grotius and Samuel Pufendorf.[148]

## ii THE CANONISTS

### Origins

The study of canon law began as rapidly and mysteriously in the Middle Ages as that of civil law. Study was based on the *Decretum*, composed, according to tradition, by Gratian in Bologna, in about 1140. The *Decretum* was a collection of excerpts from Church Councils, the writings of the fathers, and other sources that Christians regarded as authoritative. In contrast to Roman law, the number of authoritative texts increased over time as popes settled doubtful points in letters called "decretals." In the thirteenth century, a collection of papal decretals was compiled by the canon lawyer Raymond of Penafort for Pope Gregory IX, who

---

[146] Azo (n. 30), to C. 2.20, no. 9. *See Summa trecensis*, ed. H. Fitting (Berlin, 1894) (published under the title *Summa Codicis des Irnerius*), lib. 4, tit. 41; Rogerius, *Summa Codicis*, ed. A. Gaudentius (1913), to C. 4.44; Hostiensis (n. 30), iii. 17, par. 7. *See* also Gérard Fransen, *Le Dol dans la conclusion des actes juridiques* (Louvain, 1946), 49–55.
[147] *See* Chapter III, pp. 84–98.  [148] *See* Chapter IV, pp. 131–38.

promulgated it by presenting a copy to the law school at Bologna. It was supplemented by further collections. The *Decretum* and the collections of decretals composed the *Corpus iuris canonici*.

John Noonan has shown that almost everything traditionally believed about Gratian was undocumented legend built up over the centuries.[149] All that is certain, according to Anders Winroth, is that he wrote the *Decretum*, although Winroth called even that claim into question by suggesting that the *Decretum* had more than one author.[150] When it was written is a puzzle. None of the texts contained in the earliest manuscripts, with one exception, can be dated earlier than 1119.[151] The exception is a reference to a decision of the Second Lateran Council of 1139, which is cited as authority at the end of statement or dictum written by Gratian. The problem is accounting for the twenty-year gap. If Gratian had been working on the *Decretum* during the 1120s and 1130s, one would expect him to include at least some of the ecclesiastical legislation of the period. Some scholars have concluded that the *Decretum* was completed before or at the time of the First Lateran Council of 1123. They believe that the reference to the Second Lateran Council was written in the margin of a manuscript after 1139 to serve as authority for the statement made by Gratian. A copyist then inserted the marginal reference into the text. Later manuscripts, including all those extant, followed the copyist. If these scholars are right, we must imagine a manuscript tradition that vanished without a trace except for one marginal note that was incorporated into one manuscript, which became the exemplar of all those written later. Scholars who find this alternative implausible believe that Gratian was finishing the *Decretum* in 1139 as the Second Lateran Council was ending and knew enough of its proceedings to add the one reference, but not enough to add more. The difficulty is that we then have to imagine that, for twenty years, Gratian ignored contemporary ecclesiastical legislation and only then added the reference to the Second Lateran Council. Neither alternative seems plausible.[152]

There had been earlier collections, and all but a few dozen texts contained in the *Decretum* can be found in them. The *Decretum*, however, did not merely collect sources, but ordered and commented on them. It seems to have been intended as a set of teaching materials. The first section presents a series of propositions, and the texts that can be cited for and against them. The second section is composed of thirty-six hypothetical cases (*causae*), which are complicated fact patterns raising issues that are then unraveled through the use of texts excerpted from the sources. A major innovation was to place texts that seemed to conflict side by side, and then to suggest how the conflict might be resolved. Thus the *Decretum* is also entitled *The Concordance of Discordant Canons*. Gratian may have been reacting to Peter Abelard's book "Yes and No" (*Sic et Non*). Abelard had simply presented authorities

---

[149] John T. Noonan, "Gratian Slept Here: The Changing Identity of the Father of the Systematic Study of Canon Law," *Traditio* 35 (1979): 21.

[150] Winroth (n. 4), 147.

[151] Although two could be from the First Lateran Council, Winroth has shown that they could have come from an earlier council: Winroth (n. 4), 139–40.

[152] For an account of the debate, *see* Winroth (n. 4), 136–45.

that seemed to conflict, leading some to wonder whether he himself thought it was possible to reconcile them. The *Decretum* claimed that it was. The enterprise of the canon lawyers was to show how. Once again, jurists were following a new path, and one that would take them far. Yet again, had it not been for events that occurred in a short period of time for reasons that are obscure, it might have been a path not taken.

## A similar method, different authorities

The innovation of the canonists lay not in their method, but in the authorities to which they applied it. Their method was like that of the medieval civilians. Indeed, they studied law at the same schools and often earned the double doctorate, becoming *doctores utriusque iuris*, or "doctors of both laws." Distinguished civilians such as Baldus degli Ubaldi also wrote commentaries on canon law. Canonists needed to know Roman law because it was the law applied in Church courts whenever canon law sources did not furnish a solution. Together, Roman law and canon law formed the *ius commune*, the common law of much of Europe.

Nevertheless, the canonists applied this method to very different authorities. The authoritative sources for the civilians were the texts of Justinian's *Corpus iuris civilis*. Despite its size, the number of texts was small enough that all of them could be studied in the course of a legal education, and a jurist could readily find all of the texts that bore on any given problem, helped by the cross-references in the glosses. These texts were the only ones that mattered. There were no other Roman legal texts to consult and, in any event, these were ones promulgated by the Emperor Justinian.

The canonists were not studying Roman law, but the norms that should govern the Church and Christian life. Much had been said about these norms throughout the Christian tradition in scripture, the teachings of bishops, synods, councils, and popes, the admonitions of pastors, and the reflections of scholars and saints. An initial question, which the civilians did not have to face, was how thoroughly a canonist should be familiar with these sources. No single person could read them all in a lifetime even if he had access to an uncommonly good library. As we have seen, at first, the canonists relied on collections of passages excerpted from these sources. Eventually, one compilation, the *Decretum*, became authoritative. Shortly thereafter, some other texts were added to it to produce what became the standard edition. By consensus, and without any decree from any ecclesiastical authority, the texts of *Decretum* became the basis of legal education in canon law and those that the canonists cited to support their conclusions. Instead of trying to become experts on everything written in the Christian tradition, they became experts on the texts of the *Decretum*.

To collect and organize the most important texts written throughout the Christian tradition was an extraordinary task. In retrospect, the principal defect seems to have been the flaws in the manuscripts available to Gratian and the other compilers. The humanist Lorenzo Valla proved that one of them, concerning the Donation of Constantine, was forged. Other humanists pointed out that some of the texts reflected corruptions and errors that had crept into manuscripts.

As a result, in 1578, Pope Gregory XIII appointed a commission, known as the *Correctores Romani*, to produce a new version based on better texts that the philological techniques of the humanists made possible. Gratian had also included forgeries made in the mid-ninth century concerning papal power, now known as the Pseud-Isidorian Decretals, which gave a strong argument to the Protestant reformers. Nevertheless, these defects concerned what Gratian had included, not what he had left out.

The *Decretum* is a scholarly work of a kind unfamiliar today. It answered the question: if one cannot read everything, what are the most important texts to read? Today, to be accounted an expert, a scholar is usually expected to read everything in his field of expertise and judge for himself what is important. Moreover, a modern scholar is likely to interpret what St. Augustine said about one topic by examining what he said about others, not by seeing how the same topic was treated by a medieval synod. The canonists did not take this approach. If they had, their project would have been impossible. No scholar could read everything. Yet their project was to study the norms that should govern the Church and Christian life in the light of what had been said throughout the Christian tradition. Moreover, the sources were important to the canonists because of their truth value. The canonists expected to learn more about a topic by comparing what Augustine and a medieval synod had said about it than by reading what Augustine had said about something else.

The authorities of the canon lawyers differed from those of the civilians in another respect. As Katherine Christensen noted:

Whatever their contradictions, the Roman law texts were the product of one legal culture. . . . Gratian's texts came from far more diverse sources: the Bible, centuries of Church councils, the letters, sermons and treatises of the fathers, papal decretals, even penitential manuals.[153]

The texts were not only more diverse. Unlike the Roman legal texts, few of them had been formulated by jurists. They were normative in that they bore on how Church affairs should be conducted or a Christian life should be lived, but typically their authors were not trying to formulate standards to govern these matters in the manner of a jurist. Sometimes, the sources encouraged others to act virtuously or admonished them for their misbehavior. Sometimes, they reflected on a moral problem. The canonists' task was to draw legal conclusions from such texts. For example, a text taken from a sermon might denounce the sin of greed. On the basis of such a text, the canonists tried to work out the limits to an owner's legitimate use of his property. Another text might reflect on whether one must always keep one's word. The canonists would ask what the text implied about when a promise was binding. A text might denounce a sexual sin. The canonists would draw inferences as to what sexual conduct was sinful. The civilians' authorities were already legal texts. The canonists drew legal conclusions from texts that were not legal in the same sense.

---

[153] Katherine Christensen, "Introduction," in Gratian, *The Treatise on Laws*, trans. Augustine Thompson and James Gordley (Washington, D.C., 1993), ix at xv.

Yet another difference is that the civilians were always working with the same authoritative texts. As noted, although they believed that the Holy Roman Emperor, as successor of the Caesars, had the authority to promulgate new texts, the emperor rarely did so. In contrast, the texts that were authoritative for the canon lawyers became ever more numerous. New Church councils met. Popes wrote decretal letters to resolve controversies. As already noted, excerpts from these sources were added to the *Corpus iuris canonici*.

## The interaction of civil and canon law

By drawing on the canonists, the medieval civilians and their successors found solutions to problems that the Roman legal texts had not raised or resolved. Some of these solutions are still with us, and accepted in both civil and common law jurisdictions. Conversely, the canonists drew on Roman law as interpreted by the civilians to explain the norms that should govern the Church and Christian life. In doing so, they bridged two traditions: that of Roman law and that of Christianity. One can see this mutual influence even when the canonists confronted issues that had no parallel in Roman law, for example how the sacraments should be administered or how the Church should be governed. Here, we will be concerned with issues in which the concerns of the canonists and civilians overlapped—issues in which questions of moral responsibility faced by the canonists were like the questions of legal liability faced by the civilians.

Sometimes, when the canonists and civilians confronted similar questions, there was tension between the two traditions. For example, in Roman law, a person could gain title to another's property by prescription—that is, by possessing it without the owner's permission for a long enough time. Most canonists agreed that a possessor could gain title by prescription.[154] Nevertheless, in Roman law, to do so, the possessor need only be in good faith—that is, unaware that the property is another's—at the moment when he first took possession.[155] This rule was denounced in a papal decretal:

Because everything that is not according to faith is a sin ... no prescription is valid without good faith whether in canon or civil law.... Wherefore it is necessary that one who takes by prescription is at no time aware that he has that which is another's.[156]

The canonist Barthomaeus Brixiensis explained that, "in prescription, good faith is required at the beginning, in the middle, and at the end, and during the entire time of the prescription."[157] Here, the legal concept of good faith was used in a Christian sense, in which faith was opposed to sin. Even a secular court was not allowed to

---

[154] Some did not, e.g. *Die Summa des Stephanus Tornacnesis über das Decretum Gratiani*, ed. Johann Friedrich von Schulte (1891; repr. Scientia Verlag, Aalen, 1965), to C. 14 q. 6.
[155] I. 2.6.pr.   [156] X 2.26.20.
[157] *Gl. ord.* to C. 14 q. 6 c. 1 to *nisi restituatur* (unless otherwise qualified, citations to the *Glossa ordinaria* to the *Decretum* are from the Venice edition of 1595).

apply a Roman rule permitting acquisition of title in bad faith. A Roman rule had been weighed by Christian standards and found wanting.

Still, the tension was rare. James Whitman has mentioned two instances in which he believes it ran deep. One was a conflict between Christian concern for one's neighbor and the Roman text mentioned earlier, which ascribed to Pomponius the view "with regard to the price in sale that the contracting parties are naturally permitted to take advantage of each other."[158] Another was the conflict between the Christian belief that marriage is, in principle, indissoluble and the Roman law permitting divorce.[159] Certainly, Whitman is correct that these were issues over which there was a possibility of conflict. Nevertheless, even in these instances, that possibility does not seem to have much concerned the jurists.

As we saw earlier in this chapter, the medieval civilians generalized a post-classical Roman text to create a generalized remedy for a disproportionate price, for what came to be called *laesio enormis*. The text gave a remedy to one who had sold land at less than half of its "just," or "true," price. The buyer had the choice of making up the difference in price or rescinding the sale.[160] At an early date, the medieval civilians read this text broadly to give the same remedy to sellers of things other than land and to buyers as well as to sellers. They limited the text that permitted the parties to take advantage of each other. According to Accursius, the text applied to a party "unless he is deceived beyond half the just price."[161]

As noted earlier, the civilians read the texts in this way at an early date and said nothing about why they had done so. In any event, the canon lawyers did not find the rules extracted from these Roman texts troubling. They were adopted by a papal decretal that provided that, in canon law, relief would not be given unless the contract price deviated by half from the just price.[162]

The Christian principle that marriage is indissoluble did conflict with Roman law. As Alan Watson noted, Roman law traditionally kept out of marriage and divorce. There was no form prescribed for the celebration of marriage:

[T]here was complete freedom to divorce from the late third century B.C. Later, when the Empire became Christian, penalties were imposed for divorce except for a specified reason, or at other times, when the reason was insufficient. Still, the divorce itself was valid.[163]

The medieval civilians were not surprised that the law of pagan Rome could contradict Christian principles. They were surprised that Justinian, as a Christian emperor, did not set the matter right. As Iohannes Teutonicus observed in the Standard Gloss to the *Decretum*, "as Justinian was a truly Catholic emperor, it is amazing that he made rulings against the law of the Lord, for the Lord said that a

---

[158] D. 4.4.16.4; *see also* D. 19.2.22.3; Whitman (n. 42), 48–49.
[159] *See* James Q. Whitman, "The Medieval Division of the Digest," *Tijdschrift voor Rechtsgeschiedenis* 50 (1991): 269.
[160] C. 4.44.2.
[161] *Gl. ord.* to D. 44.16.4 to *naturaliter licere*.    [162] X 3.17.3.
[163] Alan Watson, *The Spirit of Roman Law* (Athens, GA, 1995), 173, citing W. W. Buckland, *A Textbook of Roman Law from Augustus to Justinian*, 2nd ed. (Cambridge, 1950), 117.

wife may be separated from her husband only on account of fornication (Matt. 5:32) C. 32 q. 2 c. 19." Yet the matter could be explained:

> But you may say, and some do say, that he allowed this out of ignorance, and therefore deserves indulgence. D. 8 c. 8. Or he erred like Jerome in D. 26. c. 1. Or he permitted this in order to avoid greater evils, as usury may be permitted to avoid robbery, or divorce may be permitted to prevent wife-killing. C. 33 q. 2. c. 9.[164]

Emperors could be ignorant, even saints could be mistaken, and sometimes one evil had to be tolerated to prevent a greater one.

Most often, the relationship of canon and Roman law was one not of conflict, but of cross-fertilization. This relationship can be seen most clearly in a branch of law that the canonists called "restitution." It raised many of the same questions as Roman private law. In its modern sense, the term "restitution" refers to the law of unjust enrichment. The canonists, however, used it to refer to the duty of a person who had wronged another to compensate his victim before he could be forgiven for the sin that he had committed. The text that they cited was a passage in the *Decretum* from a letter of St. Augustine:

> If the thing of another person on account of which sin was committed is not returned when it can be returned, there is not penance but rather pretence. If indeed it is truly done, the sin is not forgiven unless restitution is made of the thing that was taken away.[165]

The canonists understood the duty to make restitution to extend to any harm that the victim had suffered. This duty paralleled the duty of the defendant in Roman law to compensate the plaintiff. The canonists, however, were not bound by the Roman texts and found solutions to similar problems by drawing on texts of their own. They sometimes devised remedies and formulated rules not found in Roman law. Some of them passed into civil law during the Middle Ages or later, after the Roman texts had lost their force.

Conversely, the canonists drew on Roman texts to illuminate the moral principles that should govern Christian life. In Roman law, these texts concerned when particular actions could be brought. Moral principles could not depend on whether or not Roman law gave an action for their violation. Thus, for the canonists, the rules taken from Roman sources became general moral principles.

## Canon law solutions to civil law problems

In clarifying the duty to make restitution, sometimes the canonists devised remedies that were different from those given by Roman law. In the Middle Ages, the remedies of canon law were alternatives. Eventually, some of them passed into civil law.

For example, the canonists accepted the principle of Roman law that possession should be protected even when the possessor had not proven title. In Roman law, a person dispossessed of land would bring the action *unde vi*. While approving of the principle, the canonists developed an action of their own, the *actio spolii*, which was

---

[164] *Gl. ord.* to D. 10 c. 1 to *lex humana*.   [165] C. 14 q. 6 c. 1.

broader than *unde vi*. It eventually passed into the civil law and, by the seventeenth and eighteenth centuries, it had displaced the Roman action and become the standard remedy.[166]

Another example is the remedy that the canonists devised for injury to reputation or honor. In Roman law, the victim could bring an action for *iniuria*. The remedy was payment of damages. The canonists accepted the principle that a person was liable for injuring another's reputation or honor. A wrongdoer must make restitution for any harm that he had done to another,[167] including injury to another's reputation or honor. But the canonists extended the remedy. They concluded that, to make restitution, the wrongdoer must publicly declare that he had been in error, or must at least apologize for an insult.[168] They drew an analogy to other situations in which a person's sin was not absolved unless he made a declaration. According to one text, he must so declare if he posted an accusation against another at night in a public place.[169] According to another, if he was implicated in heresy, he should denounce the heresy in question at various public places.[170] In the Middle Ages, the canon law remedy was an alternative to the Roman remedy for *iniuria*. Eventually, it too was adopted by the civil law. By the sixteenth century, secular courts often allowed an action for *recantatio, revocatio*, or *palinodia* to force the defendant to confess his error or to apologize.[171]

The canonists also formulated rules not found in Roman law. These, too, sometimes passed into civil law.

In discussing property, the canonists concluded that a person could use the property of another in cases of necessity. The Romans had not formulated a general rule, although some Roman texts allowed use of another's property in discrete situations. A person could enter another's land to look for a fugitive.[172] Sometimes, he could preserve his own life and property by destroying that of another, for example if he could pull down his neighbor's house to save his own from a fire.[173] Finally, there were rules allowing the captain of a ship to jettison cargo to save the ship. The passengers whose goods had been saved had to compensate those whose

---

[166] Voet (n. 125), to lib. 43, tit. 16, p. 583 ("*Recuperandae possessionis remediis plenioribus iure Canonico utimur*"); Wolfgang Lauterbach, *Thesaurus iuris civilis sive succinta explanatio Compendii Digestorum Schützio-Lauterbachiani* (Lemgo, 1717), to lib. 43, tit. 16, p. 1400, n. 8 ("*Est hodie frequentissimum*").

[167] Raymond of Penafort cited a general text that said that a person must give back another's thing that he acquired through sin: Raimundus de Penafort, *Summa de paenitentia*, eds. Xaverio Ochoa and Alosio Díez (Rome, 1978), II.5.42, citing C. 14 c. 6 c. 1.

[168] *See* Karl Weinzierl, *Die Restitutionslehre der Frühscholastik* (Munich, 1936), 132–46.

[169] Raimundus de Penafort (n. 167), citing C. 5 q. 1 c. 2.

[170] Hostiensis (n. 30), *Quibus et qualiter; Quid de accusatoribus*, citing X 5.34.10 (vers. *precipias*).

[171] Udo Wolter, *Das Prinzip der Naturalrestitution in § 249 BGB Herkunft, historische Entwicklung und Bedeutung* (Berlin, 1985), 72. *See generally* Zimmermann (n. 28), 1072; C. von. Wallenrodt, "Die Injurienklagen auf Abbitte, Widerruf und Ehrenerklärung in ihrer Entstehung, Fortbildung und ihrem Verfall," *Zeitschrift für Rechtsgeschichte* 3 (1864): 238.

[172] These situations were summarized in the Standard Gloss to the *Decretum*: "There are cases in which one is allowed to pass through another's field: if there is a servitude, C. 3.34.11, or if one wants to dig up one's own treasure, D. 10.4.19 (at the end), if my fruit fell into your field, D. 43.27.1, when I am looking for a fugitive, D. 11.4.4 . . . and when a public road is destroyed, D. 8.6.14.1." *Gl. ord.* to D. 1 c. 2.

[173] D. 9.2.49.1.

goods were thrown overboard. These rules were similar to modern admiralty law and, indeed, were the ancestors of that law.[174]

The canonists grounded their rule on a text in which St. Ambrose denounced the sin of greed. The greedy person "sees always gold, always silver," and "asks gold even in his prayer and supplication to God."

> But, you say, what is the injustice if I diligently care for my own without seizing what is another's? Oh, imprudent saying! Your own you say? What things? From what horde did you bring them into this world? When you came into the light, when you left your mother's womb, stuffed with what possessions and goods, I ask, did you come?... Let no one call his own what is common.[175]

Such themes were salient in Ambrose's preaching: private property as a deviation from a pristine age in which all goods were in common; the usurpation of property by the rich; almsgiving, in Peter Brown's words, "as the gracious repayment to their fellow humans of an ancient debt."[176] The canonists, in search of a rule, asked in what sense private property could be "common." They said that property was not intended merely to benefit the owner, and that therefore if a person had more than enough for himself, he should give the rest away. They also said that, in a state of necessity, property became literally common. In addition to canon law texts, they cited the Roman rules on jettisoning cargo at sea.[177]

That interpretation seemed to contradict another text, taken from a penitential manual, which said that "if a person stole food, clothing or money because of necessity, being hungry or naked, he should do three weeks penance, and if he returned what he stole, he should not be compelled to fast."[178] The difficulty was to explain why a person who stole in time of necessity should have to do penance at all, even a light penance, since, by the canonists' rule, he had not committed a sin. The Standard Gloss limited the application of the text: "From the facts that penance is imposed, it may be gathered that the necessity was moderate. Penance would not have been imposed if it had been great... for in necessity all things are common."[179]

In tort, in Roman law, a person was liable for harming another under the *lex Aquilia* if he was at fault by acting intentionally or negligently. As we will see, the canonists adopted the principle that compensation was due if a person had been at fault, and that he might be at fault in either of these ways. Their innovation was to add a third reason why he might be liable: he might have been engaged in an unlawful activity and, in that event, he was liable even for harm that he did not foresee. Raymond of Penafort illustrated the doctrine by saying that a person would not be responsible for homicide if he were to throw a stone at his own animal and kill someone. He would be responsible if he were to throw the stone at another person's

---

[174] D. 9.2.2 pr.    [175] D. 47 c.8.
[176] Peter Brown, *Through the Eye of a Needle: Wealth, the Fall of Rome, and the Making of Christianity in the West, 350–550 AD* (Princeton, NJ, 2012), 133.
[177] *Gl. ord.* to D. 47 c.8 to *commune*.    [178] X 5.18.3.
[179] *Gl. ord.* to X 5.18.3. to *poenitentia* (unless otherwise qualified, citations to the *Glossa ordinaria* to the *Decretales Gregorii ix* are to the Venice edition of 1595).

horse or cow in order to steal it.[180] Similarly, a person who cut down his own tree with due care would not be responsible if it were to fall on someone. He would be responsible if he had been unlawfully cutting down another person's tree.[181]

The earlier canonists rested the principle that one was liable for the unintended consequences of unlawful acts on three texts in the *Decretum*. One was a vague statement by St. Augustine that no one can be blamed for doing what is "good and lawful."[182] Another was a ruling by the Council of Worms in 868 that a person who cuts down a tree that crushes a passerby "while carrying out some necessary work" need do penance only if he acted "by will or by negligence."[183] The third was a decision by Pope Urban I that a priest who killed a boy by throwing a stone should do penance as a homicide, but would not be suspended from his functions as those guilty of homicide usually were. The text said nothing about why the priest threw the stone.[184]

Just because their authorities said so little, the canonists found themselves improvising. The earliest canon lawyers to consider the problem said that the priest would not be guilty if he were to throw the stone for a "reason" (*causa*)[185] or "good reason" (*iusta causa*)[186] and did so with "diligence" in a place where people were not walking. Later canonists explained that the priest had a "reason" to throw the stone if he was engaged in a "lawful" activity rather than an "unlawful" one.[187] The priest would not have been guilty if he were to throw the stone to chase a wild boar or a pig out of a field of grain, unless he had been careless.[188] He would be guilty if he were to engage in an unlawful activity or fail to use the diligence that he should.[189] After the rule became generally accepted, popes referred to it obliquely in their own

---

[180] Raimundus de Penafort (n. 167), II.i.3.

[181] Raimundus de Penafort (n. 167), II.i.3. Similarly, a person need not make compensation for what we call collateral damage if he fired a ballista lawfully in time of war: Sinibaldus Fliscus (Innocent IV), *Commentaria in Apparatus in V Libros Decretalium* (Frankfort, 1570), to X 5.12.12. A less fortunate example is that of a blind man who is deemed guilty if he injured someone while hunting with a javelin: Huguccio, *Summa*, Admont, Stiftsbibliothek, MS 7, to C. 15 q. 1, *dicta Gratiani post* c. 2, f. 264rb; *Gl. ord.* to C. 15 q. 1 *dicta Gratiai post* c. 2 to *penitus*, f. 162rb. The example is unfortunate because a blind man who went hunting would be negligent, as a seventeenth-century critic noted: Leonardus Lessius, *De iustitia et iure, ceterisque virtutibus cardinalis libri quatuor* (Paris, 1628), lib. 5, cap. 9, dub. 15, no. 106.

[182] C. 23 q. 5 c. 8.  [183] D. 50 c. 50.  [184] D. 50 c. 37.

[185] Paucapalea, *Summa über das Decretum Gratiani*, ed. J. F. Schulte (1891; repr. Aalen, 1965), to D. 50 c. 37.

[186] *Summa tornacensis* (n. 154), to D. 50 c. 37.

[187] Huguccio (n. 181), to D. 50 c. 37, f. 71ra.

[188] *Glossa Palatina*, Vatican City, Biblioteca Apostolica Vaticana, Cod. palatini latini MS. 658, to D. 50, c. 37, f. 13va; Huguccio (n. 181), to D. 50 c. 37, f. 71ra; *Gl. ord.* Vatican City, Biblioteca Apostolica Vaticana, Cod. palatini latini MS 624, to D. 50 c. 37 to *Clerico*, f. 40rb.

[189] For example, *Glossa Palatina* (n. 188) to D. 50 c. 37, f. 13rb; Huguccio (n. 181), to D. 50 c. 37, f. 71ra; to D. 50 c. 44, f. 72va; to D. 50 c. 50, f. 73 ra; *Gl. ord.* Vatican City, Biblioteca Apostolica Vaticana, Cod. palatini latini MS 624 to D. 50 c. 37 to *Clerico*, f. 40rb; Guido de Baisio (Archidiaconus), *Archidiaconus super Decretum* (Lyon, 1549), to D. 50 c. 37; to D. 50 c. 44 to *casu*. For other references, *see* Stephan Kuttner, *Kanonistische Schuldlehre von Gratian bis auf die Dekretalen Gregors IX* (Vatican City, 1935), 201, n. 1, 202, n. 1.

decisions,[190] which the canon lawyers read as authority for their rule, along with other papal decisions that had never mentioned it.[191]

As we will see in a later chapter,[192] some canon law doctrines such as necessity passed into modern civil law after they had been borrowed by jurists such as Grotius and Pufendorf from late scholastic writers of the sixteenth and seventeenth centuries. The late scholastics, however, rejected the doctrine that a person was liable for the unforeseen consequences of wrongful acts. They distinguished the texts that the canon lawyers cited.[193] As we will see,[194] they claimed that liability for an unforeseen consequence was liability for a chance event. The doctrine was not taken up by Grotius and Pufendorf, and never passed into modern civil law. It did pass into English common law. It was accepted by Blackstone[195] and Hale,[196] who took it from Coke,[197] who took it from Bracton.[198] As Shulz has shown,[199] Bracton took it from Raymond of Penafort.[200]

In contrast, an innovation of the canonists in contract law did pass civil law, and it did so during the Middle Ages: the rule that a promise need not be kept under changed and unforeseen circumstances. It had no parallel in Roman contract law. The *Decretum* contained a text from St. Augustine in which he considered a question put by Cicero. Suppose one person deposits his sword with another, who promises to return it when asked to do so. If the owner of the sword asks for it after he has become insane or if he wishes to use it to hurt another, should the promise be kept? Augustine, like Cicero, answered that it should not.[201] Iohannes Teutonicus concluded: "Therefore, this condition is always understood: if matters remain in the same state."[202] As in their discussion of necessity, the canonists had found a legal standard in the moral reflections of one of the Church Fathers. As before, they supported it by citing a Roman text.[203] The text said that a formal promise (*stipulatio*) to pay money must be kept if the promisee "remains in the same position as he was when the *stipulatio* was made," but not if the promisee had been adopted, or exiled, or had become a slave, "for there appears to be in the

---

[190] X 5.12.13 (exonerating a chaplain who had gone riding to restore his appetite after an illness and killed someone when the reins broke); X 5.12.25 (exonerating a priest who was building a church and killed a coworker by dropping a load of wood on him). In both decisions, the Pope noted that the activity was a lawful one.
[191] For example, *Gl. ord.* to X 5.12.14; Raimundus de Penafort (n. 167), II.i.3; Hostiensis (n. 30), rubr. *Qua poena feriatur* sub *De homicidio voluntari, vel casuali*; Bernardus de Montemirato (Abbas Antiquus), *Commentaria ad libros Decretalium* (Venice, 1588), to X 5.12.13.
[192] See Chapter III, p. 85.
[193] Soto pointed out that the texts cited in n. 190 supported the rule only by negative inference: Domenicus Soto, *De iustitia et iure libri decem* (Salamanca, 1553), lib. 5, q. 1, a. 9.
[194] See Chapter III, p. 93.   [195] Blackstone (n. 52), *182–83.
[196] Matthew Hale, vol. 1 of *Historia Placitorum Coronae*, eds. S. Emlyn and G. Wilson (London, 1800), *471–77. See also Blackstone (n. 52), *429–30, *431, and *466.
[197] Edward Coke, *The Third Part of the Institutes of the Laws of England* (London, 1817), *56–57.
[198] Bracton, vol. 2 of *De legibus et consuetudinibus Angliae*, eds. G. E. Woodbine and S. E. Thorne (Cambridge, MA, 1968), *f. 120b–121, p. 341.
[199] F. Schulz, "Bracton and Raymond de Penafort," *Law Quarterly Review* 61 (1945): 286, 289–90.
[200] Raimundus de Penafort (n. 167), II.i.3.   [201] C. 22 q. 2 c. 14.
[202] *Gl. ord.* to C. 22 q. 2 c. 14 to *furens*.   [203] *Gl. ord.* to C. 22 q. 2 c. 14 to *furens*.

*stipulatio* the tacit agreement if he remain in the same legal position."[204] Baldus then read the rule of changed circumstances into the civil law.[205]

## From civil law actions to moral principles

Thus far, we have considered instances in which the canonists developed remedies and rules of their own to address problems like those faced by the medieval civilians. In other instances, they drew upon Roman law as interpreted by the civilians to formulate moral principles that should govern Christian life. One example is the principle that a person must make compensation for any harm that he has done another through fault, intentionally or negligently. Another is the principle that all agreements were binding as long as there was a valid reason or *causa* why they were made.

As mentioned earlier, in Roman law, one who harmed another person's property (or son, according to two texts) was liable under the *lex Aquilia* if he was at fault, intentionally or negligently.[206] As we have seen, the canonists found yet another reason why he might owe a duty of restitution: participation in an illegal activity. Nevertheless, they adopted the principle that he must make compensation if he was at fault for acting intentionally or negligently. If he was not at fault in any way, he had not committed a sin, and need not make restitution in order to be forgiven.

The proposition that a person must be at fault to commit a sin was not initially obvious. In a text included in the *Decretum*, the Eighth Council of Toledo had said that, "if an inescapable danger compels one to perpetrate one of two evils, we must choose the one that makes us less guilty."[207] In another text, Pope Gregory I had said that, "when the mind is torn between greater and lesser sins, if absolutely no path of escape lies open without sin, lesser evils are always to be chosen." He gave examples. A man swears to keep a secret that another man is about to confide to him; the secret turns out to be that he plans to murder the husband of a woman with whom he is committing adultery. A man promises obedience to a spiritual director, who then forbids him to do what is good and commands him to do what is evil. A man obtains a high position by bribery, repents, but believes that, by resigning, he will cause even greater harm to those under his authority.[208] Gratian concluded that a "dispensation ... from natural law" could be permitted "when one is compelled to choose between two evils."[209]

---

[204] D. 46.3.38.pr.   [205] Baldus (n. 32), to D. 12.4.8.
[206] *See* Chapter I, p. 20.   [207] D. 13 c. 1.
[208] D. 13 c. 2. Another example was sexual intercourse with one's wife. It might be evil, but refusing to do so would be a greater evil. On the eventual rejection of the idea that sexual intercourse with one's wife was an evil, *see* James Gordley, "*Ardor quaerens intellectum*: Sex within Marriage according to the Canon Lawyers and the Theologians of the 12th and 13th Centuries," *Zeitschrift der Savigny-Stiftung für Rechtsgeschichte Kanonistische Abteilung* 83 (1997): 305.
[209] *D.G. ante* D. 13 c. 1.

## Ius Commune: *The Medieval Jurists*

Nevertheless, the canonists soon rejected the idea that, sometimes, a person could not avoid committing a sin. According to Iohannes Teutonicus, "the Master" (Gratian) spoke "badly":

For it would then follow that necessity could make one do something evil. But the canons say that God will never punish anyone unless he has done wrong voluntarily. C. 23 q. 4 c. 23. Furthermore, if necessity really required us to do something evil, the law that prohibited this would be impossible to obey. But every law must be possible. D. 4 c. 2.[210]

The man who swore to keep the secret does not sin by revealing it, "for an oath was not invented to be a chain of iniquity."[211] The promise to obey the spiritual director "is to be understood only of whatever is lawful and honest."[212] The man in high position must give it up since he stole that office, and he can no more keep it in order to do good than a thief could keep stolen property.[213] Similar solutions had been suggested by the *Summa Pariensis* and the *Summa Lipsiensis*.[214]

Although Gratian thought that a sin could be committed without fault, nevertheless he also said that an act could not be punished when it was done *contra animum*, or "against one's will."[215] The canonists adopted the principle of the *lex Aquilia* that a person was responsible if he acted intentionally or negligently. There were three texts in the *Decretum* to support that position, although one suspects that Gratian, or someone else familiar with Roman law, had looked rather hard to find them. All of them were from the ninth century—Pope Nicolas I, the Council of Worms, and the Council of Tribourg—and all of them concerned someone who had cut down a tree that fell on another. He is not to be blamed if the harm was not the result of his "will," or "fault (*culpa*) or neglect,"[216] if it was not caused intentionally or by negligence (*negligentia*) and he was doing a "necessary work,"[217] or if he had called "look out."[218] Whatever the authors of the ninth-century texts had in mind, the Standard Gloss explained that there was no blame absent neligence (*culpa*), citing a Roman text that said that there was no *culpa*—and hence no liability under the *lex Aquilia*—if a person prunes a tree in a private place and calls out a warning, yet someone is injured by a falling branch.[219] Pope Gregory IX, in a passage that was

---

[210] *Gl. ord.* to *d.G. ante* D. 13 c. 1 to *Item adversus*. According to the *Summa Coloniensis*, the statement must be understood to describe the perplexity of a person who thinks that he has no choice except to sin, but if that were so, it would contradict the statement of St. Jerome: "Let him be anathema who says that man cannot avoid sin." The solution is for the person in question to receive wise counsel: *Summa "Elegantius in iure divino" seu Coloniensis*, eds. Gerard Fransen and Stephan Kuttner (New York, 1969), pars 1, cap. 79.
[211] *Gl. ord.* to D. 13 c. 2 to *transgressionis contagione*.
[212] *Gl. ord.* to D. 13 c. 2 to *formidat*.
[213] *Gl. ord.* to D. 13 c. 2 to *suscepti*.
[214] *The Summa Parisiensis on the Decretum Gratiani*, ed. Terence P. McLaughlin (Toronto, 1952), to D. 13 c. 2. It also suggests that the one who swore should not keep his promise, but do penance for having promised rashly: to cc. 1–2; vol. 1 of *Summa "Omnis qui iuste iudicat sive Lipsiensis,"* eds. Rudolf Weigand, Peter Landau, and Waltraud Kozur (Vatican City, 2007), to D. 13 c.2; Huguccio (n. 181), to D. 13 pr.
[215] *D.G. ante* D. 50 c. 46. [216] D. 50 c. 49 (Pope Nicolas I).
[217] D. 50 c. 50 (Council of Worms). [218] D. 50 c. 51 (Council of Triburg).
[219] *Gl. ord.* to D. 50 c. 49 to *inculpabiles*; to D. 50 c. 51 to *Si duo*, citing D. 9.2.31.

included in the *Decretals*, said, "If harm is done through your fault or injury inflicted . . . or it occurs by your lack of skill or negligence, by law you must make satisfaction for it. . . ."[220] The Standard Gloss to the *Decretals* explained, "it is necessary that fault intervenes, otherwise one is not bound," citing the *lex Aquilia*.

The Standard Gloss then placed this interpretation on four texts of the *Decretals* that had been taken from the book of Exodus. None of them mentioned fault. A man must make compensation when he leaves a pit uncovered and an ox or donkey falls into it (Ex. 21:33–34),[221] when his ox harms another's ox (Ex. 21:35),[222] when he lets his animals graze in a field or vineyard and they graze in another's field (Ex. 22:5),[223] and when his fire spreads and destroys grain (Ex. 22:6).[224] In Jewish law, the *Mishna* refers to these cases as "the four generative causes of damages." According to the *Mishna*, "what they have in common is that they customarily do damage, and taking care of them is your responsibility":[225] "In the case of anything of which I am liable to take care, I am deemed to render possible whatever damage it might do."[226] In contrast, the Standard Gloss explained them as instances of liability for negligence, citing the *lex Aquilia*.[227] In the case of the pit, it said that the person is not responsible if the pit is in a private, rather than a public, place.[228] In the case of the ox and the fire, it said that the man is responsible on account of fault *(culpa* or *negligentia)*.[229] *Culpa*, which triggered liability under the *lex Aquilia*, gave rise to a moral duty to make compensation under canon law—a duty that one must perform if one wishes to be forgiven.

In contract law, according to some modern scholars, the canonists' great innovation was the idea that, in principle, all agreements are binding if they were made for a valid reason or *causa*.[230] In Roman law, as we have seen, only certain agreements were enforceable. The canonists found support for the principle that all of them were binding in their texts. Two texts in the *Decretum* described promises as binding that would not have been binding in Roman law.[231] A text in the *Decretals* contained the general statement, "agreements are to be served, agreements are to be kept (*pacta servetur, pacta custodiantur*)."[232] The statement

---

[220] X 5.36.9.   [221] X 5.36.2.   [222] X 5.36.3.
[223] X 5.36.4.   [224] C. 5.36.5.
[225] *The Mishnah*, trans. Jacob Neusner (New Haven, CT, 1988), Babba Qamma 1:1, p. 503.
[226] Babba Qamma 1:2, p. 503.
[227] *Gl. ord.* to X 5.36.2 to *reddat pretium*; to X 5.36.3 to *reddet bovem*; to X 5.36.4 to *aestimationem restituit*; X 5.36.5 to *reddet damnum*.
[228] *Gl. ord.* to X 5.36.2 to *reddet pretium*.
[229] *Gl. ord.* to X 5.36 to *reddet damnum*.
[230] Wim Decock, *Theologians and Contract Law: The Moral Transformation of the Ius Commune (ca. 1500–1650)* (Leiden, 2013), 122–25; Jules Roussier, *Le Fondement de l'obligation contractuelle dans le droit de l'église* (Paris, 1933), 20–94, 177–216; Arrigo Solmi, "Elementi del diritto medioevale italiano," in *Contribuiti alla storia del diritto commune* (Rome, 1937), 147 at 223; Francesco Schupfer, vol. 1 of *Il diritto delle obligationi in Italia nel'età dell'Risorigimento* (Milan, 1920), 51.
[231] C. 1 q. 2 c. 66 (remuneration is promised for doing something for the Church); C. 12 q. 5 c. 3 (an archbishop's successor should keep the archbishop's promise to give goods to a monastery before he died).
[232] X 1.35.1.

had been made by a Church council in Africa to explain why a bishop should be disciplined who had promised another bishop not to attract away members of his congregation and then had broken his promise. The canonists read these texts as instances of that general rule. They concluded that agreements were binding without regard to the Roman distinctions among contracts.[233] The reason, according to the Standard Gloss to the *Decretals*, is that "God does not distinguish between simple speech and an oath."[234]

Yet the principle that all agreements are binding was not an innovation of the canonists. As we have already seen,[235] the civilians, by conflating a text that said that all contracts require consent with others that spoke of the *ius gentium*, had concluded that all contracts are binding in principle or by the *ius gentium*, although not all are legally enforceable. The civilians could deny an action while agreeing with the canonists that promises should be kept. As Guido Astuti pointed out, the differences between the civilians and canonists arose not from a difference in principle, but from a difference in the questions that they were asking. The civilians were asking what contracts were legally enforceable; the canonists were asking when breaking a promise was a sin.[236]

The canonists then limited the principle with a rule taken from the civilians: to be binding, the promise must have a *causa*. The *causa* could be liberality or the receipt of something in return. We have already seen how Bartolus read this principle into the Roman texts that had little to do with it. Baldus then read the principle into the canon law.[237]

The canonists arrived at these principles without developing a theory of tort or contract. In all of the instances that we have just examined, their method, like that of the medieval civilians, was to reconcile texts. Nevertheless, unlike the civilians, their objective was to determine when a person had sinned and must make restitution to be forgiven. That was a question that could not turn on what actions Roman law happened to recognize. Seeking an answer necessarily led them to formulate general principles of moral responsibility. Theory came later, as we will see in the next chapter, when we look at the work of the late scholastics.

---

[233] *Gl. ord.* to C. 12 q. 2 c. 66 to *promiserint*; *Gl. ord.* to X 1.35.1 to *pacta custodiantur*.
[234] *Gl. ord.* to X 1.35.1 to *pacta custodiantur*.    [235] Chapter I, pp. 47–48.
[236] Guido Astuti, "I principii fondamentale dei contratti nella storia del diritto italiano," *Annali di storia del diritto* 1 (1957): 13, 34–37.
[237] Baldus (n. 32), to C. 3.36.15, no. 3; *see* Baldus (n. 134), to X 1.35.1. The canonists were more hesitant to reject the Roman distinction between contracts of good faith and contracts of strict law. They repeated the Roman rule that, in contracts of good faith unlike those of strict law, the parties are bound to the unexpressed obligations that good faith requires: *Gl. ord.* to X 3.17.6 to *restituerent*; to X 2.25.6 to *bonae fidei*. They often described the difference in the same way as the civilians without any hint that the distinction does not matter in canon law: *Gl. ord.* to X 3.17.3 to *deceptione*; Sinibaldus Fliscus (n. 181), to X 3.17.3. Baldus finally said that, in canon law, all contracts are of good faith, but he was careful to note that he was merely giving his own opinion: Baldus (n. 134), to X 2.11.1, no. 12 ("*ego puto quod de aequitate canonica omnes contractus mundi sit bonae fidei*").

# The external and the internal forum

## Procedure in the external forum and due process of law

The canonists distinguished between the external forum, in which an offense was resolved by courts, and the internal forum, in which the offender came to a priest to confess it and receive absolution.

The Roman texts had said little about procedure. During the twelfth century, canonists, working with the civilians, developed a law of procedure for the external forum that they called the *ordo iudicarius*. Historians call it "Roman-Canonical procedure." At the time, many trials in western Europe were conducted in the manner described in the first chapter. In the first stage, a plaintiff presented his claim using a traditionally sanctioned formula and in which the least slip could be fatal. In the second stage, the issue was resolved by a procedure that did not involve the presentation and weighing of evidence, for example by ordeal, combat, the swearing of oaths by people who were not testifying to what they had heard or seen, but to their belief as to who was in the right, or by throwing the issue to a jury, which would decide it without hearing evidence.

In the Roman-Canonical procedure, a lawsuit began with a formal complaint, an *accusatio*, which did not have to conform to a set formula, and a summons to the defendant to appear in court. The defendant could present a formal answer to the complaint, an *exceptio*, or give reasons why there should be a delay before he appeared. Evidence was taken from witnesses who testified as to what they had seen and heard. The court then made a decision, which the losing party could appeal, based on the law and the evidence presented. Some key features of the *ordo iudicarius* were summarized by Stephan of Tournai:

> Briefly, it is to be seen that by the *ordo iudicarius* a person must be called before his own judge by three summonses, or one which is peremptory and serves for all. He must be allowed to present legitimate reasons for delay. The accusation must be made formally in writing. Legitimate witnesses must be produced. A decision may be made only after he has been convicted or has confessed. The decision must be in writing.[238]

The accused person had to be summoned unless, as Stephan of Tornai said, his offense was "notorious."[239] Until he was summoned, according to a decretal of Pope Innocent III, no witnesses could be heard against him.[240] As Stephan said, he had to be convicted according to the *ordo iudicarius* unless he confessed.

From the beginning, the canonists regarded the *ordo iudicarius* as more than a means of ascertaining the facts of case and applying the appropriate rule of law. Unless the guilt of the accused was notorious or the accused confessed, it was a procedure that had to be applied even if the truth of the matter might be known in some other way. Some early canonists saw the procedure as the way in which God

---

[238] *Summa Tornacensis* (n. 154), to C. 2 q. 1.
[239] *Summa Tornacensis* (n. 154), to C. 2 q. 1.
[240] X 1.6.34.

himself would judge a case, even though one might not think that an omniscient being would be concerned with how facts are established. According to Paucapalea, the *ordo* began in Paradise when, before God judged Adam, although he knew of Adam's guilt, He first summoned him and then listened to his defense: that the woman had given him the fruit to eat.[241] Stephen of Tornai explained that the summons was like an *accusatio*, the formal complaint by which a suit under the *ordo iudiciarius* was begun, and Adam's reply was like an *exceptio* or defense.[242] Indeed, Gratian included in the *Decretum* a letter from Bishop Eleuterius to the bishops of France that observed that although Jesus knew that Judas had been stealing money, "no *accusatio* had been made, and so he was not dismissed."[243] Most likely, the canonists looked for instances in which procedure mattered to God because the procedure mattered to them.

In the thirteenth century, as Pennington noted, they went further. They began to conceive of elements *ordo iudicarius* as confirming rights so basic that even popes and emperors could not easily deny them. A major step was taken by Sinibaldus Fliscus, later Pope Innocent IV, in his commentary on the *Decretals*. He began with a statement with which, as Pennington notes, no jurist would have disagreed.[244] If a person held a right by natural law, even the emperor could not take it away: "Even in secular matters, a rule cannot be enacted when the rule injures the rights of another, and the right concerned is acquired by natural law, such as property, obligations, and rights of this sort."[245] Other jurists made similar statements, but they must be understood in context. Although not even the emperor had the right to violate natural or divine law, no secular court could judge whether he had done so and refuse to enforce his edicts. Imperial authority was imagined by the civilians and some canonists as like the authority of Parliament as it has been conceived in England. No judicial authority can set aside law enacted by Parliament, although, many would agree, there are principles of justice that the Parliament must not violate.

As Pennington pointed out, the innovation of Sinibaldus Fliscus was to include the right of procedure among natural rights. Accursius had said that "actions," as distinguished from contracts, are based on the civil law.[246] According to Sinibaldus Fliscus:

Where, indeed, a rescript or rule injures the right of another in that which pertains to the civil law, as in actions that arise from the civil law, if it completely destroys a right or completely removes the power to act, it is not valid, unless it is added "any law notwithstanding." ... Some would say that although it is to be maintained that [the prince] may take away an action, nevertheless, he cannot take away [the duty] that he do justice, as that would be contrary to natural law.[247]

According to this statement, to take away a civil action may violate the natural law since it may destroy a right that belongs to a person according to the natural law.

---

[241] Paucapalea, *Summa* (n. 185), Prologue.  [242] *Summa* (n. 154), *Tornacensis Introductio*.
[243] C. 2 q. 1 c. 4.
[244] Kenneth Pennington, *The Prince and the Law 1200–1600: Sovereignty and Rights in the Western Legal Tradition* (Berkeley, CA, 1993), 149.
[245] Sinibaldus Fliscus (n.181), to 1.2.7, no. 2.  [246] *Gl. ord.* to D. 1.1.5 to *obligationes*.
[247] Sinibaldus Fliscus (n.181), to 1.2.7, no. 3 (citations omitted).

If the emperor fails to say that he is doing so "any law notwithstanding," a court can refuse to enforce the rescript. If he does include that phrase, the court must enforce it even if, in the court's judgment, it does violate natural law.

That is as close as the future pope thought he could go in allowing a court to judge the acts of an emperor. The leading canonist Hostiensis thought that a pope (and presumably an emperor) might violate a procedural right for a variety of reasons: the right of action might be delayed in order to prevent scandal; moreover, "the utility of public matters and most importantly of the Church of God and the salvation of souls is in all things to be preferred to private utility."[248] Otherwise, he took the same view as Sinibaldus.[249]

The civilian Odofredus de Denariis went still further, as Pennington has noted.[250] Odofredus relied on a text in Justinian's Code in which the Emperor Anastasius decreed that no rescript or pragmatic sanction should be observed if it seemed to prejudice any litigant.[251] According to Odofredus, "[i]f there is a rescript against the natural law, or close, it is not acknowledged because all the emperors that ever were or will be cannot take away the natural law." Suppose, then, that the emperor took away the action of *vindicatio* by which, in Roman law, an owner reclaimed his property. Some would say that "the emperor can take away a civil action if he says 'any law notwithstanding.'" But Odofredus claimed that the emperor could not do so even if he added that phrase.[252] According to Odofredus, then, a court could disregard a rule made by the highest lawmaking authority if it denied a sufficiently basic procedural right, even if that authority declared expressly that he intended to deny that right.

Pennington concluded that the thirteenth-century jurists thus arrived at a conception of procedural rights that we can best translate as "due process of law," a conception that they might have described by the phrase *servare ordinis iuris*.[253] Indeed, according to Hostiensis, the devil himself would have the right to a trial.[254]

There were two exceptions that neither the canonists nor the civilians tried to abrogate.[255] One, as noted, was that the formalities of the *ordo iudicarius* could be suspended if the offense was notorious. Pennington describes a dispute that arose from this rule. Without using the regular judicial procedure, Pope Innocent IV declared that the Emperor Frederick II was deposed. The pope's allies argued that the emperor's crime was notorious and their adversaries, that the pope could not act as he did without the regular procedure.[256]

---

[248] Hostiensis, *In decretalium libros lectura*, Oxford, New College MS 205 to X 3.34.7.
[249] Hostiensis (n. 248), to X 1.2.7.   [250] Pennington (n. 244), 151–52.
[251] C. 1.22 [vulg. 25].6.
[252] Odofredus, *In primam Codicis partem...praelectiones* (Lyon, 1552, repr. in vol. 6 of *Opera Iuridica Rariora*, Bologna, 1968) to 1.22 [vulg. 25].6, no. 9.
[253] Pennington (n. 244), 145.
[254] Hostiensis (n. 248), to X 2.25.4 to *sed equitas*.
[255] Although Hostiensis also thought that the use of the *ordo iudicarius* could be deferred in cases in which, for example, an immediate proceeding might cause scandal. His reason was that "public utility.... is to be preferred over private utility in all things": Hostiensis (n. 248), to X 3.34.7.
[256] Pennington (n. 244), 146–47.

## Ius Commune: *The Medieval Jurists*

The other exception was that the accused need not be convicted by regular judicial procedure if he confessed—a proposition that appeared in the *Decretum*.[257] The horrible result was that people who could not be convicted by that procedure were often tortured until they did confess. It is one of the glories of our own and other modern societies that we abhor the use of torture. In earlier civilizations, whether Roman, Chinese, Muslim, or Western, torture was a common method of investigation even though the evidence gathered was unreliable, as the Romans themselves understood. Ulpian said that:

[R]eliance should not always be placed on torture, although not never, because it is a chancy and risky business, and one which may be deceptive. For there are a number of people who, by their endurance or their toughness under torture, are so contemptuous of it that the truth can in no way be squeezed out of them. Others have so little endurance that they would rather tell any kind of lie than suffer torture....[258]

To obtain accurate information through torture, according to Ulpian, one should not ask questions that suggest the answer that the victim of torture should give: "The person who is going to conduct the torture should not ask whether Lucius Titius committed a homicide, but in general terms who did it; for the former seems rather that of someone suggesting [an answer] than seeking [the truth]."[259]

As these passages suggest, however, the Romans were torturing people to obtain information, and sometimes these were people whom they did not suppose to be guilty. It is harder for us to understand torture by medieval courts. Its purpose was to obtain a confession when the courts did not have enough evidence to convict under the rules of the *ordo iudiciarius*. Under these rules, one could only convict a person on the evidence of two eyewitnesses, and never on circumstantial evidence alone. As John Langbein observed: "It does not matter, for example, that the suspect was seen running away from the murdered man's house and that the bloody dagger and the stolen loot are found in his possession. The court cannot convict him of the crime."[260] "No society," according to Langbein, "will long tolerate a legal system in which there is no prospect of convicting unrepentant persons who commit clandestine crimes. Something had to be done...."[261] The something was torture. A court could order a person to be tortured on the evidence of one eyewitness or circumstantial evidence. As Langbein noted, "torture was supposed to be employed in such a way that the accused would confess to details of the crime," thus providing information that no innocent person could know, such as where he had hidden the murder weapon.[262] One does not know how torture was employed in practice.

Pennington thought that the use of torture was in flat contradiction to the recognition of procedural rights by the thirteenth-century jurists: "Torture fundamentally undermines any idea of due process."[263] He then argued that although

---

[257] C. 2 q. 1 c. 1.    [258] D. 48.18.1.23.    [259] D. 48.18.1.21.
[260] John Langbein, *Torture and the Law of Proof: Europe and England in the Ancien Régime* (Chicago, IL, 1976), 4.
[261] Langbein (n. 260), 7.    [262] Langbein (n. 260), 5.    [263] Pennington (n. 244), 157.

torture was described in academic works, we do not know to what extent it was used in practice, and we do know that Italian city states put strict limits on its use. Hard as it may be for us to accept, however, from the standpoint of the medieval jurists, the use of torture did not contradict a commitment to due process. They thought of it as a consequence of that commitment. The object of due process was to ensure that an innocent person was not convicted. To avoid that result, suspects were tortured to determine whether they were innocent.

There is a parallel in England. At the Fourth Lateran Council in 1215, priests were forbidden to participate in trial by ordeal. The English were then at a loss how to try persons accused of crime. With some misgivings, they decided that such persons could be tried by jury, even though that meant that twelve neighbors could hang a man. That procedure seemed so repugnant that the English decided that a man could not be tried by jury unless he accepted a jury trial by "putting himself on the country." If he refused to do so, from the Middle Ages through the eighteenth century, stones were piled on his chest until he either waived his right not to be tried by a jury or he died. Some died—heroically—so that, since they had not been convicted, their property would not be confiscated, and could pass to their wives and children. Torture was not used to find out who committed a crime. Rather, it was used to maintain due process, as the English perceived it.

## The relationship between the external and internal forums

### Interdependence: the possibility of cooperation by the offender

To the extent that an offender could be trusted to submit himself to the internal forum, the rules of the external forum could be relaxed.

An example is a decretal of Pope Alexander III dealing with usury. It was considered usurious to loan someone a sum of money to be repaid at a later time with interest. But was it usurious to sell someone goods to be paid for at a later time for more than the price prevailing when the goods were sold? According to Alexander III, it all depended on what the price of such goods was estimated to be at the later time. He wrote:

> You say that in your city it often happens that some people buy pepper or cinnamon or other merchandise which then is not worth more than five pounds and promise payment of six pounds at the end of a fixed term to those from whom they receive the merchandise. A contract of this type is permissible and cannot be censured according to its form as usurious. Nevertheless, the sellers will commit sin unless there is doubt as to whether the merchandise will be worth more or less at the time of payment. And therefore let your citizens reflect well on their salvation, whether they will refrain from such contracts as no human intentions are hidden from almighty God.[264]

In effect, the Pope said, there is no way to prove in the external forum whether the transaction was really a sale or a camouflaged loan at interest, since that

---

[264] X 5.19.6.

depended on whether there was doubt in the "seller's" mind about the external price. He must examine his own intentions, which could not be hidden from God, and so not make such a contract. If he had done so, he must confess the sin in the internal forum and make restitution. To the extent that one could trust the internal forum, its rules could act as substitutes for rules in the external forum.

*Separation: the distinction between crime and sin*

To the extent that an issue could not be tried in the external forum, it could be resolved only in the internal forum. The canonists consequently drew a distinction between crime and sin that previous jurists had not. All sins had to be brought to the internal forum of the confessional if the penitent sought to be forgiven. Crimes were sins, but sins that could be tried in the external forum. Other sins could be brought only to the internal forum.

As Reinhard Zimmermann has said, although the distinction between crime and tort "goes back to the Roman notions of *crimen* and *delictum*... the boundary between the two was not drawn along the same lines as it is today."[265] A variety of tort actions were penal in that they allowed the plaintiff to recover a penalty from the defendant in addition to the compensation to which he was entitled. Examples were actions for theft, robbery, and, in some cases in later law, *iniuria*.[266] In contrast, "[th]e term 'crimen' was used to designate offences prosecuted in the public interest and punishable by a public penalty upon accusation and subsequent condemnation in a special court and according to a strict and largely state controlled procedure."[267] In the Republic, the list of such offenses was small. It increased greatly during the Empire. To know whether an offense constituted a crime, one had to know what was on the list. The Roman jurists did not need to concern themselves with the concept of crime. Moreover, as Schulz noted, by the time the jurists turned their attention to these offenses, "it was too late for the development of a jurisprudence of criminal law which might rank with that of private law." In any event, "criminal law... was so undefined, arbitrary and authoritarian, that any juristic construction of concepts and principles would have been devoid of practical significance."[268] Only three of the fifty books of Justinian's *Digest* dealt with criminal matters.[269]

The canonists did consider what sort of offense constituted a crime. The commission of a crime carried certain legal consequences. One who committed a crime was subject to ecclesiastical penalties such as excommunication.[270] He could also be barred from ecclesiastical office or removed from an office that he already held. As Stephen Kuttner has shown, the canonists' discussion of what constituted a

---

[265] Zimmermann (n. 28), 917.   [266] Buckland (n. 163), 592.
[267] Zimmermann (n. 28), 917–18.
[268] Fritz Schulz, *History of Roman Legal Science* (Oxford, 1946), 140.
[269] D. 47.11–49.13.   [270] Kuttner (n. 189), 4.

crime turned on the issue of when a person's action subjected him to these consequences.²⁷¹

In his letter to Titus (1:7), St. Paul said that a bishop should be ἀνέγκλητος—a difficult word to translate, which can mean "not accused," "void of offense," or "without reproach." The King James Bible translates it as "blameless"; the Jerusalem Bible, as "irreproachable."²⁷² St. Jerome, in his Latin translation, in standard use in the Middle Ages, translated the phrase as *sine crimine*, or "without crime." St. Augustine, in a text that was included in the *Decretum*, said that the requirement that Paul had set for the appointment of a bishop applied to "a priest or deacon or anyone else to be placed in a position of trust in the Church." Such a person also must be "without crime."²⁷³ Gratian and commentators on the *Decretum* concluded not only that one must be "without crime" to be eligible for ecclesiastical office, but also that one found guilty of crime after his appointment could be deposed.²⁷⁴ According to the Standard Gloss to the *Decretum*, some thought that an ecclesiastic could be deposed for the commission of a single crime and others thought that he must be "incorrigible."²⁷⁵ But they agreed that he could not be deposed unless he had committed a crime. So it mattered greatly what offenses were considered to be crimes.

For the canonists, as Stephan Kuttner said, "[t]he concept of sin was the object of all accountability before God and the Church."²⁷⁶ Yet St. Augustine noted in the text just quoted that, when St. Paul said that a bishop must be "without crime," he could not have meant that he must be without sin, since everyone has sinned:

The Apostle Paul did not say ... "if one is without sin," for if he had, every man would be rejected, but he said, "if one is without crime," such as homicide, adultery, some foul fornication, theft, fraud, sacrilege and other things of this kind. Crime, indeed, is a serious sin deserving of accusation and condemnation.²⁷⁷

Nevertheless, as Kuttner observed, "when the [Christian] fathers spoke of *crimina*, they were not trying to formulate a juridical concept." "In the old Church, the concept of crime did not have a particular legal meaning."²⁷⁸ Thus here, as elsewhere, the canonists' task was to formulate a legal standard based on a text that was normative, in that it described how Church affairs should be conducted, but in which the author had not tried to formulate a standard in the manner of a jurist.

The task was complicated by the fact that the word crime (*crimen*) meant different things in different canonical texts, and some of these meanings of the word were inapposite to the problem of interpreting the passage in St. Paul. Gratian tried to identify and distinguish these different meanings, and the canonists

---

²⁷¹ Most of this account is based on Kuttner (n. 189), 3–22.
²⁷² The *Summa Lipsiensis* takes the passage to mean that a bishop must be "irreprehensible," but adds afterward that a sinner may be a bishop: *Summa Lipsiensis* (n. 214), to *d.G. post* D. 25 c.3 to *Nunc autem*; to *cuius sententia*.
²⁷³ D. 81 c. 1.
²⁷⁴ *D.G. post* D. 81 c. 1; *Die Summa magistri Rufini zum Decretum Gratiani*, ed. Johann Friedrich von Schulte (Giessen, 1892), to *d.G. post* D. 81 c. 1; *Summa Parisiensis* (n. 214), to *d.G. post* D. 81 c. 1; *Summa Coloniensis* (n. 210), pars 2, cap. 6.
²⁷⁵ *Gl. ord.* to D. 81 c. 1 to *damnatione*.   ²⁷⁶ Kuttner (n. 189), 3.
²⁷⁷ D. 81 c. 1.   ²⁷⁸ Kuttner (n. 189), 8.

preserved his distinctions.²⁷⁹ Nevertheless, as Kuttner noted, the result may have been confusion rather than clarity.²⁸⁰

According to Gratian, crime (*crimen*) might mean "any sin" (*quodlibet peccatum*), or "deliberate sin" (*peccatum ex deliberatione procedens*), or mortal sin (*peccatum quod semel commissum sufficit ad damnationem*), or a "criminal sin or criminal infamia" (*criminale peccatum vel criminalis infamia*).²⁸¹

The canonists agreed that the "crime" in the letter of St. Paul could not carry the first meaning. As Huguccio said, "the word crime ... understood as any sin" is "not to be accepted this way in what was set forth by the authority of Paul [for] then, indeed, every man is to be rejected since no one is without sin."²⁸²

Neither, in this context, could "crime" mean a sin committed after deliberation. As Huguccio observed, this criterion would not even distinguish serious from minor sins: crime would include "any moral or venial sin as long as it was committed with deliberation."²⁸³

As to mortal sin, the canonists agreed that, "broadly, all mortal sin is a crime because it is worthy of accusation and condemnation as concerns God."²⁸⁴ Mortal sins may be termed crimes "because they are deserving of incrimination, that is, of confession and satisfaction."²⁸⁵ But although a person who was a criminal, in this sense, had to confess his sin and do penance, the question was whether he was disqualified for ecclesiastical office or could be deposed. Some canonists thought that he could be.²⁸⁶ But then, as one canonist pointed out, a person who had committed fornication before entering orders could be deposed from an ecclesiastical office that he held thereafter.²⁸⁷ A person would be disqualified from holding office or could be deposed if he had committed some serious sexual sin, but only in his thoughts, for example by coveting his neighbor's wife. Huguccio concluded that, so far as Paul's letter was concerned, "every crime is a mortal sin but not every mortal sin is a crime."²⁸⁸

Huguccio explained the difference by another meaning of the term "crime" that Gratian had identified. Crime entailed *infamia*. When "the term *crimen* is understood to mean any mortal sin that committed once is sufficient for damnation,

---

²⁷⁹ *Summa Lipsiensis* (n. 214), to *d.G. post* C. 25 c. 3 to *cuius sententia*; *Summa Parisiensis* (n. 214), to *d.G. post* D. 25 c. 3 to *quod autem*; *Summa Coloniensis* (n. 210), pars 2, cap. 5 (but leaving out deliberate sin).
²⁸⁰ Kuttner (n. 189), 7–8.      ²⁸¹ *D.G. post* D. 5 c. 3.
²⁸² Huguccio (n. 181), to *d.G. post* D. 25 c. 3.
²⁸³ Huguccio (n. 181), to *d.G. post* D. 25 c. 3.      ²⁸⁴ Huguccio (n. 181), to D. 81 c. 1.
²⁸⁵ Huguccio (n. 181), to *d.G. post* D.25 c. 3. Similarly, "Criminal, that is, worthy of incrimination and satisfaction before a priest": *Summa Lipsiensis* (n. 214), to D. 25 c. 3 to *criminale*.
²⁸⁶ *Summa Lipsiensis* (n. 214), to *d.G. post* C. 25 c. 3 to *cuius sententia*; *Summa Tornacensis* (n. 154), to *d.G. post* D. 25 c. 3 to *nomine autem criminis*. Raymond of Penafort distinguished according to the seriousness of a moral sin. It was a bar to appointment or grounds for removal if it was very great (*enorme*), or if it was moderate and manifest, or moderate and not manifest if the offender persevered in the crime. It was not when it was light, as long as the offender repented: *Summa iuris* pars 2, iv. Other canonists said that a crime must be a mortal sin without saying whether this is a necessary or a sufficient condition for barring a person from office or deposing him: *Summa Rufini* (n. 274), to *d.G. post* D. 25 c. 3 to *dum placet*.
²⁸⁷ *Summa Tornacensis* (n. 154), to *d.G. post* D. 81 c. 1.
²⁸⁸ Huguccio (n. 181), to *d.G. post* D. 25 c. 3.

nevertheless it does not impose *infamia*."²⁸⁹ Here, he was following the opinion of other canonists and, it would seem, of Gratian himself. According to Gratian, in the epistle to Titus, what is called crime is criminal sin, or criminal *infamia*.²⁹⁰

The term *infamia* was taken from Roman law and, at first sight, might seem to have little to do with the problem that the canonists were trying to resolve. In Roman law, *infamia* referred to the status of persons who were subjected to legal disabilities on account of wrongful or unseemly conduct. For example, they could not hold office or bring an accusation in a criminal case. A criminal conviction could make a person *infames*, although not any criminal conviction would do so. So could liability imposed in certain private actions. As one Roman text explained: "One is not made *infames* by every criminal conviction but by one which is made by public judgment (*ex iudicii publici causam habet*)." The text went on to say that one could be made *infames* by private actions such as those for theft, robbery, or *iniuria*.²⁹¹ Another text explained that the term "public judgment" referred to criminal proceedings brought under certain statutes:

> ... such as the *lex Julia* on treason, the *lex Cornelia* on murderers and poisoners, the *lex Pompeia* on parricide, the *lex Julia* on embezzlement, the *lex Cornelia* on wills, the *lex Julia* on public and private force, the *lex Julia* on electoral corruption, the *lex Julia* on extortion, and the *lex Julia* on the grain dole.²⁹²

Thus, in Roman law, *infamia* was a penalty that was attached to the commission of certain criminal offenses and certain private wrongs as well. There was one parallel between *infamia* in Roman law and the problem that the canonists were confronting: a consequence of *infamia* was ineligibility to hold public office. Nevertheless, although the canonists borrowed the term from Roman law, they used it in a different way: to limit the category of sins that were "crimes" within the meaning of Paul's letter to Titus, and therefore were barriers to holding ecclesiastical office and grounds for deposition.

The question then was what sort of *infamia* constitutes a crime. One possibility was to say that it is "such *infamia* as arises from a sin deserving of accusation and deposition."²⁹³ But that answer is circular: one must know which sins call for accusation and deposition to know which entail *infamia*. Nevertheless, there was a characteristic of *infamia* that suggested another way in which to distinguish crime from sin. *Infamia*, in Roman law, was the consequence of a formal legal proceeding. One might conclude that, to constitute a crime, an offense had to be one that could be tried in a formal legal proceeding.

That was the conclusion that many canonists reached, whether or not it was inspired by the Roman law of *infamia*. St. Augustine had said that "[c]rime ... is a serious sin deserving of accusation and condemnation." Huguccio explained that "accusation" meant "judicial, that is, for which one can be brought before the court

---

²⁸⁹ Huguccio (n. 181), to *d.G. post* D. 25 c. 3.
²⁹⁰ *Summa Lipsiensis* (n. 214), to *d.G. post* C. 25 c. 3 to *cuius sententia* ("*sine crimine, id est, sine infamia criminalis peccati*"), although the *Summa* also said that crime in the epistle could mean any mortal sin.
²⁹¹ D. 48.1.7.   ²⁹² D. 48.1.1.
²⁹³ *Summa Rufini* (n. 274), to *d.G. post* D. 25 c. 3 to *criminalis infamia*.

# Ius Commune: *The Medieval Jurists*

of a judge":[294] "[N]ot every mortal sin is a crime but one for which one may be tried before the court of a judge."[295] Some believed a further limit was necessary: "a sin that scandalizes the church is called a crime" and so the sin must be one that "causes scandal."[296] But a sin that could not be tried before a court was not a crime.

The requirement that a crime must be an offense that could be tried before a court limited the sins that could be considered crimes. One limit, as Kuttner observed, was "that a sin is only a crime when it proceeds to an act... and does not remain a mere sinful desire... or a mere decision of the will."[297] A court could not judge what was hidden. As Huguccio said, "God and not man is the judge of secret things."[298] Consequently:

[S]ometimes sins are in thoughts that delight and please and are mortal; nevertheless, one cannot be accused and condemned because they did not proceed to an outward act; those which are mortal and do proceed to an outward act are crimes.[299]

Huguccio was following his predecessors, who had said, for example, that the offense cannot be one that "only consist[s] in the will,"[300] or one that, although committed "knowingly and with deliberation," is "confined to the intentions of the will."[301]

Thus the canonists concluded that a crime was not only a sin, but also one that could be tried in court in the external forum. This conclusion is at odds with the modern idea that whether an action is a crime depends on whether the state has prohibited and penalized it. It is in harmony with the belief underlying much of modern criminal law that people can be convicted only for an act, not a thought, and that the act must be one that can be proved against a person in court.

## The internal forum

### *The role of jurists and laypeople*

In Rome, we have seen, the jurists were the only ones with specialized legal training. The administration of justice was in the hands of laypeople: the praetor, the iudex, and the advocates or oratores. The jurists had to present their opinions to these people in language that they could understand. In contrast, in the medieval Roman-Canonical procedure, the administration of justice was in the hands of legal specialists. The advocates and judges were graduates of university law schools. They addressed each other in language that might be opaque to the public.

In the internal forum, however, canonists, unlike civilians, found it necessary to express their conclusions in language that non-jurists could understand. Laypeople

---

[294] Huguccio (n. 181), to D. 81 c. 1.   [295] Huguccio (n. 181), to D. 81 c. 1.
[296] *Summa Lipsiensis* (n. 214), to D. 81 c. 1 to *Crimen est grave*.
[297] Kuttner (n. 189), 19.
[298] Huguccio (n. 181), to *d.G. post* D. 25 c. 3.
[299] Huguccio (n. 181), to *d.G. post* D. 25 c. 3.
[300] *Summa Lipsiensis* (n. 214), to D. 81 c. 1 to *Crimen est grave*; *Summa Coloniensis* (n. 210), pars 2, cap. 6.
[301] *Summa Parisiensis* (n. 214), pars 2, cap. 6.

confessed their sins to priests, who themselves might have no legal training. Consequently, manuals appeared in which canon lawyers explained the law of the internal forum in a manner that would help priests to advise laypeople as to what sins they might have committed and consequently might need to confess. The law had to be presented in these manuals in a way that laypeople could grasp.

An example of such a presentation is the discussion of culpability in the *Summa on Penance* of Raymond of Penafort, one of the greatest medieval jurists, which became a model for later manuals. We have seen how the canonists developed their ideas on culpability, partly on their own and partly with the aid of Roman law. The following passage includes almost all of Raymond's discussion of the culpability of a person who kills another:

> Homicide may occur by chance, as when someone throws a stone at a bird and someone else unexpectedly passing by is struck and dies, or when someone cuts down a tree which, by chance, crushes someone, and so forth. Here one must distinguish whether he was carrying on an unlawful work, or a lawful one. If the work was unlawful, then the killing is imputed to him as, for example, if he threw the stone toward a place where men are accustomed to pass, or when a horse or cow is raged and someone is struck by the horse or cow, and in similar instances. *Dicta Gratiani ante* C. 15 q. 1 c. 3; D. 50 c. 37; c. 44; X 223.1. If, however, the work was done lawfully, the killing is not imputed to him if he uses the diligence that he should, namely, in looking about and calling out, not too late or too softly but at an appropriate time, and loudly, so that if someone were there he could escape and look out for himself, or if a teacher does not go beyond due measure in beating a student. It is otherwise if, engaged in a lawful work, he does not use due diligence. As has been said, then the killing is imputed to him. This distinction is proved from D. 50 c. 50; c. 51; X 5.12.25. Finally, some homicide is voluntary. It may be said without distinction that voluntary homicide is a mortal sin and a very great one. D. 50 c. 44.[302]

If a man were to confess to a priest that he had killed someone, the priest could ask him about his intentions, his degree of diligence, and the type of activity in which he had been engaged. The priest might, in the end, tell the man that he had not committed a sin at all. The priest could do so, guided by this passage, without himself knowing the many sources, Roman and Christian, on which it was based.

## *Offenses that cannot be tried in the external forum: the beginnings of international law*

Another consequence of the canonists' exposition of the law of the internal forum was a huge extension of the range of human affairs of concern to jurists. The rules of the internal forum applied to all forms of sin, to all violations of the law of God, whether or not they could be tried before a court.

An example that I have discussed elsewhere[303] is the law governing relations between husband and wife—in particular, sexual relations. The canonists regarded certain forms of sexual behavior, which they called "unnatural acts," as sinful.[304]

---

[302] Raimundus de Penafort (n. 167), II.1.  [303] Gordley (n. 208).
[304] *Gl. ord.* to C. 32 q. 2 c. 3 to *ab adulterio*.

But they also considered whether and when it might be sinful for a married couple to have sexual relations in the normal fashion. Such a question was unlikely to arise in the external forum. Yet, as I have described elsewhere, the canonists regarded it as a legal problem to be resolved with the same care and by the same method as that which they applied to other legal problems. In the end, they arrived at a rule that could be applied only in the internal forum: a man committed a moral sin with his wife, or she with him, if the spouse in question was so exclusively moved by desire that, although the two were married, he or she would have had intercourse even if they were not. This solution was adopted very early by Huguccio, Rolandus, and the *Summa Parisiensis*.[305] It was later accepted by the *Summa Lipsiensis*, the *Glossa Palatina*, and the Standard Gloss.[306] John Noonan and Pierre Payer have said that this solution is "impractical."[307] It turned on an inward state of mind rather than an outward act. But that does not mean, as Payer suggested, that "for a confessor...the principle, of course, is useless."[308] Quite the opposite. A key difference between the external and the internal forum was that, in the internal forum, the penitent who wished to be absolved could be asked to consider his state of mind.

In other cases, an offense could not be tried in the external forum because there was no court with jurisdiction over both parties. The example that we will consider in some detail is a dispute between kings or principalities. It might happen that no court had jurisdiction over them both. Unless the dispute could be resolved by agreement, it had to be resolved by war. The canonists considered when it was a sin to make war—a matter to be judged in the internal forum, for want of any other. Since the time of the Romans, it had been recognized that there were just and unjust causes for war. But it had not been the concern of the jurists. Now, for the first time, it was.

The Romans, although not the Roman jurists, had been much concerned with what they called the law of war and peace. According to Livy, the manner of declaring war with which he was familiar was ancient:

When an envoy arrives at the frontier of the state from which satisfaction is sought, he covers his head with a woolen cap and says: "Hear me, Jupiter! Hear me, land of So-and-so! Hear me, O righteousness! I am the accredited spokesman of the Roman people. I come as their envoy in the name of justice and religion, and ask credence for my words." The particular demands follow, and the envoy, calling Jupiter to witness, proceeds: "If my demand for the restitution of those men, or those goods, be contrary to religion and justice, then never let me be a citizen of my country." The formula, with only minor changes, is repeated when the envoy crosses the frontier, to the first man he subsequently meets, when he passes to through the gate of the town, and when he enters the public square.[309]

---

[305] Huguccio (n. 181), to C. 32 q. 4 c. 5 to *amator*; Rolandus, *Die Summa Magis Rolandi nachmals Papstes Alexander II*, ed. F. Thaner (Innsbruck, 1874), to C. 32 q. 4 to *adulteram*; *Summa Pariensis* (n. 214), to C. 32 q. 2 c. 3.

[306] *Summa Lipsiensis* (n. 214), to C. 2 q. 4 c. 5 to *ardentior*; *Glossa Palatina* (n. 188), to C. 32 q. 4 c. 5; *Gl. ord.* to C. 32 q. 4 c. 5 to *amator*.

[307] John Noonan, *Contraception: A History of its Treatment by Catholic Theologians and Canonists* (Cambridge, MA, 1965), 251; Pierre Payer, *The Bridling of Desire: Views of Sex in the Later Middle Ages* (Toronto, 1993), 128.

[308] Payer (n. 307), 128.

[309] Livy, *The Early History of Rome*, trans. Aubry de Sélincourt (Baltimore, MD, 1960), I.3.

If the demands were not met after thirty-three days, the envoy called upon Jupiter and Janus Quirinus, and all of the gods "in heaven, on earth, and under the earth," to witness that "the people of So-and-so are unjust and refuse reparation." He then recited a formula to the "elders" of Rome asking them if war should be declared. Each person voting for war responded: "I hold that these things be sought by means of a just and righteous war. Thus I give my vote and my consent." If a majority voted in favor of war, a fetial priest was sent to the frontier in the company of at least three men of military age. He recited another formula, which included the lines "the Roman people hereby declare and make war," and threw a spear across the border.[310]

For the Romans to make war, then, they had to affirm that their cause was just—for example for "the restitution of those men, or those goods"—and they had to declare war formally. Cicero referred to both elements when he said that "no war is just unless it is conducted for the recovery of things (*rebus repetitis*) and declared in advance...."[311] He also mentioned as a just cause of war the punishment (*ultio*) of the enemy's offenses.[312]

Cicero said little that was more definite about what constituted a just cause of war. Indeed, in the procedure just described, the matter was left to the judgment of those who had the power to vote for war, unguided by any definite set of rules. The law of war was not a body of substantive rules, but a procedure by which they gave their judgment, after invoking the gods, and then made a formal declaration of war. Certainly, it was not an affair of the jurists. The jurists were developing the law to be applied to disputes resolved by a iudex on instructions from a praetor. In the late Republic, when the Romans were considering the justice of going to war, no one expected Q. Mucius Scaevola, in his capacity as a jurist, to weigh in on the subject. In the classical period, the activities of the jurists remained as they had been and, in any event, concerns about the justice of a war became less significant when Rome became a world empire. A change from Republican practice was noted by Ulpian: the emperor now had the authority to declare war; consequently, "the use of arms without the knowledge of the *princeps*," meaning the emperor, "is forbidden."[313]

The canonists worked out rules about when it was a sin to go to war. Their key text was a paraphrase of Cicero by Isidore of Seville that had been included in the *Decretum*: "A war is just which is conducted by edict (*edicto*) and for the cause of the recovery of things (*rebus repetendis*) or the repelling of enemies."[314]

The canonists paraphrased this text, sometimes in ways that seemed to broaden it. Rufinus spoke not of "the recovery of things," but of *vindicta*, a word that was larger in that it could include punishment as a just cause of war (as Cicero had done), although it might refer to recovering what was one's own.[315] The *Summa Parisiensis* was explicit: a just war could be fought "to recover things taken by force" and so that injuries could be punished (*ulsciscuntur*).[316] Iohannes Teutonicus spoke of

---

[310] Livy (n. 309), I.3. [311] *De officiis* 1.11.36. [312] *De republica* II.23.35.
[313] C. 11.47 [vulg. 46]. [314] C. 23 q. 2 c. 1.
[315] *Summa Rufini* (n. 274), to C. 23 q. 1. [316] *Summa Parisiensis* (n. 214), to C. 23 q. 2.

"the recovery of things or the defense of one's country (*patria*),"[317] perhaps because he thought that defending one's homeland meant more than repelling an enemy. None of them went beyond what Cicero said, or easily might have said.

Since the canonists were speaking about the law of the internal forum, however, the question before them, properly speaking, was not what constituted a just war, but whether a person engaged in war had committed a sin that he needed to confess. He had done so if he knowingly engaged in an unjust war. But what if he engaged in a just war, but for the wrong reasons, or in an unjust war without knowing it to be unjust? Some of the wrong reasons were mentioned in a text by St. Augustine, also included in the *Decretum*, for example "greed, the cruelty of vengeance, a warlike and unappeasable spirit, savage rebellion, [and] the lust to dominate."[318] The canonists paraphrased Augustine[319] or cited the text as instances of an "unjust spirit" that made it sinful to wage war.[320] Conversely, a person might engage in war for good motives, believing the war to be just when it actually was not. Rolandus and Stephen of Tornai gave the example of an innocent prince who went to war because he had received false testimony from others. In their view, such a prince had not sinned.[321] Another question was whether those who fought under a prince who engaged in an unjust war were guilty of sin. Gregory had said, in a text included in the *Decretum*, that "the just man, if by chance he fights under a king who is sacrilegious, can rightly fight upon command if only in service of the order of peace which is commanded him...."[322] According to the Standard Gloss, that was so when the man in question had legitimate doubts about the justice of the war, but not when the injustice of it is clear: "When matters are doubtful, one is always to obey."[323]

This entire discussion presupposed that the dispute could not be decided in the external forum by a court with jurisdiction over both parties or that the purpose of the war was not simply to enforce such a decision. The idea that there might be no court with jurisdiction broke with prior ideas of the locus of political authority.

Typically, the medieval civilians claimed that the emperor was the only legitimate source of authority. They drew that conclusion from their Roman texts.[324] It was also backed by canonical authority. A text in the *Decretum*, ascribed to Gregory, but by the *Correctores* to Jerome, said that just as there was one emperor, so there cannot be more than one prelate in a church.[325] According to the Standard Gloss to the *Decretals*, the emperor "is the *princeps* of the world and its lord."[326] The text by Isadore quoted earlier said that "[a] war is just which is conducted by edict (*edicto*)," which the canonists read to mean that a war must be declared

---

[317] *Gl. ord.* to *d.G. ante* C. 23 q.2 c. 1 to *Quod autem*. Similarly, Hostiensis spoke of a war fought "for the defense of your own or your country (*patria*)": Hostiensis (n. 30), 1, rubr. *De treuga et pace, Quid sit iustum bellum*.
[318] C. 23 q. 1 c. 4.
[319] *Summa Coloniensis* (n. 210), pars 12 *iterum*, cap. 5.
[320] *Gl. ord.* to *d.G. ante* C. 23 q. 2 c. 1 to *Quod autem*. Similarly, *Summa Tornacesis* (n. 154), to C. 23 q. 2.
[321] *Summa Rolandi* (n. 305), to C. 23 q. 2; *Summa Tornacensis* (n. 154), to C. 23 q. 2.
[322] C. 24 q. 1 c. 4.     [323] *Gl. ord.* to C. 24 q. 1 c. 4.
[324] C.1.17.1; Bartolus (n. 57), to D. 1.1.9, no. 4; Baldus (n. 32), to D. 1.1.9.
[325] C. 7 q. 1 c. 41.     [326] *Gl. ord.* to X 1.6.34 to *in Germanos*.

by the *princeps*.³²⁷ It would seem, then, that the only *princeps* who could declare war was the emperor and that he would necessarily be doing so against people who, in principle, were subject to his authority.

This view was actually taken, according to Huguccio, by a jurist to whom he refers as "Johannes"—perhaps Johannes Bassianus or Johannes Faventinus.³²⁸ But it was rejected by others. Huguccio did so, citing the text from Gregory mentioned earlier in which it was said that "war was to be taken up on the authority and counsel of *principes*," a plural noun, best translated as "princes."³²⁹ He concluded that "any prince may do this."³³⁰ "Princes" meant "emperors, kings and other princes."³³¹ Others said that war might be declared "by those who direct the public power to carry on war."³³² Rolandus spoke of disputes in which no one had jurisdiction over both parties.³³³

The question then remained: who counted as "princes" who had the authority to declare war? It was not informative to say "those who direct the public power to carry on war," or that "princes" are "those to whom the counsel and command of war is committed by law,"³³⁴ or "those to whom the authority and counsel to make war belongs."³³⁵ To say that war must be declared by one with the authority to so declare did not answer the question of who possessed that authority.

The closest approach to an answer was given by Sinibaldus Fliscus, later Pope Innocent IV, in his commentary on the Decretals. He explained that people had first settled the earth wandering in groups, sometimes separating and taking separate ways, as Abraham and Lot did when their group had been large and their herdsmen began to quarrel. As they traveled, anything that they chose to appropriate became their own on the Roman legal principle that anyone who takes

---

³²⁷ According to the *Summa Parisiensis*, the text meant that a just war "must be conducted by edict of the prince against those who have been determined to be public enemies. . . .": *Summa Parisiensis* (n. 214), to C. 23 q. 2. The Standard Gloss took the same position in a note to a different text, C. 23 q. 1 c. 4 to *principes*. It cited in support the text from Ulpian quoted earlier prohibiting "the use of arms without the knowledge of the *princeps*": C. 11.47 [vulg. 46]. Isidore had been paraphrasing Cicero, who had not been describing who within the Roman state had the power to declare war, but rather insisting that war must be declared. The *princeps* to whom Ulpian was referring, however, was the emperor.

³²⁸ Frederick H. Russell, *The Just War in the Middle Ages* (Cambridge, 1975), 101, n. 46, citing Huguccio, *Summa*, to C. 23 q. 2 c. 1 B.N. Lat. MS. 15397. The passage does not appear in Huguccio (n. 181), to C. 23 q. 2 c. 1 (Admont, Stiftsbibliothek, MS 7). As yet, there is no critical edition of Huguccio.

³²⁹ C. 23 q. 1 c. 4.

³³⁰ Russell (n. 328), 101, n. 46, citing Huguccio, *Summa*, B.N. Lat. MS. 15397 to C. 23 q. 2 c. 1. See n. 328.

³³¹ Huguccio (n. 181), to C. 23 q. 1 c. 4.

³³² *Summa Rufini* (n. 274), to C. 23 q. 1 ("*publicae potestas bello gerando praesideant indicto mandato sive permissa licentia a principibus*"). Similarly, *Summa Coloniensis* (n. 210), pars 12 *iterum*, cap. 4 ("*auctortas imperantis, ut videlicet publice potestas bello presideant, principes scilcet apud quos secumdum iura belli commitendi consilium et preceptum est*"). According to Russell, Rufinus and the *Summa Coloniensis* thought that imperial authorization was necessary for a declaration of war: Russell (n. 328), 101. But that view is not supported by the passages just quoted. The *Summa Coloniensis* does speak of the authority of the emperor to declare war, but in a passage that is part of a quotation: pars 12 *iterum*, cap. 7.

³³³ *Summa Rolandi* (n. 305), to C. 23 q. 2.

³³⁴ *Summa Coloniensis* (n. 210), pars 12 *iterum*, cap. 4.

³³⁵ *Summa Rufini* (n. 274), to C. 23 q. 1.

possession of a *res nullius*—a thing that belongs to no one—becomes its owner. At some point, some person or persons acquired "just jurisdiction" over the group. Sinibaldus admitted that he did not know just how this power was acquired, but said that it must have been acquired at some point since, according to his authorities, the secular power wields the sword. One possibility is election, as when the Israelites chose to have a king.[336] In any event, the rational nature of man suggested that there should be a secular power with "just jurisdiction" over a group. He concluded that "ownership, possession, and jurisdiction may be lawful and without sin for infidels, and not only for the faithful, because they belong to every rational creature."[337] One could not make war on them or despoil them without a just cause.[338] The Crusades were lawful only because they were waged to reconquer territory taken by Muslims in unjust wars.[339] Sinibaldus did not reach this conclusion because of a concern about religious tolerance. He did agree with other canonists that "it is not lawful to use force to coerce infidels to accept the faith, because all things have been left to free will, and in this call only the grace of God is effective."[340] But the reason was not the modern idea that adherents of different religions were entitled to equal treatment. Infidels can be coerced "to admit preachers of the Gospel in lands of their own jurisdiction because all rational creatures were made to give praise to God."[341] But the reverse did not hold. Must one "admit those who wish to declare the law of Mohammed? I say no. We ought not to judge them as equal with us as they are in error and we are in the path of truth...."[342] Nevertheless, he concluded that infidel princes might have legitimate authority and one could not wage war on them without a just cause.

The canonists thus laid the foundations that made international law possible. They said that instead of one Church and one Empire, there was one Church and a plurality of secular powers with the authority to declare war, each, according to Sinibaldus Fliscus, with legitimate jurisdiction. They discussed when it was legitimate for these powers to settle their differences by war. Their authorities, and consequently the canonists themselves, said little about what constituted a just cause for war and who had the authority to declare it. Nevertheless, they recognized the basic premise of international law: that there is a plurality of secular powers that can declare war and that there are rules that govern when it is legitimate to do so. For the canonists, these rules governed in the internal forum in which those who wage war can be called to account.

---

[336] Sinibaldus Fliscus (n.181), to X 3.34.8, nos. 1–3.
[337] Sinibaldus Fliscus (n.181), to X 3.34.8, no. 3.
[338] Sinibaldus Fliscus (n.181), to X 3.34.8, no. 3.
[339] Sinibaldus Fliscus (n.181), to X 3.34.8, no. 7.
[340] Sinibaldus Fliscus (n.181), to X 3.34.8, no. 8.
[341] Sinibaldus Fliscus (n.181), to X 3.34.8, no. 8.
[342] Sinibaldus Fliscus (n.181), to X 3.34.8, no. 10.

# III

## *Ius et Iustitia*

## The Late Scholastics

## Origins

In 1503, Pierre Crockaert, a professor at the University of Paris, underwent an intellectual conversion. He rejected the nominalist philosophy of William of Occam in which he had been educated and turned to that of Thomas Aquinas. He joined the Dominican order of friars to which Aquinas himself had belonged. In 1512, he published a commentary on the last part of Aquinas' *Summa theologiae*, with the help of his pupil Francesco de Vitoria. Vitoria returned to his native Spain, where, as a professor at the University of Salamanca from 1526 until his death in 1546, he founded the school of theologian-philosopher-jurists that historians call the "Spanish natural law school," or the "late scholastics." As Wim Decock noted, others had prepared the way. In 1508, Tomasso di Vio, known as Cardinal Cajetan, started to publish what became the standard commentary on the *Summa theologiae*. The late scholastics drew on it. A Thomist revival had already begun at Salamanca in the later fifteenth century with the work of Pedro Mariniez de Osma and his student Diego de Deza. "Probably the decisive moments in the move toward Thomism," according to Decock, "were the reformation of the Dominican monastery in Vallodolid in 1502 and the foundation of an establishment for higher learning called Santo Tomás in 1517."[1] The seed sown by Vitoria fell on fertile soil. Vitoria published nothing himself and his ideas are known only through the handwritten notes of his lectures that have survived. Nevertheless, he trained scores of highly influential pupils, among them Domingo de Soto, a fellow Dominican who had been his pupil at Paris and who became his colleague at Salamanca. The enterprise started by the Dominicans was later taken up by the Jesuits, notably Luis de Molina, Leonard Lessius, and Francisco Suárez. Much of the work of Suárez concerned legal philosophy, and will be taken up in a later chapter.[2]

The project of the late scholastics was to synthesize Roman and canon law with the moral philosophy of Aquinas and Aristotle. The works of Aristotle on metaphysics, physics, ethics, and politics had been rediscovered in the late twelfth and

---

[1] Wim Decock, *Theologians and Contract Law: The Moral Transformation of the* Ius Commune *(ca. 1500–1650)* (Leiden, 2013), 51.
[2] *See* Chapter VIII, pp. 166–75.

early thirteenth centuries. They became a staple of the medieval curriculum. Aristotle came to be recognized, in the words of Dante, as "the teacher of all those who know." Aquinas used Aristotelian philosophical principles to explain Christian teaching on faith and morals. Some of the medieval civilians, such as Bartolus and Baldus, were familiar with both Aristotle and Aquinas. They sometimes read an Aristotelian meaning into their Roman texts.[3] Yet their use of philosophy was occasional.[4] Their project remained the same as that of their predecessors: to understand the Roman legal texts by reconciling each text with every other. The late scholastics used the principles of Aristotelian and Thomistic philosophy to explain Roman and canon law as interpreted by the medieval jurists.

Vitoria began his work "On Civil Power" by claiming: "The office and duty of a theologian appear to be so large that no argument, no problem, and no topic seems foreign to it."[5] Soto began his treatise, *Ten Books on Justice and Law*,[6] with a defense of why a theologian and philosopher such as himself should be writing about law:

Nor is to be accounted a fault of a theologian to take on territory that might seem more appropriate for those skilled in law as, indeed, canon law proceeds from the womb of theology and civil law by means of the precepts of philosophy. It is for the theologian to adjust the decreta of canon law to the norms of the Gospel, and for the philosopher to examine the civil law according to the principles of philosophy. Wherefore Cicero in book 1 of *The Laws* judges the discipline of law to derive not from the Praetor's Edict nor the Twelve Tables but far more from the most profound philosophy.[7]

The philosophy and theology that he intended to bring to this task, as he explained a few lines later, was principally that of Aquinas, "saint among the saints," who "in moral studies chiefly the schools universally honor as the brilliant star."[8]

We saw in the first chapter how, in the ancient world, the philosophy of Aristotle and the work of the Roman jurists had little to do with each other. Now, in the sixteenth century, that philosophy was used to explain their work.

The late scholastics could explain only some legal norms by means of their philosophical principles. Those that they could explain belonged, they said, to the natural law. Those that they could not explain by these principles belonged to the positive law.

---

[3] James Gordley, *The Philosophical Origins of Modern Contract Doctrine* (Oxford, 1991), 39–40, 50–55, 59–60; Diego Quaglioni, "'Regnativa prudentia': Diritto e teologia nel 'Tractatus testimoniorum' bartoliano," in *Atti del convegno "Theologie et droit dans la science politique de l'Etat moderne," Roma, 12–14 novembre 1987* (Rome, 1992), 155; Luigi Chiapelli, "Le idee politiche del Bartolo," *Archivio giuridico* 28 (1881): 433, 433–34; but see C. N. S. Woolf, *Bartolus of Sassoferrato: His Position in the History of Medieval Thought* (Cambridge, 1913), 384–87. On Baldus, see Gordley, *Philosophical Origins* 39, 50–56, 60–67; Norbert Horn, "Philosophie in der Jurisprudenz der Kommentoren: Baldus Philosophus," *Ius Commune* 1 (1967): 104, 124, 134; Walter Ullmann, "Baldus' Conception of Law," *Law Quarterly Review* 58 (1942): 386, 387.
[4] Gordley (n. 3), 49–67; Donald Kelly, "Science in the Renaissance: Jurisprudence Italian Style," *Historical Journal* 22 (1979): 777, 781–82.
[5] Franciscus de Vitoria, *De potestate civili*, 2nd ed., cited in "Prologue," in vol. 1 of *Relecciones Teológicas del Maestro Fray Francisco de Vitoria*, ed. Luis Alonso Getino (Madrid, 1934), 294.
[6] Domenicus de Soto, *De iustitia et iure libri decem* (Salamanca, 1553).
[7] Soto (n. 6), *Proemium*.   [8] Soto (n. 6), *Proemium*.

These norms might have been established for sound pragmatic reasons, but they lacked a principled justification. Consequently, the late scholastics had greater freedom in dealing with their legal texts than the medieval jurists. Every text did not have to be reconciled with every other. Every text did not have equal authority.

## Commutative justice and private law

The late scholastics wrote about *iustitia*, the virtue of justice, and *ius*, the just action that is the object of that virtue. The starting point for the late scholastics was an Aristotelian and Thomistic view of man. For them, as for Aristotle and Aquinas, human happiness consists in living a distinctively human life, a life that realizes, so far as possible, one's potential as a human being. It is a life unlike that of other animals because a human being can act not only by appetite, but also by reason and will. He can understand that an action contributes to the distinctively human life that he should live, and he can choose it for that reason. Living such a life is the ultimate end to which all well-chosen actions are a means, either instrumentally or as constituent parts. To identify the actions that contribute to such a life, a person exercises an acquired ability—a virtue—that these writers called "prudence." In following the dictates of prudence, he may need other virtues as well, such as the courage to face pain and danger, or the temperance to forgo pleasure.

Because man is a social animal, part of living such a life is helping others to live it well. For such a life, a person needs not only virtues, but also external things. He should try to acquire the things that he needs and help others to do so. The object of distributive justice is to ensure that each person has the resources to acquire what he needs. The object of commutative justice is to enable him to obtain them without depriving others of their share of resources.

The late scholastics explained the law of property, unjust enrichment, tort, and contract in terms of commutative justice. In the case of property, one could violate commutative justice by keeping what belonged to another. In the case of unjust enrichment, one could do so by keeping a gain made by using what belonged to another. In the case of tort, one could do so by harming what belonged to another. In the case of contract, one could do so by reneging on an agreement or by exchanging on unfair terms. As we have seen, in such cases, the canonists had said that a person must make "restitution" by compensating the other party if he is to be forgiven.[9] Aquinas described restitution as an act of commutative justice.[10]

The late scholastics rebuilt Roman and canon law on this ground plan. Instead of writing commentaries on texts as did the medieval jurists, they organized their work by discussing each field of law in turn, taking separately property, unjust enrichment, tort, and contract. In discussing each field, they laid down general principles, and then used these principles to explain as much of Roman and canon law as they could.

[9] *See* Chapter II, p. 57.  [10] Aquinas, *Summa theologiae* II-II, Q. 62, a. 1.

When they discussed property, they explained that a person would violate commutative justice by having something that belonged to another person—as Aquinas put it, *ipsa res accepta*—regardless of how he obtained it. The late scholastics explained, in the same way as Aristotle and Aquinas, why things should belong to people. Aristotle rejected the view of his teacher Plato that all property should be in common. If it were, Aristotle said, "Those who labor much and get little will necessarily complain of those who labor little and receive or consume much."[11] Aquinas gave a similar explanation.[12] The late scholastics concluded that, although all things were in common ideally, or in principle, or in the beginning, private property was instituted to remedy the defects of common ownership that Aristotle and Aquinas had described.

It followed that the right to property was not absolute. Rather, it was limited by the purposes for which private property was instituted. The late scholastics explained the canonists' rule that one could use another's property in time of necessity[13] in terms of those purposes, borrowing again from Aquinas. He had said that despite "the division of things . . . man's needs have to be remedied by these very things. . . . " Therefore, if the need is "manifest and urgent," then "it is lawful for a man to meet his own need by means of another's property. . . . "[14] Lessius explained:

[O]ne may take another's thing when one is in extreme necessity because, in extreme necessity, one needs what is necessary to preserve one's life . . . The reason for this is that the end of inferior things is to serve men through necessity, so that through them men may preserve and maintain their lives. Therefore this right belongs to all by nature. Nor can the division of things introduced by the law of peoples take away this right, for the law of peoples presupposes the law of nature and does not destroy it particularly as to what is necessary to preserve life. The division of things must therefore be deemed to have been made with a reservation to each person of this natural right to whatever is necessary to maintain his life. Otherwise the division would not have been done in a rational way.[15]

Soto and Molina took the same view.[16] As we will see, their conclusion that, in cases of necessity, one could take another's property was accepted by the seventeenth-century founders of the northern natural law school, Hugo Grotius and Samuel Pufendorf,[17] whence it passed into later law.

A person could violate commutative justice *ipsa res accepta* by having property that belonged to another. He could also do so if he had made a gain by once having had it. He then owed the owner the amount by which he had been enriched.[18] For example, according to Lessius, if he spent ten gold pieces belonging to another, but

---

[11] Aristotle, *Politics* II. v.    [12] Aquinas (n. 10), II-II, Q. 66, a. 2.
[13] *See* Chapter II, pp. 58–59.    [14] Aquinas (n. 10), II-II, Q. 66, a.7.
[15] Leonard Lessius, *De iustitia et iure, ceterisque virtutibus cardinalis libri quatuor* (Paris, 1628), lib. 2, cap. 12, dub. 12.
[16] Soto (n. 6), lib. 5, q. 3, a. 4; Ludovicus de Molina, *De iustitia et iure tractatus* (Venice, 1614), disp. 20.
[17] Hugo Grotius, *De iure belli ac pacis libri tres* (Amsterdam, 1646), II.ii.6–7; Samuel Pufendorf, *De iure naturae et gentium libri octo* (Amsterdam, 1688), II.vi.5.
[18] Molina (n. 16), disp. 718, no. 2; Lessius (n. 15), lib. 2, cap. 14, dub. 1, no. 3.

saved only five of his own, because he would have spent five otherwise, then he was enriched by only five gold pieces.[19] According to Molina and Lessius, if he bought and then resold property that belonged to another, he was enriched only if he resold at a profit.[20] They thus recognized unjust enrichment as a distinct ground for relief.[21] Roman law gave relief for specific instances of unjust enrichment. A Roman text did say that that no one should be enriched at another's expense.[22] Nevertheless, as Robert Feenstra pointed out, the late scholastics were the first to recognize this principle as the foundation of a law of unjustified enrichment on a par with contract and tort.[23] As we will see, through the work of Grotius and Pufendorf, that conclusion also made its way into later law.[24]

As we saw in an earlier chapter,[25] although Gaius had mentioned the categories of tort and contract (*delictus* and *contractus*), Roman law was a law of particular torts and contracts, each with its own rules. As noted, modern scholars believe that the categories themselves were taken from Aristotle, since they correspond to two types of commutative justice that he discussed. He said that, in involuntary transactions, in which one person has deprived another of what belonged to him, commutative justice requires that the victim recover the amount of his loss. In voluntary transactions, in which people exchange resources, commutative justice requires that they exchange resources of equivalent value so that neither gains at the other's expense.[26] Although Gaius introduced these categories, he did not try to work out the consequences of conceiving of tort and contract in terms of commutative justice. Instead, he discussed the particular torts and contracts recognized by Roman law.

The late scholastics identified *delictus* and *contractus* with commutative justice in involuntary and voluntary transactions. Unlike Gaius, they used the concept of commutative justice to explain as much of Roman and canon law as they could.

In discussing tort, they said, like the canonists, that a person owes compensation if he deprived another of whatever belonged to him.[27] Thomas Aquinas had described what belongs to a person and the types of harm that he could consequently suffer. The harm might be to a "thing" that belongs to him. It might be to his "person," and then either to his person itself or to his dignity. It might be to his relationship with another person, such as his wife or his slave.[28] The late scholastics concluded that the Roman distinctions between different actions were mere matters of Roman positive law. In principle, and as a matter of commutative justice, a person should recover whenever he has been deprived of what belongs to him. Sometimes, the late scholastics merely stated this principle[29] and sometimes they

---

[19] Lessius (n. 15), lib. 2, cap. 14, dub. 1, no. 5.
[20] Molina (n. 16), disp. 718, no. 2; disp. 721, no. 6; Lessius (n. 15), lib. 2, cap. 14, dub. 1, no. 4.
[21] Molina (n. 16), disp. 718, no. 2; Lessius (n. 15), lib. 2, cap. 14, dub. 1, no. 3.
[22] D. 50.17.206.
[23] Robert Feenstra, "Grotius' Doctrine of Unjust Enrichment as a Source of Obligation: its Origin and its Influence on Roman-Dutch Law," in vol. 1 of *Unjust Enrichment: The Comparative Legal History of the Law of Restitution*, ed. E. J. H. Schrage (Berlin, 1995), 197.
[24] Grotius (n. 17), II.x.9; Pufendorf (n. 17), IV.xiii.9.   [25] See Chapter I, p. 19.
[26] Aristotle, *Nicomachean Ethics* V.ii 1130$^b$–1131$^a$; V.i 1131$^b$–1132$^b$.
[27] See Chapter II, p. 58.   [28] Aquinas (n. 10), II-II, Q. 61, a. 3.
[29] For example, Soto (n. 6), lib. 4, q. 6, a. 5; Molina (n. 16), disps. 315, 724; Lessius (n. 15), lib. 2, cap. 12, dubs. 16, 18; cap. 20, dubs. 10–11.

classified types of harm in much the same way as Aquinas.³⁰ Similarly, Grotius explained, "Damage is when a man has less than what is his....":

Things which a man may regard as his by nature are his life... body, limbs, fame, honor, and his own acts. In the previous part of our treatise we have shown how each man by property right and by agreements possesses his own not only with respect to property but also with respect to the acts of others....³¹

As we have seen, under the *lex Aquilia*, a person could recover if he had been deprived of his property. But suppose he had been prevented from obtaining something that might have been his: was he entitled to compensation then? Aquinas had said that he was, as a matter of commutative justice, but that the amount of compensation would not be the same:

[A] man is bound to make compensation (*restitutio*) for whatever of another's he harmed. But one is harmed in two ways. One way is that he is harmed because that which he actually has is taken, and compensation must always be made for such a harm by payment of an equivalent. For example, when one person harms another by destroying his house, he is bound to pay the amount that the house is worth. The other way is that someone harms another by preventing him from acquiring what he was on the way (*in via*) to having. And compensation of an equal amount need not be made for such harm, for it is less to have such a thing virtually than to have it actually. One who is on the way to acquiring a thing has it only virtually or potentially. Consequently, if he is paid as though he had the thing actually, he would not receive the value of what was taken as compensation but more, which is not required in making compensation, as noted in article 3. He is bound, however, to make compensation according to the condition of persons and affairs.³²

In article 3, cited here, Aquinas had put the case of someone who unjustly prevents another from obtaining a benefice. He said that compensation must be paid, but not for its entire value, "because the man had not yet obtained the benefice and might have been prevented from doing so in many ways."³³ Similarly, if one person destroys seeds that belong to another and which have not yet grown, he need not make compensation for the value that the crop would have had at harvest.³⁴

Disagreeing with Aquinas, the sixteenth-century theologian Cajetan had tried to distinguish the case of the seeds from that of the benefice. The person claiming compensation for the seeds had a right to them and it was because of this right that he hoped to profit at harvest time. The claimant of the benefice never had the right to it and Cajetan concluded that he was not entitled to compensation:

[N]o reason can be seen why I am bound to make compensation in whole or in part for impeding someone from seeking a benefit to which he never had any right. It follows from

---

[30] Lessius (n. 15), lib. 2, caps. 3, 9–12.
[31] Grotius (n. 17), II.xvii.1–2. For similar conclusions by other natural lawyers, *see* Pufendorf (n. 17), III.i.2, III.i.3; III.i.6; Jean Barbeyrac, *Le Droit de la nature et des gens... par le baron de Pufendorf*, 5th ed. (Amsterdam, 1734), n. 1 to III.i.2, n. 1 to III.i.3, n. 4 to III.i.6. See generally Reinhard Zimmermann, *The Law of Obligations: Roman Foundations of the Civilian Tradition* (Cape Town, 1990), 1032–34.
[32] Aquinas (n. 10), II-II, Q. 62, a. 4.     [33] Aquinas (n. 10), II-II, Q. 62, a. 3 ad 4.
[34] Aquinas (n. 10), II-II, Q. 62, a. 4 ad 1 & 2.

this – that he never had any right in anything – that nothing was his, and consequently it follows that no compensation is due him. And if it be said that he has a right hoped for (*ius in spe*), that is not a valid consideration because a right in hope is not a right, just as wealth hoped for is not wealth. Moreover, compensation for a thing hoped for is given when a person is deprived of a right on which that hope is founded, as is shown when seeds are destroyed or the tools of a craft are taken away through the use of which a person's family is supported, and in similar cases.[35]

The late scholastics rejected Cajetan's position. Whether or not a person presently was entitled to the benefice, if he was unjustly deprived of it, he was owed compensation. To be unjustly deprived of it, some right that he presently has must have been violated. But Cajetan assumed that a person who does not yet have the right to the benefit that he is seeking had no rights at all. Lessius answered that a person could have a right to something that he had not yet acquired, for example to a gift that had not yet been made to him. Such a right was not "absolute," but "conditional." The recipient's right to a gift, for example, was "conditional" on the decision of the potential donor to give it to him.[36] Molina distinguished two meanings of the phrase "having a right":

[A] person is said to have a right (*ius*) to something in two different ways. First, because it is in some way his or owed to him. When right is used in this sense, we distinguish right in a thing (*ius in re*) and right to a thing (*ius ad rem*). In another sense, a person is said to have a right to something, not because it is owed to him, but because he has the capacity (*facultas*) for it, so that one who contravenes that right does him an injury. In this sense, everyone can be said to have the right to use his own things, for example, to eat his own food, so that injury and injustice is done to him if he is impeded. Indeed, we say that the poor have the right to beg for alms, that one who works for pay has the right to hire out his services, and that everyone has the right to hunt and fish in places where it is not prohibited. Consequently, if anyone impedes them in these matters, he does an injury and injustice and has the duty to make compensation. . . .[37]

Thus a person could have the right to seek what he had not yet acquired and the violation of this right entitled him to compensation.

Aquinas said that if someone harmed another person "by preventing him from acquiring what he was on the way to having," he should receive less.[38] The late scholastics considered whether he should receive less and, if so, what he ought to receive.

According to Soto, he should not receive less. If the landowner had wanted to sell his crop in the ear, he would have done so. If he did not, it was so that he could reap the harvest to come and his loss was therefore the value of the harvest. As Soto put it:

---

[35] Cajetan, *Commentaria to Thomas Aquinas, Summa theologica* (Padua, 1698), to II-II, Q. 62, a. 2 ad 4.
[36] Lessius (n. 15), lib. 2, cap. 12, dub. 18.   [37] Molina (n. 16), III, disp. 726.
[38] Aquinas (n. 10), II-II, Q. 62, a. 4.

If the person who has the object in hope (*res in spe*) does not want to sell it only in hope but to await all risks until he has it, therefore, he who destroys another's thing against his will is not only bound to restore the amount that it is worth in hope but, it appears, the amount it will be worth.[39]

Inconsistently, however, Soto said that a person who negligently destroys another's crop really should not have to pay the full value of the grain at harvest time. He claimed that only a person who does harm intentionally should have to pay full compensation. A negligent person should pay only the amount that Aquinas had described.[40]

Lessius and Molina disagreed with Soto. They thought that the amount of compensation to be paid should be the same whether harm is done negligently or intentionally. Lessius explained that if the owner did not want to sell his crop in the ear, admittedly, the wrong done to him was greater than if he did. He was forced against his will to give up his crop and to receive its value in money before he wished to sell it. But however great the wrong a person suffers, commutative justice entitles him to recover only an amount equivalent to the harm actually done.[41] That harm, according to Lessius, is the value of the crop at the time it was destroyed, "taking in account the circumstances prevailing then."[42] Molina argued that if the owner were paid the value of the crop at harvest time, he would be overcompensated. The further off the time of harvest, the less the crop is worth, since the perils to the crop and the labor necessary to produce it are greater.[43] For Molina, this conclusion followed from general principles that determine the value of a thing at any given time. For example, one who destroys a thing need not pay both for the thing and for the fruits that it was expected to produce, "because the value of a thing at the time at which is destroyed is evaluated with regard to the fruits which can be received from it and with regard to the use and benefit that can be received from it in the future."[44] The value of a crop thus reflects its value at maturity, as well as the risk and labor of producing it. Molina consequently came close to the concept that modern economists call the "expected value" of an asset, although he did not express it mathematically, as they do.[45]

If a person were physically harmed, the medieval jurists had concluded that he could recover by generalizing two Roman texts.[46] If his dignity was harmed, he could recover in an an action for *iniuria*. The late scholastics described both Roman actions as instances in which, as Aquinas had said, one who harmed another's person, property, or dignity owed him compensation as a matter of commutative justice.

Consequently, they regarded the limits that Roman law imposed for recovery for physical harm to a person under the *lex Aquilia* as mere matters of Roman positive

---

[39] Soto (n. 6), lib. 4, q. 6, a. 5.   [40] Soto (n. 6), lib. 4, q. 6, a. 5.
[41] Lessius (n. 15), lib. 2, cap. 12, dub. 19, no. 137.
[42] Lessius (n. 15), lib. 2, cap. 12, dub. 19, no. 137.
[43] Molina (n. 16), III, disp. 726, no. 4.   [44] Molina (n. 16), III, disp. 726, no. 3.
[45] So did Soto and Lessius in discussing wagers and insurance: James Franklin, *The Science of Conjecture Evidence and Probability before Pascal* (Baltimore, MD, 2001), 286–88.
[46] *See* Zimmermann (n. 31), 1024–25.

law. As we have seen, one Roman text denied recovery for physical harm suffered by the plaintiff on the ground that no price could be put on a free man.[47] Medieval jurists limited this text by allowing the victim an *actio utilis* under the *lex Aquilia*.[48] The late scholastics said that, in principle or, as they put it, as a matter of natural law, compensation should be made as far as possible. According to Soto, the duty to make restitution extends to "everything whatsoever of which a person can be unjustly deprived."[49] In cases of personal injury, for example, in which it was impossible to restore the limb that a person had lost, compensation was still due. As Aquinas had said, "when that which has been taken away cannot be restored in equivalent compensation should be made as far as possible."[50]

For the late scholastics, the action for *iniuria* was another instance of the principle that commutative justice required a person who harmed another to make compensation. In this case, the harm was to a person's dignity—either to his honor or to his reputation. The victim was entitled to compensation just as if his property had been taken. Indeed, his claim to compensation is stronger because, Aquinas said, reputation is worth more than wealth.[51] The late scholastics agreed. They also agreed with the canonists that the remedy that Roman law gave for *iniuria* was inadequate. Roman law required payment of damages. As we have seen, the canonists had concluded that, to make restitution, a party who had injured another's honor or reputation must publicly admit that he had been in error, or he must at least apologize.[52] According to Aquinas, he had to restore the loss of honor or reputation by taking such an action as a matter of commutative justice.[53] Again, the late scholastics agreed.[54]

The late scholastics explained why honor and reputation should be protected in Aristotelian and Thomistic terms. They defined honor as deference, acknowledgment, testimony, or recognition of the excellence of another person.[55] It is due "most properly" to virtue.[56] Nevertheless, it is due to any sort of excellence, to "every perfection of rational nature."[57] A Christian, it might seem, should bear insults patiently, and so he should, said Aquinas, unless vindicating his honor was good either for the perpetrator or for himself.[58] We should vindicate our honor, according to Molina,[59] if by doing so we can do good to others; according to Lessius, if by doing so we can better perform our office.[60] Reputation is the esteem of others for one's excellent qualities.[61] It "most properly" concerns esteem for another person's "virtue and wisdom," since they are the qualities most proper to a human being, but in a secondary sense, reputation concerns the opinion that

---

[47] G. 9.3.7; D. 9.3.1.5.  [48] *See* Chapter II, p. 34.
[49] Soto (n. 6), lib. 4, Q. 6, a. 3.  [50] Aquinas (n. 10), II-II Q. 62, a. 2 obj. 1.
[51] Aquinas (n. 10), II-II, Q. 73, a. 3.  [52] *See* Chapter II, p. 58.
[53] Aquinas (n. 10), II-II, Q. 62, ad. 2, 3.
[54] Molina (n. 16), IV, disp. 44; Lessius (n. 15), lib. 2, cap. 11, dub. 20.
[55] Soto (n. 6), lib. 5, Q. 9, a. 1 (*reverentia*); Lessius (n. 15), lib. 2, cap. 11, dub. 1, no. 2 (*testificatio*); Molina (n. 16), IV disp. 1, no. 1 (*testimonio ac recognitio*).
[56] Soto (n. 6), lib. 5, Q. 9, a. 1.  [57] Lessius (n. 15), lib. 2, cap. 11, dub. 1, no. 2.
[58] Aquinas (n. 10), II-II, Q. 72, a. 3.  [59] Molina (n. 16), IV, disp. 20, no. 1.
[60] Lessius (n. 15), lib. 2, cap. 11, dub. 14, nos. 124, 126.
[61] Lessius (n. 15), lib. 2, cap. 11, dub. 1, no. 1.

people hold of one's "eloquence, nobility, strength, beauty, power, and the like."[62] Like honor, reputation is worth having because it pertains to human perfection and enables one to do good.

These considerations allowed the late scholastics to explain a conclusion about the action for *iniuria* that, as we have seen, had been reached by the medieval civilians.[63] Except for certain cases in which disclosure was in the public interest, it was not a defense that the plaintiff did not deserve honor or a good reputation, and that the defendant had only told the truth about him or treated him as he deserved. Having an undeserved reputation, like having an undeserved fortune, is still of value because of the good that it enables a person to do. Aquinas had said that it would be a violation of commutative justice to deprive a person of an undeserved reputation.[64] Lessius compared such a person to one in possession of goods that he did not own.[65] Under Roman law, as noted earlier,[66] he was entitled to redress against someone who deprived him of possession. Despite some doubts, Lessius thought that it would be wrong to deprive someone even of a reputation that he had preserved by fraud and lies. Although such a person did not have the right to have his lies believed, he did have the right to keep his wrongdoing a secret.[67]

There were difficulties, however, in using the Aristotelian principle of commutative justice to explain compensation for harm done to one person by another. Two of the most formidable had been resolved to the satisfaction of the late scholastics by Aquinas. Aristotle had said that, when commutative justice is violated, "the judge tries to equalize things by means of the penalty," taking away the "gain" of one party and restoring the "loss" of the other.[68] If one person has harmed another's property, person, or honor without any profit to himself, it would seem that he has not gained. Aristotle had admitted that it seems odd to speak of a "gain" when one person has wounded another. Nevertheless, he maintained that, "when the suffering has been estimated, the one is called loss and the other gain."[69] The reason, according to Aquinas, is that a "person striking or killing has more of what is evaluated as good, insofar, that is, as he fulfills his will, and so is seen to receive a sort of gain."[70] "To gain," in this sense, is to fulfill one's will. A person who has voluntarily harmed another in pursuit of his own ends has "gained" and therefore must pay compensation, whether or not his ends were achieved, and whether or not he had made a financial gain by pursuing them.

A second difficulty is that Aristotle had been speaking only of intentionally inflicted harm, as David Daube has shown and as Aquinas himself noted.[71] For

---

[62] Lessius (n. 15), lib. 2, cap. 11, dub. 1, no. 1.   [63] *See* Chapter II, pp. 39–40.
[64] Aquinas (n. 10), II-II, Q. 62, a. 2 ad 2; Q. 73, a. 1 ad 3.
[65] Lessius (n. 15), lib. 2, cap. 11, dub. 10, no. 67.   [66] *See* Chapter I, pp. 10–11.
[67] Lessius (n. 15), lib. 2, cap. 11, dub. 10, nos. 65–67.
[68] Aristotle (n. 26), V.iv 1132$^a$.   [69] Aristotle (n. 26), V.iv 1132$^a$.
[70] Thomas Aquinas, *In decem libros Ethicorum Aristoteles exposition*, ed. A. Pirotta (Turin, 1934), lib. V, lectio vi, no. 952. He was following his teacher, Albert the Great, who had said that "the one who acts has more of what he wants, and the one who suffers has less ... and this is appropriately designated by the name gain and loss": Albertus Magnus, *Ethicorum libri decem*, lib. V, tract. ii, cap. 6, no. 25, in vol. 7 of *Opera Omnia*, ed. A. Bourgnet (Paris, 1891).
[71] David Daube, *Roman Law: Linguistic, Social and Philosophical Aspects* (Edinburgh, 1969), 131–56; Aquinas (n. 70), lib. V, lectio. xiii, no. 1043.

Aristotle and Aquinas, one could be responsible only for an action one performed voluntarily, since a human being acts through reason and will. *Qua* human being, he is not the cause of chance events that do not proceed from his reason and will. As we have seen, under the *lex Aquilia* and in canon law, a person also owed compensation for harm that he caused by negligence. The question thus arose whether a person who negligently harmed another had acted voluntarily. Aquinas answered that he had.[72] He failed to exercise prudence.[73] Prudence, like all virtues, is acquired by voluntary action: by taking the consequences of one's actions into account, and by doing so over and over until it becomes habitual. Aquinas and the late scholastics concluded that a person owed compensation for harm done negligently, as well as intentionally.

According to writers in the Aristotelian tradition, a prudent person weighs the magnitude of the good result that he seeks against that of the evil one that he avoids. As Aquinas said, "any prudent person will accept a small evil in order not to obstruct a great good."[74] A prudent person must concern himself with probabilities, with "what happens in the greater number of cases."[75] Cajetan gave an example of how such factors might be taken into account in his commentary on Aquinas' *Summa theologiae*. A canon law text in Gratian's *Decretum* said that parents are negligent if they fall asleep with children in their bed, and the children die because they are suffocated or crushed.[76] According to Cajetan, whether a nurse would be responsible in such a case depended on the circumstances:

> [If] the bed is large and there is nothing else near it, the nurse is always accustomed to find herself in the same place and position in which she put herself to begin sleeping, and the implacability of the infant required it, she seems to be excused, because it is not reasonable when these things concur to fear the risk.[77]

Most of the late scholastics believed that, as a matter of principle, a person owed compensation only for harm done intentionally or negligently. As noted earlier,[78] Roman law sometimes imposed liability on a person who was not at fault. For example, the defendant was liable for harm done by animals, or when objects were thrown out of windows or hung over the street, or when harm was suffered by a guest at an inn. These were instances of what in modern law is called strict liability. Nearly all of the late scholastics concluded that, although the defendant was liable in such cases according to Roman positive law, he was not required to make

---

[72] Aquinas (n. 10), II-I, Q. 68, a. 8.
[73] More technically, negligence (*negligentia*) was a lack of solicitude (*sollicitudo*) or diligence (*diligentia*). Solicitude or diligence was the virtue that enables the alert, adroit performance of the "chief act" of prudence, *praecipere*, which could be translated as "to command" or "to execute." Prudence required three "acts": to take counsel or to consider what should be done (*consiliari*); to judge or decide what should be done (*iudicare*); and to execute this decision (*praecipere*). See Aquinas (n. 10), II-II, Q. 47, aa. 8–9; Q. 54, aa. 1–2; Q. 64, a. 8.
[74] Thomas Aquinas, *De Veritate*, Q. 5, a. 4 ad 4, in vol. 9 of *Opera omnia. Secundem impressionem Petri Fiaccadori Parmae 1852–1873, photolithographice reimpressa* (New York, 1948–50), 5.
[75] Aquinas (n. 10), II-II, Q. 49, a. 1; a. 8 ad 3.
[76] C. 2 q. 5 c. 2.   [77] Cajetan (n. 35), *post* Q. 64, a. 8.
[78] *See* Chapter I, p. 19.

compensation as a matter of commutative justice and consequently not by natural law. Molina was an exception. He suggested that there were some activities so dangerous that one should not undertake them unless one was willing to pay for any harm that they caused, even if one was not negligent.[79] It was a fruitful idea, but it was not taken up by others.

Most of the late scholastics rejected the conclusion of the canon lawyers that a person must make compensation not only for harm caused intentionally or through negligence, but also for the unforeseen consequences of wrongful acts. They did so even though Aquinas had accepted this conclusion.[80] In the sixteenth century, Cajetan had already observed that there were cases in which the doctrine did not give the right result. A person who was forbidden for religious reasons to ride a horse[81] or to hunt[82] should not be responsible if he killed someone when his horse bolted or his arrow missed its mark. Soto gave another example: a priest should not be liable if he killed a coworker while repairing a church on a religious holiday when he was forbidden to work.[83] Molina and Lessius denied that a person should ever be liable for chance consequences, even if they were the consequences of an unlawful act. As Lessius put it, they "were willed neither themselves nor as to their cause."[84] They were simply a matter of "chance."[85]

The late scholastics thus gave tort law a structure that it previously lacked. So much of it has passed into modern law that the structure of the civil law of tort more closely resembles the natural law as described by the late scholastics than it does the Roman law. The late scholastics had described the distinctions among Roman actions as matters of Roman positive law, along with the limits of the *lex Aquilia* on the types of harm for which one could recover. Except in Molina's opinion, liability for harm caused without fault was a matter of Roman positive law as well. In principle, or, as the late scholastics would say, as a matter of natural law, compensation was due for "everything whatsoever of which a person can be unjustly deprived," provided that the loss was caused intentionally or negligently. Grotius was merely summarizing their conclusions when he made a statement that was to affect all modern codes: "From ... fault, if damage is caused, an obligation arises, namely, that the damage should be made good. ... Damage ... is when a man has less than what is his. ..."[86]

The late scholastics restructured the law of contract in a similar way. According to Aristotle and Aquinas, in voluntary transactions, commutative justice required that the parties exchange resources that are equivalent in value.[87] Commutative

---

[79] Molina (n. 16), disp. 698, no. 3.   [80] Aquinas (n. 10), II-II, Q. 64, a. 8.
[81] Cajetan (n. 35), to II-II, Q. 64, a. 8; Soto (n. 6), V.i.9.
[82] Cajetan (n. 35), to II-II, Q. 64, a. 8.
[83] Soto (n. 6), V.i.9.   [84] Lessius (n. 15), lib. 2, cap. 8, dub. 18, no. 103.
[85] Lessius (n. 15), lib. 2, cap. 8, dub. 18, no. 102. For a discussion of the history of the rule and its modern significance, *see* James Gordley, "Responsibility in Crime, Tort, and Contract for the Foreseeable Consequences of an Intentional Wrong: A Once and Future Rule?" in *The Law of Obligations Essays in Celebration of John Fleming*, eds. Peter Cane and Jane Stapleton (Oxford, 1998), 175.
[86] Grotius (n. 17), II.xvii.1–2. For similar conclusions by other natural lawyers, *see* Pufendorf (n. 17), III.i.2, III.i.3; III.i.6; Barbeyrac (n. 31), n. 1 to III.i.2, n. 1 to III.i.3, n. 4 to III.i.6. *See* generally Zimmermann (n. 31), 1032–34.
[87] Aristotle (n. 26), V.iv 1131ª.

justice required, then, that an exchange be voluntary and that it take place at just price.

In explaining what it meant for an exchange to be voluntary, the late scholastics were guided by the Roman jurists and the medieval civilians, who had listed different mistakes that would vitiate consent, and by the canon lawyers, who had said that the consent of one who made a promise extends only to the circumstances that he could have contemplated. The late scholastics explained their conclusions by means of the principles of Aristotle and Aquinas.

As we saw previously,[88] the Roman jurists explained when a mistake vitiated consent by putting particular cases: copper sold as gold; lead sold as silver; vinegar sold as wine. Ulpian had said that, in such cases, the error that would vitiate consent was one as to the substance (*substantia*) or essence (*ousia*) of what one was buying. Although "substance" and "essence" were terms drawn from Greek philosophy, they did not have a definite meaning for Ulpian, philosophical or otherwise. For him, they were labels attached to the cases in which a mistake would void consent. In Aristotelian philosophy, however, the world is composed of individual things termed substances, and the substantial form or essence of each thing makes it what it is. Gold is gold because it has the substantial form of gold. It can change its "accidental" qualities, such as its temperature, and still remain gold. A person who wanted to buy a thing, but was wrong about its substance or essence, did not wish to buy that thing, but something else. Lessius explained that if, for example, a party sold a gem as glass, "the substance of consent is lacking because he did not consent to this thing but to another which he believed to underlie its accidents."[89]

The canon lawyers had said that, in every promise, there was an implied condition "that things remain as they are."[90] Aquinas used Aristotle's theory of equity to explain why. According to Aristotle, whenever a law is made, particular circumstances may arise in which the lawmaker would not want it to be applied. As a matter of "equity," the law should not be applied in those circumstances. Aquinas concluded that, similarly, promises are a kind of law that one gives to oneself, and they are not binding in circumstances in which the promisor would not have intended to be bound.[91] This explanation was adopted by the late scholastics.[92] Once again, the conclusion that the promisor was not bound when the circumstances had changed sufficiently was preserved by Grotius and Pufendorf, and passed into modern law.[93]

The principle of commutative justice applied to one type of contract: a contract of exchange. One might, instead, agree to do someone a favor or to make him a gift. Accordingly, following Aquinas, the late scholastics distinguished two types of voluntary arrangement: exchange, which was an act of commutative justice, and

---

[88] *See* Chapter I, pp. 11–12.
[89] Lessius (n. 15), lib. 2, cap. 17, dub. 5. *See* Molina (n. 16), disps. 340, 342; Gordley (n. 3), 85–87.
[90] *See* Chapter II, pp. 61–62.   [91] Aquinas (n. 10), II-II, q. 88, a. 10; q. 89, a. 9.
[92] Lessius (n. 15), lib. 2, cap. 17, dub. 10; cap. 18, dub. 10. *See* Decock (n. 1), 202–08.
[93] Pufendorf (n. 17), III.vi.6.

gratuitous transactions, which were based on another Aristotelian virtue, "liberality." They used this distinction to restructure the Roman law of particular contracts.

Aristotle had described giving one's resources to another as the act of "liberality." Liberality did not simply mean giving resources away. According to Aristotle, it meant giving "to the right people, the right amounts, and at the right time, with all the other qualifications that accompany right giving."[94] Aquinas put these ideas together: when one person transfers a thing to another, either it is an act of commutative justice that requires an equivalent, or it is an act of liberality.[95]

There were, then, two kinds of voluntary arrangements: those based on commutative justice, in which each party obtained an equivalent for what he gave, and those based on liberality, in which one party chose to enrich the other at his own expense. In drawing this distinction, the late scholastics were helped by the fact that Bartolus and Baldus, as we have seen,[96] had identified two kinds of *causa*, or good reasons, why a contract should be binding: the receipt of something in return, and liberality. Both jurists were familiar with Aristotle and Aquinas and, as I have shown elsewhere, drew on their ideas in arriving at this interpretation of the Roman texts.[97] Their goal, however, was to interpret those texts. They were willing to draw on Aristotle and Aquinas insofar as it helped them to do so. The goal of the late scholastics, in contrast, was to explain the law in philosophical terms.

They reclassified the particular contracts of Roman law as either acts of liberality or acts of commutative justice. Aquinas had said:

If a man transfers [his thing to another person] simply, so that the other incurs no debt, it is an act, not of justice, but of liberality. A voluntary transfer belongs to justice insofar as it includes the notion of a debt. This may occur in many ways. First, one may simply transfer his thing to another in exchange for another thing, as happens in sale. Second, one may transfer this thing to another so that the other may have the use of it with the obligation of returning it to its owner. If one grants the use of it gratuitously, the transaction is called usufruct (*usufructus*) in things that bear fruit, and simply loan for consumption (*mutuum*) in things that do not bear fruit such as money, pottery, and so forth. If, however, not even the use is granted gratis, the transaction is called lease. Third, one may transfer his thing to receive it back again, not so that it can be used but so that it can be kept safe, as in a deposit, or because of an obligation, as when one assumes an obligation by pledging his thing, or stands surety for another. In all these actions...the mean is taken in the same way, as equality in repayment. Thus all of them belong to one species of justice: commutative justice.[98]

For the most part, the late scholastics took over Aquinas' classification, changing it to conform more closely to Roman law. For example, while the loan of money would have been *mutuum* or loan for consumption, the loan of pottery would have been a *commodatum* or loan for use if the same pottery were to be returned. Usufruct was not a loan for use, but a transfer of an interest in land resembling the common law life estate. Otherwise, their changes were minor. Molina and

---

[94] Aristotle (n. 26), IV.i, 1119$^b$–1120$^a$.  [95] Aquinas (n. 10), II-II, Q. 61, a. 3.
[96] *See* Chapter II, pp. 48–49.   [97] Gordley (n. 3), 77–79.
[98] Aquinas (n. 10), II-II, Q. 61, a. 3.

Lessius found a place for the feudal fief and a Roman contract that resembled it, *emphyteusis*: neither ownership nor use was transferred, but something in between, which they and the medieval jurists had called *dominium utile*.[99] Lessius classified deposit as a lease of one's services in caring for an object.[100] Soto subclassified contracts that transferred the use of a thing for recompense. It is a lease if the thing could be used without consuming it, and a usurious contract if it could not.[101] Later, Grotius developed a more elaborate classification in which, after distinguishing contracts of liberality from those in which the parties conferred benefits on each other, he subdivided the latter into contracts like partnership, in which equality meant that each party received benefits in proportion to his contribution, and contracts like sale and lease, in which equality meant that each party gave something of equivalent value to what he received.[102]

The late scholastics then dismissed the Roman distinctions between nominate and innominate contracts, and contracts *consensu* and *re*, as mere matters of Roman positive law. Molina concluded that "everything, indeed, concerning... nominate and innominate contracts that was invented and introduced by the pagans more subtly than usefully should be abolished."[103]

The question then arose: were all voluntary commitments binding in principle? Cajetan, in his commentary on Aquinas, had argued that a person who had been promised a gift could not demand as a matter of commutative justice that the promise be kept. Certainly, the promisor acted wrongly by breaking his promise and, in that sense, the promise was binding. But making a gift is a matter of liberality, not of commutative justice. The refusal to perform leaves the disappointed party no worse off than if the promise had never been made.[104] Cajetan concluded that the promisee could claim that the promisor acted unjustly towards him only if he had become worse off by changing his position in reliance on the promise.[105]

The leading late scholastics disagreed with Cajetan. Molina pointed out that if the donor had given something away and delivered it to the donee, it would belong to the donee. Under the Roman law, the donor could not then take it back unless the donee were guilty of gross ingratitude.[106] But there is nothing magical about the moment of delivery. In principle, Molina argued, the donor ought to be able to transfer the right to a thing, or the right to claim it, in advance of delivery. If he did so, then depriving him of that right by failing to perform violates commutative justice.[107]

---

[99] Molina (n. 16), disp. 259; Lessius (n. 15), lib. 2, cap. 17, dub. 3.
[100] Lessius (n. 15), lib. 2, cap. 17, dub. 3.
[101] Soto (n. 6), lib. 3, q. 5, a. 3.   [102] Grotius (n. 17), II.xii.1–7.
[103] Molina (n. 16), disp. 258. See Thomas Duve, "Kanonisches Recht und die Ausbildung allgemeiner Vertragslehren in der Spanishen Spätscholastik," in *Der Einfluss der Kanonistik auf die Europäische Rechtskultur Bd. 1: Zivil- und Zivilprozessrecht*, eds. Orazio Condorelli, Franck Roumy, and Mathias Schmoeckel (Cologne, 2009), 389 at 404–05.
[104] Cajetan (n. 35), to II-II, Q. 88, a. 1; Q. 113, a. 1.
[105] Cajetan (n. 35), to II-II, Q. 88, a. 1; Q. 113, a. 1.
[106] The rule is described by Lessius (n. 15), lib. 2, cap. 18, dub. 8, no. 52, and Molina (n. 16), disps. 272, 281.
[107] Molina (n. 16), disp. 262.

Lessius agreed that the question was one of intent, but he claimed that "to promise is not merely to affirm that one will give or do something but beyond that to obligate oneself to another, and consequently to grant that person the right to require it."[108] By this definition, all promises conferred a right on the promisee and were therefore actionable as a matter of commutative justice. Had Cajetan's position prevailed, something like the American doctrine of promissory reliance might have passed into civil law. But Grotius agreed with Molina, and later writers followed Grotius.[109]

Because contracts of exchange were acts of commutative justice, the parties had to exchange at a just price—a price that enriched neither party at the other's expense. The late scholastics did not conceive of this requirement as something imposed from the outside, as it were, as a constraint on the will of the parties. If one of the parties had wanted to enrich the other at his own expense, he would have made a gift. The very nature of a contract of exchange is that the parties exchange equivalents.

As we have seen,[110] according to the medieval civilians, a party was entitled to relief for an unjust price that exceeded the just price by one half. For Aquinas and the late scholastics, the principle of commutative justice explained why relief was given at all. According to Aquinas, relief was given only for large deviations from the just price, because human law could not command all acts of virtue.[111]

The late scholastics accepted the conclusion of the medieval civilians[112] that, absent public regulation, the just price was the market price under competitive conditions at the time and place of the transaction.[113] It has puzzled modern scholars that these writers expected exchange at such a price to preserve equality.

It is not surprising that the medieval civilians regarded that price as just. They had no theory about why a price would be fair. Consequently, they had almost no choice but to identify the fair price with the market price. Any other conclusion would have called into question thousands of seemingly normal market transactions.

The late scholastics had more of a theory. Like modern economists, they thought that the market price had to fluctuate to reflect factors that they called need, scarcity, and cost. "Need" meant the value that people place on goods. It might be quite different than their intrinsic worth or usefulness. "Scarcity" meant the quantity available. "Cost" meant the labor, expenses, and risk entailed in producing the goods.[114] These factors are like those that determine supply and demand in

---

[108] Lessius (n. 15), lib. 2, cap. 18, dub. 8, no. 52.
[109] Grotius (n. 17), II.xi.1.3–4; Pufendorf (n. 17), III.v.5–7; Jean Barbeyrac, *Le Droit de la guerre et de la paix de Hugues Grotius* (Amsterdam, 1729), n. 2 to II.xi.1, n. 1 to II.xi.3; Barbeyrac (n. 31), n. 10 to III.v.9.
[110] See Chapter II, pp. 35–36.    [111] Aquinas (n. 10), II-II, Q. 77, a.1 ad. 1.
[112] See Chapter II, pp. 35–36.
[113] John Noonan, *The Scholastic Analysis of Usury* (Cambridge, MA, 1957), 82–88; Raymond de Roover, "The Concept of the Just Price and Economic Policy," *Journal of Economic History* 18 (1958): 418; Ambrosetti, "Diritto privato ed economia nella seconda scolastica," in *La seconda scolastica nella formazione del diritto privato modern*, ed. Paolo Grossi (Milano, 1973), 28.
[114] Gordley (n. 3), 94–102; Soto (n. 6), lib. 6, q. 2, a. 3; Molina (n. 16), disp. 348. All of these factors had been mentioned, albeit cryptically, by Thomas Aquinas (n. 70), lib. 5, lec. 9; Aquinas (n. 10), II-II, Q. 77, a. 3 ad. 4. They were discussed by medieval commentators on Aristotle: Odd Langholm, *Price and Value in the Aristotelian Tradition* (Bergen, 1979), 61–143.

modern economic theory. Unlike modern economists, however, these writers did not think of supply and demand as separate schedules that clear at a unique equilibrium price.[115] Their explanation of how the market responds to need, scarcity, and cost was a simpler one. Buyers and sellers make a judgment as to the price that adequately reflects these factors. The market price is set by their common judgment (*communis aestimatio*). The common judgment could be wrong. If the public authorities thought it was wrong, they might fix a different price at which everyone must trade. But unless they did so, the just price was the market price, which reflected the judgment of buyers and sellers generally.[116] Monopoly prices were unfair because they reflected not the common judgment, but the efforts of a small group to get rich.[117]

The late scholastics discussed why prices change, not why a fluctuating market price preserves equality. But the fact that they thought this explanation sufficient suggests how they conceived of equality. Prices had to change to reflect need, scarcity, and cost. When and if these fluctuations need not be tolerated, public authority can fix a price. If it does not do so, then the market price preserves equality to the extent feasible. There is no need to tolerate the further inequalities that arise when, as Lessius put it, one party takes advantage of the other's "ignorance" or "necessity" to sell to him for more than the market price or to buy for less.[118]

Moreover, as Soto observed, a party who gains if prices rise might well have lost. A merchant must bear his losses if "bad fortune buffets him, for example, because an unexpected abundance of goods mounts up," and he may sell for more if "fortune smiles on him and later there is an unexpected scarcity of goods": "For as the business of buying and selling is subject to fortuitous events of many kinds, merchants ought to bear risks at their own expense, and, on the other hand, they may wait for good fortune."[119] Similarly, Lessius noted that "this is the condition of merchants, that as they may gain if they receive goods at small expense, so they lose if the expense was disproportionate or extraordinary."[120]

For the late scholastics, the requirement of equality in exchange also explained terms that the law read into a contract when the parties had made no provision themselves. In Roman law, as interpreted by the medieval jurists, a seller was bound to warrant his goods against undisclosed defects. According to Aquinas, equality would be violated if he did not.[121] The late scholastics agreed.[122] Consequently, the parties could exclude such a term only if equality was preserved in some other way. According to Molina, the law would enforce a contract in which the seller refused to provide a warranty, provided that he reduced the price to preserve equality.[123]

---

[115] Langholm (n. 114), 116.
[116] Soto (n. 6), lib. 6, q. 2, a. 3; Molina (n. 16), disp. 348; Lessius (n. 15), lib. 2, cap. 21, dub. 2.
[117] Soto (n. 6), lib. 6, q. 2, a. 3; Lessius (n. 15), lib. 2, cap. 21, dub. 21.
[118] Lessius (n. 15), lib. 2, cap. 21, dub. 4.
[119] Soto (n. 6), lib. 6, q. 2, a. 3.   [120] Lessius (n. 15), lib. 2, cap. 21, dub. 4.
[121] *See* Aquinas (n. 10), II-II, Q. 77, aa. 2–3.
[122] Soto (n. 6), lib. 2, cap. 21, dub. 11; lib. 6, q. 3, a. 2; Molina (n. 16), disp. 353; Lessius (n. 15), lib. 2, cap. 21, dub. 11.
[123] Molina (n. 16), disp. 353.

## The late scholastics and Roman law

It is hard to underrate the achievement of the late scholastics. They synthesized two great intellectual traditions of the ancient world: Roman law, as interpreted by the medieval civilians, and Aristotelian philosophy, as understood by Thomas Aquinas. They incorporated elements of the Christian tradition taken from canon law. They gave private law a doctrinal structure that it previously lacked and explained it by means of higher principles. Modern civil law has kept much of that structure, even though the philosophical principles of the late scholastics have fallen out of favor.

Nevertheless, one of the risks of such a project is that aspects of each tradition may be neglected in the effort to bring them together. Without quarreling with their higher principles, a Roman jurist might think that much of Roman law had been neglected or lost.

The late scholastics had explained why there should be a right to private property and why that right should be limited in cases such as necessity. The Roman jurists did not. Nevertheless, a Roman jurist might also have thought that the late scholastic account of ownership was less instructive than the Roman. Although the introductions to property in the *Digest* and the *Institutes* of Justinian did not consider why there should be private ownership, as we have seen,[124] they did describe the different rights that an owner might have. For example, everyone could use "common things," such as a seashore,[125] "civic things," such as a theater or stadium,[126] and "public things," such as rivers.[127] Yet sometimes, by using such things, a person acquired a right against a would-be user who might build a hut on the beach[128] or take a seat in the theater.[129] Sometimes, the user acquired a right over the private property of another: for example, anyone using the river could beach boats, dry nets, and haul fish on the privately owned land on the riverbank, and could tie up to trees that belonged to the landowner.[130] "Consecrated things" (*res sacrae*), such as places of worship, and "hallowed" things (*res religiosae*), such as tombs, belong to no one, but a private person can make property "hallowed" by burying a body on it,[131] although he cannot make place of worship "consecrated."[132] Much was lost, a Roman might think, by asking why there should be property, but not what sorts of property there might be.

It is likely that the late scholastics did not discuss these differences in ownership because they saw no easy way in which to explain them by means of higher philosophical principles. Anything that they could not explain in this way they either neglected or dismissed as matters of Roman positive law. They used their account of the purpose of private property to explain the canon law rule that a person could use another's goods in time of necessity. But they did not discuss limitations on the rights of an owner when they did not see a principled way in

---

[124] *See* Chapter I, pp. 18–19. [125] I. 2.1.1; I. 2.1.5. D. 1.8.2.1.
[126] I. 2.1.6; D. 1.8.6.1. [127] I. 2.1.2; D. 1.8.5.pr.
[128] I. 2.1.5; D. 1.8.3. [129] D. 47.10.15.7.
[130] D. I. 2.1.4; D. 1.8.5.pr. [131] D. 1.8.6.4; I. 2.1.9. [132] I. 2.1.8; D. 1.8.6.3.

which to explain them. They did not discuss the rights of an owner who was bothered by another's owner's use of his land, for example by the smoke from his hearth or his cheese shop.[133] They did not explain why a possessor who was not the owner should be protected.

An achievement of the late scholastics was to formulate a general principle of unjust enrichment. Nevertheless, a Roman jurist might think that, in doing so, they lost track of the concrete cases in which an action should arise, for example when a payment had been made that was not due,[134] and when a person incurred expenses looking after another's property when he had not been authorized to do so.[135]

Without contesting the late scholastics' principles, a Roman jurist might have had difficulty seeing why, to understand negligence, one needed to explain fault in terms of voluntary action, or to identify negligence with a lack of the virtue of prudence. He might think that negligence was better understood by putting cases of pruners cutting branches over a public way,[136] itinerant barbers shaving customers near sports grounds,[137] farmers burning stubble on windy days,[138] unskillful muleteers,[139] and physicians who prescribe the wrong medicine.[140]

A Roman jurist might have objected strongly to neglecting the differences between the *lex Aquilia* and the action for *iniuria*. For the late scholastics, both actions were instances of the general principle that a person owes compensation for harming another's person, property, or dignity. Without disagreeing, a Roman jurist might think that they ignored the limitations that ought to placed upon this principle. Nearly all of the Roman texts that deal with recovery under the *lex Aquilia* concern recovery for the loss of property, not for harm to one's body. As noted, according to one text, "a value cannot be placed on the body of a free man."[141] A Roman jurist might think that a judge should not try to value bodily harm and treat it as though a sum of money could compensate the plaintiff.

A Roman jurist might also think that the late scholastics ignored the limitations that should be placed on compensation for harm to dignity. The Roman jurists had dealt case by case with the types of offense for which a plaintiff might recover. As we have seen, he could recover for lies told about him and possibly for an embarrassing truth. He could sometimes recover for offensive language, as when the defendant assembled people at his house and raised a clamor,[142] but not for any vituperation.[143] A woman could recover if she was "accosted" and propositioned,[144] or if she was followed "assiduously."[145] The plaintiff could recover if his slave were beaten,[146] but not if he were struck lightly.[147] He could recover if someone entered his house without permission,[148] but not if someone entered his temporary lodging or his room in a brothel.[149] A Roman jurist might have had trouble seeing how one could decide when dignity should be legally protected except by putting cases. Moreover, he might have had difficulty with the idea that the law should

---

[133] D. 8.5.8.5–6. [134] Zimmermann (n. 31), 834–38
[135] Zimmermann (n. 31), 875–78. [136] D. 9.2.31. [137] D. 9.2.11.pr.
[138] D. 9.2.30.3. [139] D. 9.2.8.1. [140] D. 9.2.8.pr. [141] D. 9.3.7.
[142] D. 47.10.15.2. [143] D. 47.10.15.11. [144] D. 47.10.15.20.
[145] D. 47.10.15.22. [146] D. 47.10.15.34. [147] D. 47.10.15.44.
[148] D.47.2.21.7. [149] D. 47.10.7.5.

treat liability for offensive conduct in the same way as it treats recovery for physical harm. "An insult," according to Ulpian, "resides in the will of the culprit"; "Thus one can suffer an insult even though he is unaware, but no one can perpetrate one unless he knows what he is doing."[150] Nor is compensation due in the same circumstances. According to Ulpian, again, the action "is based on what is good and equitable," and therefore "if someone ignores the insult... he cannot, on second thought," recover for it.[151]

Moreover, a Roman jurist might think that a person should sometimes be liable if he was not at fault. Except for Molina, the late scholastics found no principled explanation of why he should be. They thought that if harm is not caused by voluntary action, it is caused by chance, and no one should be liable for chance. To a Roman jurist, it might still seem sensible that a person who keeps wild animals or hangs signs over the street should do so at his peril, and that one who was hurt by an object thrown from the window of another's house, or who had his property stolen at another's inn, should recover regardless of fault.[152] If the higher principles of the late scholastics could not explain why he should be liable, then, a Roman jurist might think, so much the worse for the principles.

The late scholastics rejected the Roman distinctions among consensual and "real" contracts, and between nominate and innominate contracts. The Roman jurists agreed that consent is required in every contract, and that the parties could make any agreement binding in advance of performance by making a *stipulatio*, thereby indicating their intention to do so formally. A Roman jurist might still have insisted that only some contracts should be binding upon consent, such as sale, lease, partnership, and mandate. Others should be binding on delivery of an object loaned, deposited, or pledged, and others only when one side had performed. The Roman might have said that the question of whether the parties wished to be committed to such an arrangement in advance of performance, when they had not formally and expressly committed themselves, should not be resolved by higher principles, but by judgment and experience. He might think that the distinctions of Roman law were founded on judgment and experience.[153]

## The development of international public law

As noted in the last chapter,[154] the law of war and peace, although of concern to the Romans, was not the concern of the Roman jurists. Nor was it the concern of the medieval civilians. As we have seen, typically, the civilians believed that there was only one legitimate authority on earth, the emperor, who was lord of the entire world.[155] Although there were canonical authorities in support of that position, as

---

[150] D. 47.10.3.1–2.   [151] D. 47.10. 11.1.   [152] *See* Zimmermann (n. 31), 1126–28.
[153] In support of this view, *see* James Gordley, "The Origins of Sale: Some Lessons from the Romans," *Tulane Law Review* 84 (2010): 1.
[154] *See* Chapter II, pp. 77–78.
[155] *See* Walter Ullmann, "Juristic Obstacles to the Emergence of the Concept of the State in the Middle Ages," *Annali di storia del diritto—rassegna internazionale* 12–13 (1968–69): 43, 62.

we have also seen,[156] some canonists broke with it when they considered the just causes of war. A just war must be declared by a civil authority with the power to do so. Some canonists, such as Sinibaldus Fliscus (later Pope Innocent IV), concluded that there had to be a plurality of civil authorities with such a power. Otherwise, every war would be, in effect, a rebellion. So it became possible for jurists to write about the law of war and peace.

The late scholastics flatly rejected the proposition that the emperor was the only legitimate authority. Vitoria said "this contention is baseless,"[157] Soto and Suárez that it was wrong,[158] and Molina that it was "obviously ridiculous."[159] They objected on the basis of the ideas they took from Aristotle and Aquinas. A human being is a political and social animal. To live the distinctively human life that is his end, he must live in association with others. It followed that, by their very nature, human beings could form a society and institute a government.[160] Because authority originated with each society, the Roman Empire was not universal. The *Corpus iuris* said that, by the *lex regia*, the Roman people transferred their authority to the emperor. But that did not mean that other peoples had done so.[161] Hugo Grotius, who is also acknowledged as one of the great founders of international law, agreed with their conclusion.[162]

The reason for their difference from the medieval civilians was not the late scholastics' familiarity with Aristotle and Aquinas. Bartolus and Baldus knew both philosophers well, and sometimes read their ideas into Roman texts.[163] Nevertheless, Bartolus claimed that anyone who denied that the emperor was lord of the whole world was a heretic. Baldus claimed that the emperor had universal authority. He did so even though he believed, like the late scholastics, that each society by its very nature—initially at least—had the power to institute government and to make law. Like them, he grounded that conclusion on Aristotelian principles that he read into the Roman texts.[164]

Possibly, although paradoxically, to concede universal dominion to the emperor may have seemed to have more practical significance to the sixteenth-century late scholastics than to the fourteenth-century civilians, and therefore to be more dangerous. In the fourteenth century, in practice, the emperor was exercising little of the authority that the jurists ascribed to him. In the sixteenth century, conceding such authority to Charles V, who was both emperor and the king of Spain, would have disturbed late scholastics such as Vitoria and Soto. If he were lord of the world,

---

[156] See Chapter II, pp. 79–81.
[157] Franciscus de Vitoria, *De Indiis insulanis relectio prior*, 2nd ed., no. 25, in *Relecciones Teológicas* (n. 5), 2: 348.
[158] Soto (n. 6), lib. 4, q. 4, a. 2; Franciscus Suárez, *Defensio fidei catholicae et apostolicae adversus Anglicanae errores* (Coimbra, 1613), lib. 3, cap. 2.
[159] Molina (n. 16), II, disp. 30.
[160] Vitoria (n. 5), nos. 3–4; Soto (n. 6), lib. 4, q. 4, a. 1; Molina (n. 16), II, disp. 22; V, disp. 3; Suárez (n. 158), lib. 3, cap. 2.
[161] Soto (n. 6), lib. 4, q. 4, a. 1; Molina (n. 16), II, disp. 30; Suárez (n. 158), lib. 3, cap. 5.
[162] Grotius (n. 17), II. xxii. 13.   [163] See n. 3.
[164] James Gordley, "The Achievement of Baldus de Ubaldis (132?–1400)," *Zeitschrift für Europäisches Privatrecht* 4 (2000): 820, 821–27.

he would be legitimate ruler of the inhabitants of the newly discovered lands of the Americas. Virtually all of Vitoria's writings, which are regarded as laying the foundations of international law, were delivered as lectures showing that Spanish domination of the newly discovered lands was unlawful.

In any event, Molina and Suárez concluded that, because in principle the government derived its authority from the people, the people could abolish a government that became tyrannical and subversive of the ends that it should serve, and could institute a new government.[165] They went considerably further than Grotius was later to do. According to Grotius, the people could resist the government only in circumstances of "dire and immediate peril," for, in establishing government, they would not have intended "to impose on everyone the heavy duty of preferring death under all circumstances to armed resistance to the violence of their superiors."[166] Modern scholars have said that the late scholastics anticipated the concept of the social contract.[167] Nevertheless, their theory was not a democratic one. The people might institute any of the legitimate forms of government that Aristotle had described: democracy, aristocracy, or monarchy. If they instituted a monarchy, they could not depose the monarch or reject his decisions if they did not like them.[168] Otherwise, as Molina observed, the form of government would not be a monarchy, but a democracy.[169]

Although the late scholastics discussed the basis of what we would call constitutional law, they had little to say about the rules appropriate to each form of government. They did discuss the rules that should govern relations among different states, each possessed of legitimate authority. Vitoria is considered one of the founders of international law.

Vitoria followed the lead of the canonists. As we have seen,[170] according to a key text in the *Decretum*: "A war is just which is conducted by edict (*edicto*) and for the cause of the recovery of things (*rebus repetendis*) or the repelling of enemies."[171] The canonists had said that a war conducted by edict was one declared by the *princeps* in the sense of the person or persons in charge of a state. Rufinus and the *Summa Parisiensis* had said that the just war could be fought not only to recover what was one's own, but also to punish those responsible for a wrong.[172] Vitoria then drew on Aristotle and Aquinas to explain why the *princeps* had the exclusive power to declare war and the reasons for which a war could be fought. According to Vitoria, a private person, as well as the state, had the right to defend his person and his goods:

But, a state has the right not only to defend itself but also to avenge itself and its subjects and to redress wrongs. This is proved by what Aristotle said in the third book of his *Politics*, namely,

---

[165] Molina (n. 16), V, disp 3; Suárez (n. 158), lib. 3, cap. 5.    [166] Grotius (n. 17), I.iv.7.
[167] See John Neville Figgis, *Studies of Political Thought from Gerson to Grotius 1414–1625* (Cambridge, 1956), 154–55; Quentin Skinner, vol. 2 of *The Foundations of Modern Political Thought* (Cambridge, 1978), 174.
[168] Vitoria (n. 5), no. 8.    [169] Molina (n. 16), II, disp. 25.
[170] See Chapter II, pp. 79–80.    [171] C. 23 q. 2 c. 1.
[172] *Die Summa magistri Rufini zum Decretum Gratiani*, ed. Johann Friedrich von Schulte (Glessen, 1892), to C. 23 q. 1; *The Summa Parisiensis* on the *Decretum Gratiani*, ed. Tenence P. McLaughlin (Toronto, 1952), to C. 23 q. 2.

that a state ought to be sufficient unto itself. But it cannot adequately protect the public good and the position of the state if it cannot and take measures against its enemies, for wrongdoers would be more ready and daring to do wrong if they could do so with impunity.[173]

He was relying on an Aristotelian conception of the state that he explained a few paragraphs later. The state was a "perfect whole" in the sense of a community from which "nothing was wanting."[174] He was also relying on Aquinas' conclusion that, because the punishment of a wrongdoer "is directed to the welfare of the whole community... [it] belongs to him alone who has charge of the community's welfare."[175] Consequently:

> ... as the care of the common good is committed to those who are in authority, it is their business to watch over the common good of the city, kingdom or province subject to them. And just as it is lawful for them to have recourse to the sword in defending the common good against internal disturbances when they punish evildoers... so, too, it is their business to have recourse to the sword in defending the common good against external enemies.[176]

Vitoria then considered the rules that govern the conduct of war. Some followed from the legitimate objectives of war: "[I]t is lawful to retake everything that has been lost" to the enemy;[177] "[I]t is lawful to avenge the wrong received from the enemy and to take measures against him and to impose punishment on him for the wrongs he has done," for there must be "a power and authority to deter wrongdoers and to prevent them from injuring the good and innocent."[178] The innocent should be spared, but only when to do so was consistent with these objectives; "If the enemy refuse to return things wrongfully seized by them and the injured party cannot otherwise compensate himself, he may do so wherever satisfaction is obtainable, whether from the guilty or from the innocent."[179] With qualifications, Grotius agreed.[180]

A just war may be conducted by whatever means are necessary to secure victory. Again, the innocent should be spared, but only insofar as is consistent with that goal. "The deliberate slaughter of the innocent is never lawful in itself," Vitoria said, since "the basis for a just war is a wrong done" and "wrong is not done by an innocent person":[181] "[E]ven in a war with Turks it is unlawful to kill children... and the same holds with the women of unbelievers."[182] The same is true with "harmless agricultural people and... the rest of the civilian population...."[183] An exception must be made for what is now known as collateral damage, which he called "collateral circumstances," "as when a fortress or city is stormed... and it is known that... cannon... cannot be discharged... without destroying the innocent together with the guilty,"[184] "although it is never right to slay the guiltless,

---

[173] Vitoria, *Relectio posterior de Indis, sive de iure belli Hispaniorum in Barbaros*, no. 5, in *Relecciones Teológicas* (n. 5), 1: 393.
[174] Vitoria (n. 173), no. 7.   [175] Aquinas (n. 10), II-II, Q. 64, a. 3.
[176] Aquinas (n. 10), II-II, Q. 40, a. 1.   [177] Vitoria (n. 173), no. 16.
[178] Vitoria (n. 173), no. 19.
[179] Vitoria (n. 173), no. 41.   [180] Grotius (n. 17), III.ii.1–2; III.xiii.1.
[181] Vitoria (n. 173), no. 35.   [182] Vitoria (n. 173), no. 36.
[183] Vitoria (n. 173), no. 36.   [184] Vitoria (n. 173), no. 37.

even as an indirect and unintended result, except when there is no other means of carrying on the operations of a just war...."[185] "It is...lawful," however, "to despoil the innocent of goods and things which the enemy would use against us, such as arms, ships, and engines of war."[186] Indeed, "[o]ne can burn and destroy their grain and kill their horses if this is necessary to sap the enemy's strength."[187] Nevertheless, "[i]f a war can be carried on effectively without spoliation of an agricultural population and other innocent folk, they ought not be despoiled."[188] Grotius agreed in principle,[189] but, surprisingly, with doubts as to such matters as the sparing of women and children.[190]

## The late scholastics and canon law

Starting from canon law, the late scholastics rejected the idea of the medieval jurists that the emperor was lord of the world. They recognized the independent authority of a plurality of secular states and grounded their authority on philosophical principles. They justified the right of a people to overthrow a government that was subversive of the proper ends of a state. They clarified the right to make war in a just cause. They laid down rules for the conduct of war. Again, it is hard to understate their achievement.

As mentioned earlier, however, when several traditions are combined, there is a risk that aspects of one of these traditions will be neglected or distorted. A medieval canon lawyer might have been concerned about the late scholastic's work. He might think that, when Vitoria discussed the law to be observed in fighting a war, he laid down rules to cover matters that depended far more on the circumstances. By and large, the canonists had not formulated such rules except for commenting on an ineffective decree of the Fourth Lateran Council that banned the crossbow as a terror weapon.

A medieval canon lawyer might also have thought that a shift had taken place in the locus of authority. As we have seen, the canon lawyers had described the justice of a war as a question to be resolved in the internal forum of the confessional, not the external forum of the courts. It had to be so because the Church courts did not wield secular power, and there were no courts that had jurisdiction over the parties. That was why, if a dispute could not be settled in any other way, it had to be settled by war. According to Gratian's *Decretum*, the priests who heard confessions had a duty to be familiar with the canons of the Church.[191] They did not need to hold a degree in canon law. As we have seen, the canon lawyers wrote manuals for the benefit of priests who had no such qualification. Yet the authority on which the canons were based was that of the scriptures, saints, church councils, and popes, whose statements were contained in the *Decretum* and *Decretals*.

[185] Vitoria (n. 173), no. 37.
[186] Vitoria (n. 173), no. 39.
[187] Vitoria (n. 173), no. 39.
[188] Vitoria (n. 173), no. 40.
[189] Grotius (n. 17), III.xii.1.
[190] Grotius (n. 17), III.iv.9.
[191] D. 38 c. 1.

Two changes had taken place by the time of the late scholastics. One was that there were now Protestant powers. To the extent that international law was based on natural law, they were morally bound to obey it. But they could not be judged in the internal forum. The question had arisen that has bedeviled international law ever since: how to enforce it when there was no forum able to do so.

Second, when questions were to be resolved among Catholics in the internal forum, the late scholastics and Vitoria in particular seemed to put less emphasis on the authority of the canons of the Church and more on that of moral theologians, such as themselves. As we have already seen, Soto said:

> Nor is to be accounted a fault of a theologian to take on territory that might seem more appropriate for those skilled in law as, indeed, canon law proceeds from the womb of theology.... It is for the theologian to adjust the decreta of canon law to the norms of the Gospel....[192]

Vitoria explained that the questions of international law on which he was writing were to be resolved, not by princes, but by *sapientes*, the wise and learned:

> In all of these matters, if one previously deliberates and legitimately considers an act to be permissible... nevertheless he would sin and not be excused by ignorance because it is apparent that the ignorance is not invincible since afterward he did not do what he could to examine what is permissible and what is not.... [I]t is necessary if the matter is not otherwise certain that he act according to the definition and determination of the *sapietes*. This indeed is the condition of a good act [citing Aristotle, Ethics II] that if he does not consult the learned (*sapientes*) in doubtful matters, he cannot be excused. Indeed, given that the act is permitted in itself (*secundum se*), if there is doubt later as to its merits, every person is held to consult the judgment of the *sapientes* and to act accordingly, even, indeed, if they are mistaken.[193]

He knew that "in the forum of conscience it belongs to the priests to judge...."[194] Yet, "in the forum of conscience, one is obliged to judge, not according to his own inclination, but according to probable reason or the authority of the learned (*sapientes*); otherwise it is a judgment made with temerity and he exposes himself to the risk of error, which itself is an error."[195] Authority to resolve "doubtful matters" belonged "to those whom the Church has constituted for this purpose: prelates, preachers, confessors, and experts in divine and human law."[196] But among the learned and the experts he surely considered men like himself and Soto. He had said, as we have seen, that "[t]he office and duty of a theologian appears to be so large that no argument, no problem, and no topic seems foreign to it."[197] Theologians' views should be consulted by those to whom the Church had entrusted the resolution of doubtful matters, and laymen such as princes should follow them. An earlier canonist might have said that the law of the Church is based on its canons and that the work of a canon lawyer was simply to reconcile them. Now, as Decock has noted, "The theologians... claimed to be superior to the...

---

[192] Soto (n. 6), *Proemium*.
[193] Vitoria (n. 157), no. 1.
[194] Vitoria (n. 157), no. 1.
[195] Vitoria (n. 157), no. 1.
[196] Vitoria (n. 157), no. 1.
[197] Vitoria (n. 5), Prologue.

canonists. They vindicated the power to evaluate... the law of the Church... from the perspective of natural law."[198]

As we have seen, medieval canon law counted on the cooperation of the penitent. It was he, for example, who must examine his own state of mind. As Vitoria describes the inner forum, it seems more like a place where one comes to receive instructions on how to behave, which he must follow, right or wrong. Aquinas said that a person who followed his conscience did not sin even if he was in error, provided that the error was "invincible," in the sense that he was not negligent or otherwise at fault for making the error.[199] Vitoria left little room for invincible ignorance. One who was ignorant should always ask the learned. Cajetan, quoted by Vitoria, said that a person does not sin if he was told incorrectly by preachers or his confessor that a permissible act is impermissible, and he disobeys them, having formed his conscience according to his own view. Vitoria disagreed. He thought it a sin to disobey preachers and confessors even when they happened to be wrong.[200]

In fairness, Vitoria expressed these opinions in a treatise denouncing the legitimacy of the Spanish Empire in the New World, the enslavement of the inhabitants, and the theft of their property. His view would not prevail if the king of Spain could decide the matter for himself even after listening to learned advisers. But Vitoria did not limit his opinions to this treatment of the inhabitants of the Americas. These opinions suggested that conscience lay more within the domain of experts and, among the experts, more in the domain of theologians.

## The late scholastics and metaphysics

As noted, the starting point for the late scholastics was an Aristotelian and Thomistic view of man. For them, as for Aristotle and Aquinas, a person's happiness consists in living a distinctively human life that realizes, so far as possible, one's potential as a human being. It is a life unlike that of other animals, because a human being can act not only by appetite, but also by reason and will. He can understand that an action contributes to the distinctively human life that he should live and he can choose it for that reason. Living such a life is the ultimate end to which all well-chosen actions are a means, either instrumentally or as constituent parts of such a life. To live such a life, he must live in association with others. It follows that, by their very nature, human beings could form a society and institute a government.[201] That was the starting point of late scholastics when they discussed the authority and purpose of the state. To live such a life, a person also needs external things. The object of distributive justice is to ensure that each person has the resources that he needs to acquire them. The object of commutative justice is to enable him to obtain them without depriving others of their share of resources.

---

[198] Decock (n. 1), 43.     [199] Aquinas (n. 10), I–II, Q. 18, a. 6.
[200] Vitoria (n. 157), no. 1.
[201] Vitoria (n. 5), nos. 3–4; Soto (n. 6), lib. 4, q. 4, a. 1; Molina (n. 16), II, disp. 22; V, disp. 3; Suárez (n. 158), lib. 3, cap. 2.

That was the starting point for the late scholastics when they explained property, tort, contract, and unjust enrichment in terms of commutative justice.

In the Aristotelian and Thomistic tradition, these views rested on more fundamental ideas about what was real. For Aristotle, the real world is composed of individual things that he called "substances." People, animals, and plants are substances, as are the elements of the inorganic world, which he believed to be earth, air, fire, and water.

Each of these things tends to behave in a definite way rather than in any way whatsoever. A pear tree has a tendency to produce pears and no tendency to chase cats. If something had no tendency to behave in any definite way, it would not be an individual thing. The way in which a thing tends to behave is called its "final cause," or "end." The "end" of a thing in this sense is not a conscious purpose, but the characteristic way in which it behaves. The pear tree has no conscious purposes, and its end is a distinctive manner of growth and reproduction, not the production of pears for people to eat. Unlike plants, animals do what contributes to their end out of an awareness of what is around them and a desire to obtain what contributes to it. But they are not conscious of the end that they achieve when they follow their desires: to nourish themselves or to reproduce. The distinctive feature of a human being is that he can be conscious of the purposes that he pursues and how they contribute to the distinctively human life that is his end. He can act through reason and will.

Each thing behaves as it does because of something within it. If it did so because of something completely outside itself, the behavior in question would not be that of the individual thing itself but of the something outside it. That within a thing which is responsible for how it behaves is its "nature." Things with a different nature are different kinds of things. Those features that a thing must have to be the kind of thing it is belong to its "substantial form." It cannot gain or lose these features and yet remain the kind of thing it is. The substantial form of a thing, which corresponds to its nature, is captured by the definition of a thing. A human being is a rational animal, an animal whose nature it is to act by reason and will.

A thing can have many parts and many activities, and yet, to be an individual thing, it must have one substantial form and one end. It can do so because of the way in which its parts and activities are related. Each part has an end of its own that itself is a means to the end of the whole either because it is instrumental to achieving that end or because it is a constituent of the end to be achieved. Each part of a pear tree has an end that contributes to the characteristic manner of reproduction and growth that is the end of the pear tree. Anything attached to a pear tree that does not contribute to this end, for example a pebble embedded in its bark, is not, properly speaking, part of the pear tree. As Aquinas said in one of his commentaries on Aristotle, there are two sorts of order, the order of part to whole and the order of means to ends, and the first is based upon the second.[202]

---

[202] Aquinas (n. 70), lib. 1, lec. 1.

A thing is defined, then, in terms of its substantial form, which corresponds to its end. Its parts and activities can then be analyzed in terms of that definition. The same is true of man-made things, which are defined by the end they are built to serve. A house is built to live in; a bed, to lie down on and sleep. Their structure can be explained in terms of their parts, each of which has an end that contributes to their ultimate end. Consequently, the method is similar whether one is analyzing an animal or a couch. As Aristotle said:

[T]he true method is to state what the definitive characteristics are that distinguish the animal as a whole; . . . and to deal after the same fashion with its several organs; in fact, to proceed in exactly the same way we should do, were we giving a complete description of a couch.[203]

Aristotle applied this method to every subject that he investigated. In *Politics*, he called it "the method that has hitherto guided us"[204] and "our usual method."[205]

In this method, concepts and purposes go hand in hand. Corresponding to the definition of what a thing is, there is an end or purpose to which all of its parts and activities are means. Knowing that definition and purpose, one can analyze the parts and their activities. This is the method that we have seen the late scholastics use in their analysis of natural law. It belongs to the nature of a human being to live the distinctively human life that was his end. He can best do so in association with others. The late scholastics defined the end of the state in terms of this end, and drew conclusions as to its authority, the right of citizens to overthrow their government if it subverted this end, and the right of the state to protect itself against other states that thwarted its purpose. Distributive justice was defined in terms of the end of giving each citizen a fair share of the resources that he needed to preserve that share, and commutative justice in terms of the need to preserve that share so far as possible. Property, tort, contract, and unjust enrichment, and the limitations of private rights, were then explained in terms of their role in achieving commutative justice. The method was like that of a biologist analyzing the organs of an animal or an engineer analyzing the parts of a machine. It rested, however, on a metaphysics in which the world was made up of substances, each substance had an end, and its parts and their activities could be analyzed in terms of that end.

As mentioned already, one of the risks of combining several traditions is that aspects of one or another of them may be distorted or neglected. As we will see in a later chapter,[206] so it was with the late scholastics and the philosophy of Aristotle and Aquinas. In that philosophy, the real world consisted of individual things or substances. That meant that the natural law could not exist apart from those substances. The natural law had to exist within human beings and nowhere else, just as the instinct for nest building exists within birds and nowhere else. As we will see, some of the late scholastics lost track of this idea and began to conceive of the natural law as consisting of principles that existed apart from the minds of particular human beings deciding how to act in the situations in which they found themselves.

---

[203] Aristotle, *Parts of Animals* I.i 641ᵃ.
[205] Aristotle (n. 11), I.viii 1256ᵃ.
[204] Aristotle (n. 11), I.i 1252ᵃ.
[206] *See* Chapter VIII, p. 000.

Moreover, the natural law is the rule that a person must follow in choosing those actions that contribute to the distinctively human life that is his end in the circumstances that he is confronting. A person depends upon reason to know the action he should take under those circumstances. The sort of reason upon which he depends is not deductive reason, which proceeds with demonstrative certainty from premise to conclusion, but rather practical reason or prudence, which proceeds without such certainty from the ends that he seeks to the means with which to achieve them. Natural law, according to Aquinas, is a decree of prudence.[207] Certainty is often impossible because the number of circumstances that matter may be greater than a person can take into account. The number that matter may be infinite. Thus prudence is in large part concerned with selecting rules that are appropriate, given a person's limited knowledge of what happens in the majority of cases. As we will see, some of the late scholastics lost track of this idea as well.

For example, Molina and Lessius believed that the rules of natural law could take account of all of the circumstances that might matter. Suárez went further. He imagined the natural law as a set of immutable rules that already took into account every circumstance that might arise. Since no human mind could do so, he imagined the natural law as having an ideal existence independent of any existing person who was confronting a problem. He thus broke with an idea of how the natural law existed and the certainty of its conclusions that was implicit, at least, in Aristotle and explicit in Aquinas.

Yet he did so without troubling other late scholastics who based their work on Aristotle and Aquinas. Perhaps the reason was that the late scholastics had become accustomed to writing only about part of the Aristotelian and Thomistic tradition. Cajetan had written a commentary on the entire *Summa theologiae*. The late scholastics wrote about "justice and law." Their treatises did not include the underlying metaphysics. Moreover, the late scholastics wrote, in large part, about rules in abstraction from particular circumstances. They may have lost sight of why particular circumstances matter and why prudence is necessary to take them into account. At any rate, Suárez developed a new metaphysics to support his position. That innovation was the beginning of rationalism. With the coming of rationalism, concepts and purposes no longer went hand in hand. A discussion of rationalism and its effect on the work of jurists must wait, however, until we examine the influence of humanism.

---

[207] Aquinas (n. 10), I–II, Q. 91, a. 3.

# IV

## *De Iure Civile in Artem Redigendo*
### The Humanist Ideal

We have seen how three traditions were reconciled in the work of the late scholastics: Roman law, as understood by the medieval civilians; the Christian tradition, as understood by the canonists; and the Aristotelian philosophical tradition, as understood by Aquinas. There was another tradition in the ancient world, described in the first chapter, which had not been reconciled. It was the ideal of Cicero—that law could be the object of *ars*, in the Greek sense, and so become part of liberal education. This ideal was revived by the humanists, who then tried to reconcile it with Roman law.

## i *STUDIA HUMANITATIS*: THE RENAISSANCE HUMANISTS

In the fourteenth century, prevailing ideals of scholarship and education were challenged by the group that we call the humanists. They hoped to achieve a "renaissance" of classical learning, which, they thought, had been forgotten or corrupted in the "middle ages," as they called the period that separated them from the ancient world.[1] Their innovation was not to stress the importance of ancient authors. Legal studies had been based on the *Corpus iuris* since the twelfth century. The study of philosophy had been based on works of Aristotle since their rediscovery in the thirteenth century. One could speak of a twelfth-century renaissance in law and a thirteenth-century renaissance in philosophy. The goal and method of the humanist program set their renaissance apart. The goal was to promote the *studia humanitatis*, the sort of learning that would produce, in Cicero's words, a *vir virtutis*, a complete man, cultivated and fit for an active role in public life. Their method was to inculcate moral virtue, practical wisdom, and a correct and eloquent command of language through the study of classical languages and authors. The humanists, as Quentin Skinner noted, gave "birth to a doctrine that was to be almost embarrassingly long-lived: the doctrine that

---

[1] Quentin Skinner, "The Renaissance," vol. 1 of *The Foundations of Modern Political Thought* (Cambridge, 1998), 110–11.

a classical education not only constitutes the only possible form of schooling for a gentleman, but also the best possible preparation for an entry into public life."[2]

Petrarch, one of the founders of humanism, had studied law for seven years at Montpellier and Bologna. "I regret and will regret," he said, "as long as there is breath in me that so large a part of my life passed by" in this way.[3] According to Petrarch, the problem was not the Roman texts. He praised the Roman jurists as "the fathers of jurisprudence."[4] The problem was the way in which Roman law was taught in his own time:

> The greater part of our legists... care nothing for knowing about the origins of law and about the founders of jurisprudence, have no other preoccupation than to gain as much as they can from their profession, and are content to learn whatever is written in the law about contracts, judgments or wills....[5]

His opinion was shared by Lorenzo Valla, one of the first humanists to write about Roman law. It was a "golden science" (*disciplina aurea*).[6] The problem was to recover the original sense of the Roman texts. Corruptions had been introduced by Justinian's compiler Tribonian, who "knew neither law nor letters."[7] But far worse errors had been introduced by the medieval civilians.

As Donald Kelley observed, Valla, in his efforts to recover the original sense of the texts of the *Corpus iuris*, "promoted philology to the level of a science"[8] and thereby "transformed the study of Roman law":[9]

> [H]is procedure was to pick out difficult or ambiguous terms; to illustrate the usage of the jurists (Ulpian was his favorite); then to compare this with other authors, such as grammarians or poets... and finally to resolve the problem through the authority of the major classical writers, that is, Quintilian and Cicero.[10]

His near-contemporary Poliziano prepared a critical edition of the *Corpus iuris* by comparing the version in common use, now called the vulgate, with the one extant manuscript on which all others had been based.

In the following century, humanist jurists built on the work of Valla and Poliziano to arrive at a still more exact reconstruction of the Roman texts. Guillaume Budé, Andrea Alciato, Jacques Cujas, and their followers discovered many instances in which the text of the *Corpus iuris* was corrupt. Errors had been made either by Justinian's compilers or by copyists. They also gained a more accurate understanding of the meaning of the words of the *Corpus iuris* by seeing how these words were used in nonlegal texts. Often, by failing to do so themselves, the medieval jurists had blundered.[11] A notorious example is Accursius' interpretation

---

[2] Skinner (n. 1), 88.
[3] Francesco Petrarca, *Epistolae de rebus familiaribus et variae* (Florence, 1859), III, 14–15.
[4] Petrarca (n. 3), III, 47.   [5] Petrarca (n. 3), III, 14–15.
[6] Lorenzo Valla, "II: *Antidoti in Poggiam*," vol. 1 in *Opera omnia*, ed. E. Garin (Torino, 1962), 286.
[7] Valla, "VI: *Elegantia latinae linguae*" (n. 6) 1: 216.
[8] Donald R. Kelly, *Foundations of Modern Historical Scholarship: Language, Law and History in the French Renaissance* (New York, 1970), 45.
[9] Kelly (n. 8), 42.   [10] Kelly (n. 8), 42.
[11] Klaus Luig, "Humanismus und Privatrecht," in *Vestigia iuris romani. Festschrift für Gunter Wesener zum 60. Geburtstag am 3. Juni 1992*, eds. Georg Klinenberg et al. (Graz, 1992), 285 at 289.

## De Iure Civile in Artem Redigendo: *The Humanist Ideal* 113

of a text that said that "proconsuls are entitled to no more than six *fasces*."[12] Not knowing what *fasces* meant, Accursius guessed that the text referred to a term of office. He translated six *fasces* as "six months,"[13] citing another text that prescribed a term for the office of dictator.[14] As Budé showed, the reference was to the bundles of rods carried by the lictors who attended the proconsuls.[15]

If the humanists had merely been seeking a more accurate version of the *Corpus iuris* and a better understanding of the meaning of its words in its ancient context, their methods and those of the medieval civilians could have been accommodated. We have already seen[16] that the jurists who prepared the vulgate version of the *Corpus iuris* had tried to reconstruct the text as it had been promulgated by Justinian, although they lacked the humanists' techniques for doing so. As Roderick von Stinzing has said, the traditional exegetic methods could have been reconciled with those of humanists, for whom:

> ... it was enough that scholarly work be done in better taste, and in purer Latin, that the authorities be handled with more independence of judgment, that the dialectical subtleties be moderated and a greater use made of antiquarian learning. All this could be combined with exegesis and a pure analytic method without disturbing its essence....[17]

Indeed, the work of the humanists could have helped the civilians to do their own work better.[18] As Domenico Maffei observed, "[t]he philological method [could assist in] the application of Roman law as positive law." His example is a Latin phrase that the civilians misunderstood, but which, as the humanists showed, meant "ten percent interest."[19] The humanists themselves liked to point out that apparent contradictions among texts that perplexed the civilians were sometimes the result of mistakes that philological methods could correct. Canon lawyers eventually combined humanist textual criticism with their traditional methods of interpretation. As mentioned previously, in 1578, Pope Gregory XIII appointed a commission of learned men, generally referred to as the *Correctores Romani*, to find and eliminate corruptions in the texts that Gratian had collected in the *Decretum*. A new edition published in 1582 became the standard text within the Catholic Church. The text was printed along with the medieval Standard Gloss. Only minor changes were made in the Gloss.

Nevertheless, the relationship of the humanists and the medieval civilians was hostile. They had different goals, and that difference led to a conflict bordering on

---

[12] D. 1.6.14.
[13] Accursius, *Glossa ordinaria* (Venice, 1569), to D. 1.6.14 to *fascibus*.   [14] D. 1.2.18.
[15] Guillaume Budé, *Annotationes... in quatuor et viginti Pandectarum libros* (Paris, 1535), 166.
[16] See Chapter II, pp. 29–30.
[17] Roderick von Stinzing, vol. 1 of *Geschichte der deutschen Rechtswissenschaft* (Munich, 1880), 139. Kelly claims that "legal methods forbade alleging an error in the law" on "historical and philological grounds": Donald R. Kelly, "Civil Science in the Renaissance: Jurisprudence Italian Style," *Historical Journal* 22 (1979): 777, 785. But there is no reason why traditional jurists could not say that the wording of a text was wrong or should be understood differently. The editors of the vulgate had done so.
[18] James Gordley, "Humanists and Scholastics," in *Essays on Law and Religion: The Berkeley and Oxford Symposia in Honour of David Daube* 13 (Berkeley, CA, 1993): 13.
[19] Domenico Maffei, *Gli inizi dell'umanisimo giuridico* (Milan, 1956), 156.

war. One difference was that the humanists were trying to recapture not simply the original text, but also its original meaning to its author.[20] The civilians were trying to apply a text to situations that the text did not expressly cover and which its author may not have considered. To do so, as we have seen, the civilians sometimes generalized a text, or limited it, or applied it by analogy in ways that the author had not envisioned. For some humanists, these interpretations were simply wrong. They deviated from the meaning of the text to its author. As Domenico Maffei noted, "just by the process of restoring the original significance of various norms, the Roman law was transformed from positive law to historic law...."[21] Similarly, Hans Schlosser observed that, "at the very moment when the humanists, whether jurists, literati, or archaeologists, put their hand to the reconstruction of the institutions of [the ancient world], they accomplished the disconnection of the past and the present."[22]

Modern historians often assume that, on this point, the humanists were right. According to Julian Franklin, the interpretations of the medieval civilians were "distortions" that permitted "a creative adaptation of the Roman concepts to the legal needs of Europe." "But it is apparent," he concluded:

... that the achievement of medieval jurisprudence depended upon a pair of premises which it had never attempted to establish scientifically: the assumption, first, that the Roman Law is intrinsically perfect; and second, that the Roman Law as it was taught to medieval students was identical with the law of Rome as it was understood by Justinian. Neither of these premises, of course, could survive a critical appraisal.[23]

To an historian such as Franklin, whose task is to understand the past, any interpretation that does not recapture the original meaning of a text is necessarily a "distortion." Therefore medieval jurists must have failed to realize that the law they taught was not "identical with the law of Rome as it was understood by Justinian." Moreover, they must have assumed that the Roman law was "perfect." Otherwise, why would they have thought that its concepts could be adapted to the legal needs of Europe?

The medieval jurists, however, were engaged in a different task—one like that of modern lawyers: to apply authoritative texts to situations with which the texts do not deal expressly. That task presupposes that the texts are authoritative, but not that the law that they embody is perfect. It presupposes that to apply a text to a situation with which the text does not expressly deal is not a distortion, even if the situation is one that its author did not consciously envision. If it were a distortion, it would be impossible for a legal text to govern situations that the lawmaker did not have in mind. It would be impossible for there to be a rule by law unless the

---

[20] Hans Schlosser, *Grundzüge der neureren Privatrechtsgeschichte*, 9th ed. (Heidelberg, 2001), 71; Hans Erich Troje, "Zur Humanistischen Jurisprudenz," in *Festschrift für Hermann Heimpel zum 70. Geburtstag am 19. September 1971* (Göttingen, 1972), 110 at 111.
[21] Maffei (n. 19), 156.   [22] Schlosser (n. 20), 157.
[23] Julian H. Franklin, *Jean Bodin and the Sixteenth-Century Revolution in the Methodology of Law and History* (New York, 1963), 17.

lawmakers were to consider every situation that might arise. To recapture the meaning of a text as consciously understood by its author is a different task, and one for which the methods developed by the humanists are indispensable. Because their methods are suited to this different task, the humanists, despite their intellectual prominence, had little influence on how law was actually applied even in their own day. As Franz Wieacker said:

> [W]hile the humanist lawyers were able to find a new legitimation for Roman law, to purify and refine the way the texts were read... they did nothing to change the idea of law or the methods used by lawyers in the late Middle Ages, especially not in the countries of the reception.[24]

Nevertheless, the humanists and the civilians themselves did not see their differences as arising from a difference in the tasks that they had undertaken. Humanists often considered the civilians to be ignorant, and the civilians often regarded the humanists as grammarians rather than jurists.

A second source of antagonism concerned the kind of learning that a legal education should impart. The goal of the medieval civilians was to train professionals in law. The goal of the humanists was to realize the Ciceronian ideal of a *studia humanitatis*, a liberal arts education suitable for every gentleman.[25] In 1422, Cicero's work *De oratore* was rediscovered through the efforts of the humanists.[26] In that work, as we have seen,[27] Cicero proposed that the civil law should become an *ars*, an art or science, that would be "magnificent and copious but neither inaccessible nor mysterious,"[28] and which could be part of the education of a complete man. As we saw, according to Cicero, an "[a]rt is the synthesis of disciplined observations for some purpose useful to life."[29] In *De oratore*, his character Licinius Crassus explained that one could arrive at a "perfect art of the civil law" by "dividing the entire civil law into its genera, which are very few, and next distributing what I may call the members of those classes, and after that making plain by definition the proper significance of each...."[30] It was clear that the medieval civilians were not presenting law as an art or science in Cicero's sense. As Stinzing noted:

> The question... was this: whether one could succeed in advancing synthesis to an effective component of scholarly treatment [of law], so that a mass of detail could be joined in a higher unity and traced back to principles....
>
> Gellius' report of a lost work of Cicero, "*de iure civile in artem redigendo*"... and his own discussion of the task of legal knowledge "*in artem redigere*"... led to the question, to what extent this task had been abandoned so far or could be realized after all. Without taking precise account of its meaning, one understood that the traditional [medieval] scholarship

---

[24] Franz Wieacker, *A History of Private Law in Europe*, trans. Tony Weir (Oxford, 1995), 200.
[25] Schlosser (n. 20), 69–70.
[26] Neal W. Gilbert, *Renaissance Concepts of Method* (New York, 1960), 96.
[27] *See* Chapter I, pp. 16–18. [28] Cicero, *De oratore* I.xli.191.
[29] Volume 1 of *Storicorum Veterum Fragmenta*, ed. Johannnes ab Arnim (Lipsiae, 1905), 21 ll. 19–20.
[30] Cicero (n. 28), I.xli.191.

wholly failed to provide an "*ars iuris*" for the law it taught was not a systematically organized whole but a disorganized mass of particularities, not easy to survey, and set forth without leading principles.[31]

Nevertheless, Petrarch praised the Roman jurists as the "founders"[32] and "fathers of jurisprudence."[33] Valla said that they had produced a "golden science."[34] An integral part of the humanist program for the revival of learning was to recover the original wording and sense of classical texts. Petrarch and Valla seem to have thought that this program could be applied to law as well. Once the original sense of the Roman legal texts had been recovered, all would be well. Later jurists in the humanist tradition then had to wrestle with the problem of achieving an art or science of civil law on the basis of texts written by jurists who, as Cicero said, had no such project in mind.

The humanist's project was like that of the late scholastics in one respect: they both wanted to explain law as a systematically organized whole. Given their program, however, the humanists could not approach that project in the same way. The late scholastics were trained in philosophy and wrote for moral philosophers. They drew their principles from the philosophy of Aristotle and Aquinas. The humanists were trained in classical literature and history, which they regarded as the core of the liberal arts. Their goal was not a philosophical account that used a technical vocabulary, and which presupposed that the reader had the training and capacity for abstraction of a philosopher. Rather, their goal was an *ars* that would be part of the education of a gentleman, which would inculcate moral virtue, practical wisdom, and a command of language that would enable him to play an active role in public life.

Humanists such as Petrarch and Valla saw the conflict between such an *ars* and the philosophy of Aristotle in much starker terms than Cicero. As noted earlier,[35] by an *ars*, Cicero did not mean a science, as Aristotle conceived it, in which knowledge was obtained by abstracting first principles and working out their implications. Instead, Cicero meant an orderly and systematic presentation of practical knowledge, like a Greek treatise on rhetoric. Indeed, Cicero may not have had much idea of what Aristotle meant by a science. Aristotle had described scientific knowledge in his so-called esoteric works or school writings, which are those that have come down to us. He also wrote dialogues and other works intended for a general audience. These popular works have since been lost and yet they seem to have been the ones with which Cicero was familiar.[36] So far as one can tell, he paid little attention to Aristotle's school writings, and, indeed, they may have been rediscovered only in Cicero's lifetime.[37]

---

[31] Stinzing (n. 17), 140.   [32] Petrarca (n. 3), III, 14–15.   [33] Petrarca (n. 3), III, 47.
[34] Valla (n. 6), 286.   [35] *See* Chapter I, p. 17.
[36] W. K. C. Guthrie, *A History of Greek Philosophy VI: Aristotle—An Encounter* (Cambridge, 1981), 63.
[37] Scholars have noted that the surviving works of Aristotle look more like lecture notes than a treatise that one would publish. According to Strabo, they survived in manuscripts that, on Aristotle's death, were left to his friend and collaborator Theophrastus, who left them to his heir Neleus of Scepsis, who left them to his heirs, who stowed them in a cellar where they remained unread until Sulla

That lack of familiarity with the works of Aristotle, as known to medieval philosophers and late scholastics, may explain why Cicero, unlike Petrarch, had a positive attitude toward philosophy in general and Aristotle in particular. Cicero did believe, as did the humanists, in the central importance of eloquence: "[T]he wise control of the complete orator is that which chiefly upholds not only his own dignity, but the safety of countless individuals, and of the entire State."[38] Still, he praised philosophy, because eloquence should combine wisdom with mastery of language, and philosophy provided wisdom. He said that, of all philosophies, he was closest to the Aristotelians.[39] Nevertheless, he had his character Crassus say of philosophers that, without the skill of an orator, "that knowledge of theirs is nothing at all. For this is the essential concern of the orator, as I have often said before—a style that is dignified, graceful, and in conformity with the general modes of thought and judgment."[40] Cicero thought that while his son Marcus should not neglect the books of the philosophers, he should read those that Cicero himself had written, because "by reading my philosophical writings you will be sure to render your mastery of the Latin language more complete."[41]

For Petrarch and Valla, the philosophy of Aristotle as found in the esoteric works, which were the only ones extant and taught in the medieval universities, was impossibly far from the Ciceronian ideal. While Cicero had contrasted a true learning with "the 'yawning and drowsy wisdom' of the jurists,"[42] Petrarch applied these words to the philosophers of his day who "reject [eloquence] as unworthy of learned men, and honor only a babyish and puzzled babbling, and a wisdom that relies on arrogant frowns and 'yawns drowsily,' as Cicero puts it."[43] "Aristotle teaches more," Petrarch said, "but Cicero moves our minds more":[44]

> [Aristotle] teaches us the nature of virtue. But reading him offers none of those exhortations, or only a very few, that inflame our minds to love virtue and hate vice. Anyone looking for such exhortations will find them in our Latin authors, especially in Cicero and Seneca....[45]

---

took them to Rome as war booty. They were edited and published in Rome by the scholar Tyrannio, and finally edited and published by the philosopher Andronicus of Rhodes sometime in the mid first century BC. Scholars disagree as to how much was lost in the interval. Zeller claimed that copies had survived of all of these works except for three works on biology and some "minor" anthropological treatises: Eduard Zeller, vol. 1 of *Aristotle and the Earlier Peripatetics*, trans. B. C. Costelloe and J. H. Muirhead (New York, 1962), 123–36. His claim was refuted by P. Moraux, *Les listes anciennes des ouvrages d'Aristote* (Louvain, 1951). Since then, as Guthrie noted, "the pendulum of scholarship has tended to swing toward the view that the school writings were largely unknown until these manuscripts were rediscovered": Guthrie (n. 36), 62, n. 1. Cicero does not mention their rediscovery, but, according to Guthrie, his failure to do so is not surprising. "Cicero confessed that he had more respect for a philosophy if it were wedded to a decent prose style. He had no reason to be excited over the news that some moth-eaten lecture-notes had turned up by the man whose published dialogues he was already wont to read with pleasure....": Guthrie (n. 36), 63.

[38] Cicero (n. 28), I.viii.33–34.  [39] Cicero (n. 28), I.i.1.  [40] Cicero (n. 28), I.xii.54.
[41] Cicero (n. 28), I.i.2.  [42] Cicero (n. 28), I.xxxiii.144.
[43] Francesco Petrarca, *De sui ipsius et multorum ignorantia*, ed. L. M. Capelli (Paris 1906), III.11.
[44] Francesco Petrarca, *Invectum contra eum qui maledixit Italie*, in Francesco Petrarca, *Invectives*, ed. David March (Cambridge, MA, 2003), 364.
[45] Petrarch (n. 44), X.108.

Valla called himself an "orator" rather than a philosopher or jurist.[46] He doubted that much "practical knowledge" and "political wisdom" could be learned from "any philosophers."[47] When asked to give an oration "In Praise of St. Thomas Aquinas," he said that the knowledge of Aquinas "was for the most part of trifling consequence," since he devoted himself to "the petty reasonings of dialecticians" without seeing that such preoccupations are "obstacles in the way of better kinds of knowledge."[48] Like Petrarch, Valla placed the highest value on studies that would lead men to virtue. Moral philosophy was valuable when it exhorted them to virtue by precept; history was more valuable because it moved them to virtue by example.[49] "Without Latin eloquence," he said, "learning is blind"—especially "in civil law."[50] As Hans Troje has noted, for some of the later humanist jurists, "true wisdom ... consisted more in feeling than in argument" and "its goal was the transformation of men."[51]

The program of the humanist jurists, as it was originally conceived, was therefore a difficult one. They were to remain faithful to the Roman texts, as understood by their authors. They were to construct an art or science of law that could be part of a liberal education, as Cicero had recommended, but on the basis of these texts written by jurists who, Cicero said, had no such goal in mind, and who, indeed, were less interested in transforming men than in giving them legal advice. In doing so, the humanist jurists were to explain law in terms of principles, but by means of principles that were accessible to those with a general education, and not abstract or technical like those of Aristotelian philosophy. Eventually, it became clear that not all elements of this program could be realized.

## ii *MOS GALLICUS*: THE FRENCH HUMANISTS

The humanist program led, in Julian Franklin's words, to "the sixteenth-century revolution in the methodology of law and history."[52] Since most of the jurists who took the new approach were French,[53] it came to be called the "French style," or *mos gallicus*. It was contrasted with the traditional Bartolist approach, which still prevailed in Italy and was known as the *mos italicus*.

One element of the humanist program was the recovery of the original texts of the *Corpus iuris* and their meaning to the jurists that wrote them. This effort, begun in Italy by Valla and Poliziano, and Alciato, was carried on by French jurists, and

---

[46] Valla (n. 6), 286.
[47] Lorenzo Valla, *De rebus a Ferdinando Hispaniarum rege et majoribus ejus gestis*, Proemium in *Opera* (n. 6), 2: 6.
[48] Lorenzo Valla, "In Praise of St. Thomas Aquinas," trans. M. Esther Hanley, in *Renaissance Philosophy*, ed. Leonard A. Kennedy (The Hague, 1973), 17 at 22, 23, 24.
[49] Valla (n. 47), 2: 5–6.
[50] Lorenzo Valla, *Elegantia latinae linguae* III, Praefatio in *Opera* (n. 6), 1: 80.
[51] Troje (n. 20), 120. [52] That is the subtitle of his book: Franklin (n. 23).
[53] Troje (n. 20), 110 at 123.

## De Iure Civile in Artem Redigendo: *The Humanist Ideal*     119

most notably Budé and Cujas. Franklin referred to the French jurists engaged in this task as "the philologists."[54]

As noted earlier, in and of themselves, the philological methods of the humanists were not incompatible with the traditional exegetical methods of the medieval civilians. One source of tension, however, was that the humanists aimed at recapturing the meaning of the legal texts to their authors, while the civilians aimed at applying them to new situations. To some humanists, the interpretations of the civilians were simply wrong. The result, in France, was a change in the way in which law was taught. The new teaching method was consistent with the premises of the humanists: a text should be taught by explaining the meaning of the text in philological context. Although this innovation gave rise to the French style, the innovator was an Italian jurist, Andrea Alciato. As Donald Kelly explained, "[h]e dispensed with the old-fashioned practice of reciting the interminable opinions of the Bartolists and substituted the humanist method of *explication de texte*, which in effect meant returning to the method endorsed by Justinian himself." Justinian had thought that the texts of the *Digest* needed no refined interpretation. For the humanists, once the techniques of philology had reconstructed the text and its meaning in its original context, there was little left to do. They stated the text and paraphrased its meaning in elegant Latin—a practice that earned the French school another name, the school of *elegantia iuris*, "elegant jurisprudence."

As we have seen, another source of tension was that part of the humanist program was to realize the Ciceronian ideal of an art or science in which civil law was explained clearly and systematically. Franklin referred to the humanists who attempted this task as "the systematizers."[55]

By the sixteenth century, it had become clear that it was one matter to recover the original meaning of the texts of the *Corpus iuris*; it was quite another to present them as a clear and systematic whole. As Franklin said, there was a "painful gap" between the "length and complexity" of legal studies and humanist demand for "clarity and ease of comprehension."[56] Many believed that the remedy was to realize Cicero's plan of presenting civil law as an art or science. Few made a sustained effort to do so. As Peter Stein has said, Franciscus Connanus and Hugo Donellus were "[a]mong the few humanists to move from the stage of planning programs to actual rearrangements."[57] And yet their efforts were to show that systematizing Roman law did not lead to the clarity and ease of comprehension one would expect of a Ciceronian *ars*.

While their ideal was Ciceronian, unlike Cicero, neither Connanus nor Donellus disparaged the Roman jurists. Connanus thought that they had achieved Cicero's

---

[54] Franklin (n. 23), 18.     [55] Franklin (n. 23), 27.     [56] Franklin (n. 23), 27.

[57] Peter Stein, *Roman Law in European History* (Cambridge, 1999), 80. *See* Peter Stein, "Donellus and the Origins of Modern Civil Law," in *Mélanges Felix Wubbe*, eds. J. A. Ankum et al. (Fribourg, 1993), 439. Stapelfeldt describes them as the two in France who achieved a systemic reordering of Roman law: K. Stapelfeldt, "Hugo Donellus," in *Deutsche und Europäische Juristen aus neun Jahrhunderten*, eds. Gerd Kleinheyer and Jan Schröder, 4th ed. (Heidelberg, 1996), 112 at 113. On the influence of Cicero's ideal of an *ars* of law on Connanus, *see* Christoph Bergfeld, *Franciscus Connanus* (Cologne, 1968), 66–67.

ideal, although their thought needed to be clarified. He said, in a remarkable passage:

> The ancient jurists made an art or science (*ars*) of law, or a close replica of an art or science, so that all the law would be distributed in genera, each genus divided into so many members, and then each indicated by the force of a definition and by examples. Why this should not be accounted among the arts or as science I do not see at all....[58]

Connanus' claim that the Roman jurists had made civil law into an art or science, which he described in the words of Cicero, was the very proposition that Cicero denied. All that remained to be done, Connanus seemed to think, was to bring order and clarity to what the ancient jurists had already achieved.[59]

Donellus described his objective in words of Cicero: *de iure in artem redigendo*.[60] He quoted Cicero as to how this goal was to be attained: a subject is to be divided into parts, which are to be explained by definitions.[61] He asked:

> What more belongs to art than order, the comprehension and then the arrangement of the matters according to an end, so that each is treated in its proper place, and the result at last is reached that those things that are first by nature are in first place, and those in second place that are second, and so, successively, each of them, situated in its right order, is explained distinctly and without confusion?[62]

Unlike Connanus, Donellus did not think that the Roman jurists themselves had reduced civil law to an art or science. But he did not challenge their work. The Roman law was superb.[63] The problem was that Justinian's compilers had thrown quotations from the jurists together in a helter-skelter fashion without order or system—a charge that had been made by Valla[64] and by Donellus' contemporary François Hotman.[65]

The elaborate multivolume works of Connanus and Donellus influenced later jurists in the same way as a failed experiment in physics. It proved impossible to give a systematic and principled account of Roman law that was faithful to the legal texts, accessible, and free from abstract and technical principles. To see why the enterprise failed, we must pay attention to their work in some detail.

Connanus and Donellus tried to turn civil law into an art or science in different ways. Connanus looked for principles that could explain the Roman texts. If a statement by a Roman jurist was correct, Connanus assumed that there was some reason why it was correct, and he tried to find that reason. Donellus drew a series of

---

[58] Franciscus Connanus, *Commentariorum iuris civilis libri x* (Naples, 1724), I.i.7.
[59] Vincenzo Piano Mortari, "La sistema come ideale umanistico dell'opera di Francesco Connano," in *La storia del diritto nel quadro delle scienze storiche*, ed. Leo S. Olschki (Florence, 1966), 521 at 530.
[60] Hugo Donellus, *Commentariorum de iure civili libri viginti octo* (Florence, 1840–47), I.i.1.
[61] Donellus (n. 60), I.i.xi.    [62] Donellus (n. 60), I.i.13.
[63] "Of the dignity and excellence of the Digest and the Code it is impossible to say enough." The Roman law "has been received by nearly all peoples and in nearly all ages from the time of Justinian to this day that they all use it in all matters in which the laws of their country is not an obstacle": Donellus (n. 60), *Praefatio* viii.
[64] Lorenzo Valla, "*Elegantia latinae linguae* VI.35," in vol. 1 of *Opera omnia*, ed. E. Garin (Torino, 1962), 216.
[65] François Hotman, *Antitribonianus sive dissertatio de studio legum* (Paris, 1603).

distinctions by which general categories were broken down successively into more particular ones to which the Roman texts could be assigned. Unlike Connanus, he was not trying to identify principles that would explain the correctness of the texts. Rather, he was trying to classify them.

Connanus took many of his principles from Aristotle, which was not surprising since, in Connanus' age, Aristotelian philosophy still dominated the universities. He encountered two difficulties. One was that he wanted an account of law that, in Cicero's words, was "magnificent and copious," but yet "accessible." As mentioned earlier, if Connanus were to work out the consequences of his principles systematically as the late scholastics had done, his work, like theirs, would have been a treatise on moral philosophy accessible to specialists in that field. Consequently, he applied his Aristotelian principles loosely, and, indeed, so loosely that they explained little. Another problem was that he was trying to explain Roman law. The late scholastics had been trying to explain the natural law. Unlike Connanus, they did not have to explain every Roman rule. When they could not, they ignored the rule or dismissed it as one of Roman positive law.

Connanus' difficulties can best be shown by example. Like the late scholastics, he identified the distinction between tort and contract with Aristotle's distinction between commutative justice in involuntary and voluntary transactions.[66] Commutative justice requires the party who gains to compensate the party who loses, so that equality may be maintained. Aristotle himself noted that it seemed "inappropriate" to speak of a "gain" when one person wounds another, although it is "called" a gain.[67] As we have seen,[68] Aquinas had said that the person who harmed another had gained in the sense of doing as he willed. That explanation made sense in the context of a moral philosophy in which anyone who wills an action does so in pursuit of an apparent good. But Connanus did not entangle himself in a theory of moral choice. Instead of suggesting an explanation, he said that when one person kills or beats another, "equality" should be restored because "it is said, even if it is not sufficiently appropriate, that in some way he who violates gains, and he who suffers the violation loses...."[69]

In contract, as we have seen, the late scholastics concluded that any contract could be binding in advance of performance, because a party could transfer a right to another party by consent and before delivery. To fail to perform would then violate commutative justice. They dismissed the Roman rules to the contrary as matters of Roman positive law. Connanus did not dismiss the Roman rules, but tried to explain them by means of higher principles. He did not manage to do so systematically. He drew upon Aristotle by distinguishing synallagmatic contracts, or contracts of exchange, from gratuitous contracts. But he gave no systematic account of how this distinction applies to the binding force of contracts. Promises of gifts, he said, are not binding in advance, but his reason was not that the promisee has no claim as a matter of commutative justice. The promisor may have acted "from ostentation"; there would be "danger... if men were bound by

---

[66] Connanus (n. 58), V.i, no. 3.　　[67] Aristotle, *Nicomachean Ethics* V.iv 1132$^a$.
[68] *See* Chapter III, p. 91.　　[69] Connanus (n. 58), V.i, no. 3.

anything whatever that they said or promised"; and it would be "iniquitous" to ask a party to perform who could not do so "without great harm" to himself.[70] Other promises are binding "if a synallagma intervenes." Otherwise, "an obligation does not arise." But Connanus claimed that a synallagma "intervened" only upon delivery.[71] That was why some contracts of exchange, such as barter, were not binding in advance of delivery in Roman law. He did not explain why delivery should matter on Aristotelian principles. Moreover, his explanation of why contracts such as sale and lease were binding before delivery in Roman law was thin. The reason, he said, is that "something else intervenes in its place, as, for example, in sale, the estimation that is made of the thing in money... so that it began, although not [yet] perfected and compensated as though (*quasi*) by delivery."[72]

Like the late scholastics, Connanus said that consent to a contract is vitiated by an error in substance (*substantia*). The term had been used by Ulpian. The late scholastics had taken it in the Aristotelian sense to mean a mistake about the substantial form or essence of an object.[73] A party who made such a mistake literally did not know what he was doing. Connanus apparently thought that the term "substance" would be familiar to his readers, as, indeed, it was in a world in which educated people had a general familiarity with Aristotelian philosophy. But when he described why a contract is void for an error in substance, it is not clear what he could have meant by the term. Sometimes, he applied it loosely, and sometimes he twisted it to explain the Roman texts. An error in substance could be a mistake about a quality that "adds or subtracts" from the "price or goodness of a thing." It could be a mistake absent which a party "would not have bought," in which case it concerns the "cause" (*causa*) that led a person to contract.[74] There is no error in substance in Ulpian's case, in which wine had soured "naturally and spontaneously" to vinegar, because the vinegar is "true wine but acidic" and so "one thing is not deemed to be given for another but for one which is worse than it ought to be." But there is an error in substance if the wine was turned to vinegar by "human industry," because then "one thing is said to be sold for another" because "even if the wine and vinegar are truly of the same substance, nevertheless the use of them is different."[75]

The problem was not that Connanus was a poor philosopher. One problem was that he was not writing for philosophers, and so he did not define his principles precisely and work out their implications. He wanted to explain law by principles that were accessible without abstraction or technical definition. His other problem

---

[70] Connanus (n. 58), V.i, no. 5.

[71] Connanus (n. 58), V.ii, no. 1. His reason was that "[i]t is a matter of natural equity that no one should be obligated by words or by consent alone against his will, but he is able by contrary words and dissent to dissolve it if matters have not changed."

[72] Connanus (n. 58), VII.vi, no. 2. *Stipulatio* was also binding before performance. Connanus' only explanation was that "the bond of *stipulatio* was developed so that there would be some faith and constancy in promises without which society would not exist": Connanus (n. 58), VI.i, no. 1.

[73] *See* Chapter III, p. 94.

[74] Connanus (n. 58), V.vi, no. 4. Connanus made these statements to explain why an error in the name of a field usually would not matter, but sometimes could void a contract.

[75] Connanus (n. 58), VII.vi, no. 5.

was that he was trying to explain all of Roman law by means of higher principles, and not only those features of it that supposedly belonged to natural law. He found himself in difficulty giving a principled explanation of which contracts Roman law would enforce or why it mattered how wine had changed to vinegar.

Donellus had a different idea of how to construct an art or science of civil law. What was needed above all was order. "What have I wished for in this work?" he asked. Nothing great, he answered, "if the question is about the subject matter. If about order and composition, I demand everything."[76]

"What, then," someone will say. "Do you repudiate the civil law compiled by Justinian or, rather, by the most excellent jurist Julian?" The truth is that I scarcely repudiate the civil law passed on to us by the old writers and, as it is now, compiled by order of Justinian. On the contrary, I am striving to the greatest extent to retain it for I endeavor to explain it by my work and, as it were, to bring it more and more into the light.... The authority of law comes from princes, but the true method of its teaching comes from those who are intelligent and skilled.[77]

The art or science that he constructed was a forking tree of distinctions by which general categories were broken down successively into more particular ones, to which Roman texts were then assigned. One problem that he faced was that he wanted to present these distinctions as founded on the authority of the Roman texts. To do so, he often had to twist the meaning of the texts, thereby violating the humanist commitment to seeking the original meaning of a text to its author. Another problem concerned what he sought to achieve by drawing these distinctions. Aristotelian higher principles, whether invoked by the late scholastics or by Connanus, were supposed to explain those matters to which they applied. Donellus' distinctions, as we will see, were not supposed to explain Roman rules by means of higher principles. Rather, they were supposed to sort the elements of Roman law into categories that were neither over- nor under-inclusive, regardless of any principles that might lie behind the sorting. Supposedly, that would realize the Ciceronian idea of law by dividing it into genera or classes. But, in Cicero's words, the distinctions should make the art "copious," but not "inaccessible."[78] For Donellus, it proved impossible to give an account of Roman law without drawing so many distinctions that the account became inaccessible indeed.

To synopsize considerably, Donellus began by claiming that all of private law is based on the maxim of Gaius, *suum cuique tribuere*, "give to each his own."[79] Private law therefore deals with what is one's own, with one's rights to his person and his things, and with the means for protecting these rights by bringing actions. It is therefore divided, as Gaius said, into the law of persons, of things, and of

---

[76] Donellus (n. 60), *Praefatio* I.i.1.
[77] Donellus (n. 60), I.i.12. He had a good deal to say about the deficiencies in the order of the Justinian *Corpus*. "Nothing is more perverse and preposterous" than the order in which the compilers treated obligations: Donellus (n. 60), I.i.8. In treating contracts, "it would seem that the compilers wanted to apply themselves to confusing those of every species": Donellus (n. 60), I.i.8. Even in single titles, one can find "only fragments ... which are better said to have been thrown and stuffed together than organized": Donellus (n. 60), I.i.10.
[78] *De oratore*, I.xli.191.    [79] Donellus (n. 60), II.ii.1.

actions.[80] Rights to one's person include the rights to life, bodily integrity, freedom, and honor (*existimatio*).[81] Rights to one's things include the rights to external things and to the performance of obligations, which are things that a person is owed.[82] Donellus distinguished among external things according to who can own and use them. Things that cannot be owned or used by anyone include *res sacrae*, such as churches, *res religiosae*, such as tombs, and *res sanctae*, such as city gates and walls.[83] Things that cannot be privately owned, but which can be privately used, include common things (those that can be used by everyone, such as air, flowing water, the sea, and the seashore),[84] public things (those that can be used by more than a single people, such as ports, rivers, riverbanks, and riverbeds),[85] and civically owned things (such as theaters, squares, and streets).[86] Finally, there are things that can be privately owned.[87] Donellus distinguished among privately owned things according to how they are acquired. Some physical things are acquired by the *ius gentium*. Other physical things and all incorporeal things are acquired by the *ius civile*.[88] By the *ius gentium*, a thing is sometimes acquired by one's own act in taking possession of it and sometimes by the act of another.[89] When a thing is not previously owned by anyone, as in the case of a wild animal or fish, acquisition by possession takes place when it is captured. When a thing is previously owned by another, acquisition takes place when it has been sold or given as a gift and is then delivered (delivery being necessary in Roman law for ownership to be transferred).[90] Following Justinian's *Institutes*, Donellus classified obligations, or things that are owed us, according to how they arise: by contract (*contractum*), as though by contract (*quasi contractum*), by wrong (*maleficium*), or as though by wrong (*quasi maleficium*).[91] By a series of further distinctions, Donellus moved from this fourfold classification to the particular obligations recognized by Roman law.

One can see from this synopsis how his attempt to systematize led to tension with the Roman texts, which is not surprising, since the jurists who wrote the texts had not been seeking a system. They had explained their concepts by putting particular cases. Donellus took the more general remarks of the Roman jurists and used them to draw his distinctions. For example, according to Justinian's compilers, Gaius had said "the precepts of the law [are] these: live honestly; harm nobody; give everyone his due."[92] Donellus, unlike Gaius, elevated the third into the basic principle of private law. Gaius had distinguished the law of persons, things, and actions.[93] For Gaius, the law of persons concerned matters of personal status such as freeman and slave, or parent and child. For Donellus, it concerned rights to life, bodily integrity, freedom, and dignity. Donellus explained, rather lamely, that Gaius had discussed personal status because the rights that Donellus described

---

[80] Donellus (n. 60), II.ii.2.
[81] Donellus (n. 60), II.viii.3.
[82] Donellus (n. 60), II.viii.1.
[83] Donellus (n. 60), IV.i.5.
[84] Donellus (n. 60), IV.ii.4.
[85] Donellus (n. 60), IV.iii.1.
[86] Donellus (n. 60), IV.iv.1.
[87] Donellus (n. 60), IV.v.1–2. On these distinctions in Roman law, *see* Chapter I, pp. 18–19.
[88] Donellus (n. 60), IV.v.7.
[89] Donellus (n. 60), IV.vii.1.
[90] Donellus (n. 60), IV.vii.2.
[91] Donellus (n. 60), XII.v.2.
[92] I. I.1.3.
[93] I. I.2.12; G. I.8.

could depend upon one's status.⁹⁴ At one point, Donellus admitted that his distinctions among the law of persons, things, and actions was not necessarily that of Gaius. Still, he said, "[e]ither Gaius felt the same way that we have explained, or if he did not feel that way, nevertheless, he expressed himself in the words that we would wish."⁹⁵ He thus deviated from the humanist principle of interpreting words according to their meaning in their original context.

When Donellus could not support his distinctions by reading them into a general text, he read them into texts that made more limited points. To show that Roman law recognized a right to bodily integrity, he cited a text that gave a remedy when a slave was physically beaten.⁹⁶ To show that Roman law protected a right to personal freedom, he cited texts that gave remedies when a person was prevented from fishing in a public place or prevented from pressing his own grapes.⁹⁷ To show that Roman law protected the right to dignity, he cited texts that dealt with specific situations in which one could recover for *iniuria*.⁹⁸ Again, he drifted away from the humanist idea that interpretation should find what a text meant to its author.

Another difficulty concerned the purpose served by his classifications. They rarely elucidated the texts. Often, unless one already knew the texts, one could not understand his classification. He had no qualms about presenting a certain number of subclassifications without explaining why there should be these and no others. He did not explain, for example, why external things that cannot be owned or used by anyone should be classified as *res sacrae*, *res religiosae*, and *res sanctae*, or why external things that a private person can use, but cannot own, should be classified as common, public, or civic. To know what things were *sacrae*, *religiosae*, *sanctae*, common, public, or civic, one would have to look to the texts that mention such things as churches, tombs, city gates, city walls, air, flowing water, the sea, the seashore, ports, rivers, riverbanks, riverbeds, theaters, squares, and streets. Indeed, sometimes one would have to look at the texts simply to understand the meaning of his classifications. For example, contract is said to be "the consent of two or more that one person gives or does something, and is bound to this performance by law."⁹⁹ One would have to know when Roman law made an agreement binding to know whether the agreement is a contract. Similarly, "a quasi contract is an act which is not wrongful by which the one who acts is obligated to another, or the one who does not act is obligated to him, without consent."¹⁰⁰ To determine which nonwrongful acts give rise to such an obligation, one would have to look to the texts.

---

⁹⁴ Donellus (n. 60), II.xi.1.    ⁹⁵ Donellus (n. 60), II.vii.4.
⁹⁶ Donellus (n. 60), XV,.xxv.3, citing D. 47.10.5.pr.
⁹⁷ Donellus (n. 60), XV.xxv.3, citing D. 47.10.3.1; D. 19.1.25.
⁹⁸ Donellus (n. 60), XV.xxv.2, taking issue with a distinction reported by Ulpian between unwelcome physical contract, for example striking a person, affronts to dignity, for example abducting the female attendant with whom an upper-class Roman woman was supposed to be attended, and committing a disgrace, for example by propositioning a woman: D. 47.10.1.
⁹⁹ Donellus (n. 60), XII.vi.3.    ¹⁰⁰ Donellus (n. 60), XV.xiv.1.

This system of classification reflected Donellus' own idea of how an art or science of law should be constructed. In the Aristotelian tradition, higher principles were supposed to explain the things to which they applied. For Donellus, it was enough that a higher category was neither over- nor under-inclusive. Donellus classified *res sacrae*, *res religiosae*, and *res sanctae* as things that cannot be owned or used by anyone because they were the only things in Roman law that fit that description. He classified common, public, and civic things as things that a person cannot own, but can use, because they are the only ones in Roman law that fit that description. Similarly, his category "contract" included all of the contracts recognized by Roman law as binding, and no others. His category "quasi-contract" included all of the nonwrongful acts recognized by Roman law as giving rise to an obligation, and no others. But the categories did not explain why certain things were subject to private ownership or use, certain agreements were binding, and certain nonwrongful acts were actionable. It is like defining the members of a graduating class by enumerating all of the students entitled to graduate. The list is neither over- nor under-inclusive, but it does not explain why they are entitled to graduate, and in order to tell if a student belongs to the graduating class, one must look at the list.

Nevertheless, Donellus' method of classification conformed to Cicero's own statements about how an art or science should be constructed.[101] In *De oratore*, Cicero had his character Crassus say that an *ars* of the civil law should be constructed by "dividing the entire civil law into its genera ... and after that making plain by definition the proper significance of each...."[102] In his *Topica*, Cicero explained that a genus or species was correctly defined if the definition included everything within the category and nothing that lay outside it. Similarly, "[t]he species are the classes into which a genus is divided without omitting anything, as, for example, if we should divide law (*ius*) into statutes (*leges*), mores, and equity."[103] A definition could be made in two ways: by "enumeration" or by "analysis."[104] A definition was made in the first way "when a thing is divided into its members," "for instance," he said, "if one should define the civil law as made up of statutes, decrees of the Senate, judicial decisions, the authority of those expert in law, the edicts of magistrates, mores, and equity":[105] "Definitions by analysis include all the species that come under the genus which is being defined in this way: alienation of a *res mancipi* is either done by *mancipatio* (a formal ceremony) or by *in iure cessio*

---

[101] Some modern scholars have thought that he was inspired not by Aristotle or Cicero, but by the logic of his contemporary Petrus Ramus: Stinzing (n. 17), 148; Heinz Hübner, "Jurisprudenz als Wissenschaft im Zeitalter des Humanismus," in *Festschrift für Karl Larenz zum 70. Geburtstag*, eds. G. Paulus et al. (Munich, 1973), 41 at 54. That is unlikely. As Neal Gilbert noted: "Ramus pronouncements on the subject of method proceed generally according to the method of dichotomies for which the Ramists later became notorious." Distinctions are to be drawn by using a single criterion so that the objects to be classified are always divided in two—those that meet the criterion and those that do not: Gilbert (n. 26), 143. He notes that while "Ramus himself does not seem to have specifically defended this practice," with rare exceptions, he followed it: Gilbert (n. 26), 143. Donellus, however, often does not use a single criterion and will draw threefold distinctions, for example among *res sacrae*, *res religiosae*, and *res sanctae*, or among common, public, and civic property.

[102] Cicero (n. 78), I. xli.191.  [103] Cicero, *Topica* VII.31.
[104] Cicero (n. 103), VII.28.  [105] Cicero (n. 103), VII.28.

(a fictitious suit)."[106] Donellus' distinctions are like these. They are meant to include everything that falls within a certain category and nothing else. But they are not based on a reason or principle that explains why the category should contain these particular elements.

Donellus' method spared him the problems that Connanus encountered in trying to find a principled explanation of all of the elements of Roman law. Nevertheless, if his distinctions did not explain why each category should contain the elements it does, or help one to understand better the elements that it contains, one might wonder what was the point of such an art or science. For Cicero, the point seemed to be clarity and simplicity. The genera would be "few,"[107] yet the *ars* would be "magnificent and copious."[108] At the same time, it would be "neither inaccessible nor mysterious."[109] Indeed, "no *ars* would be easier of attainment."[110] Although Cicero may have thought that one could arrive at such an art by a method of classification like that of Donellus, Donellus' attempt showed that it could not be done, not if one wanted to explain the Roman texts. It took him five volumes and seemingly innumerable distinctions to systematize Roman law. Often, one had to know the Roman texts to understand his classifications, and so one needed an extensive knowledge of Roman law to read his work. The task of constructing an art or science of civil law that would be "magnificent and copious, and yet neither inaccessible nor mysterious," had proved harder than Cicero thought.

Looking backward, modern scholars have found much to praise in the humanist program as it was applied to law. The philological methods developed by humanists such as Valla have proven invaluable. Humanist scholars learned how to distinguish between the meaning of texts to their authors and the application of these texts to problems that their authors did not have distinctly in mind. They read the texts of the *Corpus iuris* in conjunction with nonlegal texts and so placed them in historical context. Nevertheless, there is a gap between the humanists' achievements, as they appear in retrospect, and the goal that they had set for themselves. They had expected to integrate legal studies into the *studia humanitatis*, the education that a man should have if he is to be cultivated and play a part in public life. Their program was to be realized in law, as elsewhere, by recovering the meaning of classical texts. The texts were to be integrated into an art or science of law, such as Cicero had envisioned, based on clear principles and distinctions, and accessible to nonjurists. As it had happened, the better one understood the texts, the more they became an obstacle to such an art or science of law.

---

[106] Cicero (n. 103), VII.28. Cicero said at the beginning of the *Topica* that he was explaining Aristotle's *Topica* I, 1–2, but his explanation is so un-Aristotelian that modern scholars think he must have had some other Greek philosopher in mind: H. M. Hubbell, *Cicero: De inventione De optimo genere oratatorum Topica* (Cambridge, MA, 1949), 377.
[107] Cicero (n. 78), I.xli.185.   [108] Cicero (n. 78), I.xli.191.
[109] Cicero (n. 78), I.xli.191.   [110] Cicero (n. 78), I.xli.185.

# V

## *Ius Naturae et Gentium*
### The Iusnaturalists

The attempt to realize the Ciceronian ideal of an *ars*, an art or science, of law might have ended with the humanist jurists of the sixteenth century. Instead, it was given new life and direction by Hugo Grotius and jurists who followed his example, notably Samuel Pufendorf and Jean Barbeyrac. They wrote about what they called "the law of nature and of nations." Cicero had hoped that the civil law could be reduced to an art or science. They claimed, instead, to have made an art or science of natural law. Historians sometimes refer to them as members of the "natural law school," which can be misleading because the late scholastics also wrote about natural law, as did seventeenth- and eighteenth-century rationalists whose work will be described in a later chapter. We will refer to them as the "iusnaturalists."

Strangely enough, the iusnaturalists pursued the humanist ideal by borrowing from the late scholastics.[1] As noted in an earlier chapter, the principal conclusions of the late scholastics concerning the laws of property, unjust enrichment, tort, and contract, were taken over by Grotius and Pufendorf. So were the principal conclusions of Vitoria on public international law. Like the late scholastics, the iusnaturalists tried to give a systematic presentation of the law and the principles upon which it was based. The late scholastics, however, presented the law as resting on the moral philosophy of Aristotle and Aquinas. The iusnaturalists did not.

Even in an age in which the humanist ideal of learning was avidly pursued, Grotius was a prodigy. He graduated from the University of Leiden at the age of eleven. At the age of fourteen, he completed an edition of the *Satyricon* of the late Roman author Martianus Capella.[2] It was a fantasy about the ascension of Philologia into heaven to be married to Mercury, who symbolized eloquence, accompanied by personifications of the liberal arts. In order to understand the author's comments about the liberal arts, Grotius compared them with classical texts that

---

[1] *See* Thomas Duve, "Kanonisches Recht und die Ausbildung allgemeiner Vertragslehren in der Spanishen Spätscholastik," in *Der Einfluss der Kanonistik auf die Europäische Rechtskultur Bd. 1: Zivil- und Zivilprozessrecht*, eds. Orazio Condorelli, Franck Roumy, and Mathias Schmoeckel (Cologne, 2009), 389 at 390; Robert Feenstra, "L'influence de la scholastique espagnole sur Grotius en droit privé," in vol. 1 of *La seconda scolastica nella formazione del diritto privato modern*, ed. Paulo Grossi (Milan, 1975), 377.

[2] Also known as *De nuptiis Philologiae et Mercurii* or *De septem disciplinis* and not to be confused with the *Satyricon* of Petronius, which concerns the adventures of the narrator, Encolpius, and his boy lover Giton.

dealt with rhetoric, grammar, logic, and so forth. It seemed impossible that a boy could produce such a book. When he was sixteen, he published a translation into Latin verse of a Greek work on astronomy, the *Phaenomena* of Aratus of Soli, including with it the Latin translation made by Cicero. In various places in which lines from Cicero were missing, Grotius added his own, imitating Cicero so well that he was said to have equaled him. The year before, despite his age, he had been chosen to accompany a diplomatic mission to King Henry IV of France. It is said that the king greeted him by announcing to his courtiers: "Here is the miracle of Holland!" Before he returned from France a year later, Grotius had completed a law degree at the University of Orléans.

In 1625, he published the work that changed the study of law, *De iure belli ac pacis libri tres*. He had written it in about a year.[3] It was a huge success, and understandably so. It promised to realize the humanist ideal. Grotius presented law as a series of principles that could be understood by educated people who did not have the specialized training of jurists. He wrote elegant Latin and ornamented his work with references to classical literature. Although Grotius himself was a lawyer of considerable experience, the purpose of the book was not to aid lawyers or judges in the disposition of actual cases. Its purpose, as the humanist ideal required, was to produce a cultivated man suited for public life.[4] "There is nothing more worthy of a gentleman (*homo nobilis*)," Grotius said, "than the study of law."[5] It was particularly important for him to understand the law of war and peace:

Inasmuch, therefore, as I am convinced on the grounds I now have that there is a common law (*ius commune*) among nations that is valid for war and in war, there are many grave reasons why I should undertake to write on the subject. Throughout the Christian world I have seen a lawlessness in warfare that even barbarian races would think shameful. On trifling pretexts, or none at all, men rush to arms, and when once arms are taken up, all respect for law, whether human or divine, is lost, as though by some edict a fury had been let loose to commit every crime.[6]

Pufendorf imitated Grotius in his chief work, *De iure naturae et gentium libri octo*. Barbeyrac translated both of their treatises into French, adding notes of his own. Like Grotius, Barbeyrac intended his work for gentlemen—for "young men who are aiming at political and ecclesiastical careers,"[7] and for "men of letters" who would be able to acquire "all of the knowledge that they need to conduct themselves."[8] Pufendorf, because of a flirtation with rationalism that will be described in a later chapter, seems to have intended his work primarily for other academics.[9]

---

[3] Charles S. Edwards, *Hugo Grotius: The Miracle of Holland—A Study in Political and Legal Thought* (Chicago, IL, 1981), 7.
[4] *See* Stephan Meder, *Rechtsgeschichte Eine Einführung*, 2nd ed. (Cologne, 2005), 243.
[5] *Epistolae ad Gallos* (Leipzig, 1684), clvi.
[6] Hugo Grotius, *De iure bellis ac pacis* (Amsterdam, 1646), *Prolegomena* 28.
[7] Jean Barbeyrac, *Le Droit de la nature et des gens... par le baron de Pufendorf*, 5th ed. (Amsterdam, 1734), *Préface du traducteur* XXXII.
[8] Barbeyrac (n. 7), II.
[9] Although "the natural law is known to all men who have the use of reason," nevertheless only some were "capable of methodically demonstrating its maxims." Their knowledge would trickle down

According to Barbeyrac, however, he had done more than Grotius to state the law in simple principles accessible to every educated person. Grotius had written with "purity and exactness," and "marvelous elegance and facility," but, according to Barbeyrac, he was "too concise": "He assumes matters that demand rather great study so his work is for few beyond the savants, in contrast to that of Pufendorf, which is within the reach of all."[10] They would find Pufendorf's book comprehensible and free from "the subtleties of the bar."[11] Barbeyrac's translations were intended to make their work even more accessible. Speaking of the young men preparing for political and ecclesiastical careers, Barbeyrac acknowledged that "one will perhaps tell me that that they can read [Pufendorf] in Latin and will have no need of my translation. But... an exact knowledge of the most necessary languages is again something which is much neglected...."[12] Now, they could read his book in French.

Although the iusnaturalists shared the humanist ideal of law as an art or science, they broke with the humanist program. Although they tried to realize this ideal by borrowing the conclusions of the late scholastics, they unmoored these conclusions from the Aristotelian and Thomistic philosophical principles that had anchored them.

The humanists had studied the Roman texts in order to reduce the civil law to an art or science. The iusnaturalists sought an art or science of natural law. Grotius said, "Many before me have endeavored to give it the form of an *ars*. None have succeeded." They had failed because they had written about "what came *ex constituto*," from enacted law. They had not separated it from "natural law":

> For the natural law, as it is always the same, can easily be brought together into an *ars*, but those things that are enacted, as they always change, and are different in different places, lie outside of an *ars*, as do other notions of particular things.[13]

"Everyone knows," Pufendorf said:

> ... that most of the material in the books of the Roman law concerns the subject of the law of nature and of nations but there is interspersed with it much that is positive, and of application to the special nature of the Roman state. If the two elements have not been carefully separated, any knowledge of law cannot avoid being confused, unstable and fraught with idle controversies.[14]

Barbeyrac thought that the Roman jurists had failed "to develop and apply, as one should, the principles and rules of natural equity":

> Their definitions and distinctions are in general so far from exact and their style is so obscure that one cannot reasonably persuade oneself that they had precise and distinct ideas of these

---

to others. "The more mediocre spirits can at least comprehend these demonstrations when they are proposed to them, and recognize the truth of them clearly by comparing them to their natural condition": Samuel Pufendorf, *De iure naturae et gentium libri octo* (Amsterdam, 1688), II.ii.13.

[10] Barbeyrac (n. 7), *Préface du traducteur* XXXI.   [11] Barbeyrac (n. 7), XXXII.
[12] Barbeyrac (n. 7), XXXII.   [13] Grotius (n. 6), *Prolegomena* 30.
[14] Pufendorf (n. 9), *Praefatio*.

things and that that had brought greater profundity to the study of their subject. They were the most fertile in fictions and vain subtleties that they transported from civil law to natural law.[15]

What one needed, then, was not *ius civile in artem redigendum*, as Cicero had thought. Instead, one should make an *ars* of the natural law.

The humanists had been committed to the revival of classical sources. For the iusnaturalists, the Roman texts became an obstacle. Ironically, the work of the humanists convinced Grotius that there could not be an *ars* of Roman law. In the preface to his work, he acknowledged his debt to three groups of jurists: to the Roman jurists, to the medieval civilians ("the successors of Irnerius, Accursius, Bartolus, and so many other names...."), and to those "who have combined the study of classical literature with that of law."[16] The jurists of the last group, the humanists, were of limited use for his purposes because they "confine themselves within the limits of Roman law...."[17] Grotius did not doubt that they had faithfully reconstructed Roman law and that the medieval jurists had misunderstood it: "[T]he unfortunate condition of their times [the Middle Ages] was frequently a handicap that prevented their complete understanding of laws." As a result, the medieval jurists were "bad interpreters of the laws laid down." Nevertheless, they were "skillful in tracing out the nature of that which is fair and good," and therefore "often very successful in establishing the basis of law."[18] Paradoxically then, for Grotius, the humanists' clearer understanding of the Roman texts limited the usefulness of their work, while the misunderstandings of the medieval civilians enhanced the value of their own.

In these respects, the work of the iusnaturalists was humanism turned upside down. Barbeyrac's translations were a further break. If gentlemen were unequal to the elegant Latin of Grotius and Pufendorf, the solution was not to teach them better Latin, but to put these works into French. Paradoxically, however, by breaking with the humanist program, the iusnaturalists came closer to realizing the Ciceronian and humanist ideal of an art or science of law that could take its place in the education of a gentleman and prepare him for public life.

In pursuit of the humanist ideal, the iusnaturalists borrowed much from the late scholastics. The late scholastics, however, tried to work out with precision the implications of ideas that they had taken from Aristotle and Aquinas, while the iusnaturalists did not. One reason is that, unlike the late scholastics, they were not writing for those with technical training in Aristotelian philosophy. Grotius, like Cicero and the humanists, wanted an account of law that could be part of a nonspecialized liberal education. As we have seen, there had been a long-standing tension between the pursuit of that ideal and the use of the technical and abstract philosophy of Aristotle.

Another reason is that, in the seventeenth century, Aristotelian philosophy no longer commanded the same respect. The founders of modern critical philosophy

---

[15] Barbeyrac (n. 7), *Préface du traducteur* XXVIII.  [16] Grotius (n. 6), *Prolegomena* 53.
[17] Grotius (n. 6), *Prolegomena* 55.  [18] Grotius (n. 6), *Prolegomena* 54.

were in revolt against it. Others who professed to admire Aristotle still objected to the authority that the Aristotelian tradition had exercised. Grotius was an example. Although some modern scholars such as Richard Tuck believe that Grotius took part in the revolt, for reasons given elsewhere, I disagree.[19] The passages that Tuck cites to show antipathy to Aristotle display, at the most, occasional disagreement.[20] Grotius believed that, "[a]mong philosophers, Aristotle takes the foremost place, whether you take into account his order of treatment, or the subtlety of his distinctions, or the weight of his reasons." The trouble was that "this preeminence" had been "turned into a tyranny," as though the authority of Aristotle could not be questioned.[21]

Pufendorf was influenced by the philosophical revolt, as we will see in a later chapter. Nevertheless, he and Barbeyrac spoke of Aristotle in much the same way as Grotius. The problem was not so much that Aristotle was wrong, but that, for centuries, people had thought that he was invariably right. Pufendorf jeered at those who regarded Aristotelian philosophy as a limit beyond which the human mind could not go.[22] Nevertheless, he cited Aristotle frequently and often with approval. Barbeyrac's primary concern was to show that Aristotle could make mistakes, and, indeed, had made many.[23] His point, however, was that Aristotle had often been wrong, not that his fundamental principles were wrong.

The late scholastics wrote at a time when Aristotle still dominated university curricula.[24] The iusnaturalists regarded Aristotle as one philosopher among many and one whose authority had been exaggerated. They did not try to support their conclusions by drawing explicitly on Aristotelian principles, although many of these conclusions had been borrowed directly or indirectly from the late scholastics. The question then arose: if their conclusions were not based on the principles of Aristotelian philosophy, on what higher principles were they based?

That question was never satisfactorily answered. The iusnaturalists all claimed that their conclusions were based on higher principles. Grotius said that he had arrived at an art or science of law. Pufendorf's first work on natural law, *Elementorum*

---

[19] James Gordley, *The Philosophical Origins of Modern Contract Doctrine* (Oxford, 1991), 22–25.

[20] For example, Tuck characterized a fairly minor disagreement with Aristotle over the meaning of "right" (*ius*) as "an open attack on the basis of Aristotelian ethics": Richard Tuck, *Natural Rights Theories: Their Origin and Development* (New York, 1979), 74. The disagreement, if it can be called one, is that Grotius thought that, as a matter of commutative justice, a person had a "perfect right" to what he was owed—for example to the payment of a debt—although, as matter of distributive justice, he had only a "imperfect right" or "aptitude," which entitled him to be considered for an office, but not necessarily to receive it. Grotius's innovation was to impress into service a scholastic distinction between perfect and imperfect rights with which Aristotle, of course, was unfamiliar. A more serious disagreement, in my view, is his charge that Aristotle was mistaken to consider virtue to be "a mean in passions and actions." It is hard to know what Grotius had in mind from the three short paragraphs that he devoted to the subject, but he seems to have thought of virtue as a rule of right conduct, unlike Aristotle for whom virtue was an acquired ability to conduct oneself rightly: Grotius (n. 6), *Prolegomena* 42.

[21] Grotius (n. 6), *Prolegomena* 42.   [22] Pufendorf (n. 9), I.ii.1.

[23] Gordley (n. 19), 125.

[24] In the mid-seventeenth century, Hobbes complained that his philosophy still dominated "the Philosophy-schooles, through all the Universities of Christendome": Thomas Hobbes, *Leviathan* (Cambridge, MA, 1935), I.i.2.

*Iurisprudentiae universalis libri duo*, was organized into sixteen definitions, two axioms, and five "observations" from which he said that his conclusions logically followed.[25] In his later work, *De naturae et gentium libri octo*, although he imitated the style and manner of presentation of Grotius,[26] he still claimed to be "methodically demonstrating [the] maxims"[27] of natural law by logical deduction from axioms.[28] Barbeyrac said that the proper method is:

... to follow step by step the natural principles of this science and to pursue them to their full extent [and so] deduce, by consequences tied one to the other in a demonstrative manner, all the duties of man in whatever state he is to be found....[29]

Nevertheless, the higher principles from which they supposedly derived their conclusions about property, unjust enrichment, tort, and contract, as well as international law, were far from clear. Some of them seem to be the principles of the late scholastics, but formulated more loosely, and applied ad hoc and unsystematically. Some of them seem vague and unexplained. Sometimes, no higher principle was mentioned.

Like Aristotle, Aquinas, and the late scholastics, the iusnaturalists explained that private property was instituted to remedy the disadvantages that would ensue if property were held in common. They also said that, in a state of necessity, one person was entitled to take the property of another.[30] For the late scholastics, these conclusions were linked to specifically Aristotelian principles about the nature and end of man, which were linked in turn to others concerning what it meant to have a nature and an end. The iusnaturalists believed that man had a nature and an end, but were not concerned with explaining how it was related to the law of property.

Instead, Grotius gave a theological and historical account of how property rights first arose: "At the first creation of the world, God gave to mankind a general dominion over all things of an inferior nature." At first, people lived in "innocence and simplicity," but then art and industry appeared, "lawless passions" arose, "the remoteness of the places to which men had wandered prevented them from bringing their products to a common stock," people wished "to know what others wanted to have for their own so as not to encroach on it; many too may have desired to possess the same thing." So, "before any division had taken place, we must suppose that all agreed that whatever anyone had already taken in his possession he should keep as his own."[31] Grotius incorporated in his story events of the Book of Genesis, such as the stories of Cain and Abel, the Nephilim, the Flood, the tower of Babel, and so forth,[32] to which Barbeyrac added notes from Justin, Horace, and Seneca on the condition of early man, and some comments about Adam and the

---

[25] Samuel Pufendorf, *Elementorum Iurisprudentiae universalis libri duo* (Cambridge, 1672).
[26] Wolfgang Rod, *Geometrischer Geist und Naturrecht* (Munich, 1970), 81.
[27] Pufendorf (n. 9), II.ii.13.     [28] Pufendorf (n. 9), I.ii.1–2.
[29] Barbeyrac (n. 7), *Préface du traducteur* II.
[30] Grotius (n. 6), *libri tres* II.ii.6–7; Pufendorf (n. 9), II.vi.5; Pufendorf (n. 25), I, def. v, n. 15; II, Obs. iv, nn. 6–7; *see* Barbeyrac (n. 7), II.ii.9, n. 1.
[31] Grotius (n. 6), II.ii.2.     [32] Grotius (n. 6), II.ii.1–4.

Fall.³³ Biblical narrative and history had not replaced philosophy, but the philosophical principles that they are meant to ornament or illustrate were unclear.

In the *Elementorum iurisprudentiae universalis*³⁴ and in *De iure naturae et gentium*, Pufendorf explained that private property was instituted to avoid quarrels. In the latter work, he added that it also provides an incentive for labor, cited Aristotle with approval,³⁵ and added that private property also enables an owner to exercise the virtue of liberality by giving things to people who, if everything were held in common, would not need anything to be given to them.³⁶ Strangely enough, however, these arguments, which are supposed to explain the foundation of private property, were made in a paragraph or two in the middle of long chapters filled with other matters to which they are not clearly related. The doctrine of necessity was discussed elsewhere and was no longer clearly linked to the reason why private property should exist. In the *Elementorum iurisprudentiae universalis*, Pufendorf claimed that the principle at stake was that, "on the basis of the law of humanity, any one is bound... to the extent of his power to come to the aid of another person placed in extreme necessity...."³⁷ This obligation resembles one in the Boy Scout oath by which a scout promises "to help other people at all times"; it is imprecise, if it is not meant literally, and frightening, if it is. In contrast, in *De iure naturae et gentium*, Pufendorf leaves in doubt whether the doctrine of necessity might rest, as Grotius had thought, on the limited purposes for which property was established,³⁸ or instead on a duty to be charitable with one's property, which creates a right in a sufficiently deserving beneficiary.³⁹

As we have seen, building on Aristotle and Aquinas, the late scholastics had reached a conclusion that became basic to the modern law of unjust enrichment: a person was obligated not only to return another's property, but also any profit that he had made from its use. The Roman actions for money paid by mistake and for benefits conferred on another without a mandate were merely instances of the general principle. Grotius and Pufendorf agreed.⁴⁰

Again, however, the philosophical principles at stake became less distinct. The late scholastics explained the relationship of the law of tort and of unjust enrichment by the Aristotelian principle that it is a violation of commutative justice for one person to be enriched at another's expense. Following Aquinas, they said that one might violate commutative justice in two distinct ways: by wrongfully depriving another of his property, or by profiting from its use, however innocently.

Grotius explained liability for the use of another's thing in three sentences. According to the first sentence, one must make compensation to the extent that he was spared the use of his own resources. According to the second, the reason for the rule is that "in that degree he is judged to be richer." The third sentence tells an anecdote about the emperor Caligula.⁴¹ The rule and the reason are still, in

---

33 Barbeyrac (n. 7), II.ii.2, nn. 1, 3, 5, 8.   34 Pufendorf (n. 25), I, def. v, n. 15.
35 Pufendorf (n. 9), II.vi.5.   36 Pufendorf (n. 9), IV.iv.7.
37 He states the principle in Pufendorf (n. 25), II, Obs. vi, n. 6, and applies it at II, Obs. vi, n. 7.
38 *See* Pufendorf (n. 9), II.vi.5; IV.iv.5.   39 *See* Pufendorf (n. 9), II.vi.6.
40 Grotius (n. 6), II.x.5; Pufendorf (n. 9), IV.xiii.6, 9.   41 Grotius (n. 6), II.x.5.

abbreviated form, those of the late scholastics. What is missing is an account of the basis in commutative justice, or some other higher principle, of why one should not get richer at another's expense and whether the same principle explains why one must pay compensation for harming another's props.

According to Pufendorf, the rule as to the use of another's thing was correctly stated by Grotius. But Pufendorf severed the link between the rule and the principle that one person should not be enriched at another's expense. The reason was not that he rejected the idea of commutative justice. Elsewhere, he described it with seeming approval.[42] Nevertheless, he said that the reason why one must pay for benefits derived from the use of another's thing is not to maintain "equality, so that ... insofar as another profits from what is mine, he has more while I have less...."; the reason instead is that the "thing.... still belongs to me, as does also whatever comes of it."[43] Pufendorf does not explain why, if the principle of commutative justice is valid, the reason given by Grotius is wrong. He does not explain why, if his own reason is correct, unjust enrichment is an independent ground for liability. It would seem that the law of unjust enrichment would be absorbed by the law of property. The same can be said of Barbeyrac's explanation. He thought that one who had profited by possessing another's goods in good faith need not disgorge the profit because the good-faith possessor has the same rights as the owner.[44]

As we have seen, building on Aristotle and Aquinas, the late scholastics had concluded that recovery in tort was based on the principle that one who harmed another through his own fault owed compensation, although Molina thought that there were some activities so dangerous that one is liable without fault because one should not undertake them unless one was willing to pay for any harm that they caused. The distinction between the Roman actions was a matter of Roman positive law. Grotius, Pufendorf, and Barbeyrac agreed,[45] although Pufendorf, like Molina, thought that one should sometimes be liable without fault, since, as he had profited from an activity, he should pay its cost.[46]

Again, however, the philosophical principle underlying this conclusion became obscure. For the late scholastics, the principle was commutative justice. As Aristotle had said, in involuntary transactions, when a person harmed another, commutative justice required that he make compensation. As Aquinas had said, the person through whose fault he was harmed had gained in the sense that he had fulfilled his own objectives at the other's expense.

Grotius simply said that "a fault by the law of nature creates an obligation to repair the damage...." A fault was "an act or omission in violation of the duties required of all men...."; "By damage ... is meant every diminution, when a man has less than belongs to him." That which belongs to him is his "life ... body, limbs,

---

[42] Grotius (n. 6), I.vii.12.    [43] Pufendorf (n. 9), IV.xiii.6.
[44] Jean Barbeyrac, *Le Droit de la guerre et de la paix de Hugues Grotius* (Amsterdam, 1729), II.x.5, n. 1; Barbeyrac (n. 7), IV.xiii.6, n. 1; IV.xiii.8, n. 2.
[45] Grotius (n. 6), *libri tres*, II.xvii.1–2; Pufendorf (n. 25), II, Obs. iv, no. 30; Pufendorf (n. 9), III.i.2, III.i.3; III.i.6; Barbeyrac (n. 7), III.i.2, n. 1; III.i.3, n. 1; III.i.6, n. 4.
[46] Pufendorf (n. 9), III.i.6.

reputation and actions."[47] He did not explain why fault should matter or identify any larger principle on which this obligation rests.

Pufendorf gave a muddled account of what that principle might be. In the *Elementorum iurisprudentiae universalis*, he said that the reason why "a man [must] make good the damage he has caused to another person by his fault" is that "I should be in an inferior status if the malice or folly of another person could bring it about that I am compelled against my will to go without my property gratis."[48] He thus rested tort law on a principle that he did not seek to clarify: that no one should put another person in an inferior status. In *De iure naturae et gentium*, he did not mention that principle. He said that, by the law of nature, there are two great duties: "I. No one should hurt another; and II. If he has caused another a loss, he should make it good." The basis for the first duty is that "without it society could not exist." Indeed, "we desire nothing more than this from most of mankind.... But how can I live at peace with him who does me an injury, since nature has bred into each man so tender a love for himself...?"[49] The basis of the second duty is that:

[I]t is surely a vain thing to have given orders that a person receive no hurt if, when such hurt befalls him, he must accept the hurt at his own cost, while the man who offered him the hurt may enjoy the fruit of his injury in peace without making restitution. For men are so depraved that they will never refrain from hurting each other unless they are forced to make restitution....[50]

Pufendorf does not explain why, if the object is to prevent one person from harming another and enjoying whatever benefits he gains by doing so, the defendant must pay the amount that will compensate the plaintiff for the harm that he suffered. Indeed, if Pufendorf were correct, it would seem that the law of tort would be absorbed by criminal law.

In discussing contract, the late scholastics identified two ways in which consent might be flawed. A person might have made an error in substance, in which case he did not consent because he did not understand the nature of what he was doing. Alternatively, he might have consented, but he would not have done so had he envisioned circumstances that later arose—that is, he consented to be bound, but not under these circumstances.

Although their discussion owed much to the late scholastics, Grotius and Pufendorf lost track of this distinction. Grotius thought that the problem of mistake could be solved in the same way as that of changed circumstances: "[I]f a promise is founded on the presumption of some fact that is really otherwise, by nature, the promise has no force because the promisor does not consent except upon a certain condition..."[51] Grotius does not discuss the possibility that the promisor might be so mistaken that he did not consent at all.

Pufendorf, like Grotius, said that "a promise... will have no force" if it is "based on the presumption of some fact" and if the promisor "based and conditioned [his]

[47] Grotius (n. 6), II.xvii.1–2.   [48] Pufendorf (n. 25), II, Obs. iv, no. 30.
[49] Pufendorf (n. 9), III.i.1.   [50] Pufendorf (n. 9), III.i.2.   [51] Grotius (n. 6), II.xi.6.

consent entirely upon that fact," although he claimed, in that event, that "[c]onsent... is entirely nullified by error."[52] He said that an "error in essentials" was an instance of consent conditioned upon some fact, adding that the "essentials" included not only those things that enter into the "physical essence," but also "those qualities which the maker of the pact has especially before his eyes."[53] It is not clear whether he meant to distinguish consent given conditionally from the absence of consent.

Barbeyrac was even less clear. He made the surprising statement that, on Aristotelian principles, the effect of an error would depend on the sorrow that a person felt afterward.[54] Rejecting that idea, he said that, to void a contract, an error had to be "efficacious" rather than "accidental."[55] He did not explain why some errors were "efficacious." According to one Roman text, consent to a sale was void if the buyer was in error as to the sex of a slave, but not if he was in error as to whether a female slave was a virgin.[56] According to Barbeyrac, the reason why the one error was "efficacious" and the other was not is that it is easier to tell the sex of a slave from outward appearance than whether a slave is a virgin.[57]

In discussing whether a contract is binding upon consent, the late scholastics rejected the position of Cajetan, who claimed that that there was no reason for a promise to be binding before the promisee had changed his position. They concluded, that, in principle and if the parties so intended, all contracts should be binding upon consent. Grotius, Pufendorf, and Barbeyrac agreed.[58]

Cajetan and the late scholastics had been considering the implications of the principle of commutative justice that no one should be enriched at another's expense. Cajetan's argument was that the promisee was no poorer if the promise was broken unless he had changed his position on account of it. Molina and Lessius answered that the promisor could, if he wished, give the promise a right to claim performance, and that if he did so, the promisee would be poorer if the promise was broken, since he would have been deprived of this right.

Grotius used Molina's argument. "Why," he asked, "may there not be transferred a right *in personam* either that ownership be transferred or that something be done?"[59] Nevertheless, he did not use it to explain when it would be unjust to break a promise. He used it to attack Connanus' position, which was, as we have seen, that it would be rash to make a promise that is binding upon consent or to trust one who does, although it is not clear what the argument has to do with Connanus' position.

---

[52] Pufendorf (n. 9), III.vi.6. Similarly, in Pufendorf (n. 25), I, def. xii, no. 19, he said that "if consent is founded on a presumption as to [some] matter, and if the matter turns out to be otherwise, there was no consent at all."
[53] Pufendorf (n. 9), III.vi.7. He made a similar statement in Pufendorf (n. 25), I, def. xii, no. 19.
[54] Barbeyrac (n. 7), I.iii.10, n. 2.   [55] Barbeyrac (n. 7), II.vi.7, n. 4.
[56] D. 18.1.11.1.   [57] Barbeyrac (n. 7), II.vi.7, n. 5.
[58] Grotius (n. 6), *libri tres* II.xi.1.3–4; Pufendorf (n. 9), *libri octo* III.v.5–7; Barbeyrac (n. 44), II.xi.1, n. 2; Barbeyrac (n. 7), III.v.9, n. 10.
[59] Grotius (n. 6), II.xi.1.3. So did Barbeyrac: "[I]f a purely gratuitous promise can confer a true right, then the one to whom the promise was made has certainly lost a right that he had acquired": Barbeyrac (n. 7), III.v.10, n. 10. Like Grotius, he did so without discussing commutative justice.

In *De iure naturae et gentium*, Pufendorf, like Grotius, attacked the position of Connanus, not that of Cajetan. His arguments were more diffuse: "Connanus's position would destroy all possibility of kindness and liberality...";[60] "why should I not love and trust" one who promises a gift?[61] "[T]he obligation to keep promises should not be taken from the relations of men just because some few men of muddled wits...would ruin themselves...by making too many promises."[62] All that seems to be clear is that Pufendorf, like Grotius, believed that promises were binding upon consent. Nevertheless, in the *Elementorum iurisprudentiae universalis*, he muddied that conclusion.[63]

Grotius' account of international law, when compared with that of Vitoria, shows a similar propensity to borrow conclusions while blurring the higher principles on which they had been based. Grotius endorsed the same basic propositions as Vitoria. There are "three justifiable causes for war: defense, recovery of property and punishment...";[64] "[P]ublic war should not be waged save by the sovereign ruler of each state."[65] In the conduct of war, "we have a right to do whatever is necessary to maintaining our right."[66] He developed these propositions with the care of Vitoria and in greater detail, thus earning his place with Vitoria as one of the founders of international law.

For Vitoria, because a human being is a political and social animal by his very nature he should live in a society that enables him to live the life of a human being.[67] The state was a "perfect whole" in the sense of a community from which "nothing was wanting" that was necessary to promote the common good.[68] Therefore "a state has the right not only to defend itself but also to avenge itself and its subjects and to redress wrongs."[69] One can find propositions like these in Grotius, but they are scattered, rather than presented systematically, and called into service as needed to support a point under discussion. Interspersed with them are other propositions that might or might not be reconcilable with them, but no effort is made to explain how these propositions can be reconciled. We are told that law exists because "man [has] a desire for society, that is...for life in a community...that is peaceful and organized to suit the measure of his intelligence with persons of his own kind..."[70] Yet we are also told that "the end of society is...to preserve to everyone his own, [a] rule [which] would hold even if what we now call private property had not been introduced."[71] We are

---

[60] Pufendorf (n. 9), III.v.9.  [61] Pufendorf (n. 9), III.v.9.
[62] Pufendorf (n. 9), III.v.10.
[63] Pufendorf (n. 25), I, def. xii, no. 7. He said that, in the case of a gratuitous promise: "I am able to demand the fulfillment of [a man's] promise, and in that way I have a right by the law of nature alone, at least where it is clear that the man who made the promise is fraudulently and insolently trying to slip out of it, and I have based my calculations upon that promise and would suffer some loss in consequence." It is not clear whether he is taking the position of Molina, Lessius, and Grotius, or that of Cajetan.
[64] Grotius (n. 6), II.i.2.   [65] Grotius (n. 6), I.iii.5.   [66] Grotius (n. 6), III.1.2.
[67] Franciscus de Vitoria, vol. 2 of *Relecciones Teológicas del Maestro Fray Francisco de Vitoria*, ed. Luis Alonso Getino (Madrid, 1934), *Relectio de potestate civili*, nos. 4–5.
[68] Vitoria, "*Relectio posterior de Indis, sive de iure belli Hispaniorum in Barbaros*," no. 7, in Vitoria (n. 67).
[69] Vitoria (n. 67), no. 4.   [70] Grotius (n. 6), *Prolegomena* 6.   [71] Grotius (n. 6), I.ii.1.

Ius Naturae et Gentium: *The Iusnaturalists* 139

told that the state "is a perfect association of men."[72] Yet we are also told that "it is not universally true that all government was created for the benefit of the governed..."[73] We are told that "[t]he public authorities [alone] have not only the right of defense but of punishment as well."[74] But we are not told why.

The reason why the higher principles underlying private and public international law became obscure in the work of the iusnaturalists was not that they had tried and failed to clarify them philosophically. Grotius is regarded as a genius. Pufendorf and Barbeyrac were as intelligent as the outstanding jurists of any age. But their project was not that of the late scholastics. The late scholastics were trying to give a rigorous and consistent philosophical account of law. Grotius and Barbeyrac wanted a simple account. While it is less clear what Pufendorf wanted, according to Barbeyrac, he achieved an even simpler account than Grotius.

The price that the late scholastics paid for their rigor was that they could write only for those with the capacity and training to do formal philosophy. Moreover, since they based their work on the philosophical tradition of Aristotle and Aquinas, it was appreciated only as long as that tradition was in favor. Grotius, Pufendorf, and Barbeyrac claimed to have emancipated themselves from the authority of Aristotle. Even though they had taken some of their principles from the late scholastics, they had formulated them more simply. The price that they paid for simplicity was that the meaning of these principles became obscure.

Simplicity, however, was of the essence of the *ars* that Cicero desired and that Grotius thought he had achieved. Law was to be set forth as a series of simple principles that could form part of the liberal education of the nonspecialist. It is no wonder that Grotius believed himself to be the first to have achieved such an art or science of law, and that, in Barbeyrac's opinion, Grotius "first broke the ice" and "raised the science of morality from the dead."[75] No one before him had explained law in a series of simply formulated principles shorn of the complexities of formal philosophy, on the one hand, and of Roman law, on the other. Indeed, if these seemingly simple principles truly constituted an art or science, then, Grotius thought, the complexities were unnecessary. He believed that the principles of natural law were simple. Concern for these complexities could muddy the otherwise pristine waters. According to Pufendorf, the late scholastics were engaged in "idle and trivial logic-chopping," and had "devote[d] futile labor to utter trifles."[76] According to Barbeyrac, as noted earlier, the Roman jurists were "fertile in fictions and vain subtleties." Their thinking was "so far from exact and their style...so obscure that one cannot reasonably persuade oneself that they had precise and distinct ideas of these things."[77]

If, on the other hand, for law to be an art or science, its principles must have a precise meaning and a clear relationship to higher principles, then, as we have seen, the iusnaturalists did not arrive at an art or science of law. It may not be possible in law, any more than it is in mathematics, economics, physics, or philosophy, to

---

[72] Grotius (n. 6), I.iii.7.  [73] Grotius (n. 6), I.iii.8.  [74] Grotius (n. 6), II.i.16.
[75] Barbeyrac (n. 7), *Préface du traducteur* XXIX.  [76] Pufendorf (n. 9), *Praefatio*.
[77] Barbeyrac (n. 7), *Préface du traducteur* XXVIII.

formulate principles that are simple, in the sense that they can be understood by the nonspecialist, and precise, in the sense that they have the definite meaning that one would expect of scientific or philosophic principles. Nevertheless, the achievement of the iusnaturalists was a great one in its own right. Grotius, like Cicero, wished to bring an understanding of law within the reach of anyone with a liberal education. A liberal education enabled a person to understand the world in which he lived and to participate fruitfully in public life. To Grotius, as to Cicero, it seemed bizarre to think that a liberal education would not include a knowledge of law. The iusnaturalists brought law within the grasp of nonspecialists even if they did not do so with the exactness that a specialist would expect.

At that task, they succeeded. Their books were widely read by educated men and became staples of university curricula throughout Europe. Like Cicero, Grotius thought that a knowledge of law should prepare men for public life. To judge by the foundation of the American Republic, very likely it did. In America, two books that a well-educated gentleman was likely to have in his library were Grotius and Pufendorf in Latin or in Barbeyrac's translation. In comparison, even the works of Locke were a rarity. Gary Wills had noted how comparatively few copies there were in colonial libraries of Locke's *Two Treatises on Government* and how little evidence there is of its influence on the founders.[78] He quotes John Dunn: "There is no evidence that the Two Treatises figured in the set curriculum of any American college before the Revolution...It never held the unimpeachable authority of works of Grotius or Pufendorf."[79] The founders drew their knowledge of the larger principles of law from Grotius and Pufendorf, and with it their confidence that law was a subject within the powers of gentlemen like themselves and not the specialty of jurists.

---

[78] Gary Wills, *Inventing America: Jefferson's Declaration of Independence* (New York, 1978), 169–74.
[79] John Dunn, "The Politics of Locke in England and America in the Eighteenth Century," in *John Locke: Problems and Perspectives*, ed. J. W. Yolton (Cambridge, 1969), quoted in Wills (n. 78), 170.

# VI

## *Droit Civil Français*
### The French Alternative

## i *DROIT CIVIL SELON L'ORDRE NATUREL*

The iusnaturalists were not trying to change the way in which jurists were educated. They brought the law within the reach of educated nonspecialists. Paradoxically, in France, their work transformed the education of jurists. The change was brought about principally by Jean Domat and Robert Pothier.

Unlike Grotius, they were writing not for liberally educated gentlemen, but for legal professionals, although Domat hoped that his book would be of use not only to those "charged with the administration of justice," but also to churchman in resolving "questions of conscience" and to "individuals" in guiding "their own conduct" and "avoid[ing] wrongful lawsuits." Most of all, he wished to make it "easy to learn the laws solidly and in little time, and the study, being easy, will be agreeable." At present, he complained, the study of law "is so difficult and thorny" that "among those whose profession obliges them to know [it] many are ignorant, or only become adept after a long and painful study." The solution, for Domat and Pothier, was to give a clear and orderly account of law. They made the study of it all the more agreeable by writing in French. The reason Domat gave was not, like Barbeyrac, the difficulty of reading Latin. Instead, it was the superiority of French, which "today is in a state of perfection that equals and even surpasses the ancient languages in many ways."[1]

Like the iusnaturalists, Domat believed that a clear and orderly account of law could be given because law was a "science" that could be presented in a series of simple principles. He described this science much as they did, and indeed much as Cicero had done. "The plan I propose for this book is therefore to put the civil law in order, to divide each subject into its parts, and to present in each part the details of its definitions, its principles and its rules...." Unlike the iusnaturalists, Domat was writing about Roman law. Indeed, he claimed to be treating Roman law comprehensively: "[I]t is not the making of an abridgment that is proposed here... but the effort is made to include all the detail of the material that is dealt with."

---

[1] Jean Domat, *Les Loix Civiles dans leur ordre naturel* (Paris, 1771). Except as otherwise noted, the quotations here and in the next eight paragraphs are from the short preface to this work.

Moreover, he claimed to have been faithful to the Roman texts. He "ha[d] not failed to preserve an exact fidelity, so as not to turn any text from its meaning, and at no time to proceed without authority...." The reason, he said, was that although "the texts of the laws have the character of the truth from the natural equity that inspires them," nevertheless they also have "authority."

His goal, then, was a science of civil law based on simple principles and faithful as well to the Roman texts. Given what we have seen of the work of the French humanists, one might wonder how this goal could be achieved. The sixteenth-century French humanists sought a science of civil law, but, as we have seen, the texts were a continual obstacle. The iusnaturalists gave an account of law in terms of simply formulated principles, but they were writing about natural, rather than civil, law. Yet Domat succeeded in giving an account of Roman law that was clear and reasonably short, while remaining sufficiently close to the Roman texts that his book could be used in law schools and by judges.

One reason for his success was that, unlike the humanists and, for that matter, unlike the medieval civilians, Domat could dismiss some Roman texts entirely, while still claiming to give a comprehensive and accurate account of the Roman texts in force. In the opinion of French jurists, France had never belonged to the Holy Roman Empire. Roman law had authority in France only insofar as it had been received as French law. As Domat noted, there were "two different and even conflicting" views as to how much had been received:

On the one hand, as [the Roman texts] contain natural law and written reason, they are cited before courts, they are taught publicly, and the study of them is the basis on which degrees are given and those who wish to practice law are examined.

On the other hand, because texts are sometimes "contrary to our laws and customs in France [there] are just causes why they do not have a fixed and absolute authority in France." Consequently, jurists commonly fell into one of two errors. Because of the prestige of the texts, "many use them without discernment and take for principles either subtleties which do not belong to our usage or rules that are badly understood." Because the authority of the texts was not absolute:

...others err by regarding these books as having only the authority of custom and ordinance, rejecting often the best rules, and not acknowledging the authority of natural law because they only regard as laws those which have been promulgated and registered as law.

The correct approach was to adhere faithfully to those Roman texts that had been received into French usage. According to Domat, for the most part, those texts coincided with natural law. Certainly, some Roman rules were "arbitrary" in the sense that they governed matters that the natural law did not "precisely" determine. Examples are the law fixing the age of majority or the period of time necessary to gain title to property by prescription; "But these arbitrary rules are very few in number in the civil laws, and, of all the Roman law that belongs to our usage, nearly all pertains to natural law and very little consists of arbitrary laws." In writing about Roman law, then, Domat was in a position like that of a late scholastic writing about natural law. If a text conflicted with natural law, Domat might dismiss it as not part of the law of France, or he might interpret it to correspond to what he regarded as natural law and written reason.[2]

Another reason for Domat's success was that he had a different idea than the humanists of what it meant "to preserve an exact fidelity" to the Roman texts. As we have seen, in the humanist tradition, a faithful interpretation was one that recovered the meaning of the text in its original context. Domat's idea of correct interpretation was more like that of the medieval civilians. Like them, he would sometimes generalize a text that dealt with one situation so that it could be applied to a new one. He noted that "[a]mong all the rules [of Roman law] ... most are encased in particular facts without the rules appearing." He interpreted these texts by moving from a particular case to a more general rule. At other times, he would limit the scope of a text framed in general terms by distinguishing situations to which it would and would not apply. Thus "[o]ther [rules] are separated from the exceptions necessary to limit their sense which is too vague and extended."[3] These methods gave Domat a greater freedom than the humanists to accommodate the texts to simple principles by extending the meaning of some texts and limiting that of others. Yet, by his own standards, he was faithful to the texts.

Still another reason for Domat's success was that he had a different idea of what a science of law entailed than the late scholastics or the iusnaturalists. They thought that the lower-level principles of a science were supposed to be derived from the higher-level principles. So did the rationalists, whose work will be discussed in a later chapter. Some modern scholars have thought that Domat's principles were like those of the rationalists.[4] But Domat did not try to derive lower-level principles from higher ones. As we have seen, neither did Donellus, who tried to classify the Roman texts into categories that were neither under- nor over-inclusive. But Domat's principles were not like those of Donellus. To Domat, principles were important for pedagogical reasons. If Roman law could be learned through principles rather than through the texts, it would be "easy to learn the laws solidly and in little time." His aim was "brevity by cutting out the useless and superfluous, and clarity by the simple effect of the arrangement." Because he aimed at brevity, he had no use for a text that could not be summarized by a principle. Because he aimed at clarity, he had no use for a principle that was hard to understand. His rule was "never [to present] anything that is not clear in itself or that is not preceded by that which is necessary to understand it." Some principles had to be introduced first not because those introduced later could be derived from them, but because those introduced later would then be easier to understand.

Pothier followed Domat's example. His account of Roman law was also written in French for the use of legal professionals. Like Domat, he stated the law, so far as

---

[2] See H. Nitschke, "Jean Domat," in *Deutsche und europäische Juristen aus neun Jahrhunderten*, eds. Gerd Kelinheyer and Jan Schröder, 4th ed. (Heideberg, 1996), 108 at 109.

[3] Similarly, "it happens that the meaning of a law, evident as it seems from its terms, would lead to false consequences and to decisions that would be unjust if it were applied without distinction to everything that seems to be included in its expression": Domat (n. 1), liv. I, tit. i, sec. 1.

[4] Nitschke (n. 2), 110.

he could, in clear simple propositions, as the iusnaturalists had tried to do, although unlike them, he did not claim that the lower-level propositions were derived from the higher-level ones. Like Domat, he often extended or limited his interpretation of the texts beyond their express meaning in a way that might have been congenial to a medieval civilian, but offensive to a humanist. Like Domat, and unlike the medieval civilians, he ignored texts that he did not regard as part of French usage. Because of these features of their method, Domat and Pothier could give a clear and simple presentation of Roman law.

Nevertheless, they sought clarity in different ways. Domat held firmly to his program: he had no use for a text unless it could be brought under a principle, and no use for a principle "that is not clear in itself or that is not preceded by that which is necessary to understand it." Pothier was more relaxed. He would mention cases put by the Roman jurists because they illustrated a point that he was making. He would mention principles because he thought that they were interesting and important without trying to explain them precisely or tie them closely to a point of Roman law.

One can see the difference in approach in the Roman texts that they chose to disregard. As we have seen, the Roman jurists had explained negligence by putting one case after another. Pothier neglected nearly all of them.[5] Apparently, he thought the matter was clear enough without the need for examples. He simply paraphrased Grotius: a person was liable for an act by which "he causes damage to another through intent or malice" or "without malice but by inexcusable imprudence."[6] Domat did his best to subsume as many of the Roman cases as he could under separate principles. For example, the case of the man who prunes branches over a public street and that of the man who digs a bear pit in a public place appear under a rule that states: "Those who do works and operations which may cause harm to other persons are liable if they do not use the necessary precautions to prevent it."[7] The unskillful doctor and the carter who loaded stones improperly appear under a rule that states: "One is liable for ignorance of what one ought to know," such as "an artisan for not knowing what belongs to his profession."[8] The man who fell asleep after stoking a furnace and the man who burned stubble on a windy day were liable because they made "[f]ires which occur nearly always through fault."[9]

As we have seen, the Roman jurists put cases to explain the mistakes that would vitiate consent to a sale. Consent was absent when there was an error as to whether one was selling, an error in price, an error as to which field was to be bought and sold, or an error as to whether an object was gold or copper. Neither Domat nor Pothier had much success at formulating a general principle, let alone one that would fit all of these cases. Domat, finding himself unable to do so,

---

[5] Robert Pothier, *Traité des obligations*, §§ 116–22, in vol. 1 of *Oeuvres de Pothier*, ed. M. Siffrein nouv. ed. (1821), 1.

[6] Pothier (n. 5), §§ 116, 118.   [7] Domat (n. 1), liv. II, tit. viii, sec. 4, § 4.

[8] Domat (n. 1), liv. II, tit. viii, sec. 4, § 5.   [9] Domat (n. 1), liv. II, tit. viii, sec. 4, § 6.

disregarded the cases.[10] Pothier, finding that the best way in which to explain the effect of mistake was to give particular examples, described all of these situations, sometimes modernizing the facts.[11]

Either approach entailed a change in the study of Roman law. Hitherto, Roman law had been learned by studying the texts. Now, it was to be learned by reading about principles that, for the most part, were not mentioned in the texts, although Domat claimed to have subsumed the texts under his principles and Pothier used the texts selectively to illustrate the principles. Neither Domat nor Pothier thought that their work was a substitute for reading the Roman texts. Each of them tried to make the original texts more accessible. Domat published a collection of his favorite texts for use in law schools and in courts.[12] Pothier published a rearrangement of the Roman texts.[13] Nevertheless, the object of their treatises was to make the study of Roman law less difficult because one could understand it without reading the texts. The advantage sought and gained, as Domat said, was that the study of law became more "easy... and, being easy,... agreeable." The price paid for this advantage was that the student learned Roman law as described by Domat and Pothier, not as presented by the Roman jurists.

The work of Domat and Pothier led away not only from the Roman texts, but also from a principled explanation of law as the late scholastics and iusnaturalists had conceived it. Here again, in the search for ease of exposition, Domat and Pothier went different ways. Domat required that his principles be clear. The order in which he presented them was important not because the lower-level principles were derived from the higher-level ones, but because some principles were easier to understand when others were presented first. Consequently, although the doctrinal structure of Domat's work is like that of the late scholastics and iusnaturalists, many of their principles do not appear in his work or are marginalized. Their principles often reappear in the work of Pothier, albeit without much explanation of their meaning or their significance. For Pothier, a principle was worthy of mention if it seemed interesting and important. Anyone seeking a further acquaintance with it could read Grotius, Pufendorf, and Barbeyrac, whose works he cited continually.

Again, the advantage gained was ease of exposition. The price paid for this advantage was not to attempt a principled explanation of law as the late scholastics and iusnaturalists conceived it. In a principled explanation, the less basic principles would depend upon more basic ones. Domat's principles were useful pedagogically, but not in explaining why the law should be as it is. Sometimes, they were merely classificatory, like those of Donellus. They assigned Roman rules to a category, but analyzing the category would not help in understanding the Roman rules. Sometimes, he could not identify a clear principle and made do with a muddy one. Pothier reintroduced some of the principles of the iusnaturalists. But he mentioned them ad hoc and without much explanation of what they meant. There are limits to what an unexplained principle can be expected to explain.

---

[10] Domat (n. 1), liv. I, tit. i, sec. 5, § 10.  [11] Pothier (n. 5), §§ 17–20.
[12] Jean Domat, *Legum delectus, ex libris Digestorum et Codicis ad usum scholae et fori* (Paris, 1771).
[13] Robert Pothier, *Pandectae Justinianeae in novum ordinem digestae* (Paris, 1748–52).

For example, in discussing property, the iusnaturalists took from the late scholastics an account of the origins and purposes of property. Domat did not discuss the origin of private property;[14] Pothier presented a loose version of the account of the iusnaturalists.[15] Neither of them discussed the doctrine of necessity.

The late scholastics and iusnaturalists had reached a conclusion basic to the law of unjust enrichment: a person was obligated to return not only another's property, but also any profit that he had made from its use. Domat did not mention either this principle or the category of unjust enrichment. He merely discussed the two Roman actions in which one party recovered when the other was enriched: when money had been paid by mistake, and when benefits had been conferred on another without his authorization. He classed them, along with "obligations that arise by accident," as "obligations that arise without an agreement."[16] Pothier assigned both Roman actions to a general category: "quasi-contract." He hinted at the principle underlying them. The actions are based on "natural equity"[17]—an expression that he used elsewhere to describe the imbalance that results from an unjust price.[18] As before, however, he mentioned the principle without exploring its implications or discussing whether it extends beyond these two actions.

In tort, the late scholastics and iusnaturalists had formulated the principle that a person owes compensation for harm that he causes by fault, whether intentionally or negligently. Domat[19] and Pothier[20] agreed that one who was at fault should be liable. As we have seen, Grotius and Pufendorf were less clear than the late scholastics about a larger principle on which this principle rests. Domat and Pothier did not identify one. Pothier merely described the obligation to make compensation for harm caused intentionally as "delict," and for harm caused negligently as "quasi-delict."[21] Domat did not even classify such cases as instances of liability in tort: they were one more instance of "obligations that arise without agreement."[22]

Molina and Pufendorf had suggested that there were exceptional cases in which a person could be liable without fault.[23] Pothier and Domat were unclear as to whether there were such exceptions. According to Pothier, although parents, guardians, and teachers were not liable for torts committed by those under their authority that they could prevent, masters were liable for torts committed by their servants even when they could not prevent them. Yet Pothier added: "This has been established to render masters careful to employ only good servants."[24] Pufendorf had said that one who owned animals was liable for their escape because since he had the profit of owning them, so he should bear the loss. Domat made a similar argument to explain the liability of person who has custody (*garde*) of fierce animals, such as "lions, tigers and bears":

---

[14] *See* Domat (n. 1), liv. I, tit. iii.
[15] Robert Pothier, *Traité du droit de domaine de propriété*, § 21, in *Oeuvres de Pothier*, ed. M. Siffrein nouv. ed. (Paris, 1821), 10, 1.
[16] Pothier (n. 15), liv. II, tits. iv, vii.   [17] Pothier (n. 5), § 113.
[18] Pothier (n. 5), § 33.   [19] Domat (n. 1), liv. II, tit. viii, sec. 4, § 1.
[20] Pothier (n. 5), § 116.   [21] Pothier (n. 5), § 116.   [22] Domat (n. 1), liv. II, tit. viii.
[23] *See* Chapter V, p. 000.   [24] Pothier (n. 5), § 121.

# Droit Civil Français: *The French Alternative*

[A]s he profits from the use he can make from this animal, being its owner, and as he can obtain possession of it again, having acquired it for money or by his own efforts, and having expended time and trouble to acquire some profit, he should answer.

But he made this argument in parallel with another: he should be liable as a matter of "equity and public interest" "because it is by his fault" that the animal escaped.[25]

All contracts, according to the late scholastics and iusnaturalists, are binding on consent. Domat and Pothier agreed.[26] Like them, Domat and Pothier rejected the Roman rules as to when different contracts became binding. But unlike the late scholastics and iusnaturalists, Domat and Pothier did not try to explain why it should be so. Domat merely said that rules are "subtleties which do not belong to our usage and are a useless encumbrance."[27] Pothier said that "[t]he principles of Roman law on the different types of agreements, and on the distinction between contract and simple agreement, not being founded on natural law, and being very distant from its simplicity, are not recognized in our law."[28]

Domat and Pothier had achieved their goal of providing an account of Roman law that was solid enough to be used by professional jurists and far simpler to read than the texts themselves. To that extent, they could claim to have realized the Ciceronian ideal of an art or science of civil law that was copious, but accessible. So far as civil law is concerned, they may have come closer to realizing this ideal than anyone before them. As we have seen, however, like many achievements, it had its price. The students, judges, and other professors who relied on their treatises would be learning their Roman law secondhand, not from the texts, but from their general statements about the law. Moreover, unlike the iusnaturalists, Domat and Pothier did not offer a principled account in which lower principles are supposed to be derived from higher ones.

## ii *CODE CIVIL*

The quest for clarity culminated in the nineteenth century with the drafting and enactment of the French Civil Code. It was a short document—far shorter than the treatise of Domat or of Grotius. It summarized all of private law in a series of clear principles formulated so elegantly that the novelist Stendhal, it is said, read the Code to improve his style.

The proponents of the Code were seeking clarity for two different reasons. Some believed that it was required by the principles of the French Revolution and that these principles made a clear statement of the law possible for the first time. Every citizen should be aware of his rights and, in a republic, these rights could be simply stated. Grotius thought that the natural law should be stated so clearly that a gentleman could understand it; the French revolutionaries thought that the civil

---

[25] Domat (n. 1), liv. II, tit. viii, sec. 2, § 8.
[26] Domat (n. 1), liv. I, tit. i, sec. 1, § 8; Pothier (n. 5), § 3.
[27] Domat (n. 1), liv. I, tit. i, sec. 1, § 7, n. u.      [28] Pothier (n. 5), § 3.

law should be stated so clearly that every citizen could understand it. In contrast, Portalis, the chairman of the drafting committee that produced the Code, thought that the Code could be clear because Domat had shown how law could be reduced to a science. Nevertheless, he did not believe that the Code would enable ordinary citizens to understand the law without the help of legal professionals, nor that it could be interpreted without the commentaries of jurists. The clash between these ideas almost led to the rejection of the draft of the Code that Portalis' committee prepared. It was enacted only through the direct intervention of Napoleon Bonaparte.

The republican ideal of clarity was rooted in the principle that a citizen should be bound only by law that he or his representatives had enacted and which he could understand. The tribune Mallia-Garat explained:

> The law in a republic is an emanation of sovereignty. It is the work of the people by itself or through its representatives, by the power that the constitution has established to make law. Law is the national will.... [T]hat is why it is the only power that free human beings can acknowledge....[29]

Because the laws were to be the sole measure of the rights and duties of the citizen, they had to be transparently clear. Every citizen must be able to understand them and no one must interpret or add to them. Mallia-Garat concluded: "The origin of the law in a republic does not permit any human power to change the law or to modify it in its execution or to supplement its insufficiency, let alone its silence." One who judges without a statute is not truly a judge. He is a despot.[30] Cambacérès, who chaired an earlier committee charged with drafting a code, explained that a code should contain:

> ...a collection of precepts where everyone could find the rules for his conduct in civil life.... Where judges are not legislators, it is not sufficient to insure the authority of law by justice; it is also necessary that the laws be so disposed as to eliminate doubt by clarity and to prevent exceptions by foresight.[31]

The tribune Savoie Rollin described the way in which a code would satisfy the republican ideal in much the same way as earlier writers had explained the meaning of an art or science of civil law. Because the Code would prescribe all of the private rights required by civil liberty and appropriate to man in a state of society, "[i]t is therefore necessary that a civil code contain a reasoned system of all these rights; and as they are necessarily linked among themselves, because they advance the same end, it is necessary that the system demonstrate this linkage."[32]

---

[29] Tribunat, Opinion du Tribun Mallia-Garat, séance du 19 frimaire, an X (December 10, 1801), in vol. 6 of *Recueil complet des travaux préparatoires du Code civil*, ed. P. A. Fenet (Paris, 1827; reprinted 1968), 151, 162.

[30] Opinion du Tribun Mallia-Garat (n. 29).

[31] Cambarcérès, Discours préliminaire prononcé par Cambacérès, au Conseil des cinq cents, lors de la présentation du 3ᵉ projet de Code civil, messidor, an IV, in Fenet (n. 29), 1: 140–41.

[32] Discussion devant le Corps legislative, Discours prononcé par le tribun Savoie Rollin, 4 pluviose, an XII (January 25, 1804), in Fenet (n. 29), 11: 48.

# Droit Civil Français: *The French Alternative*

As we have seen, each stage in the quest for clarity was marked by a new reason why clarity was possible for the first time. It was possible, according to the sixteenth-century humanists, because they were returning to the original meaning of the Roman texts that had been distorted by the medieval civilians and ill-ordered by Justinian's compilers. It was possible, according to Grotius, because he was writing about natural, rather than civil, law. It was possible, according to Domat, because most of the civil law received in France corresponded to the natural law. In the republican vision, the Code could be clear and self-sufficient because its rules would describe simple, natural relationships based on reason. In a republic, according to Mallia-Garat, the enacted laws can determine the relations among citizens with precision because these relations are natural, whereas in a monarchy, they are arbitrary.[33]

Like many revolutionary ideologies, the republican vision of a code had the defect that it did not correspond to anything humanly possible. No one could have made a code with the logical coherence, universal intelligibility, and comprehensiveness that the vision demanded. Certainly, Cambarcérès could not do so. His committee produced three drafts. The disappointment that ensued is the best explanation of why none of them were enacted.

His first draft was a collection of legal maxims and rules—some quite abstract, some very particular—taken from earlier authors. In presenting his draft to the National Convention, he tried to explain that the republican ideal did not require anything more systematic:

Far from us is the presumption to have invented a theory or a system. A system! ... [W]e do not have it. Persuaded that all sciences have their chimera, nature is the only oracle that we have consulted. Happy, one hundred times happy, the filial return to this common mother![34]

To the members of the National Convention, the sprawling collection of rules that Cambacérès claimed to have received from their common mother seemed uncomfortably long. Even at that, he admitted, the Code would not foresee everything. To do so, it would have to add more laws, and a large number of laws was itself an evil.[35] Cambarcérès' draft was voted down. The reason given in the drafting history is that it was "too complicated, showing the effects of the habits of lawyers and the maxims of courts. More simple and more philosophical conceptions were wanted."[36] Although historians have speculated about other factors that may have influenced the vote, this explanation seems to be the most persuasive. The draft simply did not match the republican vision of what a code should be.[37]

---

[33] Opinion du Tribun Mallia-Garat (n. 29), 6: 157.
[34] Rapport fait à la convention nationale par Cambacérès sur le 1er projet de Code civil, séance du 9 août 1793, in Fenet (n. 29), 1: 10.
[35] Rapport fait à la convention nationale par Cambacérès (n. 34), 1: 2.
[36] Discussion devant le conseil des cinqs cents, sur le 3e projet de Cambacérès, séance du 9 pluviose, an V, in Fenet (n. 29), 1: liv.
[37] Halpérin finds this explanation plausible not only because it is the only one found in the drafting history, but because Cambacérès' first draft was rejected during an anti-lawyer campaign begun in September, 1792, when Danton called lawyers a "revolting aristocracy": Jean-Louis Halpérin,

A year later, in September, 1794, Cambarcérès was back with a new draft that he hoped would match that vision more closely. This one was much shorter than the first and consisted almost entirely of laconic, very general principles—one might almost say, of banalities. In defending this draft, Cambacérès presented his ideas as though they were a series of consequences inferred from principles. For example:

Three things are necessary and sufficient for man and society:
To be master of his person;
To have goods to meet his needs;
To be able to dispose of his person and his goods in his greatest interest.
All civil rights reduce themselves therefore to the rights of liberty, of property, and of contract.[38]

The National Convention voted this draft down as well. The reason given in the drafting history is that it was too short, resembling a table of contents rather than a civil code.[39] The delegates seemed to realize that it would leave too much open. Moreover, as they examined Cambarcérès' attempt to deduce one banality from another, they may have doubted that his draft was the incarnation of reason that they were seeking.[40]

He eventually returned with a third draft, longer than the second, which aroused so little enthusiasm that it died without a reason for its rejection being recorded.

The project might have ended there had not Bonaparte seized power and decided to revive it. He appointed a four-man drafting committee chaired by Portalis, which produced the draft that ultimately was enacted. Portalis made it clear that this draft was not supposed to conform to the republican ideal. One could try to make the laws as simple as possible, but in a great state such as France, both agrarian and commercial, with so many different professions, the laws could not be as simple as those of a less-complicated society.[41] Nor would the Code make the dangerous

---

*L'Impossible Code civil* (Paris, 1992), 135. Nevertheless, he is not entirely convinced, since the Convention had already adopted the parts of the draft without any real debate, and indeed had found the provisions on marriage too revolutionary rather than too moderate: Halpérin, 136. Nevertheless, it seems quite consistent with the explanation in the drafting history that the members of the Convention would have no objection to the draft's content and still believe it failed to satisfy the revolutionary ideal. Halpérin suggests that the adoption of a civil code at that point would have signaled an end to revolutionary government: Halpérin, 140. Similarly, Debbash suggests that, because of the revolutionary upheaval, it did not seem a time for laws: Roland Debbasch, *Le Principe révolutionnaire d'unité et d'indivisibilité de la république* (Paris, 1988), 257. But it is hard to see why the adoption of a code answering to revolutionary republican principles would have done any such thing.

[38] Rapport fait à la convention nationale sur le 2$^e$ projet de Code civil, par Cambacérès, séance du 23 fructidor, an II (September 9, 1794), in Fenet (n. 29), 1: 100.

[39] Discussion devant le conseil des cinqs cents (n. 36), 1: liv.

[40] Halpérin thinks that the defeat of the draft may have been caused by the reaction against the radicals: Halpérin (n. 37), 214. They, however, were by no means the only ones to subscribe to a republican vision of a code and it is hard to think that Cambacérès' draft answered to this vision.

[41] Portalis, Discours préliminaire prononcé lors de la présentation du projet de la Commission du gouvernement, in Fenet (n. 29), 1: 467–68.

attempt "to govern all and to foresee all": "Whatever one does, positive law can never completely replace the use of natural reason in the affairs of life."[42]

As a result, the judge would constantly confront problems that he could not resolve merely by applying the texts of the Code. Indeed, he would confront such a problem in virtually every case that came before him, since "no one pleads against a clear statutory text":[43]

> Few cases are susceptible of being decided by a statute, by a clear text. It has always been by general principles, by doctrine, by legal science, that most disputes have been decided. The Civil Code does not dispense with this learning but, on the contrary, presupposes it.[44]

In Turkey, the magistrate can "declare whatever he wishes," because "legal studies are not an art." In France, "[i]t is only too fortunate that legal studies form a science" to which "[a]n entire class of men devotes itself," becoming a "sort of seminary of magistrates."[45] The cultivation of this legal science "presupposes compendia, digests, treatises, and studies and dissertations in numerous volumes."[46]

It followed that the Code, by itself, would not inform each citizen what his rights and duties were:

> The people, one may say, cannot in this labyrinth [of commentaries] discern what they must avoid and what they must do to be certain of their possessions and their rights. But would a code, even the simplest, be within the reach of every class in society?[47]

Portalis had rejected the republican vision, but shared the ideal of stating the law in a set of clear principles. Like Domat, he believed that it was possible to do so because "[l]aw (*droit*) is universal reason, supreme reason founded on the very nature of things. Enacted laws (*lois*) are or ought to be only the law (*droit*) reduced to positive rules, to particular precepts."[48] Since legislators were simply laying down particular precepts of a higher law based on reason—principles implicit in earlier legislation and discovered through legal scholarship—there was no great cause for concern if the legislator left a question open. The judge could simply consult natural reason with the "natural light of justice and good sense."[49] He would consult not his own conscience alone, but the learning of the "entire class of men" trained in legal science that had produced "compendia, digests, treatises, and studies and dissertations in numerous volumes." "If the foresight of legislators is limited," Portalis argued, "nature is infinite. It may be applied to everything that could concern men. Why would one wish to ignore the resources that she offers us?"[50]

---

[42] Portalis (n. 41), 1: 469.
[43] Corps législatif, Discours prononcé par Portalis, séance du 23 frimaire, an X (December 14, 1801), in Fenet (n. 29), 6: 269.
[44] Portalis (n. 41), 1: 471.    [45] Portalis (n. 41), 1: 471.    [46] Portalis (n. 41), 1: 471.
[47] Portalis (n. 41), 1: 471.    [48] Portalis (n. 41), 1: 476.
[49] Présentation au Corps législatif, Exposé des motifs, par Portalis, séance du 4 ventose, an XI (February 23, 1803), in Fenet (n. 29), 6: 360.
[50] Présentation au Corps législatif (n. 49), 360.

This higher law was reflected in those "valuable collections for the science of laws" made by the Roman jurists.[51] The Romans, however, never systematically formulated the principles on which their law was based and, for centuries, the task of doing so was neglected. It was neglected by the humanists, "[l]iterary people [who] only looked to the ancients for what was pleasant," and by the "philosophers [who] limited themselves to that which concerned the speculative sciences." "Unfortunately," the Roman texts were studied only by "those destined to the bench or the bar."[52] A true science of law began in the seventeenth century with the work of jurists such as Domat. These jurists examined enacted laws with "a reason exercised by observation and by experience," "compared enacted laws to enacted laws," and "studied them in their relationship to the rights of man and the needs of society."[53] What was needed was a distillation of the principles of jurists such as Domat. Two-thirds of the provisions of the Code that Portalis' committee drafted, as finally enacted, were taken from Domat and Pothier, verbatim or in paraphrase. Among them were virtually all of the texts that concerned the law of obligations.

Republican convictions were sufficiently alive in 1801 for Portalis' opinions to provoke a major battle. His claim that a code could not decide all cases was supported by many,[54] including his colleagues on the drafting committee Tronchet[55] and Bigot-Préameneu.[56] A concern that the judges would enjoy too much authority was raised by the courts of Lyon and Rouen[57] when the draft was circulated to the appellate courts for comment. When it was debated in the *Conseil d'état*, Cambacérès, now elevated to the post of Second Consul, warned that "it could facilitate usurpations by the courts of legislative power."[58] Roederer, another leader of the *Conseil*, raised similar concerns.[59]

The draft was approved by the *Conseil* and submitted to the *Tribunat*, a body of one hundred members appointed by a senate controlled by Bonaparte's supporters. Under the Bonaparte constitution, it could debate laws, but only recommend that

---

[51] Portalis, Présentation et exposé des motifs devant le Corps-Législatif, 28 ventose, an XII, in Fenet (n. 29), 1: xcv.

[52] Portalis (n. 51), xcvi–xcvii.   [53] Portalis (n. 51), xcvi–xcvii.

[54] For example, Jaubert, Discours prononcé devant le Corps législatif, 30 ventose, an XII, in Fenet (n. 29), 1: cxvi; Tribunat, Opinion du Tribun Démeunie, séance du 18 frimaire, an X (December 9, 1801), in Fenet (n. 29), 6: 93; Tribunat, Opinion du Tribun Ludot, séance du 18 frimaire, an X (December 9, 1801), in Fenet (n. 29), 6: 106–07; Tribunat, Opinion du Tribun Huguet, séance du 19 frimaire, an X (December 10, 1801), in Fenet (n. 29), 6: 138–39; Tribunat, Opinion du Tribun Portiez (de l'Oise), séance du 21 frimaire, an X (December 12, 1801), in Fenet (n. 29), 6: 228; Discours prononcé par le conseiller d'état Berlier, séance du 24 frimaire, an X (December 15, 1801), in Fenet (n. 29), 6: 335; Communication officielle au Tribunat, Rapport fait au nom de la section de législation par le Tribun Grenier, séance du 9 ventose, an XI (February 28, 1803), in Fenet (n. 29), 6: 375; Corps législatif, Discours prononcé par le Tribun Faure, séance du 14 ventose, an XI (March 5, 1803), in Fenet (n. 29), 6: 162.

[55] Conseil d'état, Procès-verbal de la séance du 14 thermidor, an IX (2 août 1801), in Fenet (n. 29), 6: 23.

[56] Conseil d'état (n. 55).

[57] Observations présentées par les commissaires nommés par le tribunal d'appel de Lyon, in Fenet (n. 29), 4: 34; Observations arrêtées par le tribunal d'appel séant à Rouen, d'aprés et sur le rapport de sa commission, in Fenet (n. 29), 5: 455–56.

[58] Conseil d'état (n. 55), 6: 21.   [59] Conseil d'état (n. 55), 6: 21.

# Droit Civil Français: *The French Alternative* 153

they be enacted or not enacted. In the *Tribunat*, Mallia-Garat attacked the draft, describing the rule of law in a republic in the words quoted earlier. He described the power granted the judge as "despotic,"[60] "without break, without measure, without guarantee, without precaution."[61] The *Tribunat* voted a negative recommendation on the portions of the Code submitted to it. These portions were then submitted to the *Corps Législatif*, a legislative body of three hundred members, also chosen by the senate, which voted in secret and without debate, and had the power to decide if a law should be enacted. The *Corps Législatif* rejected a portion of the draft submitted to it. Bonaparte then withdrew the remaining portions from further consideration, reduced the *Tribunat* to fifty members by eliminating his opponents, and resubmitted the draft. This time, the Code was approved and enacted.

It was a great intellectual achievement to produce as simple and elegant a statement of private law as the French Civil Code. In its elegance, its simplicity, and its comprehensiveness, the Code is perhaps the finest expression of the ideal first described by Cicero. It was the culmination of centuries of effort spent in pursuit of that ideal.

The Code did not bring the law within the reach of every citizen or even of every well-educated person. But by providing a clear exposition of law, it made the law far more accessible. Although the republican ideal could never have been realized, a citizen actually could read the provisions of the Code and understand them in a general way. In nineteenth-century novels, characters whose rights are questioned will say, "[S]how it to me in the Code." The Code made the study of law, as Domat had wished, "more easy and agreeable." Students were first taught a general principle and then, once it had been explained, they could address the problems that it raised. By providing a comprehensive statement of private law, the Code made law more accessible to the professionally trained. Most of the world is now governed by codes, most of which, directly or indirectly, were modeled on or inspired by the French. Other European jurisdictions have seen the advantage of the clear exposition that a code can provide. Outside Europe, codes have facilitated the importation of Western law. It has been easier and more fruitful to begin with a code and a few commentaries than it would have been to study the Latin texts to which the provisions of the French Code can ultimately be traced.

To this extent, then, the French Civil Code realized the humanist ideal of a clear exposition of law. Nevertheless, its enactment as law began a new era. Its provisions were authoritative texts. They were not simply expositions of an art or science of civil law that commended itself without need of enactment. Cicero hoped that the principles of such an art or science could replace the particularities of the jurists, but he did not think of enacting its principles. Neither did the humanists, the iusnaturalists, or Domat and Pothier. Donellus had said that, although he had to respect the substance of the Roman texts, even an emperor could not require him to respect the exposition of them found in the *Corpus iuris*: "The authority of law

---

[60] Opinion du Tribune Mallia-Garat (n. 29), 6: 151.
[61] Tribunat, Opinion du Tribun Chazal, séance du 18 frimaire, an X (December 9, 1801), in Fenet (n. 29), 6: 76.

comes from princes, but the true method of its teaching comes from those who are intelligent and skilled."[62] With the enactment of the Code, civil law was to be taught—forever, unless the Code was amended—in the manner of Domat and Pothier, as abridged by the drafters.

Moreover, unless one believed in the republican ideal—and the drafters did not—once the provisions of the Code were enacted, they would have to be interpreted. If the interpreter looked only to the texts of the Code, none of the methods of interpretation that had been used by jurists in the past would serve him very well.

For the Romans, explaining the meaning of concepts such as possession, fault, and consent was not done by interpreting authoritative texts; it was done when the jurist, on his own authority, tested a concept against a particular case. If a Roman jurist could have read the Code, he would recognize the basic concepts of private law with which he was familiar, such as possession, negligence, and contractual consent. But he would not see how one could determine the meaning of these concepts without putting myriad cases about people stepping onto land or gazing at it from a turret, or pruners cutting down branches, or athletes practicing with javelins, or copper sold as gold, or vinegar as wine.

The medieval civilians developed methods for interpreting authoritative texts by reconciling each text with every other. Their method presupposed that there were texts to reconcile. For them to use these methods to clarify concepts such as possession, fault, or consent, the texts must indicate what constitutes possession or fault and when a mistake will vitiate consent. Then they could generalize some texts, limit others, and apply still others by analogy. The texts of the French Civil Code, however, simply provide that possession is to be protected (arts. 2282–83), that compensation is to be made for harm caused by fault (arts. 1382–83), and that no valid consent is given when a person makes an error in substance (arts. 1109–10). A medieval jurist would have trouble seeing how one could clarify these provisions without other texts to enable one to do so.

The late scholastics and iusnaturalists claimed that the principles by which they explained law were linked together like those of a philosophical system, so that the lower-level principles could be derived from the higher ones and explained by them. Whether or not they succeeded, it is difficult to imagine that the principles contained in the Code are linked in this way. The Code was not based on a coherent set of philosophical principles. Rather, it was based on the work of Domat and Pothier. Domat's principles, as we have seen, were pedagogical rather than philosophical. Pothier's were loose and unexplained references to the principles of Grotius, Pufendorf, and Barbeyrac, which were themselves often vague and unsystematic. The drafters completed their work in a few months. They did not have time, even if they had wished to do so, to rework the materials that they found in Domat and Pothier to bring them into line with some new set of principles.

---

[62] Hugo Donellus, *Commentariorum de iure civili libri viginti octo* (Florence, 1840–47), I.i.12.

A late scholastic or iusnaturalist would have trouble seeing how the texts of the Code could be interpreted by looking to higher-level principles.

A Roman or medieval jurist, a late scholastic, or a iusnaturalist might agree that the law was now stated more clearly than ever before. But he might think that clarity had been achieved at an excessive price, much as one could make pea soup clear by leaving out the peas.

Objections like these would not have troubled Portalis. As we have seen, he believed that "[l]aw (*droit*) is universal reason, supreme reason founded on the very nature of things. Enacted laws (*lois*) are or ought to be only the law (*droit*) reduced to positive rules, to particular precepts."[63] For him, the precepts of the Civil Code were based on a coherent set of principles grounded in universal reason. To interpret them, the judge could consult natural reason with the "natural light of justice and good sense."[64] He could also consult the "valuable collections for the science of laws" made by the Roman jurists, which reflected this higher law.[65] He could draw upon the learning of the "entire class of men" trained in legal science who had produced "compendia, digests, treatises, and studies and dissertations in numerous volumes."[66] He was referring to compendia, digests, treatises, and studies and dissertations that had already been written on Roman law, not to new ones that were yet to be written and based solely on the texts of the Civil Code. Portalis did not expect the Civil Code to be the sole authoritative source of French law.

[63] Portalis (n. 41), 1: 476.
[64] Présentation au Corps législatif (n. 49), 6: 360.
[65] Portalis (n. 51), 1: xcv.
[66] Présentation au Corps législatif (n. 49), 6: 360.

# VII

## *Usus Modernus Pandectarum*
### The German-Dutch Alternative

We have seen how new schools arose in the sixteenth century that broke with the method of the medieval jurists. Particularly in France, the humanists tried to reconstruct the original meaning of the Roman texts, founding a school known as the *mos gallicus*, as distinguished from the *mos italicus*, which taught in the manner of the medieval jurists. The late scholastics took a philosophical approach. They explained the Roman texts with ideas drawn from Aristotle and Aquinas. In the seventeenth century, Grotius and his followers developed a new school, which we have called that of the iusnaturalists, by drawing on the conclusions of the late scholastics, and trying to express them with humanist simplicity and elegance.

Wherever Roman law was in force, however, it was taught to those who were to practice or administer law. Their needs were not met by the work of the humanists, or that of the late scholastics or the iusnaturalists. The humanists reconstructed the meaning of these texts to the ancient Romans, but did not explain how to apply them to situations that the Romans themselves had not considered.[1] The late scholastics were interested in the light that the Roman texts shed on the natural law. When they could not explain a text with the ideas that they took from Aristotle and Aquinas, they said that the text belonged to Roman positive law rather than natural law. They were not concerned with explaining Roman positive law. Neither were the iusnaturalists. Thus the question arose: how was the Roman law to be understood and taught?

We have already seen how this question was answered in France. Domat and Pothier drew on the work of the iusnaturalists to write simple elegant treatises on the Roman law as it had been received in France, which, according to Domat, largely coincided with the natural law.

In the Netherlands and Germany, jurists took a different approach, founding what historians have called the *usus modernus pandectarum*, "the modern use of the Digest."[2] The phrase is taken from the title of a book by Samuel Stryk published in

---

[1] *See* Hans Schlosser, *Grundzüge der neureren Privatrechtsgeschichte*, 9th ed. (Heidelberg, 2001), 71, 73.

[2] On other parts of Europe, *see* Klaus Luig, "Institutionenlehrbücher des nationalen Rechts im 17. und 18. Jahrhundert," *Ius Commune* 3 (1970): 64; Karl Wieacker, *Privatrechtsgeschichte der Neuzeit*, 2nd ed. (Göttingen, 1967), 215.

1690, but the distinguishing features of this approach had already appeared in the sixteenth century.³

The school of the *usus modernus pandectarum* was long-lived and its achievements have been greatly underrated. One of the greatest was to preserve the study of law based on the Roman texts, and the enterprise of harmonizing them and applying them to problems that their Roman authors had not directly confronted. Nevertheless, the project of these jurists is most easily described in negative terms. Unlike the late scholastics, the iusnaturalists, Pothier, Domat, and the later rationalists, they did not try to resolve legal problems by means of higher principles.⁴ An exception was Heineccius, whose work will be discussed later.⁵ Unlike the humanists, their goal was not to recapture the meaning of the texts to their Roman authors. Like the medieval jurists, they harmonized the Roman texts, but they did not have the same commitment to extracting a meaning from each text and reconciling it with every other.

Typically, they did not dismiss the importance of the higher principles of natural law or of philosophy, although they did not apply them to legal problems. They began their treatises with accounts of law and justice that were squarely in the Aristotelian tradition, although these accounts became sketchier as time went on. Yet they rarely drew on these accounts to explain the Roman law.⁶

For example, Wesenbeck, like Aristotle, distinguished general or universal justice from particular justice, and distributive from commutative justice, noting that the one follows a geometric proportion and the other, an arithmetic. He distinguished theoretical from practical reason, saying that practical reason is based on the awareness (*notitia*) implanted in our minds of certain principles of right and wrong, and that the natural law is an awareness of these practical principles and the conclusions to be drawn from them.⁷ Although Wesenbeck's account was brief compared with that of a late scholastic, that of Vinnius was still sketchier, and that of Brunnemann sketchier still, even though they introduced the same concepts.⁸ Voet does little more than distinguish distributive and commutative justice, and explain that there is a law of nature that Grotius grounded on the rational and social nature of man, and Pufendorf on human sociability.⁹

---

³ Or earlier: Klaus Luig, "Samuel Stryk (1640–1710) und der 'Usus modernus pandectarum'," in *Die Bedeutung der Wörter: Studien zur europäischen Rechtsgeschichte. Festschrift für Sten Gagnér zum 70. Geburtstag*, eds. Michael Stolleis et al. (Munich, 1991), 219 at 219–20.
⁴ *See* Wieacker (n. 2), 211, 228–29.
⁵ *See* Chapter VIII, pp. 182–83.   ⁶ *See* Wieacker (n. 2), 216–17.
⁷ Matthew Wesenbeck, *Commentarii in Pandectas Juris Civilis et Codicem Justinianeum olim dicti Paratitla* (Amsterdam, 1665), 1.1, §§ 11–15.
⁸ Arnold Vinnius, *In quatuor libros Institutionum Imperialium commentarius academicus et forensis* (Amsterdam, 1703), 1, §§ 2–4 (expressing the same concerns as Grotius about the distinction between distributive and commutative justice); Johannes Brunnemann, *Commentarius in quinquaginta libros Pandectarum opus theoretico-practicum*, nouv. ed. (Wittenberg, 1731), 1.1.6; 1.1.10, no. 3.
⁹ Johannes Voet, *Commentarius ad Pandectas* (Naples, 1827), 1.1, §§ 9, 15, 17–18. Lauterbach, perhaps more wisely, devoted most of his introduction to discussing the importance to jurists of positive law, drawing on Aristotelian conceptions of equity and prudence: Wolfgang Lauterbach, *Collegium theoretico-practici ad...Pandectarum libros* (Tübingen, 1707), I.1, §§ 1–4. As with the others, however, his introductory remarks had little to do with his discussion of legal problems.

One reason why these introductions were progressively more summary is that the jurists made little effort to apply philosophical ideas to the legal issues that they discussed. Like the late scholastics, they concluded that all agreements are actionable in principle, but without discussing the Aristotelian principle of commutative justice. They ignored the basic distinction that the late scholastics had drawn between contracts based on commutative justice and those based on liberality. They did not mention commutative justice when they discussed the remedy for *laesio enormis*.[10] It is as though, having mentioned commutative justice in their introductions, they found no further use for the idea. When he discusses error in contract formation, Wesenbeck repeats the term "essence" (*ousia*) in the Roman text, but he does not explain it.[11] Brunnemann made the un-Aristotelian claim that an error in "matter" is an error in "substance,"[12] and Voet, that vinegar is different is substance depending on whether or not wine was deliberately soured to produce it.[13] The philosophical principles that they claimed to accept were often the same as those of the late scholastics, but they ignored these principles when they discussed legal doctrine.

Cornelis van Bijnkershoek took a similar approach to public international law. His purpose was practical. He did not write a systematic treatise, but one focused, he said, "on questions of most frequent use," "questions" that, although they "may have interest in any state, ... are all closely connected with the affairs of the Belgic Confederation." His method, he said, "was to appeal first and foremost to sound reason," to which he "added the treatise of nations, edicts and decrees of our own States-General and also, and not infrequently, cited precedents from the history of our own or other nations. ..."[14] By reason, as Arthur Nussbaum noted, he meant "common sense in finding the best and most equitable solution": "The law of nature is practically ignored in his discussion."[15] Consequently, he has been called the "precursor" of "the modern school of jurists which recognizes the positive value of rules in treaties and customs [and] the self-sufficiency of positive law which cannot be superseded but only guided" by reason, but not in the sense of Grotius.[16]

Similarly, the jurists of the *usus modernus pandectarum* were interested in the conclusions of the humanists concerning the meaning of the Roman texts in historical context,[17] so much so that some historians have said that the work of the Dutch jurists in particular was marked by that of the "elegant" jurisprudence of the humanists.[18] As Reinhard Zimmermann has noted, however:

---

[10] Wesenbeck (n. 7), 18.5, §§ 4–6; Vinnius (n. 8), III.14, § 5; Brunnemann (n. 8), 18.5.4, no. 10.
[11] Wesenbeck (n. 7), 18.1, § 6.
[12] Brunnemann (n. 8), 18.1.9, § 2.    [13] Voet (n. 9), 18.1, § 5.
[14] Cornelius van Bynkershoek, *Questionum iuris publici libri duo* (Leiden, 1737), Ad lectorem 2–3.
[15] Arthur Nussbaum, *A Concise History of the Law of Nations* (New York, 1947), 143–44.
[16] Coleman Phillipson, "Cornelius van Bykershoek," in *Great Jurists of the World*, eds. Sir John Macdonnell and Edward Manson (Boston, MA, 1914), 395–96.
[17] A. M. M. Canoy-Olthoff and P. L. Nève, *Holländische Eleganz gegenüber deutschem* Usus Modernus Pandectarum (Nijmegen, 1990), 4.
[18] Hans E. Troje, "Die Literatur des gemeinen Rechts unter dem Einfluss des Humanismus," in *Handbuch der Quellen und Literatur der neuen Europäischen Privatrechtsgeschichte* 2(1) (Munich, 1977): 615, 634.

It can safely be maintained that the Dutch, in their capacity as humanists, were mere successors of the French.... Had their jurisprudence been merely "elegant" it hardly deserved to be remembered as a particularly fruitful era of the *ius commune*.[19]

The jurists of the *ius modernus* differed because, unlike the humanists, their goal was not to recapture the historical meaning of the texts, but to apply the texts to legal problems that the Romans did not consciously consider. Indeed, they prided themselves on considering contemporary problems and avoiding the pedantry of the humanists. Voet said that his treatise would go "beyond the principles of Roman law" to treat "modern law" and "modern questions."[20] Stryk attacked those scholars who "acutely think out subtleties of Roman law which are abandoned by the courts." He said that a jurist is "[n]either to fear when the courts recede from the written law, nor to say facilely that something has fallen into desuetude."[21] Böhmer complained of those who "spend their time all their life ferreting out subtleties in law...." "I do not condemn all critical study of Roman law," he said, "so far as sometimes it can shed light on interpretation...." But:

[W]here the matter takes away time from the actual law of today, and if the question is asked, for the use of whom? I answer that it is vain to pursue of such glorious erudition. Is this not, truly, to bring the greatest pedantry to law?[22]

In both of these respects—in their disinclination to use philosophical principles to resolve legal problems, and in their willingness to go beyond the historical meaning of their texts—their work was like that of the medieval jurists, whom they often cited with favor.[23] Indeed, their method of interpreting texts was similar. Like the medieval jurists, they would sometimes generalize a text, sometimes limit its scope, and sometimes work by analogy from one text to another. As Georg Struve explained, unless the text of a law was clear or had been clarified by usage, it had to be interpreted "by extension" or "by restriction." In the former case, the law is "extended... by words that are not expressed in it": "The legislator wanted more, but wrote down less." In the latter case, "a law which seems to be general according to its words is given a narrower sense." Then "it appears that the legislator, although wrote more, meant less." Struve seems to have regarded the drawing of an analogy from a particular case to other cases as a form of extensive interpretation. In the case of a *ius singulari*, a law dealing with a particular situation, "if it appears that the legislator would want to include not only the case expressed [in the text] but others as well an extension will also take place."[24]

---

[19] Reinhard Zimmermann, "Roman-Dutch Jurisprudence and its Contribution to European Private Law," *Tulane Law Review* 66 (1992): 1685, 1713.
[20] Voet (n. 9), subtitle and Preface.
[21] Samuel Stryk, *Specimen usus modernus Pandectarum ad libros v. priores* (Magdeburg, 1739), Preface.
[22] Justus Hennig Böhmer, *Introductio in ius Digestorum* (Luca, 1791), Preface to 1st ed.
[23] Canoy-Olthoff and Nève (n. 17), 4.
[24] Georg Adam Struve, *Syntagma jurisprudentiae, secundum ordinem Pandectarum concinnatum* (Jena, 1692), II, § 49.

Consequently, some historians have described the *usus modernus* as a victory of the "Bartolist" *mos italicus* over the humanist *mos gallicus*.[25] Nevertheless, jurists of the *usus modernus* did not write like medieval jurists. As Wieacker said, they broke with the *mos italicus*.[26] Indeed, as Canoy-Olthoff and Nève put it, "in this period the great distinction between the *mos italicus* and the *mos gallicus*, as it had been since the inception of legal humanism, no longer existed."[27] As Zimmermann said, "the Roman-Dutch jurists reinvigorated the *mos italicus* on the basis and level of the humanistic learning provided by the *mos gallicus*."[28]

Again, the difference from the medieval jurists can best be described in negative terms. The jurists of the *usus modernus* did not have the same commitment to interpreting every Roman text in terms of every other. They no longer used the extreme care that the medieval jurists had taken to reconcile the texts. One reason, as Zimmermann's remark suggests, is that they had learned from the humanists. Understood in its historical context, the *Corpus iuris* was an accretion of texts laid down over time. Moreover, the jurists of the *usus modernus* had learned from the late scholastics and the iusnaturalists that only some of the texts could be explained by philosophical principles. Again, they were writing to serve the needs of practicing judges and lawyers.[29] They were interested in those aspects of Roman law of practical importance in their time, whereas the medieval jurists had been interested in every aspect. Finally, they no longer regarded the Roman texts as having the same authority that the medieval jurists ascribed to them. The texts were not in force because they had been promulgated by the emperor, but because some, although not all, of them had been received by usage.[30]

Instead of a careful reconciliation of texts, one typically finds in treatises on the *usus modernus* an assertion about Roman law followed by citation of authority. The authority cited is most often a Roman text. Frequently, it is another jurist. In early works, the jurist might be a medieval civilian, such as Bartolus, Baldus, Cinus, or Azo. In later works, it is usually another jurist of *usus modernus*. The medieval civilians had also cited the opinions of other jurists. But, in presenting them, they described a range of opinions to be considered in turn, before presenting their own. The jurists of the *usus modernus* often simply state their conclusions and cite authority to back them up. Even admirers of this school have confessed that it lacks the brilliance of others.[31]

Neither did the jurists of the *usus modernus* impose order on the law by linking the texts together in medieval fashion. Like the medieval jurists, they typically discussed the titles into which the Digest and the Institutes were divided one title at time. Unlike the medieval jurists, however, they typically did not proceed one text at a time in discussing each title. Rather, they organized their discussion as a series

---

[25] Schlosser (n. 1), 76.    [26] Wieacker (n. 2), 208, 214.
[27] Canoy-Olthoff and Nève (n. 17), 3.    [28] Zimmermann (n. 19), 1711.
[29] Canoy-Olthoff and Nève (n. 17), 76–77; Wieacker (n. 2), 208.
[30] Wieacker (n. 2), 205–07; Karl Kroeschell, *Deutsche Rechtsgeschichte (seit 1650)* (Opladen, 1988), 3. They credit much of the change to Hermann Conring, *De origine iuris Germanici liber unus* (Helmstadt, 1643).
[31] Wieacker (n. 2), 214.

of questions suggested by each title, and answered each question, citing texts to support the answers that they gave. One could follow their discussion without reading the texts. Reading the texts was necessary only to check the author's claim that they supported whatever point he had made.

According to some scholars, the distinctive contribution of the jurists of the *usus modernus* was that they paid more attention to the usage of their own day. Certainly, they claimed to be doing so and, with time, the claim became stronger. Wesenbeck appealed to usage cautiously in the commentary he wrote in 1565. In 1690, Stryk, in the treatise for which the school is named, *Specimen usus moderni Pandectarum*, did not begin, like his predecssors, with a discussion of the nature of law and justice. Instead, he discussed the authority of positive law. It depended, he said, on usage and right reason. The law of Justinian was accepted as *ius commune*, common law, throughout Europe "not by necessity of statute but by equitable reason."[32] It was common law in Germany, but that did not mean that only Roman law is in force. Customary law was also in force, not "promiscuously but only insofar as it conforms to right reason";[33] "From this it follows that the civil law is to be observed in cases decided in the Empire insofar as it is not opposed to an honest and reasonable custom or to a more recent Imperial law."[34] The civil law is to be followed unless a custom is proven:[35]

In the same way one ought to decide: what is to be accepted if, when civil law is invoked, it is objected that it is not in use or that what the Roman law proposed has never before been received in Germany.... And clearly if the authority of law depends upon... common reception, the decision is clear: when the use of a law ceases so does its force (*dispositio*).... Thus if for a thousand years, no one in Germany made a testament, one would say that in Germany the permission to make a testament is gone.[36]

Wieacker concluded:

[T]he *Usus modernus* was of especial value: instead of echoing the sources, literature and rules of a *ius commune* imported from the rest of Europe it incorporated into its doctrine the whole positive law obtaining in Germany. No longer in thrall to the *Corpus iuris* as glossed by Accursius and the Commentators it examined the laws... as actually applied in the higher courts. It is to the legal science of this age—a legal science based on German decision-making, set out in books both learned and practical... that we owe the particular kinds of law teaching and writing with which we are familiar today. The *Usus modernus* really saw the birth of legal science as we still know it....[37]

One should be careful. The jurists of the school did emphasize the authority of usage. Some of them may have looked to the law in force. Byndershoek cited the decisions of the Dutch Estates General on matters of international law on which there were few Roman texts. Others may have relied on a general knowledge of what courts were doing. As Zimmermann noted, many of them had practical

---

[32] Stryk (n. 21), § 42.   [33] Stryk (n. 21), § 27.   [34] Stryk (n. 21), § 28.
[35] Stryk (n. 21), § 33.   [36] Stryk (n. 21), § 34.
[37] Wieacker (n. 2), 214; *A History of Private Law in Europe with particular reference to Germany*, trans. Tony Weir (Oxford, 1995), 167.

experience.³⁸ But they did not to reach their conclusions about civil law by analyzing the decisions of higher courts. By the time jurists began to do so, the *usus modernus* was forgotten. As John Dawson has pointed out, the practice of "the publication of reasoned judicial opinions, prepared by the judges themselves... was not generalized until well after 1800."³⁹ The citation of these opinions even by nineteenth-century German jurists was a rarety: "Germany's case law revolution," which led to academic writing as we now know it, took place in the twentieth century.⁴⁰

The jurists of the *usus modernus* occasionally cited a statute. Simon van Groenewegen, in his *Treatise on Laws that are Abrogated or Not Used in Holland*, referred to the decisions of courts.⁴¹ But when most jurists referred to usage, they either cited no authority for their sometimes contradictory claims about what it was, or they cited each other. Often, they may have appealed to usage because it enabled them to get rid of features of the Roman law that they regarded as wrong or archaic. As Nanz noted, Wesenbeck, in his commentary in 1565, was the first to make the claim that, according to usage, all agreements are enforceable, for which he miscited Bartolus and Baldus.⁴² He also noted that all agreements are actionable in canon law, and said that "today the same is true in every forum in which matters are decided according to what is equitable and good and adjudged by the supreme power as are the high courts of princes, arbitrators, merchants, and so forth."⁴³ He also appealed to principles—not those of the late scholastics, but those that had been accepted by medieval canonists and civilians, although never taken so far:

> For as every agreement is naturally obligatory by what is good and fair... it follows that he who does not observe an agreement acts against nature, conscience, and the duty of a good man, and sins mortally, as the canonists want it to be.⁴⁴

Later jurists simply said that modern usage was to give an action,⁴⁵ some mentioning that the rule had been taken from canon law.⁴⁶ The appeal to *usus* had become final. Yet it was not backed up by citations to what courts actually did, but to other jurists who held the same view.

Another example is the assessment of damages for injury to property under the *lex Aquilia*. According to the *lex Aquilia*, the judge was to award damages for the amount that the object harmed had been worth during the preceding year.⁴⁷

---

³⁸ Zimmermann (n. 19), 1712–13.
³⁹ John P. Dawson, *The Oracles of the Law* (Ann Arbor, MI, 1968), 432.
⁴⁰ Dawson (n. 39), 432–502.
⁴¹ Zimmermann (n. 19), 1693, citing Simon van Groenewegen, *Tractatus de legibus abrogatis et inusitatis in Hollandia* (Leiden, 1664) to C. 2.3.10.
⁴² Klaus-Peter Nanz, *Die Entstehung des allegmeinen Vertragsrechtsbegriff in 16. bis 18. Jahrhundert* (Munich, 1985), 85; see Italo Birocchi, "La questione del patti nella dottrina tedesca dell'Usus modernus," in *Toward a General Law of Contract*, ed. John Barton (Berlin, 1990), 146–55, 197–213.
⁴³ Wesenbeck (n. 7), 2.14, § 9.  ⁴⁴ Wesenbeck (n. 7), 2.14, § 9.
⁴⁵ Vinnius (n. 8), 3.14.2, § 11; Voet (n. 9), 2.14, § 9; Böhmer (n. 22), 2.14, § 25; Stryk (n. 21), 2.14, §§ 1–3. An exception was Lauterbach, who denied that an action could be brought on a mere agreement: Lauterbach (n. 9), 2.4, §§ 19–20.
⁴⁶ Brunnemann (n. 8), 2.14.7, no. 6.   ⁴⁷ D. 9.2.2.pr.

Wesenbeck, citing medieval authority, interpreted the rule to mean that if the value of the object had increased during the year, the plaintiff should recover the higher value.[48] Other jurists were content to say that this rule was no longer recognized in practice.[49] Again, the jurists cited each other, but not judicial opinions, and so got rid of a rule that they may not have liked.

They appealed to *usus* or custom in a similar way when they discussed the extent to which the plaintiff can recover under the *lex Aquilia* for bodily injury. Wesenbeck, Brunnemann, and Vinnius accepted the solution that, as we have seen, had been reached by Azo and Accursius by reading a Roman text broadly. He could recover not in an *actio directa*, but in an *actio utilis*.[50] Voet agreed, although he rejected a limitation, accepted by Vinnius and Lauterbach,[51] which, as he admitted, was supported by the Roman texts: that one could not recover for pain and suffering.[52] Stryk said that, today, no attention is paid to the distinctions between an *actio directa*, *utilis*, and *in factum*;[53] "The present use of this title [on the *lex Aquilia*] is most ample as the reparation of all damages may be demanded, if in any way they proceed from another's fault."[54] He said that recovery for pain and suffering was "reasonable." He admitted that the Roman texts were opposed to this conclusion, but said "that practice is not iniquitous which allows an estimation of the pain according to the character of the wound as determined by the arbitration of the judge...."[55] The jurists had moved from accepting conclusions on the basis of Roman texts, as the medieval jurists had done, to rejecting the texts themselves if they conflicted with practice. As before, they appealed to practice to eliminate a Roman rule that seemed unreasonable. Again, they did so without citing the decisions of courts, although, in the passage just quoted, Stryk did refer to a criminal statute that required a judge who had wrongfully tortured someone to make compensation.

The jurists of the *usus modernus* did not found "legal science as we still know it," based on "the examination of laws ... as actually applied in the higher courts." They claimed, as Domat did in France, that Roman law had been partially received in Germany. Consequently, like Domat and unlike the medieval jurists, they had the flexibility to disregard texts that seemed unreasonable by claiming they had not been received. They were no more interested than Domat in testing that claim against actual court decisions.

The achievement of the *usus modernus* was not to found a new legal science. As we have seen, their project can best be described in negative terms. Nevertheless, it was inspired by a positive vision. The jurists of the school respected the immense intellectual wealth of Roman law, and wished to preserve and apply it. Even their appeals to usage seemed to perfect it by eliminating archaisms. They could not teach the Roman texts with the conviction of the medieval jurists that every word

---

[48] Wesenbeck (n. 7), 9.2, § 5.
[49] Böhmer (n. 22), 9.2, § 4; Stryk (n. 21), 9.2, § 2. Vinnius made this point in his notes to the commentary of Wesenbeck: Wesenbeck (n. 7), 9.2, § 9.
[50] Wesenbeck (n. 7), 9.2, § 7; Brunnemann (n. 8), 9.2.7, no. 1; Vinnius (n. 8), 4.3, § 2.
[51] Vinnius (n. 8), 4.3, § 2; Lauterbach (n. 9), 9.2, § 6.   [52] Voet (n. 9), 9.2, § 11.
[53] Stryk (n. 21), 9.2, § 6.   [54] Stryk (n. 21), 9.2, § 1.   [55] Stryk (n. 21), 9.2, § 10.

and phrase was pregnant with truth—not after the work of the humanists, late scholastics, and iusnaturalists. But they did not teach in the manner of the humanists. To do so would have deprived the texts of their significance for their own times, of their permanent value, and of a significance that transcended their historical context. As Zimmermann has said:

> [T]he Roman-Dutch lawyers, by combining these two mainstreams of tradition, succeeded in rejuvenating the *ius commune* at a time when the *mos italicus* had become fossilized and the *mos gallicus* had reached a state of purely antiquarian overrefinement that was, more often than not, devoid of any practical significance.[56]

Nor did these jurists teach in the manner of the late scholastics or iusnaturalists. Although they believed in a natural law, to do so would be to teach natural law, not Roman law. Thus the negative features of their project were by-products of a positive ideal: to preserve the heritage of Roman law, and to keep it from becoming either a mere matter of history or an approximation of the principles of natural law.

As a result, on the eve of the nineteenth century, the French and German jurists were in different positions. They agreed that only part of the Roman law had been received in France and in Germany. In France, however, Domat and Pothier had presented law with humanist elegance and simplicity, insisting that its principles reflected those of the natural law as described by the iusnaturalists. The esteem for elegance and simplicity, and the belief that the law was based on a coherent set of principles, persisted in the nineteenth century, outliving the belief in natural law. In Germany, the jurists of the *usus modernus* had separated the examination of the legal text from higher principles. As John Dawson noted, however, during this same period, the seventeenth and eighteenth centuries, Germany made a commitment to legal science in the sense of a systematic account of law based on philosophical principles then prevailing.[57] This enterprise, so different from that of the *usus modernus*, was undertaken by a different school of jurists, the rationalists—in particular, Gottfried Wilhelm Leibniz and Christian Wolff. They attempted to deduce their conclusions from abstract concepts, not to ground them on legal texts. Thus in Germany, unlike France, a chasm emerged between two approaches to law: that of the *usus modernus*, based on texts unsupported by principles, and that of the rationalists, based on principles unsupported by texts. It was only in the nineteenth century that German jurists tried to bring texts and principles back together.

[56] Zimmermann (n. 19), 1711.  [57] Dawson (n. 39), 148–262.

# VIII

## *Mos Geometricus*
### The Coming of Rationalism

Rationalism originated in the seventeenth century and flourished in the eighteenth. It has been presumed dead since its condemnation by the nineteenth-century jurists. Yet its tenets lived on to cause problems for jurists in the nineteenth century—problems that later jurists recognized, but which continued, and still continue, to plague their work.

Rationalists believed that law is based on concepts that are eternally and immutably grounded in human nature—an innovation in metaphysics that began with the late scholastic Francesco Suárez. They believed that the only proper method to reach legal conclusions is to deduce them logically from these concepts—an innovation in method that began with René Descartes. They defined these concepts without regard to the purposes that they served. For example, the rights of states in international law and the rights of property owners or contracting parties in private law were defined without regard to the purposes that these institutions serve. Concept and purpose no longer went together as they had in the earlier natural law tradition. This innovation can be traced to the German philosophers Gottfried Wilhelm Leibniz and Christian Wolff.

Mainline nineteenth-century jurists rejected rationalism. They were positivists. They did not believe that legal concepts were founded on human nature—or, at any rate, that jurists should be concerned about such concepts. Their business as jurists was to interpret the law established by human authority. These jurists were also conceptualists. They believed that underlying the statutes and cases enacted or decided by human authorities were legal concepts that they could identify and the content of which they could logically explore. For that reason, the statutes and cases could be interpreted. Nevertheless, the work of the nineteenth-century jurists incorporated the features of rationalism that have just been described.

These features were the focus of the attack on their work launched in the late nineteenth century by critics such as Oliver Wendell Holmes in the United States, François Gény in France, and Rudoph von Jhering in Germany, and carried forward by their successors. These critics complained that the nineteenth-century jurists treated legal concepts as though they had a transcendent and eternal existence. Holmes objected that "law is not a brooding omnipresence in the sky."[1] The mistake, Gény said, was to regard legal principles as "predetermined, basically

---

[1] *Southern Pac. Co. v. Jensen*, 244 U.S. 222 (1916).

immutable, governed by inflexible dogmas, and therefore not susceptible of adjustment to the varied and changing exigencies of life."[2] Jhering described an imaginary heaven in which nothing existed but pure legal concepts, cut off from anything on earth.[3] The critics also complained that one could not begin with concepts and, by logic alone, arrive at legal conclusions. Moreover, in reflecting on the meaning of concepts, the nineteenth-century jurists had ignored the purposes that legal institutions serve.[4]

In later chapters, we will see how the work of the nineteenth-century jurists incorporated these features of rationalism and the problems that then emerged. We will see that their critics found it easier to identify these problems than to find an alternative approach that resolved them. In this chapter, we will see how rationalism arose.

## An innovation in metaphysics

The pioneer of the rationalist approach was the late scholastic, Francesco Suárez, who broke with the metaphysical tradition that he inherited, although, as we will see, other late scholastics had already moved in that direction. Legal scholars, such as John Finnis and Germain Grisez, and philosophers, such as Etienne Gilson, regard it as the point at which the earlier approach to natural law taken by Aquinas was abandoned.[5]

Suárez agreed with Aquinas that living a distinctively human life is the ultimate end to which all well-chosen actions are directed, and that they are directed to that end by the precepts of natural law: "[A]ll these precepts tend to the same end, truly, the due conservation and natural perfection or happiness of human nature; consequently, they belong to the natural law."[6] Like Aquinas, Suárez defined perfection in terms of the fulfillment or completion of one's being, and goodness in terms of perfection.[7]

---

[2] François Gény, *Methode d'interpretation et sources en droit privé positif*, 2nd ed. (English translation, Louisiana, 1963), no. 62.

[3] Rudolf von Jhering, "Im juristischen Begriffshimmel," in *Scherz und Ernst in der Jurisprudenz* (Leipzig, 1884), 350.

[4] Oliver Wendell Holmes, Jr., "The Path of the Law," in *Collected Legal Papers* (1920), 167 at 182, 186; Gény (n. 2), nos. 23, 68, 159; Rudolf von Jhering, *Der Zweck im Recht* (Leipzig, 1877), preface.

[5] John Finnis, *Natural Law and Natural Rights* (Oxford, 1980), 45; Germain Grisez, *Christian Moral Principles* (Quincy, IL, 1997), 106; Etienne Gilson, *Being and Some Philosophers* (Toronto, 1952), 211.

[6] Suárez, *Tractatus de legibus et de legislatore deo* (Coimbra, 1612), lib. 2, cap. 7, no. 7.

[7] Suárez, *Disputationes metaphysicae* in vol. 25 of *Opera omnia*, ed. C. Berton (Paris, 1861), disp. 10, sec. 1, no. 11. Unlike Aquinas, he did not think that one can define good in terms of perfection alone; one must add the idea (*ratio*) of appropriateness or concord (*convenientia*) with the nature perfected: Suárez, *Disputationes metaphysicae*, no. 12. Yet although Finis, Grisez, and Pauline Westerman have their doubts, like Aquinas, Suárez did think of natural law teleologically, as precepts that guide a human being to the fulfillment that is his ultimate end: Grisez (n. 5), 106; Finnis (n. 5), 45; Pauline C. Westerman, *The Disintegration of Natural Law Theory: Aquinas to Finnis* (Leiden, 1997), 101.

The difference is that, for Aquinas, natural law does not exist apart from the mind of a person who is applying it. In so doing, that person applies a general principle of natural law to arrive at a specific precept that covers his own situation. The most general principles direct a person toward the ultimate end that he should pursue. A person following the natural law recognizes, without further thought, that pursuit of this end is worthwhile.[8] He then decides how to act by applying these principles to the circumstances in which he finds himself. When he does so, the specific precept at which he arrives exists "in act." When he is not actually doing so but is able to do so, the precept exists as a "habit" or capacity, in the same way as a knowledge of French irregular verbs exists in the mind of a person who can speak French, but is not doing so at present. For Aquinas, the natural law exists in the mind of a human being, either in act or as habit. It is like the way in which nest building exists in the mind of a bird. It exists "in act" when the bird is building its nest and as a "habit" when it is not so doing, but is able to do so. The natural law does not exist apart from the mind of a human being any more than a nest-building instinct exists outside the mind of a bird. The difference is that a bird does not reflect on how to build a nest, but if a human being is to follow the natural law, he must reflect on the precepts by which he should be guided if he is to realize his end as a human being.

Suárez thought otherwise. One can see the difference in the way in which he and Aquinas treated a case put by Cicero and Augustine. One person entrusted his sword to another, who promised to give it back when the owner asked for it. Cicero and Augustine said that if the owner asked for it back under normal circumstances, the person entrusted with the sword must return it. He should not do so, however, if the owner has gone mad or wishes to use the sword to injure someone. Aquinas and Suárez agreed that both the person who returned the sword in the one case and the person who refused to do so in the other acted in accordance with the natural law.

They disagreed over whether the natural law is different for the one person than for the other. For Aquinas, the natural law exists in act when a person is actually applying its most general principles to his own situation. Consequently, the natural law varies according to the circumstances in which a person finds himself. Although "[t]he natural law as to general principles is the same for all," Aquinas said, as to the "conclusions ... of those general principles, it is the same for all [only] in a majority of cases. ..."[9] Accordingly, the natural law can change, not as to "its first principles" or so that "what it prescribes is not correct in most cases," but it can change with the circumstances.[10] The natural law is the same everywhere as to its "general principles," but not as to its conclusions.[11]

Suárez denied that the natural law can ever change. He acknowledged that there were "some"—meaning Aquinas—who thought that the natural law is the same only as to its "universal principles," but not as to the "conclusions" to be drawn from these principles.[12] But for Suárez, "granted that in this case [the sword] is not

---

[8] Aquinas, *Summa theologiae*, Q. 94, a. 2.   [9] Aquinas (n. 8), a. 4.
[10] Aquinas (n. 8), a. 5.   [11] Aquinas (n. 8), a. 6.   [12] Suárez (n. 6), lib. 2. cap. 8, no. 7.

to be returned, the reason is not that the natural precept has changed, for the principle was not posited for this case but for others....":[13]

[I]t is no objection that the matter is variable.... For [natural law] prescribes one thing as to the matter in one situation, and another for that in another, and so in itself it remains always unchanged, although according to our way of speaking and when it is spoken of extrinsically, it seems as though it varies.[14]

Suárez did not conceive of the natural law as consisting only of the precept that the person entrusted with the sword was actually using to guide his conduct, since the precept in the one case was different than the precept in the other. He conceived of the natural law as a precept that prescribes how a person should act under various circumstances, even though a person deciding how to act may have in mind only the application of the precept to his own circumstances.

The difference can be seen again in their discussions of societies that are ignorant of some precept of natural law. Their example was the ancient Germans, who, according to Caesar, did not know that it is wrong to steal. Aquinas and Suárez agreed that the ancient Germans were mistaken as to what the natural law requires of them, although they might not be to blame for being mistaken.[15] Had they not been mistaken, they would have acted more justly and so lived better lives. According to Aquinas, however, the precept of natural law forbidding theft did not exist among them. It had been "abolished" or "blotted out from their hearts."[16] Although the general principles of natural law are known by all people, including the ancient Germans, this "secondary precept" was not known by them and could not be applied by them. Since the natural law does not exist apart from the mind of a person who is applying it, or who is able to do so, this precept did not exist among them. For Suárez, the natural law prescribes the right course of action in a given set of circumstances. Theft is wrong for the Germans under their circumstances, as it is in any other society. Therefore the precept prohibiting theft had not been abolished whether or not the Germans were or could have been aware of it.[17]

For Aquinas, then, the natural law is like a plan that a person has in mind when he considers how to get from point A, where he is located, to point B, where he wishes to go. It is like a recipe that a person is following when he bakes a cake. The plan would be different for a person starting in a different place or with a different destination, as would the recipe in the mind of someone who is cooking something other than a cake. In the same way, the natural law varies from one person to another. For Suárez, the natural law is like a road map or cookbook. The map indicates not only how a person who wishes to do so can get from point A to point B, but also how a person who wishes to do so could get to point B from point C, or could get from point A to point D. The cookbook not only indicates how a person who wishes to do so should bake a cake, but also what he should do if he wishes to cook something else. The road map and the cookbook remain the same,

---

[13] Suárez (n. 6), lib. 2. cap. 13, no. 6.   [14] Suárez (n. 6), lib. 2. cap. 13, no. 9.
[15] Aquinas (n. 8), I–II, Q. 94, a. 4; Suárez (n. 6), lib. 2, cap. 8, no. 7.
[16] Aquinas (n. 8), I–II, Q. 94, a. 6.   [17] Suárez (n. 6), lib. 2, cap. 8, no. 7.

like the natural law. They would be the same if a person in need of a route or a recipe were unable to consult them, just as the natural law would be the same for a person who was unable to know and apply one of its precepts.

Suárez' view that the natural law is invariable and immutable was shared by some of his contemporaries, such as Luis de Molina[18] and Gabriel Vasquez.[19] But it raised a question with which Suárez dealt more cleverly than they:[20] how, or in what way, does such a road map or cookbook exist if not in the mind of a traveler or a cook?

Suárez agreed with "the common opinion of the Thomists" that, most properly speaking, the natural law was an "act": "The natural law exists most properly in an actual judgment of the mind."[21] Nevertheless, the precepts of natural law existed even when no one had them in mind. According to Suárez:

[I]t is one thing to speak of the existence of precepts ... and another to speak of their actual obligation or exercise. Therefore, although one can postulate a state in which one precept is in use and another is not, nevertheless, the law of nature is always the same, and made up of the same precepts, because they are either principles or conclusions necessarily elicited from them which are not defective in any situation.[22]

The precepts exist even when they are not "exercised" by anyone or capable of being followed by anyone.

That is not possible in Aquinas' metaphysics. For Aquinas, as for Aristotle, the world consists of things that actually exist, such as human beings. For a precept of the natural law to exist, it must exist in the mind of a human being, either in "act" or as a "habit." In the metaphysics of Suárez, "being ... has a double meaning, by which it signifies either being as prescinding from actual existence or being as actual existence";[23] "[B]eing primarily seems to signify a thing having a real and actual

---

[18] Ludovicus de Molina, *De iustitia et iure tractatus* (Venice, 1614), V, disp. 49, no. 3.
[19] Gabriel Vasquez, *Commentariorum ac disputationum in primam partem sancti Thomae*, ed. novissima (Lyon, 1631), disp. 231, cap. 4, no. 16.
[20] According to Molina, the natural law "is nothing else but the intellectual power (*potentia*) itself and the natural light of the intellect...." The precepts of the natural law would exist even in a society in which every person was ignorant of them, because "this power of the intellect cannot be abolished in us": Molina (n. 18), V, disp. 49, no. 6. Suárez agreed that the "natural light of reason" was a human capacity, but he pointed out that a capacity was not a precept, and the question was whether the precepts of natural law can change: Suárez (n. 6), lib. 2, cap.5, nos. 2, 5; *see also* no. 9. Gabriel Vasquez identified the natural law with the rational nature of a human being, since "that is said to be good which is harmonious or appropriate to rational nature, and evil which is inappropriate....": Vasquez (n. 19), disp. 231, cap. 4, no. 16. The natural law did not change because human nature did not change. Suárez objected, as he had with Molina, that human nature is not a precept, and the question is whether the precepts of natural law can change. "[R]ational nature,... neither prescribes, nor shows what is honest or evil, nor directs, nor illuminates, nor has any other effect that is proper to law....": Suárez (n. 6), lib. 2, cap. 5, no. 14.
[21] Suárez (n. 6), lib. 2, cap. 5, no. 14.     [22] Suárez (n. 6), lib. 2, cap. 8, no. 9.
[23] Suárez (n. 7), disp. 2, sec. 4, no. 9. Wishing to emphasize the centrality of actual existence in Suárez's philosophy, José Pereira noted that Suárez spoke of "actual and real existence" as the "primary" signification of the term "being," that "existence, as existence, corresponds to being as such"—Suárez (n. 7), disp. 50, sec. 12, no. 7—and "being and existence are the same"—Suárez (n. 7), disp. 2, sec. 4, no. 1. For similar texts, *see* José Pereira, "'The Existential Integralism of Suárez': Re-evaluation of Gilson's Allegation of Suarezian Essentialism," *Gregorianum* 85 (2004): 660, 665–66. But Pereira

existence...; thence the word was transferred to signify that which has a real essence [*essentia realis*]."²⁴ This idea of a real essence or *essentia realis*, as José Pereira noted, "is original in Suárez."²⁵ As a result, Suárez could consider the precepts of natural law while prescinding from whether anyone actually knows of a particular precept or is applying it. The precepts can be invariable and immutable even though they actually exist only intermittently and partially in the minds of actual human beings. The precept requiring one to return a deposit under some circumstances and not under others, with a full specification of the circumstances that could matter, can exist in this secondary sense even though no one actually has the complete precept in mind.

In order to take this position, Suárez had to reject an idea that had been of fundamental importance in the Aristotelian tradition: that practical reason operated differently than theoretical reason and did not reach its conclusions with the same degree of certainty. For Aristotle, theoretical reason and practical reason both proceeded from first principles to conclusions, but, as W. K. C. Guthrie observed, "as Aristotle never tires of insisting, [practical reason] can never offer the cast iron certainty" of theoretical truths.²⁶ In the *Nicomachean Ethics*, Aristotle explained:

[T]he whole discussion of human action must proceed in general terms and not with precision... [A]ccounts must conform to their subject matter, and there is no permanence about what is to be done, and what is profitable, any more than about what is healthy. Such being the exposition in general, in particular cases it must be even less precise. These do not fall under any art or rule but the agents themselves must consider what suits the present situation as with medicine and seamanship.²⁷

According to Aquinas, "all acts of virtue belong to the law of nature" because "everything belongs to the law of nature to which a man is inclined according to his nature."²⁸ In order to decide how to act, a person needs to apply the general principles of the law of nature to his particular situation. He does so by exercising a capacity that Aristotle called *phronesis* and Aquinas called *prudentia*, or prudence, which is often translated as "practical reason." Aristotle explained that "*phronesis* is not [theoretical or scientific] knowledge, for it is concerned with the ultimate particular... since such is the thing that has to be done."²⁹ Aquinas explained that, to act rightly, a person had to apply general or universal principles to "actions," which "are in singular matters."³⁰ Since "an infinite number of singulars cannot be comprehended by human reason,"³¹ a person might have to apply

---

acknowledged that, for Suárez, a being was not only "a thing having a real and actual existence," but also, albeit in a secondary sense, "being as prescinding from actual existence," which is the point at issue here.

²⁴ Suárez (n. 7), disp. 50, sec. 12, no. 7.   ²⁵ Pereira (n. 23), 667.
²⁶ W. K. C. Guthrie, *A History of Greek Philosophy VI: Aristotle—An Encounter* (Cambridge, 1981), 346.
²⁷ Aristotle, *Nicomachean Ethics* II.ii 1103$^b$ 34, translation from Guthrie (n. 26), 78.
²⁸ Aquinas (n. 8), I–II Q. 94, a. 3.
²⁹ Aristotle (n. 27), VI.ix 1142$^a$ 23–27, following the translation of Guthrie (n. 26), 346–47.
³⁰ Aquinas (n. 8), II–II, Q. 47, a. 3.   ³¹ Aquinas (n. 8), II–II, Q. 47, a. 3 ad. 2.

general principles in a situation in which the circumstances that matter are more than he can comprehend.

To do so, a person needs prudence and several kindred virtues that limit the circumstances he considers. "Memory" and "experience," which are parts of prudence, suggest to him "what is true in the majority of cases."[32] He can seek advice from experienced people, and, indeed, "stands in great need of being taught by others especially old folk...."[33] In doing so, he employs the related virtue of *eubolia*, which is the seeking of counsel. Another virtue, *sinesis*, enables him to apply "common rules" that have been devised for similar situations. Nevertheless, he needs another virtue, *gnome*, to make exceptions to the common rules and to "judge... according to higher principles." *Gnome* is necessary because:

> [I]t happens sometimes that something has to be done which is not covered by the common rules of actions, for instance, in the case of the enemy of one's country, when it would be wrong to give him back his deposit [of a sword].[34]

Nevertheless, despite the use of these virtues, Aquinas concluded, "'our counsels are uncertain' (Wis. 9: 14) because an infinite number of singulars cannot be comprehended by human reason."[35]

Suárez continued to speak of theoretical and practical reason. But he believed that they reached their conclusions in basically the same way. The law of nature consists "of principles [and] conclusions necessarily elicited from them." These conclusions were certain and immutable. Since the "natural law... is posited by right reason... [it] cannot deviate from the truth, for if it does deviate, it is not right reason...."[36] That was so, at least, when all of the circumstances on which these conclusions depend were specified:

> Granted that the propositions of physics [referred to earlier as "natural and speculative science" as contrasted with "moral and practical"[37]] may be said to fail sometimes, nevertheless, scientific conclusions do not fail because they are not to be taken absolutely but with some limitation, at any rate as to what will arise from certain causes in themselves unless there is an impediment. So it is with the present natural precept [on the return of deposits] which, as I said, does not prescribe absolutely as to this matter, for example, that deposits are to be returned but under due circumstances that are understood, as I explained sufficiently before.[38]

Since the natural precept took account of all of the circumstances that matter, no virtue such as *gnome* was needed to make an exception when new circumstances arose. Suárez did not discuss *gnome*. He did discuss the related virtue of *epikeia*, or "equity." According to Aristotle and Aquinas, *epikeia* corrects the application of a human law when the law fails to take account of some circumstance.[39] Aquinas'

---

[32] Aquinas (n. 8), II–II, Q. 49, a. 1.    [33] Aquinas (n. 8), II–II, Q. 49, a. 3.
[34] Aquinas (n. 8), II–II, Q. 51, a. 4.
[35] Aquinas (n. 8), II–II, Q. 47, a. 3 ad. 2. The contrast is noted by Westerman (n. 7), 105–07.
[36] Suárez (n. 6), lib. 2, cap. 16, no. 9.    [37] Suárez (n. 6), lib. 2, cap. 16, no. 9.
[38] Suárez (n. 6), lib. 2, cap. 16, no. 9.    [39] Aristotle (n. 27), V.x.

example, again, is the return of the sword to a lunatic or malefactor.[40] According to Suárez, there was no place for *epikeia* in natural law: "[N]atural law cannot be corrected, as it is posited by right reason, which cannot deviate from the truth, for if it does deviate, it is not right reason...."[41] To see that the sword should not be returned to the lunatic or malefactor requires not *epikeia*, but interpretation.[42]

Although Aquinas himself seems to have thought that *epikeia* is a virtue concerned with the application of human, rather than natural, law,[43] nevertheless, as we have seen, in dealing with moral choice, he gave a similar account of the virtue of *gnome*.[44] Whatever precepts we use to guide our actions will not hold invariably, because "it happens sometimes that something has to be done which is not covered by the common rules of actions," as in the case of the sword.[45] For Suárez, there could not be exceptions, because the precepts of natural law took all of the circumstances that could matter into account.

Suárez does not say whether, as Aquinas thought, the circumstances that might matter are infinite in number so that the human mind cannot grasp them all. Nevertheless, it is doubtful that he thought that they were. If these circumstances were infinite, the natural precept that took proper account of them would be infinitely long. It is hard to see how it could actually exist in any human mind and, consequently, how it could exist in Suárez' secondary sense—that is, prescinding from whether or not it actually exists.

Moreover, the examples that he does give are cases such as the return of the sword in which it seems, on the surface, that only a few circumstances would matter, such as whether its return is demanded by a lunatic or malefactor. He

---

[40] Aquinas (n. 8), II–II, Q. 120, a. 1.    [41] Suárez (n. 6), lib. 2, cap. 16, no. 9.

[42] Suárez (n. 6), lib. 2, cap. 16, no. 7. Farrell seems to think, I believe incorrectly, that Aquinas looked at the precepts of natural law in the same way—that "a full statement of the precept" would include the way in which it would be applied under different circumstances: Walter Farrell, *The Natural Moral Law According to St. Thomas and Suarez* (1930), 116.

[43] He did say that *epikeia* "corresponds properly to legal justice": Aquinas (n. 8), II–II, Q. 121, a. 2 ad. 1; that "legal justice...directs man immediately to the common good...": Aquinas (n. 8), II–II, Q. 58, a. 7; and that all law, human or natural, directs man to the common good: Aquinas (n. 8), I–II, Q. 90, a. 2. Nevertheless, *epikeia* "moderates the observance of the letter of the law": Aquinas (n. 8), I–II, Q. 120, a. 2 ad 3. Only human law is written in letters. So *epikeia* must concern human law, which is law promulgated by public authority to direct a community to its common good: Aquinas (n. 8), I–II, Q. 90, a. 3. In contrast, Cajetan said that *epikeia* concerns "law, both positive and natural": Cajetan (Tomasso di Vio), *Commentaria* to *Thomas Aquinas, Summa theologica* (Padua, 1698), to II–II, Q. 120, a. 1. In speaking of natural law here, he may have meant only those human laws that restate natural law, as suggested by Angel Rodriguez Luño, "La virtù dell'epicheia. Teoria, storia e applicazione (I). Dalla Grecia classica fino a F. Suárez," *Acta philosophica* 6 (1997): 197, 222–23. In any event, Aquinas did not take the position of Suárez. To show that he did, Suárez cited a passage in his commentary to the *Sentences* of Peter Lombard, 4. D. 33, q. 1, a. 2, where Aquinas discussed dispensation from the natural law prohibiting polygamy. But in that passage, he did not mention *epikeia*: Suárez (n. 6), lib. 2, cap. 16, no. 1.

[44] The parallel is noted by Luño (n. 43), 221–22. But it does not follow that "*gnome*...is the part of prudence that regulates the virtue of *epikeia*....": Luño (n. 43), 222. *Gnome* moderates the application of "common rules" for making moral decisions; *epikeia* "moderates the observance of the letter of the law." In both cases, there is a need to moderate, and for the same reason and in the same way. But that does not show that one virtue regulates the other.

[45] Aquinas (n. 8), II–II, Q. 51, a. 4.

avoids mentioning cases in which the number and complexity of the circumstances that might matter is apparent. One such case was put by Aquinas. Suppose that one person has a high opinion of another and wishes to become friends: should he tell that person just how high his opinion is? In the majority of cases, Aquinas observed, to do so would promote friendship. Sometimes, however, it would reinforce conceit or arouse a suspicion of flattery.[46] Any number of circumstances might affect what one ought to say. Finding the right words would be easier for a person with more experience, better advice, a familiarity with common rules of social intercourse, and an ability to apply them flexibly. Suárez does not mention this case. It may be that he did not think that precepts of natural law apply in situations of this complexity.[47] If he had, his immutable precepts would have been extraordinary. They would have to prescribe, immutably, what to say to another person under all of the circumstances that could matter: the situation, their previous relationship, and the possibilities for that relationship to develop fruitfully. There would have to be as many precepts as there are friendships or love stories, and, indeed, as many precepts as there are possible friendships or possible love stories.[48]

Given his metaphysics, we can see why Suárez thought that the precepts of natural law are invariable and immutable, and why they could be applied with certainty. Nevertheless, other late scholastics had arrived at similar conclusions before Suárez developed a metaphysics that would explain them. Molina believed that the precepts of natural law were invariable and immutable.[49] He defined natural law as "that which has the same force everywhere and not because it is seen or unseen...."[50] In the case of the promise to return the sword:

[T]here is no dispensation or variation of the law as stated and interpreted by the light of the intellect, for the law remains in itself as it was before, not to be understood in the event that such circumstances intervene. It was never the natural law that that a thing deposited be returned when a madman demands it, but rather the natural law always prescribed the contrary.[51]

According to Leonard Lessius, *epikeia* or equity had no application:

... if the natural law is considered properly, namely, with those circumstances to which the reason of the natural law applies. Then, indeed, it is to be followed in every case as it is just and right in itself, wherefore no *epikeia* is admitted.[52]

---

[46] Aquinas (n. 8), II–II, Q. 49, a. 7.

[47] Because of its failure to take account of more complex situations in which an action contributes to human flourishing, Suárez's account has been attacked by natural law scholars such as Germain Grisez and John Finnis. Grisez criticizes its "negativism and minimalism," its concern with "issuing a few prohibitions [rather] than at directing people's lives toward growth and flourishing," and its failure to recognize that "although essential human nature does not change, in the course of human history new possibilities do open up and humankind acquires powers to act in new, more complex ways." "[I]t is too much concerned with laws and too little with persons": Grisez (n. 5), 104–06. *See* Finnis (n. 5), 45.

[48] Gilson thought that this possibility showed the fundamental problem with Suárezian metaphysics. "[T]here are no such things as fully determined essences prior to their existential actualization.... The Mattheus Passion was not an essence hovering in a limbo of possible essences where Johann Sebastian Bach caught it, so to speak, on the wing": Gilson (n. 5), 211. Nor do friends catch on the wing a possible dialogue.

[49] *See* n. 20.    [50] Molina (n. 18), I, disp. 4.    [51] Molina (n. 18), I, disp. 4.

[52] Leonardus Lessius, *De iustitia et iure, ceterisque virtutibus cardinalibus libri quatuor* (Paris, 1628), lib. 2, cap. 47, dub. 9.

Indeed, Lessius thought that the precepts of natural law could be applied with certainty:

> Even though demonstrations are not made immediately concerning singulars but universals... nevertheless, one can have certain knowledge (*certa notitia*) of singulars, of what and how they are or ought to be, as that this house is correctly built, or not correctly, and that for it to be correctly built, it requires this and that.... So there can be certain knowledge (*notitia*) of singular actions, of whether they are honest or not, and of what it required for them to be done honestly.[53]

To make such a statement, Lessius, like Suárez, must have regarded the circumstances that matter as limited. Presumably, Lessius did not mean that an architect can have "certain knowledge" that he has provided the ideal protection against storms, or found the best places for windows and balconies, or achieved the right combination of simplicity and elegance. Presumably, Lessius meant that the house is built correctly if it is suitable for its purposes and not defective, for example if it large enough for human habitation and the roof does not leak. To build correctly is to follow rules so lacking in complexity that one can be certain whether or not the architect complied with them.

One does not find these opinions about natural law a generation or so earlier, for example with Cajetan,[54] Francisco de Vitoria,[55] and Domingo de Soto,[56] none of whom believed that the precepts of natural law are invariable and immutable, or that one can have certain knowledge of how to apply them. In the course of the sixteenth century, these opinions seem to have become more plausible. If they had not, Suárez's metaphysics might have seemed less plausible.

One reason for the change may have been the intellectual achievement that had taken place in the interval. As we have seen, the late scholastics had synthesized Roman and canon law with philosophical principles taken from Aristotle and

---

[53] Lessius (n. 52), lib. 1, c. 1, dub. 1, no. 4.

[54] *See* his comments on Aquinas' discussion of natural law: *Commentaria* to I–II, Q. 94, aa. 1, 4, 5, 6. He agreed with Aquinas that since prudence makes judgments as to singulars, "our counsels are uncertain," "because of the uncertainty of the outcome and because of what is hidden from us": *Commentaria* to II–II, Q. 47, a. 3. *See* also his discussion of prudence. He does not differ from Aquinas on the need for prudence and kindred virtues in the application of the most general moral principles to a particular situation. For his position on *epikeia*, see *Commentaria* to II–II, Q. 120.

[55] His discussion of the need for prudence follows Aquinas. *See* Francisco de Vitoria, *Comentarios a la secunda secundae de Santo Tomás*, ed. V. Beltrán de Heredia (1932) (Latin text, despite the Spanish title) to II–II, Q. 47, a. 3; Q. 49, Q. 51. Nevertheless, unlike Cajetan, he does not discuss in what way judgment as to singulars makes our counsels uncertain. He explains the need for making a judgment as to singulars by pointing out that it is not enough to eat or drink: one must decide what to eat; and even then, if one wants to eat an apple and to eat bread, one must decide which to eat first: Vitoria, *Comentarios*, to II–II, Q. 47, a. 3. John Finnis noted that Vitoria already deviated from Aquinas in another respect—by claiming that "an obligation can derive only from the will of a superior": Finnis (n. 5), 350. As Finnis also noted, Suárez held that view, and it is another major difference between his approach to natural law and that of Aquinas: Finnis (n. 5), 45–46. But it not the one with which we are dealing here.

[56] His discussion of natural law follows Aquinas. The natural law exists in man as a habit that makes possible the act, which is the dictate of reason as to what to do. It is the same everywhere and at all times as to its general principles, but not as to the conclusions drawn from them: Dominicus de Soto, *De iustitia et iure libri decem* (1556), lib. 1, Q. 4, aa. 1, 4, 5.

Aquinas. Molina and Lessius modeled their treatises on natural law on those of their predecessors, such as Soto. Suárez read their treatises. They may all have moved too quickly from the proposition that these books described natural law to the conclusion that the natural law was what these books described. The natural law may have seemed to consist of the precepts that they could formulate that would explain their legal texts—or at least, those of texts that they deemed to reflect natural, rather than positive, law. The number of texts was limited, and certainly did not raise the full range of problems that a human being would address in seeking to live a fulfilled life. The Romans jurists were not explaining how to live a fulfilled life. Rather, they were explaining when a person could be held liable for such things as depriving another of possession of his property, failing to observe good faith in a sale, or damaging another's property. The canon lawyers were concerned with human perfection. Nevertheless, when they wrote about the external forum, they described rules that could be applied in Church courts. When they wrote about the internal forum, they wrote about general rules that the priest could explain to the penitent, but which often had to be applied to the penitent's situation by the penitent himself. The late scholastics were more concerned with explaining the general rules than with how they might vary with the circumstances. Molina, Lessius, and Suárez may have lost touch with the approach to natural law of Aquinas because of the nature of the intellectual project of the late scholastics and the sources with which they were working.

Then, too, although the late scholastics were trained in metaphysics and moral philosophy, with the exception of Suárez, they were writing treatises on only one aspect of moral philosophy, the virtue of justice (although Lessius said a bit about other cardinal virtues). Unlike Aquinas or Cajetan, they were not writing a unified work in which what was said about metaphysics was related to what was said about natural law, which had to be related in turn to a theory of moral choice, and not only to justice, but also to other virtues such as prudence. In paying close attention to what Aristotle and Aquinas had said about justice, they may have lost track of what else they had said.

The synthesis of the late scholastics was an extraordinary intellectual achievement. There is a risk, however, when traditions are combined, that aspects of one tradition or another may be distorted or neglected. We saw earlier how the late scholastics lost touch with certain aspects of Roman and canon law. They may have lost touch with some basic principles of Aristotelian and Thomistic metaphysics by concerning themselves too exclusively with the project of synthesizing moral philosophy with Roman and canon law.

In any event, Suárez cast a long shadow. His metaphysics influenced two of the most important rationalists to write about law, Gottfried Wilhelm Leibniz and Christian Wolff. As Leroy Loemker noted, in the seventeenth century "Suárez's *Disputationes Metaphysicae* had become the academic standard of doctrine for Protestant and Catholic Europe alike."[57] Leibniz claimed that, as a student, he

---

[57] Leroy E. Loemker, "Introduction" to vol. 1 of *Gottfried Wilhelm Leibniz: Philosophical Papers and Letters*, ed. and trans. Leroy E. Loemker (Chicago, IL, 1956), 1 at 17.

had read Suárez like a novel.[58] The metaphysics that he developed owed much to Suárez' concept of possible being. According to Leibniz, there are certain propositions that are "absolutely necessary, whose contrary implies contradiction [such as] occurs in the eternal verities like the truths of geometry."[59] These propositions will be valid in any possible world.[60] Which possible world will come into actual existence depends upon the will of God. Because God is good, however, he will call into existence the best of all possible worlds.[61] Which world is the best depends upon "principles of goodness, of justice and of perfection that follow from his understanding, and do not depend upon his will any more than does his essence."[62]

Before incorporating these propositions in his system of metaphysics, however, Leibniz had already accepted the principle of Suárez that concerns us here. He worked out his system from 1680 to 1697.[63] He wrote, in 1666–67, in an essay on *The Elements of Natural Law*:

> The doctrine of law (*doctrina iuris*) belongs to those sciences that depend on definitions and not on experience, on demonstrations of reason and not of sense, and are matters of law, one can say, and not of fact. As, indeed, justice consists in some congruity and proportionality, we can understand that something is just even if there is no one who is acting justly, or who is being treated justly, in the same way that the concepts (*rationes*) of numbers are true even if there were no one to count and nothing to be counted, and we can predict that a house will be beautiful, a machine efficient, or a commonwealth happy if it comes into being even if it should never do so. We need not wonder, therefore, that the principles of these sciences possess eternal truth.[64]

Leibniz wrote this passage at the age of twenty.

"And then," as Gilson said, "Suárez begat Wolff."[65] In his work *First Philosophy or Ontology*, Wolff said:

> Being is what can exist, and consequently, that with which existence is not incompatible.... [A] right triangle with acute angles drawn on paper is a being, as it exists in act, but no less is a triangle that can be drawn a being, because it exists when it is first drawn, and therefore it can exist. If a stone is exposed to fire or to the rays of the sun in summer, it is hot. Therefore, a hot stone can exist, and therefore it is a being, not inasmuch as it exists in act, but inasmuch as existence is not incompatible with it. The idea of being taken generally scarcely involves

---

[58] Stuart Brown and N. J. Fox, *Historical Dictionary of Leibniz's Philosophy* (Lanham, MD, 2006), v. Suárez, 221.
[59] Gottfried Wilhelm Leibniz, *Discours de métaphysique* (Paris, 1907), xiii.
[60] Leibniz (n. 59), iii.  [61] Leibniz (n. 59), i–iii.  [62] Leibniz (n. 59), ii.
[63] C. D. Broad, *Leibniz: An Introduction* (Cambridge, 1975), 2.
[64] Gottfried Wilhelm Leibniz, *Elementa juris naturalis*, in *Philosophische Schriften Erster Band 1663–1672*, ed. Akademie der Wissenschaften der DDR (Berlin, 1990), 459 at 460. Loemker notes that this passage "already presupposes the distinction between possibility and existence made in his later thought....": *Gottfried Wilhelm Leibniz: Philosophical Papers and Letters*, ed. and trans. Leroy E. Loemker (Chicago, IL, 1956), 138, n. 5. Leibniz wrote several short treatises with the title *Elementa iuris naturalis*. Two will be cited here: this one, which appears at page 459 of *Philosophische Schriften Erster Band 1663–1672*, and another, which appears at page 433. They will be cited by the first page followed by the page on which the reference is to be found.
[65] Gilson (n. 5), 112.

existence but only a lack of incompatibility with existence, or, which is the same, the possibility of existing.⁶⁶

Because what is possible can exist, what is possible is a being.

This idea not only resembles the *essentia realis* of Suárez, but is the same idea expressed in different words. Wolff said that it "must be agreed, among the scholastics," that Suárez "most profoundly meditated matters of metaphysics."⁶⁷ What is more surprising is that, according to Wolff, this conception of being was also that of Aquinas.⁶⁸ The actual position of Aquinas was now off the radar screen: as Gilson said, "Suárezianism has consumed Thomism."⁶⁹

## An innovation in method

Although Suárez said that the natural law consists of principles that are known of themselves or those that are necessarily inferred from them,⁷⁰ he was not clear about the method to be followed to arrive at them or to draw the necessary inferences. Some scholars have said that "Suárez narrows down the scope of reason to that of theoretical reason only...overlook[ing] the importance of practical reason as distinct from theoretical reason...."⁷¹ Certainly, he overlooked the importance of practical reason, as Aristotle and Aquinas had understood it.⁷² But he could not have thought of theoretical reason as they did either. As we have seen, he seems to have thought that theoretical and practical reason worked in basically the same way, although he did not explain how they worked.

An innovation in method was made by René Descartes.⁷³ In 1637, Descartes published, anonymously, his first work: *Discourse on the Method of Rightly Conducting the Reason and Seeking for Truth in the Sciences*. Reflecting on his own education, he said:

[S]o soon as I had achieved the entire course of study at the close of which one is usually received into the ranks of the learned...I found myself embarrassed with so many doubts and errors that it seemed to me that I had drawn no other profit from the effort to instruct myself than, increasingly, to have discovered my ignorance.⁷⁴

Although "philosophy...has been cultivated for many centuries by the best minds that have ever lived, nevertheless, no single thing is to be found in it which is not an

---

⁶⁶ Christian Wolff, *Philosophia prima sive ontologia*, ed. Johannes Ecole (Helesheim, 1962), §§ 134–35.
⁶⁷ Wolff (n. 66), § 169.   ⁶⁸ Wolff (n. 66), § 169.   ⁶⁹ Gilson (n. 5), 118.
⁷⁰ Suárez (n. 6), lib. 2, cap. 13, no. 3.   ⁷¹ Westerman (n. 7), 97.
⁷² According to Germain Grisez and John Finnis, Suárez's precepts concern "theoretical" or "self-evident relations of conformity or non-conformity to human nature": Grisez (n. 5), 104; Finnis (n. 5), 48.
⁷³ Jan Schröder traces the break with the earlier natural law approach of the iusnaturalists to this innovation: Jan Schröder, *Recht als Wissenschaft Geschichte der juristischen Methodenlehre in der Neuzeit (1550–1933)* (Munich, 2012), 170–71.
⁷⁴ René Descartes, "Discours de la méthode pour bien conduire sa raison et chercher la vérité dans les sciences," in vol. 1 of *Oeuvres philosophiques*, ed. Ferdinand Alquié (Paris, 1963), 567 at 571.

object of dispute, and in consequence which is not doubtful...."[75] "As to the other sciences, inasmuch as they borrow their principles from philosophy, I judged that one could have built nothing on foundations so infirm."[76] "For that reason," he explained, "I entirely quitted the study of letters."[77] "I employed the rest of my youth in travel..."[78] Yet, when "I considered the manners of other men...I remarked in them almost as much diversity as I had formerly seen in the opinions of the philosophers."[79]

Descartes had been "pleased above all" by one branch of study: "mathematics because of the certainty of its demonstrations and the evidence of its reasoning."[80] During his travels, he concluded that one could obtain certainty "in all those things which fall under the cognizance of man" by "accepting nothing as true which I did not recognize to be so," and then employing those "chains of reasoning, simple and easy as they are, which geometricians use to arrive at the most difficult demonstrations...."[81] Thereafter, "I always remained firm in the resolution I had made...to accept nothing as true which did not appear to be more clear and more certain than the demonstrations of the geometricians had formerly seemed."[82] Four years later, he published his *Meditations on First Philosophy*, in which he sought certainty by doubting everything that could be doubted, including the existence of the physical world, and then working out the logical consequences of the one proposition that he could not doubt—that is, that he was doubting.

By Aristotle's method, one was able to grasp higher principles by accumulating experience and finding the common element in the particular cases that have been observed. One could not use that method if one accepted nothing as true until it had been proven with the certainty of the demonstrations of geometry. Experience could no longer be a starting point.

Erhard Weigel, a professor at the University of Jena, became a convinced Cartesian. Like Descartes, who had discovered analytic geometry, Weigel was a mathematician. He was also an accomplished astronomer. A crater on the moon is named for him. He saw the conflict between the Aristotelian position that one could not have certain knowledge in ethics and the Cartesian program of accepting "nothing as true which did not appear to be more clear and more certain than the demonstrations of the geometricians." He concluded that, since ethical knowledge did exist, it must consist of propositions demonstrable by the methods of geometry.[83] Indeed, he claimed that Aristotle himself would have agreed. Aristotle's work had been misunderstood for centuries. In 1648, Weigel published these conclusions in a work entitled *Aristotelian Analysis Restored through Euclid*.[84]

---

[75] Descartes (n. 74), 576.
[76] Descartes (n. 74), 576.
[77] Descartes (n. 74), 576–77.
[78] Descartes (n. 74), 577.
[79] Descartes (n. 74), 578.
[80] Descartes (n. 74), 574.
[81] Descartes (n. 74), 587.
[82] Descartes (n. 74), 613–14.
[83] Although he did not demonstrate these propositions: Wolfgang Rod, *Geometrischer Geist und Naturrecht* (Munich, 1970), 77.
[84] Erhard Weigel, *Analysis Aristotelica ex Euclide restituta*, in vol. 3 of *Werke* (Stuttgart, 2008).

Samuel Pufendorf studied law at Jena, where he became Weigel's pupil and close friend. Inspired by Weigel, he wrote the book discussed in an earlier chapter,[85] *Elementorum jurisprudentiae libri duo*, a title based on Euclid's *Elements* of geometry. His conclusions were organized under a series of definitions, axioms, and "observations," much as one might organize a treatise on geometry.[86] In the Preface, he explained that it was Weigel, "an honored friend of mine ... who first exhorted me to attempt something in this field."[87] He said that "the science of law and equity ... has hitherto not been cultivated to the extent that its necessity and dignity demand," because of "a common conviction that in matters of morality, by their very nature, there is no firm and infallible certainty, and that all knowledge of such matters rests on probable opinion only." Many subscribed to that opinion because it had been held by "Aristotle himself, who, I do not know by what fatal favor, has hitherto appeared to the majority of mankind to surpass the summit of human genius...." But he considered it:

... utterly absurd for men to have been denied sure knowledge of those things which they were enjoined by the authority of their Creator to put into action, while at the same time, one may have definite and clear knowledge of things that can be safely ignored....

In any event, Aristotle had been misunderstood. Correctly interpreted, "even by the decrees of the Stagirite, law will be allowed to claim its place in among the sciences which are called demonstrative."[88] "All this was set forth not long ago in the most clear and convincing fashion in a special treatise by that illustrious man, Herr Eberhard Weigel...."[89]

Pufendorf differed from Suárez because he accepted the Cartesian method. Suárez' ideas about method were less clear. In addition, Pufendorf's metaphysics could not have been more different. Pufendorf believed that an action was right or wrong by "imposition" of the will of God.[90] According to Leibniz, Pufendorf might as well say that "the reason a triangle has three sides ... is that God has willed it so."[91] As Leibniz noted, Descartes had actually taken such a position. He had said:

God did not will the three angles of a triangle to be equal to two right angles because he knew that they could not be otherwise. On the contrary, it is because he willed the three

---

[85] See Chapter V, pp. 132–33.
[86] Thus Wieacker classes him as a progenitor of the new geometric method in contrast to the older method of Grotius: Karl Wieacker, *Privatrechtsgeschichte der Neuzeit*, 2nd ed. (Göttingen, 1967), 270–71.
[87] Samuel Pufendorf, *Elementorum jurisprudentiae libri duo* (Cambridge, 1672), *Praefatio* 7.
[88] Pufendorf (n. 87), 4–5.   [89] Pufendorf (n. 87), 6–7.
[90] Pufendorf (n. 87), I.i.
[91] Gottfried Wilhelm Leibniz, "Opinion on the Principles of Pufendorf," in *The Political Writings of Leibniz*, ed. Patrick Riley (Cambridge, 1972), 64 at 71–72.(For the original, see Gotofredus Guillielmus Leibniz, *Opera omnia 4*, ed. Louis Dutens (Geneva, 1769), iii, 275.) On their disagreement, see J. B. Sneewind, "Barbeyrac and Leibniz on Pufendorf," in *Samuel Pufendorf und die europäische Frühaufklärung Werk und Einfluss eines deutschen Bürgers der Gerlehrtenrepublik nach 300 Jahren (1694–1944)*, eds. Fiamemetta Paladini and Gerald Hartung (Berlin, 1996), 184–85; René Sève, *Leibniz e l'école modern du droit naturel* (Paris, 1989), 101.

angles of the triangle to be necessarily equal to two right angles that it is true and cannot be otherwise.[92]

According to Leibniz, that statement showed "how great can be the errors of great men."[93] The principles of arithmetic and geometry are "immutable," and "justice follows certain rules of equality and proportion [which are] no less founded on the immutable nature of things...."[94]

As we have seen, Leibniz subscribed to a metaphysics like that of Suárez. He also subscribed to a method like that of Descartes and Weigel. In 1663, at the age of seventeen, he spent a year studying law at the University of Jena, where he heard Weigel lecture.[95] Four years later, he published a book entitled *A New Method of Learning and Teaching Jurisprudence*. "Demonstration (*analytica*) or the art of judging," he explained, "seems to me to be almost completely reducible to two rules: (1) no word is to be admitted unless it is explained, (2) and no proposition unless it has been proven."[96] By the use of these rules, it would be possible, he said, to arrive at the "elements" of "didactic jurisprudence," consisting of "the explication of terms or definitions" and of "propositions or precepts"—"aptly called by the name of elements in imitation of Euclid...."[97] "To reduce law to an art or science (*ius in artem redigendi*) was an ancient concern" raised by Cicero.[98] One could do so by means of the "new method." "The new method would bring incredible advantages": "A compendium of that which is to be learned would marvelously appear," in which "an infinity of special rules would be learned at once by means of general ones," and in which one "would descend in order from the premises of genera to species" through "an accurate definition of terms." "The way would be open for undecided cases in law to be determined by universal principles (*rationes*)."[99]

Although Leibniz' metaphysics was like that of Suárez, his confidence in the power of demonstration from general rules seems to have led him to a different view of what the precepts of natural law are like. For Suárez, as we have seen, a precept of natural law, properly interpreted, took account of every circumstance that could matter. For that reason, as we have seen, he seems to have thought that the number of circumstances that could matter was limited. For Leibniz, law will comprise "an infinity of special rules." From a limited number of general and universal principles, one can derive an infinite number of special rules to cover all of the circumstances. In the same way, the definition of a triangle or a circle might lead to innumerable consequences.

Leibniz wrote the *New Method* to attract the attention of John Philip of Schönborn, the Elector of Mainz. He succeeded in doing so. Leibniz was appointed, with

---

[92] René Descartes, *Objections faites par des personnes très doctes contre les précédents méditations avec les réponses de l'auteur, Réponses aux sixièmes objections* no. 6, in Descartes (n. 74), 507 at 872–73.
[93] Leibniz (n. 91), 71.    [94] Leibniz (n. 91), 71.
[95] Consequently, although I agree with Hartmann that Leibniz's ideas on method were not derived from Ramus or Donnellus, I do not think they were the original product of youthful genius: Gustav Hartmann, *Liebnitz als Jurist und Rechtsphilosoph* (Tübingen 1992), 25–26.
[96] Gottfried Wilhelm Leibniz, *Nova methodus discendae docendaeque jurisprudentia*, in Leibniz, *Philosophische Schriften Erster Band* I, § 25.
[97] Leibniz (n. 96), II. § 6.    [98] Leibniz (n. 96), II, § 8.    [99] Leibniz (n. 96), II, § 11.

Herman Lasser Andrew, to codify the law, with results that will be described shortly.

Christian Wolff, like Leibniz, was a mathematician. He was appointed a professor of mathematics at the University of Halle, although he lectured there on philosophy as well. His method was like that of Leibniz. He described it in the Preface to his treatise *Institutions of the Law of Nature and of Nations*:

> As the love of truth was instilled in me as it were by nature, as I have often taught, I applied my mind to the study of mathematics for no other reason than to understand the great certainty to be found in geometry. I had nothing more at heart than once having known it, to put its truth in plain light, and to yield to it not as one persuaded but convinced. In that spirit I turned to the explication of law. The source of every law is in human nature, as the ancients taught and the moderns have repeated though not demonstrated....
>
> All of this can only be put in the light by following in the track of Euclid... that is, explaining each term by an exact definition, and making a sufficient determination of the meaning of each proposition, and arranging the definitions so that those that come before allow one to fully understand those that follow.[100]

As Claes Peterson has said, what Wolff means:

> ...is clearly not that logic is an analytic disentangling of legal argument. Instead, logic is the way to a synthetic understanding of the legal system. With the help of logic, a logically coherent system of norms can be constructed and even the norms can be derived from it.[101]

## An innovation in principle

As we have seen, the late scholastics explained property, unjust enrichment, tort, and contract by means of the principles of distributive and commutative justice taken from Aristotle and Aquinas. In the work of the rationalists, these principles dropped from view. In the case of Pufendorf, the innovation was negative: he did not replace these principles with any others. In the case of Leibniz and Wolff, the innovation was to identify a higher principle from which the law could supposedly be derived, but one that they did not link—and could not link—to distributive or commutative justice as traditionally understood.

As we have seen,[102] unlike the late scholastics, Pufendorf did not base the doctrines of private law on principles of distributive and commutative justice. The question arose: on what higher principles were they based? His critics objected that there was little relationship between his conclusions and any higher principles. His *Elements of Universal Jurisprudence* was organized into definitions, axioms, and

---

[100] Christian Wolff, *Institutiones juris naturae et gentium*, in Christian Wolff, *Gesammelte Werke* 26, ed. M. Thomann (Hildesheim, 1972), *Prefatio*.
[101] Claes Peterson, "Zur Anwendung der Logik in der Naturrechtslehre von Christian Wolff," in *Entwicklung der Methodenlehre in Rechtswissenschaft un Philosophie vom 16. bis zum 18. Jahrhundert*, ed. Jan Schröder (Stuttgart 1998), 177 at 177.
[102] *See* Chapter V, pp. 134–36, 138.

"observations" from which he claimed his conclusions logically followed. Nevertheless, his account of private property appears under Definition V, which defines property in the "affirmative" sense as that which is subject to private or common ownership, and in the "negative" sense as that which is "no man's." He did not explain how to move from there to the doctrine of necessity. The rules of tort law supposedly followed from Observation IV: "Right reason dictates that a man should care for himself in such a way that human society be not thrown into disorder." But he did not explain what his conclusions had to do with that Observation. His conclusions as to contract law were supposed to follow from Definition XII: "Principles of human action are those things from which it springs and on which it depends, and by which a human action is brought to completion." But it was not clear how they followed.

The complaint of Leibniz and Wolff was that Pufendorf had accepted much of the legal learning of his time without ever explaining how it could be derived from higher principles. Leibniz said, speaking of Pufendorf's *Duties of Man and the Citizen*, "the greater part of the thoughts expounded in the course of the work are not consistent with the principles, and are not logically deduced from them, but rather are borrowed from elsewhere...."[103] Wolff observed:

It is commonly said that Pufendorf used the demonstrative method. Indeed, those who think so sufficiently show themselves to be unacquainted with the demonstrative method, and those who are versed in mathematics or in our philosophical works abundantly understand how far this judgment is from the truth.[104]

They might have said the same about the "axiomatic method"[105] of Johannes Gottlieb Heineccius, who was a professor of philosophy before becoming a professor of law.[106] He wrote a commentary on the *Digest* and is usually classed by

---

[103] Leibniz (n. 91), 65.

[104] Christian Wolff, *Jus naturae method scientific pertracta*, published as *Jus Naturae*, in ed. Marcellus Thomannus, vols. 17–24 of *Gesammelte Werke II. Abteilung Lateinishce Schriften*, eds. J. École, J. E. Hofmann, M. Thomann, and H. W. Arndt (Hildesheim, 1972), *Prolegomena* § 2. The inconsistency is noted by modern scholars. See Thomas Behme, "Gegensätzliche Einflüsse in Pufendorfs Naturrecht," in *Samuel Pufendorf und die europäische Frühaufklärung Werk und Einfluss eines deutschen Bürgers der Gerlehrtenrepublik nach 300 Jahren (1694–1944)*, eds. Fiamemetta Paladini and Gerald Hartung (Berlin, 1996), 74; Hans Wehberg, "Introduction," xiii, to Samuel Pufendorf, *The Elements of Universal Jurisprudence*, trans. William Abbott Oldfather (Oxford, 1931). The inconsistency is not surprising given Pufendorf's limitations as a philosopher, which have been acknowledged by his biographers. Denzel said that that he was "a man of broad learning," but with "no philosophical mind": Horst Denzel, *Moralphilosophie und Naturrecht bei Samul Pufendorf: Eine geistes- und wissenschaftsgeschictlich Untersuchung zur Geburt des Naturrechts aus der praktischen Philosophie* (Munich, 1972), 7. According to Krieger, "Pufendorf possessed, as a secondary thinker, a great comparative advantage over his mentors. He was an occasional philosopher—that is, he worked up philosophical analyses only on those occasions in which his more mundane concerns required footing....": Leonard Krieger, *The Politics of Discretion: Pufendorf and the Acceptance of Natural Law* (Chicago, IL, 1965), 50.

[105] Karl Droeschell, *Deutsche Rechtsgeschichte (seit 1650)* 3 (Opladen, 1989), 17; Klaus Luig, "Heineccius," in *Juristen Ein biographisches Lexikon Von der Antike bis zum 20. Jahrhundert*, ed. Michael Stolleis (Munich, 1995), 579 at 579; Klaus Luig, "Die Anfänge der Wissenschaft vom deutschen Privatrecht," *Ius Commune* 1 (1967): 195, 219.

[106] Luig, "Heineccius" (n. 105), 579.

Mos Geometricus: *The Coming of Rationalism* 183

historians as a jurist of the *usus modernus pandectarum*. As Christoph Bergfeld noted, although the content of his commentary was much the same, his method was new: he wished to derive legal rules syllogistically from higher principles. His model was mathematics.[107] As he said, one must "find definitions which are most evident, clear axioms, and, necessary conclusions which thereafter flow spontaneously from these definitions, and which can be reduced to their principles."[108] He had the same difficulty as Pufendorf in extracting necessary conclusions from his definitions. Sometimes, he packed the conclusions he wanted into the definitions, and then ceremoniously unpacked them. For example, he defined the elements of the *lex Aquilia* in such a way that two "axioms flowed from these definitions. I. An action under the *lex Aquilia* lies whenever harm (*damnum*) is done intentionally or through negligence. II. This law requires that our assets be destroyed or diminished by physical action on a physical thing."[109] These axioms did indeed follow, since he had defined the *lex Aquilia* to require "unlawfulness" (*iniuria*), which meant "any international wrong or negligence," and "harm" (*damnum*), by which "we understand the corruption of a physical thing by a physical action."[110] Sometimes, he simply inserted a conclusion without explaining how it was derived. For example, after the passage just quoted, he added that his definition applied only to a direct action under the *lex Aquilia*, and that an *actio utilis* or *in factum* would be given in cases in which the damage was done not by physical action on a physical thing.[111] Similarly, he defined sale as consent to give an object for a price,[112] "from which it easily appears" that the substance of a sale requires consent, an object, and a price.[113] Then, in discussing the price, he explains that it must not be "manifestly iniquitous,"[114] without explaining where that principle comes from.

Some modern scholars have said that the "geometric paradigm in law" originated with Leibniz.[115] Certainly he, rather than Pufendorf or Heineccius, was the first to take it seriously. He and Wolff did identify higher principles from which they attempted to derive basic rules of law. But the principles had no relation to distributive and commutative justice, as traditionally understood. For Leibnitz and Wolff, the highest principle, grounded in human nature, was one of pure altruism. Everyone should do whatever he can to perfect both himself and everyone else. According to Leibniz, "[s]ince justice aims at the good, and wisdom and goodness together form justice and refer it to the good, we may ask what is the true

---

[107] Christoph Bergfeld, "Pufendorf und Heineccius," in *Samuel Pufendorf und die europäische Frühaufklärung Werk und Einfluss eines deutschen Bürgers der Gelehrtenrepublik nach 300 Jahren (1694–1944)*, eds. Fiamemetta Paladini and Gerald Hartung (Berlin, 1996), 225 at 227.
[108] Johannes Gottlieb Heineccius, *Elementa iuris civili secundum ordinem pandectorum* (Venice, 1746), *Prefatio* (dated 1727) xxii.
[109] Heineccius (n. 108), 9.2, § 183.  [110] Heineccius (n. 108), 9.2, § 182.
[111] Heineccius (n. 108), 9.2, § 186.  [112] Heineccius (n. 108), 18.1, § 252.
[113] Heineccius (n. 108), 18.1, § 253.  [114] Heineccius (n. 108), 18.1, § 293.
[115] H. M. Hoeflich, "Law and Geometry: Legal Science from Leibniz to Langdell," *The American Journal of Legal History* 30 (1986): 99; Roger Berkowitz, *The Gift of Science: Leibniz and the Modern Legal Tradition* (Cambridge, 2005), 17; Rod (n. 83), 100.

good. I reply that it is merely whatever serves the perfection of intelligent substances":[116]

A good man is one who loves all men so far as reason permits. Therefore ... we may most fittingly describe justice ... as the charity of the wise man, that is, as charity which follows from the dictates of wisdom. ... Charity is universal benevolence.[117]

Borrowing from Leibniz,[118] Wolff said that each person has the right and the duty to do whatever will perfect himself, and, unless it conflicts with this duty, whatever will perfect other people:

Without doubt, every man as an ultimate end should seek his perfection and that of others, and therefore to make all use of his faculties that is required for this end to be pursued. The perfection of others, then, should be no less dear and of concern to us than our own.[119]

Thus "[e]very man must give what he is able to any other man who does not have it in his power to the extent that he can without neglecting his own duties."[120]

The problem was how to move deductively from this principle of pure altruism to doctrines of property, contract, tort, and the like, all of which concern private right. As Klaus Luig has said, to explain the relationship of the higher principles and private right was "the most difficult task" for Leibniz,[121] and also, one could say, for Wolff. Leibniz did not even attempt it. Despite the rationalist program, as Hans-Peter Schneider observed, Leibniz did not try to move deductively from the one to the other, and if he had, he could not have succeeded.[122] The same can be said of Wolff. Instead, for them, the relationship between altruism and private right was one of radical disjunction. Private right was defined negatively by its difference from altruism. It was a right that was private, and therefore not altruistic, and therefore self-regarding.

Leibniz and Wolff maintained that private rights must exist because human beings were too imperfect to adhere to the ultimate principle of altruism. Thus they defined private right not in terms of this ultimate principle, but in opposition to it. Having done so, they could not move from this principle to concepts of property,

---

[116] Gottfried Wilhelm Leibniz, "Reflections on the Common Conception of Justice," in *Leibniz*, ed. Loemker (n. 57), 911 at 917.

[117] Gottfried Wilhelm Leibniz, "Codex iuris gentium diplomaticus," *Praefatio*, in *Leibniz*, ed. Loemker (n. 57), 690 at 690. Similarly, "the good man is one who is benevolent toward all. ... The ultimate rule of law is everything is directed to the maximum general good or common happiness": "De tribus juris praeceptis sive gradibus," in Gottfried Wilhelm Leibniz, *Textes inédits*, ed. Gaston Grua (New York, 1985), 606 at 607.

[118] Clemens Schwaiger, "Ist Wolffs Ethik leibnianisch? Ein Beitrag zur Wiederbelebung der Glücksthematik," in *Leibniz und Europa VI: Internationaler Leibniz-Kongress* (Langenhagen 1994), 727 at 728.

[119] Wolff (n. 104), I, § 609.   [120] Wolff (n. 104), I, § 608.

[121] Klaus Luig, "Leibniz als Dogmatiker des Privatrechts," in *Römishes Recht in der europäischen Tradition Symposion aus Anlass des 75 Geburtstages Franz Wieacker*, eds. Okko Behrends, Malte Diesselhorst, and Wulf Eckart Voss (Ebelsbach, 1985), 213 at 220.

[122] Hans-Peter Schneider, *Justitia Universalis Quellenstudien zur Geschichte des "christlichen Naturrechts" bei Gottfried Wilhelm Leibniz* (Frankfort-am-Main, 1967), 366.

tort, and contract. These concepts had to be defined, and their content explained, independently of any higher principle. The rationalist program was thus transformed. Its proponents had claimed that they could begin with higher principles and move deductively to rules of law. But the rules came to depend upon concepts that had to be defined and explained independently of such principles.

We will consider first the higher principle, then the disjunction between that principle and private right, and then the consequences of that disjunction.

## The higher principle

A first question is how far one could get by applying the methods of deductive logic to the principle of altruism alone. In the short treatise mentioned earlier, *Elements of Natural Law*, Leibniz defined jurisprudence (*iurisprudentia*) as "the science of the just." "I call it a science, albeit a practical one," he said," because from the definition of a good man all of its propositions can be demonstrated, and do not depend upon induction or examples...."[123] Yet the propositions that he demonstrated concern justice in the abstract rather than the private rights of individuals. Moreover, they do not add much to one's understanding of justice, or even of justice conceived as altruism. They seem tautological. Reading them is like watching a boat with its rudder jammed, which is endlessly turning in circles. Leibniz, however, thought that he was steering a straight course.

The following are some of his twenty-six definitions:

Justice is the habit of loving everyone.

| | | |
|---|---|---|
| Right (*ius*) is the power | | of a good man |
| Obligation the necessity | | |

| | | | |
|---|---|---|---|
| Just, licit | | is whatever is | possible |
| Unjust, illicit | | impossible | to be done |
| Fair, due | | necessary | |
| Not due | ommisible | by a good man | |

A person is one who loves himself or one who may be affected by pleasure (*voluptatis*) or pain (*dolor*)....
A good man is one who loves everyone....
We love those in whose happiness (*felicitas*) we take pleasure (*delectio*)....
Happiness (*felicitas*) is the optimum state of a person....
...
Optimum is the maximum of the good.
Good is that which is desired by one who thoroughly knows which is not only the cause of the pleasing (*jucundus*) but its cause, requisite, and support; and the contrary of evil.[124]

---

[123] Leibniz, *Elementa iuris naturalis* (n. 64), 459, 466–67.
[124] Leibniz (n. 64), 459, 466–67.

Leibniz then proposed "theorems" or "combinations of terms," which, he said, followed by demonstration (*analysis*) from the definitions. Some of these concerned the relation of legal terms to each other. Some combined legal terms with the idea of the possible. The following are some examples of the former:

Nothing just is unjust.
Nothing unjust is just.
Nothing that is omissible and not due is due (*debitum*).
Nothing that is due is omissible and not due.
Nothing unjust is due.
Nothing due is unjust.[125]

Leibniz then showed how further propositions could be demonstrated by replacing certain terms with others with the same meaning. For example, for "one who loves everyone," one could substitute "one who takes pleasure in the happiness of everyone," "who feels harmony at the happiness of everyone."[126] By a series of substitutions, he arrives at propositions such as the following:

Everyone who loves undertakes to benefit the person loved. . . .
Everyone who loves benefits the person loved unless he is not able, or unless he is impeded by an opposing love.
If several loves concur, the undertaking accomplishes the maximum of harmony that can be produced in the present state.
If two loves occur, the greater one prevails.[127]

One wonders how Leibniz could hope to move deductively from definitions and theorems like these to any propositions about what should govern the law of property, unjust enrichment, contract, and tort. In fact, neither he nor Wolff were able to do so.

## The disjunction between the higher principle and private right

Leibniz and Wolff distinguished sharply between altruism and what Leibniz called "strict right" and Wolff called "perfect right." The principle of altruism could not be realized.[128] Strict or perfect rights existed because people are too imperfect to abide by that principle. As Leibniz said, although "it behooves us to bear the greatest pains for the sake of others," most people will not do so.[129] According to Wolff, "[i]f men maintained integrity, they would have remained in the original

---

[125] Leibniz (n. 64), 459, 470, 473.
[126] Leibniz (n. 64), 459, 477.   [127] Leibniz (n. 64), 459, 479.
[128] *See* Klaus Luig, "Die Würzeln des aufgeklärten Naturrechts bei Leibniz," in *Naturrecht—Spätaugklärung—Revolution*, eds. Otto Dann and Diethelm Klippel (Hamburg, 1995), 61 at 65; Klaus Luig, "Die Plichtenlehre des Privatrechts in der Naturrechtsphilosophie von Chistian Wolff," in Klaus Luig, *Römisches Recht Naturrecht Nationales Recht* (Goldbach, 1998), 259 at 261.
[129] Liebnitz, "Codex iuris gentium" (n. 117), *Praefatio* 693. *See* Werner Schneiders, "Naturrecht und Gerechtigkeit bei Leibniz," *Zeitschrift für philosophische Forschung* 20 (1966): 607, 622; Patrick Riley, *Leibniz' Universal Jurisprudence Justice as the Charity of the Wise* (Cambridge, MA, 1996), 202–03.

state [in which there were no perfect rights]. Because they are corrupted, at least in part... common utility persuades that they recede from it...."[130]

Leibniz and Wolff then explained strict or perfect rights negatively by their contrast with altruism. A strict or perfect right is self-regarding. No one is obligated, as a matter of strict or perfect right, to help anyone else and no one, as a matter of strict or perfect right, can require him to do so. As a matter of strict right, according to Leibniz, one person is not obliged to help another even if that meant relieving him from great distress by a slight effort, for example by throwing a rope to a drowning man or allowing him a drink from a "healing fountain" capable of relieving his pain.[131] According to Wolff, no one is under a legal duty to use a perfect right for the benefit of others.[132] Moreover, the enjoyment of a strict or perfect right does not depend on the goodwill of others. A strict right or perfect right could be enforced against one who violated it "by legal action if [the victim is] a member of a state, or the right of war if he is outside a state."[133]

Both Leibniz and Wolff acknowledged that a person ought to help others, although he was not bound as a matter of strict right to do so. Although Leibniz said that he should do so as a matter of justice, his definition of justice extended beyond strict right. He thus distinguished three "precepts," or "grades," of justice. As a matter of strict right, one must not harm another—a precept that he identified with the Roman maxim "injure no one" (*neminem laedere*). As a matter of "equity," he ought to help others—a precept that Leibniz identified with the maxim "give each his due" (*suum quique tribuere*). The third precept was to act according to the pure altruism that, as we have seen, was for Leibniz the ultimate principle of justice. It meant "to hold this life itself, and that which makes it desirable second to the great advantage of others, so that it behooves us to bear the greatest pains for the sake of others."[134] He identified it with the Roman maxim "live honorably" (*honeste vivere*), which he translated as "live piously."[135] Wolff said that a person could be under a moral duty to use his perfect right for the benefit of others. But that was left to his conscience. He could exercise a perfect right as he chose without any questions being asked about whether he was using it well.[136]

## Private law

In the work of Leibniz and Wolff, as we have seen, there was a disjunction between the altruism and private right. Although the deductive method was supposed to derive lower-level principles from higher-level ones, one could not move deductively from the principle of altruism to the concept of private right. One had to define

---

[130] Wolff (n. 104), I, § 129.   [131] Leibniz (n. 117), 923.
[132] Wolff (n. 104), III, § 397.
[133] Liebnitz, "Codex iuris gentium" (n. 117), *Praefatio* 691. Wolff said the same: Wolff (n. 104), III, §§ 396–97. In the best of states, duties of equity—shortly to be described—could also be enforced by positive law: Schneiders (n. 129), 638.
[134] Leibniz, "Codex iuris gentium" (n. 117), *Praefatio* 693.
[135] Leibniz, "Codex iuris gentium" (n. 117), *Praefatio* 691.
[136] *See* Wolff (n. 104), III, § 397.

private rights negatively, by what they were not. They were not altruistic. As we have seen, Leibniz and Wolff explained their ultimate principle teleologically, in terms of the end of human perfection.[137] Nevertheless, they could not define private rights in terms of the purpose that these rights served. Rather, they defined them by their contrast to the altruism and in abstraction from any purpose that they served. Concept and purpose no longer went hand in hand.

As a result, there was also a disjunction between their concept of private rights and rules to determine their scope and content. Leibniz and Wolff defined tort, property, and contract in the same way as they defined private right. These rights are not altruistic, but self-regarding. Only a right holder is protected, and protected in any use that he chooses to make of a right. These rights were defined in abstraction from the purposes for which rights in property, tort, and contract were established.

Tort was defined in terms of harming another by depriving him of a private right. Leibniz said that a person is harmed if he is deprived of whatever he has, whether acquired by "fortune or industry."[138] According to Wolff, "[t]he one to whom harm has been done has less than he ought to have."[139] There was a disjunction between this definition and any rules to specify what counted as a harm or violation of a right for which compensation must be made. Unlike the late scholastics or Grotius, Leibniz and Wolff did not identify the different types of harm that the law would redress, or the principles or purposes for which it might do so.

Leibniz and Wolff agreed that if one person was at fault for harming another, he owed compensation. They did not explain why in terms of a larger theory of accountability for one's actions. They recognized that there must be some link between the harm that a person had done and his obligation to repair it. This link was fault. Leibniz said that what was not the result of fault was the result of "chance."[140] But he did not explain what distinguished "fault" from "chance," or why one should not be liable for causing harm by chance. Indeed, he thought that one should be liable, but not to the same extent. If no one was at fault, the damages should be divided between the parties.[141] Wolff explained fault as a failure to act as one ought to act: "[W]e are obligated to avoid any fault," because "we are obligated to act rightly... and consequently to avoid any defect of rectitude the avoidance of which is in our power...."[142] One was therefore liable in tort for any failure to "act rightly" that leaves someone with "less than he ought to have." There was a gap between this definition and any rules that could determine when one acted rightly and what one ought to have.

Property was defined as a right that is private and self-regarding. For Leibniz and Wolff, a property right is conceptually unlimited in the sense that the owner can do

---

[137] Rod (n. 83), 130; Bénédict Winger, *Das rationale Pflichtenrecht Christian Wolffs Bedeutung un Funcktion der transcendalen, logischen und moralischen Wahrheit im systemtischen und theistischen Naturrecht Woffs* (Berlin, 1992), 273–79.
[138] Leibniz, "De tribus juris..." (n. 117), 606 at 607.
[139] Wolff (n. 104), II, § 580.   [140] Leibniz (n. 64), 433 at 434.
[141] Leibniz (n. 64), 433 at 435.   [142] Wolff (n. 104), I, § 299, cited II, § 490.

whatever he wishes with his property. As Luig said, for Leibniz, "the thing [is] the object of an absolute right."[143] Similarly, according to Wolff, the owner "has the right to dispose of rights over a thing subjected to him according to his own judgment (*arbitrio*)." The right "of disposing of a thing by one's own decision, indeed, as one sees fit, we call ownership":[144]

By nature, no one is held to give another a reason concerning in what way a thing is used, nor does anyone have the right to impede an abuse of things, so long as whoever is abusing the thing does nothing against the right of another.[145]

There was a gap between that definition and any rules that could determine who, besides the owner, could use a thing and how the owner's right to do so could be limited.

Similarly, Leibniz and Wolff described the freedom of the parties to contract on any terms they choose as conceptually limitless. There was a gap between this definition and any rules limiting that right or binding the parties to terms to which they had not assented. As Luig observed, for Liebnitz, contract law is:

...fundamentally governed by the principle of the freedom and equality of the citizens. This equality is also realized in the freedom to make a law for one's own contractual relations through the *lex contractus*, of which the material fairness is not, at least in principle, controlled by the state.[146]

"In contracts" Leibniz said:

...we have the right to gain either according to the principle that it is licit for the parties to circumvent each other...or according to the principle that one may benefit without harming another (*innoxia utilitas*) as when the house that I buy from you is of more use to me, for example, if I am a brewer.[147]

Similarly, Wolff said:

No man can be forced to exchange for another's thing, the price of things, especially those that are useful and to the extreme those that are pleasant is to be determined so that one can charge the other as much of a price as he wishes.... Indeed, in the initial state, the price of things cannot be determined except by mutual consent.[148]

Nevertheless, Leibniz and Wolff recognized that, sometimes, there are limits to the owner's right to use his property and the terms on which the parties can contract. Leibniz' solution was to say that a right might be unlimited conceptually or in principle, but yet the law might have a reason, extrinsic to the definition of the right, for imposing a limit. To speak of property or contract is necessarily to speak of an unlimited right, because that is what these terms necessary mean. An architect

---

[143] Klaus Luig, "Leibniz als Dogmatiker des Privatrechts," in *Römishes Recht in der europäischen Tradition Symposion aus Anlass des 75 Geburtstages Franz Wieacker*, eds. Okko Behrends, Malte Diesselhorst, and Wulf Eckart Voss (Ebelsbach, 1985), 213 at 231.
[144] Wolff (n. 104), I, § 609, cited II, § 496; II, § 118.
[145] Wolff (n. 104), II, § 169. [146] Luig (n. 143), 239.
[147] Leibniz, "Varia," *Textes inédits* (n. 117), 2: 811 at 814.
[148] Wolff (n. 104), IV, § 319.

could not speak of a square without meaning a plane figure with four equal sides and four equal angles. But there might be a particular reason why the law would limit an unlimited right or the architect would design a room that was less than perfectly square. Liebnitz said that an owner's property is "what is in his power, or what he may deal with in every way according to his will unless for some particular reason there is an exception."[149] Similarly, although, conceptually, the parties could contract on whatever terms they chose, there might be particular reasons to make an exception. "The judge will order performance," he said, "unless there is a serious reason to the contrary, as, indeed, when there is the hindrance of great difficulties in value. By law, *laesio* is deemed to be grave when it goes beyond half."[150]

Wolff did not try to find particular reasons for limiting the conceptually unlimited. Wolff found a collision between a conceptually unlimited right and a different, but higher, right that could be played as trump. Wolff defended the doctrine that one may use another's property in time of necessity by saying that there is a right extraneous and superior to the owner's right: the right of self-preservation. That right can never be given up, because it is "connatural,"[151] in the sense that it is inseparably joined to human nature.[152] Therefore one could use another's property, but only when one's life was at stake. The right of self-preservation also trumped the rule that a party could sell at any price he chose: the price must not be so high that someone would starve.

Similarly, Leibniz and Wolff explained how rights of property and contract come into being without reference to purposes that these rights serve. They identified an act that creates these rights without explaining why it should. Property rights were created by *occupatio*, a right arising in Roman law from first possession. Leibniz said, "[i]f one begins to possess a thing then belonging to no one, he acquires it." He gave examples from Roman law, such as wild animals, gems found on the beach, property that has been abandoned, and treasure.[153] According to Wolff, anyone, acting in his own interest, could take possession of goods, or cultivate land, and thereby acquire a perfect right to what he possessed.[154] But neither explained why property rights should originate that way. Grotius had said that rights arise in this way because, as people lived further apart, it was inconvenient to bring goods together to divide them.[155] Leibniz and Wolff did not explain. Their idea seems to be that, because these rights must arise in some way, they arise by first possession.

In contract, the act that gave rise to a right was a declaration by the parties of their will to be bound. Leibniz defined a promise as a "declaration that something to your benefit is to be done by me." He defined an agreement (*conventio*) as a

---

[149] Leibniz, "De iustitia et novo codice," *Textes inédits* (n. 117), 2: 621 at 621.
[150] Leibniz, "De utilitate innoxia," *Textes inédits* (n. 117), 2: 870 at 877–78.
[151] Wolff (n. 104), I, § 609, cited II, § 496; VI, § 562.
[152] Wolff (n. 104), II, § 10; I, § 64.
[153] Leibniz, "Annotationes ad methodi vigelianae librum de rerum dominio," *Textes inédits* (n. 117), 2: 858 at 858.
[154] Wolff (n. 104), I, § 609, cited II, § 496; II, §§ 171–73.
[155] *See* Chapter V, p. 133.

"promise and its acceptance taken together." He defined a contract as an "agreement producing an action."[156] According to Wolff:

One who sufficiently declares that he wishes to make a performance (*praestare*) to another, whether to give or to do, and to transfer the right to him to require that he perform, is said to make a promise. A promise, therefore, is a declaration of our will to perform to another joined to the right to require the transfer of that to be performed.[157]

Neither of them explained why a promise ought to be binding. Their idea seems to have been that, since there must be some way to acquire contract rights, they may be acquired by a declaration of will. Wolff said that, "[b]y an internal obligation resting on conscience, men are obligated to each other to do just as each needs the thing or the work of another."[158] Given the imperfection of human nature, however, it must be possible to transform such an obligation into one that is "external" and enforceable against one who violates it.[159] He concluded "that men acquire a right of this sort from the promise of another when they have need of it."[160]

For Leibniz, limits to the price at which the parties could exchange were read into a contract for unspecified particular reasons. For Wolff, they were read in so that people would not starve. Since they did not have a principle of commutative justice, it is not surprising that they did not define contract as an exchange that would enrich neither party at the other's expense. For the same reason, they found no place for the law of unjust enrichment. No right was violated merely because one party was enriched at another's expense.

## Public international law

There was also a disjunction between the higher altruistic principles that govern relations among nations and the strict or perfect rights that a nation possesses. According to Wolff, "[e]ach nation ought to love and care for every other nation as itself."[161] It ought "to promote the happiness of other nations and to do all it can to make them happy...."[162] Accordingly, nature has established a "society" (*societas*) among nations.[163] "The purpose" of that society is for each nation "to give mutual assistance in perfecting itself and its condition."[164] To promote this end, "all nations are understood to have come together in a state whose individual members are individual nations or particular states."[165] "In the supreme state, the nations as a whole have the right to coerce individual nations if they are unwilling to perform their obligations...."[166] Indeed, the supreme state has a form of government.

---

[156] Leibniz, "Definitionum iuris specimen," *Textes inédits* (n. 117), 2: 721 at 733.
[157] Wolff (n. 104), III, § 361.   [158] Wolff (n. 104), III, §§ 396–97.
[159] Wolff (n. 104), III, § 396.   [160] Wolff (n. 104), III, § 397.
[161] Christian Wolff, *Ius gentium methodo scientifica pertractatum* (Frankfurt, 1764), §161.
[162] Wolff (n. 161), § 162.   [163] Wolff (n. 161), § 7.
[164] Wolff (n. 161), § 8.   [165] Wolff (n. 161), § 9.   [166] Wolff (n. 161), § 11.

Since it "consists of nations as a whole" and "each individual nation is free," its government is "popular" or "democratic" (*popularis*).[167]

Then, as before, Wolff uncoupled altruistic duty from strict or perfect right: "If one nation does not wish to do for another that which it is naturally obligated to do, that is wrongful but does not do the other an injury." The right of that nation is "imperfect."[168] Consequently, "no nation can coerce another to do for it those things that nations are naturally obligated to do for each other."[169] Perfect rights belong to a nation in the same way as they belong to an individual in private law. One nation can acquire the perfect right to require another nation to do something for it only by "stipulation," or mutual agreement,[170] as in contract law. Otherwise, a nation has a perfect right "not to permit itself to be injured by another,"[171] as in tort law. Within a nation, violations of perfect right are grounds for a civil action; between nations, they are grounds for war.

Erich Vattel adopted Wolff's main conclusions, and presented them in French and in a more readable form. He was an admirer of Wolff and Leibniz, and published simplified explanations of Liebnitz' philosophy.[172] In his treatise on international law, he rejected Wolff's idea that there was a supreme state, a *maxima civitas*, composed of all states.[173] Nevertheless, there was a "Society established by Nature among all Nations," and "the end of this great Society ... is that of mutual assistance in order to perfect themselves and their condition."[174] "The first general Law, which is shown us by the end of the Society of nations itself, is that each nation must contribute all that is within its power to the happiness and perfection of the others."[175] But then he distinguished, like Wolff, between perfect and imperfect right: "A perfect right is one which is united with the right to constrain those who will not satisfy the obligation to which it corresponds; an imperfect right is one that is not accompanied by this right of constraint." The right of each nation to have others contribute to its happiness and perfection is an imperfect right.[176] Violation of a perfect right is an injury that is a just cause for war.[177]

In contrast to Wolff, Vattel, like Grotius, pursued the humanist ideal of a polished work on law that gentlemen could read without specialized training. In realizing this idea, Vattel borrowed from Wolff just as Grotius had borrowed from the late scholastics. Vattel wished "to facilitate a knowledge of the brilliant ideas contained [in Wolff's treatise] for a greater number of readers."[178] Wolff had written "in the method and even the form of works on geometry," which made the work "almost useless" to the people whom Vattel wished to address.[179] Since "the Law of Nations is the Law of sovereigns ... one should write especially for

---

[167] Wolff (n. 161), § 19. [168] Wolff (n. 161), § 159. [169] Wolff (n. 161), § 158.
[170] Wolff (n. 161), § 192. [171] Wolff (n. 161), § 252.
[172] Emerich de Vattel, *Défense du système Leibnizien* (1741).
[173] Emerich de Vattel, *Le Droit des gens ou principes de la loi naturelle appliqués à la conduite et aux affaires des nations et des souverains* 1 (London, 1758), Préface xvii.
[174] Vattel (n. 173), *Préliminaires* § 12. [175] Vattel (n. 173), *Préliminaires* § 13.
[176] Vattel (n. 173), *Préliminaires* § 17. [177] Vattel (n. 173), 3: § 28.
[178] Vattel (n. 173), *Préface* xiv. [179] Vattel (n. 173), *Préface* xv.

them and for their ministers."[180] His motives for writing, like those of Grotius, were to educate them and so lead them away from the barbarities of war:

> Whoever takes up arms without legitimate cause... is answerable for all the evils and all the horrors of the War. The bloodshed, the desolation of families, the pillaging, the violence, the devastation, the conflagrations are his works and his crimes. Guilty towards the enemy, whom he attacks, oppresses and massacres without cause; guilty towards his people, whom he leads into injustice, whom he imperils without necessity, without reason; towards those of his subjects who are overwhelmed by the war, who suffer, who lose their lives, their goods or their health; and finally, guilty towards the entire human Race, whose peace he disturbs and to whom he gives a pernicious example. What a dreadful list of miseries and crimes!... [I]f our weak voice should in all the course of centuries, prevent only one war, what more glorious recompense could we desire for our tireless labor?[181]

Like Grotius, Vattel achieved his goal of writing a book that would be read widely by educated people and particularly by statesmen. By 1840, sixteen editions had been published in French and fifteen in English translation.[182] Like Grotius, he was highly regarded by the founders of the American republic. At the outbreak of the Revolution, "Vattel was the latest and most popular... of Continental writers," according to Jesse Reeves.[183] His influence was "unrivaled," according to Peter and Nicholas Onuf.[184] George Washington checked out a copy from the New York Society Library shortly after his inauguration, which, it seems, he failed to return.[185] Benjamin Franklin said that an English edition of Vattel sent to him by the publisher "has been continually in the hands of the members of our Congress now sitting...."[186]

## Conclusion

Leibniz and Wolff believed that their rationalist program had succeeded. Like Suárez, they sought immutable principles. Like Descartes, they wished to establish them by deductive logic. They believed that they had deduced immutable principles of law from concepts invariably attached to human nature. As we have seen, there was a gulf between their higher principles and such concepts as property, tort, and contract. It was not clear how those concepts were to be applied. As Peter König observed, Leibniz had sought a set of principles that would be "short, clear

---

[180] Vattel (n. 173), *Préface* xxiii.  [181] Vattel (n. 173), §§ 183–84.
[182] Albert de Lapradelle, "The Law of Nations: Bibliography of the Different Editions," in *The Law of Nations or the Principles of Natural Law*, ed. E. de Vattel (Washington, D.C., 1916), lvi at lvi–lix.
[183] Jesse S. Reeves, "The Influence of the Law of Nature upon the Law of the United States," *American Journal of International Law* 3 (1909): 547, 549.
[184] Peter Onuf and Nicholas Onuf, *Federal Union: Modern World: The Law of Nations in an Age of Revolution 1776–1814* (Madison, WI, 1993), 11.
[185] To make up for the loss, a copy, although not the one borrowed by Washington, was returned to the Library from Mount Vernon on May 20, 2010: *The Week*, May 21, 2010.
[186] Letter by Franklin to Dumas (Philadelphia, PA, December 19, 1775), in vol. 2 of *The Revolutionary Diplomatic Correspondence of the United States*, ed. Francis Wharton (Washington, D.C., 1889), 64.

and easily surveyed (*überschaubar*) by help and guidance of which any possible case that arises for judicial decision can be decided quickly and with certainty."[187] Leibniz thought that he had succeeded. Writing to Herzog Johann Friedrich, he declared:

> *The Elements of Natural Law* would be such a small book but so much would be included in it with such clarity and brevity that the most important questions of the law of nations and public law could be explained by any reasonable man if only he follows the method described in it.[188]

Writing to Louis Ferrand, he claimed that "I can lead everything out of these definitions...."[189] Yet, as König observed, "Although in his own opinion... this plan had largely succeeded, in reality, it never arrived at a conclusion."[190]

In the eighteenth century, many others thought that the rationalist program had succeeded. As John Dawson said:

> [T]he influence of Wolff was enormous even among those who reacted against it. His admirers set themselves to perfecting his system and working out its consequences; his opponents could not escape the net it cast. Its influence reached more gradually, and, in the end, incompletely to "half-learned" or unlearned judges and practitioners; in the abundant legal literature that still poured forth, there was much that followed older styles and gave only a pale reflection of the Wolffian synthesis. The agents for the transmission of his ideas were overwhelmingly law professors.[191]

Nevertheless, by the nineteenth century most jurists believed that the rationalist program had failed. Yet, as we will see, that was not the end of the conceptualist approach that the rationalists had pioneered.

---

[187] Peter König, "Das System des Rechts und die Lehre von der Fiktionen bei Leibniz," in *Entwicklung der Methodenlehre in Rechtswissenschaft und Philosophie vom 16. Bis zum 18. Jahrhundert*, ed. Jan Schröder (Stuttgart, 1998), 137 at 137. Similarly, Schneider (n. 122), 358–59.

[188] Leibniz, Letter to Herzog Johann Friedrich, October 1671, in "Philosophischer Briefwechsel," in vol. 1 of *Sämliche Schriften und Breife* (Leibniz-Forschungstelle Münster, Darmstadt, 1926), 162.

[189] Leibniz, Letter to Louis Ferrand, January 31, 1672, in "Allgemeiner Politischer und Historischer Briefwechsel," in vol. 1 of *Sämliche Schriften und Breife* (Leibniz-Forschungstelle Münster, Darmstadt, 1926), 181.

[190] König (n. 187), 137. Similarly, Schneider (n. 122), 358–59.

[191] John P. Dawson, *The Oracles of the Law* (Ann Arbor, MI, 1968), 237.

# IX

## *Novus Ordo*

### Positivism and Conceptualism

Before the nineteenth century, jurists concentrated on bodies of law that had an authority that transcended political boundaries. The Roman texts were regarded as a *ius commune*, in force everywhere according to the medieval civilians. They were in force in France insofar as they had been received there and, according to Domat, the texts received for the most part reflected natural law. According to the *usus modernus pandectarum*, the Roman texts were in force in Germany and the Netherlands by custom because they rested on reason. The late scholastics, the iusnaturalists, and the rationalists had written about natural law—a law with an authority which was independent of the texts in force.

In the nineteenth century, jurists came to believe that they should interpret texts without regard to any higher principles on which they might rest. If there were such principles, it was not the task of jurists to investigate and apply them. The texts were authoritative simply because they were the law of a particular region, enacted or accepted by those with authority in that region. We can speak of this approach as "positivism," if we use the word with caution. The positivism of the jurists was not a philosophical view of the nature and sources of law. Rather, it was a belief about where the law was to be found so far as their work was concerned.

French jurists sought the law in French legislation such as the French Civil Code. German jurists centered their work on the Roman texts that were now regarded as a *gemeines Recht*, or German common law. Common lawyers thought that their law rested on the authority of decided cases. Certainly, they had always thought so, but now a change occurred in how the cases were understood. The common law ceased to consist of bodies of lore organized about writs or forms of action. As we will see, it was organized according to legal doctrines, many of which were borrowed from the Continent. Nevertheless, the Continental sources from which the doctrines were borrowed were not recognized as authoritative in themselves. Rather, the doctrines were thought to rest on the authority of the decided cases.

The jurists systematized law by concepts that they claimed to find in their sources. We can speak of this endeavor as "conceptualism," if, again, we are careful about the word. Conceptualism was not a philosophy. Rather, it was a method of explaining the law by identifying basic concepts and deriving from them as many rules as possible.

Thus the jurists began a new project that united positivism and conceptualism. Although work on the project began in the late eighteenth century and continued into the twentieth, for convenience we will call it the "project of the nineteenth-century jurists."

The project may have originated, in part, because of the jurists' disillusionment with the attempt to explain law by means of higher principles founded on human nature. That attempt seemed unlikely to succeed after the rise of modern critical philosophy, and all the more unlikely because of the efforts of jurists over the previous two centuries. In the work of the iusnaturalists, and of Domat and Pothier, the higher principles had become so indistinct and their links to legal doctrines so unclear that they may have seemed like platitudes and non sequiturs. The work of the rationalists may have seemed like a series of tautologies leading nowhere. The alternative seemed to be positivism: if the law did not rest on higher principles grounded in human nature, then it rested on texts with legal authority.

Positivism was linked to conceptualism. If the texts were the ultimate source of law, then a jurist must be able to derive his conclusions from the texts. If he could not do so, he was presenting his own opinions as if they were law. He was usurping legal authority. Therefore there must be concepts underlying the texts from which his conclusions could be derived.

These considerations help to explain why the project of the nineteenth-century jurists made sense to them. Yet, as with other projects that we have examined, this one too need not have been. Positivism and conceptualism were not the only possible response to the situation of the jurists, nor were they an obvious response.

## Positivism

The nineteenth-century jurists' commitment to positivism depended on a new understanding of legal texts that was far from obvious. The French jurists now regarded legislation as the exclusive source of French law, and their Civil Code as one exclusive source of private law. In contrast, Portalis had thought that, to interpret the Code, one must look beyond it to Roman and natural law. German jurists came to regard Roman texts that were once accepted as the *ius commune* of Europe as forming a German *gemeines Recht*, the authority of which rested on the German *Volksgeist*—the "mind," or "spirit"—of the German people. Common lawyers restructured their law by borrowing extensively from Continental authorities, while claiming that their work rested on the authority of their own decided cases.

### *L'ecole de l'exégèse* in France

The nineteenth-century French jurists implicitly rejected the view of Portalis, the chairman of the committee that drafted the French Civil Code. As we have seen, Portalis did not expect the Civil Code to be the sole authoritative source of French law.¹ To interpret it, the judge could turn to the "natural light of justice and good sense," since law is based on "universal reason, supreme reason," founded on the very nature of things. He could also consult the "valuable collections for the science of laws" made by the Roman jurists. He could draw upon the learning of the "entire class of men" trained in legal science who had produced "compendia, digests, treatises, and studies and dissertations in numerous volumes." He was referring to compendia, digests, treatises, and studies and dissertations already written, not new ones concerned only with the texts of the Civil Code.

In the nineteenth century, however, the conviction grew that the Code should be interpreted exegetically without looking beyond its own texts. Thus the Code was treated as self-sufficient even though its drafters had not intended it to be, and even though, as we have seen, its drafter-in-chief had risked the defeat of his project rather than abandon his conviction that self-sufficiency was an unnecessary and impossible goal.

Charles Toullier, who wrote the first commentary on the Code soon after its enactment, tried to interpret it according to jurists who had written on natural law.² Later nineteenth-century authors did not. They usually said that they believed in a natural law, but their protestations were sentimental introductions to exegetical commentaries. The natural law, according to Alexandre Duranton, was promulgated by God and known to man through the light of natural reason.³ According to Antoine Marie Demante, it was given by God, engraved on our hearts, inseparable from our reason, and invariably attached to our nature.⁴ Charles Demolombe acknowledged its divine origin, its universality, and its immutability.⁵ To deny that such a law exists, François Laurent said, would be to deny that there is a God and to deny that man is a spiritual being, thereby reducing man to a brute and law to a chain.⁶ Raymond-Théodore Troplong said that to deny that the Creator engraved such a law on our hearts would be false and degrading.⁷ Auguste Valette claimed that all nations recognize such a higher law and that the only people who do not are certain metaphysicians whose systems need not be considered.⁸ Charles Aubry and Charles Rau defined the natural law as the ensemble of rules that would permit restraining a citizen by force.⁹

But their commentaries were innocent of any real attempt to determine what the natural law was or to interpret the Code in its light. Demante said that the Code

---

[1] *See* Chapter VI, pp. 150–53.
[2] Charles Bonaventure Marie Toullier, *Le Droit civil français suivant l'ordre du Code*, 4th ed. (Paris, 1824–37). As Ghestin and Goubeaux have observed, the fact that Toullier did not regard the texts as self-sufficient is good evidence that the drafters did not either: Jacques Ghestin and Gilles Goubeaux, vol. 1 of *Traité de droit civil*, 2nd ed. (Paris, 1983), §§ 142–45.
[3] Alexandre Duranton, vol. 13 of *Cours de droit français suivant le Code civil*, 3rd ed. (Paris, 1834), §§ 15–16.
[4] Antoine Marie Demante and Edouard Colmet de Santerre, vol. 1 of *Cours analytique de Code Civil* (Paris, 1883), § 4 (by Demante).
[5] Charles Demolombe, vol. 1 of *Cours de Code Napoléon* (Paris, 1854–82), §§ 6, 8.
[6] François Laurent, vol. 1 of *Principes de droit civil français* (Paris, 1869–78), § 4.
[7] Raymond-Théodore Troplong, vol. 1 of *De la vente* (Paris, 1837), Preface, xvii, n. 1.
[8] Auguste Valette, *Cours de Code Civil* (Paris, 1872), 2.
[9] Charles Aubry and Charles Rau, vol. 1 of *Cours de droit civil français* (Paris, 1869–71), § 2.

had to be interpreted in light of the natural law,[10] but his works were an echo of the natural law tradition rather than an effort to explain and apply the natural law. Duranton said that recourse to natural reason and equity should be the last resource of the interpreter.[11] Demolombe took as his motto "The texts before all else."[12] From the point of view of a jurist, he explained, there is only one true law: the positive law.[13] Troplong praised the jurist who measured his writings by the inflexible text of the Code.[14] Valette advised restraint in using principles of equity to interpret it.[15] Laurent claimed that the jurist should merely note defects in the Code, thus leaving to the legislator the task of bringing it into accord with natural law.[16] Aubry and Rau gave an account of interpretation that made no reference to natural reason or equity.[17]

They gave quite different reasons for reaching what was essentially the same conclusion. Duranton explained that, while natural law speaks to all men of virtue and intelligence, these men were simply too prone to make mistakes as to its secondary precepts.[18] Laurent thought that the natural law is revealed to the human conscience progressively as a people approaches perfection. The legislator, however, was supposed to prepare for it by interpreting statutes and noting their defects.[19] Troplong[20] and Valette[21] contented themselves with general remarks about the perfection and comprehensiveness of the Code. Demolombe agreed that, with a Code so complete, humane, and equitable, a case could scarcely arise in which natural law would be any different from positive law. Moreover, while there was a pre-existent, universal, and immutable natural law, to think about such a law was more appropriate to a philosopher or a moralist than a jurist. For a jurist writing about the Code, the one true law was the positive law.[22] Aubry and Rau claimed that, while there were absolute and immutable principles such as the personality of man, the right of property, the constitution of the family, and the liberty and obligatory force of contracts, one could not determine a priori the rules by which these principles should be developed. While the principles were immutable, the rules were contingent and variable.[23] The only point on which the French did agree, then, was that their task was to interpret the Code exegetically and insofar as

---

[10] Demante and Colmet de Santerre (n. 4), 1: § 23 (by Demante). On the other hand, he seems to have thought that recourse should be had to general principles of law or natural equity only in the rare instance in which a case is not covered by the letter or spirit of the statute, or the statutory text is so obscure as to have no true sense: Demante and Colmet de Santerre (n. 4), 1: § 28.

[11] Duranton (n. 3), 1: § 96.   [12] Demolombe (n. 5), 1: 1st preface, vi.
[13] Demolombe (n. 5), 1: § 8.53.   [14] Troplong (n. 7), 1: Preface, viii.
[15] Valette (n. 8), 1: 4. While acknowledging that the judge must consult general principles of law to find a solution when statutory provisions are absent, Valette maintained that it would be astonishing to find a case in which these provisions were wholly lacking, given the legislation enacted in the previous seventy years: Valette (n. 8), 1: 34–35.
[16] Laurent (n. 6), 1: §§ 5, 30. For a judge to decide a case by natural law is permissible only when the texts are insufficient, and then it is a necessary evil: Laurent (n. 6), 1: §§ 256–57.
[17] Aubry and Rau (n. 9), 1: §§ 40–41.   [18] Duranton (n. 3), 1: § 96.
[19] Laurent (n. 6), 1: § 5.   [20] Troplong (n. 7), 1: Preface, xii.
[21] Valette (n. 8), 1: 34–35.   [22] Demolombe (n. 5), 1: §§ 8–10.
[23] Aubry and Rau (n. 9), 1: § 2, n. 2.

possible without recourse to the natural law in which many said that they believed.²⁴ Although Philippe Rémy dislikes the phrase "school of exegesis" (*école de l'exégèse*), he notes that these jurists, "despite their great diversity," shared the same "work" or task. It was the "'explanation' or development of the Civil Code." He praises them for having undertaken it: "Sixty-five years of explanation are not too much to make a Code of 2000 articles of daily use to a civil lawyer."²⁵ Like these jurists, he considers French law to be an elaboration of the rules of the Code—a movement, as he describes it, "from the rule to the problems."²⁶

As Portalis had said, however, many cases could not be covered by the express language of a Code provision. He expected that these provisions would be interpreted by the principles of a higher law. If that was not possible, then the question arose: by what principles could they be interpreted? As we will see, the answer of the nineteenth-century jurists was to extract principles from the texts that made sense to them, but which were quite different from those that had made sense to Domat, Pothier, or the drafters of the Code.

## *Pandektenrecht* in Germany

In Germany, the view that became orthodox was developed by Friedrich Carl von Savigny. Like the jurists of the *usus modernus pandectarum*, Savigny regarded the Roman texts as authoritative as received and modified in Germany. Together with borrowings from canon law and customary law, they constituted the *gemeines Recht*, or German common law. For the jurists of the *usus modernus* school, as we have seen, these texts had authority because they rested on universal principles, and because they had been accepted by usage or custom, which, like legislation, was a source of law. Savigny did not believe that the texts rested on universal principles. He thought that there were no universal principles sufficiently definite to be of use to a jurist.²⁷ The texts were authoritative and had been received in Germany because the *Geist*—the mind, or spirit—of the German people had accepted them.²⁸ The *Volksgeist*—the unconscious mind or spirit of a people—is the source of its law.²⁹ It is manifested in "the common conviction of the people, the kindred consciousness of an inward necessity, excluding all notion of an accidental and arbitrary origin."³⁰ The authority of the *gemeines Recht* did not rest on mere custom.

---

²⁴ *See* André-Jean Arnaud, *Les Juristes face à la sociétè du XIX 2e siècle à nos jours* (Paris, 1975), 53–60.
²⁵ Philippe Rémy, "Eloge de l'exégèse," *Droits Revue française de théorie juridique* 1 (1985): 115, 119.
²⁶ Rémy (n. 25), 121.
²⁷ Friedrich Carl von Savigny, vol. 1 of *System des heutigen Römischen Rechts* (Berlin, 1840–48), § 8.
²⁸ *See* James Whitman, *The Legacy of Roman Law in the German Romantic Era: Historical Vision and Legal Change* (Princeton, NJ, 1990), 125–31.
²⁹ Savigny (n. 27), 1: § 8.
³⁰ Friedrich Carl von Savigny, *Vom Beruf unsrer Zeit für Gesetzgebung und Rechtswissenschaft* (Heidelberg, 1840), 8.

Because the *gemeines Recht* was based on this common conviction, it possessed authority. For the same reason, it possessed unity. Savigny, Georg Friedrich Puchta, and Bernhard Windscheid described the *gemeines Recht* as a "natural whole."[31] Windscheid observed that "[t]he concept of *gemeines Recht* is related... to the extraordinarily important concept of the whole which is not the sum but the unity of its parts."[32]

Because it possessed unity, the *gemeines Recht* could be interpreted. The French Civil Code could not, because its provisions lacked unity. Their unity could not come from higher principles of "natural equity," as Portalis had thought.[33] There were no principles of natural law or equity that were sufficiently definite to be of use.[34]

Nor could unity come from the foresight of the legislator. Savigny argued, like Portalis, that it would be impossible for the Code to provide for "each [particular case] by a corresponding provision.... [T]his undertaking must fail because there are positively no limits to the actual variety of actual combinations of circumstances."[35]

In principle, Savigny said, it would be possible to draft provisions that could extend to any case that might arise. A code might then have another kind of unity—or, as Savigny put it, "a perfection of a different sort"—which one might call logical, or conceptual, unity:

> [It] may be illustrated by a technical expression of geometry. In every triangle, there are certain given features from the relations of which all the rest are deducible: thus, given two sides and the included angle, the whole triangle is given. In like manner, every part of our law has points by which the rest may be given: these may be termed leading axioms.[36]

The difficulty was that "to distinguish them, and to deduce from them the internal connection... is one of the most difficult problems of jurisprudence. Indeed, it is peculiarly this that gives our work a scientific character."[37] The drafters of the French Code had achieved nothing of the kind. Their Code was an amalgam of texts lacking this technical perfection.

Savigny and his followers believed that the *gemeines Recht* was a natural whole because it was an expression of the *Volksgeist*, and for that reason it had a logical or conceptual unity that allowed jurists to identify its legal axioms and to deduce their internal connections. The axioms and their connections were not rooted in human nature, as the rationalists had thought. Rather, they were rooted in the *gemeines Recht*. That was so even though, as Savigny and his followers recognized, the *gemeines Recht* was an amalgam of Roman, canon, and customary law, and even though, as the humanists had shown, the *Corpus iuris* was an amalgam of the opinions of different jurists writing at different times. Thus the school that Savigny founded has been called *Pandektenrecht*, because it regarded the Roman texts of the

---

[31] Savigny (n. 27), 1: § 10.
[32] Bernhard Windscheid, vol. 1 of *Lehrbuch des Pandektenrechts*, 6th ed. (Frankfurt am Main, 1887), § 1.
[33] Savigny (n. 30), 74–76.  [34] Savigny (n. 30), 74–76.  [35] Savigny (n. 30), 38.
[36] Savigny (n. 30), 38.  [37] Savigny (n. 30), 38.

Digest or Pandects as authoritative. It has been called *Begriffsjurisprudenz* because its object was to understand the concepts underlying the Roman texts. It has been called the "historical school" because of its belief that the conceptual or logical unity to be found in the texts was the product of an historical process in which each text carried a deeper meaning than its author personally understood.

The rationalists had thought that, because the law possessed a logical unity, like mathematics, it must be based on concepts that, in their view, were as eternal and immutable as those of mathematics. Savigny used the analogy of mathematics to illustrate the conceptual or logical unity of the *gemeines Recht*. Neither Savigny nor his followers explained in a distinct way why the *Volksgeist* should produce a law with this conceptual or logical unity.[38]

Savigny believed that there is a *Menschengeist*, a mind or spirit of humanity. According to Savigny, "what operates in a particular people in only the general *Geist* of man (*Menschengeist*) which reveals itself in particular ways."[39] But the *Menschengeist* for Savigny did not play the same role as that of human nature for the rationalists. It was not a repository of coherent principles. As Okko Behrends observed, for Savigny it was "mystical," in the technical sense that its precepts, if there were any, transcend human understanding.[40]

Savigny never explained why, if the *Menschengeist* reveals itself in the *Geist* of particular peoples in particular ways, the German *Volksgeist* happened to manifest itself in a law in which the elements logically cohere and which jurists could show to be coherent. Did he mean that the *Menschengeist*, operating elsewhere, through the *Geist* of another people, might operate in a different way? Could there be a people, led by the *Menschengeist* and therefore human, that had no law? Or a people that had no coherent law? Or could there be a law that was coherent, although based on different concepts than the *gemeines Recht*? Savigny was not a philosopher seeking answers to these questions. He was instead a jurist defending the Roman texts and the jurists' role in expounding them against French ideas that he thought were unsound.

Savigny seemed to think that, because the *gemeines Recht* was a natural whole, then *ipso facto* it was a logically or conceptually coherent whole. Puchta came close to distinguishing the two. He said that the authority of legal concepts or principles does not depend exclusively on the *Volksgeist*.[41] They would have an intellectual authority even if they had not been received anywhere. He came close to the rationalist position that these concepts are invariable and timeless:

---

[38] Joachim Bohnert, *Über die Rechtslehre Georg Friedrich Puchtas* (Karlsruhe, 1975), 138–45. On the different explanations of Savigny and his followers, see Jan Schröder, *Recht als Wissenschaft Geschichte der juristischen Methodenlehre in der Neuzeit (1550–1933)* (Munich, 2012), 198–200.
[39] Savigny (n. 27), 1: § 21.
[40] Okko Behrends, "Geschichte, Politik und Jurisprudenz in F. C. v. Savigny's System des heutigen römischen Rechtens," in *Römisches Recht in der europäischen Tradition: Symposion aus Anlass des 75. Geburtstages von Franz Wieacker*, eds. Okko Behrends, Malte Diesselhorst, and Wulf Eckart Voss (Ebelsbach, 1985), 257 at 264.
[41] See Walter Wilhelm, *Zur juristischen Methodenlehre im 19. Jahrhundert: Die Herkunft der Methode Paul Labands aus der Privatrechtswissenschaft* (Frankfurt am Main, 1958), 78–79.

A law which did not originally develop among a people either has only inner scientific authority (as *raison écrite*) or also outer authority like that of indigenous law (or 'received law'). In the states in which Roman law does not have the latter authority today, it at least possesses the former, which is by no means insignificant. In most German states, however, it possesses both.[42]

Puchta was fortunate that Roman law did possess both forms of authority. If it possessed only the authority of received law, there would be another law, like that of the rationalists, which rested on reason alone and was not the law of any particular people. It is not surprising that some scholars have thought that Puchta returned to some form of natural law—although, as Hans-Peter Haferkamp has noted, that claim is hard to establish.[43]

Windscheid seems to have thought that, because the Roman law was built upon coherent principles and concepts, it had an intellectual force that explained both why it was accepted in Germany and why it could be interpreted by jurists. Like Savigny, Windscheid believed that the source of law was the *Volksgeist*. Nevertheless, he said, Roman law was received "by the custom, not of the *Volk*, but of the jurists," who were "directed by the overpowering intellectual force with which the Roman law confronted them."[44] Indeed, the Roman law had a decisive influence on all of Europe:

> ...because its content in large part does not relate to the particularities of the Roman *Volksgeist* but is nothing else than the expression of general human relations, developed, however, with a mastery that no case law or legislation has since known how to achieve, and therefore of immediate value where civilized people live together.... The concepts of Roman law are always sharp and precise, and yet they are always elastic, always capable of opening to needs in life that are newly arisen and of making room for their requirements.[45]

Here, the German *Volksgeist* seems to mean a national genius for appreciating, appropriating, and developing concepts that are of significance "wherever civilized people live together." Nevertheless, for Windscheid, unlike the rationalists, these concepts were not universal:

> Roman law is not absolute law. There is no absolute law. In the area of law, as in other areas, truth is revealed only in the progressive work of the human spirit (*Menschengeist*). Nevertheless, Roman law resulted from the legal effort of that part of humanity which, among all other peoples that previously appeared in history, participated in the greatest contribution to legal culture. Roman law is not law, as little as Greek art is art, but the spiritual summit of humanity was reached by Greek art in no greater measure than by Roman law.[46]

While believing that the *gemeines Recht* possessed conceptual unity, the German jurists also recognized that it was based on Roman, canon, and customary law, and

---

[42] Georg Friedrich Puchta, *Lehrbuch der Pandekten* (Leipzig, 1838), § 3.
[43] Hans-Peter Haferkamp, *Georg Friedrich Puchta und die "Begriffsjurisprudenz"* (Frankfurt am Main, 2004), 444. See Christoph-Eric Mecke, *Begriff und System des Rechts bei Georg Friedrich Puchta* (Göttingen, 2009), 589–638; Bohnert (n. 38), 143–45.
[44] Windscheid (n. 32), 1: § 1.    [45] Windscheid (n. 32), 1: § 6.
[46] Windscheid (n. 32), 1: § 6.

that, as the humanists had shown, the Roman texts themselves had been written and understood in different ways at different times by different jurists. Puchta explained that, although elements had been taken from Roman, canon, and indigenous law, "each of these elements had to suffer modification" so that the *gemeines Recht* would form a "whole."⁴⁷ According to Heinrich Dernburg, they had been received "according to the German *Geist*, uniting ancient Roman legal ideas with German and modern ones," to form the *gemeines Recht*, which "was not established by legislation but formed in the womb of the *Volk* by custom, legal practice and science...."⁴⁸ The *Volksgeist* was therefore responsible for the historical development of the *gemeines Recht* as a unified body of law that jurists could understand in terms of its underlying principles. Savigny said:

> With the progress of civilization, national tendencies become more distinct, and what would otherwise have remained common becomes appropriated to particular classes. The jurists now become an increasingly distinct class of this kind. The law perfects its language, takes a scientific direction, and, as formerly it existed in the consciousness of community, now it devolves upon the jurists who thus, in this department, represent the community.⁴⁹

In taking this scientific direction, the jurists were identifying principles that the law already contained and which were evidenced by the historical development in the way in which these texts were understood.⁵⁰

Consequently, Windscheid described the school founded by Savigny as the heir of the humanists. It had taken a "new step in the science of Roman law"—a step that began "from the same point as in the 16th century."⁵¹ Like the humanists, the German jurists understood the texts in their historical context. Yet they understood their historical meaning better by understanding the principles underlying the texts:

> Roman law was conceived as the result of a development that stretched over many centuries, and in this development one sought and found the explanation of the true sense of the *Corpus iuris*. Accordingly, the new school that arose [in the nineteenth century] is called the historical school. Its greatest name and acknowledged head is Friedrich Carl von Savigny. This school is principally distinguished from the historical school of the 16th century by the energy of its effort to understand legal principles (*Rechtssätze*) and powers (*Kräfte*) underlying actual relations and in this way to discover their inner life increasing attention to the sharp expression of concepts and to the demonstration of the systematic relationship between particular principles of Roman law. As to the last, the role of Georg Friedrich Puchta, the most significant of Savigny's students, is well known.⁵²

Windscheid believed that, like the humanists, his contemporaries were engaged in an historical enquiry. Yet their enterprises seemed different. As Ernst Böckenförde noted, Savigny's belief that the *Volksgeist* was responsible for such an historical

---

⁴⁷ Puchta (n. 42), § 5.
⁴⁸ Heinrich Dernburg, vol. 1 of *Pandekten*, 5th ed. (Berlin, 1892), § 1.
⁴⁹ Savigny (n. 30), 28.  ⁵⁰ *See* Wilhelm (n. 41), 22–23, 25–27.
⁵¹ Windscheid (n. 32), 1: § 9.  ⁵² Windscheid (n. 32), 1: § 9.

development was not based on the study of history.⁵³ Rather, it was an attempt to resolve theoretical problems about why the law had authority and how it could rest on principles that were neither those of a higher law nor the prescriptions of a human legislator. He and his followers did not seek the historical meaning of texts, as the humanists did, by asking what the texts meant to their authors. They identified principles that made sense of the texts and therefore, they said, illuminated their historical meaning. As we have seen,⁵⁴ initially the humanists believed that when they recaptured the original meaning of the Roman texts, they would arrive at an art of science of law unified by common principles. Savigny and his followers thought that when they identified principles that were coherent and made the best sense of the texts, they were understanding historical meaning of the texts.

## Anglo-American common law

In France, although the texts of the Civil Code remained the same, jurists changed their view of the authority of these texts. These texts were the private law of France sanctioned by the authority of the state. The German *Pandektists* interpreted the same texts as the *usus modernus pandectarum*, but now understood their authority differently. They were expressions of the German *Volksgeist* with a conceptual or logical unity that the jurist could investigate. In common law jurisdictions, the authoritative texts were the decisions of judges. But, again, the authority of these texts was now understood differently. The decided cases were understood to be authority for a restructured common law, with a structure and doctrines borrowed in large part from Continental jurists, although the writings of these jurists did not have comparable legal authority.

As mentioned earlier, English law had not traditionally been organized around general concepts such as ownership, possession, tort, or contract. English judges used cases to determine the scope of the writs recognized by the courts. Until the nineteenth century, to obtain relief, the facts of the plaintiff's case had to fit one of the existing writs, or "forms of action."

Frederic William Maitland predicted that, when the history of the common law is finally written, we will understand how the common lawyers arrived at "the great elementary conceptions, ownership, possession, contract, tort and the like."⁵⁵ Yet, as Charles Donahue has said, "[r]elatively little of the history of the forms of action seems to deal with 'the great elementary conceptions,' like ownership, possession, tort and contract."⁵⁶ In the nineteenth century, these conceptions and much else were borrowed by common lawyers from Continental authors. The common law

---

⁵³ Ernst Böckenförde, "Die Historische Rechtsschule und das Problem der Geschichtlichkeit des Rechts," *Collegium Philosophicum: Studien Joachim Ritter zum 60. Geburtstag* (Basel, 1965), 9 at 16. See Wilhelm (n. 41), 36–37.

⁵⁴ See Chapter IV, p. 116.

⁵⁵ Frederic William Maitland, "Why the History of English Law is Not Yet Written," in vol. 1 of *The Collected Papers of Fredric William Maitland* (Cambridge, 1911), 480 at 484.

⁵⁶ Charles Donahue, "Why the History of Canon Law is Not Written," Selden Society lecture, Old Hall of Lincoln's Inn, London, July 3, 1984 (London, 1986), 6.

was still said to rest on the authority of the decided cases. The decided cases were interpreted to support the borrowings.

As we have seen, the English courts were never clear about whether they were protecting ownership or possession until the Court of Queen's Bench decided *Asher v. Whitlock* in 1865.[57] They were not clear until the nineteenth century about whether the fault of the defendant mattered when the plaintiff sued for some harm that he had suffered. Before then, as Milsom and Fifoot pointed out, they failed to distinguish fault and strict liability.[58] It was not until 1865, in the now-famous case of *Raffles v. Wichelhaus*,[59] that an English court finally said, like the Roman jurists, that mistake could prevent the formation of a contract because the parties must consent to the same thing. These concepts had been basic to civil law since the time of the Roman jurists. The common lawyers were now seeking a more systematic account of their own law. These Roman concepts made sense to them.

In some areas of law, the systematization of the common law could not go as far as others. In property law, for example, it would have been hard to make sense conceptually of the common law estates in land and future interests, the rule against perpetuities, or the distinctions among easements, covenants, and equitable servitudes.

The same can be said of the law of restitution before twentieth-century scholars tried to fill the breach.[60] As John Dawson said, "any suggestion that the continuities [the courts] were creating added up to a 'law' of restitution would have been met for decades with disbelief."[61]

Tort and contract, however, were reorganized so far as possible along Continental lines. Here, the common lawyers were not borrowing Roman concepts. As we have seen, Roman law was a law of particular torts and contracts. Intead, they were borrowing from the structure that had been built by the late scholastics and passed on by iusnaturalists such as Grotius.

The late scholastics gave tort law a structure that it previously lacked. They described the distinctions among Roman actions as matters of Roman positive law, as well as the limits that the *lex Aquilia* placed on the types of harm for which one could recover. In principle, liability for harm was based on fault, which could be intentional or negligent, although Molina found room for strict liability. If harm was caused by fault, the defendant owed compensation for, as Soto said, "everything whatsoever of which a person can be unjustly deprived."[62] Grotius summarized their conclusions in words that affected the structure of all modern codes:

---

[57] 1 L.R. 1 Q.B.
[58] S. F. C. Milsom, *Historical Foundations of the Common Law* (London, 1981), 392–98; C. H. S. Fifoot, *History and Sources of the Common Law Tort and Contract* (London, 1949), 189, 191.
[59] 2 H. & C. 906, 159 E.R. 304 (1858).
[60] *See* pp. 261, 273–74. *See* D. J. Ibbetson, *A Historical Introduction to the Law of Obligations* (Oxford, 1999), 299–302.
[61] John P. Dawson, "Restitution without Enrichment," *Boston University Law Review* 61 (1981): 563, 564.
[62] Domenicus de Soto, *De iustitia et iure libri decem* (Salamanca, 1553), lib. 4, Q. 6, a. 3.

"From... fault, if damage is caused, an obligation arises, namely, that the damage should be made good... Damage... is when a man has less than what is his... "[63]

The common lawyers borrowed this structure and used it to explain what they now called the common law of tort. They classified, as actions in tort, such traditional writs as trespass in assault and battery, trespass to land, trespass to chattels, libel, and slander. They adopted, as an organizing principle, the doctrine that a person was liable for harm caused by fault, drawing on Continental writers.[64] As on the Continent, fault meant "wrongful intent or culpable negligence."[65] "Negligence" was now recognized as a separate tort by common law judges,[66] with the approval of most of the treatise writers.[67] If negligence was actionable under this new tort, then the older forms of action—or many of them—had to be classified as "intentional torts" in which liability was based on wrongful intent. Sir Frederick Pollock, who would have been the last to acknowledge his great role in reshaping English law, claimed that, in the case of "personal wrongs," such as battery, assault, false imprisonment, slander, and libel, "generally speaking, the wrong is wilful or wanton. Either the act is intended to do harm, or, being an act evidently likely to cause harm, it is done with reckless indifference to what may befall by reason of it."[68] He concluded that "the Roman conception of delict agrees very well with the conception that appears really to underlie the English law of tort."[69]

One element of the Continental model was that, typically, liability rested on fault. Another element was that the defendant must have deprived the plaintiff of something to which he had a right. The common lawyers incorporated this second element by identifying the remedies provided by the traditional writs with different rights that the law sought to protect.

This step had already been taken by Blackstone. He distinguished actions that protected personal property (trespass to chattels and trover), those that protected real property (trespass to land), and those that protected the "personal security of individuals" against injuries to "their lives, their limbs, their bodies, their health or their reputations."[70] Injuries to personal security were redressed by actions for

---

[63] Hugo Grotius, *De iure belli ac pacis* (Amsterdam, 1646), II. xvii. 1–2.
[64] Ibbetson (n. 60), 164–68.
[65] Sir John Salmond, *The Law of Torts: A Treatise on the English Law of Liability for Civil Injuries*, 4th ed. (London, 1916), 8.
[66] A first step was to hold that the plaintiff could not recover for bodily injuries that the defendant caused accidentally and without negligence. In the United States, this step was taken in *Brown v. Kendall*, 60 Mass. 292 (1850), in England, in *Stanley v. Powell* (1891) 1 Q.B. 86. As Prosser noted, it was then illogical not to do the same with damage to property: William L. Prosser, *Handbook of the Law of Torts* (St. Paul, MI, 1941), 77–78.
[67] For example, Francis Hilliard, vol. 1 of *The Law of Torts or Private Wrongs* (Boston, MA, 1866), 83–84, 104–05, 109; Salmond (n. 65), 9; Sir Frederick Pollock, vol. 6 of *The Law of Torts: A Treatise on the Principles of Obligations Arising from Civil Wrongs in the Common Law*, 8th ed. (London, 1908), 8. Addison was an exception: C. G. Addison, vol. 2 of *Wrongs and Their Remedies: A Treatise on the Law of Torts*, ed. F. S. P. Wolferstan, 4th English ed. (Albany, NY, 1876), 691.
[68] Pollock (n. 67), 9.   [69] Pollock (n. 67), 17.
[70] William Blackstone, vol. 3 of *Commentaries on the Laws of England* (London, 1776), 119.

menace and assault in the case of threats, and, in the case of actual injury, by actions of battery for harm to life and limb, actions of malpractice and nuisance for harm to health, and actions of libel and slander for harm to reputation.

Although the treatise writers of the nineteenth and early twentieth centuries proposed different solutions, like Blackstone, they looked for a correspondence between forms of action and harms for which the plaintiff should be compensated. Francis Hilliard and C. G. Addison, who wrote two of the earliest treatises on tort law, explained that, for the plaintiff to recover, he must have suffered some "injury"[71] or "damage."[72] Pollock and Salmond, in their more systematic works, said that he must have suffered some "harm."[73] Later writers, such as Fowler Harper and William Prosser, spoke of the violation of "interests demanding protection"[74] or "legally recognized interests."[75]

A paradox of the enterprise was that the Anglo-Americans were drawing on Continental authority while, for the most part, insisting that only their decided cases had genuine authority. Not surprisingly, the traditional case law did not sit easily with Continental ideas either about fault or about rights in need of vindication.

Under the common law forms of action, the plaintiff could sometimes prevail when the defendant clearly was not at fault. He was liable for trespass to land even if, in good faith, he had thought that the land was his own. The defendant could not escape liability for battery, assault, false imprisonment, or defamation by proving that he had been innocently mistaken as to the identity of the victim, or the existence of a privilege, or whether a statement was defamatory. The treatise writers were in a difficult position. They could not scrap these rules without admitting that their conclusions were not supported by the decided cases, although Pollock at one point considered making that admission.[76] So instead they improvised.

According to Pollock, "[a] man can but seldom go by pure unwitting misadventure beyond the limits of his own dominion."[77] In all but "exceptional cases," strict liability would not result in "real hardship."[78] According to Lawrence Vold, the defendant was liable for mistakes in identity because "the risk ... should be placed on the intentional wrongdoer rather than his innocent victim."[79] He did not explain why an actor who made a reasonable mistake should count as a wrongdoer. According to Jeremiah Smith, "an *intentional* entry standing alone and unexplained involves fault."[80] He did not ask why the law will not let such a person make an explanation. Sir John Salmond thought that the reason lay in "the evidential difficulties in which the law would find itself involved if it consented to make

---

[71] Hilliard (n. 67), 1: 83–84.   [72] Addison (n. 67), 2.
[73] Pollock (n. 67), 6; Salmond (n. 65), 8.
[74] Fowler Vincent Harper, *A Treatise on the Law of Torts: A Preliminary Treatise on Civil Liability for Harms to Legally Protected Interests* (Indianapolis, IN, 1933), 5.
[75] Prosser (n. 66), 8–9. Similarly, *Restatement of Torts* § 1 cmt. d (1934) ("legally protected interests"); *Restatement (Second) of Torts* § 1 cmt. d (1965) (same).
[76] Pollock (n. 67), 15.   [77] Pollock (n. 67), 16.   [78] Pollock (n. 67), 11.
[79] Lawrence Vold, "Note," *Nebraska. Law Review* 17 (1938): 149.
[80] Jeremiah Smith, "Tort and Absolute Liability: Suggested Changes in Classification—II," *Harvard Law Review* 30 (1917): 319 (emphasis original).

any inquiry into the honesty and reasonableness of a mistaken belief which a defendant set up as an excuse for his wrongful act."[81] He did not say why the defendant was held liable even if there were no evidential difficulties.

A different approach was taken by Warren Seavy, Harper, Prosser, and the *Restatements*.[82] They said that the intent that mattered was not one to do wrong or harm. According to Seavy, it was the intention "to deal with the things or with the interests of others." He claimed that "[t]he liability of one whose words unexpectedly prove to be defamatory can be based, in most instances, on his intent to deal with another's reputation."[83] Similarly, Harper claimed that the intention that matters is "to violate a legally protected interest of the plaintiff."[84] In the case of trespass to land or chattels, the defendant need merely intend "the immediate effect of his act which constituted the interference with plaintiff's possession."[85] To be liable for defamation, "the defendant must have intended to publish the defamatory matter, i.e., he must have voluntarily published the statement which harms the plaintiff's reputation and thus invades his legally protected interests." But he need not have intended that anyone's reputation be harmed.[86] Similarly, Prosser said that the intention that matters is not a desire to do harm, but "an intent to bring about a result which will invade the interests of another in a way the law will not sanction."[87] He drew the same conclusions as Harper. So, too, did the *Restatements*.[88]

Neither were the common law writs a list of harms against which the law had decided to protect the plaintiff. Again, there was a problem of fit.

For example, the defendant was liable in battery if he had not hurt the plaintiff. A person who had been struck, but not physically harmed, could recover.[89] Some writers said that the reason was "the very great importance attached by the law to the interest in physical security,"[90] or that the interest "in bodily integrity" is one of the "most highly protected."[91] Salmond described the interest in question as "not merely that of freedom from bodily harm, but also that of freedom from such forms of insult as may be due to interference with his person."[92] Harper,

---

[81] Salmond (n. 65), 116.

[82] Beale had yet another explanation. He said that someone who enters land mistakenly thinking it is his own "acts on a mistake as to his own authority." The mistake cannot "give him an authority which in law or in fact he lacks": Joseph H. Beale, "Justification for Injury," *Harvard Law Review* 41 (1928): 553. He did not explain why one who enters land without authority and without believing that he has authority is liable only if the entry is negligent but one who makes such a mistake is liable without negligence.

[83] Warren Seavey, "Principles of Torts," *Harvard Law Review* 56 (1942): 72.

[84] Harper (n. 74), 41.  [85] Harper (n. 74), 55.

[86] Harper (n. 74), 504.  [87] Prosser (n. 66), 40–41.

[88] *Restatement of Torts* § 13, § 13 cmt. d, § 158, § 158 cmt. e, § 577, § 580 (1934); *Restatement (Second) of Torts* § 13, § 13 cmt. c, § 158, § 158 cmt. f (1965). In response to the constitutional challenges to no-fault liability, the *Second Restatement* changed its rules to include a requirement of fault for liability in defamation: *Restatement (Second) of Torts* §§ 580, 581.

[89] For example, Melville M. Bigelow, *Elements of the Law of Torts for the Use of Students*, 3d ed. (1886), 101 ("any forcible contact may be sufficient"); Salmond (n. 65), 382 (force may be "trivial").

[90] George L. Clark, *The Law of Torts* (Columbia, MO, 1926), 10.

[91] Seavey (n. 83), 72.  [92] Salmond (n. 65), 383.

# Novus Ordo: *Positivism and Conceptualism*

Prosser, and the *Restatements* agreed,[93] and so they were able to redefine battery in a way that fit the cases and also corresponded to the harms that Salmond had identified: the plaintiff could recover for "unpermitted unprivileged contacts with [his] person,"[94] and for "harmful or offensive touching."[95]

A plaintiff could recover in an action of assault even if he had not been touched. According to the earlier treatise writers, the reason was the violation of a "right not to be put in fear of personal harm."[96] Yet the plaintiff could not recover always or only when he had been put in fear. As before, some, such as Seavy, said that the reason was the importance of personal security, as though that explained the matter.[97] Harper, Prosser, and the *Restatements*, however, redefined the right at stake as "the interest in freedom from apprehension of a harmful or offensive contact."[98] That interest corresponded to their more precise definition of assault: it required the "apprehension of a harmful or offensive contact," in which apprehension simply means the awareness that such a contact may imminently occur.[99] The law, then, was protecting a rarefied state of mind.

Similarly, the plaintiff's property was supposedly protected by an action for trespass to land, and his reputation by actions for libel and slander. Yet the plaintiff could recover for trespass if the defendant entered his land even if he did no physical damage. He could recover for libel and certain types of slander if the defendant "published" a defamatory statement, whether or not the plaintiff's reputation had suffered, or had suffered with anyone whose opinion mattered to him. This time, none of the treatise writers managed to describe the interest as stake so as to make it conform to the circumstances under which the plaintiff could recover. Some of them found reasons why the law would impose liability when no harm was done. Some said that the law "presumes,"[100] or "implies,"[101] damage. According to Cooley, it does so in the case of defamation because it would be "unjust" to deny recovery to a plaintiff who could not prove that he had been harmed.[102] According to Salmond, "[t]he explanation [is] that certain acts are so likely to result in harm that the law prohibits them absolutely and irrespective of the actual issue."[103] According to Seavy, the reason was that, like the interest in bodily integrity, the

---

[93] Prosser (n. 66), 44–45; Harper (n. 74), 38; *Restatement of Torts* ch. 2, titles of topics 1 & 2 (1934); *Restatement (Second) of Torts* ch. 2, titles, topics 1 & 2 (1965).
[94] Prosser (n. 66), 43.
[95] Harper (n. 74), 39. See *Restatement of Torts* §§ 13, 15, 18–19 (1934); *Restatement (Second) of Torts* §§ 13, 15, 18–19 (1965).
[96] Thomas M. Cooley, *A Treatise on the Law of Torts or the Wrongs which arise Independent of Contract* (Chicago, IL, 1907), 161. *See* Francis M. Burdick, *The Law of Torts: A Concise Treatise on the Civil Liability at Common Law and Under Modern Statutes for Actionable Wrongs to Person and Property* (Albany, NY, 1913), 266.
[97] Seavey (n. 83), 72.
[98] Prosser (n. 66), 48; Harper (n. 74), 43 (same, but speaking of a "harmful or offensive touching"); *Restatement of Torts* ch. 2, title of topic 3 (1934); *Restatement (Second) of Torts* ch. 2, title of topic 3 (1965).
[99] Prosser (n. 66), 48; Harper (n. 74), 43; *Restatement of Torts* § 21 (1934); *Restatement (Second) of Torts* § 21 (1965).
[100] Hilliard (n. 67), 1: 87.
[101] Burdick (n. 96), 338.
[102] Cooley (n. 96), 30–31.
[103] Salmond (n. 65), 12.

interests in "reputation, together with those in the possession and ownership of land, are the most highly protected."[104] Some merely let the matter pass.

In a similar way, the common lawyers reclassified their actions of covenant and assumpsit as actions in contract. David Ibbetson notes that:

As occurred with the law of torts at the same time, English lawyers began to use theoretical models to give a structure to contractual liability, and by 1800 the law of contract could be treated as an abstract entity distinct from the forms of action.[105]

Again, Ibbetson notes, the common lawyers borrowed from Continental authors.[106] As we have seen, Roman law was a law of particular torts and contracts. Again, the common lawyers borrowed this time from the structure that had been built by the late scholastics and passed on by iusnaturalists such as Grotius.

According to the late scholastics and iusnaturalists, there were two kinds of voluntary arrangements made for a *causa*, or reason, that the law would respect: contracts of exchange, and gratuitous contracts in which one party assisted another without recompense. In principle, both were binding. Still, if one party gratuitously enriched another by making a gift, the late scholastics and iusnaturalists believed that the law sensibly required a formality for the promise to be binding, which, in their ages, was notarization. They reclassified the particular contracts of Roman law as either acts of commutative justice or of liberality.

In common law, one could bring an action on almost any promise if one used a formality called "seal." Originally, a wax impression was made on a paper on which the promise was written. No formality was required to bring an action in assumpsit, and yet not every promise was enforceable. The promise, it was said, must have "consideration."

The treatise writers identified "consideration" with bargain or exchange. That gave the common law a structure that looked like the civil law. Gratuitous promises required a seal, just as gifts, in civil law, required the formality of notarization. As in civil law, exchanges did not.

Nevertheless, there were difficulties with identifying the civil law distinction between the two *causae* with the common law actions of covenant and assumpsit. One problem was that seal was an antiquated formality, unlike notarization on the Continent. Another problem was that "consideration" had never meant "bargain," or "exchange." The courts had found consideration in a variety of cases. Some were bargains or exchanges in the normal sense; some were not, for example promises of gratuitous loans and bailments.[107] The gratuitous loans and bailments were like the types of arrangement that Roman law had called loan for consumption (*mutuum*), loan for use (*commodatum*), and deposit (*depositum*). In the first two cases, the recipient of the loan was receiving a favor. He could consume or use the object, and

---

[104] Seavey (n. 83), 72. [105] Ibbetson (n. 60), 215.
[106] Ibbetson (n. 60), 215, 217–21.
[107] A. W. B. Simpson, *A History of the Common Law of Contract* (Oxford, 1975), 416–52.

later return the same amount or the object itself. In the last case, the recipient was doing the favor of looking after another's object for a while without charge.[108] To refuse to enforce these contracts in assumpsit would have been odd. A person who had borrowed from another would then be liable only if he made such a promise under seal. Similarly, a promise made to a prospective son-in-law was enforceable even though it was not a bargain. English courts wanted to enforce such a promise, and so they said that the consideration was "natural love and affection."

Beginning with Blackstone, Anglo-American treatise writers identified "consideration" with the *causa* of a contract of exchange.[109] As Simpson said, they regarded consideration as a local version of the doctrine of *causa*.[110] Consequently, the common law treatise writers were faced with three alternatives. They could compromise their positivism by saying that the courts were wrong in claiming that such gratuitous arrangements had consideration. They could compromise their effort to systematize the common law by refusing to identify consideration with any specific concept such as bargain or exchange. Or they could say that there really was a bargain or exchange when a promise was made to a prospective son-in-law or by the recipient of a gratuitous loan or bailment.

The last of these alternatives might seem the least likely, but Pollock achieved it. He devised an ingenious definition of bargain or exchange that is still with us. He said that "whatever a man chooses to bargain for must be conclusively taken to be of some value to him."[111] To say that the parties had entered into a bargain or exchange therefore meant that the promisor was induced to give his promise by some change in the position of the promisee.[112] In the case of the prospective son-in-law, according to Pollock, the parent was induced to promise by a change in the promisee's position: marriage. In the case of the gratuitous loan, the borrower was induced to promise to repay the loan or to look after and return the object loaned by the lender's change in position: he parted with the object. One anomaly remained: the recipient of a deposit was not promising to look after an object because he wanted to be entrusted with something that he could not use. Yet, in the early case of *Coggs v. Bernard*, in which a carter agreed to transport a keg of brandy free of charge, the court said that "a bare being trusted with another man's goods, must be taken to be a sufficient consideration."[113] Otherwise, Pollock seemed to have succeeded. Pollock's doctrine was adopted in America by Oliver Wendell

---

[108] On the Roman contracts, *see* Chapter I, pp. 20–21.
[109] Blackstone (n. 70), 2: 442; John J. Powell, vol. 1 of *Essay Upon the Law of Contracts and Agreements* (London, 1790), 331; William Taylor, *A Treatise on the Differences Between the Laws of England and Scotland Relating to Contracts* (London, 1849), 16; William Wentworth Story, *A Treatise on the Law of Contracts* (Boston, MA, 1851), 431, n. 1; S. Comyn, vol. 1 of *Contracts and Agreements not under Seal* (Flatbuch, 1809), *8; James Kent, vol. 2 of *Commentaries on American Law* (Boston, MA, 1884), *630.
[110] A. W. B. Simpson, "Innovation in Nineteenth Century Contract Law," *Law Quarterly Review* 91 (1975): 247, 262.
[111] Pollock, *The Law of Torts or Private Wrongs*, 10th ed. (1936), 172.
[112] Pollock (n. 111), 164.
[113] 2 Ld. Raym. 909, 920, 92 Eng. Rep. 107, 114 (K.B. 1703).

Homes,[114] whence it passed by way of Williston[115] into the *First*[116] and *Second*[117] *Restatement of Contracts*. It is taught today as the "bargained for detriment" formula for consideration.

The formula is still used in the United States even though the cases that Pollock sought to explain are now dealt with by a new doctrine, that of promissory reliance. According to that doctrine, a promise is enforceable without either a formality or consideration if it induced the promisee to change his position in reliance that the promise would be kept. The parent is liable, supposedly, because the son-in-law married in reliance on his promise of financial assistance. The borrower's promises are binding, supposedly, because the lender relied upon them in making the loan. This is not the place to pursue the question, but one may doubt whether the doctrine of promissory reliance really resolves these cases.[118] Would a court really deny relief to a son-in-law who would have married for love, even if he had been promised nothing? The *Second Restatement* waffles by saying that the son-in-law will be assumed without proof to have relied.[119] Suppose that when Antonio, the merchant of Venice, loaned Bassanio money to woo the fair Portia, he was convinced he would never be paid back and made the loan only because he preferred to lose the money than to risk Bassanio's friendship. Should Antonio not be entitled to recover if Bassanio refuses to repay him, although, having won the fair Portia, Bassanio can afford to do so?

## Conceptualism

The project of the nineteenth-century jurists was to find the law in authoritative texts and to understand the texts, so far as possible, by a set of concepts that were thought to underlie them. It combined positivism and conceptualism.

As noted earlier, both elements went together. They did not believe that, as jurists, their task was to understand the law through means of higher principles rooted in human nature. Rather, it was to find the law in texts invested with legal authority. If a jurist's conclusions were to have the same legal authority, they must

---

[114] The language just quoted is from later editions of his treatise on contracts, but the core of his theory of consideration was presented in the first edition, published in 1876, which he had sent in manuscript form to his friend Oliver Wendell Holmes. Holmes wrote back that the account of consideration "was the best which I had seen": Letter from Pollock to Holmes, December 16, 1875, in vol. 1 of *Holmes–Pollock Letters*, ed. M. Howe, 2nd ed. (Cambridge, MA, 1961), 276; Letter from Holmes to Pollock, June 17, 1880, in *Holmes–Pollock Letters*, 1: 14, 15. Holmes then published his own theory of consideration, which was similar: Oliver Wendell Holmes, *The Common Law* (Boston, MA, 1881), 293–94.

[115] Samuel Williston, "Consideration in Bilateral Contracts," *Harvard Law Review* 27 (1914): 503, 516–18.

[116] *Restatement of Contracts* § 75 (1932).

[117] *Restatement (Second) of Contracts* § 71(1) (1979).

[118] *See* James Gordley, "Enforcing Promises," *University of California Law Review* 83 (1995): 547, 574–78, 584–89.

[119] *Restatement (Second) of Contracts* § 90(2) (1979).

follow logically from these texts. Therefore there must be concepts underlying these texts from which conclusions can be deduced.

The nineteenth-century jurists rejected rationalism. Yet Karl Wieacker observed a parallel between rationalism and the conceptualism of nineteenth-century German *Pandektists*:

> [They] borrowed the method of forming a system and concepts and logically deducing legal decisions from the system and concepts from their predecessor Christian Wolff.... The subsequent development of [their] legal science shows that it never surrendered in principle the formalism of natural law, descending *more geometrico* from axioms to general concepts and from these to particular concepts and particular principles.[120]

There was a similar parallel between the method of the rationalists and that of nineteenth-century French and Anglo-American jurists, although they did not write with the logical rigor of the Germans. As noted earlier,[121] in Germany, a chasm had emerged between two approaches to law: that of the *usus modernus*, which was based on texts unsupported by principles, and that of the rationalists, which was based on principles unsupported by texts. The *Pandektists* tried to combine close attention to texts with the logical rigor of rationalism. In France, the humanist tradition was too strong. As Rémy observed, the French jurists wrote "often more oratorically, always more rhetorically," than a jurist would today.[122] They were more relaxed about principles and texts both before and after the Code was enacted. In England and America, the attempt to systematize law according to principle was too new. The holdings of the decided cases continually got in the way of attempts to explain them logically. Yet the French jurists and the common lawyers, like the Germans, based their conclusions on concepts supposedly extracted from their authoritative texts, in the same way as the rationalists based theirs on concepts that were supposedly immutable. Contemporary French and Anglo-American jurists, like the Germans, look back on the nineteenth century as an age of conceptualism.

At first sight, the parallel seems surprising. The starting points of the rationalists were at the other extreme from those of the nineteenth-century jurists. The rationalists believed that there is a higher law based on principles rooted in human nature. Leibniz and Wolff, following Suárez, thought that these principles are immutable. Correctly understood, they already prescribed the correct course of conduct under all possible circumstances. These ideas were based on philosophical principles that the rationalists understood and defended. As we saw, their idea of immutable principles depended on a metaphysical innovation: their idea of what it means for a thing to exist. Their idea that conclusions must follow with deductive certainty was based on an innovation in method or epistemology: their idea of how truth is known.

---

[120] Franz Wieacker, *Privatrechtsgeschichte der Neuzeit unter besonderer Berücksichtigung der deutschen Entwicklung* (Göttingen, 1967), 373–74; Mecke (n. 43), 594. Bohnert noted that, despite all of the debate over the work of Savigny and his followers, one point of agreement has been its resemblance to that of the rationalists: Bohnert (n. 38), 125.
[121] See Chapter VII, p. 164.    [122] Rémy (n. 25), 119.

The nineteenth-century positivists thought that there were no principles of natural law—or at least none that jurists need to consider. The law is found in texts with legal authority. They were not philosophers, and avoided the metaphysical and epistemological questions. Yet we have seen the resemblance in their work. A jurist's conclusions were to follow from authoritative texts rather than immutable principles, yet they must follow deductively or they would not have the same authority as the texts. Therefore it must be possible to demonstrate the correct application of higher principles under any circumstances that might arise. The nineteenth-century jurists seem unaware of the metaphysical and epistemological ideas that had led to a similar approach among the rationalists. They took a similar path not because they adhered to such ideas, but because they seemed to see no alternative.

Another innovation of the rationalists, as we have seen, was to disjoin legal concepts from higher principles that could give them content. The rationalists did so even though they thought that such concepts were to follow logically from the higher principles. The gap arose because, once the rationalists had defined the higher principles in terms of altruism, they were unable to get from those principles to concepts of private right. So they defined these concepts negatively in terms of their contrast to altruism.

In private law, for Leibniz and Wolff, the higher principle was that everyone should act for the happiness and perfection of others.[123] Private rights, such as tort, property, and contract, were defined negatively in terms of their contrast to altruism and in abstraction from any purpose that they served. Only a right holder is protected, and protected only in any use that he chooses to make of a right.

In international law, according to Wolff, "[e]ach nation ought to love and care for every other nation as itself."[124] Then Wolff uncoupled altruistic duty from strict or perfect right: "If one nation does not wish to do for another that which it is naturally obligated to do, that is wrongful but does not do the other an injury." The right of that nation is "imperfect."[125] Consequently, "no nation can coerce another to do for it those things that nations are naturally obligated to do for each other."[126]

Here, again, there was a parallel with the work of the nineteenth-century jurists. As we will see, the concepts that the French, the German, and the Anglo-American jurists used to interpret their law were not only much like each other, but also much like those of the rationalists. They were much like each other even though the French claimed that their law was based on legislation, the Germans, on the *gemeines Recht*, as received through the *Volksgeist*, and the Anglo-Americans, on their cases. Yet, like the rationalists, in private law, they defined property, tort, and contract in terms of rights that the right holder could use as he chose and in abstraction from the purposes served by recognizing these rights. In international law, they said that each state had the right to do as it chose, provided that it did no

---

[123] *See* Chapter VIII, pp. 183–84.
[124] Christian Wolff, *Ius gentium methodo scientifica pertractatum* (Frankfurt, 1764), § 161.
[125] Wolff (n. 124), § 159.   [126] Wolff (n. 124), § 158.

wrong. "Wrong" was defined without regard to the purposes for which states are established and the reasons why they should have the rights that they do.

One reason why the rationalists came under fire was that they did not show how to get from concepts thus defined to concrete rules. The nineteenth-century jurists put considerable effort into doing so. Yet they encountered a series of problems that they took seriously, but were unable to resolve. Their failure to do so made them targets for critics in the twentieth century. Indeed, it became the project of twentieth-century jurists to expose this failure, and to find an alternative to positivism and conceptualism.

In the remainder of this chapter, we will see how the nineteenth-century jurists faced these problems. We will see that twentieth-century jurists were better at pointing to their predecessors' failures than finding alternative solutions. In the next chapter, we will examine the efforts of the twentieth-century jurists to find an alternative to positivism and conceptualism.

We will look first at some problems of international law, and then of private law.

## International law

Positivism in itself created problems for the understanding of international law. If the law did not rest on higher principles, but on the legal authority of the state, what law could bind the state? How could the state bind itself, or be bound by another state's law?

Conceptualism added to the difficulty. The nineteenth-century jurists defined the rights of the state negatively, in terms of the right of the state to do as it chose, in abstraction from the purposes for which states were founded and on account of which they should have rights. The rationalists could not get to a more positive concept because there was a gap between their higher principle of altruism and one that could give content to the rights of states. The nineteenth-century jurists could not do so from any higher principle at all. There was no principle to obligate the state to act otherwise than it chose, and no reason why it should choose to apply another state's law.

### International public law

One might conclude that, on such premises, there could not be an international law binding upon national states. Indeed, John Austin said that the "law of nations" is "law improperly so called." It consists only of "the opinions current among nations":[127]

> Every positive law, or every law simply and strictly so called, is set by a sovereign person, or a sovereign body of persons, to a member or members of the independent political society wherein that person or body is sovereign or supreme.[128]

---

[127] John Austin, *The Province of Jurisprudence Determined* (London, 1832), 146–47.
[128] Austin (n. 127), 136–37.

Many scholars agreed with Austin, although some reached his conclusions by a different route.[129] Those who genuinely believed that international law did not exist did not write treatises about it. Beginning in the early nineteenth century, those who did write treatises generally dealt with the problem in one of three ways.

Some bypassed the question of the theoretical foundations of international public law. The leading American jurist, Henry Wheaton, when considering whether international law rests on "principles of natural justice," answered:

> It may, indeed, have a remote foundation of this sort; but the immediate visible basis on which the public law of Europe, and of the American nations which have sprung from European stock, has been erected, are the customs, usages, and conventions observed by that portion of the human race in their mutual intercourse.[130]

The same approach has been taken by some treatise writers ever since.

Other jurists said that international law rests on the consent of the sovereign, which is manifested in a treaty or custom. The sovereign does bind itself—or at least agrees to do so. According to August Wilhelm Heffter, author of a leading German treatise, "[t]he truth is...that States do not admit any laws to be obligatory among them but those that result from reciprocal consent."[131] Today, some treatise writers also take that approach.[132]

A third approach was to claim that international law must be based on transcendent moral principles, yet without attempting to identify and apply these principles. The principles are posited simply so that international law can exist. This approach resembles that of certain nineteenth-century French jurists mentioned earlier, who, after declaring that there is a natural law, treated the Civil Code as comprehending all of the private law of France.[133] Thus, Robert Phillimere said in his leading English treatise on international law, there was "a moral sanction conferred on [it] by the fundamental principle of Right,"[134] by "natural law,"[135] which was part of God's law.[136] Similarly, according to Paul Pradier-Fodéré, author of a leading French treatise, one must grant "the necessary principle of a moral order superior to the human will which binds individuals, and makes nonobservation of a received custom or treaty a violation of law." To deny that principle would

---

[129] Austin's route was to define law as a command "distinguished from other significations of desire...by the power and purpose of the party commanding to inflict an evil or pain in case the desire be disregarded": Austin (n. 127), 6. One can believe that international law is not law without subscribing to this definition. Moreover, only if one subscribes to this definition need one deny that international law is law. The iusnaturalists and Vattel recognized, and often bemoaned, the fact that international law could not be enforced.

[130] Henry Wheaton, *Elements of International Law*, 3rd ed. (Philadelphia, PA, 1846), 40–41. At one point he did say that one source of international law is "the rules of conduct which ought to be observed between nations and deduced from reason": Wheaton, *Elements*, 47.

[131] August Wilhelm Heffter and F. Heinrich Geffcken, *Das Europäisches Volkerrecht der Gegenwart auf den bisherigen Grundlagen*, 8th ed. (Berlin, 1888), § 3. Similarly, *see* George Grafton Wilson, *Handbook of International Law*, 2nd ed. (St. Paul, MN, 1927), §§ 2, 5.

[132] For example, Karl Doehring, *Völkerrecht Ein Lehrbuch* (Heidelberg, 1999), § 2; Louis Henkin, *International Law: Politics and Values* (Dordrecht, 1995), 27–28.

[133] *See* pp. 197–99.

[134] Robert Phillimore, vol. 1 of *Commentaries upon International Law* (London, 1859), § 62.

[135] Phillimore (n. 134), § 22.   [136] Phillimore (n. 134), §§ 33, 42.

"transform law into a simple science of material observation."[137] As before, a similar position is taken by some contemporary treatise writers.[138]

The jurists who took these positions wrote the same sort of books. After a short introduction on the foundation of international law, they discussed the same problems, looking for solutions to treaties, customs, and the opinions of other jurists—mostly their contemporaries. Even those who said that there were higher moral principles did not describe these principles systematically and use them to solve these problems.

For that reason, James Lorimer, a Scottish jurist, attacked them and almost everyone else who had written about international law since Vattel. According to Lorimer, Wolff and Vattel, despite their distinction between imperfect and perfect rights,[139] had preserved the great work of Suárez, Grotius, Pufendorf, and Barbeyrac,[140] which had been founded on that of "the scholastics":

The value of what was indirectly effected by Thomas Aquinas, who, as in ethics and theology, stands out in solitary majesty, and by Soto, whom we may regard as the immediate founder of the dynasty of jurists which culminated in Grotius, when contrasted with the labours of the civilians—from Bartolus and Baldus down even to Bijnkershoek—consisted in this: that . . . the scholastic jurists remounted to nature, and sought to discover laws of which the validity was universal.[141]

"The conception of a law that had no deeper roots than 'sovereignty'" came later, said Lorimer, citing Austin:[142]

From Vattel's time . . . till our own . . . the effort has been made to determine the consuetude, which is accepted as the common law, without reference to any absolute or necessary standard, and positive law is criticized or amended only in accordance with prevailing sentiments, or with such experience of its results as recent events are supposed to afford.[143]

Lorimer defined "the law of nations" as "the law of nature, realized in the relations of separate political communities."[144] He tried to develop and apply the principles of that law, while avoiding the "real fault of the elder jurists [which] was that they were not careful enough in circumstances of the State life in which they sought to realize the necessary law. . . ."[145] To do so was his project. It was not that of his contemporaries.

## International private law

International private law, or conflict of laws, deals with the question of which law a court should apply when the laws of different jurisdictions differ. The nineteenth-

---

[137] Paul Pradier-Fodéré, vol. 1 of *Droit international publique Européen et Américain* (Paris, 1885), 21.
[138] For example, Charles Rousseau, *Droit international public*, 11th ed. (Paris, 1987), no. 13.
[139] James Lorimer, vol. 1 of *The Institutes of the Law of Nations: A Treatise of the Jural Relations of Separate Political Communities* (Edinburgh, 1883), 77–78.
[140] Lorimer (n. 139), 68–77.   [141] Lorimer (n. 139), 68.
[142] Lorimer (n. 139), 75–76, 76, n. 1.   [143] Lorimer (n. 139), 81.
[144] Lorimer (n. 139), 19.   [145] Lorimer (n. 139), 80.

century pioneers were Joseph Story, who has been called "the father of American and English conflicts of law,"[146] and Friedrich Carl von Savigny, who has been credited with a "Copernican revolution."[147] They both tried to resolve the problem by reference to the same principle: the principle of territorial sovereignty.[148] "It is plain," Story said, "that the laws of one country can have no intrinsic force, *proprio vigore*, except within the territorial limits and jurisdiction of that country":[149]

For it is an essential attribute of every sovereignty, that it has no admitted superior, and that it gives the supreme law within its own dominions on all subjects appertaining to its sovereignty. What it yields, it is its own choice to yield....[150]

According to Savigny: "1. Every state can require that only its own law (*Gesetz*) is valid within its boundaries. 2. No state can require that its own law be accepted as valid beyond its boundaries."[151]

Nevertheless, both thought that, in choosing which law to apply, a court should consider such factors as where the suit was bought, where a person had lived or acquired a certain status, where a tort or crime was committed or harm done, where a contract was made or to be performed, and where property was located. As we have seen, these were much like the factors that the medieval jurists had identified. They had been repeated by later jurists. Story and Savigny knew of them through the seventeenth-century works of the Dutch jurists Ulrich Huber and Paul Voet.[152]

Neither Huber nor Voet, nor the medieval jurists, had tried to solve the problem by an appeal to the principle of territorial sovereignty. Some scholars believe that Huber did so.[153] He said that "the laws of each state have force within that state and bind all those who are subject to it but not others."[154] Yet, although different states might adopt differing particular laws, they might recognize the authority of bodies of law that extend beyond their boundaries and are the same in other states. "It often happens," he said, "that a transaction that occurs in one place is of

---

[146] *See* Albert A. Ehrenzweig, *Private International Law: A Comparative Treatise on American International Conflicts Law, Including the Law of Admiralty General Part* (Leyden, 1967), 53.
[147] *See* Friedrich K. Juenger, *Choice of Law and Multistate Justice* (Dordrecht, 1992), 37–38.
[148] Joseph H. Beale, vol. 3 of *A Treatise on the Conflict of Laws* (New York, 1936), § 72.
[149] Joseph Story, *Commentaries on the Conflict of Law, Foreign and Domestic* (Boston, MA, 1841), § 7.
[150] Story (n. 149), § 8.     [151] Savigny (n. 27), 8: § 348.
[152] Harrison said of Huber's short essay "that in the whole history of law there are probably no five [quarto] pages that have been so often quoted, and possibly so much read": Frederick Harrison, *On Jurisprudence and the Conflict of Laws* (Oxford, 1919). According to Lorenzen, "they had a greater influence upon the development of the Conflict of Laws in England and the United States than any other work": Ernest G. Lorenzen, "Huber's De Conflictu Legum," in *Celebration Essays to Mark the Twenty-fifth Year of Service of John H. Wigmore* (Buffalo, NY, 1987), 199 at 199.
[153] Donald Earl Childress III, "Comity as Conflict: Resituating International Comity as Conflict of Laws," *University of California at Davis Law Review* 44 (2010): 11, 20 (he "established conflict of laws as a discipline concerned with sovereign interests"); Alfred Hill, "Governmental Interest and the Conflict of Laws: A Reply to Professor Currie," *University of Chicago Law Review* 27 (1960): 463, 482 (he "stat[ed] unmistakably that the basic objective of the law of conflict of laws is to advance the governmental interests of the forum").
[154] Ulrich Huber, "De conflictu legum in diversis imperiis," Appendix III in Friedrich Carl von Savigny, *A Treatise on the Conflict of Laws*, trans. W. Guthrie (Edinburgh, 1880), § 2.

different use and effect in others," because "after the dispersion of the Roman imperial provinces, the Christian world was divided into entirely different peoples, who are not subject to each other...." Absent such a difference, one could apply the Roman *ius civile*. One could apply the *ius gentium* or law of nations. Indeed, one of Huber's first questions is which of these two bodies of transnational law should determine what to do when different local rules have emerged. The "fundamental rules," he said, "seem to have been sought in Roman law, but... they have more to do with the *ius gentium* than with civil *ius civile*."[155] Similarly, Voet discussed what to do when "statutes" conflict. A "statute" belongs to the *ius particulare* or *ius municipale*—to particular or local law—as distinguished from the *ius commune* or common law:

> The particular law is enacted by another legislator than the Emperor. I say particular law as opposed to the common law (*ius commune*), not insofar as [common law] is natural or international law, but insofar as it is the civil law of the Romans....[156]

As we have seen, the medieval jurists thought that the Roman law was an *ius commune* in force everywhere absent local statutes or custom. Indeed, although they developed the rules that passed into "international private law," they did so without believing that there were any nations that possessed sovereignty. Principalities and states might vary the *ius commune* with the express or tacit permission of the emperor. But, as we have seen, in their eyes, the emperor was sovereign of the world.

As a result, Story and Savigny were using rules about conflict of laws that were devised to resolve quite a different problem. The rules had been fashioned to deal with local differences from a common legal system, not to decide which legal system to apply to a transaction. The problem of deciding what law to apply when a statute of Modena differed from one of Parma was simple by comparison. One would look to the law of Modena if it had a special rule about acquiring citizenship, or driving carts within the city, or the witnesses needed for a contract of sale, or the height to which a person could build—an example used by Iacobus, Cinus, and Bartolus.[157] Such variations aside, a court would apply the general law of persons, torts, contracts, or property of the *ius commune*. Story and Savigny were using rules like these to decide which general body of the law of persons, torts, contract, or property to apply. The result has been that, since the time of Story and Savigny, many applications of the rules of conflict of laws have seemed arbitrary. That is not

---

[155] Huber (n. 154), § 1.
[156] Paul Voet, *De statutis eorum concursu* (Leyden, 1700), § 1, c. 4, §§ 1–2. Story quoted these words to show that civilian writers used the word "statutes" to "mean, not... positive legislation [but] in contradistinction to the imperial Roman law, which they are accustomed to style, by way of eminence, the COMMON LAW, since it constitutes the general basis of the jurisprudence of all of continental Europe, modified and restrained by local customs and usages, and positive legislation": Story (n. 149), § 12.
[157] Iacobus de Arena Parmensis, *Super iure civile* (Lyon, 1541), to C. 8.53.1; Cinus de Pistoia, *Super codice cum additionibus* (Frankfort-am-Main, 1493), to C. 8.53.1; Bartolus de Saxoferrato, *Commentaria Corpus iuris civilis* (Venice, 1615), to C. 1.1 no. 26. *See* Chapter II, pp. 44–45.

surprising since rules devised to resolve one problem were now applied to a different one.

Another problem that has troubled scholars is that it hard to see how to get from Story and Savigny's principle of territorial sovereignty to the list of factors that they believed should determine which law to apply. In view of that principle, why should one country apply the laws of another in preference to its own? As Story acknowledged, "[e]very nation must be the final judge for itself" of when it should do so.[158] Savigny said that "the strict right of sovereignty might certainly go so far as to require all judges of the land to decide the cases that come before them solely according to the national law, regardless of the rules of some foreign law...."[159]

Here, again, we see the gap between a basic concept defined negatively and in abstraction from purpose—the right of the state to do as it chooses—and any way in which to establish the content of that right. According to Story and Savigny, the concept of territorial sovereignty does not, of itself, lead to the rules that govern conflict of laws. They must be based on some other consideration.

For Story, the consideration that explained why one state would apply another's law was "comity":[160]

Whatever extra-territorial force [laws] are to have, is the result, not of any original power to extend them abroad, but of that respect, which from motives of public policy other nations are disposed to yield to them, giving them effect... with a wise and liberal regard to common convenience and mutual benefits and necessity.[161]

For Savigny, the consideration was that "[t]he more multifarious and active the rule between different nations, the more will men be persuaded that it is not expedient to adhere to such a stringent rule...." Consequently, nations have adopted the "opposite principle" of "equality in judging between natives and foreigners":

[I]t is a consequence of this equality, in its full development, not only that in each particular state the foreigner is not at a disadvantage to the native... but also that, in cases of conflict of laws, legal relations are decided in the same way, whether the judgment is pronounced in this state or that.[162]

Thus the rules of international private law did not follow from the concept of sovereignty. They limited the implications of that concept on account of comity or expediency.

If Story and Savigny were right, then comity and expediency had led states not only to rules to govern conflict of laws, but also to the same rules—to rules the application of which often seemed arbitrary to the nineteenth-century jurists themselves, and which, we can see in retrospect, were designed for quite a different problem.

But the very fact that these rules did not follow from the concept of territorial sovereignty was troubling in an age of conceptualism. In the twentieth century, the American jurist Joseph Beale tried to show how such rules could be derived from

---

[158] Story (n. 149), § 33.
[159] Savigny (n. 27), 8: § 348.
[160] Story (n. 149), § 33.
[161] Story (n. 149), § 7.
[162] Savigny (n. 27), 8: § 348.

that concept, even though, in his day, a conceptualist approach to law was under attack. Drawing on A. V. Dicey,[163] Beale claimed that, because law is the creation of a sovereign state, it can never operate outside the territory of the state that created it. Therefore, when a state makes use of another state's law, it is not applying foreign law. Rather, it is enforcing a right that had vested in the plaintiff in a foreign territory according to foreign law: "The primary purpose of law being the creation of rights... the chief task of the Conflict of Laws [is] to determine the place where a right arose and the law that created it...."[164] In the case of a tort, for example, that right arose in the state where the last event occurred necessary to give rise to the right. When the plaintiff sues successfully in another state, he is merely enforcing a right that already exists. Beale wrote this approach into the *Restatement of Conflict of Laws* of 1934, for which he served as Reporter. It was adopted by Oliver Wendell Holmes[165]—although he was one of the first critics of conceptualism.

Beale was attacked, notably, by Brainerd Currie, who started a revolt that has also been called a "Copernican revolution" in the conflict of laws.[166] Currie claimed to oppose Beale's conceptualist approach. Like Story and Savigny, he believed that the decision of one state to apply the law of another must rest on expediency—or, as he put it, on policy. Paradoxically, his analysis was based on the same principle as that of Story, Savigny, and Beale: the principle of territorial sovereignty. The power of Currie's attack was that he turned this principle against them. A state had the right to decide what law to apply within its own territory. Therefore it had the right to make its own judgment concerning expediency. Beale, like Story and Savigny, had assumed that their rules for resolving conflicts of laws subordinated every other policy of the state to whatever unclear policy underlay these rules. Their approach:

> ...attributes to the choice-of-law rule a policy content of far greater importance than is normally attributed to the municipal law of the forum. This is a strange inversion of values. A choice-of-law rule is an empty and bloodless thing. Actually, instead of declaring an overriding public policy, it proclaims the state's indifference to the result of the litigation [although] the law of the state points to the *result* which alone can advance the social and economic policy embodied in that law.[167]

Before applying foreign law, Currie said, the state should consider the interest or policy on which that law was based and whether it conflicted with an interest or policy underlying its own law. The alternative would be to base international private law not on considerations of expediency, but, as Beale did, on what Currie called "metaphysical" conclusions about where a cause of action really arose.

---

[163] A. V. Dicey, *A Digest of the Law of England with Reference to the Conflict of Laws*, 5th ed. (London, 1932), 17–25.
[164] Beale (n. 148), 1: § 8A.8; 3: § 73.
[165] *Cuba R. R. v. Crosby*, 222 U.S. 473, 478 (1912) ("when an action is brought upon a cause arising outside of the jurisdiction... the duty of a court administering justice is not to administer its notion of justice but to enforce an obligation that has been created by a different law..."). See Brainerd Currie, "On the Displacement of the Law of the Forum," in *Selected Essays on the Conflict of Laws by Brainerd Currie* (Durham, NC, 1963), 3 at 4–5; Ehrenzweig (n. 146), 55.
[166] *See* Juenger (n. 147), 146.   [167] Currie (n. 165), 52 (emphasis original).

The problem was, as Currie's critics pointed out, that it is hard to see what could be meant by the "interest" or "policy" of a state.[168] The state can enact whatever laws it deems to be expedient. It would seem, then, that there is a state "interest" or "policy" behind every law it enacts. But then, as David Cavers pointed out, the word "interest" merely expresses "the conclusion that the purposes of a statute or common law rule would be advanced by its application.... Since the rule emanates from the state, ... the rule's purposes may reasonably be ascribed to the state."[169] If, however, the word "interest" is understood narrowly as that of the government, as distinct from that of a private party, the state often does not have an interest of its own in a law that it makes. As Albert Ehrenzweig noted, "'governments' are ... 'interested' in the solution of conflicts problems in such exceptional cases as tax or currency matters."[170] Once again, it had proven impossible to bridge the gap between the concept that, by definition, the state can do as it chooses, and any way of giving content to this concept by explaining or limiting what the state should choose to do.

As Mathias Reimann has pointed out, for various reasons Currie's approach has had little impact in Europe. One reason is a belief that the state cannot act as it chooses. There are limits to the extent to which it can prefer its own interests over those of others. In the absence of any way in which to analyze these limits, European scholars have preferred the traditional rules because they, at least, seem to be neutral.[171]

## Private law

According to the nineteenth-century jurists, the law was to be found by the exegesis of authoritative texts, not by examining higher principles on which these texts were based. As we have seen, for the French, the texts were those contained in legislation such as the Civil Code; for the Germans, they were found in *Corpus iuris*; in Anglo-American jurisdictions, in the decisions of common law courts. Despite the disparity in these sources, the French, the Germans, and Anglo-Americans arrived as the same basic concepts, supposedly based on their texts. Property was an unlimited right of the owner to use a thing as he chose. Any restraints on its exercise were limitations imposed by the law on a right that was, in principle or by definition, unlimited. A person was liable in tort if, by fault, he harmed another person. Contract was defined in terms of the will or consent of the parties. The parties' contractual obligations were those that they had willed to assume.

---

[168] Friedrich K. Juenger, "Conflict of Laws: A Critique of Interest Analysis," in *Selected Essays on the Conflict of Laws* (Ardsley, NY, 2001), 131 at 163–65.
[169] David F. Cavers, *The Choice of Law Process* (Ann Arbor, MI, 1965), 100.
[170] Ehrenzweig (n. 146), 63.
[171] Mathias Reimann, *Conflict of Laws in Western Europe: A Guide through the Jungle* (Irving, NY, 1995), 105, 109.

Having defined property, tort, and contract in the same way as the rationalists, the nineteenth-century jurists faced similar problems. There was a disjunction between the definitions of property, tort, and contract and any way in which to determine the limits or the content to the concepts so defined. One could not explain these rules in terms of the purposes of property, tort, and contract because these concepts had been defined without reference to any purpose that they served.

If property is defined as the exclusive and unlimited right of the owner to use what he owns as he chooses, it is hard to move from that definition to rules that protect a nonowner's use of a thing that belongs to another or limit the owner's use of it. If tort is defined by saying that a person owes a duty to compensate those whose rights he violates through his own fault, then there is a gap between this definition, and rules, and an account of why fault triggers a duty to compensate and what constitutes the violation of a right. If a contract is the will or consent of the parties, then there is no clear way in which to get from this definition to rules that sometimes bind the parties to obligations that they did not will or which bind them despite their wants, hopes, and expectations.

As we have seen, these problems arose for the rationalists. They dealt with them briefly. The nineteenth-century jurists, however, considered them closely. They wished to show that their concept explained the rules found in their authoritative texts.

The obstacles that they encountered drew the fire of twentieth-century jurists. One can better understand the efforts of the nineteenth-century jurists by considering the twentieth-century jurists' criticism. The twentieth-century critics, as we will see, did a good job of pointing out the nineteenth-century jurists' failures to resolve them, but never arrived at generally accepted solutions to these same problems. In the rest of this chapter, we will finish considering the project of the nineteenth-century jurists and also begin to consider that the twentieth century. The twentieth-century jurists sought an alternative to nineteenth-century conceptualism. In this chapter, we will discuss their difficulties finding generally accepted ways in which to resolve the problems that the nineteenth-century jurists faced. In the next, we will consider why they could not do so.

A word of caution, however: to say that jurists have not arrived at a generally accepted solution to these problems is not to disparage their work or to deny that some of their ideas, if followed up by others, might have led to generally accepted solutions. I particularly admire the work of Peter Birks, Melvin Eisenberg, Jacques Ghestin, and Hein Kötz. Nevertheless, jurists in the twentieth and early twenty-first centuries are still facing the same problems.

## Property

The nineteenth-century conceptualists defined property in terms of the will of the owner. It is, in principle, the absolute and exclusive right of an owner to do as he chooses with what he owns.

In France, Aubry and Rau said that:

[P]roperty... expresses the Idea [sic] of the most complete legal power of a person over an object and can be defined as the right by virtue of which a thing is submitted in an absolute and exclusive manner to the will and the conduct of a person.[172]

Laurent explained that a proprietor could use his thing however he wished until prohibited by law or until he injured the rights of others.[173] According to Demolombe, as "an absolute right property confers upon the master a sovereign power, a complete despotism over the thing."[174]

They claimed to have taken this concept of property from article 544 of the Civil Code.[175] It states: "Property is the right to enjoy and to dispose of things in the most absolute manner provided that one does not make a use of them that is prohibited by laws (*lois*) or regulations (*règlements*)."

This provision paraphrased a passage in Pothier: property is "the right to dispose of a thing at [the owner's] pleasure, provided he does not violate the laws or the right of another: *ius de re libere disponendi* or *ius utendi et abutendi*."[176] The meaning seems to be that an owner can use his right of property as he chooses, but that does not imply that the right is unlimited. Pothier was describing the rights of the holder of a French feudal estate, which were limited and not only by natural law: he was entitled to use and alienate the land freely, but he was liable for feudal rents and duties. Pothier did not have a principle of unlimited property rights in mind. There is no reason to think that Portalis did.[177]

The drafters of the Code do not tell us much about their theories of property. One has the sense that they wished to leave theoretical issues aside as much as possible.[178] So far as one can tell, however, they subscribed to the ideas of the iusnaturalists, and of Domat and Pothier. Portalis and Cambacérès explained the origins of property in the same way as did Grotius. The common ownership of all things gave way to a system in which property was acquired by taking possession

---

[172] Aubry and Rau (n. 9), 2: § 190.   [173] Laurent (n. 6), 6: § 101.
[174] Demolombe (n. 5), 9: § 543.
[175] A belief that is held by some legal historians: André-Jean Arnaud, *Les Origines doctrinales du Code civil français* (Paris, 1969), 180; Jean-Louis Halpérin, *L'Impossible Code civil* (Paris, 1992), 278; Adolphe Lydie, *Portalis et son temps "Le Bon génie de Napoléon"* (Paris, 1936), 275.
[176] Robert Pothier, "Traité du droit de domaine de propriété," § 4, in vol. 9 of *Oeuvres de Pothier*, ed. Bugnet (Paris, 1861). For similar passages, see Pothier, "Traité du droit de domaine de propriété," § 14; Pothier, "Introduction générale aux coutumes," § 100, in vol. 1 of *Oeuvres de Pothier*, ed. Bugnet (Paris, 1861).
[177] See Alfons Bürge, *Das französische Privatrecht im 19. Jahrhundert zwischen Tradition und Pandektenwissenschaft, Liberalismus und Etatismus* (Frankfurt-am-Main, 1991), 2–8. Villey and Arnaud found no evidence that earlier jurists who used language like that in article 544 had in mind a modern, individualistic conception of the proprietor's rights: M. Michel Villey, *La Formation de la pensée juridique moderne* (Paris, 1968), 239; Arnaud (n. 175), 180–83.
[178] Cambacérès explained, when presenting his first and third drafts, that it was not his task to decide theoretical controversies about the origin of property: Rapport fait à la convention nationale par Cambacérès sur le 1$^{er}$ projet de Code civil, séance du 9 août 1793, in vol. 1 of *Recueil complet des travaux préparatoires du Code civil*, ed. P. A. Fenet (Paris, 1827; reprinted 1968), 7; Discours préliminaire prononcé par Cambacérès, au Conseil des cinq cents, lors de la présentation du 3$^{e}$. Projet de Code civil, messidor, an IV, in Fenet, *Recueil*, 1: 161.

of it.[179] The Tribunal of Lyon attacked the provision that became article 544 for failing to say that property rights were unlimited. According to the Tribunal, property rights should be based on the principles of "laisser faire" and "laisser passer." It is difficult to find all of these rights clearly enough expressed in the words "to enjoy and dispose of one's thing...."[180] The court would have been more alarmed had it heard the Tribune Gillet defending the article before the *Corps Législatif*: "There is no property so absolute that it is not subordinated in some way to the interests of the property of another."[181]

The principle that property rights are unlimited is missing not only in the drafting history of the Code, but also in the early commentaries. Toullier and Duranton gave a traditional natural law account of property. It was once held in common, but private rights were established, according to Toullier, because otherwise no one would labor[182] and, according to Duranton, because of long, continued possession, which created a "moral relationship" between possessor and thing possessed.[183] Both cited jurists in the natural law tradition.

In Germany, jurists defined property rights in the same way as did their French contemporaries. According to Windscheid, property is the power to dispose of what belongs to a person according to his "will";[184] according to Puchta, it is "the exclusive authority to use and dispose of a thing,"[185] "the full legal subordination of a thing,"[186] and its "total legal subjection";[187] according to Friedrich Keller, the perfect and complete right over a thing.[188] Dernburg explained that "[t]he right to property grants, according to its definition, every power over a thing which is possible according to nature and law."[189] Arndts explained that "[p]roperty, according to its basic concept, is the right of a subject to complete domination over a physical thing."[190]

This concept of property was said to rest on the Roman texts. We have seen enough of the Roman texts concerning ownership to realize how differently the Roman jurists described property. The introductions to the *Digest* and the *Institutes* described a variety of less-than-absolute rights that a person could have in various sorts of things.[191]

---

[179] Portalis, Présentation au Corps législatif 28 ventose, an XII, in Fenet (n. 178), 11: 112–14; Cambacérès, *Discours préliminaire*, in Fenet (n. 178), 1: 164. For similar remarks by Tribune Grenier, see Discussion devant le Corps législatif. Discours prononcé par le tribun Grenier, 6 pluviose, an XII (January 27, 1804), in Fenet (n. 178), 11: 157.

[180] Observations présentées par les commissaires nommés par le tribunal d'appel de Lyon, in Fenet (n. 178), 4: 95–96. See Bürge (n. 177), 7–8.

[181] Discussion devant le Corps législatif, discours prononcé par le tribun Gillet, 10 pluviose an XII (January 31, 1804), in Fenet (n. 178), 11: 331.

[182] Toullier (n. 2), 3: 41–46.   [183] Duranton (n. 3), 4: 202–03.
[184] Windscheid (n. 32), 3: § 167.   [185] Puchta (n. 42), § 123.
[186] Puchta (n. 42), § 122.
[187] Georg Friedrich Puchta and A. Rudorff, vol. 2 of *Cursus der Institutionen*, 3rd ed. (Leipzig, 1851), § 231.
[188] Friedrich Ludwig Keller, *Pandekten* (Leipzig, 1861), § 112.
[189] Dernburg (n. 48), 1: § 192.
[190] Ludwig Arndts, *Lehrbuch der Pandekten*, 9th ed. (Stuttgart, 1877), § 130.
[191] See Chapter I, pp. 18–19.

In fact, as mentioned earlier,[192] the nineteenth-century German jurists defined property in the same way as the eighteenth-century rationalists. The rationalists did not base this definition on Roman texts. Rather, they defined property and other private rights by contrasting them with the ultimate moral principle of altruism. It would be surprising if a definition of property arrived at in this way also happened to be embodied in the Roman texts.

Nineteenth-century Anglo-American jurists defined property rights in much the same way. According to Sir Frederick Pollock, a complete property right was the "exclusive and effective control of a thing in the highest degree possible, for this includes the power to deal with the thing, within the bound of what nature allows, at one's will and pleasure."[193] Christopher Columbus Langdell defined a property right formally, "as one which does not imply a correlative duty in another."[194]

In England and the United States, some legal historians have seen the failure of the nineteenth-century jurists to impose a principled limit on the rights of an owner as a result of the economic forces unleashed in the nineteenth century by capitalism and industrialization. One difficulty with this explanation was suggested in the Prologue. These historians explain the nineteenth-century jurists' ideas about property by means of events that happened to occur at the same time—the rise of capitalism and industrialization—without evidence that the two were linked in the minds of people then alive. Rarely, if ever, do these historians cite a jurist who defended his ideas about property by claiming that they would foster a free enterprise economy or the growth of industry. It is hard to see why the jurists would be so reticent about the real reasons why they were writing.

Another difficulty is that the attention of these historians has often been confined to Anglo-American law. As we have seen,[195] in the nineteenth century, the common lawyers began thinking in terms of bodies of law, such as property, tort, and contract, and organizing them systematically into doctrines with the help of many ideas borrowed from Continental authors. Thus, if one looks only at the law of England and America, it is easy to think that everything new in the common law was brand new, rather than borrowed, and then to identify it with the new economic conditions of the nineteenth century.

For example, Patrick Atiyah thought that property law changed in the nineteenth century as people began to think of themselves as owners with a right to dispose of their property as they chose.[196] But people had long had such a right: how, one wonders, did they think of their right to dispose of their property before the nineteenth century? According to Morton Horwitz, pre-nineteenth-century common lawyers had a "physicalist" conception of property "derived from land,"

---

[192] *See* Chapter VIII, pp. 188–89.
[193] Sir Frederick Pollock, *A First Book of Jurisprudence for Students of the Common Law*, 6th ed. (London, 1929), 172–73.
[194] Christopher Columbus Langdell, *Harvard Law Review* 13 (1900): 527, 537–38.
[195] *See* pp. 204–12.
[196] Patrick S. Atiyah, *The Rise and Fall of Freedom of Contract* (Oxford, 1979), 84–85.

which disappeared with the "abstraction of the legal idea of property."[197] But the abstraction of that legal idea dates at least to the late scholastics.[198]

Horwitz himself quoted the pre-nineteenth-century definition of Blackstone: property is the "sole and despotic dominion ... in total exclusion of the right of any other individual."[199] He thought that Blackstone meant that an owner could use his property as he chose however much his use might interfere with that of others.[200] This conception of property was tolerated before the modern era because "the low level of economic activity made conflict over land use extremely rare."[201]

As we have seen, however, Pothier's definition in the eighteenth century was like Blackstone's. Neither Pothier nor Blackstone meant that there were no limits to an owner's right to interfere with others. Like Pothier, Blackstone drew on the iusnaturalists. He said that he was describing property not as generally conceived, but as it was in natural law. He gave a standard natural law account of how all things had once been in common and how private property rights had been instituted because of the disadvantages of this state, citing Grotius, Pufendorf, and Barbeyrac.[202]

People have noticed that uses of land may conflict ever since they began living near each other. The early common law cases forced pigsties[203] and breweries[204] out of villages. When the medieval civilians discussed conflicting uses of land, they were interpreting a Roman text that prohibited a cheese shop from discharging smoke that bothered people living upstairs.[205] Blackstone himself said that if one person's use interferes with another, "it is incumbent on him to find some other place to do that act, where it will be less offensive."[206]

Once the nineteenth-century jurists, like the rationalists, defined property as the right of the owner to do as he wished with what he owned, there was a gap between this definition and any rules that would protect nonowners or limit an owner's rights.

In some cases, the nineteenth-century jurists bypassed the problem. An example is the doctrine that one can use another's property in time of necessity. The doctrine was overlooked in France, although a few recent treatise writers have tried to read it into the Code.[207] It was ignored in Germany, and added to the German Civil

---

[197] For example, Morton Horwitz, *The Transformation of American Law 1870–1960: The Crisis of Legal Orthodoxy* (Oxford, 1992), 145.
[198] See Chapter III, p. 85.   [199] Blackstone (n. 70), 2: *2.   [200] Horwitz (n. 197), 31.
[201] Horwitz (n. 197), 31.   [202] Blackstone (n. 70), 2: *2–5.
[203] *Aldred's case*, 77 Eng. Rep. 816, 9 Co. Rep. 57b (K.B. 1611).
[204] *Jones v. Powell*, Palm. 536 (K.B. 1628); *Rex v. Jordan*, cited in *Rex v. Pierce*, 89 E.R. 967, 2 Show. K.B. 327 (1683).
[205] D. 8.5.8.5.   [206] Blackstone (n. 70), 3: *217–18.
[207] François Terré, Philippe Simler, and Yves Lequette, *Droit civil: Les Obligations*, 7th ed. (Paris, 1999), no. 704; Boris Starck, Henri Roland, and Laurent Boyer, "Obligations," vol. 1 in *Responsabilité délictuelle*, 4th ed. (Paris, 1991), nos. 300–01. The cases they cite do not show an acceptance of the doctrine by the courts. They concern what the Germans call *Notstand*, in which one person is threatened by another's property: Cour de cassation, 2$^e$ ch. civ., November 26, 1986, D.S. 1987 (defendant protected a spaniel by shooting two dogs that were attacking it). Or they are cases of negligence in which a person chose to risk the lesser of two harms: Cour de cassation, 2$^e$ ch. civ., April 8, 1970, JCP 1970. J.136 (defendant broke a glass pane to rescue the plaintiff, a

Code[208] only in one of the last drafts justified by an appeal to justice unsupported by theory.[209] In the United States, it was recognized without benefit of theory in judicial decisions at the turn of the century.[210] It is recognized in England, although the authority is scanty.[211]

At other times, the nineteenth-century jurists saw the problem clearly and tried energetically to resolve it. Despite the definition of property rights, sometimes the owner was not the only one protected: the possessor was protected as well. Despite the definition of property rights, sometimes the owner could not use his property as he wished: he could not do so because his use interfered with a neighbor.

*The protection of a nonowner* The problem of why a possessor who is not the owner should be protected was debated by two of the greatest nineteenth-century German jurists, Friedrich Carl von Savigny and Rudolph Jhering. Protection of the possessor without title seemed to contradict the proposition that the owner had the exclusive right to the use of property. The question, as Savigny put it, is "how possession, without any regard to its own lawfulness, can be a basis for rights."[212]

Savigny said that, by dispossession:

An independent right of the person ... is not violated but the situation of the person is altered to his disadvantage; the unlawfulness, which consists in the use of force against this person, can only be eliminated with all of its consequences by the restoration and protection of the factual situation to which the force extended.[213]

That answer is not perfectly clear. It suggests two rather different explanations for the protection of possession, each of which had its champions among the nineteenth-century German jurists. According to the first, the law protects the peace and order of society against unlawfulness and force. According to the second, the law protects the victim himself. The victim has a legally protectable claim against unlawful interference even though he does not have a legally protectable claim to possession.

The first explanation was accepted by Savigny's contemporary Rudorff.[214] Supposedly, relief is given merely because public order has been disrupted and

---

child, who was locked in the bathroom, and a fragment struck the child's eye); Trib. Charolles, March 13, 1970, JCP 1970. J.16354 (truck driver swerved to avoid hitting a third party and struck plaintiff's car).

[208] German Civil Code (*Bürgerlichesgesetzbuch*) § 904.
[209] *Protokolle der Kommission für die zweite Lesung des Bürgerlichen Gesetzbuches* VI, § 419, 214 (Berlin, 1899).
[210] *Vincent v. Lake Erie Transportation Co.*, 124 N.W. 221 (Minn. 1910); *Ploof v. Putnam*, 71 A. 188 (Vt. 1908).
[211] John Murphy, *Street on Torts*, 12th ed. (Oxford, 2007), 305–06; W. V. H. Rogers, *Winfield and Jolowicz on Tort*, 17th ed. (London, 2002), § 25.29; K. M. Stanton, *The Modern Law of Tort* (London, 1994), 69.
[212] Friedrich Carl von Savigny, *Das Recht des Besitzes*, 6th ed. (Berlin, 1837), 9.
[213] Savigny (n. 212), 41.
[214] Rudorff, "Über den Rechtsgrund der possessorischen Interdicte," *Zeitschrift für geschichtliche Rechtswissenschaft* 7 (1831): 90, 110–14.

not because the plaintiff has a protectable interest. German critics objected that if the plaintiff has no protectable interest, then the unlawfulness or disruption of public order cannot merely consist in the fact that the plaintiff was deprived of possession. It must also be found in the unlawful or disruptive way in which the defendant deprived him of it. But, as Jhering noted, relief is given when there has been dispossession without violence or a breach of the peace,[215] for example when the defendant took the plaintiff's hat by mistake in place of his own.[216]

In the nineteenth century, most German jurists turned to the second explanation instead: the possessor should be protected against interference even though possession in itself is not worthy of protection. According to Gans, Puchta, Windscheid, Bruns, and Randa, the reason was that the possessor's will was actualized or expressed in his exercise of dominion over an object. The will was worthy of protection without regard to whether this exertion of dominion was rightful or wrongful.[217] To interfere with another's exercise of will was to interfere with his freedom or personality,[218] or to violate the principle that each person is the equal of every other.[219]

The advantage of this approach, as Puchta observed, is that the victim is protected simply because the act of dispossession itself interferes with his will, not because the act that interferes is unlawful in any other respect.[220] The difficulty is that the law does not protect people against any interference with their will. Rather, it protects them against dispossession. German critics made this point in various ways. Jhering argued that the law does not protect the will regardless of what is willed, but rather defines the circumstances in which the will is protected.[221] Heck noted that while one can always expand a word such as "personality" to cover any instance in which one gives relief, doing so does not explain why relief is given.[222]

Indeed, if the possessor is not the owner and is acting without right, the law is protecting the will to do something wrongful. Jhering objected that even if, in the abstract, the will should be protected, it is hard to see why the will to do wrong should be.[223] Moreover, the law is not simply protecting the will of the possessor,

---

[215] Rudolph von Jhering, *Über den Grund des Besitzschutzes Eine Revision der Lehre vom Besitz*, 2nd ed. (Jena, 1869), 8.
[216] Philippe Heck, *Grundriß des Sachenrechts* (Tübingen, 1930), §§ 3, 6.
[217] Eduard Gans, *System des römischen Civilrechts* (Berlin, 1827), 211–12; Georg Friedrich Puchta, vol. 2 of *Cursus der Institutionen*, 3rd ed. (Leipzig, 1851), § 224; Georg Friedrich Puchta, vol. 1 of *Vorlesungen über das heutige römischen Recht*, ed. Rudorff, 2nd ed. (Leipzig, 1849), § 122; Georg Friedrich Puchta, "Zu welcher Classe von Rechten gehört der Besitz?," in *Kleine Zivilistische Schriften*, ed. F. Rudorff (Leipzig, 1851), 239 at 255–56; Windscheid (n. 32), 1: § 148; Carl Georg Bruns, *Das Recht des Besitzes im Mittelalter und in der Gegenwart* (Tübingen, 1848), § 58; Anton Randa, *Der Besitz mit Einschluß der Bestzklagen nach österreichem Recht*, 3rd ed. (Breitkopf, 1879), § 8.
[218] Puchta, *Vorlesungen* (n. 217), § 122, 243; Randa (n. 217), § 8.
[219] Windscheid (n. 32), 1: § 148, n. 6.    [220] Puchta, *Vorlesungen* (n. 217), § 122.
[221] Jhering (n. 215), 31–34.    [222] Heck (n. 216), Excurs I, 488.
[223] Jhering (n. 215), 31–34.

but settling a conflict among different people's wills. By taking an object, a dispossessor allows his will to override that of the earlier possessor. By keeping it, the earlier possessor allows his own to override the will of all those who come later. As Dernburg noted, respect for the will does not explain why the earlier possessor should win.[224] Nor does it explain why physical possession matters. If the law were merely protecting a person's will to appropriate an object, Jhering objected, it would protect that will however it were expressed, whether or not physical possession was taken.[225]

Jhering recognized that, to explain protection, one needed to identify some substantive right in need of protection. Like his contemporaries, however, he thought that the substantive right could not be possession itself. Instead, it was ownership. By protecting possession, the law gave a more effective protection to ownership.[226] The owner would not have to prove his title when dispossessed.[227] The protection given to possessors who were not owners was an "unavoidable consequence"—a "price" paid for protecting owners.[228]

Critics pointed out that Jhering's theory does not explain why a possessor is protected when he clearly is not the owner[229]—indeed, why he is sometimes protected even against the owner.[230] Moreover, it rests on the assumption that the person dispossessed is most often the owner—an assumption that Jhering himself had questioned.[231]

Dernburg recognized that the difficulty with all of these theories is a feature that they have in common: they give no reason to protect possession as such. According to Dernburg, possession should be protected because it is "the factual order of society (*tatsächliche Gesellschaftsordnung*), the given division of physical goods. It grants the individual directly the instruments of his activity, the means for the satisfaction of his needs."[232] If so, one might wonder, why is possession not a right belonging to the possessor? Dernburg denied that it is.[233] He explained that the owner, and not the possessor, has the right to possess. But if that is so, why should possession be protected?

Two common law jurists, Oliver Wendell Holmes and Sir Frederick Pollock, approached the problem by claiming that possession was a right, although it was not the same as ownership. Like the owner, the possessor has the right to deal with a thing as he chooses. The owner's rights, however, are good against all of the world, while the possessor's rights are good against everyone except the owner.[234] In Pollock's words, the possessor "may have all or most of the advantages of ownership against every one but the true owner, in other words, it may confer a relatively good title":[235] "[w]e treat the actual possessor not only

---

[224] Dernburg (n. 48), § 170.
[225] Jhering (n. 215), 37–38.
[226] Jhering (n. 215), 45–46.
[227] Jhering (n. 215), 47–54.
[228] Jhering (n. 215), 55.
[229] Randa (n. 217), § 8; Dernburg (n. 48), § 170; Heck (n. 216), Excurs I, 488.
[230] Randa (n. 217), § 8; Heck (n. 216), Excurs I.
[231] Jhering (n. 215), 25–27.
[232] Dernburg (n. 48), § 170.
[233] Dernburg (n. 48), § 169.
[234] Holmes (n. 114), 210–11.
[235] Pollock (n. 193), 178.

as legal possessor but as owner, as against every one who cannot show a better right...."[236]

Pollock's idea avoided all of the troubles that German scholars had encountered once they denied that the possessor had a right to possess. To accept it, however, one can no longer define property as the conceptualists did: as the exclusive and unlimited right of the owner to do as he chooses with his own. Pollock did not suggest an alternative theory of property to replace the will theory.

The twentieth-century project was to find an alternative to the conceptualism of the past. Yet today, when French and German jurists explain why the possessor is protected, they merely recapitulate the theories of Savigny and Jhering.[237] It is as though the discussion was frozen a century ago, and on the conceptualist premise that only an owner can have the right to the use of a thing.

English jurists typically accept the theory of Pollock. Curiously, they have forgotten that it was developed by him in response to a German debate provoked by a will theory of property. They regard it as ancient and indigenous to the common law. In medieval English law, it is said:

[T]he estate in land is based on the right of seisin or possession, of the land.... This reliance on possession as the basis of land ownership resulted in the common law taking the view that the acquisition of possession was itself the acquisition of a title to the land. Possession was the *root of title*.[238]

That view of English jurists is surprising since, as we have seen,[239] for much of the nineteenth century, English courts had said that possession was protected only because it was evidence of title. Moreover, Pollock himself did not claim that he had merely explained English law. He had developed a theory of why both English and Roman law protected possession:

It may be worth remarking that in general terms the relations of possession and ownership in Roman and English law, the difficulties arising out of them, and the devices resorted to for obviating or circumventing those difficulties, offer an amount of resemblance even in detail which is much more striking than the superficial and technical differences. We cannot doubt that these resemblances depend on the nature of the problems to be solved and not on any accidental connection. One system of law may have imitated another in particular doctrines and institutions, but imitation cannot find place in processes extending over two or three

---

[236] Pollock (n. 193), 172.

[237] Jean-Louis Bergel, Marc Bruschi, and Sylvie Cimamonti, *Traité de droit civil: Les biens*, 4th ed. (Paris, 2000), nos. 124–25, 127; Henri Mazeaud, Léon Mazeaud, Jean Mazeaud, and François Chabas, *Leçons de droit civil, II. Les Biens: Droit de la propriété et ses démembrements*, 8th ed. (Paris, 1994), nos. 1413–14. Others give no explanation: *see*, e.g., Guy Raymond, *Droit civil*, 3rd ed. (Paris, 1996), no. 513.

[238] E. H. Burn and J. Cartwright, *Cheshire and Burn's Modern Law of Real Property*, 18th ed. (Oxford, 2011), 13 (emphasis original). Similarly, Kevin Gray and Susan Francis Grey, *Elements of Land Law*, 4th ed. (Oxford, 2005), § 3.23; Kevin Gray and Susan Francis Grey, "The Idea of Property in Land," in *Land Law: Themes and Perspectives*, eds. Susan Bright and John Dewar (Oxford, 1998), 15 at 18–19.

[239] *See* Chapter I, p. 24.

centuries, and whose fundamental analogies are externally disguised in almost every possible way.[240]

Contemporary English jurists have not recognized that Pollock was trying to resolve a problem that German conceptualists had created by their definition of property right. He was trying to do so by redefining that right. Conceptualism was redescribed as traditional common law.

*The rights of an owner* The problem of when an owner can use his land in a way that interferes with another was raised by the Romans and discussed by the medieval civilians.[241] It was bypassed by the late scholastics and iusnaturalists. It did not seem to be the sort of problem that could be resolved by their higher principles. But neither were they bothered by it.

The nineteenth-century conceptualists realized that restricting how an owner could use his land seemed to contradict their definition of property as the exclusive right of an owner to do as he chooses with what he owns.

French jurists acknowledged the contradiction. Limits to the owner's right had to be tolerated for pragmatic reasons. Life would become impossible if the law were to allow owners to exercise the rights that belonged to them in principle. According to Aubry and Rau, the "respective rights of [the] proprietors" of adjacent land were in a "conflict [that] cannot be resolved except by means of certain limits imposed on the natural exercise of the powers inherent in property."[242] Demolombe observed that if all proprietors could "invoke their absolute right, it is clear that none would have one in reality." What would be the result? "It would be war! It would be anarchy!" Similarly, Laurent thought that:

According to the rigor of the law, each proprietor would be able to object if one of his neighbors released on his property smoke or exhalations of any kind, because he has a right to the purity of air for his person and his goods.[243]

If that were so, he admitted, the existence of towns would be impossible.[244] Thus they arrived at the curious position that, in principle, the law conferred rights on proprietors that they should not have and which the law prohibited them from exercising.

The nineteenth-century German jurists, like Liebnitz,[245] thought that the law might confer a right that was unlimited, by definition or in principle, and then limit the use of it. They described the Roman text that prohibited the owner of a cheese

---

[240] Pollock (n. 193), 179.   [241] *See* Chapter II, pp. 37–39.
[242] Aubry and Rau (n. 9), 2: § 194.   [243] Laurent (n. 6), 6: § 144.
[244] Laurent (n. 6), 6: § 144. In a later volume of his work, Laurent finally decided that "[t]he Code was wrong to say that the owner has the right to enjoy and to dispose of his thing in the *most absolute manner*....": Laurent (n. 6), 20: § 417. Nevertheless, he did not suggest any other way in which property could be defined.
[245] *See* Chapter VIII, pp. 189–90.

shop from sending smoke onto upstairs premises[246] as a limitation of ownership by positive law (*gesetzliche Beschränkung des Eigenthums*).[247] According to Windscheid, the limitation was a good one because "reckless realization of the consequences of the concept of ownership is not possible without serious disadvantages." But the right to use one's property as one wishes is still a "consequence of ownership."[248] Positive law limited the owner's rights, as though the law no sooner conferred property rights on the owner than it had to take some of them back.

Jhering, who, as we will see, was one of the first to revolt against conceptualism, broke with the definition of the right of property as an unlimited right. Property rights would be worthless if a property owner either could disturb his neighbor at will or could not disturb him at all. An owner who could disturb his neighbors at will could make their land valueless by some pestilential use of his own. An owner who could not disturb them at all could not cook or use heat if his neighbors objected to the odors or smoke. Jhering concluded that an owner's rights must depend on the degree of interference and the normal use of land.[249] As we have seen, such a limitation had been proposed by Bartolus.[250] It was accepted even by nineteenth-century conceptualists such as Windscheid, who maintained that, in principle or by definition, an owner could use his property as he wished and the restraints imposed on him were statutory limitations of this right.[251] Jhering did not accept that definition of property, but neither did he propose another.

Jhering's rule was adopted by the German Civil Code.[252] A similar rule was adopted, independently it would seem, by the French and the common lawyers. The French Civil Code contained no general provision about disturbances among neighbors. French courts give relief, however, when a disturbance exceeds that which is "normal" among neighboring properties. What is normal is judged by the character of the locality.[253] In common law jurisdictions, an interference with a neighbor is actionable as a "nuisance" when it is "unreasonable."[254] Everyone agrees, however, that an interference may be "unreasonable" even when an owner was

---

[246] D.8.5.8.5. *See* Chapter II, pp. 37–39.
[247] Puchta, *Cursus* (n. 217), 2: § 231; Karl Vangerow, *Leitfaden für Pandekten-Vorlesungen* (Marburg, 1847), § 297 Anm. II; Windscheid (n. 32), 1: § 169.
[248] Windscheid (n. 32), 1: § 169.
[249] Rudolph von Jhering, "Zur Lehre von den Beschränkungen des Grundeigenthümers im Interesse der Nachbarn," *Jahrbücher für die Dogmatik des heutigen römischen und deutschen Privatrechts* 6 (1863): 81, 94–96.
[250] *See* Chapter II, p. 38.
[251] Windscheid (n. 32), 1: § 169. *See* Vangerow (n. 247), § 297 Anm. II.
[252] German Civil Code (*Bürgerlichesgesetzbuch*) § 906.
[253] Gérard Cornu, *Droit civil Introduction Les Personnes Les Biens*, 4th ed. (Paris, 1990), § 1096; Murad Ferid and Hans Sonnenberger, vol. 2 of *Das Französische Zivilrecht*, 2nd ed. (Heidelberg, 1986), § 3 C 191; Boris Starck, Henri Roland, and Laurent Boyer, *Droit civil: Obligations Responsabilité délictuelle*, 2nd ed. (Paris, 1985), § 310; Alex Weill, François Terré, and Philippe Simler, *Droit civil Les Biens*, 3rd ed. (Paris, 1985), § 309.
[254] For example, in England: Murphy (n. 211), 420; Rogers (n. 211), § 14.6; Margaret Brazier, *The Law of Torts*, 8th ed. (London, 1988), 32; Sir Basil Markesinis and Simon F. Deakin, *Tort Law*, 3rd ed. (Oxford, 1994), 419; in the United States: *Restatement (Second) of Torts* §§ 822, 826 (1965); William Keeton, Dan Dobbs, Robert Keeton, and David Owen, *Prosser and Keeton on the Law of Torts*, 5th ed. (St. Paul, MN, 1984), 629.

not careless, and so his conduct was not "unreasonable" as the term is understood in the law of negligence.[255] Although English and American jurists list several considerations that determine the "reasonableness" of an interference, the ones that matter are the extent of the interference and whether land is used in the way that is normal in a given locality.[256] The *Restatement (Second) of Torts* confused matters by suggesting that a court should consider "whether the gravity of the harm outweighs the utility of the actor's conduct."[257] But few courts have followed that suggestion.[258]

Again, however, it has been difficult for contemporary jurists to explain the rule that their legal systems have adopted. German jurists occasionally describe their law of *Immissionen* as a limitation on ownership, but they seem to have in mind not an abstractly defined concept of property, but the rights conferred on a proprietor by § 903 of the German Civil Code. They do not explain why such limitations should be imposed.[259] Some have pointed out that if neighbors could use their property in any way that they wish, one use would interfere with the other and both properties could become valueless.[260] That is the argument that Jhering made in the nineteenth century. But it is a purely negative argument that shows why the rights of owners cannot be absolute. It does not explain why their rights should depend on whether the interference is large and abnormal.

Some French jurists have said that the reason why a remedy is given is that to interfere with one's neighbors is an abuse of right (*abus de droit*).[261] As we will see in the next chapter, the doctrine of *abus de droit* was developed by twentieth-century jurists in revolt against conceptualism. Conceptualism, they said, had neglected the purposes for which the law recognizes rights. One has abused his

---

[255] In England: Murphy (n. 211), 420; Rogers (n. 211), § 14.6; Brazier (n. 254), 321; Markesinis and Deakin (n. 254), 419; in the United States: *Restatement (Second) of Torts* § 826(b)(1965); Keeton, Dobbs, Keeton, and Owen (n. 254), 629. See generally James Gordley, "Introduction," in *The Development of Liability between Neighbours*, ed. James Gordley (Cambridge, 2010), 23–24.

[256] In England: Murphy (n. 211), 425–26, 428–29; Rogers (n. 211), § 14.7; Brazier (n. 254), 322–27 (extent of the harm and suitability of the locality; she also says that the impracticability of preventing the interference and the social value of the plaintiff's activity bear on reasonableness, but she clearly does not mean that the plaintiff loses if his activity is of purely personal value and it is impracticable to prevent the interference); Markesinis and Deakin (n. 254), 427–33 (duration of interference and character of neighborhood; they also mention fault, but say that a nuisance is actionable without fault; they do mention the abnormal sensitivity of plaintiff's activity as bearing on reasonableness); Rogers (n. 211), 407–08 (extent of the harm and nature of the locality); in the United States: *Restatement (Second) of Torts* §§ 829, 831 (1965); Keeton, Dobbs, Keeton, and Owen (n. 254), 629 (amount of harm and nature of the locality; they mention the possibility of spreading losses by insurance or by shifting a loss to the general public, but they do not cite any cases that turned on this consideration).

[257] *Restatement (Second) of Torts* § 826(1) (1965).

[258] Jesse Dukeminier, James E. Krier, Gregory S. Alexander, and Michael H. Schill, *Property*, 7th ed. (Austin, TX, 2010), 734–35.

[259] For example, P. Bassenge, in Palandt, *Bürgerliches Gesetzbuch*, 5th ed. (Munich, 1996), to § 906, no. 1.

[260] H. Roth, in J. von Staudinger, *Kommentar zum Bürgerlichen Gesetzbuch*, 13th ed. (Berlin, 1996) to § 906, no. 1.

[261] Their opinions are described by Starck, Roland, and Boyer (n. 207), §§ 315–25, and by Weill, Terré, and Simler (n. 253), § 313.

right to use his property as he chooses when he interferes with a neighbor's use of his own. As we will see, critics of the doctrine have pointed out that if the law does not give the proprietor the right to interfere with his neighbors, then one cannot say he is abusing a right when he does. Indeed, proponents of the doctrine seem to think that the right to property must be defined as the conceptualists said: as the right of the proprietor to do as he chooses without regard to the purposes that the law wishes to serve by recognizing such a right. Only when the right is defined as a conceptualist would define it is it possible for the proprietor to abuse it. Nor do the French jurists explain why an interference with another counts as an abuse only when it is large and abnormal for the area. Some French jurists have said that liability should be imposed because one person should not be allowed to create or profit from the risk that his activity will injure others.[262] They do not explain why he may not do so only when the interference is abnormal. Other French jurists have criticized this explanation without offering one of their own.[263]

In the United States, the most serious attempts to explain the law of nuisance have been made by members of the law and economics movement. We will discuss this at a later point.[264]

## Tort

In tort law, for the nineteenth-century jurists, the defining or organizing principle was that one who harms another through fault, whether intentionally or negligently, is obligated to make compensation.

For the French jurists, fault was the only principled explanation of tort liability.[265] They based this conclusion on articles 1382–83 of the French Code, which imposed liability on one who intentionally or negligently caused another person a harm (*dommage*). René Savatier and Jean-Louis Halpérin regarded this provision as another instance of the individualism of the Code. According to Savatier, it was "the corollary of the liberty of the individual."[266] Halpérin traced it from the Code to what he calls the individualism of the seventeenth- and eighteenth-century natural lawyers.[267]

The drafters of the Code had paraphrased Pothier, who said that a person is liable for an act by which "he causes damage to another through intent or malice," or "without malice but by inexcusable imprudence."[268] Pothier, in turn, had been

---

[262] Bergel, Bruschi, and Cimamonti (n. 237), no. 109.
[263] Mazeaud, Mazeaud, Mazeaud, and Chabas (n. 237), no. 1341.
[264] *See* Chapter X, pp. 303–05.
[265] Toullier (n. 2), 11: 138; Duranton (n. 3), 13: 741; Aubry and Rau (n. 9), 4: § 446; M. L. Larombière, vol. 5 of *Théorie et pratique des obligations* (Paris, 1857), 738, 767; Laurent (n. 6), 20: §§ 387, 550, 639.
[266] René Savatier, *Les Métamorphoses économiques et sociales du droit privé d'aujourd'hui*, 2nd ed. (Paris, 1959), § 2, 6.
[267] Halpérin (n. 175), 57.
[268] Robert Pothier, "Traité des obligations," §§ 116, 118, in vol. 1 of *Oeuvres de Pothier*, ed. M. Siffrein, nouv. ed. (Paris, 1821), 1.

paraphrasing Grotius.[269] As we have seen, although iusnaturalists such as Grotius, as well as Domat and Pothier, believed that a person should be liable for harm caused by fault, they did not subscribe to the same principles as the nineteenth-century jurists. They believed that liability for fault rested on higher principles concerning human duty, although they were often unclear about what these principles were.

Moreover, according to some of the earlier jurists, fault was not the only principled basis for liability. According to Molina, some activities were so dangerous that a person engaged in them should be liable without fault. Pufendorf claimed that a person who profited from an activity should be liable for the harm that it caused others absent fault. As we have seen, Pothier and Domat were not clear.[270] According to Pothier, masters were liable for torts committed by their servants even when they could not prevent them. Yet he added: "This has been established to render masters careful to employ only good servants."[271] Domat said that when harm is done by fierce animals that escape from a person's cutody (*garde*), that person is liable because, "as he profits from the use he can make from this animal... he should answer." But Domat said that he should also be liable as a matter of "equity and public interest," "because it is by his fault" that the animal escaped.[272]

This ambiguity passed into articles 1384 and 1385 of the Civil Code, which were based on the passages from Domat and Pothier just described. Article 1384 provides that "a person is liable not only for the damage he causes by his own act but also for that caused for the acts of persons for whom he is responsible or things that he has under his care (*garde*)." The article goes on to provide for the vicarious liability of parents, artisans, teachers, masters, and employers. Parents, artisans, and teachers may escape liability by proving that they could not have prevented the act that caused damage. No such privilege is given to masters and employers. Article 1385 imposes liability on those who own or use animals. Whether fault is the exclusive principle of liability is as ambiguous under these provisions as it is in the original texts of Domat and Pothier.

One can see the ambiguity in the legislative history of these provisions.[273] Bertrand de Greuille explained why masters and employers cannot escape liability for acts that they could not prevent in the same way that Domat had explained the liability of the owner of wild animals: "Is it not the service from which the master profits that has produced the evil that he is condemned to repair?" But he immediately followed this question by another that suggests that liability is based on fault: "Does he not have to blame himself for having given his confidence to men who are bad, clumsy, or imprudent?" He explained the liability of the owner of animals by stating the "general thesis" that "nothing that belongs to a person can

---

[269] *See* Chapter V, pp. 135–36.   [270] *See* Chapter VI, pp. 146–47.
[271] Pothier (n. 268), § 121.
[272] Jean Domat, *Les Loix Civiles dans leur ordre naturel* (Paris, 1771), liv. II, tit. viii, sec. 2, § 8.
[273] John Bell and David Ibbetson, *European Legal Development: The Case of Tort* (Cambridge, 2012), 60–62; James Gordley, "Myths of the French Civil Code," *American Journal of Comparative Law* 42 (1994): 459, 480–81.

injure another with impunity."²⁷⁴ Tarrible and Treilhard, in contrast, seem to base liability exclusively on fault.²⁷⁵

The nineteenth-century jurists found it puzzling that masters and employers cannot escape liability by proving the absence of fault. Duranton and Larombière said that the masters could have been more careful in choosing whom to employ.²⁷⁶ Laurent, Aubry, and Rau gave no explanation.²⁷⁷ Laurent discussed the explanation of Bertrand de Greuille that the master profits from the work that gave rise to the injury, but he rejected it on the ground that the work "is the occasion, not the cause."²⁷⁸ Thus even if one were disposed to see the recognition of fault as the sole basis of liability as an individualistic development, one does not find it unambiguously in the Code, but, again, one does in the commentators.

The German jurists explained liability in tort as the French nineteenth-century jurists did. Fault, for them, was a principle of accountability, but they did not explain why it gave rise to a duty to compensate the plaintiff. Windscheid simply said that a person is liable in tort "because he was at fault";²⁷⁹ Puchta, that "every tort presupposes a relationship of accountability";²⁸⁰ Arndts, that "every tortious act" presupposes "the element... indicated by the word fault."²⁸¹ All of them agreed that a person might be at fault through intention or negligence.²⁸² Arndts said that "what lies beyond [fault] is chance...." But they did not explain what distinguished fault from chance, except to say that it was the basis for accountability.²⁸³ Nor did they explain why one should

---

²⁷⁴ Rapport fait par Bertrand-de-Greuille, Communication officielle au Tribunat, 10 pluviose an XII (January 31, 1804), in Fenet (n. 178), 13: 477.
²⁷⁵ According to Tarrible, vicarious liability and liability for animals are based on the principle that "damage, to be subject to reparation, must be the effect of a fault or an imprudence on the part of someone," since otherwise "it is only the work of chance": Discours prononcé par le Tribun Tarrible, Discussion devant le Corps-Législatif, 18 pluviose, an XII (February 8, 1804), in Fenet (n. 178), 13: 488. According to Treilhard, some are liable for weakness, others, a bad choice, "all [for] negligence": Présentation au Corps Législatif, et exposé des motifs par Treilhard, 9 pluviose, an XII (January 30, 1804), in Fenet (n. 178), 13: 468. If so, one wonders why the Code does not include masters and employers when it enumerates the people who can escape vicarious liability by proving that they could not have prevented the act that causes damage. Treilhard does not mention them, and Tarrible seems to be unaware that masters and employers have not been included. After enumerating them and all of the other people who may be liable for the acts of another, Tarrible says that liability "is at an end with regard to all of them if they prove that they could not prevent the act that gives rise to it": Tarrible, Discussion devant le Corps-Législatif, in Fenet (n. 178), 13: 489.
²⁷⁶ Duranton (n. 3), 13: 741; Larombière (n. 265), 5: 767.
²⁷⁷ Aubry and Rau (n. 9), 4: § 447; Laurent (n. 6), 20: § 88.
²⁷⁸ Laurent (n. 6), 20: § 588.
²⁷⁹ Windscheid (n. 32), 1: § 101. He also said there that, sometimes, the defendant could be liable without fault: "Conduct may be tortious (*unerlaubt*) on account of its result in itself...."
²⁸⁰ Puchta (n. 42), § 255.   ²⁸¹ Arndts (n. 190), § 85.
²⁸² Windscheid (n. 32), 1: § 101; Puchta (n. 42), § 255; Arndts (n. 190), § 85.
²⁸³ Arndts did say that fault entailed "a relationship to the will of the party on the basis of which responsibility can be imputed to him": Arndts (n. 190), § 85. That relationship seems clear enough in the case of intentionally inflicted harm. But Arndts did not try to explain why it extended to negligent acts in which the harm was not intended—a problem that, as we have seen, writers in the Aristotelian tradition had resolved by considering the connection between the will and the virtue of prudence.

owe compensation. Windscheid simply noted that "[a] particularly important consequence of tortious acts (*unerlaubte Handlungen*) is the obligation to make reparation for the harm they have caused."[284]

Windscheid explained harm as a "*Rechtsverletzung*, that is the violation of a right." The conduct is not allowed because it is in conflict with the right of another person.[285] Ludwig Arndts explained that "[e]very tortious act...presupposes, objectively, a violation (*Verletzen*)...."[286] Again, there was no higher principle to explain the sorts of rights one should have and consequently the harms for which one should be compensated.

We have seen how differently the Roman authors of their texts had approached tort law.[287] Their law recognized particular torts, only one of which, an action under the *lex Aquilia*, required the defendant to have acted intentionally or negligently. In most of the texts, when the plaintiff can recover, he has been deprived of his property. Two texts implied that a father could recover for harm suffered by his son. There were other harms for which he could not recover, such as physical injury to the plaintiff himself.

As with property law, the German jurists defined tort in the same way as the rationalists. As we have seen, Leibniz and Wolff agreed that a person owed compensation if he harmed another through fault. Leibniz said that what was not the result of fault was the result of "chance."[288] He explained harm as depriving someone of what he ought to have—that is, as violating a private right. Leibniz said that a person is harmed if he is deprived of whatever he has whether acquired by "fortune or industry."[289] According to Wolff, "[t]he one to whom harm has been done has less than he ought to have."[290] The rationalists did not base this definition on the Roman texts. Again, it would be surprising if a definition of tort arrived at in this way were to be embodied in them.

As we have seen, nineteenth-century Anglo-American treatises on torts arrived at the principle that liability was based on fault by borrowing from Continental jurists. They recognized a tort of negligence and classified the traditional writs as "intentional torts." That distinction had been foreign to the case law that was said to support it.[291]

---

[284] Windscheid (n. 32), 1: § 102.
[285] Windscheid (n. 32), 1: § 101. A secondary principle was that one might be liable anyway if the defendant acts in a way that the law forbids: Windscheid (n. 32), 1: § 101.
[286] Arndts (n. 190), § 84.
[287] See Chapter I, p. 20.
[288] Gottfried Wilhelm Leibniz, "Elementa juris naturalis," in *Philosophische Schriften Erster Band 1663–1672*, ed. Akademie der Wissenschaften der DDR (Berlin, 1990), 433 at 434.
[289] Gottfried Wilhelm Leibniz, "De tribus juris praeceptis sive gradibus," in vol. 2 of *Textes inédits*, ed. Gaston Grua (New York, 1985), 606 at 607.
[290] Christian Wolff, *Jus naturae methodo scientific pertracta*, published as *Jus naturae* in ed. Marcellus Thomannus, in vols. 17–24 of *Gesammelte Werke II. Abteilung Lateinishce Schriften*, eds. J. École, J. E. Hofmann, M. Thomann, and H. W. Arndt (Hildesheim, 1972), II, § 580.
[291] *See* pp. 205–10.

*Liability for fault* Most nineteenth-century jurists regarded fault as the master principle on which liability in tort must depend. By "fault," they meant an action that is morally culpable. Like the rationalists, they did not explain why moral culpability should give rise to duty of compensation. Like the rationalists,[292] they did not tie the principle to any larger theory of human accountability. Nils Jansen has noted the tension between liability based on wrongdoing and liability based on compensation for harm done to another.[293] In my view, this tension has not marked the entire history of tort law. It is the result of a modern problem that arose with the rationalists and passed into the work of the nineteenth-century jurists.

The difficulties were seen at the end of the nineteenth century and became a target for critics. Jurists such as Josserand said that they could see no reason why the duty to make compensation should depend on whether a person who harmed another had been morally at fault.[294] The critics then found themselves on the other horn of a dilemma. If the fault is irrelevant to the duty to make compensation, then is all liability strict liability? If fault is relevant, but does not entail moral responsibility, then what can fault mean?

The dilemma is best understood by looking at the efforts that French jurists have made to escape it. Most jurists have concluded that fault, but not culpable misconduct, is required for liability under articles 1382–83 of the Civil Code. As Alain Bénabent has noted, the requirement of fault in the "moral" sense has been "abandoned": "[F]ault has become a purely objective idea consisting only of factual conduct that is juridically described as abnormal."[295] According to Boris Starck, Henri Roland, and Laurent Boyer, morality cannot matter since, on the one hand, "to cause a harm to another and then to abandon him to a miserable state because one was not at fault is inhuman, and in our sense, not moral...." On the other hand, "it is not moral to place a burden on the author of an involuntary fault—negligence or imprudence—that can amount to millions of francs in damages."[296]

If a defendant need not be at fault in the ordinary or "moral sense," and, indeed, if he can be "juridically" at fault for events that he could not possibly prevent, the question is how to explain why liability is imposed by articles 1382–83. "Unfortunately," according to Starck, Roland, and Boyer, "authors are not in agreement among themselves as to the new basis of responsibility."[297] They describe three popular theories.[298] One is the theory of *risque-profit* according to which whoever

---

[292] See Chapter VIII, p. 188.
[293] Nils Jansen, "Duties and Rights in Negligence: A Comparative and Historical Perspective on the European Law of Extracontractual Liability," *Oxford Journal of Legal Studies* 24 (2004): 443.
[294] Louis Josserand, *De la responsibiité du fait des choses inanimées* (Paris, 1897), 6–8, 103–08.
[295] Alain Bénabent, *Droit civil: Les Obligations*, 12th ed. (Paris, 2010), no. 542.
[296] Starck, Roland, and Boyer (n. 207), no. 8.
[297] Starck, Roland, and Boyer (n. 207), no. 41.
[298] These theories are also described by François Terré, Philippe Simler, and Yves Lequette, *Droit civil: Les obligations*, 9th ed. (Paris, 2005), no. 685; Philippe Malaurie and Laurent Aynès, "Obligations," vol. 1 in *Responsibilité délictuelle*, 11th ed. (Paris, 2001), no. 25.

profited from an activity should be liable for the damages that activity caused.[299] This theory resembles the explanation of strict liability proposed by Molina on the basis of ideas of commutative justice, and in looser form by Pufendorf and Domat.[300] Indeed, it would serve better as justification for strict liability than for liability for fault.

The objection of Stark, Roland, and Boyer was that the theory did not go far enough. It imposed liability on a defendant engaged in a profit-making activity, not one conducted for other purposes.[301] Unlike the late scholastics, they did not regard any object that one pursued voluntarily as a gain.[302] For the French jurists, one solution has been to broaden the theory so that the defendant would be liable for any *risque crée*—any risk that he had created.[303] The difficulty is that if a person is liable for creating a risk, prudently or imprudently, regardless of its size, then, as Starck, Roland, and Boyer have noted, "it would be necessary to conclude that a person is always responsible," including "the victim of the harm ... himself...."[304]

The problem with these theories, according to Starck, Roland, and Boyer, is that they look at the question of liability "only from the standpoint of whoever caused the harm....":

> That way of reasoning is incomplete because it leaves out the point of view of the victim.... Everyone has the right to his life and his physical integrity, ... to the physical integrity of the property that belongs to him, and more generally, to his physical and moral security.[305]

They concluded that the ultimate question is balancing a "right to act" against a "right to security."[306] They did not explain how a balance is to be struck. If the actor's conduct is normal and blameless, what will turn the balance? If it is abnormal and blameless, why should the abnormality matter?

All of these theories have been attacked by Henri Mazeaud, Léon Mazeaud, Jean Mazeaud, and François Chabas. According to these jurists, when proponents of a risk theory speak of "abnormal conduct," they do not mean conduct that is unusual or even unusually dangerous. For the proponents of risk theories, "abnormal conduct" means conduct that a prudent person would avoid. But if fault in the sense of imprudence does not matter, why should it matter what a prudent person would have done? If the criterion of abnormality is abandoned, according to the Mazeauds and Chabas, the only other is the creation of a risk. But that eliminates all criteria.[307] They have noted that, "except in a few cases" such as children and the insane, the law persists in imposing liability for fault in the ordinary sense, whatever

---

[299] Labbé, "Note," S. 1890.4.18, described by Starck, Roland, and Boyer (n. 253), no. 42.
[300] *See* Chapter VI, pp. 146–47.   [301] Starck, Roland, and Boyer (n. 253), no. 43.
[302] *See* Chapter III, p. 91.   [303] Described by Starck, Roland, and Boyer (n. 253), no. 44.
[304] Starck, Roland, and Boyer (n. 253), no. 45.
[305] Starck, Roland, and Boyer (n. 253), no. 58. For a similar criticism of the risk theories, *see* Terré, Simler, and Lequette (n. 207), no. 685, 686.
[306] Starck, Roland, and Boyer (n. 253), no. 58.
[307] Henri Mazeaud, Léon Mazeaud, Jean Mazeaud, and François Chabas, *Leçons de droit civil II. Obligations: théorie générale*, 5th ed. (Paris, 1998), no. 430.

the jurists may say.[308] That is as it should be, they have said, since there is no reason why it is more equitable to shift the loss to the innocent actor.[309]

The conceptualist's principle of liability for culpable misconduct has been discredited. Yet the French jurists have not found a coherent alternative. As Terré, Simler, and Lequette have observed, "[l]ogic has not necessarily received its due, either as to the sources of the rules, or as to a harmony which has vanished."[310]

Since the nineteenth century, leading German treatise writers have also denied that, in principle, liability for fault is based on moral culpability. According to Josef Esser, liability is imposed because of the "act," not the "actor," and without "the reproach of fault."[311] The reason is "a plausible division of risks," "an acceptable compromise between the interests of the injuring and the injured party."[312] It has been objected that the German Civil Code requires not only that the defendant act intentionally or negligently, but also that his action is "unlawful." For example, he is not liable if he intentionally struck the plaintiff in self-defense since it was not unlawful to do so. If he is liable for negligence, not because he was at fault, but simply because he behaved in the wrong way, it would seem that his liability is really for unlawful behavior.[313] The more fundamental problem is what the "interests" of either party have to do with imposing liability for conduct that the defendant could not help, except in the trivial sense that the defendant always has an interest in escaping liability and the plaintiff in holding him liable.

Today, leading English treatise writers also deny that, in principle, liability for fault is based on moral culpability. Heuston and Buckley, in their revision of Salmond's treatise, claim that "[t]here is no necessary element of 'fault' in the sense of moral blameworthiness...."[314] According to K. M. Stanton, "the compensatory purpose" of tort law should not be "undermined by arguments founded on moral responsibility...."[315] Unlike the French, they do not explain how fault should be reinterpreted.

Since the time of Oliver Wendell Holmes, American jurists have proposed theories to explain why fault in the moral sense should not matter. Holmes argued that if "a man is born hasty and awkward... his slips are no less troublesome to his neighbors than if they sprang from guilty neglect."[316] Leading contemporary

---

[308] Mazeaud, Mazeaud, Mazeaud, and Chabas (n. 307), no. 432.
[309] Mazeaud, Mazeaud, Mazeaud, and Chabas (n. 307), no. 429.
[310] Terré, Simler, and Lequette (n. 207), no. 673.
[311] Josef Esser and Eike Schmidt, *Schuldrecht I Allgemeiner Teil 2 Vertragshaftung, Schadensersatz, Personmehrheit im Schuldverhältnis Ein Lehrbuch*, 5th ed. (Heidelberg, 1976), 35. *See* Hans Brox, *Allgemeines Schuldrecht*, 10th ed. (Munich, 1982), no. 219.
[312] Esser and Schmidt (n. 311), 35.
[313] *See* Brox (n. 311), no. 219.
[314] R. F. V. Heuston and R. A. Buckley, *Salmond and Heuston on the Law of Torts*, 19th ed. (London, 1987), 216.
[315] Stanton (n. 211), 69.   [316] Holmes (n. 114), 108.

jurists, such as Stephen Perry[317] and Jules Coleman,[318] have argued that the defendant should be liable if he deviated from the standard of conduct that a reasonable person would normally observe, whether or not he is personally at fault. Their claim is like that of the French jurists who believe that the defendant should be liable, even if was not personally imprudent, if his conduct was abnormal. They then describe abnormal conduct as conduct that a prudent person would avoid. Richard Epstein has claimed that liability should be imposed regardless of fault if a case falls within one of four "causal paradigms." The paradigms, however, describe actions that people typically do not perform unless they are at fault:[319] the defendant applied force to the plaintiff's person or thing; he frightened the plaintiff; he compelled the plaintiff to act; or he created a dangerous condition that injured the plaintiff.[320] Epstein then described defenses by which the defendant can escape liability. They look like typical cases in which a person ordinarily would not be at fault. For example, he is not liable if the plaintiff blocked his right of way, and whether the plaintiff did so depends on applicable state traffic laws.[321]

These theories have not been generally accepted, perhaps because they are subject to criticisms like those of the Mazeauds and Chabas in France. The abnormal conduct for which liability is imposed is that which a prudent person would and could avoid. It is not merely conduct that is unusually dangerous, like that of person who unwittingly carries a contagious disease or who is blown off a building into a crowd. But if the personal fault of the defendant does not matter, why should it matter what a prudent person would have done?

In France, England, and the United States, the views of the jurists have had little effect on the results reached by courts. Whatever theory one adopts, the man born hasty and awkward would not escape liability. How could he prove that he was born that way or that, if he had tried, he could not have overcome his limitations? In France, the few cases in which a person is held liable for conduct that he demonstrably could not help are those of children and insane persons. Imposing

---

[317] Stephen Perry, "The Moral Foundations of Tort Law," *Iowa Law Review* 77 (1992): 449, 451–52; Stephen Perry, "Loss, Agency and Responsibility for Outcomes: Three Conceptions of Corrective Justice," in *Tort Theory*, eds. Ken Cooper-Stephenson and Elaine Gibson (North York, ON, 1993), 24.

[318] Jules L. Coleman, "Tort Law and the Demands of Corrective Justice," *Indiana Law Journal* 67 (1992): 349, 357. See Jules L. Coleman, *Risks and Wrongs* (Cambridge, 1992), 333–35; Jules L. Coleman, "The Mixed Conception of Corrective Justice," *Iowa Law Review* 77 (1992): 427, 428, 442; Jules L. Coleman, "Mental Abnormality, Personal Responsibility and Tort Liability," in *Mental Illness: Law and Public Policy*, eds. B. Brody and H. T. Engelhardt, Jr. (Dordrecht, 1980), 107; Jules L. Coleman, "Moral Theories of Torts: Their Scope and Limits: Part I," *Law and Philosophy* 1(3) (1982): 371, 376–78.

[319] On the normative character of Epstein's paradigms, *see* Ernest J. Weinrib, "Causation and Wrongdoing," *Chicago-Kent Law Review* 63 (1987): 407, 417; Perry, "Moral Foundations" (n. 317), 464; Gary T. Schwartz, "The Vitality of Negligence and the Ethic of Strict Liability," *Georgia Law Review* 15 (1981): 963, 988–89.

[320] Richard A. Epstein, "A Theory of Strict Liability," *Journal of Legal Studies* 2 (1973): 151, 166–89.

[321] Richard A. Epstein, "Defenses and Subsequent Pleas in a System of Strict Liability," *Journal of Legal Studies* 3 (1974): 165, 176.

liability on them is a recent development. The insane were not held to the standard of conduct of a normal person until the enactment of the Law of January 3, 1968, now article 489–2 of the Civil Code. By analogy, children were held to an adult standard by the *Assemblée plénière* of the *Cour de cassation* in 1984.[322] Despite the opinion of leading jurists, English courts have held children to the standard of care appropriate to their age,[323] and Canadian courts, applying English common law, have refused to impose liability on the insane.[324] American courts do not hold children to an adult standard, although, according the *Second Restatement of Torts*, they should hold the insane to the standard of a normal person. That was a question on which the *First Restatement* had reserved judgment. In any event, whether to impose liability on children or the insane is not the same question as whether other people should be liable for conduct that they cannot help. People whose conduct is the result of a physical disability are not held liable. The German Civil Code of 1900, while acknowledging that children and the insane are not at fault for failing to meet the standard of a normal adult,[325] holds them liable if, in the court's judgment, fairness requires that the damage be made good.[326]

Again, critics were more successful in discrediting the conceptualists' principle than in finding an alternative of their own.

The one great change has been the development of strict liability alongside liability for fault. Technological changes made it possible, without any fault at all, to cause ever greater amounts of harm. It seemed imperative to impose strict liability whether or not one had a good theoretical reason for doing so. To find such a reason would have been difficult for earlier jurists, although, as we have seen, Molina, Pufendorf, and Domat had justified strict liability on the ground that it prevented one person from taking risks for his own benefit that harmed another.[327] The task was particularly difficult for the nineteenth-century jurists. They had neither the theory of commutative justice relied on by Molina, nor the more indefinite higher principles of Pufendorf and Domat. Moreover, they had defined tort liability as a duty to make compensation for harm caused by fault.

In the end, courts and jurists recognized that nineteenth-century conceptual analysis could not deal with the problem. More acceptable results were reached. Yet no alternative and generally accepted explanation was found for these results.

American courts arrived at a coherent rule: the defendant is liable for harm caused by ultra-hazardous or abnormally dangerous activities. This rule was accepted by American courts and by the *Restatements of Torts*.[328] Yet American jurists did not find a coherent and generally accepted explanation for it. The most serious effort has been made by members of the law and economics movement,

---

[322] Cass., Assemblée plénière, May 3, 1984 (4th case), D.S. 1984. J.529.
[323] *Gough v. Thorne* [1966] 2 All E.R. 398 (C.A.).
[324] *Att'y Gen'l of Canada v. Connolly* [1989] 64 D.L.R. 4th 84 (Sup. Ct. British Columbia); *Buckley & Toronto Transp. Com'n v. Smith Transport Ltd.* [1946] 4 D.L.R. 721 (Sup. Ct. British Columbia).
[325] German Civil Code (*Bürgerlichesgesetzbuch*) §§ 827–28.
[326] German Civil Code (*Bürgerlichesgesetzbuch*) § 829.
[327] See Chapter VI, pp. 146–47.   [328] *Restatement (Second) of Torts* § 519 (1965).

which we will consider later. English courts have rejected the American rule. They adopted an odd one: a property owner is liable if he brought a "non-natural" thing on his land that "escaped" and did damage.[329] The language is taken from the nineteenth-century case of *Rylands v. Fletcher*.[330] The rationale is not at all clear. The French adopted a rule that seems stranger. As we have seen, article 1384 of the Civil Code imposes liability on a person for harm done by objects in his "custody." The meaning of the passage to the drafters is not clear.[331] The nineteenth-century French jurists interpreted it as a special case of liability for fault. Strangely, French courts have now interpreted it to mean that a person is liable without fault for harm done by any object in his "custody," however dangerous or innocuous the object may be, unless the harm was caused by *cas fortuit* or *force majeure*.[332] German courts have not adopted any general rule. They impose strict liability only as provided by a patchwork of special statutes. For example, the defendant is liable for the operation of trains,[333] aircraft,[334] automobiles,[335] and electric and gas installations.[336]

What is missing—and has been missing since the nineteenth century—is an explanation of why liability is imposed, sometimes for fault, and sometimes regardless of fault.

*Harm* For the conceptualists, as for the rationalists,[337] recovery in tort is based on the principle that one owes compensation for harm caused by fault. The rationalists said little about what constitutes a harm, except that it is a violation of another person's rights. The conceptualists tried to explain what constituted such a violation. The results of their efforts puzzled later jurists, but are still with us.

The nineteenth-century jurists saw two alternatives. One that prevailed in France was to say that the plaintiff could recover for any sort of harm that he might suffer. He had the right not to suffer harm. The other, which prevailed in Germany and then in common law jurisdictions, was to define a violation of rights for which one could recover in a more limited way. There must be a violation of an absolute right such as property, which is a right held against all of the world. There is no liability for violation of a relative right, such as one based on contract, which is a right against a particular person. Although this was a conceptualist solution, it is still with us, overlaid by efforts to account for it by considerations of policy.

Applying their broad definition of harm, French courts have allowed a plaintiff to recover for any harm that he has suffered, including economic losses, even though neither his body nor his physical property were harmed. Factory owners

---

[329] *Cambridge Water Co Ltd v. Eastern Counties Leather plc.* [1994] 2 A.C. 264; *Read v. J. Lyons & Co., Ltd.* [1947] A.C. 156 (H.L.).
[330] *Fletcher v. Rylands* (1866) L.R. 1 Ex. 265; *Rylands v. Fletcher* [1868] L.R. 3 H.L. 330.
[331] See pp. 236–37.
[332] The rule dates from Cass. ch. réun., February 13, 1930, D. 1930.1.57.
[333] *Haftpflichtgsetz* § 1(1).      [334] *Luftvehkehrgesetz* § 33.      [335] *Strassenverkehrgesetz* § 7.
[336] *Haftpflichtgsetz* § 2(1).      [337] See Chapter VI, p. 188.

have recovered for profits that they lost when defendants cut off their supply of gas by breaking a pipe belonging to a third party.[338] A soccer club has recovered for profits that it lost when the defendant negligently killed a star player.[339] A bus company has recovered for the profits that it lost when defendants negligently caused a traffic jam and their potential customers either walked or took cabs to their destinations.[340]

Nevertheless, applied consistently, this approach would lead to results that the French courts have been unwilling to accept. They have limited recovery even though they cannot explain why it should be limited. For example, they did not allow a partnership to recover for the deals that were not consummated because the company president who was negotiating them was negligently injured.[341] They did not allow creditors to recover the sums that they would never be repaid because the borrower was negligently killed.[342] In each case, they denied relief without admitting that they were limiting the definition of harm. But it is hard to know how seriously they took the reasons that they gave. Although French law allows recovery for "the loss of a chance," according to the *Cour de cassation*, the partnership could not recover because consummation of the deal under negotiation was not "certain." Although a plaintiff is not denied relief because he could have insured himself against a loss, the creditor was denied relief because he could have purchased insurance on the life of the debtor.

The preliminary draft of the German Civil Code contained a provision like that of the French: "One who has caused another harm (*Schaden*) by intention or by negligence by an unlawful (*widerrechtlich*) act or omission is obligated to make him compensation."[343]

The members of the First Commission accepted the *Pandektists*' general principle governing recovery in tort law: the plaintiff could recover for a violation of a right.[344] A question raised at its first meetings was:

[W]hat is to be understood as the "violation of a right": only the violation of a right which receives an absolute protection or any violation of the legal order by an act prohibited by law as contrary to the legal order . . . ?[345]

The Commission chose the first alternative. As a general principle, the plaintiff could recover only for the violation of an "absolute right." It noted that a "right of

---

[338] Cass., 2ᵉ civ. ch., May 8, 1970, Bull. civ. 1970. II. no. 160.
[339] Cour d'appel, Colmar, April 20, 1955, D. 1956.Jur.723.
[340] Cass., 2ᵉ civ. ch., April 28, 1965, 1965 D.S.Jur.777.
[341] Cass., 2ᵉ civ. ch., June 12, 1987, JCP 1987. IV. 286.
[342] Cass., 2ᵉ civ. ch., February 21, 1979, JCP 1979. IV. 145.
[343] *Teilentwurf des Vorentwurfs zu einem BGB, Recht der Schuldverhältnisse* no. 15, § 1.
[344] *Die Vorlagen der Redaktoren für die erste Kommission zur Ausarbeitung des Entwurfs eines Bürgerlichen Gesetzbuches, Recht der Schuldverhältnisse*, Teil 1, *Allgemeiner Teil* I, ed. Werner Schubert (Berlin, 1980), 657 ("the sphere of rights of each person must be respected and left untouched by all other persons; whoever acts contrary to this general command of the law without there being any special grounds for justification has by that alone committed a tortious act [literally, a nonpermitted act, *unerlaubte Handlung*]").
[345] *Protokolle der Kommission zur Ausarbeitung eines Bürgerlichen Gesetzbuchs* (1881–89), in vol. 3 of *Die Beratung des Bürgerlichen Gesetzbuchs*, eds. H. H. Jakobs and Werner Schubert (Berlin, 1983), 971–72.

obligation" (*obligatorisches Recht*), such as a contract right, is not "absolute." An absolute right could be violated by anyone. A right of obligation "cannot be violated by anyone except the debtor."[346] That conclusion followed, supposedly, from the definition of the violation of a right.

The result, after several amendments, was § 823(1) of the German Civil Code, which enumerated certain of the absolute rights: "One who intentionally or negligently unlawfully violates the life, body, health, freedom, property or similar right (*sonstiges Recht*) of another is obligated to compensate him for the harm that thereby ensues."[347]

This provision does not permit recovery for pure economic harm—harm that results when none of these enumerated rights has been violated—as the *Reichsgericht* held soon after the Code was enacted.[348] That limitation is the result of the conceptualist approach that the Commission had taken from the nineteenth-century jurists: one defines a right and then deduces the consequences.

In the early twentieth century, the same approach was taken by jurists in England and the United States. According to J. F. Clerk and W. H. B. Lindsell, "interference with rights of service or with rights of contract generally is not actionable." In that respect, such rights differed from rights such as property, which were "unqualified."[349] A similar principle was adopted in the eighth edition of C. G. Addison's treatise on torts, which was published in 1906 after his death by William Gordon and Walter Griffith.[350] They said that because negligence is the breach of a duty, the plaintiff is therefore liable only "where there is an obligation toward the plaintiff." "It follows," they said, "that if there is no duty to be careful there is no action for negligence."[351] Similarly, in 1910, Sir John Salmond said that

---

[346] *Protokolle der Kommission zur Ausarbeitung eines Bürgerlichen Gesetzbuchs* (n. 345), 984, 986–87.

[347] Section 704(1) or an earlier draft provided: "The violation of life, body, health, freedom and honor are also [along with property] to be regarded as the violation of a right." The provision was changed by adding the phrase "similar right," since it had proved impossible to enumerate all of the absolute rights, and deleting the right to one's honor, since it had been decided on independent grounds that a plaintiff should not recover money damages for violations of his honor, a view that has since been corrected by decisions of the *Bundesgerichtshof*: *Bundesgerichtshof*, 1954, EBGHZ 13, 334.

[348] *Reichsgericht*, April 11, 1901, ERGZ 48, 114; *Reichsgericht*, February 27, 1904, ERGZ, 58, 24.

[349] John Frederick Clerk and William Harry Barber Lindsell, *The Law of Torts*, ed. W. Paine, 3rd ed. (London, 1904), 11. They cited *Cattle v. The Stockton Waterworks Co.* (1875) L.R. 10 Q.B. 453, in which the plaintiff was not allowed to recover the extra expenses that he incurred when the defendant's negligence caused the flooding of a third party's land on which he was building a tunnel. In that case, however, the court had rested its decision on different considerations—that the damage was "remote" and that recovery would unduly multiply the number of possible plaintiffs: *Stockton Waterworks*, 457, as noted by Robby Bernstein, *Economic Loss*, 2nd ed. (London, 1998), 11. At another point, Clerk and Lindsell do suggest that the case turned on the remoteness of the damage: *Law of Torts*, 133.

[350] Charles Greenstreet Addison, *A Treatise on the Law of Torts or Wrongs and their Remedies*, eds. William Gordon and Walter Griffith, 8th ed. (London, 1906). Although they styled themselves "editors," Gordon and Griffith had found it necessary to rewrite the treatise extensively because it was unsystematic, they said, compared with the treatises of Sir Frederick Pollock, and Clerk and Lindsell. Since it contained "little or nothing about the law of Negligence," they had written the chapter on that subject from scratch: Addision, *Law of Torts*, viii. They also cited *Stockton Waterworks* (n. 349) as an illustration.

[351] Addison (n. 350), 701.

## Novus Ordo: *Positivism and Conceptualism*  247

"nuisance is actionable only at the suit of the occupier or owner of the land affected by it; not at the suit of strangers whatever pecuniary interest they may have in the non-existence of the nuisance."[352] He also said that "[n]egligent injury to property gives an action to the owner of that property, or to other persons having some proprietary interest therein, but not to mere strangers who are thereby subjected to pecuniary loss."[353] In later editions, Salmond generalized the principle: "He who does a wrongful act is liable only to the person whose rights are violated."[354] Thereafter, the same principle was endorsed in a long series of English cases stretching from 1911 to 1969.[355]

It made its way to the United States in 1927 in the landmark opinion of Oliver Wendell Holmes in *Robbins Dry Dock and Repair v. Flint*,[356] in which Holmes once again adopted a conceptualist solution despite his complaints about conceptualism. In that case, while a steamer was in dry dock, its propeller was damaged as a result of the defendant's negligence. The plaintiff had chartered the steamer and sued for the profits that he lost during the delay resulting from the repair of the propeller. Reversing the circuit court, Holmes held that he could not recover because "[t]he injury to the propeller was no wrong to the [plaintiff] but only to those to whom it belonged."[357]

In some cases, applying the rule straightforwardly leads to results that courts are not willing to permit. They have either refused to apply the rule or done so less than

---

[352] John William Salmond, *The Law of Torts: A Treatise on the English Law of Liability for Civil Injuries*, 2nd ed. (London, 1910), 10. For that principle, he cited there *Stockton Waterworks* and *Anglo-Algerian Steamship Co. Ltd. v. The Houlder Line, Ltd.* [1908] 1 K.B. 659, in which the defendant had negligently damaged a third party's dock and the plaintiff was not allowed to recover for the loss he suffered when his ship was unable to use it. As in *Stockton Waterworks*, the court had not mentioned this principle, but spoken of the remoteness of the harm (at 665) and the danger of multiplying possible plaintiffs (at 668). Indeed, the court noted that the plaintiff could recover: at 664–65. Salmond was speaking of what are now called cases of public nuisance if the plaintiff were specially affected. The rule is now said to be different in nuisance than in negligence, but the court was writing before that difference came to be accepted.

[353] Salmond (n. 352), 10.

[354] Salmond, *Law of Torts*, ed. W. T. S. Stallybrass, 8th ed. (London, 1934), 133. Whether the English treatise writers who first put forward this argument knew that German jurists had already done so is another question. That is certainly a possibility for Salmond. He was surely familiar with the German Civil Code and may have known of the work of the First Commission as well. His select bibliography in his book *Jurisprudence* shows a thorough knowledge of German writing on private law and a special admiration for Bernard Windscheid, one of the most distinguished members of the First Commission. He described Windscheid as "one of the most distinguished German exponents of modern Roman law" and his book, *Lehrbuch des Pandektenrechts*, as "an admirable example of the scientific study of a legal system": John William Salmond, *Jurisprudence or the Theory of the Law* (London, 1902), 654. Stone has suggested that he used ideas taken from Windscheid in that book: Julius Stone, *Legal Systems and Lawyers' Reasonings* (London, 1964), 141. See Alex Frame, *Salmond Southern Jurist* (Wellington, New Zealand, 1995), 63.

[355] *La Société Anonyme de Remorquage à Hélice v. Bennets* [1911] 1 K.B. 243, 245–46, 248; *Elliott Steam Tug Co. Ltd. v. Shipping Controller* [1922] 1 K.B. 127, 140; *Morrison Steamship Co. Ltd. v. Greystoke Castle* [1947] A.C. 265, 280, 305–06 (H.L.); *Best v. Samuel Fox & Co. Ltd.* [1952] A.C. 716, 730–31; *Attorney-General for New South Wales v. Perpetual Trustee Co. (Ltd.)* [1955] A.C. 457, 484; *Electrochrome Ltd. v. Welsh Plastics Ltd.* [1968] 2 All E.R. 205, 206; *Margarine Union GmbH v. Cambray Prince Steamship Co. Ltd.* [1969] 1 Q.B. 219, 251.

[356] 275 U.S. 303 (1927).   [357] *Robbins Dry Dock* (n. 356), 308.

straightforwardly. In *People's Express Airlines v. Consolidated Rail Corp.*,[358] a commercial airline recovered when it was forced to evacuate its premises because the defendant negligently allowed a dangerous chemical to escape from a railway tank car. The court refused to apply the rule that denies recovery when no physical harm has occurred. "The challenge," the court said, "is to fashion a rule that limits liability but permits adjudication of meritorious claims."[359]

In other cases, German and English, as well as American, courts have refused to apply the rule. The best known are those in which plaintiffs lost money that they loaned or invested in the enterprise of a third party on the basis of false information on its financial condition negligently furnished them by a defendant with which they did not have a contract.[360] German courts, however, have claimed that the plaintiff was not recovering in tort, but on a contract, even though the two had never entered into a contract.

Once again, although later jurists found the conceptual analysis of the nineteenth century to be inadequate, they did not find an alternative. The court in *People's Express* did not suggest one. Lord Denning defended the old rule by an appeal to a miscellany of policy considerations, some of them conclusory, such as "this is a hazard that we all run," or "the risk of economic loss should be suffered by the whole community," or "the law provides for deserving cases."[361] One commentator has said that the purpose of the rule is to avoid "indeterminate liability," that there is no reason why a person should protect another's "business interests" as distinct from his "property," and that an "individual's property is to some extent constituted by his property."[362] These are attempts ex post to defend a rule that ex ante rested on conceptual reasoning that is not acceptable today.

## Contract

The nineteenth-century jurists defined contract in terms of the will of the parties.

According to the French jurists, and many modern scholars, that definition was enshrined in the Civil Code. They pointed to article 1134: "Agreements legally formed take the place of law for those who have made them. They can only be

---

[358] 495 A.2d 107 (N.J. 1985).

[359] *People's Express Airlines* (n. 358), 111. In contrast, in Germany, when the defendant negligently blocked the only passage to a canal leading to a mill, a shipper under contract to pick up grain at the mill recovered for the profits that he lost because one of his ships could not leave the canal, but not for those that he lost because another one could not enter and pick up the grain. The court treated the ship trapped in the canal as one that had been physically disabled, and so claimed that it was applying the rule: *Bundesgerichtshof*, December 21, 1970, BGHZ 55, 153.

[360] *Hedley Byrne & Co. Ltd. v. Heller & Ptnrs., Ltd.* [1964] A.C. 465 (H.L.); *White v. Guarante*, 372 N.E. 315 (N.Y. 1977); *Bundesgerichtshof*, February 13, 1979, NJW 1979, 1565; *Oberlandesgericht*, Munich, July 13, 1956, BB 1956, 866. The courts stressed that the information was prepared or supplied to a definite person or group. Plaintiffs have not recovered when information was prepared for general circulation among an indefinite number of actual or potential investors or creditors: *Credit Alliance Corp. v. Andersen & Co.*, 483 N.E.2d 110 (N.Y. 1985).

[361] *Spartan Steel & Alloys Ltd. v Martin & Co (Contractors) Ltd.* [1973] 1 Q.B. 27 (C. A.).

[362] Murphy (n. 211), 96.

revoked by mutual consent or for reasons authorized by law. They must be executed in good faith."

The statement that agreements "take the place of law" for the parties was a paraphrase of a passage in Domat, who himself had taken it from a collection of decretals promulgated by the medieval Pope Boniface VIII,[363] who in his turn had taken it from the *Corpus Juris Civilis*.[364] As Alfons Bürge observed, the passage says that agreements take the place of law; it does not say anything about autonomy.[365] Yet, according to many modern scholars, this text proclaimed the autonomy of the will[366] and the freedom of contract.[367] Indeed, it exalted contract to the same level as law.[368]

It is not clear to what extent the makers of the Code understood and accepted the principles of the iusnaturalists, and of Domat and Pothier. These jurists had believed that, while a party entered into a contract by consent or will, nevertheless the terms of the contract were not merely expressions of their will. Rather, they were—or ought to be—terms consistent with justice. Nevertheless, the articles of the Code and the remarks of the drafters are more consistent with that understanding of contract than the one that emerged later in the century. Articles 1108 and 1131 require the contract to have a lawful *cause*. Article 1104 explains that, when a contract is "commutative" (*commutatif*), "each of the parties commits himself to give or do a thing that is regarded as the equivalent of that which is given or done for him." Article 1135 provides: "Agreements are obligatory not only as to that which is expressed in them but also as to all the consequences that equity, usage or statute give the obligation according to its nature." Apparently, we are still in a world in which contracts have a "nature," in which certain consequences follow according to "equity" from that "nature," and in which the nature of some contracts requires, in principle, an exchange of equivalents.

The drafters may have drawn on the ideas of the earlier jurists more on account of familiarity than understanding or conviction. Yet, on the rare occasions on which they speak about the basic principles of contract law, their statements are consistent with these ideas. According to Portalis:

The freedom to contract cannot be limited except by justice, good mores and public utility....

There are situations as to which justice is clearly manifested. A partner, for example, wishes to divide all of the profits of a partnership without taking part in the risks. The claim

---

[363] VI 5.13.85. [364] D. 50.17.23. [365] Bürge (n. 177), 64–65.
[366] For example, Cornu (n. 253), 1: § 289; Halpérin (n. 175), 279; Christian Larroumet, vol. 3 of *Droit civil: Les obligations Le contrat*, 4th ed. (1998), § 116; F. Marty and P. Reynaud, vol. 1 of *Droit civil: Les Obligations*, 2nd ed. (Paris, 1988), § 33; Mazeaud, Mazeaud, Mazeaud and Chabas (n. 307), 1: § 43; 2: § 116.
[367] For example, Ghestin and Goubeaux (n. 2), § 137; Marty and Reynaud (n. 366), 1: § 33; Alex Weill and François Terré, *Droit civil: Les Obligations*, 4th ed. (Paris, 1986), § 10.
[368] For example, Jean Carbonnier, vol. 2 of *Droit civil*, 11th ed. (Paris, 1977), 66, and vol. 4: 35; Mazeaud, Mazeaud, Mazeaud, and Chabas (n. 307), 1: § 43; Savatier (n. 266), § 2; Weill and Terré (n. 367), § 18; Alex Weill and François Terré, *Droit civil: Introduction Générales*, 4th ed. (Paris, 2979), § 96.

is revolting. One need not look outside such an agreement for an iniquity that is perpetrated by the letter of the agreement itself.[369]

Cambarcérès explained: "Every contract is essentially an exchange; it presupposes therefore the return of an equivalent...."[370] Portalis said that, "undoubtedly... good faith, reciprocity, and equality are required in contracts...."[371]

Again, the Code itself said that the parties were bound to all of the consequences that the laws, equity, and custom attach to their agreement,[372] paraphrasing Domat.[373] As we have seen, Domat, like the late scholastics and iusnaturalists, had said that terms are read into contracts according to "natural equity," such as a warranty into the contract of sale.[374] The seller might disclaim the warranty if the "equity" of the contract was preserved by lowering the price.[375] That was hardly the view that the will of the parties in and of itself is the source of such terms. The drafters seem to have held the earlier view. Bigot-Préameneu said that the provisions of the Code were based on features that were "inherent in the contract, which differentiate its nature and effects."[376] Lacuée, a critic of the draft, objected that the Code might "extend obligations well beyond the limits the contract debtor consented to give them" by "imposing on the debtor obligations that he could not have foreseen." Tronchet, for the drafting committee, answered:

The contract of sale, for example, admits obligations that are the natural result of the contract because they are drawn from its essence, and that they have their effect although they are not expressed at all. Such, among others, is the warranty.[377]

These remarks, it must be emphasized again, are scraps of thought thrown out as the occasion demanded, and while they indicate a familiarity with the work of the earlier jurists, they do not imply a serious commitment to it or even anything more than a superficial understanding of it. Nevertheless, they certainly do not indicate that the old theory had been abandoned for a new one that contract is merely the will of the parties, and that the justice or injustice of the terms does not matter.

According to Halpérin, the Code magnifies the importance of the individual will, since it allows property to be transferred as soon as the parties assent to a sale, rather than upon delivery, as Roman law provided. He acknowledges that the drafters took this provision from iusnaturalists such as Grotius,[378] but he believes,

---

[369] Portalis, Discours préliminaire prononcé lors de la présentation du projet de la Commission du gouvernement, in Fenet (n. 178), 1: 510.

[370] Rapport fait à la convention nationale sur le 2ᵉ projet de Code civil, par Cambacérès, séance du 23 fructidor, an II (September 9, 1794), in Fenet (n. 178), 1: 107.

[371] Portalis (n. 369), 1: 513.    [372] Code civil art. 1135.

[373] Jean Domat, Les Loix civiles dans leur ordre naturel, 2d ed. (Paris, 1713), liv. I, tit. i, sec. 3, § 12.

[374] Domat (n. 373), liv. I, tit. i, sec. 3, § 12.

[375] Domat (n. 373), liv. I, tit. i, sec. 4, § 2.

[376] Présentation au Corps-Législatif, et exposé des motifs, par M. Bigot-Préameneu, in Fenet (n. 178), 13: 329.

[377] Tronchet, Discussion du Conseil d'état, Procès-verbal de la séance du 7 pluviose an XII (January 28, 1804), in Fenet (n. 178), 14: 54–55.

[378] Hugo Grotius, De iure belli ac pacis libri tres (Amsterdam, 1646), II. xii. 15.1. See Samuel Pufendorf, De iure naturae et gentium libri octo (Amsterdam, 1688), V.v.3; Domat (n. 373), liv. I, tit. ii, § 7.

partly for this reason, that Grotius espoused a new theory of contract that stressed the will.[379] We have seen, however, that Grotius took this principle, and many others, from the late scholastics.[380]

Similarly, the nineteenth-century German jurists defined contract in terms of the will, or consent or agreement, of the parties, without limiting, in principle, what could legitimately be willed.[381] Contract, they said, is a type of *Rechtsgeschäft*—a term that is virtually untranslatable, but which English writers have called a "legal transaction," a "juristic act," or an "act-in-law." A *Rechtsgeschäft*, in the words of Windscheid, is "a private declaration of will (*Willenserklärung*) intended to produce a legal effect." The legal effect "is always the production, extinction, or modification of legal rights." *Rechtsgeschäft* includes more than contract. A last will and testament also is a private declaration of will intended to produce a legal effect. Windscheid explained:

> The most important distinction to be drawn among *Rechtsgeschäfte* is that between unilateral and bilateral acts. Either the *Rechtsgeschäft* comes into being through the declaration of one person's will [as in the case of a last will and testament], or the agreement of several persons' wills is necessary. More precisely, in the latter case the will declared by one person must be grasped and held firm by the will manifested by others. A bilateral *Rechtsgeschäft* is commonly termed a contract.[382]

Although they claimed to be interpreting the Roman texts, these ideas were distant from the Roman law of particular contracts in which only some contracts bound the parties upon consent, and in some the parties were bound to whatever good faith required. Again, their ideas were like those of the rationalists. As we have seen,[383] Leibniz and Wolff described the freedom of the parties to contract on any terms they choose as conceptually limitless. In Leibniz's view, Luig observed, contract law is "fundamentally governed by the principle of the freedom and equality of the citizens. This equality is also realized in the freedom to make a law for one's own contractual relations through the *lex contractus*...."[384] Again, it would be surprising had the Roman texts happened to embody these same ideas.

In common law jurisdictions, contract was defined as mutual assent.[385] As A. W. B. Simpson has said, the will of the parties became "a sort of Grundnorm

---

[379] Halpérin (n. 175), 57, 130, 207.   [380] *See* Chapter III, p. 97; Chapter V, p. 137.
[381] Savigny (n. 27), 3: § 134; Puchta (n. 42), §§ 49, 54; Windscheid (n. 32), 1: § 69.
[382] Windscheid (n. 32), 1: § 69. For similar accounts, *see* Savigny (n. 27), 3: § 134; Puchta (n. 42), §§ 49, 54; Arndts (n. 190), § 58.
[383] *See* Chapter VIII, p. 189.
[384] Klaus Luig, "Leibniz als Dogmatiker des Privatrechts," in *Römishes Recht in der europäischen Tradition Symposion aus Anlass des 75 Geburtstages Franz Wieacker*, eds. Okko Behrends, Malte Diesselhorst, and Wulf Eckart Voss (Ebelsbach, 1985), 213 at 239.
[385] Kent (n. 109), *477; Dodd, "On the Construction of Contracts: Assent—Construction," *The Legal Observer* 12 (1836): 249, 249–50; Peter Carey, "A Course of Lectures on the Law of Contract: Lecture I," *The Law Times* 4 (1845): 463, 505; Theophilus Parsons, vol. 1 of *The Law of Contracts* (Boston, MA, 1860), *399; Theoron Metcalf, *Principles of the Law of Contract* (New York, 1878), 14; Sir Frederick Pollock, *Principles of Contract* (London, 1885), 23–24; Samuel Leake, *Elements of the Law of Contract* (London, 1867), 12; William Anson, *Principles of the English Law of Contract* (London, 1889), 13; Louis Hammon, *General Principles of the Law of Contract* (St. Paul, MN, 1912), 38.

from which as many rules of contract law as possible were to be inferred."[386] As a consequence, the terms of a contract were whatever the parties chose them to be. Thus, as Joseph Story said:

[E]very person who is not from his peculiar condition under disability is entitled to dispose of his property as he chooses; and whether his bargains are wise and discreet or profitable or unprofitable or otherwise are considerations not for courts of justice but for the party himself to deliberate upon.[387]

Again, the common lawyers claimed to have found this principle in their sources. But as we have seen,[388] before the rise of conceptualism, the common lawyers had not been thinking in terms of contract, let alone a will theory of contract. They had been thinking in terms of writs such as covenant and assumpsit.

As in the case of property, English and American historians have tended to assume that whatever was new in the common law of contract was a nineteenth-century innovation rather than a borrowing. Grant Gilmore said that contract, as a legal category, was invented by Christopher Columbus Landgell.[389] Atiyah claimed that the idea of will was new. "[T]raditionally," he said, "a contract was primarily conceived of as a relationship involving mutual rights and obligations; there was not necessarily an implication that the relationship was created by a conscious and deliberate act of will...."[390] Horwitz believes that the generic sale was first recognized in the nineteenth century. Before that time, he thinks, contract was simply a means of transferring title to specific property. As we have seen, however, contract was systematically organized as a distinct body of law by the late scholastics.[391] The idea that all contracts are entered into by consent goes back to the Romans.[392] The generic sale was recognized in the Middle Ages and subjected to papal legislation.[393] Again, a source of difficulty is that their familiarity with Anglo-American law leads historians to assume that what changed in the common law in the nineteenth century was brand new, and changed because of nineteenth-century conditions, not because of borrowing from abroad.

In any event, in the United States, the definition of contract as the will of the parties touched off a constitutional crisis. American courts have the power to review the constitutionality of legislation. The American Constitution contains a clause providing that no one can be deprived of life, liberty, or property without due process of law—a clause that was construed to protect contract rights. From 1905,

---

[386] Simpson (n. 110), 266.
[387] Joseph Story, vol. 1 of *Commentaries on Equity Jurisprudence as Administered in England and America*, 14th ed. (Boston, MA, 1918), 337.
[388] *See* p. 210.
[389] For example, Grant Gilmore, *The Death of Contract* (Columbus, OH, 1974).
[390] Atiyah (n. 196), 37.    [391] *See* Chapter III, pp. 93–98.
[392] *See* Chapter I, p. 20; Chapter II, pp. 47–48.
[393] Accursius, *Glossa ordinaria* to C. 4.48.2 to *veneant* (Venice, 1581), X 5.19.6; James Gordley, "The Origins of Sale: Some Lessons from the Romans," *Tulane Law Review* 84 (2010): 1437, 1456–57. *See* generally Wolfgang Ernst, "Gattungskauf und Lieferungskauf im romischen Recht," *Zeitschrift der Savigny-Stiftung für Rechtsgeschichte, Romanistische Abteilung* 114 (1997): 303.

when the Supreme Court decided *Lochner v. New York*,[394] until 1937, when it retreated in *West Coast Hotel v. Parrish*,[395] the Court held that the terms on which parties contract were up to them unless some public interest was at stake. Otherwise, their right to contract on whatever terms they chose was violated. For example, the state could require a ten-hour day for railway engineers because safety depended on their alertness, but it could not do so for bakers, since the wholesomeness of their bread did not depend upon how long they worked.[396]

In a famous dissent, Oliver Wendell Holmes objected that "[t]he Fourteenth Amendment does not enact Mr. Herbert Spencer's Social Statics."[397] The majority of the Court would have denied that its decision depended on the theories of Herbert Spencer or anyone else. It may be that the majority was sympathetic to Spencer's theories, or opposed to social legislation, for the same reasons as many conservatives who were not jurists. But the majority claimed to be deciding the case according to law. Nineteenth-century contract law had provided the Court with the minor premise of its argument. The major premise was that the US Constitution protected contract rights. The minor premise might have been taken from Joseph Story: whether one's "bargains are wise and discreet or profitable or unprofitable or otherwise are considerations not for courts of justice but for the party himself to deliberate upon." Judge Peckham, speaking for the Court in *Lochner*, affirmed "the general right of an individual to be free in his person and in his power to contract...."[398]

When he stated that principle, Story was not thinking of the problems of industrialization or capitalism. The principle was that of his European and American contemporaries, and of the rationalists before them. Like them, he could see no other source of contractual obligations than the will of the parties, and no limits in principle to what the parties might will. Neither could the majority of the Supreme Court.

Indeed, the critics of the Supreme Court themselves could see no source of contractual obligations other than the will of the parties. Their criticism was not that some terms of a contract are substantively unfair and that legislation may be needed to provide fair ones. Rather, it was that the party with stronger bargaining power could impose his will on the other. Charles McCurdy has pointed to Richard Ely's *Studies in the Evolution of Industrial Society* in 1903 as typical of the reform literature of the time.[399] Assume that people are equal, Ely argued, and "each one can guard his own interests individually, providing only the hampering fetters of law should make way for a reign of liberty." But instead behind the contract lies "inequality in strength of those who form the contract.... Wealth and poverty, plenty and hunger, nakedness and warm clothing, ignorance and learning, face each other in contract, and find expression in and through contract."[400] These

---

[394] 198 U.S. 45 (1905).   [395] 300 U.S. 379 (1937).
[396] *Lochner v. New York*, 198 U.S. 45, 57–59 (1905).   [397] *Lochner* (n. 396), 75.
[398] *Lochner* (n. 396), 57.
[399] Charles W. McCurdy, "The 'Liberty of Contract' Regime in American Law," in *The State and Freedom of Contract*, ed. Harry N. Scheiber (Stanford, CA, 1998), 161 at 162.
[400] Richard Ely, *Studies in the Evolution of Industrial Society* (New York, 1903), 402.

arguments were tracked by Roscoe Pound in his famous essay in 1909, "Liberty of Contract."[401] As McCurdy noted, Oliver Wendell Holmes wanted to say in an opinion that "to suppose that every other force may exercise its compulsion at will but that the government has no authority to counteract the pressure with its own is absurd." He backed down when his fellow justices objected.[402] One can see why they did. According to Ely and Pound, the terms of all contracts are determined by relative bargaining power, much as the motions of particles are determined by the vectors of opposing forces. They proposed no standard for determining which interplay of forces was just or unjust, any more than a moral standard could apply to the motion of a particle. Consequently, they proposed no standard as to when the state could justly intervene. It is no wonder that, in the opinion of the *Lochner* majority, there was no middle ground between holding all state intervention to be unconstitutional or allowing the state to change the terms in any contract where there had been a difference in bargaining power—which is to say, in almost any contract. The constitutional protection of contract would be meaningless.

*Relief from terms to which one consented* Having defined contract in terms of the will of the parties, the nineteenth-century jurists, like the rationalists,[403] believed that, in principle, the parties could contract on whatever terms they chose. They then had to explain why the texts that they regarded as authoritative did give relief from unfair terms, at least under some circumstances. As the previous remarks suggest, that task was not easy. We will consider one example: relief for an unjust price.

In France, despite the arguments by Berlier,[404] the French Civil Code provided that the seller can rescind a sale of land when he has received less than five-twelfths of its value,[405] the value to be determined as of the time of sale.[406] As we have seen, Portalis, Cambacérès, and Tronchet explained that the nature of a commutative contract required equality.[407]

In Germany, relief for an unjust price had been curtailed in Prussia in 1794. It was abolished in Bavaria in 1861, in Saxony in 1863, and in commercial matters by the *Allgemeines Handelsgesetzbuch* of 1861. Nevertheless, Roman law remained the

---

[401] Roscoe Pound, "Liberty of Contract," *Yale Law Journal* 18 (1909): 454.
[402] McCurdy (n. 399), 183.   [403] *See* Chapter VIII, p. 189.
[404] J. Locré, vol. 12 of *La Legislation civile, commerciale et criminelle de la France* (Paris, 1826–31), 65.
[405] French Civil Code (*Code civil*), art. 1674.
[406] French Civil Code (*Code civil*), art. 1675.
[407] Portalis, Discussion du Conseil d'état, Procès-verbal de la séance du 21 nivose an XII (January 12, 1804), in Fenet (n. 178), 14: 46–47. He had made the argument about the nature of a commutative contract in Portalis, Discussion du Conseil d'état, Procès-verbal de la séance du 30 frimaire an XII (December 22, 1803), in Fenet (n. 178), 14: 43; Cambacérès, Discussion du Conseil d'état, Procès-verbal de la séance du 30 frimaire an XII (December 22, 1803), in Fenet (n. 178), 14: 43; Tronchet, Discussion du Conseil d'état, Procès-verbal de la séance du 7 pluviose an XII (January 28, 1804), in Fenet (n. 178), 14: 63. *See* pp. 249–50.

chief object of university study, and with it the Roman text on which the doctrine of *laesio enormis* had been based.[408]

Anglo-American courts of equity refused to enforce an "unconscionable" contract. I have shown elsewhere that nineteenth-century American courts regularly refused to do so when an exchange was one-sided.[409] Although a party denied relief in equity could still sue for damages at common law, his damages would be awarded by a jury that might be reluctant to award much on such a contract. In any event, one historian has found only two reported cases in which a plaintiff who was denied specific performance still managed to recover damages.[410]

Nevertheless, many of the nineteenth-century jurists said that, in principle, there should be no relief for an unjust price. According to Demolombe, value was "subjective," "variable," and "relative."[411] Laurent said that the value of things was not "absolute": things worth one amount "from a commercial point of view" might be worth a different amount to the parties because of the "needs, tastes and passions."[412] Duranton, Colmet de Santerre, and Marcadé claimed that the relief supposedly given for an unjust price was really given for some "defect in consent" — for fraud, mistake, duress, or some sort of moral constraint.[413] Glasson thought that although relief violated the "principle of freedom of contract," it was an exception justified on grounds of "humanity."[414]

German jurists regarded relief as an exception to the normal rules of contract law. The basic principle was contained not in the Roman text that gave relief to one who sold land at less than half its just price, but in another text, mentioned earlier, which said that "it is permitted by nature for one party to buy for less and another to sell for more, and thus each is allowed to outwit the other."[415] That text must state the general principle, they said, because contracts are made by the will of the parties, and hence relief for an unjust price is contrary to the nature of a contract. Consequently, that text, according to Windscheid, stated a principle rooted "in the nature of a contract of sale":[416] according to Vangerow, one "lying in the nature of things."[417] It must be so, Holzschuer said, because relief for a disparity in price interfered with "the binding force of contracts."[418] Nevertheless, as in other situations, once the German jurists declared a principle, they were willing to make exceptions to it. Windscheid asked: "Are there not limits to the advantage one contracting party can take of the other?"[419] Some jurists pointed to the

---

[408] See Chapter I, p. 35.
[409] James Gordley, *The Philosophical Origins of Modern Contract Doctrine* (Oxford, 1991), 154–58.
[410] Ralph A. Newman, "The Renaissance of Good Faith in Contracting in American Law," *Cornell Law Review* 54 (1969): 553, 559.
[411] Demolombe (n. 5), 24: § 194.   [412] Laurent (n. 6), 15: § 485.
[413] Duranton (n. 3), 10: §§ 200–01; Demante and Colmet de Santerre (n. 4), 5: § 28 *bis*; Victor Marcadé, *Explication théorique et pratique du Code Napoléon* (Paris, 1859), 357–58.
[414] Ernest Glasson, *Eléments du droit français* (Paris, 1884), 550, 553.
[415] D. 19.2.22.3.   [416] Windscheid (n. 32), 3: § 396, n. 2.
[417] Vangerow (n. 247), 3: § 611, n. 1.
[418] Rudolf von Holzschuher, vol. 3 of *Theorie und Casuistik des gemeinen Civilrechts* (Leipzig, 1864), 729–30.
[419] Windscheid (n. 32), 2: § 396, n. 2.

language of the text that provided a remedy to the seller of land: relief was given because "it is equitable" (*humanum est*).[420] They disagreed about how broadly to read the Roman text that provided for relief. Some jurists wished to limit relief to sellers of land because it was an exception.[421] Others wished to extend it to buyers and to kindred contracts because such relief would be equally equitable.[422] They agreed, however, that to give relief was to make an exception to the normal rules of contract law.

English and American jurists also thought that, in principle, relief should not be given because a price was unjust. Some made arguments about value like those of Demolombe and Laurent. Value, according to Joseph Story, "must be in its nature fluctuating and will depend upon ten thousand different circumstances. One man in the disposal of his property may sell it for less than another man would."[423] According to Chitty and Metcalf, there were "no means" for determining whether an adequate price had been paid.[424] William Wentworth Story thought that the determination would require "a psychological investigation into the motives of the parties,"[425] a view also held by Addison.[426] Pollock quoted Hobbes' attack on Aristotle's concept of a just price: "The value of all things contracted for is measured by the appetite of the contractors, and therefore the just value is that which they be contented to give."[427]

Moreover, to give relief would interfere with the freedom of the parties to contract on whatever terms they chose. As noted earlier,[428] Joseph Story said that whether a person's bargains are wise and discreet, or profitable or unprofitable, or otherwise, are considerations not for courts of justice, but for the party himself to deliberate upon.[429] A similar argument was made, along with the argument about value, by Chitty, Addison, Metcalf, and William Wentworth Story.[430] It was also advanced in one form or another by Leake, Taylor, Bishop, Smith, Newland, and Hammon.[431]

The Anglo-American treatise writers then had to explain why courts of equity refused to enforce an "unconscionable" contract. As A. W. B. Simpson observed,

---

[420] Vangerow (n. 247), 3: § 611, n. 1 (describing the views of others); Carl von Wächter, vol. 2 of *Pandekten* (Leipzig, 1881), § 207, 472–73.
[421] Holzschuher (n. 418), 3: 729–30; Vangerow (n. 247), 3: § 611; Wächter (n. 420), 2: § 207. Some wanted to limit relief to sellers on the grounds that sellers who accepted a low price were more like to have been needy than buyers who paid a high one: Puchta (n. 42), § 364; Keller (n. 188), 333.
[422] Johann Seuffert, vol. 2 of *Praktisches Pandektenrecht* (Wurzburg, 1852), § 272.
[423] Story (n. 387), 1: 339.
[424] Joseph Chitty, *A Practical Treatise on the Law of Contracts Not Under Seal and upon the Usual Defences to Actions Thereon* (London, 1826), 7; Metcalf (n. 385), 163.
[425] Story (n. 109), 435.
[426] Charles Greenstreet Addison, *A Treatise on the Law of Contracts* (London, 1911), 12.
[427] Pollock (n. 385), 172, quoting Thomas Hobbes, *Leviathan* I.xv. 102.
[428] *See* p. 252.    [429] Story (n. 387), 1: 337.
[430] Chitty (n. 424), 7; Addison (n. 426), 12; Metcalf (n. 385), 163; Story (n. 109), 435.
[431] Leake (n. 385), 311–12; William Taylor, *The Laws of England and Scotland Relating to Contracts* (London, 1849), 17; Joel Prentiss Bishop, *Commentaries on the Law of Contracts* (Chicago, IL, 1907), 18; John William Smith, *The Law of Contracts* (Philadelphia, PA, 1847), 96; John Newland, *Contracts within the Jurisdiction of Courts of Equity* (1821), 357; Hammon (n. 385), 692.

they did so by inventing a new rationale. They claimed that a disparity in price matters because it is considered as "evidence of fraud, not as an independent substantive ground, and not as constituting hardship."[432] If the courts of equity had acted in accordance with this rationale, they would have stopped giving relief almost entirely. When a fraud is committed, there will often be a disparity in price, but it will rarely be the only evidence of fraud or the best evidence. The victim of fraud in any normal sense will know what the other party did to defraud him. A court concerned only about fraud would hear the testimony of both parties, and consider the disparity in price in deciding who to believe. As I have shown elsewhere, most often, when courts of equity found a contract to be unconscionable, there was no allegation of fraud in the ordinary sense. No one claimed that a fact had been concealed or misrepresented. Yet the courts gave relief anyway.[433] Indeed, had it been otherwise, the courts would not have needed a doctrine of unconscionability, but only one that gave relief for fraud.

In support of their principle, the Anglo-American treatise writers cited a common law rule that a contract was enforceable only if it had consideration and that a court would not examine the adequacy of consideration. Most of the statements quoted earlier about the indeterminacy of a fair price and the interference with parties' freedom were made in discussing this rule. Yet, as Simpson observed, the rule was made by judges who were not dealing with hard bargains.[434] As we have seen, the judges found consideration not only in contracts of exchange, but also in gratuitous promises such as gifts to prospective sons-in-law, and gratuitous loans and bailments.[435] They found consideration in promises that involved multiple parties, in which the transaction was not one-sided when the role of all of the parties is taken into account. In these cases, to require consideration to be adequate would have defeated the very purpose that the judges were trying to achieve, which was to enforce a promise in which consideration was not recompense. Thus it came to be said, in a famous passage from *Sturlyn v. Albany*,[436] that "when a thing is done, be it never so small, this is a sufficient consideration to ground an action." In *Sturlyn*, the plaintiff had leased to a third party, who had granted his estate to the defendant. The plaintiff asked the defendant to pay the rent, which he promised to do if the plaintiff would show him a deed proving that the rent was due. The showing of the deed was said to be consideration for the paying of the rent. As Simpson noted, the case has nothing to do with the enforcement of hard bargains.[437] As I have shown elsewhere, neither did practically all of the cases in which American courts invoked the rule against examining the adequacy of consideration. In some cases, the price had been set by a procedure designed to prevent questions of unfairness from arising. Some involved aleatory contracts, in which the price does not seem unfair considering the risk involved. In

---

[432] A. W. B. Simpson, "The Horwitz Thesis and the History of Contracts," *University of Chicago Law Review* 46 (1979): 533, 569.
[433] Gordley (n. 409), 154–57.
[434] Simpson (n. 107), 445–49.
[435] Simpson (n. 107), 416–52.
[436] Cro. Eliz. 67, 78 Eng. Rep. 327 (Q.B. 1587).
[437] Simpson (n. 107), 447.

some, one party received a benefit de facto, although the rights that he purchased were legally invalid. Some involved gifts, for example made by a dying man to those who had cared for him in his illness, or by a philanthropist to a college that would name a fund after her. Some involved reliance, as when one person guaranteed another's credit. As noted, some involved three-party situations in which the consideration was not inadequate given the role of the third party.[438] The enforcement of hard bargains has been no more than the occasional consequence of a rule that the courts used to make more promises enforceable.

In the twentieth century, relief has become more accepted. In France, special statutes have been enacted that give a remedy to those who pay an excessive amount for fertilizer, seeds, and fodder,[439] or for a rescue at sea,[440] or after an aviation accident,[441] or to those who receive too little when selling artistic or literary property.[442] Sometimes, courts have given relief despite the limitations of the Civil Code by declaring that the contract was procured by fraud, duress, or mistake, even though the victim had neither been told a lie nor threatened, and his only mistake concerned the value of what he bought or sold.[443]

The first draft of the German Civil Code of 1900 abolished relief for a one-sided bargain entirely. But in the final version, § 138(2) gave a remedy whenever one party obtained a "disproportionate advantage" by exploiting the difficulties, indiscretion, or inexperience of the other party. Since 1936, German courts have been willing to give relief for a violation of "good morals" (§ 138(1)) if the contract is sufficiently one-sided, even if such a weakness was not exploited.[444]

In the United States, § 2–203 of the Uniform Commercial Code allows a court to give relief in law or equity when a contract to sell goods is severely unfair. Section 208 of the *Second Restatement of Contracts* provides for similar relief in other types of contract. American courts have held the price to be unconscionable when home appliances were sold for over three times their usual retail price,[445] and when homeowners were charged extravagant amounts for windows and side walls.[446]

Although English courts are more conservative,[447] they have given relief, for example, when a woman was not compensated for signing a release of her interests in her house.[448] The judge quoted with favor the requirements set down in a nineteenth-century case: "What has to be considered is, first, whether the plaintiff

---

[438] Gordley (n. 409), 151–54. [439] Law of 8 July 1907.
[440] Law of 29 April 1916, art. 7. [441] Law of 31 May 1925, art. 57.
[442] Law of 11 March 1957.
[443] Cass. req., January 27, 1919, S. 1920. I. 198; Cass. civ., November 29, 1968, Gaz. Pal. 1969. J. 63; Cour d'appel, Douai, June 2, 1930, Jurisp. de la Cour d'appel de Douai 1930.183; Cour d'appel, Paris, January 22, 1953, Sem. jur. 1953. II. 7435.
[444] *Reichsgericht*, March 13, 1936, ERGZ 150, 1. Although, according to the courts, paragraph one will be applied when there is not only a "disproportionate advantage," but also a "reproachable intent" on the part of the advantaged party, where the advantage is disproportionate, the intent will be presumed: Hein Kötz, *Vertragsrecht* (Tübingen, 2009), no. 229.
[445] *Jones v. Star Credit Corp.*, 298 N.Y.S. 2d 264 (Sup. Ct 1969); *Frostifresh v. Reynoso*, 274 N.Y. S. 2d 757 (Sup. Ct 1966), *rev'd as to damages*, 281 N.Y.S. 2d 964 (App. 1967).
[446] *American Home Improvement Co. v. MacIver*, 201 A.2d 886 (N.H., 1964).
[447] Richard Stone, *The Modern Law of Contract*, 7th ed. (London, 2008), § 13.9.
[448] *Cresswell v. Potter* [1978] 1 WLR 255 (Ch.). *See* Chitty (n. 424), § 15-002.

## Novus Ordo: *Positivism and Conceptualism*

is poor and ignorant; second, whether the sale was at a considerable undervalue; and third, whether the vendor had independent advice."[449]

Few jurists today would claim that to give relief when an exchange is one-sided violates the basic principles of contract law. On the other hand, there is no generally accepted way of explaining relief.[450]

A frequent explanation is one that we saw earlier:[451] that the parties are in an "unequal bargaining position."[452] Those who favor this explanation owe more than they admit to the will theories. They account for relief not by explaining how the terms of a contract could be unjust, but by suggesting that one person is imposing his will on another unless the two parties have equivalent bargaining strength. Yet parties very rarely have equal bargaining strength in the sense meant by these authors. One cannot give relief every time such parties contract. Even if one could, it would impossible to tell what terms they would have agreed upon had their strength been equal. In any event, courts give relief only when the price deviates from the one that would be set in a competitive market. Yet that price has nothing to do with bargaining strength: in a competitive market, the parties do not bargain.

These points have been made by members of the law and economics movement. Again, they have their own explanation why relief is given, which we will consider later.[453]

*Consent* The nineteenth-century conceptualists said that contracts are formed by will or consent. Like the rationalists, however, what they said about consent was negative. Consent was private and self-regarding. A party was free to choose as he wished, consulting only his own expectations and desires. That definition raised a problem. Suppose a contract defeats a party's wants and desires. Did he consent? It seems odd to say that he consented to something he did not want. But if a party can escape whenever his wants and expectations are defeated, contracts would not be binding. Here, again, jurists did not find—and have not yet found—a solution on which they can agree.

---

[449] *Fry v. Lane* (1888) 40 Ch.D. 312.

[450] Charles Fried endorses "the liberal principle that the free arrangements of rational persons should be respected": Charles Fried, *Contract as Promise: A Theory of Contractual Obligation* (Cambridge, MA, 1981), 35. Yet even he concedes that "some bargains, though they meet all the tests I have set out so far, seem just too hard to enforce": Fried, *Contract as Promise*, 109. His explanation is that a random event has caused the breakdown of what he calls a "functioning social system," or "political system of social redistribution," within which exchange normally takes place: Fried, *Contract as Promise*, 109–10. He seems to be groping toward the idea of a system of commutative and distributive justice without getting there.

[451] *See* pp. 253–54.

[452] Bénabent (n. 295), nos. 165, 173; Lawrence Koffman and Elizabeth Macdonald, *The Law of Contract* (London: 1992), 3, 5; W. David Slawson, *Binding Promises: The Late Twentieth Century Reformation of Contract Law* (Princeton, NJ, 1996), 23 at 38. *See* Stefanie Rollof in Peter Westrmann, *Erman Bürgerliches Gesetzbuch Handkommentar*, 12th ed. (Cologne, 2008), §§ 305–10, no. 1.

[453] *See* Chapter X, pp. 307–08.

Article 1110 of the French Civil Code provided that "[e]rror is only a ground for the nullity of a contract when it falls on the substance itself of the object of the contract."[454] This article paraphrased Pothier,[455] who was paraphrasing Pufendorf, who was drawing either on the late scholastics or the Roman text that said that there was no consent if the parties had made an error in *substantia*. As we have seen, the Romans were impressing a philosophical word into service with no distinct idea of what it meant.[456] The late scholastics had given the text an Aristotelian meaning.[457] Things with the same substantial form or substance were the same kind of thing. A person who did not know the substance of the performance to which he consented literally did not know to what he was consenting.

The explanation of the late scholastics made sense in an Aristotelian world in which different kinds of things differ in nature, substance, or essence. It is hard to say what it could have meant to the nineteenth-century jurists. Nevertheless, some of them repeated it. Those who did not often went to one of the extremes just described. Some said that a party was not bound if the contract did defeat his wants and expectations, or, to put it another way, if he would not have contracted had he known the truth. Others said that, in principle, a mistake was irrelevant even if it did defeat a party's hopes and expectations.

Sticking with tradition, some French jurists said that an error in "substance" is one that concerns the nature or species of an object. Colmet de Santerre said that it must concern a quality absent which its "nature" would be different.[458] Demolombe said that it must concern the "principal" or "characteristic" quality of a thing that individualizes it, makes it proper to a given use, or gives it is name.[459] Aubry and Rau said that the error must concern "the properties which, taken together, determine [its] specific nature and distinguish it according to common notions from things of every other species."[460] Some French jurists take this position today.[461]

---

[454] Leading French jurists thought that this article applied only to errors regarding a property of an object: e.g. Demante and Colmet de Santerre (n. 4), 5: §§ 14 *bis*, 16 *bis*, 1; 27 *bis*, 1–3 (written by Colmet de Santerre); Demolombe (n. 5), 24: §§ 88, 124–27, 164, 171, 181–84; Laurent (n. 6), 15: §§ 450–53, 458, 484. Such an error rendered consent "impure" in contrast to an error in physical identity, in which case there was a complete absence of consent. In the former case, an action had to be brought to avoid the contract. In the latter, it was void ab initio. The Code did not say that an error in substance affected the "purity" of consent, and did not mention any other kind of error. The drafters paraphrased Pothier. They did provide that, in the case of error in substance, as in the case of fraud or duress, an action had to be brought to rescind the contract. They may have done so because they were following a Roman text that said that, in a *stipulatio*, a promise induced by mistake, fraud, or duress is not simply void, but gives rise to an *exceptio*. Or they may have done so because the requirement makes procedural sense, or because they were working in haste, or because they wanted to keep matters simple. It is not likely that they did so because they held a new view of the effect of consent that they never so much as mentioned.

[455] Robert Pothier, "Traité des obligations," § 18, in vol. 2 of *Oeuvres de Pothier*, ed. M. Bugnet, 2nd ed. (Paris, 1861), 1.

[456] *See* Chapter II, p. 94.   [457] *See* Chapter II, p. 94.

[458] Demante and Colmet de Santerre (n. 4), 5: § 16 *bis* ii (written by Colmet de Santerre).

[459] Demolombe (n. 5), 24: § 89.

[460] Aubry and Rau (n. 9), 4: § 343 *bis*.   [461] Raymond (n. 237), no. 238.

Borrowing the phrase, nineteenth-century English and American judges said that a contract is void for an error in "substance."[462] Some English courts and commentators still say that relief will be given if, because of the mistake, a performance is "essentially different" than the one contemplated.[463] It is not surprising that most contemporary jurists reject that solution.[464]

Seeing the difficulties, Laurent claimed that an error would vitiate consent if the parties would not have contracted had they known the truth. Some French jurists take that position today.[465] The error must concern a quality that the parties had principally in view[466]—one that led them to contract[467] and which was the "determining" motive.[468] A similar position was taken by the nineteenth-century German jurist Ferdinand Regelsberger[469] and by those American jurists who said that relief should be given if a mistake was "material."[470] At the turn of the twentieth century, the Italian jurist Fubini pointed out the trouble with it: "If a party could always avoid a contract because of a quality of importance to him alone, agreements will be subject to grave uncertainty."[471] Anyone who wants to escape from a contract must have made a mistake so important that otherwise he would not have contracted.

---

[462] In *Sherwood v. Walker*, 33 N.W. 919, 923–24 (Mich. 1887), the court said that a contract was void because the error was one in "substance" rather than "in some quality or accident." In England, Lord Blackburn said, in dicta, that English law was the same as civil law—relief would be given for an error in "substance": *Kennedy v. Panama Royal Mail Co.* (1867) L.R. 2, Q.B. 580, 588. This language was quoted favorably by Lord Warrington and Lord Atkin in *Bell v. Lever Brothers, Ltd.* [1932] A.C. 161, 207, 219. Lord Atkin added, in dicta, that a contract is void if the mistake concerned a quality that made the object "essentially different": *Bell*, at 218. Lord Thankerton said the mistake must concern a quality that is "essential": *Bell*, at 235.

[463] *Associated Japanese Bank Ltd. v. Credit du Nord S.A.* [1988] 3 All E.R. 902, 913; *Bell v. Lever Bros.* [1932] A.C. 161, 218 (claiming nevertheless that relief would be denied if a work believed to be by an old master were discovered to be a modern copy, at 224); Chitty (n. 424), vol. 1 in *General Principles*, 30th ed. (London, 2008), § 5–051; Michael H. Whincup, *Contract Law and Practice: The English System with Scottish, Commonwealth and Continental Comparisons*, 5th ed. (Alphen an den Rijn, Netherlands, 2006), § 10.13.

[464] Jacques Flour, Jean-Luc Aubert, and Éric Savaux, *Les obligations 1. L'acte juridique*, 14th ed. (Paris, 2010), nos. 196–97; Mazeaud, Mazeaud, Mazeaud, and Chabas (n. 307), *Leçons de droit civil II. Obligations: théorie générale* no. 166.

[465] Flour, Aubert, and Savaux (n. 464), nos. 196–97; Philippe Malaurie and Laurent Aynès, *Cours de droit civil 6 Les obligations*, 10th ed. (Paris 1999), no. 403; Bénabent (n. 295), no. 82.

[466] Ambroise Colin and Henri Capitant, vol. 2 of *Cours élémentaire de droit civil français*, 7th ed. (1932), no. 38; Georges Ripert, Jean Boulanger, and Marcel Planiol, vol. 2 of *Traité élémentaire de Planiol*, 4th ed. (1952), no. 199.

[467] Colin and Capitant (n. 466), no. 38.

[468] Colin and Capitant (n. 466), no. 40; Ripert, Boulanger, and Planiol (n. 466), no. 199; Jacques Mestre, "Obligations et Contrats Speciaux. 1. Obligations en général," *Révue trimestrielle du droit civil* 88 (1989): 736, 739.

[469] Ferdinand Regelsberger, vol. 1 of *Pandekten* (Leipzig, 1893), § 142.

[470] For example, Story (n. 387), 152; Clarence D. Ashley, *The Law of Contracts* (Boston, MA, 1911); Clarence D. Ashley, "Mutual Assent in Contract," *Columbia Law Review* 3 (1903): 71, 72. The younger Story and Bishop explained that a mistake was material if, but for the mistake, the parties would not have contracted: William Wentworth Story, *The Law of Contracts Not Under Seal* (Boston, MA, 1851), 405, 419; Bishop (n. 431), 297–98.

[471] Fubini, "Contribution à l'étude de la théorie de l'erreur sur la substance et sur les qualités substantielles," *Revue trimestrielle de droit civil* 1 (1902): 301, 309–11.

Led by Savigny, German jurists went in the opposite direction. He claimed that an error in a party's hopes and expectations could not vitiate consent. He argued that if the actual will of a party did not correspond to what he had declared his will to be, there was no genuine declaration of will and consequently no contract. Relief is given for that reason, he claimed, and not because of a mistake that the party made in deciding whether to contract.[472] In order for this solution to work, Savigny recognized that a "sharp distinction" must be drawn "between the will itself and that which precedes it in the soul of the person who wills."[473] A party might decide to buy a certain object for various reasons, but his will was his decision to buy that object. "The will itself," Savigny said, "is an independent event, and it alone is important for the formation of legal relations." One cannot "link" this event with the process of decision as though the process were part of its "essence."[474]

This solution, or a variant of it, was generally accepted by nineteenth-century German jurists.[475] It passed into § 119(1) of the German Civil Code, which provides that a *Rechtsgeschäft* is void when a party is in error as to the content of his declaration of will.

Nevertheless, some, including Windscheid, noted that Savigny's solution did not work in the cases put by Ulpian that were described earlier: copper was sold for gold, lead for silver, or vinegar for wine.[476] If a party decided to buy a certain ring or a certain cask and declared his will to do so, his declaration did correspond to his will, as Savigny had defined it. He would not have made that decision if he had known that the ring was made of copper or lead, or that the cask contained vinegar. According to Savigny, however, the will of the party was his final decision expressed in his declaration of will, not the considerations on which it had been based. Savigny tried to resolve the problem by saying that some properties of a thing were bound up with its identity. These were the properties that made it a thing of a certain kind, "according to the concepts dominant in actual commerce." If a party declared his will to buy a certain thing falsely believing that it possessed these properties, then his will did not respond to his declaration.[477]

In England, that solution was borrowed by Pollock, who said that relief should be given for a mistake in an "attribute" of an object that constituted "a difference in

---

[472] Savigny (n. 27), 3: § 135.    [473] Savigny (n. 27), 3: § 114.
[474] Savigny (n. 27), 3: § 114; similarly Puchta (n. 42), 77.
[475] Puchta (n. 42), 77; Windscheid (n. 32), 1: § 76. Among the variants were the theories of Hölder, which asked whether the will of one contacting party corresponded to that of the other: Eduard Hölder, "Die Lehre vom error," *Kritische Vierteljahresschrift für Gesetzgebung und Rechtswissenschaft*, 14 (1872): 561, 568, 574; Zitelmann, who asked whether the will of the party corresponded to the legal result that the law was now asked to bring about: Ernst Zitelmann, *Irrtum und Rechtsgeschäft* (Leipzig, 1879), 341–42; and Brinz, who made the bizarre claim that a contract was void when a party indicated that he wanted one thing, but willed another, although the reason was not the discrepancy itself, as Savigny had thought, but that such a party was unaware of what he was doing and so lacked the will to act: Aloys Brinz and Phillip Lotmar, vol. 4 of *Lehrbuch der Pandekten* (Berlin, 1894), § 525. In all of these theories, relief was granted, not because of a mistake that led a party to decide as he did but because his decision did not correspond to something else: the will of the other party, the legal result to be brought about, or the declaration of what he willed.
[476] D. 18.1.9. *See* Chapter I, p. 11.
[477] Savigny (n. 27), 3: § 137.

kind" according to "the course of dealing."⁴⁷⁸ Like Savigny, he said that, in such a case, no contract had been formed because a party's declared will differed from his true will.⁴⁷⁹ A similar approach has been taken in recent times by Werner Flume and Sir Guenter Treitel. Flume rejected the idea that a person who points to a ring or says "this ring" is merely indicating "a 'something' defined by space and time...." Rather, he has a picture (*Vorstellung*) of the object and "grasps it as having a certain composition."⁴⁸⁰ Treitel believed that "[s]ome particular quality may be so important to [the parties] that they actually use it to *identify* the thing."⁴⁸¹

At this point, as Fubini noted, the jurists had come full circle. This solution is like that of Aubry and Rau, who said that a mistake must concern a property that gives a thing its "species" or "specific nature" according to "common notions."⁴⁸² It is as hard to see why "actual commerce" would be any more likely than "common notions" to be concerned with which differences in properties constitute difference in species or kind rather than in quality or degree. Some nineteenth-century German jurists objected that Savigny's solution contradicted his own principles.⁴⁸³ If the significance of a characteristic to a party did not matter, its significance according to "commercially dominant concepts" should not matter either. Windscheid accepted Savigny's solution despite the difficulty because, he admitted, he could not think of anything better.⁴⁸⁴

A version of it passed into § 119(2) of the German Civil Code, which provides: "A mistake over those characteristics of a person or a thing that are regarded as essential in commerce counts as an error in the declaration." Modern German scholars have been unsuccessful in explaining what that might mean. It is not helpful to be told that such a characteristic includes "all factors that contribute to value,"⁴⁸⁵ unless one actually proposed giving relief for any mistake as to a factor that affects value. It is not helpful to be told that error in such a characteristic is a type of error in motive that invalidates the contract by way of exception, unless one is told why the exception is made and how widely it extends.⁴⁸⁶

Some jurists concluded that the problem was insoluble. If the will of the parties had no intelligible meaning, the contracts were not formed by the will of the

---

⁴⁷⁸ Pollock (n. 385), 436.     ⁴⁷⁹ Pollock (n. 385), 392–94.
⁴⁸⁰ Werner Flume, *Allgemeiner Teil des Bürgerlichen Gesetzbuchs 2 Das Rechtsgeschäft*, 2nd ed. (1975), 477. His position was adopted by Medicus: Dieter Medicus, *Allgemeiner Teil des BGB Ein Lehrbuch*, 7th ed. (Heidelberg, 1997), no. 770.
⁴⁸¹ Guenter Treitel, *The Law of Contract*, 10th ed. (London, 1999), 267 (emphasis original).
⁴⁸² Fubini (n. 471), 309–10.
⁴⁸³ Ernst Bekker, "Zur Lehre von der Willenserklärung: Einfluss von Zwang und Irrthum" [Review of A. Schliemann, *Die Lehre vom Zwange* (Rostock, 1861)], *Kritische Vierteljahrsschrift für Gesetzgebung und Rechtswissenschaft* 3 (1861): 180, 188–89; Achill Renaud, "Zur Lehre von Einflusse des Irrthums in der Sache auf die Gültigkeit der Kaufverträge mit Rücksicht auf v. Savigny: Der *error in substantia*," *Archiv für die Civilistische Praxis* 28 (1846): 247, 247–54; M. Hesse, "Ein Revision der Lehre von Irrthum," *Jherings Jahrbücher für die Dogmatik des heutigen römischen und deutschen Privatrechts* 15 (1877): 62, 101.
⁴⁸⁴ Windscheid (n. 32), 1: § 76a.
⁴⁸⁵ Hans Brox, *Allgemeiner Teil des Bürgerlichen Gesetzbuchs*, 11th ed. (Cologne, 1987), no. 372 ("*alle wertbildende Factoren*").
⁴⁸⁶ Medicus (n. 480), no. 744; Heinrich Palm in Peter Westrmann, *Erman Bürgerliches Gesetzbuch Handkommentar*, 12th ed. (Cologne, 2008), § 119, no. 41.

parties. Oliver Wendell Holmes in the United States and Siegmund Schlossmann in Germany developed "objective" theories in which contract was defined as a set of legal consequences that the law assigned to what the parties said, whatever they may have willed. But they, too, found it difficult to explain why the law gave relief for mistake.

According to Holmes, a mistake prevented the formation of a contract if the parties contradicted themselves outwardly. For example, if one party said that he would buy "this barrel of mackerel" and the barrel contained salt, the language was contradictory. No object was both "this barrel" and "of mackerel." Consequently, no contract was formed.[487] Holmes recognized the difficulty. A taciturn party who merely said that he wanted "this barrel" would be bound, while a loquacious one who described what he wanted in more detail would be released for the most insignificant discrepancy between the goods and his description. Holmes responded, in a famous phrase that he used more than once: "The distinctions of the law are founded on experience, not on logic."[488] To put it another way, Holmes could not see how his own solution could be logically defended.

Schlossmann thought that relief should depend on whether it is "fair and equitable to grant protection against the legal consequences of his transaction to a person who was in error as to the characteristics of an object."[489] "[T]he person in error is human, and therefore it is equitable" to help him, "insofar as it can be done without serious damage to more or less equally important interests of the other party."[490] This statement is like that of a modern French jurist. The judge must maintain "an equilibrium between the protection of the party who was deceived and a certain juridical security assured to the other party."[491] These statements seem to mean only that the protection of each party is important and that their needs for protection must somehow be accommodated.

Twentieth-century jurists have improvised. Some have said that both parties must have been mistaken about a characteristic that they knew to be important.[492] They do not explain why the mistake must be mutual if mistake vitiates one party's consent and a contract requires the consent of each party. Moreover, as French critics have noted, relief cannot be given because of what both parties happened to know. A sale of land cannot be avoided if both parties knew that the buyer intended to pay for it with money that he inherited, and in fact he inherited nothing.[493]

Others have tried to steer a path between the two extremes just described: of claiming that a party is not bound when he did not receive what he wanted or expected, or saying that his wants and expectations do not matter. It has been hard

---

[487] Holmes (n. 114), 310–11. [488] Holmes (n. 114), 312.
[489] Siegmund Schlossmann, *Irrthum* (Jena, 1903), 46.
[490] Schlossmann (n. 489), 47. [491] Bénabent (n. 295), no. 75.
[492] Raymond (n. 237), no. 236; Larroumet (n. 366), 3: no. 338. Edwin Peel, *The Law of Contract*, 13th ed. (London, 2011), 8-001; *Restatement (First) of Contracts* § 503 (1932). Allan Farnsworth notes that while that was the traditional view, courts have given relief for unilateral mistake, and not only when a mechanical error was made in compiling a bid, although that is the most frequent case: E. Allan Farnsworth, *Contracts*, 3d ed. (St. Paul, MN, 1999), 631, 635.
[493] Mazeaud, Mazeaud, Mazeaud, and Chabas (n. 307), no. 166; Paul Esmein, Marcel Planiol, and Georges Ripert, *Traité pratique de droit civil français 6 Obligations* (Paris, 1952), no. 177.

to find such a middle path. To do so, jurists have tried to identify some state of mind that influenced a party, but is not simply what he wanted or expected. Some jurists asked whether a party assumed the risk that he would be mistaken. Others have asked whether his mistake concerned a fundamental or basic assumption.

Arthur Corbin popularized the first approach, which was incorporated into the *Second Restatement*:[494] a party will not receive relief if he assumed the risk that the facts are not as he hoped. In the words of the *Second Restatement*, a party bears a risk when "he is aware... that he has only limited knowledge... but treats his limited knowledge as sufficient." P. S. Atiyah in England and Paul Kramer in Germany have taken a similar approach.[495] The trouble is that a party cannot be bound simply because he went ahead, realizing that his knowledge is limited. Anyone would do so unless he thought himself omniscient.

In the United States, Samuel Williston borrowed a solution that German jurists had developed to resolve a different problem: when relief is given for changed and unforeseen circumstances. Most of the *Pandektists* denied that relief should be given. Windscheid argued that it should on the grounds that a contract is subject to an "undeveloped condition" (*unentwickelte Voraussetzung*) that circumstances do not change.[496] His contemporaries found that phrase meaningless: a party either willed to make his contract subject to a condition or he did not. The doctrine was not included in the German Civil Code, although Windscheid warned that if it was thrown out the front door, it would come back through the window. Indeed it did. The financial upheavals of the First World War and the great German inflation led the courts to hold that relief could be given for "failure of the basis of the transaction" (*Wegfall der Geschäftsgrundlage*), although no one knew quite what it meant.[497]

Borrowing the idea, Williston said that a mistake vitiates consent if it goes to a "fundamental assumption"[498] of the parties. A version of this approach passed into the *First*[499] and *Second Restatements of Contracts*. According to the *Second Restatement*, to invalidate a contract, a mistake must concern "a basic assumption on which the contract was made."[500] The *Second Restatement* adopted the same formulation to describe when relief is given for changed circumstances.[501] A number of Anglo-American scholars have agreed.[502]

It has been as hard for the Americans as for the Germans to explain what is meant by a "basic assumption." This phrase could refer to the importance of a belief to the

---

[494] Arthur Corbin, vol. 3 of *Contacts* (St. Paul, MN, 1963), § 598.
[495] P. S. Atiyah, *An Introduction to the Law of Contract*, 5th ed. (Oxford, 1995), 227; Ernst A. Kramer, in *Münchener Kommentar zum Bürgerlichen Gesetzbuch*, ed. Franz Jürgen Säcker, 4th ed. (Munich, 2001) to § 119, no. 114.
[496] Windscheid (n. 32), 1: 75–78.
[497] Codified in 2002 at § 313 German Civil Code (*Bürgerlichesgesetzbuch*).
[498] Samuel Williston and George Thompson, *A Treatise on the Law of Contracts* (1937), § 1544.
[499] *Restatement (First) of Contracts* § 502 (1932).
[500] *Restatement (Second) of Contracts* § 152(1) (1981).
[501] *Restatement (Second) of Contracts* § 261.
[502] Melvin A. Eisenberg, "Mistake in Contract Law," *California Law Review* 91 (2003): 1573, 1624; Peel (n. 492), 8-001; Chitty (n. 424), 1 *General Principles* 5-017.

parties.[503] But then a party would not be bound by a contract when he was mistaken about something sufficiently important to him. As we have seen, that solution does not explain the binding force of contracts. Alternatively, a basic assumption could refer to an event in the mind of a party: he took something for granted and acted on it. Eisenberg and Farnsworth use the example of a person who takes it for granted that the floor exists and will support him.[504] But it is hard to see why a person should obtain relief because he took something for granted. Many losing contracts are made by people who did not question their assumptions about the durability of the market for mainframe computers, or the capacities of the equipment that they bought, or the tastes of the friends for whom they purchased presents. Moreover, the propensity to question one's assumptions varies from one person to the next. It would be odd to deny relief to the timorous and yet grant it to the sanguine.

## Unjust enrichment

As described earlier, although common law jurisdictions borrowed much else from Continental jurists in the nineteenth century, the law of unjust enrichment was an exception. Common law jurists had little to say on the subject until the twentieth century.[505] Continental writers, in contrast, had recognized unjust enrichment as an independent body of law since the time of the late scholastics. Nineteenth-century French and German writers put a good deal of thought into the subject. Their problem is that, as we have seen, the late scholastics had founded it, like the law of contract and tort, on the principle of commutative justice, taken from Aristotle and Aquinas, that no one should be enriched at the expense of another.[506] Grotius based the law of unjust enrichment on the same principle, although he did not mention commutative justice.[507] As noted earlier, however, the nineteenth-century jurists had difficulty with the idea of giving relief for an unjust price. They did not believe that, in principle, exchange required equality, nor did they believe in a theory of commutative justice. Why, then, should the mere fact that one party was enriched at another's expense be a ground for relief?

---

[503] *Restatement (Second) of Contracts* § 152 comm. b (1981).
[504] Eisenberg (n. 502), 1622; Farnsworth (n. 492), 624.
[505] In 1937, the American Law Institute published a *Restatement of Restitution*, although John Dawson noted that it merely "patched the parts together and gave the subject a name": Dawson (n. 61), 564–65. The first comprehensive American treatise was only published by George Palmer in 1978: George E. Palmer, *The Law of Restitution* (Boston, 1978). In that year, Lord Diplock insisted emphatically that "there is no general doctrine of unjust enrichment recognized in English law"; there were merely "specific remedies in particular cases": *Orakpo v. Manson Investments Ltd.* [1978] A.C. 95, 104 (H.L.). Nevertheless, Sir Robert Goff and Gareth Jones had already published a treatise on the English law of restitution, which was followed in 1985 by a still more systematic work by Peter Birks: Peter Birks, *An Introduction to the Law of Restitution* (Oxford, 1985). Perhaps impressed at the degree of order that these treatise writers had found in the decided cases, English courts have now recognized a general principle of liability for unjustified enrichment: *Lipkin Gorman v. Karpnale Ltd.* [1991] 2 A. C. 548. But skepticism has continued: *see* Chitty (n. 424), 1 *General Principles*, 30th ed. (London, 2008), § 29–011.
[506] *See* Chapter III, pp. 85–86.   [507] *See* Chapter V, 134–35.

As we have seen, in France, the idea of equality in exchange was alive in the minds of the drafters of the Civil Code and in the work of the early treatise writers. So it was with unjust enrichment. The French Civil Code did not speak of a principle of unjust enrichment. It mentioned two cases in which Roman law had given an action: when money had been paid by mistake (article 1376), and when benefits had been conferred on another without his own approval (article 1372). Here, the drafters followed Domat, who had classified these cases as obligations "that arise without an agreement," without mentioning unjust enrichment.[508] The reason was not that Domat or the drafters were breaking with the natural law tradition. As we have seen,[509] Domat was trying to classify Roman rules for pedagogical reasons in a way that facilitated learning, not in a way that corresponded to the principles on which they were based. The drafters paraphrased him.

According to Toullier, the two cases mentioned by the Code were instances of a broader principle: "the legislator commands what it just," and does so "because it is just that no one enrich himself at the expense of the other."[510] The Code, following Justinian, had classified these cases as "quasi-contracts," but it had given a bad definition of "quasi-contract." According to article 1371, "quasi-contracts are purely voluntary human acts which result in an obligation to a third party or the other party." The correct rule, according to Toullier, was that "[a]ny licit act of a man which enriches one person by a detriment to another obligates the one who this act enriches to return the thing or the amount by which he was enriched."[511] That principle explained the protection of property: one could reclaim it even from a party who had innocently come into its possession. It "completed" the Code, since the same principle explained liability for harm caused tortiously under article 1382. To that extent, the principles of the late scholastics and iusnaturalists passed into the first treatise written on the French Civil Code.

With an exception soon to be noted, an explanation of the Code in terms of a broader principle disappeared from the treatises of mainline nineteenth-century jurists. Laurent conceded that the two situations mentioned in the Code were based on "equity,"[512] but he said that these were the only two situations in French law in which the plaintiff could recover:

[O]ne cannot have a quasi-contract without law because the obligations that result are found in the law.... One invokes equity in vain: equity is a stranger to the law in the sense that by itself, it neither creates a right nor an obligation.[513]

Larombière said of the two situations mentioned in the Code that "it is not necessary to seek their source elsewhere in natural principles of good faith, justice and equity which forbid one to be enriched at the expense of another."[514] Nevertheless, he said, given the definition of quasi-contract in the Code, which

---

[508] Domat (n. 373), liv. II, tits. iv, vii.   [509] *See* Chapter VI, p. 143.
[510] Charles Bonaventure Marie Toullier, vol. 11 of *Le droit civil français suivant l'ordre du Code*, 5th ed. (Paris, 1842), no. 15.
[511] Toullier (n. 510), no. 20.   [512] Laurent (n. 6), 20: no. 308.
[513] Laurent (n. 6), 20: no. 309.   [514] Larombière (n. 265), 5: art. 1371, no. 3.

does not mention enrichment at another's expense, but defines a contract as a voluntary act, there were many other obligations in the Code that fell under the definition.[515] Similarly, Demolombe criticized Laurent, but his own examples of other quasi-contracts were drawn from the Code, like those of Larombière.[516] So were the examples that Duranton gave of additional quasi-contracts.[517]

The exception was the leading treatise of Aubry and Rau, in which they said:

> Payments made without a *cause*, that is to say (*hoc sensu*) for a future *cause* that is not realized or for an already existing *cause* which has, however, ceased to exist, as well as those that have in view a *cause* that is contrary to law, to public order, or to good mores, and, finally, those that are obtained with the aid of illicit means, give rise, in principle to an action for repayment, independently of any error on the part of the person who has made them....

Here, the principle became that a payment without a *cause* can be recovered. Aubry and Rau were doubtless aware of a Roman text that said that a plaintiff could reclaim a performance that had been made *sine causa*, or without a basis or a reason[518]—a text that the Romans neither generalized nor explained. In all likelihood, however, Aubry and Rau were following the explanation that Savigny had given in a volume of his *System des heutigen Römishen Rechts* published in 1841.[519]

Although Roman law had no general law of unjust enrichment, it recognized actions called *condictiones*. Savigny noted that these could not be classified as actions in tort, contract, or for the return of property or restoration of possession. He noted that they:

> ... are unquestionably available and they appear to us at first glance to be extremely various. Nevertheless, they allow themselves to be traced back to a very simple principle which has developed from this variety by a simple organic process of formation without the intervention of legislation.[520]

The principle is not simply that one party could not be enriched at another's expense. The principle is that he could not be enriched without a legally recognized ground—a *Grund*, a *causa*, or, as Aubry and Rau put it, a *cause*:

> Accordingly, we can employ the expression, an enrichment without ground (*grundlos*) out of our assets (*Vermögen*) provided the concept of enrichment is limited in a manner appropriate to those relationships. Specifically, the *causa* is gone or was already missing for the transfer of a right from one person to another, as is the case in a loan after notice to repay or the payment in error of what is not due.[521]

---

[515] Larombière (n. 265), 5: art. 1371, no. 6.  [516] Demolombe (n. 5).
[517] Duranton (n. 3), 13: no. 654.  [518] D. 12.7.1.3.
[519] In its first edition, their treatise was a translation of a German work on the French Civil Code by Zacariae. They themselves were from the German-speaking region Alsace, where Aubry taught at the University of Strasbourg from 1833 until its annexation by Germany in 1871. They added the treatise in subsequent editions, making it more their own work. Between the second edition (1844) and the third (1856), they added the explanation for recovery just quoted.
[520] Savigny (n. 27), 5: 511.
[521] Savigny (n. 27), 5: 526.

Despite occasional doubts about whether the various Roman actions could be subsumed under a single principle,[522] Savigny's solution became standard among German jurists.[523]

Savigny said that, for an action to lie, one party had to be enriched at another's expense without a "ground." Holzschuer said that the law "cannot tolerate the having (*Haben*) without a legal ground because one person is enriched through damage to another."[524] Seuffert said that, absent a legal ground, it was "right and equitable" for there to be an action.[525] Yet they did not explain whether the enrichment is in itself an evil to be remedied. If not, why should there be an action? If so, why, in principle, is there no remedy outside the law of unjust enrichment, for example in the law of contract for an unequal exchange?

Savigny's answer was that, in contract, there was a legal "ground" for the enrichment:

It is otherwise with a sale at a low price where, indeed, the buyer is enriched at the expense of the seller but nevertheless without any lack of a *causa*, that is, the legal ground of the alteration, but only as to the material evaluation of worth, which lies entirely outside the legal sphere.[526]

He did not explain why, if the enrichment of one party at another's expense was an evil to be remedied, the enrichment of a buyer at the expense of a seller "lies entirely outside the legal sphere."

Savigny's reliance on the concept of "legal ground" seemed circular to some jurists. It seemed to mean that the defendant must repay what he had gained unless there was a legal ground for keeping it—in other words, that the defendant is required to repay the gain except when the law does not require him to do so.

Windscheid tried to avoid the circularity by devising a different explanation. He also thought that an action would lie only when one party was enriched at the expense of another, although the principle had to be limited: "[T]he fact that one person is enriched in an unjust manner from another's assets gives rise to an obligation for him to explain to the disadvantaged person why he is richer."[527] Nevertheless, the principle that "enrichment from another's assets by itself and as such gives rise to an obligation to compensate the other person for the disadvantage . . . is incorrect at this level of generality. . . . "[528] For Windscheid, the limitation was not that there must be no legal ground for the enrichment. Rather, the enrichment must be unjust.

It is usually unjust, he said, if a person was enriched through another's assets without that other person's consent. It is not unjust if the enrichment occurred

---

[522] Vangerow merely speaks of them as actions "on grounds similar to contract" (borrowing from Justinian's term "quasi-contractus"): Vangerow (n. 247), 3: kap. 5. Wächter described the standard explanation as "usual" without expressly endorsing it: Wächter (n. 420), § 218.
[523] For example, Puchta (n. 42), § 307; Arndts (n. 190), § 340; Dernburg (n. 48), 2: § 138; Holzschuher (n. 418), 3: § 265; Seuffert (n. 422), 2: § 435a.
[524] Holzschuher (n. 418), 3: § 265, note.
[525] Seuffert (n. 422), 2: 435a.   [526] Savigny (n. 27), 526.
[527] Windscheid (n. 32), 2: § 421.   [528] Windscheid (n. 32), 2: § 421, n. 1.

with the other party's consent, although there are exceptions.[529] The law might have deprived the will of that party of its force either for his own protection, as in the case of a minor, or on account of public order, as in the case of illegally high interest rates.[530] Or the will of that party might be ineffective because it was subject to what Windscheid called an "undeveloped condition," or *unentwickelte Voraussetzung*.[531] As we have seen, this was the idea that he used to explain relief for changed and unforeseen circumstances, and one that his contemporaries rejected. Here, it enabled him to go beyond the strict view that a mistake counted legally only if there was a discrepancy between a party's conscious will and its outward expression. It allowed him to apply a broader concept of what mistakes mattered and to apply that concept to explain the law of unjust enrichment. This explanation, however, was only as sound as his concept of an "undeveloped condition," and that was an idea that his contemporaries did not accept.

Moreover, neither Savigny nor Windscheid explained why the law gave an action when one party was enriched at another's expense only sometimes and not generally. As we have seen, Windscheid, like Savigny, thought that relief for an unjust price lay beyond the principles of the law of contract.

In France, matters changed in 1892, when, despite the opinion of most nineteenth-century jurists, the *Cour de cassation* allowed recovery:

> ... because this action is based on the principle of equity that prohibits one from enriching himself through a detriment to another, and the exercise of this action, not being governed by any statutory text, is not subject to any determinate condition; it is enough, for it to be recognized, that the plaintiff alleges and offers to prove an advantage that he would have had through a sacrifice or a personal act that was obtained by the party against whom he brings the action. . . .[532]

That statement was considered too broad. The court qualified it in 1914 by imposing a limit that, as French jurists have noted,[533] was taken from Aubry and Rau: there would be an action "where the assets of one person were enriched at the expense of another without a legitimate *cause*. . . ."[534]

For there to be an action, French jurists now agree, there must be an enrichment at the expense of another that is without *cause*.[535] According to Alain Sériaux, one reason for the limitation "without cause" is that if the principle were not limited, the entire law of obligations "would be considered as a series of particular applications" of it.[536] That, as we have seen, is precisely what the late scholastics had in

---

[529] Windscheid (n. 32), 2: § 422.
[530] Windscheid (n. 32), 2: § 423.    [531] Windscheid (n. 32), 2: § 423.
[532] Cass. req, June 15, 1892, D. 1892.1.596; S. 1893.1.281.
[533] Jacques Flour, Jean-Luc Aubert, and Eric Savaux, *Les obligations* 2 *Le fait juridique*, 10th ed. (Paris, 2003), no. 37; Alain Sériaux, *Droit des obligations*, 2d ed. (Paris, 1998).
[534] Cass., May 12, 1914, S. 1918–19.1.41.
[535] Flour, Aubert, and Savaux (n. 533), nos. 38, 44; Sériaux (n. 533), no. 87; Alain Bénabent, *Droit civil: Les Obligations*, 5th ed. (Paris, 1995), nos. 486, 491; Philippe Malaurie, Laurent Aynès, and Philippe Soffel-Munck, *Droit civil Les Obligations*, 4th ed. (Paris, 2009), no. 1015.
[536] Sériaux (n. 533), no. 87.

mind when they explained the law of obligations in terms of commutative justice. Another reason is that there are instances in which an action cannot be brought even though one person was enriched at another's expense. One is a contract at an inequitable price, which the late scholastics and iusnaturalists believed to be a basis in principle for relief, but which the French jurists still regard as an exception to general principles of contract.[537] Another is a person whose business draws customers away from his competitor[538]—a case that the late scholastics would not regard as taking away anything that belonged to the competitor. They would have said that to give a remedy would take away the right of the defendant to sell what he could.[539]

*Cause* was then defined "as a legal justification for the enrichment."[540] The *cause* is "quite simply, ... the technical notion that expresses the general idea ... that the action ... must not disturb the positive legal order by permitting an alternation of its rules."[541] Thus enrichment at another's expense is prohibited unless it has a *cause*, and it has a *cause* whenever it is permitted. It need not be permitted by an express text of the Civil Code. If a person takes away business from a competitor, "the liberty of commerce and industry justify the enrichment."[542] In other words, the action can be brought except when it cannot.

Section 812(1) of the German Civil Code provided that "one who has received something through another's performance or at his expense in some other way without legal basis (*ohne rechtlichen Grund*) is obligated to give it back." It was like the solution of Savigny rather than Windscheid, except that it did not say expressly that one party must have been enriched at another's expense.

In the twentieth century, however, German jurists attacked Savigny's principle. It was incorrect to say that an action could be brought when one party was enriched at another's expense and there was no legal basis (*Grund*) for the enrichment. In 1934, Walter Wilburg claimed that it was impossible to formulate any general rule as to when enrichment is unjustified.[543] Ernst von Caemmerer argued that one cannot regard an enrichment as unjustified when the person enriched has no contractual or statutory claim to be. A person might renounce a right that is consequently acquired by someone else. Or he might open a tourist hotel in a hitherto unknown village, or build a dam, thereby enhancing the value of neighboring properties.[544] Other jurists pointed out that "enrichment may be due to the

---

[537] Flour, Aubert, and Savaux (n. 533), no. 33; Sériaux (n. 533), no. 87; Bénabent (n. 535), no. 491.
[538] Flour, Aubert, and Savaux (n. 533), no. 33; Bénabent (n. 535), no. 491.
[539] See Chapter III, pp. 87–88.
[540] Bénabent (n. 535), no. 491. Malaurie, Aynès, and Soffel-Munck (n. 535), no. 1068 ("The cause constitutes the legal title constituting justifying the enrichment or impoverishment"); Sériaux (n. 533), no. 90 ("There is enrichment without a cause ... when the person enriched cannot invoke any legal title justifying his enrichment").
[541] Flour, Aubert, and Savaux (n. 533), no. 44.
[542] Bénabent (n. 535), no. 491.
[543] Walter Wilburg, *Die Lehre von der ungerechtfertigten Bereicherung nach österreichischem und deutschem Recht* (Graz, 1934), 5–6.
[544] Ernst von Caemmerer, "Grundprobleme des Bereicherungsrechts," in vol. 1 of *Gesammelte Schriften*, ed. Hans G. Leser (Tübingen, 1968), 370 at 374–75.

display of particular skills in (lawful) competition."[545] Von Caemmerer concluded that, in many cases, "third parties are advantaged without a contractual or statutory claim to be. But they are not unjustifiably enriched, and there is no action in unjustified enrichment against them."[546]

Here, von Caemmerer is no longer conceiving of enrichment at other parties' expense as a taking or using something that belongs to the other party, or that the other party has the right to use. A party relinquishes his right to what he abandons. He does not have the exclusive right to any benefit that his use of his own property may confer on others, or to sell to his competitor's customers. As a result, von Caemmerer's approach made the problem both easier than that of Savigny and more difficult. It became easier in that von Caemmerer did not have to explain, as Savigny did, why, if enrichment at another's expense was bad, the principle did not extend throughout the legal system, mandating, for example, an equal exchange in contract law. It was harder in that one could now see no evil that the law of unjust enrichment sought to correct, or, for that matter, any general principle on which it rested.

Von Caemmerer did not seek a general principle: "[W]hen it is a question of applying a general clause that is framed in so broad and general a way as the maxim of unjust enrichment," one cannot find "abstract and general criteria of application." A jurist, "like a judge in a system of case law," must identify "groups of cases and types of claims."[547] Building on the work of Wilburg and without intending to be exhaustive, he described four major ones, of which two are important to the present discussion: (1) the defendant made an encroachment (*Eingriff*) on the plaintiff's property; (2) the plaintiff rendered the defendant a performance (*Leistung*), which was without a legal basis (*Grund*), in the sense that the purpose the plaintiff was pursuing was not achieved.[548] Today, his typology is widely accepted. It is found in most German textbooks and commentaries.[549]

It has proven hard, however, to give these categories a definite meaning without recourse to a general principle. An *Eingriff* cannot mean that the defendant destroyed the plaintiff's property or interfered with the plaintiff's use of it. If he did, that would be grounds for an action in tort. When von Caemmerer speaks of *Eingriff*, he has in mind cases in which the defendant used or consumed the plaintiff's property: for example, he consumed the plaintiff's heating oil, believing in good faith that it was his own.[550] Moreover, in order to tell whether the plaintiff has an action, one must determine whether the plaintiff had the exclusive right to the use of the resources in question. As Reinhard Zimmermann has noted, von

---

[545] Reinhard Zimmermann, *The Law of Obligations: Roman Foundations of the Civilian Tradition* (Cape Town, 1990), 889.
[546] Von Caemmerer (n. 544), 375.   [547] Von Caemmerer (n. 544), 391.
[548] The others are: the plaintiff incurred expenses (*Impensen, Aufwendungen*, today, commonly, *Verwendungen*) improving the defendant's property; and the plaintiff paid another's debt and now claims recourse (*Rückgriff*) against the defendant. The first cannot be discussed here without an excursus into the differences on the subject between modern civil law and older law. The second matters only where the law allows the plaintiff's payment to discharge the other's debt.
[549] Zimmermann (n. 545), 889–90.   [550] Von Caemmerer (n. 544), 378.

Caemmerer's category of *Eingriff* cannot be applied without asking "who was entitled to the right with regard to which there was interference."[551] But then we are back to defining *Eingriff* as an enrichment through consumption, or the use of something that belonged to the plaintiff or which the plaintiff had the exclusive right to use. That would take us back to the principle against unjust enrichment, as understood by the late scholastics and iusnaturalists.

Moreover, it would be hard to determine what belongs to the plaintiff and what he has the exclusive right to use without considering why people have exclusive entitlements to resources. Like the earlier jurists, von Caemmerer believed that the reasons why the plaintiff recovers in such cases are implicit in the very establishment of private rights to resources:

> The meaning of property law is that the owner is assigned the authority to use, to profit from and to consume the object ('*uti, frui, abuti*'). The advantage that the encroacher derives from the consumption or use of the object is therefore unjustified. The encroacher must give back to the owner the value that he would in fairness have had to pay had he known how matters were. In this group of cases, the enrichment is considered to be unjustified because it is in contradiction to the purpose pursued by the legal order in the assignment of property.[552]

Wilburg said the same.[553] If they were right, then we must determine the purpose that the legal order was pursuing in establishing property rights in order to determine whether the plaintiff had an exclusive entitlement on which the defendant has encroached. Unlike the late scholastics and iusnaturalists, however, von Caemmerer and Wilburg did not present a theory of the purposes of property law, although they acknowledged that their solution depended upon these purposes. Indeed, since the rationalists, property had been defined in abstraction from its purpose.

Von Caemmerer's category of *Leistung ohne Grund* is definite only if we can determine the meaning of *Leistung* and *Grund*. For von Caemmerer, *Leistung* does not simply mean that the plaintiff incurred expense that conferred a benefit on the defendant. He would do so by building a tourist hotel in a hitherto unknown village. It must mean that he incurred expense in order to benefit the defendant. We have come back to a principle that the defendant must be enriched at the plaintiff's expense and, in this case, that the plaintiff must have intended that he be.

The *Grund* or "legal basis of the performance," according to von Caemmerer, "is a contractual or statutory claim—also a 'natural' or 'moral' obligation."[554] To ask whether there is a *Grund* raises the problem of circularity that Windscheid may have found with Savigny and which stands out among contemporary French writers. It comes close to saying that there will be an action except when the law says that there will not. In England, Peter Birks' reason for regarding the "principle against unjust enrichment . . . with suspicion" was that "as soon as steps are taken to bring it down to earth it begins to say nothing other than that the law ought not to

---

[551] Zimmermann (n. 545), 890.   [552] Von Caemmerer (n. 544), 378.
[553] Wilburg (n. 543), 28.   [554] Von Caemmerer (n. 544).

be ignored"—that is, that "[t]here are circumstances in which the law does not permit one person to be enriched at the expense of another."⁵⁵⁵

Birks tried to explain the law not by a general principle, but by looking "downward to the cases."⁵⁵⁶ Like Windscheid, he tried to identify situations or "factors" that make it unjust for the defendant to have been enriched. In some cases, the defendant has been enriched "by subtraction" from the plaintiff's assets, and the "transfer" of wealth is unjust if it was "non-voluntary" on the part of the plaintiff or "freely accepted" by the defendant. In other cases, the defendant was enriched by committing a wrong, and the type of wrong explains why the enrichment is unjust.⁵⁵⁷

A difficulty with giving relief when a transaction is "non-voluntary" is the one that led Windscheid to speak of the failure of a *Voraussetzung*, and "undeveloped condition" of an expression of will. As Sonja Meier has pointed out,⁵⁵⁸ what sort of involuntariness will matter depends on the type of transaction in question. In a certain sense, whenever a party regrets having made a contract, the transaction was "involuntary." Circumstances have arisen—possibly including his own change of mind—which he did not anticipate when he committed himself.

Meier also pointed out that Birks cannot account for instances in which one cannot identify any unjust factor other than the enrichment itself. Her example was a payment made *ultra vires* by an entity that had no authority to authorize it.⁵⁵⁹ One might, of course, add "payments *ultra vires*" to the list of "unjust factors," but then, as Meier pointed out and as Birks realized, his approach would lose whatever explanatory power it had.⁵⁶⁰ Or one might say that such payments are recoverable for "policy reasons,"⁵⁶¹ but that explanation is not helpful unless one can say what these reasons are. Before his premature death, Birks surrendered and adopted the Continental approach that a remedy should be given when the defendant was enriched without reason—*sine causa*.⁵⁶²

---

⁵⁵⁵ Birks (n. 505), 23.   ⁵⁵⁶ Birks (n. 505), 23.
⁵⁵⁷ For a chart, *see* Birks (n. 505), 106.
⁵⁵⁸ Sonja Meier, *Irrtum und Zweckverfehlung: Die Rolle der unjust-Gründe bei rechtsgrundlosen Leistungen in englischen Recht* (Tübingen, 1999), 396–405.
⁵⁵⁹ Sonja Meier, "Unjust Factors and Legal Grounds," in *Unjustified Enrichment: Key Issues in Comparative Perspective*, eds. David Johnston and Reinhard Zimmermann (Cambridge, 2002), 37 at 62–65.
⁵⁶⁰ Meier (n. 559), 64–65; Peter Birks, *Unjust Enrichment* (Oxford, 2003), 98.
⁵⁶¹ Chitty (n. 424), 1 *General Principles* § 20-028, n. 142.   ⁵⁶² Birks (n. 560), 87–143.

# X

## *Ubinam Gentium Sumus?*
## After Positivism and Conceptualism

The project of the nineteenth-century jurists must be understood in terms of the goals that they set themselves and their success in achieving them by their own standards. We have seen the obstacles that they faced in pursuing their goals, their search for solutions, and the difficulties that they themselves found with these solutions. In international law, they had difficulty explaining how the state could itself be bound by law or why it should ever apply the law of other states. In private law, they found it hard to explain why the law sometimes protects nonowners and limits the rights of owners, if property law was based on the principle that an owner can do as he chooses with what he owns. They tried to explain tort law by means of the principle that one cannot culpably violate another's rights. Consequently, they had trouble explaining why culpability should matter, why it sometimes does not matter, and when one violates another's rights. They defined contract in terms of the will of the parties. They then found it hard to explain why the parties sometimes are bound to obligations that defeat their hopes and expectations. They had difficulty explaining the laws of unjust enrichment once they had discarded the principle that no one should be enriched at another's expense.

As we have also seen, later jurists have also failed to resolve these difficulties. Their project has been to find an alternative to conceptualism. Yet, to paraphrase Grant Gilmore, the systems remain unstuck and we see, at present, no way of sticking them back together.[1] In this chapter, we will consider their critique of conceptualism and their search for another way in which to make sense of law. We will better understand why the systems remain unstuck and the difficulties of the nineteenth-century jurists remain unresolved.

### The revolt

The critics of conceptualism concentrated their attack on three tenets of rationalism, which had been adopted by the nineteenth-century jurists despite their rejection of rationalism. As we have seen, these tenets were attacked early on by

---

[1] Grant Gilmore, *The Death of Contract* (Columbus, OH, 1974), 102.

Oliver Wendell Holmes in America, François Gény in France, and Rudoph von Jhering in Germany.[2]

One of these tenets was that legal concepts are eternal and immutable. As we have seen, this idea can be traced back through Wolff and Leibniz to Suárez. The critics of the nineteenth-century jurists claimed that they regarded legal concepts in the same way. It is a mistake, Holmes said, to think that law is "a brooding omnipresence in the sky."[3] Legal principles, Gény objected, are not "predetermined, basically immutable, governed by inflexible dogmas, and therefore not susceptible of adjustment to the varied and changing exigencies of life."[4] Jhering pictured his opponents as living in a heaven of pure legal concepts detached from anything on earth.[5] The criticism was taken up by their successors. In America, Hermann Oliphant objected that legal principles are not "endowed with a life of their own."[6] The mistake, according to Joseph Ingham, was to think that there is a "system of principles or rules existing independently of the comprehension of any individual observer."[7] In Germany, Philippe Heck denied that concepts are "primary objects of knowledge."[8] Ernst Fuchs said that there is "no finding of truth in concepts."[9] According to Ernst Stampe, "[t]he legal order as such does not exist."[10]

Another tenet of rationalism was that legal conclusions can be deduced from legal concepts. We have seen that this idea can be traced back through Wolff and Leibniz to Descartes. The nineteenth-century jurists were attacked for believing that legal conclusions could be reached by deductive logic. According to Holmes, legal questions cannot be "settled deductively, or once for all."[11] He criticized those who think "that the only force in the development of law is logic," "that a given system, ours, for instance, can be worked out like mathematics from some general axioms of conduct."[12] Gény denied that jurists could reach conclusions "by means of a strict logic."[13] Jhering complained of *Begriffsjurisprudenz*, a jurisprudence that reached its conclusions by the analysis of concepts.

A third tenet, which marked the work of Leibniz and Wolff, was the belief that one could analyze legal concepts, such as the rights of states, or owners of property, or contracting parties, without regard to the purposes that these institutions served. The nineteenth-century jurists were attacked for neglecting purpose in their search for the meaning of concepts. According to Holmes, "every rule" should be "referred

---

[2] *See* Chapter VIII, pp. 165–66.   [3] *Southern Pac. Co. v. Jensen*, 244 U.S. 222 (1916).
[4] François Gény, *Methode d'interpretation et sources en droit privé positif*, English translation, 2nd ed. (Louisiana, 1963), no. 62.
[5] Rudolf von Jhering, "Im juristischen Begriffshimmel," in *Scherz und Ernst in der Jurisprudenz* (Leipzig, 1884), 350.
[6] Hermann Oliphant, "A Return to Stare Decisis," *American Bar Association Journal* 14 (1928): 71, 76.
[7] Joseph W. Ingham, "What is the Law?," *Michigan Law Review* 11 (1912): 1, 9.
[8] Philippe Heck, "Was is diejenige Begriffsjurisprudenz, die wir bekämpfen?," *Deutsche Juristen-Zeitung* 14 (1909): 1457, 1460.
[9] Ernst Fuchs, "Die sociologische Rechtslehre: Eine Erwiderung," *Deutsche Juristen-Zeitung* 14 (1910): 283, 283.
[10] Ernst Stampe, "Rechtsfindung durch Konstruction," *Deutsche Juristen-Zeitung* 10 (1905): 417, 419.
[11] Oliver Wendell Holmes, Jr., "The Path of the Law," in *Collected Legal Papers* (1920), 167 at 182.
[12] Holmes (n. 11), 180.   [13] Gény (n. 4), no. 23.

articulately and definitely to an end which it subserves."[14] The law, according to Gény, is shaped by "two directing objectives": "justice and general utility."[15] Jhering described "purpose" as "the creator of the entire law...; there is no legal rule which does not owe its origin to a purpose."[16]

In the twentieth century, the attack on deductive logic and on the elucidation of concepts without regard to purpose was pressed in the United States, by Roscoe Pound[17] and by the American legal realists;[18] in France, it was taken up by Bonnecase;[19] in Germany, by the *Freijuristen*, the school of *Interessenjurisprudenz*, and the advocates of "legal sociology."[20]

Although there was general agreement on what legal concepts are not and on how they should not be used, there was less on what they are and how they might be.[21] To resolve that question, the critics would have had to rethink epistemological and metaphysical problems inherited from the rationalists. That would have been difficult. Like the nineteenth-century jurists, and in marked contrast to the rationalists or the late scholastics, few of them were philosophers and they were not writing for philosophers. Their quest for an alternative to nineteenth-century conceptualism had led them to the oldest problems in philosophy: in what way, if any, does a concept exist? How does a concept, which is universal, relate to a particular? How does it relate to a purpose? They jumped quickly to a variety of

---

[14] Holmes (n. 11), 186.
[15] Gény (n. 4), no. 159; *see* no. 68. See François Gény, vol. 1 in *Science et technique en droit privé postitif* (Paris, 1925), nos. 53–54.
[16] Rudolf von Jhering, *Der Zweck im Recht*, trans. Isaac Husak (Boston, MA, 1913), author's preface, liv.
[17] Roscoe Pound, "Mechanical Jurisprudence," *Columbia Law Review* 8 (1908): 605, 608; Roscoe Pound, "Law in Books and Law in Action," *American Law Review* 44 (1910): 12, 25.
[18] Ingham (n. 7), 9; Morris R. Cohen, "The Process of Judicial Legislation," *American Law Review* 48 (1914): 161; Morris R. Cohen, "On Absolutisms in Legal Thought," *University of Pennsylvania Law Review* 84 (1936): 681, 687; Walter W. Cook, "Scientific Method and the Law," *American Bar Association Journal* 13 (1927): 303, 307; Oliphant (n. 6), 74; Jerome Frank, *Law and the Modern Mind* (New York, 1930), 8–9; Karl N. Llewellyn, "Some Realism about Realism," in *Jurisprudence: Realism in Theory and Practice* (Chicago, IL, 1962), 42 at 70 (originally published *Harvard Law Review* 44 (1931): 1222); Felix S. Cohen, *Ethical Systems and Legal Ideals: An Essay of the Foundations of Legal Criticism* (Westport, CT, 1933), 33–35; Felix S. Cohen, "Review of C. K. Ogden, *Bentham's Theory of Fictions*," *Yale Law Journal* 42 (1933): 1149, 1150; Felix S. Cohen, "Transcendental Nonsense and the Functional Approach," *Columbia Law Review* 35 (1935): 809, 821 (citing in support Holmes, Gray, Pound, Brooks Adams, M. R. Cohen, T. R. Powell, Cook, Oliphant, Moore, Radin, Llewellyn, Yntema, and Frank); Hessel E. Yntema, "American Legal Realism in Retrospect," *Vanderbilt Law Review* 14 (1960): 317, 326.
[19] Julien Bonnecase, *L'école de l'exégèse en droit civil: Les traits distinctifs de sa doctrine et de ses méthodes d'après la profession de foi de ses plus illustres représentants*, 2nd ed. (Paris, 1924).
[20] Stampe (n. 10), 417; Ernst Stampe, "Rechtsfindung durch Interessenerwägung," *Deutsche Juristen-Zeitung* 10 (1905): 713, 713; Heck (n. 8), 1458; S. Rundstein, "Freie Rechtsfindung und Differenzierung des Rechtsbewusstseins," *Archiv für bürgerliches Recht* 34 (1910): 1, 5; Ernst Fuchs, "Klassische Einwendungen gegen die soziologische Rechtslehre," *Monatsschrift für Handelsrecht und Bankwesen* 20 (1911): 82, 87; Max Rumpf, *Gesetz und Richter: Versuch einer Methodik der Rechtsanwendung* (Berlin, 1906), 41; Hugo Sinzheimer, *Die soziologische Methode in der Privatrechtswissenschaft* (Munich, 1909), 5–6; Ignatz Kornfeld, *Sociale machtverhältnisse: Grundzüge einer allgemeiner Lehre vom positiven Rechte auf soziologischer Grundlage* (Vienna, 1911), 6.
[21] See Wilfrid E. Rumble, Jr., *American Legal Realism: Skepticism, Reform and the Judicial Process* (Ithica, NY, 1968), 103–04.

solutions in which one common feature was a rejection of conceptualism. They then had to conduct their search for an alternative without having arrived at a coherent and shared account of how these philosophical problems could be resolved.

When they sought a new explanation of what it meant to think with concepts, typically they tried to explain concepts as aggregations of simpler elements. German jurists such as Stampe thought that "[w]hat does exist is a collection of legal principles, each principle embracing in its legal application only a definite state of facts." The mistake was a "logical expansion" of the principle to other factual situations that "lie beyond these limits."[22] According to Sohm:

> The *ius quod est* comes first. It is the law which as such applies to the individual case. The same is true of our legal concepts. The legal concepts are not the law but a formal statement of the content they offer.[23]

Heck thought that the problem with "conceptual jurisprudence" was "inversion." Instead of regarding the precept governing a particular situation as primary, the conceptualists treated that precept as though it followed from some more general concept.[24]

Typically, the German jurists who attacked *Begriffsjurisprudenz* did not dismiss the value of concepts altogether. Sohm said:

> We think and speak in legal concepts. Why? Wherefore?... Through legal concepts we overcome the monstrous amount of material. We cannot enumerate all the rules of law. How would that be possible! We impress legal concepts into service. Every legal concept teaches us innumerably many legal rules.[25]

According to Heck, it was a mistake is to confuse the attack on *Begriffsjurisprudenz* with an attack on the use of concepts: "Without concepts no thought is possible. Legal science obviously must formulate concepts."[26] Fuchs explained: "The fight against *Begriffsjurisprudenz* is not directed at concepts as such." Every science needs them. "But concepts in all modern developed sciences are something secondary."[27]

There was a paradox in their moderation. If a legal rule governed only one situation, how was it possible to subsume a multitude of rules under a single concept? If the concept explained what a multitude of rules had in common and why they should govern many different situations, then one was explaining the rules by a concept. In that case, the concept could not be purely secondary. It was not a shorthand expression for a set of differing rules. It explained what the rules had in common and why they should be as they were. That seemed like a return to conceptual jurisprudence. If, in contrast, the concept did not explain what the rules had in common, how could it be more than an enumeration of particular rules, in which case it was a list of rules rather than a concept? This is not an ex post critique

---

[22] Stampe (n. 10), 419.
[23] Rudolph Sohm, "Über Begriffsjurisprudenz," *Deutsche Juristen-Zeitung* 14 (1909): 1019, 1022.
[24] Heck (n. 8), 1460.   [25] Sohm (n. 23), 1021.
[26] Heck (n. 8), 1457–58.   [27] Fuchs (n. 9), 283.

of the difficulties of the twentieth-century jurists. These were difficulties with which they struggled.

Some German jurists and many American legal realists took the discussion further. They spoke not only about the relationship between concepts and particular rules, but also about the relationship between concepts and any sort of particulars. According to Ignatz Kornfeld:

> In reality... [there] are only single things and events concretely limited in space and time. Concepts and rules result from knowledge of them. In reality, in "tree" nothing is present other than single trees defined in their quality and relations (by space, time, causality).[28]

Lon Fuller said that American legal realists characteristically held:

> ... the belief that the individual in his own private thinking does not employ universals and abstractions, and that these things are only convenient devices for the communication of ideas. It is the notion that in the internal economy of the mind only "things" are dealt with, and that abstractions and concepts are only packages of these "things" bundled together for export purposes as it were.[29]

According to Fuller, this belief was based on an "error in psychology"—the error that people arrive at concepts by "bundling together" things and that they mean by these concepts only the collection of things thus bundled.[30] Bingham had said, for example, that concepts "are only mental implements manufactured by the mind and senses to aid in acquiring, retaining, and communicating knowledge of the objective phenomena."[31] Morris Cohen responded that:

> Far from being absurd, as Bingham asserts, to suppose that rules and principles can exist independently of the comprehension of the individual observer, that is exactly what we all assume when we teach any science or systematic truth. And the law is no exception.

True, "everything localized in space and time is particular." Yet "all that we can ever say about things involves abstract traits, relations, or universals....":

> [I]f there is any difficulty about conceiving of them in objective nature, that difficulty is not cured by putting them into the mind. For if the nominalistic logic is good it should lead us... to deny that there can be any universals or abstractions in the mind.[32]

Other legal realists thought that the meaning of concepts is determined by the purpose for which the concept is found useful. Cook said that:

---

[28] Kornfeld (n. 20), 25–26.
[29] Lon L. Fuller, "American Legal Realism," *University of Pennsylvania Law Review* 82 (1934): 429, 444.
[30] Fuller (n. 29), 444.
[31] Ingham (n. 7), 9. Similarly Frank (n. 18), 63 ("lawyers [must] learn to stop using abstractions as substitutes for specific events...."); Herman Oliphant, "Facts, Opinions and Value Judgments," *Texas Law Review* 10 (1932): 127, 134 ("The postulates or ultimate standards of reference in the most rigidly scientific bodies or procedures are... merely categories of thought that our minds have invented for the purpose of arranging disjoined experience into... ordered patterns").
[32] Morris R. Cohen, "Justice Holmes and the Nature of Law," in *Law and the Social Order: Essays in Legal Philosophy* (New York, 1933), 198 at 210 (originally published *Columbia Law Review* 32 (1932): 352).

[W]e may for a particular purpose group together into a class a larger or smaller number of situations... conceiving that their differences are irrelevant for the purpose in view. The essential characteristic chosen as the basis of our classification will vary with our purpose and must be relevant to it. An essential characteristic of water is that it quenches thirst; another that it floats boats; another that is cleanses; another that it puts out fires.[33]

His example illustrates the difficulty. Everything that floats boats, or cleanses, or puts out fires is not water, and the reason why water can do all of these things, a chemist would say, is because of the properties that follow from what it is: $H_2O$.

Felix Cohen believed that legal concepts "which are not defined either in terms of empirical fact or in terms of ethics" are "are supernatural entities which do not have a veritable existence except to the eyes of faith":

*Corporate entity, property rights, fair value,* and *due process* are such concepts. So are *title, contract, conspiracy, malice,* [and] *proximate cause.*... Legal arguments couched in these terms are necessarily circular, since the terms themselves are creations of the law....[34]

Further, "definitions are acts of will, which are neither true nor false...."[35] It is difficult to know how seriously Cohen himself took this claim. As a critic pointed out, in the same article he criticized courts for not considering, for example, the difficulty of suing out-of-state corporations and the social importance of labor unions—the factors, he said, that really mattered. But those factors could not matter if corporations and labor unions are supernatural entities that do not have a veritable existence.[36]

Karl Llewellyn suggested at one point that concepts are reducible to their influence on behavior: "[W]ords take on an importance either because or insofar as they are behavior, or insofar as they demonstrably reflect or influence other behavior."[37] Pound accused him of calling into question "law as a body of general precepts and... the idea of a systematic legal order and rational judicial processes."[38]

The more moderate position was that concepts did matter somehow, but not in the way in which the conceptualists had thought that they did. Yntema said that "the skepticism and even disdain of various realists for systematic simplification of legal principle... is quite understandable [but it] flew in the face of the fact... that communication by general concepts is indispensible in law...."[39] According to Morris Cohen:

---

[33] Cook (n. 18), 306.   [34] Cohen, "Transcendental Nonsense" (n. 18), 820.
[35] Felix Cohen, "Fundamental Principles of the Sociology of Law," in *The Legal Conscience: Selected Papers of Felix S. Cohen*, ed. Lucy Kramer Cohen (New Haven, CT, 1960), 185 at 186.
[36] William B. Kennedy, "Functional Nonsense and the Transcendental Approach," *Fordham Law Review* 5 (1936): 272, 287.
[37] Karl N. Llewellyn, "A Realistic Jurisprudence—The Next Step," *Columbia Law Review* 30 (1930): 431, 443.
[38] Roscoe Pound, "Fifty Years of Jurisprudence," *Harvard Law Review* 51 (1938): 777, 794.
[39] Yntema (n. 18), 327–28.

Granted that traditional concepts like rights, titles, contracts, etc. have been grossly abused, it ought still to be clear that without the use of concepts and general principles, we can have no science, or intelligible systematic account of law or any other field.[40]

A similar position was taken by Pound,[41] Dickenson,[42] and Fuller.[43] That position seemed sensible and safe, but it gave no guidance as to the method by which concepts were to be taken into account.

In short, the critics of conceptual jurisprudence agreed that legal analysis could not be based on concepts. Yet they gave no clear account, or at least none upon which one could build, of how concepts were related to particular rules or to particulars of any kind. The critics had to approach problems of method while leaving this problem unresolved.

Their approaches were varied. Some thought that one could resolve legal problems by a trained legal intuition that was not arbitrary, but was not deductive logic. Some thought one could do so by considering the interests that were at stake in the new case and why one of these interests should prevail. Some thought that one could avoid the abuses to which conceptualism had led by considering the social purpose served by a legal rule and refusing to apply it in a way that thwarted this social purpose. Finally, some thought that the underlying problems could be solved only by incorporating law into the social sciences.

We will discuss each approach in turn.

## The appeal to intuition

In Germany, the so-called "free jurists" (*frei Juristen*) concluded that because one cannot reach the proper result in a new case by deduction, a judge is free to make his own determination based on his experience and on the social considerations that he deems relevant.[44] A judge, Fuchs said, must look to "men and their life together in the widest sense," and one can "no more learn that out of a book than driving or riding." What he called "[s]ociological legal decision struggles above all for what is

---

[40] Cohen, "On Absolutisms" (n. 18), 681. Similarly, Morris R. Cohen, "The Place of Logic in the Law," in *Law and the Social Order: Essays in Legal Philosophy* (New York, 1933), 165 at 165–66, 177 (originally published, *Harvard Law Review* 29 (1915): 622).

[41] Roscoe Pound, "The Call for a Realist Jurisprudence," *Harvard Law Review* 44 (1931): 697, 710 (We must reject the "absolute universalism of the last century, without losing sight of the significance of generalizations and concepts as instruments toward the ends of a legal order...").

[42] John Dickenson, "Legal Rules: Their Function in the Process of Decision," *University of Pennsylvania Law Review* 79 (1931) 841 ("a legal rule based purely on what judges have done and not on what they said must itself be reduced to, and take the form of, language before it can enter into the discussion of later cases").

[43] Fuller (n. 29), 444, 447. (He condemns "a *too* distrustful attitude toward universals and abstractions" of many realists: "Now this bias, for it is a bias, has its value in a science that has suffered for centuries from an unbridled pseudo-rationalism. But like all biases, the realist's peculiar bias may often lead sometimes lead him astray.")

[44] On the similarities and differences among them, *see* Jan Schröder, *Recht als Wissenschaft Geschichte der juristischen Methodenlehre in der Neuzeit (1550–1933)* (Munich, 2012), 348–50.

practically the most understandable, legal and equitable result."[45] Brie said that the judge should decide according to "equity" or "right law" (*richtiges Recht*);[46] Kiss, that he should decide according to "equity" or "conceptions of value" (*Werthbegriffe*).[47] According to Stampe, by the proper method, one:

... genuinely discovers the principle [to be applied] by social considerations by which the interests, private and public, which concern its content thereafter, are identified and compared with each other so that the content then may be determine by the interests worthy of protection.[48]

He was attacked by Heck, who agreed that "[t]here are gaps in the law that [must] be filled by an evaluation of interests," but who objected that Stampe left the judge free to evaluate interests as he saw fit.[49] According to Jung, however, when a case cannot be decided by a concrete existing rule, the judge must decide it by legal intuition (*Rechtsgefühl*). He contrasted his "intuitive law" with one based on deduction.[50] His approach was attacked by Kornfeld on the grounds that *Rechtsgefühl* was "insufficiently defined," that while we are told that each judge should follow it, "what is never sufficiently explained to us is the authority on which this 'should' is based nor its actual content":[51] "[T]o the attribute '*Recht*' (law) in '*Rechtsgefühl*' no definite meaning is attached...."[52] Indeed, Wolfgang Friedmann, a refugee from Hitler's Germany, said that the free jurists "anticipated in theory what has become reality in the administration of justice under National Socialism," in which "German courts ignored a specific and unambiguous provision of a statute where it was not in accord with National Socialist principles."[53]

In France, the principal advocate of an approach that combined logic and legal intuition was Gény, one of the first and greatest critics of the nineteenth-century approach to law.[54] He criticized the German free jurists. They were correct that legal conclusions could not be reached by logic alone. Nevertheless, whether they wrote about equity (*Billigkeit*),[55] legal feeling or hunch (*Rechtsgefühl*),[56] just law

---

[45] Fuchs (n. 9), 283–84.
[46] S. Brie, "Billigkeit und Recht," *Archiv für Rechts—und Wirtschaftphilosophie* 3 (1909): 526, 527.
[47] Géza Kiss, "Billigkeit und Recht mit besonderer Berücksichtigung der Freirechtsbewegung," *Archiv für Rechts- und Wirtschaftsphilosophie* 3 (1909): 536, 537, 549.
[48] Stampe (n. 10), 417.
[49] Philippe Heck, "Interessenjurisprudenz und Gesetzestreue," *Deutsche Juristen-Zeitung* 10 (1905): 1140, 1140–41.
[50] Eric Jung, *Das Problem des natürlichen Rechts* (Leipzig, 1912), 35, 47. On Jung's view, *see* Rudolf Müller-Erzbach, "Gefühl oder Vernunft as Rechtsquelle?," *Zeitschrift für das gesammte Handelsrecht un Konkursrecht* 37 (1913): 429.
[51] Kornfeld (n. 20), 100–01.   [52] Kornfeld (n. 20), 101.
[53] Wolfgang Friedmann, *Legal Theory*, 5th ed. (New York, 1967), 343.
[54] On his influence in Germany, *see* Schröder (n. 44), 337.
[55] Citing Schmölder, *Die Billigkeit als Grundlage des bürgerlichen Rechts* (1907); Brie and Reichel, "Billigkeit und Recht, mit besonderer Berücksichtigung der Freirechtsbewegung," *Archiv für Rechts- und Wirtschaftsphilosophie* 3 (1909): 526–35, and comments by Kisc, *Archiv für Rechts- und Wirtschaftsphilosophie* 3 (1909): 536–50; Rundstein (n. 20), 1–40.
[56] Citing Jung (n. 50); Müller-Erzbach (n. 50), 429–57; Berolzheimer, "Die Gefahren einer Gefühlsjurisprudenz," *Archiv für Rechts- und Wirtschaftsphilosophie* 4 (1910): 595–610.

(*richtiges Recht*),[57] or value judgment (*Werturteil*),[58] their efforts at "broadening the law appear singularly uncertain, incomplete, and, all in all, failing."[59] His method did not simply depend on intuition alone. His starting point was the authoritative sources of law. He combined intuition and logic in a way that he called "tempered deduction."

The method required a "double operation":

First, one had to rise from level of statute or the legal norms extracted from it to a higher principle.... This first operation is often carried out so easily that it appears to be the result of mere intuition rather than a true logical induction.

But, in any event, it is not a matter of logical inference: "[I]t always expresses a subjective conception which could not have been arrived at without groping if the instinct or tradition had not suggested or even imposed it in the first place."[60] The second operation is to proceed from the principle to its consequences: "This is a process of deduction, and therefore logic plays the principal role." But it does not play the entire role: "A legal consequence deduced by means of strict logic" sometimes "is openly in conflict with the sense of equity that we carry within ourselves."

[I]t sometimes happens that a legal consequence deduced by means of a strict logic, is openly in conflict with the sense of equity that we all carry within ourselves, or is irreconcilable with the practical needs which result from the conflict of legal interests.

In that event, "[f]ortunately, the sense of justice and common sense protest against it so energetically that very few lawyers, even among those who most insist on the principles, carry the strictly logical deductions to their extreme."[61] The principles that guided the entire enterprise were based on "two directing objectives": "justice and general utility."[62]

A number of American legal realists also appealed to legal intuition. Morris Cohen said that cases should be decided by "sensitively minded judges," whose "*feelings* as to right and wrong must be logically and scientifically trained."[63] Herman Oliphant described judicial decisions as "the accumulated wisdom of men" based on their intuition.[64] The most noteworthy approach was developed by Karl Llewellyn, perhaps the foremost of the legal realists. He denied that judges'

---

[57] Citing Rudolf Stammler, *Theorie der Rechtswissenschaft*, 2d ed. (Halle, 1923), 740; Lorenz Brütt, *Der Kunst der Rechtsanwendung* (Berlin, 1907), §§ 7–12.
[58] Citing Brütt (n. 57), § 4.   [59] Gény (n. 4), no. 219.
[60] Gény (n. 4), no. 22.   [61] Gény (n. 4), no. 23.
[62] Gény (n. 4), no. 159; *see* no. 68. *See* Gény (n. 15), 1: nos. 53–54.
[63] M. Cohen, "Logic in Law" (n. 40), 182 (emphasis original). Similarly, Morris R. Cohen, "Philosophy and Legal Science," in *Law and the Social Order: Essays in Legal Philosophy* (New York, 1933), 219 at 232 ("a judge's decision is, and should be, based not on existing rules, which are frequently inadequate, but rather on a sensitive perception of the actual factors in the case and a mind inventive in finding just solutions...").
[64] Oliphant (n. 6), 159. In contrast, Jerome Frank thought that judges decided cases by intuition, but in the negative sense of their own biases and predilections: Frank (n. 18), 103–06, but *see* 157, where he praises the role of the judge as arbitrator.

decisions must be based either on deductive logic or on their own opinions about policy. He told the Annual Meeting of the Conference of Chief Justices in 1959:

> There are...altogether too many people—Gentlemen Chief Justices of the various Supreme Courts of these United States—to whom the basic question about you seems to be whether you and your brethren are...mere voices with a mission only of accurate transmission, or whether, in the sharpest contrast, you and your brethren are in the nature of better-class politicians deciding cases the way you see fit while you just manipulate the authorities to keep it all looking decent.
>
> You resent that kind of misposing of the issue. I join you in resenting it.[65]

Llewellyn thought that judges decide cases in neither of these ways. They do so according to their own judgment, but it is a judgment guided by "situation sense." He spoke of "situation sense" as an "opened, reasoned, extension, restriction or reshaping of the relevant rules... done in terms of the sense and reason of some significantly seen *type* of life-*situation*." That, at least, was how he summarized in a sentence "what has cost me a 500-page book."[66] A judge, then, had the ability to see when a proposed application of a rule of positive law would lead to what he called the "right result":

> Under the Grand and Only True Manner of deciding: (a) any rule that is not leading to a right result calls for rethinking and perhaps redoing; and, also and equally, (b) any result which is not comfortably fitted into a rule good for the whole significant situation type calls certainly for a cross-check and probably for more worry and still more work.[67]

Gény and Llewellyn reached their conclusions by recognizing that the decision of new cases must depend on the authoritative sources of law, whether codes or decided cases. Otherwise, it would be meaningless to speak of the "rule of law." They recognized that one cannot get by deduction from these sources to the decision of a new case. Therefore there must be some ability by which we discriminate between better and worse results, and that is so even though no one result is indisputably right. They call this ability "tempered deduction" or "situation sense."

They thus broke with the methodological presumptions of the nineteenth-century jurists, and indeed with those of the rationalists. They claimed that a person could know the truth of certain propositions on the basis of experience and without demonstration. That is a proposition that the Roman jurists and medieval civilians had taken for granted, but which had fallen out of favor. It resembled the claim of Aristotle and Aquinas that there is an ability that they called practical reason or prudence. The resemblance is close enough that I was once asked by the Law and Economics Center of George Mason University to conduct a seminar for

---

[65] Karl N. Llewellyn, "On the Current Recapture of the Grand Tradition," in *Jurisprudence: Realism in Theory and Practice* (Chicago, IL, 1962), 215 at 215 (originally published *University of Chicago Law School Record* 9 (1960): 6). For a similar criticism, *see* Morris R. Cohen, "Rule versus Discretion," in *Law and the Social Order: Essays in Legal Philosophy* (New York, 1933), 259 at 265–66 (originally published *Journal of Philosophy* 11 (1914): 208).

[66] Llewellyn (n. 65), 210–20, referring to Karl Llewellyn, *The Common Law Tradition: Deciding Appeals* (Boston, MA, 1960).

[67] Llewellyn (n. 65), 221.

judges on the similarity between Aristotelian prudence and Llewellyn's situation sense by conference organizers who had no commitment to either.[68]

For Aristotle and Aquinas, prudence is not merely an ability to know what one cannot demonstrate. Rather, it is an ability to identify the actions that will most contribute to the distinctively human life that is one's end. Did Gény and Llewellyn suppose that there is such an end?

Gény did. As we have seen, he believed that "tempered deduction" is guided by "two directing objectives," "justice and general utility"—or, as he might have put it in the language of Aristotle, justice and the common good. To say so, Gény acknowledged, is "still far from completely enlightening us. For these two concepts are in themselves empty. . . ." There must be a source that gives them "content so we can draw from them all we expect." According to Gény:

This is exactly where the concept of the *nature of things*, as I think it should be understood, intervenes. The issue is not only to consider and to analyze all the factual elements in the life of society, observe their relations, and discern their mutual interactions. With full confidence in our conscience and reason, we must use these faculties to derive the laws from reality and thus to contribute all our resources to a truly scientific construction of the common law we seek.[69]

Because higher principles are grounded on justice and general utility, which in turn are grounded on the nature of things, the principles are not arbitrary. They are based on reality. Through the faculties of reason and conscience, human beings can see the relationship of these principles to justice and utility, and ultimately to the nature of things. Therefore they can "derive laws from reality." The operations of inferring and applying these principles do not rest on logic alone. But they are not arbitrary either. They rest on reason and conscience, which themselves are not arbitrary.

Gény acknowledged that:

When I state that the principles revealed by conscience and recognized by human reason through intuition are the first necessary directive for the free search of an interpreter of positive law, I am aware that I expose myself to the reproach of returning to an outmoded and almost forgotten doctrine of natural law.[70]

His defense was that he was not returning to natural law as understood in the seventeenth and eighteenth centuries. In those centuries:

Starting with the idea of the absolute power of human reason to discover the laws of our nature, both in principle and in detail, the school of natural law claimed to constitute a complete, immutable, immediately and universally applicable system of law by force of thought alone.[71]

---

[68] The seminar, "Llewellyn and Aristotle on the Force of Reason," was presented at a symposium for judges on "The Nature of the Judicial Function," sponsored by the Law and Economics Center of the School of Law, George Mason University, at Captiva, FL, December 3, 2006.
[69] Gény (n. 4), no. 159. *See* Gény (n. 15), 1: no. 14.   [70] Gény (n. 4), no. 160.
[71] Gény (n. 4), no. 160.

They had failed to recognize that although principles were grounded on nature of things, they were nevertheless "provisional" and "susceptible of adjustment to the varied and changing exigencies of life."[72] The result had been "an excessive and somewhat blind reaction to the 18th-century natural law doctrine."

But to deny that legal principles were ultimately grounded in reality and the nature of things is to deny them any claim to validity:

[I]n switching to the other extreme and recognizing only rules which depend on the variety of these relations alone, do we not sacrifice the permanent and immutable foundations of truth and justice which impose themselves on us? Do we not sacrifice law itself by reducing it to a pure dependency on facts? In reality, even the most rabid champions of the positivistic doctrine do not go thus far in its actual application. Despite their doctrinaire nihilism, they unconsciously return to recognizing effectively the *objectively* just, no matter how reduced in scope.[73]

One of his criticisms of his French successors and of the *frei Juristen* was that:

... because of the common feeling that it is impossible to agree on the metaphysical or ethical bases of the problem, the questions of interpretation of law have been most of the time debated in Germany as well as in France, by tacit agreement, in isolation from any genuine and profound philosophy and on the more comfortable but shaky ground of "legal positivism" which is still today the generally adopted position of legal scholars.[74]

Llewellyn also claimed to believe in a natural law, but he distinguished between natural law in the philosopher's sense and in the lawyer's sense. In the philosopher's sense, natural law is "a body of principle for the right ordering of any society,"[75] while:

A *lawyer's* Natural Law is an effort to bring the philosopher's Natural Law to bear in lawyerlike actual regulation of the multiple specific problems of human conflict.... Natural Law in the philosopher's sense bears on the work of the normal legal scholar who is concerned with Natural Law as a keystone and as a touchstone for his own labors, while it leaves those actual labors still to be done. The labors themselves must be concerned in good part with the formulation, detail by detail, of apposite rules, or apposite rules for the particular legal scholar's own society—rules which are consistent with, and perhaps crowned by the philosopher's Natural Law. But few of those rules will be dictated by the philosopher's Natural Law. Their purposes may often be, but rarely if ever their form.[76]

A lawyer's natural law varies with time and place:

[A] jurists' or lawyers' Natural Law will in a diversified world fail of its very function if its content is to be sought in formulations so broad as to apply to many times, systems and societies at once. Its very virtue lies in concretization so great as to invite its infiltration—its infiltration not only in terms of large guidance but of detailed rule.[77]

---

[72] Gény (n. 4), no. 62.   [73] Gény (n. 4), no. 161.   [74] Gény (n. 4), no. 205.
[75] Karl N. Llewellyn, "One 'Realist's View of Natural Law for Judges," in *Jurisprudence: Realism in Theory and Practice* (Chicago, IL, 1962), 111 at 111 (originally published *Notre Dame Lawyer* 15 (1939): 3).
[76] Llewellyn (n. 75), 112.   [77] Llewellyn (n. 75), 114.

Natural law, in the lawyer's sense, should shape positive law:

[I]t affords a concrete guide to the making of proper positive law, and a concrete guide for the correction of positive law which has gotten itself badly and aberrantly made.... It is the aim and function of such Natural Law is to be... drawn upon continually as a source of positive law; and this ought to hold no less as to the reading ("interpretation," "construction," "application") or development of statute law than it does in regard to the continuing reformulation of case-law and principle.[78]

Here, Gény and Llewellyn broke with the nineteenth-century jurists and the rationalists, and returned to something like the older idea of the role of prudence in applying higher principles to specific circumstances. They did not, however, return to the pre-rationalist tradition of natural law. In the pre-rationalist tradition, rules and doctrines bridged the gap between universal statements about human good, on the one hand, and actions to promote the good, on the other—actions that are always particular and performed with an incomplete knowledge of all of the circumstances that matter. Gény did not suggest how rules and doctrines could bridge that gap. Gény did not try to interpret the French Civil Code, as Portalis wished, by looking to principles of natural law identified by legal science that the Code enshrined. Although Llewellyn said that natural law in the philosophers' sense consisted of a body of principles that could inform natural law in the lawyer's sense, he did not suggest what those principles might be or in which philosophical works they might be found. At one point, he suggested that nobody knew what they are. He said that law was a "quest for Goals worth putting in the upper case." But, he said, "I cannot define them. I know nobody who can."[79] Indeed, he had so little interest in law as a body of precepts that Pound accused him of destroying the intellectual possibility of regarding law in that way.[80]

## The evaluation of interests

For Heck:

Law is only there to serve the interests of life, to weigh human interests against each other and to set boundaries to them. The investigation of the legal principles and the state of interests, the investigation of interests, is the principle task of legal science.[81]

Some who sought solutions through intuition or *Rechtsgefühl* went with him that far. According to Stampe:

Law is an order of coercion (*Zwangsordnung*) of social relations. The cause of this order of coercion is the struggle of interests that arises from human egoism. Its goal in the modern

---

[78] Llewellyn (n. 75), 113.
[79] Karl N. Llewellyn, "The Current Crisis in Legal Education," *Journal of Legal Education* 1 (1948): 211, 218–19.
[80] Pound (n. 38), 794.   [81] Heck (n. 8), 1460.

cultural state must be the mediation of this struggle in the best possible manner to serve the common good.[82]

Legal solutions are to be found "by the balancing of interests."[83] According to Jung, "an injury is not an injury because of particular rules but of interests";[84] "What is essential is [that rules] do not allow a violation of the interests and the duties that arise from them."[85]

Heck's objection was that Stampe left the judge free to evaluate interests as he saw fit. Setting boundaries to interests is to be done by society through statute:

> Stampe ... depart[s] from the previously accepted effect of a statute and so alter[s] the authority of judicial power.... The value judgment of the society only has effect when it coincides with the decision of the judge, which is to say it has no effect of its own. On this presumption, the judge is authorized to set aside a clear command in individual cases without relation to other statutes.[86]

Jung responded that "[t]here is always ... a person with opposing interests present; which of these interests is 'worthy of protection' is precisely the question. When the needs of life (or commerce, etc) are given as the reason for a legal decision, then it is virtually always the needs that appear to be correct—on whatever ground—to the decision maker."[87] Therefore, in order to balance interests, the decision maker had to rely on his own sense of a proper balance—on intuition, or *Rechtsgefühl*.[88]

Heck maintained that, when there were gaps in the law, "the judge must be bound in the filling of gaps ... to the same value judgments that are contained in the statutory law."[89] Therefore, "[o]pposition to technical *Begriffsjurisprudenz* does not presuppose a contradiction with the statutory formulation of concepts or with the obligation of the judge to follow existing law."[90] If so, it would seem, the judge is not balancing interests himself. The lawmaker has already balanced the interests and the judge has to find a balance that has already been struck. Thus Rudolf Müller-Erzbach concluded:

> What the judge has to do is decide if the interests in the case before him are the same situation as those in the struggle of interests decided by existing law.... The resolution of the question whether a particular law is to apply to concrete case requires of the judge a comparison of the state of interests, not a weighing of interests....[91]

This claim went further than that of the nineteenth-century jurists. They had been attacked for believing that the positive law contained a set of concepts that resolved cases that the lawmaker never had in mind. According to this claim, not only had the lawmaker resolved a conflict of interests in the cases that he had in mind when he made the law, even though he may not have had the conflict and the interests themselves distinctly in mind, but also his resolution of it carried over to the conflicts in other cases that he had never contemplated. Yet, for Heck, the alternative seemed

---

[82] Stampe (n. 10), 417.  [83] Stampe (n. 10), 417.  [84] Jung (n. 50), 91.
[85] Jung (n. 50), 86.  [86] Heck (n. 49), 1141.  [87] Jung (n. 50), 32.
[88] Jung (n. 50), 35.  [89] Heck (n. 49), 1142.  [90] Heck (n. 8), 1457.
[91] Müller-Erzbach (n. 50), 438–39.

to be that the judge resolved these cases by an intuition of the right result, which supposed that there was a right result, or that he resolved them however he wished.

A deeper question is what an interest is and why one interest should be preferred to another. Supposedly, rights are established to protect interests or to settle conflicts among them. But interests must be more than mere desires, or anyone who desires a diamond mine would have an interest in having one. Do interests exist, then, only when the law recognizes a desire as potentially worthy of protection? On what basis does it do so? And why should one interest prevail over another? When one balances interests, is one really deciding which interest weighs most heavily, or simply deciding which to favor? According to Max Rumpf, either the balancing of interests means an "unprincipled utilitarianism" or it means nothing at all.[92]

In the United States, "balancing the interests" became a catchphrase, although there never was a full-blown school of *Interessenjurisprudenz*. According to Llewellyn, however, no one knew what an interest is and balancing interests was arbitrary.[93] Ever since Jhering had tried to analyse the law in terms of interests, there had been a "confusion" that could now be "cleared up":

The term interests... comes to focus on the presence of social factors, and to urge that substantive rights themselves, like remedies, exist only for a purpose. That purpose is now perceived to be the protection of interests. To be sure, we do not know what interests are. [As to their] presence, extent, nature and importance... no two of us seem able to agree... The scientific advance should be obvious. Complete subjectivity has been achieved.[94]

Llewellyn continued: "The attribution of 'interest' as a quality of anything of necessity involves a value judgment over and above those that are inherent in any scientific inquiry."[95]

Jhering first spoke about the importance of interests. Yet the question of what an interest is and why it should be protected had actually concerned him more than the partisans of *Interessenjurisprudenz*. The answer that he gave to this question seemed to his successors too bizarre to be credited.

He had realized, in *The Spirit of Roman Law*, that law could not be explained in terms of the concept of will. He attempted to substitute the concept of interest. But then he realized that this concept was insufficient without a further explanation of what an interest is and why it should matter. So "[t]he concept of Interest made it necessary to consider Purpose....":

Once this question came before me, I could no longer avoid it; it always emerged again in one form or another. It was the sphinx which imposed its question upon me, and I must solve this riddle if I would regain my scientific peace of mind.... Thus the original object of my investigations was transformed into one of much greater extent....[96]

---

[92] Rumpf (n. 20), 84.   [93] For example, Pound (n. 41), 711.
[94] Llewellyn (n. 37), 441.   [95] Llewellyn (n. 37), 445.
[96] Rudolf von Jhering, *Der Zweck im Recht*, quotations and citations from the English translation by Isaac Husak, *Law as a Means to an End* (Boston, MA, 1913), author's preface, liii.

In his book *Der Zweck im Recht* [*Purpose in Law*], Jhering presented a philosophical account of purpose not only as the basis of law, but also of nature and human history: "The fundamental idea of [the book] consists in the thought that Purpose is the creator of the entire law: that there is no legal rule which does not owe its origin to a purpose, i.e., to a practical motive."[97]

For Jhering, purpose is either the object consciously sought by an animal or a human being, or it is a larger purpose of "nature," or "society," or "history." In the former sense, it is fulfilled when the animal or human being achieves the object that it sought, even though the animal or human being did not have this larger purpose in mind. Thus, he said, speaking of animals:

> Why does the animal drink?... Shall we have to answer... that the animal drinks for the purpose of self-preservation? This answer is both true and false. It is true from the standpoint of the purpose of nature. But the purpose of nature is not at the same time that of the animal. For the purpose of nature the copulation of the animal is likewise indispensible, but when the animal undertakes the act it has not in view the purpose of preserving the species, it merely follows its impulse, it desires to put an end to the discomfort which it feels. In both cases, when it drinks and when it copulates, it serves the purpose of nature, but it serves it only by serving itself, *i.e.*, the two purposes coincide, the general purpose of nature and the individual purpose of the animal....[98]

According to Jhering, it is much the same with a human being. From his own standpoint, his purpose is the objective that he consciously seeks, which is generally egoistic, egoism being "the exclusive tendency of the will to one's own self" without regard to others.[99] Indeed, he gives an almost utilitarian account of why a person acts one way rather than another. His decision:

> ... depends upon the preponderance of the reasons for the deed over the reasons against it. Without such a preponderance the will can no more move than a balance can be set in motion when there is a equal weight in both scales.... [E]very decision is preceded by an antecedent balancing.... The satisfaction which the person who wills promises himself from the act forms the purpose of his volition.[100]

But he was unwilling to adopt what Rumpf was to call an "unprincipled utilitarianism" in which satisfaction became an end in itself.[101]

Instead, Jhering asked:

> How can the world exist under a regime of egoism, which desires nothing for the world, but everything for itself alone? The answer is that the world exists by taking egoism into its service, by paying it the reward that it desires. The world interests egoism in its own purposes, and is then assured of its co-operation. This is the simple device by means of which nature, as well as humanity and the individual man, gain control of egoism for their purposes. Nature wills the existence of humanity. For the realization of this will it is

---

[97] Jhering (n. 96), liv.  [98] Jhering (n. 96), 20–21.
[99] Jhering (n. 96), 24.  [100] Jhering (n. 96), 8–9.
[101] Rumpf (n. 20), 84. For that reason, those scholars who describe Jhering as a utilitarian are mistaken, e.g. Friedmann (n. 53), 321–25.

# Ubinam Gentium Sumus? *After Positivism and Conceptualism* 291

necessary that the individual man preserve the life which nature gave him, and hand it down to others after him. How does she attain this purpose? By interesting egoism in it.[102]

Thus:

Nature can...win man for her purposes only by setting in motion the lever of his own interest within him. She herself has chosen this way; if she had not wanted it she would have had to make man different from what he is. This interest she has given him in the form of pleasure and pain.[103]

The lever of self-interest is the source of all forms of human association because nature has so contrived it:

Nature herself has shown man the way he must follow in order to gain another for his purposes: it is that of *connecting one's own purpose with the other man's interest*. Upon this principle rests all our human life: the State, society, commerce and intercourse.[104]

Nature thus "calls into being works and structures" that go far beyond the egoistic motives of human beings, indeed "with which the ego is like a grain of sand compared with the Alps."[105]

Indeed, "[o]ur whole culture, our whole history, rests on the realization of individual human existence for the purpose of the whole."[106] In that principle:

[W]e possess the *highest cultural law of history*. The cultural development of humanity is determined according to the measure in which it realizes the above principle, and we need only infer from what history *does* to what she *desires*, and prove the *manner in which* she attains what she desires.[107]

Society, in turn, is the source of law.[108]

One could speak, then, not only of the purposes of individuals, but also of those of society, history, and nature, to which those of people, and indeed of animals, are merely a means: "[T]he law of purpose as the highest world-forming principle."[109] But how is it that society, history, and nature can be said to have purposes of their own, distinct from those of individuals? Jhering answered:

[T]he assumption of purpose in the world, which, since I am simple enough not to be able to think of purpose without a conscious will, is synonymous in my mind with the assumption of a God—the assumption, I say, of a purpose in the world posited by God, or a divine idea of purpose....[110]

This divine purpose is realized not by the direct intervention in history by God or by prophets, philosophers, or leaders who understand the purposes of God. Rather, God realizes it by constituting men in the way in which they are so that their self-interest realizes man's cultural destiny and thereby realizes God's purposes, just as,

---

[102] Jhering (n. 96), 25. [103] Jhering (n. 96), 26–27.
[104] Jhering (n. 96), 28 (emphasis original). [105] Jhering (n. 96), 34–35.
[106] Jhering (n. 96), 59–60. [107] Jhering (n. 96), 65 (emphasis original).
[108] Jhering (n. 96), 33. [109] Jhering (n. 96), author's preface, lviii.
[110] Jhering (n. 96), author's preface, lvii.

by attaining its own purposes such as slaking its thirst, an animal realizes the purposes of survival and reproduction that are those of nature, and hence of God.

Jhering had devised a solution, *deus ex machina*,[111] to the problems that were to enmesh Heck. Interest was defined as purely egoistic. The reason why the law should protect an interest was simply that God had so contrived it that higher purposes than pure egoism would be thereby achieved.

## The appeal to social purpose: *abus de droit*

Yet another approach was an appeal to social purpose. For all of their discussion of legal methodology, the critics of the nineteenth-century jurists did not achieve a reconstruction of doctrine, as we saw in the last chapter. Their greatest doctrinal innovation, although it did not endure in its original form, was a super-doctrine—a doctrine that could be used to trump any other doctrine: *abus de droit*, or abuse of right. According to this doctrine, because every right and every rule of law was established to serve a larger social purpose, every right and rule could be set aside when this purpose was not served. This doctrine was developed in France and borrowed in Germany. It still exists, although it has now been defanged and declawed.

The French proponents of this doctrine claimed to be leading an attack on the thought of the nineteenth-century jurists. By regarding legal rights as "absolute," these older jurists had misunderstood them. The exercise of a right should be limited by the purpose that led the law to recognize such a right. A person abuses a right when he exercises it in a way that does not serve this purpose. René Demogue explained:

[T]he expression... "abuse of rights" indicates a problem of the limits of every right.... Does it not have limits of a kind which are teleological or social? Is it not necessary to understand, as included in every provision of law, [the qualification that] the right hereby recognized can only be exercised for motives in accordance with good social order?[112]

According to Louis Josserand, "to abuse [a right] is to proceed, intentionally or unintentionally, against the purpose of the institution of which one has misunderstood the finality and the function."[113]

They claimed that French courts had already retreated from the old view that rights are absolute in a decision by the Court of Appeal of Colmar, which they regarded as pathbreaking.[114] If rights were absolute, a property owner could not be

---

[111] Morris Cohen used that phrase to describe Jhering's solution: Morris R. Cohen, "On Continental Legal Philosophy," in *Law and the Social Order: Essays in Legal Philosophy* (New York, 1933), 286 at 306.
[112] René Demogue, vol. 4 of *Traité des obligations en général* (Paris, 1924), no. 679.
[113] Louis Josserand, *De l'esprit des droits et de leur relativité Théorie dite de l'abus des droits*, 2nd ed. (Paris, 1939), no. 245.
[114] Colmar, May 2, 1855, D. 1856.II.9. They claimed that a similar principle was at stake in cases of liability for vexatious litigation: Demogue (n. 112), nos. 635–41; Josserand (n. 113), nos. 39–62. Josserand found analogies in cases involving mortgages, family authority, and corporate and

prevented from building a false chimney to block his neighbor's window. Therefore, in denying that he could, the courts had accepted a new conception in which rights have limits that are "teleological and social," and which correspond to their "finality and function." Tacitly, the courts had accepted a doctrine of abuse of rights.

Critics of the doctrine, such as Marcel Planiol and George Ripert, claimed that the courts had done no such thing. Rather, in these cases, they had merely prevented a person from exercising a right for the sole purpose of harming another. That was nothing new. It was an application of an old principle that had been endorsed by the nineteenth-century jurists themselves.[115] No one had ever believed that rights were "absolute."[116] Consequently, the only novelty in the new doctrine was the expression "abuse" of "rights"[117]—an expression that they regarded as misleading and dangerous.

Plainiol and Ripert were correct that that there was nothing new about giving relief when a person used his land solely to harm his neighbor. The decision by the court of Colmar was neither pathbreaking nor unprecedented, as Antonio Gambaro has pointed out.[118]

Nevertheless, it was misleading to say that no one had ever believed that rights were "absolute." It depends upon what one means by "absolute." As we have seen, the nineteenth-century jurists did believe that, conceptually, property entailed an unlimited right to use what one owned as one willed. Still, as Leibniz said and as they said, there might be limits set by law to a conceptually unlimited right. Moreover, some will theorists, such as Laurent in France and Windscheid in Germany, thought that it was inconsistent with the reasons for respecting the will to allow an owner to use his property for the sole purpose of harming another.[119]

The innovation of the proponents of the doctrine of abuse of rights was not their claim that rights could be limited. Rather, it was to reject the conceptualistic approach in favor of one in which rights are understood, as they put it, "teleologically," in terms of their "finality and function." They did not mean, however, to proceed like the late scholastics, who had explained the purpose of property in terms of the reasons for which it was instituted, and those of contract and tort in terms of commutative justice, and then tried to explain doctrines of property, contract, and tort in terms of these purposes. Their approach was more general.

---

administrative law: Josserand (n. 113), nos. 33–38 (mortgages); 63–83 (family authority); 155–91 (corporate law); 192–97 (administrative law).

[115] Marcel Planiol and Georges Ripert, vol. 6 of *Traité pratique de droit civil français* (Paris, 1930), no. 573; Georges Ripert, *La Règle morale dans les obligations civiles*, 3rd ed. (Paris, 1935), no. 90.

[116] Planiol and Ripert (n. 115), no. 573.

[117] Planiol and Ripert (n. 115), no. 573.

[118] Antonio Gambaro, "Abuse of Rights in the Civil Law Tradition," *European Review of Private Law* 4 (1995): 561, 566.

[119] François Laurent, vol. 20 of *Principes de droit civil français* (Paris, 1869–78), § 411; Bernhard Windscheid, vol. 1 of *Lehrbuch des Pandektenrechts*, 6th ed. (Frankfurt am Main, 1887), § 121. The same position was taken by Karl Adolph von Vangerow, *Lehrbuch der Pandekten*, 7th ed. (Marburg, 1863), § 297. Others disagreed: Charles Demolombe, vol. 11 of *Cours de Code Napoleon* (Paris, 1854–82), § 66, and vol. 12, § 19; Carl Georg von Wächter, *Pandekten* (Leipzig, 1880), § 33.

Their doctrine authorized a judge to refuse to apply a rule or doctrine whenever he deemed it inconsistent with social purpose, a concept that remained ill-defined.

For that reason, the doctrine frightened critics such as Planiol and Ripert. They did not defend the old conceptualism. They agreed rights that were not "unlimited"[120] or "absolute."[121] They did not claim that institutions such a property entailed, in principle, an unlimited right of the owner. They ignored the fact that the nineteenth-century jurists had defined property in that way. Ripert built a theory of the inherent limitations of rights that was sufficiently close to the doctrine of abuse of rights that he admitted that the doctrine "seems in appearance like the one we are defending."[122]

No one, then, was trying to revive the old conceptualism. Planiol and Ripert rejected the new doctrine because it seemed dangerous. It was too extensive and unlimited. It suggested not merely that a court should consider the purposes for which rights are recognized, but also that it should "remedy every wrong"[123]—that "the judge can ask of each man an account of the motives of his acts...."[124]

One reason that critics such as Planiol and Ripert thought it dangerous to give a judge such a power was that they thought that individual rights would be sacrificed to judicial conceptions of social needs. One source of their fear was that the proponents of the doctrine themselves did not distinguish clearly between interpreting rights according to purposes and interpreting them to promote social purposes, which, they believed, meant promoting a society that was less individualistic and more socially concerned. When Demogue said that there must be "teleological or social" limits to rights, the two words meant much the same thing to him. For him and for Josserand, the error of the will theorists was not simply to misunderstand the nature of rights. It was to allow individual choice to trump social concerns. Demogue favored the doctrine of abuse of rights because it was "in harmony with the reaction which is taking place against individualistic ideas. Today, one wants the individual to act in the general interest."[125] Josserand described the "dogma of the absolutism of rights" not merely as formalistic, but as "egotism in its juridical form," which is "no less dangerous or less sterile than in any other form."[126] The doctrine of "abuse of rights constitutes a living and moving theory of great suppleness, an instrument of progress, a method of adapting law to social needs."[127]

Their critics responded by claiming that the doctrine would subvert individual rights. It threatened "individualistic doctrines," which, according to Planiol, "have been an effective agent in the struggle against despotism."[128] According to Ripert, Josserand's theory "tends to destroy the idea of right. Now this idea, far from being anti-social, is indispensible to the preservation of a society threatened by statism and communism."[129]

---

[120] Planiol and Ripert (n. 115), no. 574.  [121] Ripert (n. 115), no. 91.
[122] Ripert (n. 115), no. 103 *bis*.  [123] Planiol and Ripert (n. 115), no. 574.
[124] Ripert (n. 115), no. 103 *bis*.  [125] Demogue (n. 112), no. 679.
[126] Josserand (n. 113), no. 233.  [127] Josserand (n. 113), no. 247.
[128] Planiol and Ripert (n. 115), no. 574.  [129] Ripert (n. 115), no. 103 *bis*.

It would be a mistake, then, to see the doctrine of abuse of rights merely as a critique of the conceptualism of the nineteenth-century jurists. Moreover, as a critique of conceptualism, it was flawed for reasons that its critics were eager to point out. In a famous passage, echoed by Ripert,[130] Planiol argued: "To speak of an abuse of rights is... to fall into a *logomachie*; for, if I use my right, my act is licit, and when it is illicit, that is when I go beyond my right and act without right."[131] The argument was persuasive even to some, like Léon Duguit, who sympathized politically with Demogue and Josserand, and wished for a "socialization" of private law. The doctrine was a "contradiction": "To say that... one who abuses his right does not enjoy any legal protection is to say, quite simply, that he is doing a thing that he does not have the right to do."[132]

In answering this argument, Josserand reintroduced the conceptualism that he had been trying to escape. The word *droit* in French means both "right" and "law". In the one sense, as Josserand noted, it means "a determinate prerogative," such as "property, servitudes, paternal power." In the other sense, it means "the ensemble of social rules," such as "the civil law," for which he coined the unfortunate word *juricité*. "The abusive act," he said:

> ... is, quite simply, one which is done by virtue of a right whose limits have been respected, [the first meaning of *droit*] but is nevertheless contrary to law envisaged in its *juricité*, that is to say, as an obligatory body of social rules [the second meaning of *droit*].[133]

That answer makes sense, however, only if the "limits" of a right do not correspond to what Josserand called "finality and function." If they do, the scope of the right, interpreted in terms of its finality and function, would exclude the possibility of abuse. But if its scope has been defined without regard to the purposes that the recognition of the right serves, then we have returned to conceptualism. As we have seen, the conceptualists defined property and contract without regard to their purposes, and so they sometimes had to imagine that the law first granted too broad a right and then had to curtail the right that it had just granted. Josserand had to imagine that the law set the "limits" of a right too broadly to accord with its "finality and function," so that the right holder has something to abuse. The abuse of rights doctrine is then needed to curtail the right that the law had just granted. The doctrine may have appealed to its proponents less because it was a sound critique of conceptualism, than because they hoped it would be "an instrument of progress" toward a less individualistic and more socially concerned society.

Despite its weaknesses as a critique of conceptualism, the doctrine passed into Germany in the 1930s. Hans-Peter Haferkamp[134] has traced it to a book by

---

[130] Ripert (n. 115), no. 91.  [131] Planiol and Ripert (n. 115), no. 574.
[132] Léon Duguit, *Les Transformations générales du droit privé depuis le Code Napoléon*, 2nd ed. (Paris, 1920), 200 (citing Planiol).
[133] Josserand (n. 113), no. 245.
[134] Hans-Peter Haferkamp, *Die heutige Rechtsmissbrauchslehre—Ergebnis nationalsozialistische Rechtsdenkens?* (Berlin, 1995); Hans-Peter Haferkamp, in *Historisch-kritischer Kommentar zum BGB, Band II, Schuldrecht: Allgemeiner Teil §§ 241–432*, eds. Mathias Schmoeckel, Joachim Rückert, and Reinhard Zimmermann (Tübingen, 2007), to § 242, nos. 74–76.

Wolfgang Siebert published in 1934.[135] As Haferkamp notes, Siebert borrowed the doctrine from the French, among whom, Siebert himself explained, "the doctrine of the limits to the use of rights" is "best developed".[136] Siebert formulated the doctrine in the same way as the French: whether rights are abused is to be determined by "an immediate consideration of the end of the rights."[137] He called that formulation an *Innentheorie*. He discussed Plainiol's objection that the doctrine is a *logomachie*, and adopted Josserand's answer to Planiol.[138]

Siebert published his book in 1934. His theory was an immediate success. Haferkamp cites seventeen jurists who adopted it by 1942.[139] The reason, Haferkamp concluded,[140] was that these jurists thought that it would promote a society that was less individualistic and more in line with national socialist principles, just as its French proponents thought that it would promote one that was less individualistic and more socially concerned. Siebert's own allegiance is clear. He explained:

> The penetration of formal rights with legal-ethical and with social-ethical content not only accords with German legal thought but appears necessary to avoid a legal order that is foreign to the *Volk* and to the development of a unified *Weltanschauung* for the law.[141]

In support, he cited Adolf Hitler addressing the 1933 *Juristentag*: "The total state will suffer no distinction between law and morality."[142] Siebert acknowledged that the doctrine could lessen the certainty of the law. But, he said, "legal certainty matters less to the interest of the *Volk* than rightness (*Gerechtigkeit*)."[143] Moreover, "[l]egal uncertainty will vanish more and more, the stronger and surer the German national-socialist concept of law takes hold."[144]

Haferkamp believes that the doctrine of abuse of rights in Germany is still stamped by its Nazi origins. He points out that "the principal aspects of Siebert's doctrine remain." For example, abuse of rights is still explained in the way in which Siebert explained his *Innentheorie*.[145]

It is true that the doctrine has remained. It has become a peg on which German courts have hung a variety of decisions, nearly all of which can be justified independently of the doctrine.[146] But the reason why jurists still speak of the "abuse of law" is that no one thinks today that taking account of the purpose of a right commits one to building a national socialist society. It is the same in France. The doctrine disappointed those who thought it would help to forge a new social order. Consequently, it no longer seems threatening. It is not an independent doctrine, but a phrase that a court uses when it wants to limit the scope of a rule.

---

[135] Wolfgang Siebert, *Verwirkung und Unzulässigkeit der Rechtsausübung* (Marburg, 1934).
[136] Siebert (n. 135), 68.   [137] Siebert (n. 135), 155.   [138] Siebert (n. 135), 73–74.
[139] Haferkamp, *Historisch-kritischer Kommentar* (n. 134), to § 242, n. 594.
[140] Haferkamp, *Rechtsmissbrauchslehre* (n. 134).
[141] Siebert (n. 135), 155–56.
[142] *Völkischer Beobachter*, October 5, 1933, cited in Siebert (n. 135), 156, n. 8.
[143] Siebert (n. 135), 155.   [144] Siebert (n. 135), 154.
[145] Haferkamp, *Historisch-kritischer Kommentar* (n. 134), to § 242, no. 82.
[146] James Gordley, "The Abuse of Rights in the Civil Law Tradition," in *Prohibition of Abuse of Law: A New Principle of EU Law?*, ed. Stefan Vogenauer (Oxford, 2011), 33 at 41–46.

## The appeal to the social sciences

### Sociological jurisprudence and policy science

In Germany, jurists such as Ernst Fuchs called for a "sociological legal doctrine" (*soziologische Rechtslehre*). What he meant was that, because "logic does not decide controversies," their resolution must concern "sociological or practical conflict":[147] "Sociological legal decision struggles above all for what is practically the most understandable, legal and equitable result."[148] To find the right result, one must look to "men and their life together in the widest sense," and one can "no more learn that out of a book than driving or riding."[149] He was not appealing to sociology as a distinct science. Neither was Hugo Sinzheimer when he described as "sociological" a "method which makes its particular task the knowledge of legal reality."[150] Neither was Hermann Kantorowicz when he said that sociology considers "the entirety of social life in its seamless extent: economy, technology, morals, art, religion, the biological-psychological basis, and so forth...."[151] For him, sociology meant taking account of culture in its widest sense. "Legal sociology" meant "the investigation of social life in its relation to legal norms."[152]

In the United States, Roscoe Pound called for "a pragmatic, a sociological legal science"[153]—"[a] theory of interests or of the ends of the legal order based on or consistent with modern psychology."[154] He concluded that:

The modern teacher of law should be a student of sociology, economics and politics as well. He should know not only what courts and the principles by which they decide, but the circumstances and conditions, social and economic, to which these principles are applied; he should know the state of popular thought and feeling which makes the environment in which these principles apply.[155]

For Pound:

[T]he entire separation of jurisprudence from the other social sciences ... was in large part to be charged with the backwardness of the law in meeting social ends, the tardiness of lawyers in admitting or even perceiving such ends, and the gulf between legal thought and popular thought on matters of social reform.[156]

The appeal to the social sciences was taken up by others. According to Harlan Stone, the Dean of Columbia Law School:

---

[147] Fuchs (n. 20), 87.   [148] Fuchs (n. 9), 284.
[149] Fuchs (n. 9), 283–84.   [150] Sinzheimer (n. 20), 13.
[151] Hermann U. Kantorowicz, *Rechtswissenschaft und Soziologie* (Tübingen, 1911), 2.
[152] Kantorowicz (n. 151).
[153] Pound, "Mechanical Jurisprudence" (n. 17), 609.   [154] Pound (n. 41), 711.
[155] Roscoe Pound, "The Need of a Sociological Jurisprudence," *Green Bag* 19 (1907): 607, 611–12. See Roscoe Pound, "Do We Need a Philosophy of Law?," *Columbia Law Review* 5 (1905): 339, 353.
[156] Pound, "Law in Books" (n. 17), 510.

> Present day problems of legal education ... arise ... from our traditional attitude toward the law as a body of technical doctrine more or less detached from those social forces which it regulates. We have failed to recognize as clearly as we might that law is nothing more than a form of social control intimately related to those social functions which are the subject matter of economics and the social sciences generally.[157]

Oliphant urged that "[w]e should critically exercise all the methods now used in any of the social sciences and having any degree of objectivity."[158] Felix Cohen said that a tenet of "sociological jurisprudence" is "that legal science is dependent for its basic materials upon social statistics and social sciences."[159]

Pound had called for a sociological jurisprudence in the first decade of the twentieth century. Stone had done so in 1924, and Oliphant, in 1928. By the 1930s, hope had dimmed. One problem was disillusionment with the results of decades of effort to apply the social sciences to law. In 1932, Oliphant attacked the "common despair of applying scientific methods to legal and other social problems."[160] Others acknowledged it. Charles Clark, the Dean of Yale Law School, observed that "the much heralded union of law with the other social sciences lags far behind the publication of the banns betokening ultimate marriage."[161] Jerome Frank said that law schools had a "troubled conscience" on account of "something called 'sociological jurisprudence.' Its watchword is that 'law' is one of the 'social sciences.' But that didn't bring law schools back on track."[162] Brainerd Currie, writing a post mortem account of sociological jurisprudence in 1955, said that it had been "disappointing," having "produced findings without significant value."[163]

Another problem was that of "values." It was hard to see how social science, by itself, could explain which ends were worth pursuing. As Felix Cohen himself said:

> We have heard a good deal, in the last twenty years, of the need for examining the consequences of legal rules, but "sociological jurisprudence" remains in large part a pious program rather than a record of achievement. At the root of this failure is the lack of any definite criterion of importance which will dictate which of the infinite consequences of a legal rule or decision deserve to be investigated. Such a criterion of importance can be supplied only by an ethical system. But thus far, none of the advocates of sociological jurisprudence believe in any ethical system, or, if they do, no word of it is spoken before company.[164]

It seemed naive to say, as Pound had done, that a theory of the ends of the legal order could be based upon modern psychology.

A signal attempt to resolve these problems was made by Harold Lasswell and Myers McDougal. "We submit this basic proposition," they said: "if legal education

---

[157] Harlan F. Stone, "The Future of Legal Education," *American Bar Association Journal* 10 (1924): 223, 235.
[158] Oliphant (n. 6), 161.
[159] Cohen, "Review of C. K. Ogden" (n. 18), 1149.    [160] Oliphant (n. 31), 177.
[161] Charles E. Clark, "Law Professors, What Now?," *American Bar Association Journal* 20 (1934): 431, 432.
[162] Jerome Frank, "A Plea for Lawyer-Schools," *Yale Law Journal* 56 (1947): 1303, 1312–13.
[163] Brainerd Currie, "The Materials of Law Study," *Journal of Legal Education* 8 (1955): 1, 67–68.
[164] Cohen, "Review of C. K. Ogden" (n. 18), 1150–51.

in the contemporary world is adequately to serve the needs of a free and productive commonwealth, it must be conscious, efficient and systematic *training for policymaking.*"165 That meant that the law student must be taught "the social and psychological sciences," the "rapid expansion" of which had made them "more technical and exhaustive."166 The student should be taught "traditional legal skills" as well, but that is not because the skills enable him to find better solutions to problems. Rather, it is because they "set him apart from, and give him a certain advantage over other skill groups in our society."167 The lawyer is "in an unassailably strategic position to influence, if not to create policy."168 The policy that he creates will depend on his knowledge of the social and psychological sciences.

Certainly, the lawyer-policymakers would implement values, but these would be "democratic" values. Education would inculcate them: "A legitimate aid of education is to seek to promote the values of a democratic society and to reduce the number of moral mavericks who do not share democratic preferences." Indeed, supposedly, these values were in some way validated not by philosophical principles,169 but by the social sciences themselves:

The laborious work of modern science had provided a non-sentimental foundation for the intuitive confidence with which the poets and prophets of modern brotherhood have regarded mankind. Buttressing the aspirations of these sensitive spirits stands the modern arsenal of facts about the benevolent potentialities of human nature and a secure knowledge of the methods by which disturbed personality growth can be prevented or cured.170

Thus:

In a democratic society a policy-maker must determine... Which procedures actually aid or hamper the realization of human dignity? How can the institutions of legislation, adjudication, production and distribution be adjusted to democratic survival? What are the slogans and doctrines—in which contexts of experience—that create acceptance of democratic ideals and inspire effort to put them into practice?171

Llewellyn wrote a rebuttal. The purpose of legal education was not to train "some selected few key men of highly superior endowments" who can "in four or even three years' time by intimate work on the frontiers of the instructor's thinking be springboarded almost ahead of their instructors...."172 Even then, there was no social science that would equip even these few to make policy. Instead, "[w]e find suggestion after suggestion... that one something is 'an index' of something else.... And the 'index' proves to be an indicator fraught with error, if you will, in the well-known manner of social not-yet-science."173 Moreover, their method left no work for the careful craftsman-like treatment of law that Llewellyn treasured:

---

165 Harold D. Lasswell and Myers S. McDougal, "Legal Education and Public Policy: Professional Training in the Public Interest," *Yale Law Journal* 52 (1943): 203, 206 (emphasis original).
166 Lasswell and McDougal (n. 165), 217.   167 Lasswell and McDougal (n. 165), 218.
168 Lasswell and McDougal (n. 165), 209.   169 Lasswell and McDougal (n. 165), 213.
170 Lasswell and McDougal (n. 165), 225.   171 Lasswell and McDougal (n. 165), 214.
172 K. N. Llewellyn, "The McDougal and Lasswell Plan for Legal Education," *Columbia Law Review* 43 (1943): 476, 477.
173 Llewellyn (n. 172), 482.

"Where they go off, to my mind, is in a confusion between a would be 'science' and an effective art or craft."[174] Indeed, if they were right, they could attain the goal of the nineteenth-century jurists of arriving at legal results by proof from higher principles, although the proof would no longer be by logical deduction. "What McDougal and Lasswell seem to put forward... is queerly similar to Langdellian study of a body of law," Llewellyn observed: "[D]o your own synthesis from the ground up as though there were no books."[175]

## Economics

Few people now would regard "democratic values" as unitary rather than as a complex of goals often in tension with each other and in need of reconciliation. Even then, few would believe, with McDougal and Lasswell, that law could be derived from these values by a policy science.

The members of the law and economics movement believe that their approach is free from these difficulties. They have a unitary goal: economic efficiency. They have a method: economic analysis. They claim that it can explain legal doctrine.

This is a book about history. The law and economics movement is very much alive. Still, the approach of this book is to consider the projects in which jurists have been engaged—projects defined by their goals and methods. These goals and methods explain what jurists have achieved, and the limits to what they could achieve. The law and economics movement is a project in progress. One can look at where it has gone so far and where it could go.

One problem that its partisans have faced is defending the goal of economic efficiency. Another is defending the claim that the pursuit of this goal can explain the law.

Two leading members of the movement, Robert Cooter and Jody Kraus, believe that the first of these problems has yet to be successfully addressed. They note: "The economic analysis of the content of the common law... implicates the most fundamental jurisprudential questions in legal philosophy."[176] In their view, the movement has succeeded, but not because its founders answered these questions. Quite the opposite: "The account... offered by its proponents lacked philosophical sophistication, and philosophers replied with a devastating critique."[177]

The critique attacked the premise that legal doctrine should be grounded on efficiency, as economists define the term. A situation is Pareto efficient if no one can be made better off, in terms of his own preferences, without making someone else worse off, in terms of his own. A situation is Kaldor-Hicks efficient if some are made better off and others worse off, but the winners would be willing to compensate the losers even though they do not actually do so. According to Posner, Kaldor-

---

[174] Llewellyn (n. 172), 481.   [175] Llewellyn (n. 172), 481.
[176] Robert Cooter and Jody S. Kraus, "The Measure of Economics," Manuscript (April 24, 2012) (cited with permission), 55.
[177] Cooter and Kraus (n. 176), 30.

Hicks efficiency is formally identical to what he calls "wealth maximization."[178] In either case, whether an outcome is efficient does not depend on how resources are distributed. If a handful of families were to control nearly all of the resources, the outcome would be Pareto efficient as long as there were no way in which to make one person better off without making another person worse off. It would be Kaldor-Hicks efficient if there were no way to make someone sufficiently better off that he would be willing to compensate a person made worse off.

As Cooter and Kraus explained, critics claimed that efficiency, thus defined, is a normatively indefensible goal. They claimed that "[t]he use of Pareto efficiency was normatively irrelevant because no possible changes in law were Pareto efficient—every possible change necessarily made at least one person worse off."[179] As Michael Trebilcock noted, one person's preferences drive up the price of something that others want.[180] Moreover, the fact that a person gratifies his own preferences may distress others.[181] It may do so if he is hated or envied, or if his preference is for an activity, such as cock-fighting, which revolts other people.

Again, critics claimed that:

[T]he use of cost-benefit efficiency ("Kaldor-Hicks") was normatively indefensible because it justified a decision imposing actual losses on some individuals provided others could net a gain even after hypothetically paying full compensation to the losers. Merely hypothetical compensation could not transform unfair losses into fair ones.[182]

Suppose, Ronald Dworkin argued, that Derek's book is worth $2 to him and $3 to Amartya. Wealth would be maximized if somebody (an imaginary tyrant) were to transfer the book forcibly to Amartya, who then would not need to pay for it. But there is no reason to think that the transfer would be an improvement unless we assume, gratuitously, that the book will provide more satisfaction to Amartya than to Derek.[183] Posner answered Dworkin by saying that the figures chosen are deceptive. The transfer "probably will increase the amount of happiness," meaning satisfaction, if the book were "worth $3,000 to Amartya and $2 to Derek."[184] But then he is falling back on the idea that there are amounts of happiness or utility, and the objective is to maximize them. Law and economics would then be committed

---

[178] Richard A. Posner, "The Value of Wealth: A Comment on Dworkin and Kronman," *Journal of Legal Studies* 9 (1980): 243, 244.
[179] Cooter and Kraus (n. 176), 41.
[180] Michael J. Trebilcock, *The Limits of Freedom of Contract* (Cambridge, MA, 1993), 58; Richard Posner, "Utilitarianism, Economics and Legal Theory," *Journal of Legal Studies* 9 (1979): 103, 114. A similar point is made by Ronald Dworkin, "What is Equality? Part 2: Equality of Resources," *Philosophy and Public Affairs* 10 (1981): 283, 307–08.
[181] Trebilcock (n. 180), 62–63, 243. *See* Guido Calabresi, "The Pointlessness of Pareto: Carrying Coase Further," *Yale Law Journal* 100 (1991): 1211, 1216–17.
[182] Cooter and Kraus (n. 176), 41. *See* Guido Calabresi, "The New Economic Analysis of Law: Scholarship, Sophistry or Self-indulgence?," *Proceedings of the British Academy 1982* 68 (1983): 85, 89 ("whoever believed that wealth maximization without regard to its distribution could qualify as the goal of law in a just society?"); Hugh Collins, "Distributive Justice through Contracts," *Current Legal Problems* 45 (1992): 49, 51 ("what is important is the ability of each individual to pursue a meaningful life, and the fulfilment of that aim involves some sacrifice of collective prosperity").
[183] Ronald M. Dworkin, "Is Wealth a Value?," *Journal of Legal Studies* 9 (1980): 191, 197, 199.
[184] Posner (n. 178), 245.

to a philosophy of utilitarianism that even most economists have given up, and which Posner elsewhere disavows. For an economist, to maximize utility merely means to maximize preference satisfaction—that is, the extent to which a person gets more of what he prefers—regardless of why or to what extent he prefers it. Preference satisfaction is defined as the choice of one outcome in preference to another. It is defined without regard to any amount of utility or happiness that the choice may bring.

Cooter and Kraus note, "[f]inally, wealth maximization was [said to be] normatively indefensible as the sole criterion of evaluation because wealth has no intrinsic value and its maximization is a poor means of achieving normatively defensible ends, such as welfare maximization or equality."[185] Why should one maximize the ability of a few rich persons to satisfy their preferences? And suppose that someone is poor? According to Posner, a person whose "net social social product is negative" must starve.[186]

At one point, Posner said that "[w]hen wealth is maximized, people must benefit others to secure benefits for themselves," they will have "economic liberty," and they are likely to practice "traditional ('Calvinist' or 'Protestant') virtues."[187] These are appeals to values that are presumed to be higher than wealth maximization, and need to be explained and defended. More recently, however, he has said that philosophy is incapable of justifying any goal, including his own:

> My belief that moral theory lacks the necessary resources for resolving moral controversies enables me to reconcile my qualified acceptance of moral subjectivism with my qualified rejection of moral skepticism. A person who murders an infant is acting immorally in our society; a person who sincerely claimed, with or without supporting arguments, that it is right to kill infants would be asserting a private moral position. I might consider him a lunatic, a monster, or a fool, as well as a violator of the prevailing moral code. But I would hesitate to call him immoral....[188]

This discussion may clarify my position on the normativity of economics. Economists ranging from Adam Smith, Jeremy Bentham, and Alfred Marshall to Oscar Lange and Abba Lerner and thence to Friedrich Hayek, Milton Friedman, and David Friedman have sometimes tried to make economics a source of moral guidance by proposing, often under the influence of utilitarianism, that the goal of a society should be to maximize average or total utility, or wealth, or equality as a means toward maximizing utility, or freedom, or some combination of these goods. These are doomed efforts. What the economist can say, which is a lot but not everything, is that if a society values prosperity (or freedom or equality), these are the various policies that will conduce to that goal, and these are the costs associated with each.[189]

Cooter and Kraus are correct, then, that the law and economics movement did not prosper because of its philosophical strength.

---

[185] Cooter and Kraus (n. 176), 41.   [186] Posner (n. 180), 128.
[187] Posner (n. 180), 122–24.
[188] Richard Posner, "1997 Oliver Wendell Holmes Lectures: The Problematics of Moral and Legal Theory," *Harvard Law Review* 111 (1998): 1637, 1645.
[189] Posner (n. 188), 1669–70.

It prospered, they believe, because of its claim that it could make sense of legal doctrine. More particularly, "economic analysis achieved the success that launched its prominence" not in explaining doctrines "cast in economic terms," such as antitrust law, but in explaining the doctrines to which "American legal education has given pride of place": "the common law courses of torts, contracts and property."[190] Dworkin criticized the use of economics by saying that "[a] successful theory must not only fit but [also] justify the practice it interprets."[191] According to Cooter and Kraus, Dworkin thereby "concedes that economic analysis might reasonably be shown to have an acceptable level of fit with common law cases."[192]

If we look at the law of property, tort, and contract, and at the doctrinal problems that we have inventoried, we can see that philosophers such as Dworkin have made that concession too readily.

In property law, one problem that the nineteenth-century lawyers largely bypassed is the right to use another's property in time of necessity. It appeared in the German Civil Code only because it was inserted at the last minute for pragmatic reasons. In the United States, it appeared, without fuss, in the early twentieth century in *Ploof v. Putnam* and *Vincent v. Lake Erie*, in which it was held that a ship could tie up to another person's pier in a storm.[193]

Posner, in search of an economic explanation, noted that, in *Ploof*, it was the pier owner's employee who cut loose the plaintiff's ship. The pier owner was not there and so "negotiations were, in the circumstances, infeasible."[194] The negotiations, he claims, would have led to an efficient result. Suppose, however, that the owner had cut the ship loose himself. In *Ploof*, the court rested its decision not on the defendant's absence, but on the plaintiff's "necessity."[195] If it meant what it said, it would have held the pier owner liable. Suppose that the pier owner cut the ship loose out of sheer cussedness after the plaintiff offered him a fortune to refrain. Would that result be efficient? I think that an economist would have to say so. He defines efficiency in terms of preference satisfaction, whatever the preference may be, and cussedness is as much a preference as any other. It is hard to believe that a court would have relieved the pier owner from liability because of the efficiency of the result.

Another puzzle for the nineteenth-century jurists, as we have seen, is why a landowner was sometimes liable for activities that interfered with his neighbors. In France, Germany, and common law jurisdictions, he was held liable if his activity was abnormal for the area and interfered to a significant degree. But jurists had trouble explaining why.[196]

---

[190] Posner (n. 188), 31.
[191] Ronald Dworkin, *Law's Empire* (Cambridge, MA, 1986), 285.
[192] Cooter and Kraus (n. 176), 47.
[193] *Ploof v. Putnam*, 71 A. 188 (Vt. 1908); *Vincent v. Lake Erie Transportation Co.*, 124 N.W. 221 (Minn. 1910).
[194] Richard Posner, *Economic Analysis of Law*, 5th ed. (New York, 1998), 190.
[195] 71 A. at 189 ("necessity...will justify entries upon land and interferences with personal property that would otherwise be trespasses").
[196] *See* Chapter IX, pp. 232–35.

Economic explanations began with a famous article by Ronald Coase, published in 1960, "The Problem of Social Cost."[197] According to Coase, the reason for imposing liability on a person whose activity causes noise, smoke, or smells that bother his neighbor cannot be that the activity interferes with him. Imposing liability would interfere with the person conducting the activity. All one can say is that two activities interfere with one another. From an economic perspective, the problem is to ensure that the efficient level of precautions is taken. A precaution is efficient if it costs less than the expected value of the harm that will otherwise occur. Coase argued that if the parties can negotiate costlessly, it does not matter where the law places liability. If liability is placed on the party who conducts the activity, he will take any precaution that costs less than the damages that he will be required to pay. If the precaution costs more, he will not take it, because he will prefer to pay damages. If, instead, he is not held liable, then the other party will pay him to take any precaution that costs less than the damage that the other party will otherwise suffer. If it costs more, the other party would prefer to suffer the damages. But that account does not explain the law. The person who conducts the activity is held liable if it is abnormal for the area.

Guido Calabresi tried to bring Coase's conclusions into line with how the law is, and how most people think it should be, by pointing out that there usually will be costs that can best be avoided by imposing liability. The activity, for example the operation of a cement plant, may affect many people who will find it hard to speak with one voice and to agree what portion of the cost of a precaution each of them should pay. The person conducting the activity is more likely to know what precautions can be taken, how effective they are, and how much they cost. The costs entailed in determining and taking the right level of precautions will consequently be less if liability is imposed on that person.[198]

Once again, the explanation does not fit the law. The person who operates the cement plant is held liable even if it is perfectly obvious that there are no precautions that he could feasibly have taken to prevent the harm. In such a case, it does not matter whether he best knows what precaution could have been taken, or whether neighboring landowners could have costlessly negotiated with him to take them. Even if it were not so, it is odd to explain the law of nuisance as a way of optimizing the production of cement and the precautions taken in doing so. Certainly, that is not what jurists have thought ever since the Romans imposed liability on the owner of a cheese shop whose smoke bothered those living upstairs. There is something strange about explaining a rule by considerations that could not have been even vaguely in minds of those who fashioned it. By coincidence, they might have framed a rule that later proves to be appropriate for reasons that they could have envisioned. That might happen once or twice, but it cannot consistently explain a body of rules developed by those who did not have the benefit of reading

---

[197] Ronald H. Coase, "The Problem of Social Cost," *Journal of Law and Economics* 3 (1960): 1.
[198] *See* Guido Calabresi, *The Cost of Accidents: A Legal and Economic Analysis* (New Haven, CT, 1970), 135–403; Guido Calabresi, "Transactions Costs, Resource Allocation and Liability Rules: A Comment," *Journal of Law and Economics* 11 (1968): 67, 71–73.

modern articles that explain what they were doing. Indeed, the authors of these articles are often admired for the novelty and ingenuity in finding explanations that hitherto eluded even their contemporaries.

In tort, as we have seen, most nineteenth-century conceptualists regarded fault as the master principle on which liability in tort must depend. A person was not accountable for harm not caused by his fault. Such harm was the result of chance. The conceptualists never had a theory of voluntary action that would explain why a person was accountable for fault, and why fault might take the form of intentional wrongdoing or negligence.

Typically, the economic explanation is that a person is negligent if he fails to take the efficient level of precaution to prevent a loss. Liability is imposed so that he will have an incentive to do so. A precaution is efficient if its cost is less than the benefit to be gained by taking it. Costs and benefits are determined by the amount that a person would be willing to pay, given the purchasing power that he commands, to obtain or avoid what he likes or dislikes. Thus, according to Posner, if one person walks fast and smashes another's oranges, the court must judge how much the oranges were worth to the plaintiff, and how much walking fast was worth to the defendant, meaning how much each would be willing to pay for what he wants.[199]

This economic explanation is often illustrated by a formula for negligence proposed by Judge Learned Hand in *United States v. Carroll Towing Co.*[200] Hand said that a precaution should be taken if the burden it entails (B) is less than the loss that may occur (L) multiplied by the probability that the precaution will prevent the loss. Richard Epstein said that Hand may have been "unwittingly adumbrating an economic explanation" of negligence, and the Hand formula is usually taught as if he were. But is it likely that he really thought that "burden" and "loss" were definable as the amount that a person would pay to avoid them? Suppose the loss were to human life? Might Hand merely have been restating as a formula the common sense intuition that reasonable conduct depends on risk and on the importance of what is at stake? It is reasonable to drive at a lower speed when it starts to rain, because then there is a greater risk of losing control of the car. It is reasonable to drive at a faster speed when one is rushing an injured person to the hospital. Moreover, is it likely that Hand thought that the reason why negligence should be defined this way was in order to induce people to take an efficient level of precautions by threatening them with damages?

As we have seen, the idea that negligence entails a balancing of good and bad consequences, taking into account the probability that they will occur, pre-dates the economic explanation by centuries. Writers in the Aristotelian tradition explained negligence as the failure to exercise the virtue of prudence. Cajetan gave the example of a nurse who puts a crying child to sleep in her own bed, then rolls over in the night, smothering the child. Whether the nurse was negligent depends on the size of the bed, the propensity of the nurse to roll in her sleep, and the implacability

[199] Posner (n. 180), 120.   [200] 159 F.2d 169 (2d Cir. 1947).

of the child.[201] The considerations that matter are like those mentioned by Learned Hand.

What, then, does the economic explanation add that better fits the law of negligence? It defines good and bad consequences as preferences backed by cash. It claims that the purpose of imposing liability is to give people the right incentives to take the efficient level of precautions. It is hard to see how that explanation "fits" what jurists concerned with negligence, from the Romans to Learned Hand, could have had in mind even vaguely, or that it fits with a common sense understanding of what negligence law is about.

According to Posner, as we have seen, if one person walks fast and smashes another's oranges, to determine if the defendant was negligent, the court must judge how much walking fast was worth to him and compare it with how much the oranges were worth to the plaintiff, which means how much each would be willing to pay for what he wants. Now change the facts: a very rich person who does not care about harming others, or perhaps even enjoys doing so, habitually drives his Lamborghini at great speed down side streets. Fear of liability does not deter him from doing so, because driving fast is worth more to him than any damages that he will have to pay. Indeed, suppose that he is willing to pay more for the privilege of driving fast than his potential or actual victims would pay for him to drive more safely, since, while they value their lives dearly, that value, as measured by the amount that they can pay, is less than the rich man would accept in return for slowing down. It follows that he is not negligent. The "loss" to him of driving safely is greater than the "loss" to those whom he maims or kills. Because he is not negligent, it follows that he is not even obligated to compensate a victim.

Neither does the claim that the purpose of negligence law is to provide incentives to take the efficient level of precautions fit the law as we know it. It does not explain why the sanction imposed on the negligent party is liability to the defendant in damages. The negligent party may be insured against liability. One could develop ingenious explanations of why he might be deterred anyway, but they are not straightforward. Moreover, the damages that he pays may not correspond to the loss that he has occasioned others. He may pay less if he killed someone than if he crippled him. Moreover, by hurting one person, he may have hurt others. As we have seen, whether the others can recover is one of the unresolved problems left over from the nineteenth century.[202] German jurists and common lawyers said that one could recover only for violation of an "absolute" right good against all of the world, and so excluded recovery for pure economic harm. In France, although the defendant is supposed to be liable for all harm that he does, courts have cut back on his liability. The economic explanation does not fit French law, let alone German law or common law.

As we have seen, another problem in tort law that was left unresolved in the aftermath of conceptualism is the basis for liability without fault or strict liability.

---

[201] Cajetan (Tomasso De Vio), *Commentaria* to Thomas Aquinas, *Summa Theologica post* Q. 64 a. 8 (Padua, 1698).
[202] *See* Chapter IX, pp. 244–48.

For the conceptualists, it had no principled justification. They defined tort liability in terms of fault. In the nineteenth century, many jurisdictions imposed strict liability in various situations. Only American courts brought it within a general rule: that the defendant was strictly liable if he engaged in abnormally dangerous activities. But that general rule was left unexplained.

Economic explanations of strict liability have followed the same lines as those of liability for activities of a landowner that interfere with others. According to Coase, if a person dynamites to build a tunnel, or flies an airplane that crashes, or stores water in a reservoir that escapes and had been able to negotiate costlessly with his potential victims, he would take the same level of precautions whether or not he is held liable. According to Calabresi, it is better to hold him liable because negotiations are apt to be neither practical nor costless, and because he is more likely to know whether a precaution is worth taking, given the chance of harming someone. But, as before, that is not the law. Different jurisdictions impose strict liability in different situations, but no one escapes liability when it is obvious that he was without fault and that no precaution was economically feasible.

Contracts should be enforced, according to economic analysis, because a contract can make both parties better off and so lead to an efficient result. As Trebilcock and Peter Benson observed, however, a contract makes the parties better off only *ex ante*,[203] at the time that the contract is made. It need not make them both better off *ex post*, and indeed, if it did, one party would not be trying to escape liability. There is no explanation of why it is efficient for them to be better off *ex ante* even if they are not *ex post*. They call this problem the "Paretian dilemma." As Guido Calabresi has noted, as long as there are *ex post* losers:

> [W]e will not be achieving an improvement according to the strict Pareto standard.... [W]e could say that we do not *care* about these losers,... but that lack of care implies a distributional theory that has all too conveniently been kept out of sight.[204]

One could construct an answer by crediting the parties with some degree of foresight and judgment *ex ante*—that is, with exercising the virtue of prudence, and then finding a reason why the contract should be enforced if a party acted imprudently, or acted prudently but mistakenly. But that takes us beyond economic theory.

As mentioned earlier, another puzzle for the nineteenth-century jurists is why the parties are not bound, sometimes, by terms to which they did agree. The most striking case is the price.

One would think that, as long as each party knew what he was getting and what he was giving up, such a contract would be efficient and therefore, according to economic analysis, that it should be enforced. That would be so even if one person were in imminent danger and his only possible rescuer charged a fortune for a rescue that he could perform almost costlessly. That is not the law. Landes and

---

[203] Trebilcock (n. 180), 244; Peter Benson, "The Idea of a Public Basis of Justification for Contract," *Osgoode Hall Law Journal* 33 (1995): 273, 284–87.
[204] Calabresi (n. 182), 96.

Posner, however, have found an economic explanation for relief. If the rescuer could charge an excessive price, parties who might find themselves in need of rescue would spend more money trying to avoid such a situation and so there would be an economically inefficient overinvestment in safety equipment.[205] Once again, that explanation does not fit the law. The rescuer cannot charge an excessive price even if he can prove that no possible expenditure on safety equipment by the other party could have prevented the need for a rescue. Moreover, again, it is odd to explain a rule by considerations that could not have been vaguely in the mind of those who fashioned it, such as optimizing investment in rescue equipment.

One might think that it would be equally difficult to find an economic explanation of the law of unjust enrichment. If a bank mistakenly deposits $1 million in a person's account, the bank is poorer and that person is richer, but, as we have seen, in and of itself, there is nothing inefficient about the change in who commands resources. The reason why the bank must be repaid, according to Saul Levmore, is that otherwise:

> [It] would protect [itself] with more paperwork, and disbursing agents would demand more proof before paying claims. It does not require great faith in the usefulness of economic analysis in law to believe that the flat denial of restitution in these cases would lead to an inefficiently high level of care.[206]

This explanation does not fit the law. The bank will recover the $1 million even if it could be shown that no amount of extra paperwork could have prevented the overpayment. Moreover, it strains the imagination to think that those who developed and preserved ancient rules concerning the duty of restitution of money paid by mistake had any such thing remotely in mind.

This book is about history, not about the future. Cooter and Kraus hope that, in a forthcoming book, they will be able to put the law and economics movement on a sounder philosophical foundation. Perhaps they will also give a better explanation of the law. Who is to say? My own view is that one could not integrate economics and law without acknowledging that some preferences are genuinely better than others, and that people have an ability (call it prudence) to tell that they are, that if goods are to go to whoever will pay the most, there must be a reason why some people should be richer than others (call it distributive justice, qualified by incentives such as Aristotle described to labor and to use resources carefully), and that when

---

[205] William M. Landes and Richard A. Posner, "Salvors, Finders, Good Samaritans and Other Rescuers: An Economic Study of Law and Altruism," *Journal of Legal Studies* 7 (1978): 83. The same explanation is given by F. H. Buckley, "Three Theories of Substantive Fairness," *Hofstra Law Review* 19 (1990): 33, 40–48.

[206] Saul Levmore, "Explaining Restitution," *Virginia Law Review* 71 (1985): 65, 69. *See* Hanoch Dagan, "Symposium: Restitution and Unjust Enrichment—Mistakes," *Texas Law Review* 79 (2001): 1795. He analyzes how to save the costs that unjust enrichment might incur. He does not go so far as to say that, in and of itself, unjust enrichment does not matter. Quite the contrary, he thinks that, because it is an instance of "involuntariness," it runs contrary to the "autonomy" prized by "the liberal tradition": Dagan, "Symposium," 1796. Perhaps. But from the economic standpoint that he takes in his article, it is hard to see why it matters whether someone involuntarily loses purchasing power that he once had when it does not matter if he involuntarily never had it in the first place.

one person becomes richer at the expense of another, there must be a reason why the law permits it (call it a reason consistent with commutative justice). The concepts of prudence, distributive justice, and commutative justice once made it possible to relate individual to social purpose, and to explain property, tort, contract, and unjust enrichment in terms of these purposes. These concepts fell out of fashion long ago, but we have not found a viable alternative. I have argued elsewhere that we are unlikely to do so.[207]

## Whither?

"Whither are we going?" we would like to know. According to the critical legal studies movement, which flourished in the United States in the 1970s and 1980s, we are going nowhere. Many of its members made the same point as the German free jurists and the American legal realists. One cannot begin with the authoritative sources of law and conclude by deductive logic how new cases should be decided. In any new case, there is a plausible argument to be made on either side. Otherwise, the case would not be in court. Therefore, according to members of the critical legal studies movement, the judge decides cases not by law, but as he likes. There is no rule of law.

Roberto Unger gave a more sophisticated account of why he thought that the legal tradition had failed. This account was part of what he called "total criticism." All aspects of society are related. Formalism, as he called the nineteenth-century alliance of positivism and conceptualism, arose when, "[a]s a result of the dissolution of th[e] hierarchical order [in post-feudal European societies] and of the expansion of the market economy, concepts like 'just price' in exchange and distribution according to 'virtue' lost their meaning."[208] Disenchantment with formalism was one aspect of a larger change in society, which, when it is completed, will bring forth new ways of thinking that correspond to new social relationships. It is too early to say what they will be. All one can say is "that both human nature and our understanding of it can progress through a spiral of increasing community and diminishing domination."[209]

This is an approach to history that I criticized in the Prologue. There is no way to treat all aspects of a society as though they constitute a whole in which each part has meaning only in terms of the others. Nevertheless, if one considers Unger's account of the rise and fall of formalism, and of the inability of jurists to find a satisfactory alternative, much of it accurately summarizes how we came to be where we are.

---

[207] Set out in James Gordley, "The Moral Foundations of Private Law," *The American Journal of Jurisprudence* 47 (2002): 1; James Gordley, "Economics and the Cardinal Virtues: The Ethics of Profit-Seeking," in *Rethinking the Purpose of Business: Interdisciplinary Essays from the Catholic Social Tradition*, eds. S. A. Cortright and M. J. Naughton (South Bend, IN, 2002), 65.
[208] Roberto Mangabiera Unger, *Knowledge and Politics* (New York, 1975), 77.
[209] Unger (n. 208), 239.

Formalism, according to Unger, was a response to the demise of "metaphysical systems" that "taught that the mind could understand what the world is really like." In Unger's terminology, these systems:

> ... accepted the view that all things in nature have intelligible essences.... [T]he supporters of the doctrine of intelligible essences have gone on to hold that the standards of right and wrong also have essences which thought can comprehend.[210]

Positivism was "the resort to a set of public rules as the foundation of order and freedom is a consequence of the subjective conception of value. The subjective conception in turn presupposes the abandonment of the doctrine of intelligible essences."[211] But then:

> ... a difficulty arises. If there are no intelligible essences, how do we go about classifying facts and situations, especially social facts and social situations? Because facts have no intrinsic identity, everything depends on the names we give them. The conventions of naming, rather than any perceived quality of "tableness" will determine whether an object is to count as a table. In the same way, convention rather than contract will determine whether a particular bargain is to be treated as a contract.[212]

That is why one cannot proceed by defining the concepts in which a law is framed and demonstrating their consequences:

> In the absence of intelligible essences... there are no obvious criteria for defining general categories of acts and persons when we make the rules.... Nor are there clear standards by which to classify the particular instances under rules when we come to the stage of applying the rules we have made.[213]

For Unger, the same difficulty arises if one tries to apply rules not by deductive logic, but by asking about the purposes that the rules serve. If values are subjective, then interests and ends are those of individuals: "[S]ociety is artificial: groups are the products of the will and interests of individuals. For the individual, the group is characteristically a means to the satisfaction of ends he could not achieve except through membership."[214] But then "the purpose theory" of how law should be applied "leaves the regime of legal justice hanging in the air":[215]

> [T]he purpose theory of law needs some way of defining the values, policies or purposes that are to guide the judge's work. In general a rule will be thought to serve many purposes. Moreover, a judge deals with a whole system of rules, from which he must select the rule appropriate to the case before him. When he applies one of these rules to the case, he must weigh the policy of the rule he is choosing against the policies he might have applied to the case with a different result. Thus, the purpose theory of adjudication requires not only a criterion for the definition of controlling policies, but also a method for balancing them off against one another. In the absence of a procedure for policy decision, the judge will inescapably impose his own subjective preferences, or somebody else's, on the litigants.[216]

---

[210] Unger (n. 208), 30–31. [211] Unger (n. 208), 80. [212] Unger (n. 208), 80.
[213] Unger (n. 208), 80. [214] Unger (n. 208), 81. [215] Unger (n. 208), 94.
[216] Unger (n. 208), 94–95.

# Ubinam Gentium Sumus? *After Positivism and Conceptualism* 311

From what we have seen, that is not a bad summary of the way that we have come. But it is not an indictment of the possibility of law. The legal tradition, as we have seen, is not dependent on a metaphysical theory, although there are metaphysical theories that are incompatible with it. The law grew up independently of metaphysics. Moreover, the difficulties to which Unger points are those spawned by one metaphysical tradition: rationalism. He has indicted not law, but law based on rationalism—or on the attempts since the nineteenth century to escape it.

Formalism was conceived, according to Unger, in a revolt against "the doctrine of intelligible essences." He claims that "Plato's ethics and Aquinas' theory of natural law exemplify" this doctrine.[217] But the doctrine that he has in mind is not that of Plato or Aquinas; it is that of the rationalists. In a footnote to the sentence just quoted, he said, "For the development of the view, see Christian Wolff, *Philosophia Prima sive Ontologia* §143...."[218] Indeed, Unger conceives of "the doctrine of intelligible essences" in rationalist terms. He believes that "the doctrine denies any significance to choice other than the passive acceptance or rejection of independent truths. Our experience of moral judgment, however, seems to be one of at least contributing to shape the ends we pursue."[219] He speaks of "the inability of the theory of objective value to determine how we should act in particular situations."[220] Etienne Gilson, Germain Grisez, or John Finnis might have stated in exactly the same way their objection to the position of Suárez, adopted by Wolff.[221] As we have seen, it was a break with that of Aquinas, in which the natural law meant the choice by an individual as to how to apply universal, but general, precepts to a particular situation in which there might be no one right answer and more circumstances that matter than he could take directly into account.

The result is a distorted picture not only of the work of earlier jurists, but also of the problems of nineteenth-century positivism and conceptualism. Unger concludes, as the free jurists and American legal realists did, that one cannot deduce determinate results in new cases from authoritative texts. He correctly observes that, absent "criteria for defining general categories of acts and persons when we make the rules," there cannot be "clear standards by which to classify the particular instances under rules when we come to the stage of applying the rules we have made."[222] Yet, as we have seen, in assuming that such a thing could be done, the nineteenth-century jurists had accepted the premise of the rationalists. One must begin with a secure starting point: for the rationalists, a definition that had the certainty of mathematics; for the nineteenth-century jurists, a text that had the authority of positive law. One must then demonstrate logically how the concept or the text applies to a new situation. One must be able to do so or, for a rationalist, one would be introducing uncertainty; for a positivist, one would be usurping authority. The problem arises only on rationalist premises of how one reaches legal conclusions.

---

[217] Unger (n. 208), 31.  [218] Unger (n. 208), 31, n. 1.  [219] Unger (n. 208), 77.
[220] Unger (n. 208), 77–78.  [221] *See* Chapter VIII, pp. 166–77.  [222] Unger (n. 208), 80.

As Unger says, those who revolted against positivism and conceptualism wanted to understand the law in terms of purpose. Yet, as he observes, "the purpose theory" of how law should be applied "leaves the regime of legal justice hanging in the air."[223] The question is which purposes matter. As we have seen, some thought that the answer could be found by intuition, some by balancing interests, some by an appeal to social policy, and some by an appeal to social science. Yet none of them, with the exception of the law and economics movement, attempted a reconstruction of legal doctrine in which the purpose of a particular doctrine is identified and the doctrine interpreted accordingly. In the case of the law and economics movement, there is a discrepancy between the goal of efficiency and any particular doctrine that this goal is said to explain. In order to explain doctrine by purpose, one would have to bridge the gap between concept and purpose. That, as we have seen, is a problem that began with the rationalists and continued with the nineteenth-century conceptualists.

The problem is not that law is impossible. The problem is that the legacy of rationalism has made it seem so. Which brings us back to the question of whither we are going.

I have my own ideas about where we should go. I think we should re-examine ideas that were eclipsed with the rise of rationalism.[224] But if the story told in this book is accurate, the question of where we will go is unanswerable. We have described the work of jurists in terms of the projects in which they engaged—projects defined by certain goals and methods. The goals and methods enabled the jurists to achieve what they did, limited what they could achieve, and sometimes doomed their efforts to failure. But why any particular project started is a mystery. We have spent some time describing the origins of these projects and seen how historically contingent they were. There is no reason why there had to be rationalists, humanists, late scholastics, medieval civilians, or, for that matter, Roman jurists. The entire tradition might not have been.

The one thing that would surprise me is if it were to disappear. Its intellectual strength is too great. The physicist Richard Feinman, who, despite his eminence, taught first-year physics, once said that although his students were engaged, they had no idea of the intellectual power that they were being given—a power to explain by a few ideas a vast number of particular phenomena. I have the same sense teaching my first-year students. The tradition founded by the Roman jurists has lasted two thousand years. To understand and develop it has been the life work of brilliant men and now women. It has shaped the law of nearly the whole world. I doubt whether a future historian will regard it as we do the worship of god-kings in Egypt or the lore of liver divination.

---

[223] Unger (n. 208), 94.
[224] James Gordley, *Foundations of Private Law Property, Tort, Contract, Unjust Enrichment* (Oxford, 2006).

# Index

Abelard, Peter 52
*Abus de droit*/Abuse of rights 234–5, 292–6
Accursius 33, 34, 35, 36, 37, 39, 40, 41, 45, 47, 48, 49, 50, 51, 56, 67, 112–13, 131, 163
*Accusatio* 66, 67
*Actio spolii* 57
*Actio utilis* 90, 163
Addison, Charles Greenstreet 207, 246, 256
Admiralty law 59
Alciato, Andrea 112, 118, 119
Alexander III (Pope) 70
Altruism 183–4, 185, 186, 187, 188, 214, 226
Ambrose 59
Anastasius 68
Anglo–American common law *see* Common law
Appius Claudius 6
Aquinas, Thomas 21, 49, 82–8, 90–5, 97–9, 102, 103, 107–11, 118, 121, 131, 133–5,139, 156, 166–73, 175, 177, 181, 266, 284, 285, 311
Aratus of Soli 129
Aristo 38
Aristotle 12–17, 19, 21, 49, 82–5, 91–5, 102, 103, 107–11, 116–17, 121, 131–5, 137, 139, 156, 157, 169, 170, 174, 175, 177–9, 181, 256, 260, 266, 284, 285, 305, 308
Arndts, Ludwig 225, 237, 238
*Ars* 17, 11, 115, 116, 119, 126, 127, 128, 130, 131, 139
*Asher v Whitlock* 24, 205
Assumpsit 210–11, 252
Astuti, Guido 65
Atiyah, Patrick S. 226, 265
Atticus 16
Aubry, Charles 197, 198, 224, 232, 237, 260, 263, 268, 270
Augustine 54, 57, 60, 61, 72, 74, 79, 167
Augustus 5
Aulus Cascellius 5
Aulus Gellius 18
Austin, John 215–16, 217
Azo 34, 35, 50, 51, 160, 163

Baldus degli Ubaldi 31, 35, 38, 48, 49, 50, 53, 65, 83, 95, 102, 160, 162
Barbeyrac, Jean 128, 129, 130, 131, 132, 135, 137, 138, 140, 145, 154, 217, 227
Bargaining strength 259
Barthomaeus Brixiensis 55
Bartolus of Saxoferrato 31, 38, 39, 41, 42, 43, 44, 48, 49, 50, 65, 83, 95, 102, 118, 119, 131, 160, 162, 233
Battery 208–9

Beale, Joseph 220–1
*Begriffsjurisprudenz* 42, 201, 276, 278
Behrends, Okko 201
Bénabent, Alain 239
Benson, Peter 307
Bergfeld, Christoph 183
Berlier, Théophile 254
Bigot de Préameneu, Felix Julien 152, 250
Bijnkershoek, Cornelis van 158, 161
Birks, Peter 223, 273–4
Bishop, Joel Prentice 256
Blackstone, William 37, 41, 61, 206, 207, 211, 227
Blühdorn, Jürgen 16
Böckenförde, Ernst 203
Böhmer, Justus Hennig 159
Bologna 28
Bonaparte, Napoleon 148, 150
Boniface VIII (Pope) 249
Bonnecase, Julien 277
Boyer, Laurent 239, 240
Bracton, Henry de 61
Brie, S. 282
Brown, Peter 59
Brunnemann, Johannes 157, 158, 163
Bruns, Carl Georg 229
Buckley, R. A. 241
Budé, Guillaume 112, 113, 119
Bulgarus 28, 33, 34, 35
Bürge, Alfons 249
*Bürgerlichesgesetzbuch see* German Civil Code

Cajetan, Tomaso di Vio, Cardinal 82, 87–8, 92, 93, 96, 97, 107, 110, 137, 175, 305
Calabresi, Guido 304, 307
Cambacérès, Jean Jacques Régis de 148, 149, 150, 152, 224, 250, 254
Canon law
  authorities 53–5, 106–7
  contract 56, 61–2, 64–5
  crime 71–5
  due process of law 66–70
  fault 62–4
  internal forum 75–81, 107
  international law 78–81
  marriage 56–7, 76–7
  necessity 58–9
  origins 51–3
  possession 57–8
  prescription 55–6
  reputation 58
  restitution (compensation for harm done another) 57
  unlawful acts, liability 59–61

# 314    Index

Canoy-Olthoff, A. M. M. 160
Cassius 12
Catholic Church 113, 175
*Causa* 49, 60, 62, 64, 65, 95, 122, 210, 211
Cavers, David 222
Celsus 11
Chabas, François 240, 242
Charles V (Emperor) 102
Chitty, Joseph 256
Christensen, Katherine 54
Christian values 36, 54, 55–6, 57, 62, 90
Ciaralli, Antonio 28, 29
Cicero 3, 16–18, 61, 78, 79, 111, 115, 116–17, 118, 119, 120, 126, 127, 128, 129, 131, 139, 140, 141, 153, 167, 180
Cinus de Pistoia 39–40, 44, 160
Clark, Charles 298
Clerk, J. F. 246
Coase, Ronald 304, 307
*Code civil see* French Civil Code
*Coggs v. Bernard* 211
*Cognitio extraordinaria* 20
Cohen, Felix 280, 298
Cohen, Morris 279, 280, 283
Coke, Edward 61
Coleman, Jules 242
Colmet de Santerre, Edouard 255, 260
Commentators 31, 44
Common law authority of decided cases 196, 205
    contract 25–6, 210–2
    forms of action 21, 204
    positivism and conceptualism 204–12
    possession 23–4
    procedure, traditional 22–3
    Roman law contrasted 21–7
    tort 24–6, 205–10
Commutative justice 84–98, 107–8, 109, 121, 134, 135, 158, 210, 254
Conceptualism
    contract 248–66
    critics 275–81
    international private law 217–22
    international public law 215–17
    property 223–35
    tort 235–48
    unjust enrichment 266–74
Confession *see* Canon law, internal forum
Conflict of laws *see* International private law
Connanus, Franciscus 119, 120, 121, 122–3, 127, 137–8
Consensual contracts 11–12, 20, 49, 101, 136, 144, 147, 259–66
Consideration 210–11
Constitution of the United States 252–3
Contract
    *causa* 48–9, 64–5, 94–5
    consent
        common law 25–6

        conceptualists 259–66
        French jurists, *ancien régime* 144–5
        humanists 122
        iusnaturalists 136–7
        late scholastics 94
        medieval jurists 46–8, 49–50
        Roman law 11–12, 19–21
    enforceability
        canon law 64–5
        French jurists, *ancien régime* 147
        humanists 121–2
        iusnaturalists 137–8
        late scholastics 96–7, 101
        rationalists 190–1
        Roman law 19–21
        *usus modernus pandectarum* 162–3
    unfair terms
        canon law 56
        conceptualists 254–9
        economic interpretation 307–8
        late scholastics 97–8
        medieval civilians 35–6, 50–1
        rationalists 189–90
    unforeseen circumstances
        canon law 61–2
        late scholastics 94
Cook, Walter W. 279–80
Cooley, Thomas M. 209
Cooter, Robert 300–3, 308
Corbin, Arthur 265
*Correctores Romani* 54
Council of Tribourg 63
Council of Worms 60, 63
Covenant 210
*Cox v. Prentice* 27
Crime 71–5
Critical legal studies movement 309
Crockaert, Pierre 82
Crusades 81
Cujas, Jacques 112, 119
*Culpa* 10, 50, 63, 64
Currie, Brainerd 221, 222, 298

Damage *see* Tort, harm
Daube, David 6, 91
Dawson, John 162, 164, 194, 205
Decock, Wim 82, 106
*Decretum* 28, 51–3, 54, 56, 57, 60, 61, 62, 63, 64, 67, 69, 72, 79, 92, 103, 105, 113
Demante, Antoine Marie 197
Demogue, René 292, 294, 295
Demolombe, Charles 197, 198, 224, 232, 255, 256, 26
Dernburg, Heinrich 203, 225, 230
Descartes, René 165, 177–8, 179, 180, 193, 276
Deza, Diego de 82
Dicey, A. V. 221
Dickenson, John 281
Dinus de Mugello 39

Diocletian 1
Distributive justice 84, 107, 109
Divorce 56–7
*Doctores utriusque iuris* 53
*Doe dem. Carter v. Barnard* 24
Dolazalek, Gero 30, 31
*dolus* 10
Domat, Jean 141–8, 151–5, 163, 164, 195, 196, 199, 224, 236, 240, 243, 249, 250, 267
*Dominium utile* 96
Donahue, Charles 22, 204
Donellus, Hugo 119, 120–1, 123–7, 143, 153
Due process 66–70
Duguit, Léon 295
Dunn, John 140
Durandus 34
Duranton, Alexandre 197, 198, 225, 237, 255, 268
Dworkin, Ronald 301, 303

*Ecole de l'exégèse* 196–9
Economic harm 244–5, 246, 248
Economics 300–9
Efficiency 300
Ehrenzweig, Albert 222
Eisenberg, Melvin A. 223, 266
*Elegantia iuris* 119
Eleuterius 67
Ely, Richard 253, 254
*Emphyteusis* 96
*Epikeia* 171–2, 173
Epistemology, *see* Metaphysics and epistemology
Epstein, Richard 242, 305
Esser, Josef 241
Euclid 179, 180, 181
European Court of Human Rights 40
*Exceptio* 66, 67
Exchange 95, 97, 210, 211
Existence 169–70, 176–7
*Explication de texte* 119

Farnsworth, E. Allan 266
Fault *see* Tort, fault
Feenstra, Robert 86
Feinman, Richard 312
Ferrand, Louis 194
Fifoot, C. H. S. 24, 25, 205
Finnis, John 166, 311
First Lateran Council 52
Flume, Werner 263
Formalism 309–10, 311
Forms of action 21
Formulary procedure 2–3, 4, 5, 7, 22
Fourth Lateran Council 70, 105
Frank, Jerome 298
Franklin, Julian 114, 118, 119
Frederick II (Emperor) 68
*Freijuristen* 277, 281, 286
French Civil Code (*Code civil*)
  contract 248–51, 254, 260
  fault 235–6, 243
  intepretation, according to the drafters 151–4
  interpretation, according to the nineteenth century jurists 196–9
  interpretation, the Republican ideal 147–50
  necessity 227
  nuisance (*troubles de voisinage*) 233
  property 224–5
  strict liability 236–7, 244
  unjust enrichment 267
French humanists 118–27
French jurists, *ancien régime*
  contract 144–5, 147
  fault 144, 146
  property 146
  strict liability 16–17
  unjust enrichment 146
Friedmann, Wolfgang 282
Fuchs, Ernst 276, 278, 281, 297
Fuller, Lon 279, 281

Gaius 2, 3, 8, 12, 18, 19, 20, 21, 86, 123, 124–5
Gans, Eduard 229
*Gemeines Recht* 195, 196, 199–204, 214
Gény, François 165, 276, 277, 282, 284, 285, 287
Geometry 178, 179, 180, 181, 183
German Civil Code (*Bürgerlichesgesetzbuch*)
  contract 258, 262–3
  necessity 227
  nuisance 233
  property 234
  tort 243, 245–6
  unjust enrichment 271
Ghestin, Jacques 223
Gilmore, Grant 252, 275
Gilson, Etienne 166, 176, 177, 311
Glasson, Ernest 255
Glossators 31, 44
Glosses 29, 30–1, 33
Gnaeus Flavius 6
*Gnome* 171, 172
Gombrich, Ernst 43
Gratian 28, 51, 52, 53, 54, 62, 63, 67, 72, 73, 74, 92, 105, 113
Gratuitous transactions 95, 121, 210
Gregory I (Pope) 62
Gregory IX (Pope) 51, 63
Gregory XIII (Pope) 54, 113
Greuille, Bertrand de 236, 237
Griffith, Walter 246
Grisez, Germain 166, 311
Groenewegen, Simon van 162
Grotius, Hugo 21, 51, 61, 85–7, 93, 94, 96, 97, 102–5, 128–33, 135–40, 145, 146, 149, 154, 156, 157, 192–3, 205, 210, 217, 224, 227, 236, 250–1, 266
Guthrie, W. K. C. 170

Hadrian 3
Haferkamp, Hans-Peter 202, 295, 296
Hale, Matthew 61
Halpérin, Jean-Louis 235, 250
Hammon, Louis 256
Hand, Learned 305, 306
Harper, Fowler 207, 208, 209
Haskins, Charles Homer 32
Heck, Philippe 229, 276, 278, 282, 287, 288, 292
Heffter, August Wilhelm 216
Heineccius, Johannes Gottlieb 182
Henry IV of France 129
Heresy 58
Heuston, R. F. V. 241
Hilliard, Francis 207
Hitler, Adolf 282, 296
Hobbes, Thomas 256
Holmes, Oliver Wendell 165, 211–12, 221, 230, 241, 247, 253, 254, 264, 276
Holt's rule 24
Holy Roman Empire 142
Holzschuher, Rudolf von 255, 269
Homicide 59–60, 76
Horak, Franz 15
Horwitz, Morton 226–7, 252
Hostiensis 68
Hotman, François 120
Huber, Ulrich 218, 219
Huguccio 73, 74, 75, 77, 80
Humanists
 philology 112–15
 Renaissance ideal 112–13, 115–16
 systematization of Roman law 119–27
 teaching of Roman law 119

Iacobus de Arena 28, 44, 45
Iacobus de Ravanis 37, 38, 39, 40, 49
Ibbetson, David 210
*Infamia* 73–4
Ingham, Joseph W. 276, 279
*Iniuria* 7, 20, 39, 58, 71, 89, 90, 91, 100, 125
Innocent III (Pope) 66
Innocent IV (Pope) 67, 68, 80, 102
*Insinuatio* 20
*Interessenjurispudenz see* Interests, jurisprudence of
Interests, jurisprudence of 277, 287–92
Interference with neighbors *see* Nuisance
International private law (conflict of laws)
 conceptualists and their critics 217–22
 medieval civilians 43–5
International public law
 canon law 78–81
 conceptualists 215–17
 iusnaturalists 138–9
 late scholastics 101–5
 rationalists 191–3
 Roman law 77–8
 *usus modernus pandectarum* 158

Intuition 281–7, 288
Iohannes Bassianus 33
Iohannes Teutonicus 56, 61, 63, 78
Irnerius 28, 29, 30, 131
Isidore of Seville 80
*Ius commune* 28, 44, 53, 161, 195, 196, 219
 *see also* Canon law; Medieval civil law
Iusnaturalists
 contract 136–8
 international law 138–9
 natural law 128–33
 necessity 133–4
 property 133–4
 strict liability 135
 tort 135–6
 unjust enrichment 134–5

Jansen, Nils 239
Javolenus 8
Jerome 72
Jewish law 64
Jhering, Rudolf von 165, 166, 228, 229, 230, 231, 233, 234, 276, 277, 289–92
Johann Friedrich, Herzog 194
Jörs, Paul 12
Josserand, Louis 239, 292, 294, 295, 296
Junius Brutus 2, 14
Juries 23, 70
Just war 77–81, 101–2, 103–5
Justinian 1, 3, 18, 19, 29, 53, 56, 68, 71, 99, 112, 113, 119, 120, 124, 149, 161, 267

Kaldor-Hicks efficiency 300–1
Kantorowicz, Hermann 29, 31, 297
Kaser, Max 15
Keller, Friedrich 225
Kelley, Donald 112, 119
Kiss, Géza 282
König, Peter 193
Kornfeld, Ignatz 279, 282
Kötz, Hein 223
Kramer, Paul 265
Kraus, Jody 300, 301, 302, 303, 308
Kuttner, Stephan 71, 72, 73, 75

La Pira, Giorgio 13
*Laesio enormis* 35, 51, 56, 158, 255
Landes, William M. 307
Langbein, John 69
Langdell, Christopher Columbus 226, 252, 300
Larombière, M. L. 237, 267, 268
Lasser, Herman Andrew 181
Lasswell, Harold 298, 300
Late scholastics
 commutative justice 84
 contract 94–8, 101
 international law 101–5
 metaphysics 107–10, 166–75

necessity 85
nuisance 100
possession 100
property 85, 99–100
prudence 84, 91–2
tort 86–93, 100–1
unjust enrichment 85–6
Lateran Councils 52, 70, 105
Laurent, François 197, 198, 224, 232, 237, 255, 256, 261, 267, 268, 293
Lauterbach, Wolfgang 163
Law and economics movement 235, 284, 312
Leake, Samuel 256
Legal realism 279, 283
Legal sociology 277
*Legis actio* 3–5, 22, 23
Leibniz, Gottfried Wilhelm 164, 165, 175–6, 179–81, 182, 183, 184, 185–94, 213, 214, 232, 238, 276, 293
Lequette, Yves 241
Lessius, Leonard 82, 85, 86, 88, 89, 90, 91, 93, 94, 96, 97, 98, 110, 137, 173–4, 175
Levmore, Samuel 308
*Lex Aebutia* 2
*Lex Aquilia* 7, 20, 34, 59, 62, 63, 64, 87, 89, 90, 92, 93, 100, 162, 163, 183, 205, 238
*Lex regia* 102
Liberality 95, 158, 210
Lindsell, W. H. B. 246
Livy 77
Llewellyn, Karl 280, 283–4, 285, 286, 287, 289, 299–300
*Lochner v New York* 253, 254
Locke, John 140
Loemker, Leroy 175
Lorimer, James 217
Luig, Klaus 184, 189

Maffei, Domenico 113, 114
Maine, Sir Henry 22, 26
Maitland, Frederic William 22, 204
Manilius 2, 5
Marcadé, Victor 256
Marriage 56–7, 77
Martianus Capella 128
Martinus 28
*Materia Codicis* 30, 31
Mazeaud, Henri 240, 242
Mazeaud, Jean 240, 242
Mazeaud, Léon 240, 242
McCurdy, Charles 253, 254
McDougal, Myers 298, 300
Medieval civil law
conflict of laws 44–45
contract 35–6
nuisance 37–9
possession 48
tort 34–5, 39–40, 50
water rights 41–2

Meier, Sonja 274
*Menschengeist* 201
Metaphysics and epistemology
Aquinas 107–10, 166–73
critical legal studies movement 309–12
critics of conceptualism 277–81
Descartes, René 178, 179–80
late scholastics 107–10, 166–75
Leibniz, Gottfried Wilhelm 175–6, 180–1, 183–7
Pufendorf, Samuel 179–80
Suárez 166–73
Wolff, Christian 176–7, 180–1, 183–7
Metcalf, Theoron 256
Mills 41, 42–3
Milsom, S. F. C. 24, 205
*Mishna* 64
Modestinus 1
Molina, Luis de 82, 85, 86, 88–90, 93, 95–8, 101–3, 110, 135, 137, 146, 169, 173, 175, 205, 236, 240, 243
*Mos gallicus/Mos italicus* 118, 156, 160
Mucius Scaevola 2, 5, 14, 16, 78
Müller-Erzbach, Rudolf 288

Nanz, Klaus-Peter 162
Nazism 282, 296
Necessity
canon law 58–9
economic interpretation 303
iusnaturalists 133–4
late scholastics 85
rationalists 187–90
Negligence *see* Tort, fault
Netherlands: *usus modernus pandectus* 156–64, 183, 195
Nève, P. L. 160
Newland, John 256
Nicolas I (Pope) 63
Noonan, John 52, 77
Nuisance
conceptualists 232–5
economic intepretation 303–5
late scholastics 100
medieval civilians 37–9
Nussbaum, Arthur 158
*Nyal's Saga* 4

Oath helpers 22, 23
Odofredus de Denariis 28, 37, 38, 68
Oliphant, Hermann 276, 283, 298
*Ordo iudicarius* 66–7, 68, 69
Osma, Pedro Mariniez de 82

*Pandektenrecht* 199–204
Pareto efficiency 300–1
*Patrimonium* 34
Paucapalea 67
Paul (Apostle) 72, 73

Paul(us) (jurist) 1, 10, 15, 48
Payer, Pierre 77
Pennington, Kenneth 28, 67, 68
*People's Express Airlines v. Consolidated Rail Corp.* 248
Perry, Stephen 242
Petrarch 112, 116, 117, 118
Petrus de Bellapertica 39, 49
Phillimere, Robert 216
Philology 54, 112, 113, 119, 127
Placentinus 33
Planiol, Marcel 293, 294, 295, 296
*Ploof v. Putnam* 303
Policy science 297–300
Poliziano 112, 118
Pollock, Sir Frederick 206, 207, 211, 212, 226, 230–2, 256, 262
Pomponius 1, 2, 16, 28, 35, 56
Portalis, Jean-Étienne-Marie 148, 150, 151, 152, 155, 196, 199, 200, 224, 249, 250, 254, 287
Positivism 165, 195, 196, 214, 310, 311, 312
  Anglo-American common law 204–12
  French *école de l'exégèse* 196–9
  German *Pandektenrecht* 199–204, 213
  international law 215
Posner, Richard A. 300–2, 303, 305, 306, 307
Possession
  canon law 57–8
  common law 23–4
  conceptualists 227–32
  late scholastics 100
  medieval civil law 48
  Roman law 10–1
Pothier, Robert 141, 143–7, 153–5, 164, 196, 199, 224, 227, 235, 236, 249, 260
Pound, Roscoe 254, 277, 280, 281, 287, 297, 298
Practical reason *see* Prudence
Pradier-Fodéré, Paul 216
Prescription 55
Prices 35, 51, 56, 97–8
  *see also* Unjust price
Pringsheim, Fritz 13
Procedure
  archaic 3–4
  common law, traditional 22–3
  Roman 3–6
  Romano-Canonical 66–70
Promissory reliance 212
Property
  canon law 57–8
  conceptualists 223–35
  French jurists, *ancien régime* 146
  humanists 124
  iusnaturalists 133–4
  late scholastics 85, 99–100
  rationalists 188–90
  Roman law 18–9
Prosser, William 207, 208–9

Protestantism 106, 175
Prudence 84, 110, 170, 171, 177, 285, 287, 305
Public places 41, 42
Public policy 43
Puchta, Georg Friedrich 200, 201–2, 203, 225, 229
Pufendorf, Samuel 51, 61, 85, 86, 94, 128–30, 132–40, 145, 146, 154, 157, 179, 181–3, 217, 227, 236, 240, 243, 260

Radding, Charles 28, 29
*Raffles v. Wichelhaus* 26, 205
Randa, Anton 229
Rationalism
  metaphysics 166–77
  method 177–81
  natural law and 166–75, 177, 180
  parallels and contrast with nineteenth-century jurists 213–15, 276
  practical reason 170, 171, 177
  private law 187–91
  public international law 191–3
  theoretical reason 170, 171, 177
Rau, Charles 197, 198, 224, 232, 237, 260, 263, 268, 270
Raymond of Penafort 51, 59, 61, 76
*Rechtsgefühl* 282, 287, 288
*Rechtsgeschäft* 251, 262
Regelsberger, Ferdinand 261
Reimann, Mathias 222
Rémy, Philippe 199, 213
Renaissance humanists 111–18
*Res nullius* 81
Richardus Malumbra 45
Ripert, George 293, 294, 295
Robbery 20
*Robbins Dry Dock and Repair v. Flint* 247
Roland, Henri 239, 240
Rolandus 77, 79, 80
Rollin, Savoie 148
Roman law
  common law and 21–7
  contract 11–12, 19–21
  French civil law and 141–7, 153–5
  *gemeines Recht* and 200–4
  Greek philosophy and 12–18
  international law 77–8
  late scholastics and 99–101, 156
  later civil law and 18–21
  medieval jurists and 28–32
  method 7–12
  origins 1–7
  possession 10–11
  procedure 2–5
  property 18–19
  tort 11, 19–20, 100–1
Roman-Canonical procedure 66, 75
Rufinus 78, 103
Rumpf, Max 289, 290
*Rylands v. Fletcher* 244

Sacral procedures 3–4, 5–6
Salmond, Sir John William 207, 208, 209, 246–7
Savatier, René 235
Savigny, Friedrich Carl von 199–204, 218–21, 228, 231, 262, 263, 268–73
Schiavone, Aldo 13, 14
Schiller, Arthur 15
Schlosser, Hans 114
Schlossmann, Siegmund 264
Schneider, Hans-Peter 184
Schönborn, John Philip of, Elector of Mainz 180
*Scott v. Littledale* 26
Seavy, Warren 208, 209
Second Lateran Council 52
Sériaux, Alain 270
Seuffert, Johann 269
Sexual relations 54, 73, 76–7
Shulz, Fritz 1, 2, 9, 13, 14, 15, 16, 61, 71
Siebert, Wolfgang 296
Simler, Philippe 241
Simpson, A. W. B. 26, 211, 251, 256–7
Sin 71–5
Sinibaldus Fliscus 67, 68, 80–1, 102
Sinzheimer, Hugo 297
Skinner, Quentin 111
Slaves 8–9, 36
*Smith v. Jeffryes* 26
Smith, Jeremiah 207
Smith, John William 256
Social purpose 292–6
Social sciences
  economics 300–9
  sociological jurisprudence and policy science 297–300
Sohm, Rudolph 278
Soto, Domingo de 82, 83, 85, 88–9, 96, 98, 102, 106, 174, 175, 205
Spanish natural law school *see* Late scholastics
Spencer, Herbert 253
Stampe, Ernst 276, 278, 282, 287, 288
Stanton, K. M. 241
Starck, Boris 239, 240
Stein, Peter 8, 13, 14, 15, 21, 119
Stephen of Tournai 66, 79
Stinzing, Roderick von 113, 115
*Stipulatio* 20, 49, 61–2, 101
Stone, Harlan 297, 298
Story, Joseph 43, 218, 219–20, 221, 252, 253, 256
Story, William Wentworth 256
Strict liability *see* Tort, strict liability
Struve, Georg 159
Stryk, Samuel 156, 159, 161
*Studia humanitatis* 111, 115, 127
*Sturlyn v. Albany* 257
Suárez, Francisco 82, 102, 103, 110, 165–77, 179, 180, 193, 213, 217, 276, 311
Sulpicius Rufus 14

Taylor, William 256
Terré, François 241
Territorial sovereignty 218, 219, 220

Theft 14, 20
Theoretical reason 170, 171, 177
Tort
  fault
    canon law 59–61, 63–4
    conceptualists 239–44
    common law 24–6
    economic interpretation 305–6
    French jurists, *ancien régime* 144
    humanists 121
    iusnaturalists 135–6
    late scholastics 92–4, 100
    medieval civilians 50
    rationalists 188
    Roman law 11
  harm
    conceptualists 244–8
    iusnaturalists 135–6
    late scholastics 86–91, 100
    loss of an opportunity 87–9
    medieval civilians 34–5
    pure economic loss 34–5, 87–9, 245–8
    rationalists 188
    reputation 39–40, 48, 90–1, 100
    Roman law 19–20
    *usus modernus pandectarum* 162
  strict liability
    economic interpretation 306
    French jurists, *ancien régime* 146–7
    iusnaturalists 135
    late scholastics 92–3, 101
    nineteenth century jurists 243–4
    Roman law 19
Torture 69–70
Touillier, Charles Bonaventure Marie 197, 225, 267
Trebilcock, Michael 301, 307
Treitel, Sir Guenter 263
Trespass 24, 25, 206, 207, 209
Trial by jury 23, 70
Trial by ordeal 70
Tribonian 112
Troje, Hans 118
Tronchet, François Denis 152, 254
Troplong, Raymond-Théodore 197, 198
Tryphonius 8–9
Tuck, Richard 132

Ugo 28, 48
Ulpian 1, 3, 10, 11, 34, 46, 47, 48, 50, 69, 78, 94, 101, 122, 262
*unde vi* 57, 58
Unger, Roberto Mangabiera 309–10, 311, 312
*United States v. Carroll Towing Co.* 305
Unjust enrichment
  conceptualists 266–74
  economic interpretation 308
  French jurists, *ancien régime* 146
  iusnaturalists 134–5
  late scholastics 85–6
Unjust price 35, 51, 56, 97–8, 254–9

Urban I (Pope) 60
Usufruct 95
Usury 70
*Usus modernus pandectarum*
   contracts 162
   humanists contrasted 158–9
   international law 158
   medieval civilians contrasted 159–61
   natural law schools contrasted 157–8
   torts 162–3
   usage, its authority 161–3
*Uti possidetis* 7
Utilitarianism 289, 290

Vacarius 50
Valette, Auguste 197, 198
Valla, Lorenzo 53, 112, 116, 117, 118, 120, 127
Vangerow, Karl 255
Vasquez, Gabriel 169
Vattel, Emerich de 192–3, 217
Viehweg, Theodore 15, 16
*Vincent v. Lake Erie* 303
*Vindicatio* 68
Vinnius, Arnold 157, 163
Vio, Tomasso di (Cardinal Cajetan) 82, 87–8, 92, 93, 96, 97, 107, 110, 137, 174, 175, 305
Vitoria, Francesco de 82, 83, 102, 103–4, 105, 106, 107, 128, 138, 174
Voet, Johannes 48, 157, 158, 159, 218

Vold, Lawrence 207
*Volksgeist* 196, 199, 200, 201, 202, 203, 204, 214
Von Caemmerer, Ernst 271–3
Vulgate 29

Wager of law 22–3
War 77–81, 101–2, 103–5, 192–3
Watson, Alan 4, 5, 7, 8, 9, 14, 21, 41, 56
Wealth maximization 302
*Weaver v. Ward* 25
Weigel, Erhard 178, 179, 180
Wesenbeck, Matthew 157, 158, 161, 162, 163
*West Coast Hotel v. Parrish* 253
Wheaton, Henry 216
Whitman, James 56
Wieacker, Franz 115, 160, 161, 213
Wilburg, Walter 271, 272, 273
William of Occam 82
Williston, Samuel 212, 265
Wills, Gary 140
Windscheid, Bernhard 200, 202, 203, 225, 229, 233, 238, 251, 255, 262, 265, 269–70, 273, 274, 293
Winroth, Anders 28, 30, 31, 52
Wolff, Christian 164, 165, 175, 176, 177, 181–4, 186–94, 213, 214, 217, 238, 276, 311
Writs 21–2, 23, 26, 204

Zimmermann, Reinhard 71, 158, 160, 161, 164, 27

Printed and bound by CPI Group (UK) Ltd, Croydon, CR0 4YY